NEW TESTAMENT EPISTLES

1 & 2 PETER
JUDE

A CRITICAL AND EXEGETICAL COMMENTARY

by

GARETH L. REESE

HEAD OF NEW TESTAMENT DEPARTMENT
CENTRAL CHRISTIAN COLLEGE OF THE BIBLE
MOBERLY, MISSOURI

Scripture Exposition Books, LLC
803 McKINSEY PLACE
MOBERLY, MISSOURI
65270

Acknowledgment

The Scripture quotations contained herein, unless otherwise noted, are from the New American Standard Bible, copyrighted 1960, 1962, 1963, 1968, 1971, 1972, 1973, 1975, 1977, by the Lockman Foundation. Used by permission.

Reese, Gareth Lee, 1932-

New Testament Epistles: A critical and exegetical commentary on 1 and 2 Peter and Jude / by Gareth L. Reese. -- Scripture Exposition Books, c2004.

xxxvi, 164, xl, 120, xxi, 48, 20, 35 p. ; 26 cm.
Cover title: New Testament Epistles -- Peter and Jude.
Spine title: 1-2 Peter and Jude.
Includes bibliographical references and index.
ISBN 0-971-765243

1. Bible. NT. Peter--Commentaries. 2. Bible. NT. Jude--Commentaries. I. Bible. NT. Peter. English. New American Standard. 1963. II. Bible. NT. Jude. English. New American Standard. 1963. III. Title. IV. Title: New Testament Epistles--Peter and Jude.

BS 2795.53.R43

PREFACE

This present volume continues a series of commentaries on the books of the New Testament written from the unique standpoint of the Restoration Movement, a position which allows us to approach those Scriptures with no special theological doctrine or dogma to defend and explicate. The author believes this approach provides us with an unhindered freedom to listen to what the Holy Spirit would tell us within the pages of the Sacred Scriptures. By deliberately adapting the time-honored grammatico-historical method of interpretation, the Word of God is allowed to impress upon our minds the authorial intent the Divine Author had in mind. What remains for each of us readers is to consciously and deliberately and consistently put into practice the precepts and prohibitions He has spoken.

The author acknowledges a debt of gratitude to those expositors and commentators whose works are cited in the footnotes and bibliographies. They have significantly shortened the amount of time needed to master the nuances of Greek grammar and syntax that are peculiar to the writings of Peter and Jude. Though they have been carefully consulted, the use made of the conclusions and emphases of some of the newer works, written from a redaction critical or sociological or rhetorical critical standpoint, have been deliberately minimized in these notes. It seems counter-productive to this author to rely on such works, especially if the methodology used by their authors assumes there is no inspiration behind the writing of these Scriptural books.

It is greater gratification to this author to express his thanks to his students, whose sharp questions and keen minds have helped clarify notes and references in preliminary editions of this work. He also expresses heartfelt appreciation to the supporters of Central Christian College of the Bible who, by their regular giving and prayers, have made it possible for him to have the time and opportunity to keep providing for the colleges and churches these tools for in-depth Bible study.

The epistles of Peter and Jude, it appears, may play a key role in the 21st century church's attempt to correct the cultural drift and to arrest the slide into Gnostic-like New Age ideas that have become part of the average man-in-the-street's worldview. The religion taught by Jesus and His apostles is still the "grace of God." "Stand firm in it!" "Contend earnestly for the faith which was once for all delivered to the saints!"

TABLE OF CONTENTS

Commentary on 1 Peter — Page
- Introductory Studies i
- Chapter 1 1
- Chapter 2 34
- Chapter 3 65
- Chapter 4 99
- Special Study #1: Gifts of the Spirit 124
- Chapter 5 145

Commentary on 2 Peter
- Introductory Studies i
- Chapter 1 1
- Chapter 2 38
- Chapter 3 81

Commentary on Jude
- Introductory Studies i
- Chapter 1 1

Bibliography
- 1 and 2 Peter 1
- Jude 17

Index
- 1 Peter I-1
- 2 Peter I-19
- Jude I-37

Commentary On

1 Peter

1 PETER

INTRODUCTORY STUDIES

I. Preliminaries

1 Peter belongs to that group of New Testament books which are now called Catholic or General Epistles. The seven epistles written by James, Peter, John, and Jude were so designated in the Greek text issued by Stephanus in AD 1550,[1] though he was not the first to use the term. Stephanus intended by this designation to indicate to his readers that these letters were addressed generally, that is, to more than one congregation.[2] A general letter is not quite the same as an encyclical letter, for an encyclical is addressed to all churches everywhere, whereas Peter's letters were addressed to several provinces (1 Peter 1:1) in a large geographical region.

Of all these general epistles, perhaps it can be said that 1 Peter is the best known, most read, and most loved. It is one of the easiest of the New Testament letters to read and understand. Edgar J. Goodspeed called it "one of the most moving pieces of persecution literature" which men can read. If Old Testament people could turn to Job for help when facing persecution, New Testament people, while being persecuted for their faith, turn to 1 Peter for guidance and comfort.

In the NASB the title is "The First Epistle of Peter." As is true for all our New Testament books, it is generally assumed that the autographs had no titles affixed to the outside of the scroll, and that the titles presently found on the books were added by men. The letters were intended to be read in the churches; when a congregation, after making copies of neighboring church's letters, had its own collection of letters,[3] and one in particular was wanted for the day's Scripture reading, the added titles helped identify them quickly without having to open each one and begin reading to find out which letter one had in hand. Since the oldest copies we have of the New Testament letters all bear titles, it must be said that the

---

[1] Few textual editors have followed Stephanus' lead since it appears the letters of 2 and 3 John, from a reading of those epistles, were both local in destination. Nevertheless, the name "general letters" has passed into common usage in New Testament studies.

[2] The general letters are thus distinguished from some of Paul's letters which were addressed to a single individual or a single town or congregation. "Catholic" meant "universal" and carries no implication that the letters somehow were related to the ecclesiastical organization known through much of church history as the Roman Catholic Church.

[3] In the author's class notes on *New Testament -- General Introduction* (covering Canon, Text, Inspiration, and principal English Versions), it is documented that congregations began collecting the books written by apostles and New Testament prophets before Paul died (cp. 2 Peter 3:16).

titles reflect the traditional views of the early church.[4] It may also be affirmed that the older the manuscript, the shorter is the title. The oldest known Greek manuscripts have simply *Petrou a* (Peter 1) or *Petrou Epistole a* (Epistle of Peter 1).[5] The numeral added to Peter's name for this letter indicates the acceptance (at the time when the titles were added) of a second epistle by Peter. The designation "epistle" was added very early and simply reflects the epistolary formula (1 Peter 1:1,2); it indicates early Christians took this formula at face value. An *epistolē*, from which we get our word "epistle", was something sent by a messenger, whether an oral or written message. It came to be the common term for a written message from one individual or group to another, whether private or general. Such epistles arose from definite historical or life situations and were intended to address specific needs. To appreciate what these are, we shall study the historical allusions found in each letter, and also reflect on what the Bible and early Christian tradition tells us about the life of Peter.

II. HISTORICAL ALLUSIONS

A. Beginning of the letter, 1:1-7

In verse 1, the writer signs his name, "Peter," and identifies which Peter it is by calling himself an "apostle of Jesus Christ." He then names the provinces in which the intended readers live. They are "Pontus, Galatia, Cappadocia, Asia, and Bithynia."

As he continues on, Peter characterizes the readers as being "chosen," as having "obeyed Jesus Christ," and as having been "sprinkled with His blood." This identifies the readers as being Christians. Already we have learned something about the historical circumstances behind this epistle. The date of writing can be no earlier than AD 30 (that is, after Christ has died and risen, and after the gospel has begun to be preached [remember Peter's first recorded sermon in Acts 2]). The date of writing is also after AD 50, since there were no Christians that we know about (at least among ethnic Gentiles) in any of those provinces until after Paul's first missionary journey, AD 45-48.[6]

---

[4] Since there is a consistency in the wording of the titles, no matter the provenance of the manuscript one may have in hand, it can also be affirmed that there is no valid reason to question the truthfulness of the traditional titles, whether the titles give the destination of the letter (as in Paul's epistles), or whether the title (as in the general epistles, and the Gospels) denotes the author assigned to the letter. (In making this statement, it is recognized that in the case of Ephesians, some old manuscripts do not carry "in Ephesus" in the early verses, and that that letter may be called "Ephesians" because that is where the letter ended up, after making the rounds of the churches.)

[5] Later scribes expanded the titles, so that one finds "The First Catholic (or General) Epistle of Peter" (cp. the title found in the KJV), or "The First Catholic Epistle of the Apostle Peter." The scribe who copied the work we know as Codex Angelicus in the 9th century expanded the title to "The First Epistle Catholic of the holy and all-praiseworthy Apostle Peter."

[6] Paul's first journey did take the gospel to Galatia (Acts 13-14). It was not until after that date that the gospel penetrated some of the other provinces.

Peter also describes the readers as "strangers scattered" (KJV) or "who reside as aliens" in these provinces. In 2:11 he calls them "aliens and strangers." How did they come to be scattered? Were they ethnic Jews, "dispersed" by earlier anti-Jewish persecutions? Were they ethnic Jews "scattered" by earlier anti-Christian persecutions? Has a term that used to be applied to Israel now been applied to the church, so that the readers are "scattered Christians" of whatever ethnic background – strangers and pilgrims away from their heavenly homeland? Whatever the answer to these questions, already the underlying theme of persecution has surfaced. We wonder, in passing, what persecution it is the readers are enduring.

In verse 3, we are told that the "resurrection of Jesus Christ from the dead" is something that has already happened. Furthermore, there is an "inheritance which is imperishable and undefiled and will not fade away" awaiting the faithful Christian. Christians who are being persecuted and whose property is being confiscated need to hear promises like this. In fact, it is precisely those who are faithful (verse 5) who have a promise about such an inheritance. Is it not implied that the persecution was severe enough that some were tempted to quit the faith? Finally, verse 7 holds out hope of the second advent of Jesus Christ, when all the faithful will receive "praise and glory and honor." Now there is a motive to faithfulness, whatever the persecution that may be faced!

B. At the close of the letter, 5:6-14

Historical allusions are found not only in the epistolary opening, but some also were regularly included in the closing words of a first-century letter. 1 Peter 5:6 reads "humble yourselves ... under the mighty hand of God." Is this a reminder that all of the difficulties the readers faced were known by God, and even permitted by Him for their eternal good? It is a very precious reminder to His suffering children that "it matters to Him about you."

Verse 8 speaks about the devil as a roaring lion prowling about. Is it possible there is an allusion to the persecution by Nero in Rome, when Christians were thrown to the lions in the Circus Maximus? Does Peter so word his warning so that Christians will recognize that it is not just Nero who has ordered the persecution, but that behind Nero's edict lay none other than the devil's own prompting, as that evil one tried to get Christians to defect? Well, says Peter, 'Don't defect! Resist him, firm in your faith!' And you resist, not only for your own benefit, but also for the benefit which others, who being similarly persecuted, can gain from your example of faithfulness to Jesus no matter the exigencies.

Verse 10 seems to promise that after a little time of suffering (Christians should not expect to be exempt from suffering) God will restore all the missing body parts lost to the lions. In the great resurrection morning, when the dead in Christ arise, the Christians' bodies will be whole and complete.

Verse 12 introduces Silvanus as being the secretary, or amanuensis, who actually penned the letter; we know him as "Silas" in the book of Acts. Peter (1 Peter 1:1) dictated it, or gave directions for its contents, and Silas did the actual writing. Peter summarizes the whole thrust of 1 Peter in these words, "This [Christianity] is the true grace of God. Stand firm in it!" Don't let the persecution cause you to waver and lose heart and eventually quit Christ!

In verse 13, the writer tells us he is in "Babylon" when he writes, and that Mark is with him. Both "she who is in Babylon" ("the *church that* is in Babylon," KJV)[7] and "Mark"[8] send their greetings to the readers. The verse implies that several folk who were with Peter, or in whose midst he lived and traveled, knew about this letter Peter was writing, knew about the needs of the readers, and wanted the readers to know of their concern for them. If we knew for certain the identity of the place here called "Babylon," we could identify the place of writing for 1 Peter.[9]

C. Middle of the letter, 4:12-19

Sometimes in ancient letters, one can find historical allusions in the midst of the letter. 4:12 speaks of a "fiery ordeal" coming on the readers to "test" them. It will be a time when they will "share the sufferings of Christ." One wonders if "fiery ordeal" has some reference to Nero's persecution, when some Christians were covered with pitch, crucified, and then set afire to serve as street lights so Nero could see to drive his chariots through his gardens at night. Anyone who can envision the horrible experience of grease or tar on their bodies and then being set afire can appreciate the agony these crucified people went through. There would be no way they could try to rub the sticky coating off their bodies, and the coating simply made the burn more severe and painful.

Peter encourages, 'Do not be ashamed to suffer as a Christian. Instead, glorify God in that name. Let those also who suffer according to the will of God entrust their souls to a faithful Creator as you continue to do what is right!'

In fact, all through the letter are instructions about how to face persecution. Note, it

---

[7] The Greek simply reads "The (something feminine singular) in Babylon." Whoever or whatever the (something feminine) is, it is further described as being "chosen together with you" -- i.e., as being Christian. Whether it is a "church" (a word which is feminine in the Greek), or some Christian lady, will be discussed in notes at 1 Peter 5:13.

[8] This is the "John Mark" who accompanied Paul and Barnabas on the first missionary journey (Acts 13:5), who quit in the middle of the journey (Acts 13:13), and who then traveled with Barnabas when he and Paul split into two different missionary teams (Acts 15:39). He is the same Mark who is commended later by Paul (2 Timothy 4:11), and whom Paul wants Timothy to bring to Rome when Timothy himself comes to the town where Paul is when he wrote 2 Timothy.

[9] Later in these Introductory Studies we shall carefully examine this matter in detail.

is not suffering in general this letter talks about, but suffering because one is a Christian. The letter abounds with calls to heroic Christian living, being helpful to your fellow believers, submitting to your shepherd-leaders, and having your behavior winsome among the Gentiles. Non-Christians are to see in the believer's behavior that Christianity does change the way a man lives. It is a beneficial, beautiful, and lasting way to live, even if one is called on to suffer for it!

III. SURVEY OF THE LIFE OF PETER

A. His Youth – till he meets Jesus

John 1:41-44 and Matthew 8:14 tell us some details. Peter was probably as old as Jesus when they met, perhaps older. Traditionally, John was the youngest of Jesus' apostles, Peter the oldest. His father was named John (Jonas, KJV),[10] his brother was named Andrew.[11] He was born at Bethsaida,[12] a fishing village on the coast of the Sea of Galilee. He owned a house at Capernaum,[13] and he was married.[14]

What kind of boy and young man was Peter? Some say he was a rough, tough fisherman. It is true that he followed the trade of fisherman,[15] but the idea that he was a rough, tough, foul-mouthed fisherman comes from a misunderstanding of the report of Peter's denial of Christ at His trials before Annas and Caiaphas. Peter did not at that occasion use curse words but rather took a solemn oath (Matthew 26:74), calling a curse upon himself if he were lying. We get some indication of his lifestyle from the housetop experience, where Peter says he has never touched anything common or unclean (Acts 10:14). Jesus selected only good men to be his apostles.[16]

B. The Period of his association with Jesus – until Jesus' ascension

When Peter first met Jesus, Peter was already a disciple of John the Baptist. He was brought to Jesus by Andrew, his brother (John 1:40-42). On his first meeting with Jesus, he

---

[10] Matthew 16:17, John 1:42, 21:16.

[11] Matthew 10:2, John 1:40.

[12] John 1:44.

[13] Matthew 8:14, Luke 4:38.

[14] Matthew 8:14.

[15] Matthew 4:18, Mark 1:16, Luke 5:2,3.

[16] Even Judas was a good man when Jesus called him. Those identified as "zealots" were ex-zealots, whose lives had changed for the better as they became disciples of Jesus.

received the surname "Cephas" – Peter, the man of rock. After sundry lessons and discipleship sessions, in the second year of His earthly ministry, Jesus chose from among his disciples twelve men to become apostles. Peter was among this group of twelve (Matthew 4:18-20, Luke 5:10,11). In the listings of the apostles, Peter's name is the first one given. He was one of the inner three (Peter, James, and John). He was accorded the dignity of being chosen by the apostles as their spokesman, perhaps because he was older than the rest.

There are a number of memorable things recorded that involved Peter during his travels with Jesus. There are his walking on the water of the Sea of Galilee;[17] the good confession of Jesus as the Messiah;[18] his wish to build three tabernacles on the Mount of Transfiguration;[19] the question of temple tribute, when he probably got himself into trouble because of his impetuousness;[20] his inquiry as to the reward to be gained from following Christ;[21] his refusal to allow Jesus to wash his feet, hastily followed by the opposite extreme;[22] his promise to go with the loved Master into prison and death and his promise rather to die than deny his Lord;[23] his threefold denial;[24] his willful defense of Jesus with a sword;[25] the tearful repentance after seeing the look of Jesus;[26] his hurrying forth to the tomb of the risen Savior;[27] Jesus' post-resurrection appearance to him;[28] the loving zeal with which he anticipated the others in greeting the Master on the shore of the Sea of Galilee;[29] his reply to the Redeemer's question, "Peter do you love me?"[30] and Jesus' foretelling of his manner of death.[31]

---

17 Matthew 14:29-31.

18 Matthew 16:16-18.

19 Matthew 17:4-8.

20 Matthew 17:24-27.

21 Matthew 19:27-30.

22 John 13:6-9.

23 Matthew 26:35; Luke 22:33.

24 Matthew 26:31-35, 58, 69-75.

25 John 18:10,11.

26 Matthew 26:75.

27 Luke 24:12; John 20:2-7.

28 1 Corinthians 15:5, Luke 24:34.

29 John 21:7-11.

30 John 21:15-17.

31 John 21:18-19.

C. The period of apostolic ministry in the church

In the first twelve chapters of Acts, Peter is the apostle whose acts chiefly are recorded. He took the lead in suggesting a replacement for Judas;[32] it is Peter's sermon on the day of Pentecost that is recorded;[33] as God works miracles through him, the gospel is credentialed and multitudes of folk become believers through the gospel's victorious power;[34] he deems it joy to endure the reproach of Christ -- he allows neither threatenings nor ill treatment to make him falter in confessing the name of Christ;[35] he joins John in carrying the gospel to Samaria;[36] we find him on an evangelistic crusade in the coastal regions of the Mediterranean;[37] he is the first apostle, who, in consequence of a vision with which he was honored, received Gentiles into the communion of the Christian church;[38] in AD 44 he was imprisoned and about to be executed when he was miraculously delivered.[39]

In Acts 15, we find Peter at the conference on circumcision, held in Jerusalem in the year AD 51. According to Galatians 2:11-17, we next find Peter at Antioch, where his dissimulation was publicly corrected by Paul.

After this, we know little for certain about Peter's travels or life. It is clear from 1 Corinthians 9:5 that he undertook various journeys to spread the gospel of the kingdom of God. According to an ancient tradition in Origen, which may have originated from the early verses of 1 Peter, Peter is said to have preached the gospel to the Jews scattered throughout Pontus, Galatia, Cappadocia, Asia, and Bithynia.[40] A famous paragraph in Jerome's writings deals with Peter:

> Simon Peter ... himself chief of the apostles, after having been bishop of the church of Antioch and having preached to the Dispersion -- the believers in circumcision, in Pontus, Galatia, Cappadocia, Asia and Bithynia -- pushed on to Rome in the second year of Claudius to overthrow Simon Magus, and held the sacerdotal chair there for twenty-five years until the last, that is, the fourteenth year of Nero. At his hands he received the crown of martyrdom being nailed to the cross with his head towards the ground and his feet raised

---

[32] Acts 1:15-26.

[33] Acts 2:16-26.

[34] Acts 3:7 (lame man), 5:1-10 (Ananias and Sapphira), 9:34,36-41 (Aeneas and Dorcas).

[35] Acts 4:8-12, 5:29-32.

[36] Acts 8:14-17.

[37] Acts 9:32-35.

[38] Acts 10:34-48.

[39] Acts 12:3-17.

[40] Origen is quoted by Eusebius, *H.E.,* iii.1.

> on high, asserting that he was unworthy to be crucified in the same manner as his Lord. He wrote two epistles which are called catholic, the second of which, on account of its difference from the first in style, is considered by many not to be by him. Then too the Gospel according to Mark, who was his disciple and interpreter, is ascribed to him. On the other hand, the books, one of which is entitled his Acts, another his Gospel, a third his Preaching, a fourth his Revelation, a fifth his "Judgment," are rejected as apocryphal. Buried at Rome in the Vatican near the triumphal way he is venerated by the whole world.[41]

In Jerome's account, according to Huther, there are several particulars that are doubtful. (1) The episcopate of Peter at Antioch. This is reported also by Eusebius (*Chron.* AD 40) who makes Peter *found* (plant) the church at Antioch, in contradiction to Acts 11:19ff. (2) His journey to Rome to oppose Simon Magus. This also seems to come from Eusebius (*Chron.*) who appeals to Justin Martyr for it. It appears to be based on Justin's story of a statue found at Rome (then identified as being Simon's), but now known to have been a statue of the Sabine god Semo Saneus. (3) The 25 year's bishopric of Peter at Rome. This has been minutely examined by scholars and shown on chronological grounds to have been impossible and to be inconsistent with Galatians 2:7-9, according to which Peter, who by this hypothesis had been then for many years bishop in Rome, and continued so for many years after, was to go to the circumcision as their apostle.[42] (4) Huther also objected to "the peculiar manner of his crucifixion." But Huther was likely wrong in his attempted interpretation of Origen's expression (in *H.E.* iii.1) as meaning simply "capital punishment" rather than "crucified head downwards."

Peter did come to Rome late in his life. The persecution of Christians by Nero, after he blamed them for the conflagration of Rome in AD 64, was raging. Paul already has been arrested, and in time, so was Peter. From the record of the New Testament, they had not seen each other for almost 20 years. From tradition, both Peter and Paul were executed for being "Christians," falsely blamed for causing the fire that had destroyed much of the city.

---

[41] See *Nicean and Post-Nicean Fathers*, Series 2, Vol.3, edited by Philip Schaff and Henry Wace (Grand Rapids: Eerdmans, 1953), p. 61. Footnotes on p.361 tell us that "the technical term 'Dispersion'" refers to "Jews out[side] of Judea." "Circumcision" is a paraphrase for "Hebrews" in Eusebius and Rufinus [from whom Jerome gets some of his material]. "That Peter met Simon Magus in Rome is a post-apostolic legend." At the time Schaff and Wace wrote, there was a scholarly debate on whether the "Judgment" of Peter and the recently discovered "Teaching of the Twelve" were in fact the same works. Textual variations have "whole city" rather than "whole world." See also Joh. Huther, *Critical and Exegetical Handbook to the General Epistles of James, Peter, John, and Jude*, vol. 10 in *Meyer's Commentary on the New Testament* (Winona Lake, IN: Alpha Publications, 1979, reprint of 1883 edition), p. 170 for a listing of additional perspectives regarding how the quotation by Jerome is disputed.

[42] In the author's commentary on Acts, Special Study #12 is entitled "Was Peter Ever in Rome?" While the Roman church affirms he was in Rome, and some protestants affirm he never was, the evidence cited in the Special Study indicates Peter did come to Rome late in his life (but not 25 years living there), and was executed in Rome in the Spring of AD 68, the 14th year of Nero. "The evidence that Peter did spend a short time in Rome is as strong, early, and wide, as that on which we believe that Hannibal invaded Italy." A.J. Mason, in *Ellicott's Commentary*, p.3.

IV. AUTHORSHIP

A. The Reason for such a study

With Peter's signature affixed to the letter, why should there be any question about authorship? With many books the question of genuineness[43] is of secondary importance, for most books are judged by the character of their contents, and not by the author whose names they bear. With reference to the books included in our Bibles, however, the question of genuineness – of authorship – is most vital and important. In many instances the possible inspiration and authority of the book itself is based upon the authorship; the book is authoritative because it was written by an apostle (who was inspired by virtue of the baptism of the Holy Spirit) or a close associate of an apostle (who could have received spiritual gifts by the laying on of an apostle's hands, and thus been able to speak by inspiration). Where a book is ascribed to a definite writer, the historicity of the book depends on the truthfulness of the inscription. In every instance, the question of authorship has great bearing on the trustworthiness and credibility of the book itself. If 1 Peter 1:1 is not true, for example, how do we know 3:21 is?

B. Arguments for Peter's Authorship

Internal Evidences. (1) The letter is signed by "Peter, an apostle of Jesus Christ" (1:1). In view of the fact that the book claims to have been written by the apostle Peter, to say it was written by another (for example, that it is a "pseudonymous writing") is to say that the book is a forgery, and of spurious character, and of doubtful value.[44] Either 1:1 is true, or it is false. Certain modern scholars say it is false, and thus cast doubt on the whole of the book's contents. But this is opposite of all historical evidence (see below, External Evidences). In addition to signing the letter, the author calls himself "an apostle of Jesus Christ," an "elder and eyewitness of the sufferings of Christ" (5:1); he speaks of a dear one, Mark, as being with him (5:13), and he writes with the help of Silvanus (5:12).[45]

---

[43] Genuineness is a technical term dealing with authorship. A book is considered genuine if it was written by the person whose name it bears. 1 Peter is genuine only if the apostle Peter wrote it, since that is the name that appears on the letter at 1 Peter 1:1.

[44] Donald Guthrie, *New Testament Introduction* (Downers Grove, IL : InterVarsity, 1970), p.786-790, and in an appendix on "Epistolary Pseudepigraphy," p.671-684, has pointed out some of the serious problems inherent in any view of pseudonymous authorship.

[45] Ever since higher criticism has been a method of Bible study, the authorship of Bible books has been questioned and genuineness jettisoned for many of them. Our refusal to be swayed by much of what higher criticism says follows along these lines: In dealing with any ancient writing, the writer is at the outset assumed to be intelligent and straightforward. His statements of matters ostensibly lying within his knowledge, and particularly any affirmations about himself or his activities, are regarded as reliable. The given literary work is further studied for internal consistency; the writings of contemporary or later authors are scanned for direct references to this author or his work, and for possible allusions to it, quotations from it, or other evidence of their acquaintance with it. (In due time, in these Introductory Studies, we shall look at allusions, quotations, and canonical listings for 1 Peter.) The original assumption of genuineness and accuracy is not properly altered or denied unless these further studies reveal very compelling evidence to the contrary. Compelling evidence against Peter's being the author has not been produced.

(2) In the letter are expressions and terms that show the writer was a companion of Jesus during His personal ministry on earth. Examples: (a) Many writers feel that Jesus' statement to Peter, "You are Peter (*petros*) and upon this rock (*petra*) I will build My church" (Matthew 16:18), is the statement that caused Peter later to describe Jesus as "the chief cornerstone" of a spiritual house wherein His followers are "living stones" (1 Peter 2:4-8). (b) In an object lesson on humility, Peter had seen his Lord gird himself with a towel and wash His disciples' feet (John 13:1-9), and in this letter (5:5) Peter bids Christians to tie humility on themselves like a slave's apron. (c) Jesus often used the word adversary to denote one's opponent (Matthew 5:25; Luke 12:58, 18:3) and this word readily found its way into Peter's vocabulary (1 Peter 5:8). (d) Peter witnessed the Lord's submission to the shame of Pilate's judgment hall and the crucifixion, and he writes with feeling of Him who "while being reviled, He did not revile in return; while suffering, He uttered no threats, but kept entrusting *Himself* to Him who judges righteously" (1 Peter 2:23). (e) He had seen the ragged timber on which the Lord died, and to him it was a "tree" (*xulon*) on which the Savior bore our sins (1 Peter 2:24 KJV). (f) Three times bidden to feed the flock of God (John 21:15-17), Peter came to regard Jesus as "the Shepherd and guardian of souls" (1 Peter 2: 25). (g) In 1 Peter 1:19 we have Christ described as "a lamb unblemished and spotless," which reminds us that Peter was present when John the Baptist pointed out Jesus with the words, "Behold, the Lamb of God who takes away the sin of the world!" (John 1:29).[46] These indications of the author's personal experiences with Jesus are woven into the very warp and woof of 1 Peter and are indications of genuineness, which would be impossible for a forger or an imitator to have achieved. In verse after verse of the book we see vividly portrayed the influence of events in the public ministry of Jesus in which Peter participated, or at which he was present.

(3) There is a similarity existing in the language and teaching of 1 Peter and the speeches of Peter as recorded in the book of Acts. Examples: (a) The reference to the Father as judging "without respect of persons" (1 Peter 1:17) recalls Peter's earlier word to Cornelius and the group of Gentiles in his house (Acts 10:34). (b) The allusions to God as having raised Christ from the dead (1 Peter 1:21) remind one of the apostle's characteristic resurrection witness in Acts (2:32, 3:15, 10:40). (c) The proclamation of Christ as Isaiah's prophetically seen "chief cornerstone" (1 Peter 2:7,8) is very similar to Peter's words to the Sanhedrin (Acts 4:11). (d) A number of other analogies could be highlighted – compare 1 Peter 1:10-12 with Acts 3:18; compare 1 Peter 1:20 with Acts 2:23; compare 1 Peter 2:4 with Acts 4:11; compare 1 Peter 3:22 with Acts 2:33-34. (e) Compare the distinctive term *xulon* ("tree") in 1 Peter 2:4 with Acts 5:30 and 10:39. This harmony of language is indicative that the same Peter whose sermons are recorded in Acts is the one who is the writer of 1 Peter.

[46] Other fruitful comparisons include: 1 Peter 3:9 with Matthew 5:10-12 and Luke 6:22; 1 Peter 3:14, 3:17, 4:14; 1 Peter 1:13 with Matthew 5:10-12 and Luke 6:22; 1 Peter 2:12 with Matthew 5:16; 1 Peter 4:10 with Luke 12:42. See further, R. H. Gundry, "'Verba Christi' in 1 Peter: Their Implications Concerning the Authorship of 1 Peter and the Authenticity of the Gospel Tradition," *NTS* 13 (1966/67), p.336-50.

(4) Barclay has argued that the epistle shows evidences of coming from an early date (i.e., not 2nd century), and this points to the truthfulness of the signature which names Peter as the writer. Barclay calls attention to the simplicity of church organization (i.e., elders [5:1] are congregational leaders; there is no reference to "bishops" as distinct from elders such as are later found in Ignatius' letters in the first half of the 2nd century), and argues that this simplicity is strong evidence that the letter was not written at the late date suggested by some theologically liberal scholars.[47]

External evidences for the Petrine authorship of 1 Peter. External evidence for the existence and acceptance of 1 Peter as authoritative for the church comes from early Christian literature, books written by Christians between AD 96 and AD 325.

(1) Allusions and quotations.[48] Clement of Rome (AD 96) speaks of "the precious blood of Christ" (1 Cl. vii). This unusual phrase may well come from Peter's statement that we are redeemed by the precious blood of Christ (1 Peter 1:19).[49] Polycarp (AD 115) continuously quotes Peter, although he does not mention him by name. In his letter to the Philippians 2:1, Polycarp quotes 1 Peter 1:13,21, about "girding up the loins of your mind" and about "believing in God who raised Jesus from the dead and gave Him glory." In Philippians 8:1, Polycarp quotes 1 Peter 2:22,24 about how "Jesus bore our sins in His body on the cross" and "nor was any deceit found no guile." In 10:2, Polycarp alludes to 1 Peter 2:12, "keep your behavior excellent among the Gentiles." There are similar types of allusions in the Epistle of Barnabas (AD 130), the Didache (AD 140), the Shepherd of Hermas

---

47 Wm. Barclay ("The Letters of Peter," in *Daily Study Bible* [Philadelphia: Westminster, 1960], p.166) argues that the theology reflected in 1 Peter is the theology of the early church. While this is true, the argument used by Barclay to establish his claims has some serious flaws. As a Neo-liberal, Barclay tends to find three levels of material in our New Testaments -- what Jesus said and did (of which we know very little), what the apostles said and did (of which we know very little), and what the early church believed and taught (which makes up the bulk of our New Testament writings). So embedded in our books, in Barclay's thinking, is not only *kerygma* (the apostolic preaching) but also *didache* (the teaching of the early church). Barclay even has a neat five-point summary of what he perceives to be *kerygma*, the early preaching, and then he shows that both in Acts and 1 Peter the "preaching" matches; thus, 1 Peter is an early book. To postulate, as liberals do, that the apostles improved on Jesus, and that the early church improved on the apostles, and that we must carefully work our way through the New Testament books to identify what is *kerygma* and what is *didache*, is a frontal attack on the inspiration of the books, and a denial that there is any definitive, absolute doctrine to be found in those books. The results of such a method of Bible study are entirely unsatisfactory!

48 There are several types of testimony concerning the New Testament books to be found in early Christian literature. *Allusions* are references that prove the book exists. Such allusions may be ideas or language used that parallels or even paraphrases what one finds in the New Testament books. *Quotations* are references that quote a Bible text verbatim, but do not mention the author, or the Bible text may be found in more than one book. *Annotated quotations* are references that quote the text giving either or both the book and the author's name. *Canonical listings* show the book is considered to be canonical and is so designated. It must be remembered in consulting the earliest Christian writers for information, that it was not their custom to quote any books of the New Testament with scrupulous accuracy, or to name writers. In addressing the heathen, such a process would have been utterly useless, and in addressing Christians familiar with the apostolic writings, it was needless.

49 In addition, 1 Clement xxxvi has the words "marvelous light" which remind us of 1 Peter 2:9.

(AD 125),[50] and in Theophilus of Antioch (compare *ad Autolycum* ii.34 with 1 Peter 2:11, 1:18, 4:2). Eusebius tells us that Papias quoted this epistle in writings no longer extant (Eusebius, *H.E.*, iii.39, iv.14).

(2) Annotated quotations. Irenaeus (AD 180) is the first to quote 1 Peter by name. He twice quotes 1 Peter 1:8, "though you have not seen Him, you love Him, and though you do not see Him now, but believe in Him, you rejoice greatly with joy inexpressible," and he once quotes 1 Peter 2:16 with its command not to use liberty as a cloak for maliciousness.[51] Clement of Alexandria (AD 190) quotes 1 Peter 1:21, 2:11, 3:14-17, 4:12-14 as being by Peter,[52] and wrote a commentary on 1 Peter.[53] Tertullian (AD 200) identified Peter as the author of 1 Peter 2:20.[54] Origen (AD 210), in a Commentary on Psalm 3, quotes 1 Peter 3:19 and attributes it to Peter.

(3) Canonical listings. It was one of the books whose authority had never been disputed, says Origen.[55] Eusebius placed it among the canonical Scriptures which are universally acknowledged.[56] He records no evidence that the early church had any doubts concerning the Petrine authorship of 1 Peter. He explicitly says, "it was anciently used by the ancient fathers in their writings, as an undoubted work of the apostle."[57]

Internal and external evidence both point to Peter the apostle as the human author of this letter. The evidence for the genuineness of 1 Peter is of such quality as to be among the strongest of all the books of the New Testament.[58]

The patristic evidence establishes that 1 Peter was known and used as an authoritative work before the close of the first century. True, no writer names the author until Iraneus,

---

[50] *Didache* i.4 reads *apechou ton sarkikon kai somatikon epithumon*, which is very likely an allusion to 1 Peter 2:11. Hermas, *Vis.* IV.iii.4 reads *hosper gar to chrusion dokimadzetai dia tou puros kai euchreston ginetai houtos kai humeis k.t.l.*, which may be a reflection of 1 Peter 1:7, but also could come from Proverbs 17:3. Barnabas, xvi.10 has *touto estin pneumatikos naos oikodomoumenos to kurio*, which may be a reminiscence of 1 Peter 2:5.

[51] *Adv. Haer.* iv.9.2, iv.16.

[52] *Stromata* iii.11, iii.18, iv.7,20. In another work, *Paedag.* i.6, Clement quotes 1 Peter 2:1-3 as being by Peter. He often quotes 1 Peter with the introductory formula "Peter says ...."

[53] Eusebius. *H.E.*, vi.14.

[54] *Scorpiac*, chap. 12 and ch. 14.

[55] In the passage on the canon, as reported by Eusebius, *H.E.*, vi.25.

[56] Eusebius. *H.E.*, iii.25.

[57] Eusebius. *H.E.*, iii.3.

[58] Perhaps only for 1 Corinthians is the evidence of genuineness (that the writer to whom it is attributed wrote it) stronger.

but the very fact the epistle was used so early as an authoritative work without naming its author may well indicate its Petrine authorship was accepted as self-evident.

C. Arguments raised against the Petrine authorship of 1 Peter

Attacks against the Petrine authorship commenced with F. C. Baur (1762-1860), leader of the "Tubingen School" of German radical biblical criticism. Through the years critics have pointed to several anomalies they believe mitigate against Peter being the author of 1 Peter. It is needful to list them and evaluate them.

1) The excellent Greek in which 1 Peter is written. How could a fisherman from Galilee produce such excellent Greek, it is questioned. The Greek of 2 Peter is rugged, while the Greek of 1 Peter is excellent Greek, a fact almost universally acknowledged.[59] Greek was a participle loving language, and good Greek usage relies heavily on the use of participles. 1 Peter abounds in these, and the vocabulary is rich. Various avenues have been pursued in an attempt to explain the good Greek. (a) The letter as it now stands is a translation of an Aramaic original. Peter would have written in Aramaic, and someone else translated it using the excellent Greek we now see in our manuscripts. However, the fact is that the letter was written in Greek; the adjectives alone found in the book are sufficient disproof that it is a translation from an Aramaic original. (b) Galilee was bi-lingual, and Peter must have known enough Greek to carry on his fishing business. James, the Lord's brother, was never out of Palestine, yet he writes excellent Greek in his epistle. Matthew's Greek is better than most, and Matthew was a Galilean. Peter's brother bore a Greek name. No Galilean middle-class person would have been ignorant of the Greek language, it can be argued. Why should it simply be assumed that Peter could not write or speak good Greek?[60] (c) Another hypothesis is that the letter itself supplies its own solution to this problem in 1 Peter 5:12, "by Silvanus ... I have written briefly." The Greek means that Silas was Peter's agent, his instrument, his secretary, in writing this letter. It is claimed by proponents of this

---

[59] F.W. Beare (*The First Epistle of Peter* [Oxford: Blackwell, 1970], p.47) wrote, "The epistle is quite obviously the work of a man of letters, skilled in all the devices of rhetoric, and able to draw on an extensive, and even learned, vocabulary. He is a stylist of no ordinary capacity, and he writes some of the best Greek in the whole New Testament, far smoother and more literary than that of the highly-trained Paul." J. B. Mayor (*The Epistles of Jude and 2 Peter* [Grand Rapids: Baker, 1965], p.civ) said, "1 Peter has no equal in the New Testament for sustained stateliness of rhythm." Barclay (*op. cit.*, p.169-70) concludes by saying, "The Greek of 1 Peter is not entirely unworthy to be set beside the Greek of the masters of the Greek language. It is difficult, if not impossible, to imagine Peter using the Greek language like that."

[60] Certain other "evidences" have been alluded to in an effort to show Peter could not speak or write Greek. Papias says "Mark was Peter's interpreter" (Eusebius, *H.E.*, iii.39.15). "Interpreter" is taken to mean "translator," and the argument is made that Peter habitually preached in Aramaic, and Mark had to translate into Greek or Latin, whatever the needs of the audience. This argument may affirm too much. What is there to prohibit Peter from preaching in Greek, and Mark translating it into Latin because that was the vernacular of Peter's Roman audience? On a conservative dating of 1 Peter, an interval of more than 30 years separated Peter the fisherman from Peter the writer. Who can measure what facility he could have achieved in Greek over so long a period of time? In fact, there were Hellenistic Jews in Jerusalem who were unfamiliar with Aramaic. Thus, during the early years of Peter's work there among the Hellenists, he would have needed to use Greek. And then as he began to work in the Greek Diaspora, would he not have needed to cultivate its use more intensively, if he had not learned it already while still living in Galilee?

theory that Silas was more proficient in Greek than Peter was. That is an assumption, since we do not have a single line extant by Silas other than what is claimed for him in 1 Peter. We do know that Silas was one of the "leading men among the brethren" at the Jerusalem Conference (Acts 15:22), and he is styled as a "prophet" (i.e., one who could speak by inspiration, Acts 15:32). Some have affirmed that Peter dictated in rough Greek (like that found in 2 Peter) and Silas corrected and polished Peter's words as he wrote on papyrus what Peter said. Others have pictured Peter as telling Silas in general terms what he wanted written, leaving it to Silas to put the actual words into writing.[61] Peter would approve the finished product, and add the last personal paragraph to it. Thus 1 Peter reflects Silas' proficiency in Greek, while 2 Peter reflects Peter's actual ability with the language. Whichever option we adopt, the excellence of the Greek in 1 Peter, while admitted, does not prove to us to be an insuperable barrier to believing that Peter is the source of what is contained in the letter.

2) The lack of annotated quotations of 1 Peter till the 2nd century is a second evidence used to dispute the Petrine authorship. Because of this alleged paucity of evidence, Barclay has theorized that the letter made its appearance after Peter's death, and was not actually written by the apostle Peter. He argues that Eusebius' citation of earlier writers who held the Petrine authorship actually implies there were those in Eusebius' day who doubted the genuineness of 1 Peter, just as Barclay himself does. Barclay then calls attention to the fact that very few writers in the West or in Rome quote the book, and you'd expect it to be quoted in the West if Peter wrote it from Rome. He notes that Tertullian, for example, who labored in the West, has 7,258 quotes of Scripture in his extant writings, and only 2 are from 1 Peter. Barclay also appeals to the absence of 1 Peter from the Muratorian Canon (AD 170), which, he insists, was the official list of books accepted as Scripture by the Roman church. 1 Peter, he believes, was omitted, because it was not apostolic in authorship. (Of course, to affirm this, he must deny the truthfulness of 1 Peter 1:1). Barclay adds another argument to bolster his case: 1 Peter was not included in the Old Syriac Version. Syriac was one of the first languages into which at least some of the Christian Greek Scriptures were translated. Some of the first books to be so translated were translated by Tatian, who went from Rome to Syria, about AD 150. His omission of 1 Peter, Barclay argues, is precisely because the church at Rome rejected the Petrine authorship. This argument is not precisely in accordance with the known facts,[62] and should not be given much weight.

---

[61] Either way, we have not impinged on the inspiration of 1 Peter. If the apostle Peter dictated it, there is every reason to affirm its inspiration. If, on the other hand, Silas did the actual wording, we can still affirm the inspiration of the letter, since Silas was a prophet. (Some have used 1 Thessalonians. 2:6 to prove that Silas was an "apostle" of Jesus, just like Paul was, and in this way they can affirm the inspiration of any letter written by Silas.)

[62] B. F. Westcott, in his book *A General Survey of the History of the Canon of the New Testament* (London: Macmillan, 1870), p.221, teaches that 1 Peter was included in the Old Syriac. Further, perhaps all Tatian did was translate the four gospels into Syriac (the *Diatessaron*). If that is the case, what Tatian did would provide exactly no evidence on what epistles were or were not in the Syriac Canon. The argument from "paucity of evidence" and "number of quotations" is misleading. See above on pages xi-xii for allusions and quotations of 1 Peter, and the strong evidential value of these allusions and quotations.

3) The resemblance to the epistles of Paul, it is postulated, suggests 1 Peter was not written during the apostle Peter's lifetime. It is true there are "Paulinisms," resemblances and similarities to Romans and Ephesians, as well as resemblances to James.[63] Higher critics like Barclay insist the letters of Paul were not collected until about AD 90; so if 1 Peter is written in AD 66 or so, how did he know Ephesians? But if someone other than Peter wrote the letter about the turn of the century, these resemblances to and quotes of other epistles is explainable.[64] The alleged dependence of 1 Peter on the Pauline epistles should not be overdrawn. "In the case of Romans as in that of Ephesians, the resemblances to 1 Peter are quite superficial, attaching only to current commonplaces."[65] The agreements are nothing more than evidence of a shared Christian tradition, independently cited by two writers. When the argument is examined in detail, the alleged "Paulinisms" of 1 Peter are not convincing evidence against its Petrine origin.

4) The supposed lack of an occasion behind the letter. This argument against the Petrine authorship depends on the affirmation that we can find no persecution in Peter's time that would provide an occasion for such a letter from him. However, a brief review of early history shows there was indeed just such an occasion as 1 Peter implies. There was a time when Christians had little to fear from the Roman government. When Rome conquered a foreign land, they allowed the people to keep all the old religions (*religio licita*), but they could introduce no new ones (*religio illicita*). For some time, the Romans regarded the Christians as a Jewish sect; therefore, Christianity was a *religio licita*. But a change came in the days of Nero. Rome burned in July of AD 64. By October of AD 64 blame had been put on the Christians. The people who had lost all their possessions were bitter against Nero, who was rumored to have started the fire, so Nero needed a scapegoat. The Christians were

---

63 Compare 1 Peter 1:3 and Ephesians 1:3, or 1 Peter 1:13 and Ephesians 6:14, or 1 Peter 1:20 and Ephesians 1:4, or 1 Peter 3:22 and Ephesians 1:20,21. Further, the injunctions to slaves, husbands and wives in 1 Peter 2:18-20 and Ephesians 6:5-9 are very similar. The point that critics are trying to make is that 1 Peter is quoting Ephesians.

64 There are replies to all these allegations. (1) In order for Barclay to hold his AD 90 date for the collection of Paul's letters, he must arbitrarily deny the Petrine authorship of 2 Peter also – for 2 Peter 3:16 speaks of a collection of Paul's letters. If Peter wrote 2 Peter, then at least some Paul's letters are collected before Paul and Peter died in AD 68. (2) Peter and Paul were in Rome together (says early Christian literature). Why couldn't Peter have seen a copy of Paul's letters, especially his letter to the Romans (already a treasured possession of the church at Rome as early as AD 58)? Ephesians (in this commentator's judgment) was addressed to the churches of Asia Minor, one of the same provinces to which Peter is writing. Is there a problem with Peter getting a copy of the letter from Paul to see what Paul had written to the same audience? In fact, in 2 Peter 3:16, Peter indicates he has recently read some of Paul's letters. Why should not apostles study the writings of other apostles as Daniel the prophet had studied the writings of other prophets (Daniel 9:2)? Or why could not the Holy Spirit have inspired both Peter and Paul to write similar things (thus Peter need not ever have seen Paul's letters). (3) The injunctions to slaves, husbands, and wives were part of the standard ethical teaching of the church, given to all converts in all congregations. Peter need not be borrowing or plagiarizing from Paul.

65 Charles Bigg, *A Critical and Exegetical Commentary on the Epistles of St. Peter and St. Jude* (Edinburgh: T & T Clark), p.20. The affinities between Paul's writings and Peter's are not close enough to prove copying (literary dependence).

it.[66] After all, did not the Christians speak of a coming day when the world would be destroyed by fire? The persecution against them began at Rome and then spread to many of the provinces. In some places nothing would happen to the Christians for months. Then some spark might set off the explosion, and the persecution with its terror would begin. That is the situation behind 1 Peter.

5) A slight modification of the last objection says that the description of the persecutions one finds in 1 Peter reflect a date too late for Peter the apostle to have written this book. The references to persecution and suffering, so prominent in 1 Peter, have been studied closely by scholars to see how they correspond with what is known from history about the persecutions of the early Christians. Shirlesy Jackson Case distinguished three principal waves of persecution against the Christians: one occurring in the reign of Nero (AD 54-68), one in the reign of Domitian (AD 81-96), and one in the reign of Trajan (AD 98-117).[67] The one in the reign of Domitian does not fit 1 Peter, since sacrifices to the emperor are not mentioned in 1 Peter as a problem confronting the Christians. If this epistle had been written during Domitian's persecution that well-known, grave issue could not have been passed over (cf. Martial, *Epigrams*, 13:4, Pliny the Younger, *Epistle* 10, 96:5). In the persecution of Trajan, there is no doubt that Christians were liable to punishment and persecution for no

---

[66] Tacitus, *Annals* 15:44 wrote, "Neither human assistance in the shape of imperial gifts, nor attempts to appease the gods, could remove the sinister report that the fire was due to Nero's own orders. So, in hope of dissipating the rumor, he falsely diverted the charge on to a set of people to whom the vulgar gave the name Christians, and who were detested for the abominations they perpetuated. The founder of the sect, one Christus by name, had been executed by Pontius Pilate in the reign of Tiberius; and the dangerous superstition, though put down for the moment, broke out again, not only in Judea, the original home of the pest, but even in Rome, where everything shameful and horrible collects and is practiced." Tacitus tells us that a huge multitude of Christians perished, and perished in the most sadistic ways. "Mockery of every sort was added to their deaths. Covered with the skins of beasts, they were torn by dogs and perished, or were nailed to crosses, and were doomed to the flames and burned, to serve as a nightly illumination, when daylight had expired. Nero offered his gardens for this spectacle, and was exhibiting a show in the circus, which he mingled with the people in the dress of a charioteer, or stood aloft on a car. Hence, even for criminals who deserve extreme and exemplary punishment, there arose a feeling of compassion; for, it was not, as it seemed, for the public good, but to glut one man's cruelty that they were being destroyed."

The same terrible story is told by the later Christian historian, Sulipicius Severus, in his *Chronicle*. "In the meantime, the number of Christians being now very large, it happened that Rome was destroyed by fire, while Nero was stationed at Antium. But the opinion of all cast the odium of causing the fire upon the emperor, and he was believed in this way to have sought for the glory of building a new city. And, in fact, Nero could not, by any means he tried, escape from the charge that the fire had been caused by his orders. He, therefore, turned the accusation against the Christians, and the most cruel tortures were accordingly afflicted upon the innocent. Nay, even new kinds of death were invented, so that, being covered in the skins of wild beasts, they perished by being devoured by dogs, while many were crucified, or slain by fire, and not a few were set apart for this purpose, that when the day came to a close, they should be consumed to serve for light during the night." (Quoted by Barclay, *op. cit.*, p.177-78.)

[67] See his "Peter, Epistles of," in *Hasting's Dictionary of the Apostolic Church* (Grand Rapids: Baker, 1973), p.201-209.

other reason than that they were Christians (remember what 1 Peter 4:16 says).[68] But there is more information in 1 Peter about the persecution Peter's readers faced than 4:12-16. In those other passages, 1 Peter does not reflect the systematic persecution of Trajan's time.[69] Instead one sees the state of things as might be expected to exist in the provinces as a result of the Neronian persecution which began in AD 64.[70]

6) Its meager references to the Holy Spirit are used by Beare as another objection to apostolic authorship. He alleges that an important leader of the church, writing about the moral life of Christians without paying attention to the transforming power of the Holy Spirit, is impossible to believe. Hiebert replies to this by calling attention to the fact that letters admitted even by the critics to have been written by Paul have fewer references to the Holy Spirit than does 1 Peter. For example, Colossians has but one passing reference (1:8), 2 Thessalonians has but one (2:13), whereas there are four references in 1 Peter (1:2, 1:11, 1:12, and 4:14).

7) Its alleged lack of personal reminiscences. Kummel has flatly asserted 1 Peter contains no evidence at all that the writer was familiar with the earthly Jesus, His life, His

---

[68] F.W. Beare, *op. cit.*, p.26ff, advocates the idea that the persecution reflected in 1 Peter 4:12-16 is that of Trajan, and therefore the apostolic authorship has been compromised. Pliny's letters 96 and 97 to Trajan show that all one had to do to be led away to execution was to answer in the affirmative when Pliny asked them if they were Christians. Pliny asks if he were following the correct procedure, and Trajan replies that he was, and that anyone who denied he was a Christian should be asked to prove it by sacrificing to the gods. Upon such a sacrifice, they were immediately to be set free.

[69] Unlike how the persecution was going in Rome, Peter writes at a time before any systematic persecution was taking place in the provinces. For there was a possibility the Christians might disarm the fury of their persecutors by an innocent and upright life (1 Peter 3:13). There was room for hope that their good living in Christ might shame their persecutors (3:16). It was still possible to describe the Roman governors in the provinces as being "sent by Him for the punishment of evildoers, and the praise of those who do right" (2:14).

[70] All we know of the Neronian persecution is derived from the somewhat rhetorical account in Tacitus (quoted above, footnote #66), one brief sentence in Suetonius (*Nero* 16), and the allusion in 1 Clement 6:1. From these references it will not do to say that in Nero's time Christians suffered not as Christians but as those who were accused and found guilty of crime (arson). Nor may it be said that by the time of Trajan, the grounds on which Christians were condemned to suffer had changed from [allegedly] being guilty of criminal activity to simply being Christians. It seems rather evident that in Nero's time Christians suffered because of their religion. The reasons for this view include: (1) It would have ill-suited Nero's position to throw the blame of the great fire on persons who would have to be proven guilty of incendiarism before they were punished. By accusing the Christians, Nero could argue they were guilty of *religio illicita*. He had legal grounds for action, with no special edict needed, and no trial needed to prove their complicity in the burning of Rome. (2) The language of Tacitus is quite consistent with, even if it does not require, this interpretation of the situation. Thus, in regard to the clause "primum correpti qui fatebantur," the whole context refutes the idea that the confession was of incendiarism. The meaning can only be "fatebantur *se esse Christianis*." The admission of Christianity was the turning point in their case. (3) The words of Suetonius ("afflicti suppliciis Christiani, genus hominum superstitionis nouae ac maleficae") are most naturally interpreted as asserting that Christians suffered as *Christians*. If Nero was the first to act on the essential illegality of the Christian religion, and in fact stamped Christianity as illegal, Suetonius had good reason for placing (as he does) his notice of the fact among the various police regulations. (4) It is difficult to suppose that the *ingens multitudo* (cf. *polu plethos*, Clement), including, according to Clement, matrons and girls and slaves, were one and all convicted of criminal actions. But they could well all be condemned as participants in an illegal religion, especially in a time of excitement and panic.

teaching, or His death. Kummel then urges that if Peter wrote this book, you would expect personal reminiscences.[71] The only reply one can make to Kummel is that his claim is simply false. As many as thirty-two passages in 1 Peter are equivalents to the teachings of Jesus or reflect some event in His life that was witnessed by the author of 1 Peter. Instead of saying there is a lack of personal reminiscences, what should be said is that only an eyewitness like Peter could have managed to reflect so much of the life and teaching of Jesus in such a brief letter of exhortation and encouragement.

8) Its quotations from the Septuagint. Kummel also has made this objection, thinking it inconceivable for a Galilean fisherman to have written 1 Peter since the quotations and allusions to the Old Testament without exception are taken from LXX. This objection relies on the assumption that the LXX was not that well known or used in the land of Israel, an assumption that is simply contrary to all evidence. The quotations of the Old Testament in *Hebrews*, a book written to people in the land of Israel, are regularly taken from the LXX. Greek speaking members of the church at Jerusalem certainly were familiar with that version. James, the Lord's brother, who was as much Galilean as Peter, used the LXX when addressing the Jerusalem Conference (Acts 15:15-18). And years later, Justin Martyr, who grew up in Samaria, used the LXX entirely in his writings.

Most of the objections raised against the Petrine authorship of 1 Peter, with the exception of the objection regarding the good Greek of 1 Peter, appear to be unfounded attempts to invent any kind of plausible evidence to support a preconceived theory – namely, that the statement of 1 Peter 1:1 cannot be taken at face value.

D. The alternatives to the Petrine authorship are not credible.

One alternative suggested by those who reject Peter as the author is to affirm that the letter was "pseudonymous;" that is, whoever penned it wrote under a pseudonym.[72] Appeal to support this alternative is found by calling attention to the fact that New Testament apocryphal and pseudepigraphical writings were "signed" by famous men long dead, i.e., they are pseudonymous. The heretics who wrote those works deliberately attached the name of

---

[71] W. G. Kummel, *Introduction to the New Testament* (New York: Abingdon, 1966), p.424.

[72] Beare, who categorically states that "Peter" is a pseudonym, attempts to show there was no fraud involved or intended in using a false name. He dates the letter after Peter's death, and says, "The Christians of Asia Minor must have known that Peter was long since dead ... They would recognize the pseudonym for what it was -- an accepted and harmless literary device ..." (*op. cit.*, p.48). Instead of Christians knowingly accepting pseudonymity, what happened to the author of the *Acts of Paul and Thecla* (he was excommunicated and his work rejected) shows that exactly the opposite was true in the church. That such leaders as Polycarp and Papias would attribute the letter to Peter if they knew it was written long after the apostle's death, and written by someone else, impinges on their truthfulness and Christian character. Those early church leaders were keenly conscious of the unbridgeable difference between the original apostles and men like themselves who were not apostles. Is 1 Peter the only exception to this rule? Who can believe it?

some famous person to give their heresy more credibility. In the case of those books, the name "signed" on the books was a deliberate lie. Are we ready to say 1 Peter 1:1 is a deliberate lie? How has it happened that what was true of apocryphal and pseudepigraphical writings is now said to have happened to canonical writings, too? Have we lowered the books of Scripture to nothing more than fiction?

Since the pseudonymous alternative has failed to command scholarly acceptance, another has been suggested. 1 Peter was at one time a sermon that began with 1:3, and to which someone attached an epistolary opening. Of course, we do not know whose sermon it was, so 1 Peter is really anonymous. The theory is that in the second century when the canon was forming, someone attached Peter's name to the sermon to insure its inclusion in the canon. This is also said to explain why 1 Peter was alluded to in early Christian literature, but was not known to them as Petrine. Several errors have been propounded in the attempt to establish this alternative. The idea that the canon was not formed until the second century is false. Books were accepted as genuine and apostolic the moment they were first received. What was happening in the second century was the guarding of the canon. Books that did not pass apostolic authorship were excluded from the list of accepted inspired books. No one dared add an epistolary beginning to Hebrews. Why would we think someone would try it for 1 Peter? The "spin" or twist put on the evidence from early Christian literature almost depends on the listener being ignorant that what is true of 1 Peter – i.e., no annotated quotations until late in the second century – is true of most all the New Testament books, even those admitted by the critics to be genuine Pauline letters.[73] Only if we know of no other reasons for the absence of an annotated quotation until late will we accept the suggestion that the absence of annotation proves anonymity. There is no manuscript evidence of 1 Peter without the epistolary framework (i.e., no copy has been found with 1:1-3 and 5:12-14 missing). Further, the idea that these verses were added later is contradicted by the clear points of connection found in the opening and closing verses with the body of the letter itself.[74]

E. Conclusion concerning authorship

Peter, the apostle of Jesus, is the author of this letter as internal and external evidence affirms. Silas was the human penman, writing as Peter directed him to write.

---

[73] Clement of Rome alluded to as many as 22 books (not just 1 Peter) of the New Testament without identifying the source by name. Did he not know Paul was the author of many of these? Is it not more plausible to state that Clement accepted the authorship of the books he quoted as being self-evident to his readers?

[74] The openings and endings of 1st century letters regularly alluded to the contents of the body of the letter. This is true of 1 Peter, too. To see it, compare 1:2 with 1:17; 2:11 with 4:12. If the original writing had no allusion to Silvanus and Mark, why bring them into the picture, and why in a letter attributed to Peter, when those workers are known (from Paul's letters) to be Paul's helpers?

V. PLACE OF WRITING

1 Peter 5:13 is the verse that must be interpreted in order to settle the question of place of writing. The verse reads "She (the church, KJV) who is in Babylon,[75] chosen (elected, KJV) together with you, sends you greetings (salutes you, KJV), and *so does* my son, Mark." From this it is clear that Peter was in a place called "Babylon," but there has been no little difference of opinion as to what place is thus designated. Is the word "Babylon" to be explained figuratively or literally?

Two different places of writing have been suggested by those who take the term literally.

A. Babylon in Egypt

There was a Babylon situated in lower Egypt, located near the present Cairo. It began as a refugee settlement by folk fleeing the Assyrians, and the refugees gave their new settlement the name of the city from which they had come. During the first century AD, it was a Roman military garrison, an army camp on the frontier. The Coptic church has an old tradition that Peter wrote from this place in Egypt. In addition, Eusebius tells us that Mark brought Christianity to Alexandria and established churches there.[76]

It is the opinion of this commentator that Babylon in Egypt is not a very live possibility as to the place from which our letter was written. While it might be possible to show Mark was in Egypt, it is difficult to believe that Peter, Silas, and Mark all were together at that frontier camp at the same time. There is no evidence of a church in this place in Egypt for the first four centuries. If so, who is the "she who is in Babylon" if there were no congregation there? There is no traditional support for Peter's residence in this Egyptian place. His name is never connected with Egypt in early Christian literature. The evidence is so weak that few scholars adopt the Egyptian hypothesis.

B. Babylon in Mesopotamia

This view has in its favor the fact that we can take the name "Babylon" literally.[77] For

---

[75] The Greek text, with the exception of Sinaiticus and a few other manuscripts (which read "the church in Babylon"), reads simply "the co-elect (something feminine singular) in Babylon." The Latin Vulgate and the Peshitto Syriac also read "the church in Babylon." The probable meaning of this is discussed in notes at 1 Peter 5:13.

[76] Eusebius, *H.E.*, ii.16.

[77] It is a favorite among Protestants, Calvin and Erasmus among them. One supposes part of its popularity stems from the fact it helps keep Peter away from Rome, and thus weakens the claims for Peter's papacy. One must be careful lest arguments are embraced because they are self-serving, whether Coptic or Protestant or Catholic.

this hypothesis to become viable it is necessary to get both Peter and Mark to Babylon. Can that be done? Proponents believe it can, for the following reasons: (1) The order of the provinces addressed (1 Peter 1:1) is from east to west – the natural order of delivery for a letter coming from the Euphrates region. (2) "Babylon" must be taken literally since the use of the term as a figurative designation for Rome or Jerusalem was a later development.[78] (3) It is possible to have John Mark in Babylon at the time Peter wrote.[79] (4) Proponents of this theory say it is possible that Peter did journey to Babylon.[80]

Each of the reasons for taking "Babylon" literally has been answered by those who reject this interpretation of 1 Peter 5:13. (1) The regions addressed actually are a circuit – you start in the north and end up in the north. The most usual route from Babylon would have been what was called the southern route, and someone traveling by that route would have delivered the letter in a different order than 1:1 lists the provinces. (2) The argument that Peter used terms literally is not true 100% of the time. He describes the devil as a "lion" and he calls Mark his "son," which is hardly to be taken literally. If in chapter 5 there already is figurative language, why can't "Babylon" be taken figuratively, too? (3) This commentator feels there is much less chance that the reconstruction of Mark's travels that takes him (and Peter) to Babylon is correct, than the reconstruction required by the hypothesis that 1 Peter is written from Rome, and that Mark is there. (4) Peter, the apostle to the circumcision, had little need to go to Babylon, for Babylon on the Euphrates, during the days of Peter's life, had no Jews living there. The Jews were driven out about AD 40.[81] Jews from the area around Babylon were present at Pentecost (Acts 2:9) and there was a synagogue there as late as AD 36. But toward the end of the reign of Caligula (d. AD 41), the Jewish colony in Babylon

---

[78] J. Ramsay Michaels ("1 Peter," in *Word Biblical Commentary* [Waco, TX: Word, 1988], p.lxiii, 311) argued that "Babylon" was not applied figuratively to Rome until after AD 70, when because of the Roman destruction of Jerusalem the Jewish people (remembering what Babylon did to Jerusalem in 586 BC) would have some reason to speak in similar pejorative language of Rome. In reply to Michaels, there is little, if any, Jewish or Christian literature from the pre-AD 70 first-century period. This makes an argument from the use or non-use of "Babylon" less significant. The earliest use of "Babylon" in a figurative sense for Rome in early Christian writers is Tertullian (AD 200). Jerome also used "Babylon" figuratively for Rome, about AD 385. (This is documented in the *Bible Commentary* edited by Cook on "Revelation," p.754.) The Reformers also tended to identify Rome as "Babylon the harlot" when commenting on Revelation 17. (This commentator is not convinced that the continuous historical method of interpretation of Revelation used by the Reformers, which makes "Babylon" a reference to Rome, is the correct one.)

[79] When Paul wrote Colossians (AD 63), Mark was with him in Rome, but was about to begin a journey into Asia Minor (Colossians 4:10). Four or five years later, Mark was in Asia Minor, but on the verge of a trip to Rome with Timothy (2 Timothy 4:11). In those years between AD 63 and 67, Mark could have journeyed to Babylon (even accompanying Peter, proponents of this theory allege).

[80] It is affirmed that we know very little of Peter's movements between AD 51 (after the Jerusalem Conference) and AD 66 or 67 when tradition has him at Rome (after the conflagration under Nero's regime). The great commentary on the Jewish Law is called the *Babylonian Talmud*. So important was the Jewish community in Babylon that Josephus had issued a special edition of his histories for them. Since Babylon on the Euphrates was a center of Jewish life, it is affirmed, and since Peter was the apostle to the circumcision, it could be expected that he would make a trip to that city. Instead of tradition having Peter in the east, there is no local tradition of any other apostle than Thomas ever being associated with the east.

[81] Josephus, *Ant.* xvii.9.8-9.

was scattered by violent persecution and massacre. It is true that years later, in the AD 200s, we again find a colony of Jews in Babylon working on the "Babylonian Talmud" in contrast to the "Palestinian Talmud." When did Jews come back to Babylon?[82] When Rome beat Palestine to her knees (AD 70-132), there was a great migration to Babylon, as the Jews fled before the conqueror. But this was after the death of Peter. If a trip to Babylon is postulated because Peter ministered to Jews, there was not much need for a trip between AD 40 and 65.

C. Treat the term "Babylon" in a figurative sense.

Three different places of writing have been suggested by those who would take the term figuratively.

1. "Babylon" – is a figurative name for Antioch of Syria.

M.E. Boismard offered the suggestion that the place of writing was Antioch, and gave these reasons to substantiate his opinion: we know Peter was one time in Antioch (Galatians 2:11ff); the teaching of the "descent into Hades" (3:19) was a doctrine established early in the churches of Syria; the title "Christian" is found in the New Testament only at those places that speak of the Church in Syria (Acts 11:26, 26:28) and in 1 Peter 4:16; and the *Apostolic Tradition* of Hippolytus both has a Syrian background and reflects the language of 1 Peter.[83] When scholars began to interact with Boismard, Cuming countered by finding that the *Apostolic Tradition* clearly emanated from Rome, not Antioch.[84] Martin called attention to the absence of 1 Peter's influence on Ignatius of Antioch as a telling counter-objection, and also argued that 1 Peter has close affinities with 1 Clement, which emanated from Rome.[85] In the light of these evidences, it is difficult to think of Antioch as being the "Babylon" from which 1 Peter was written.

2. "Babylon" – is a figurative name for Jerusalem.

Proponents of this hypothesis suppose the name "Babylon" was given to Jerusalem because of the wickedness of that city. And some have interpreted Revelation 11:8 in such a way that they find a "Biblical" evidence that Jerusalem was sometimes given the appellation "Babylon" by Christians.

---

[82] Against the view that no Jews were in Babylon in the AD 60's, proponents of taking "Babylon" literally point to the fact that when Jews were expelled from Rome by Claudius, about AD 49, they soon returned in large numbers. Could not the same thing have happened in Babylon, too?

[83] *Review Biblique* 64 (1957), p.81.

[84] G.J. Cuming, *Hippolytus: A Text for Students*. Bramcote, Notts.: Grove Books, 1976.

[85] R. Martin, "Peter, First Epistle of" in *International Standard Bible Encyclopedia*, edited by Geo. Bromiley (Grand Rapids: Eerdmans, 1975), Vol.3, p.809.

Even if it could be shown that the name "Babylon" was sometimes given to Jerusalem, it is difficult to show that Peter was still at Jerusalem at the time (i.e., a pending persecution) this letter must have been written. Our study of Peter's travels and ministry in the AD 50's and 60's put him a long way from Jerusalem during those years.[86] Jerusalem as the possible place where 1 Peter was written is, in this commentator's opinion, not a viable option.

3. "Babylon" – is a figurative reference to Rome

The evidence marshaled to support this interpretation includes: (1) If 1 Peter was written in a time of persecution, the use of the term in a figurative sense is understandable. If Peter were writing from Rome, he would be putting himself and the Christians who were hiding him in jeopardy if the authorities got their hands on a letter in which he literally identifies the place where he is. The authorities would have left no stone unturned in their search for him. (2) The uniform, unvarying testimony of early Christian writers who spoke on the subject is that "Babylon" here is a reference to Rome.[87] It was not until the time of the Reformation that there was any attempt to identify the place of 1 Peter's authorship as somewhere other than Rome. (3) As is true with Peter, all early church tradition has Mark in Rome. No tradition has either Peter[88] or Mark in the east. (4) There is no reference to any church in Babylon on the Euphrates. If 1 Peter 5:13 ("she who is in Babylon, chosen ...") is a reference to a congregation among whom Peter is working, it is hardly Babylon.[89] The early records of Christianity, which give very full accounts of Christian churches, and which especially give prominence to those founded by apostles or under their guidance, are absolutely silent as regards the existence of a church in Babylon. We have no notice of a succession of bishops, no intimation of persecutions against Christians in that city.

---

[86] See the Special Study in the author's *Acts* commentary, "Was Peter ever in Rome?" for Peter's possible travels after the Jerusalem Conference.

[87] Papias, Clement of Alexandria, Jerome, Oecumenius, Eusebius, all state this conclusion as a well-known fact, needing no defense. What Oecumenius wrote was, "He calls Rome Babylon, on account of the pre-eminence which of old had belonged to Babylon." In the 2nd century and later, it was customary for Christians (see Tertullian, and the *Sibyllene Oracles*, and the *Apocalypse of Baruch*) to call Rome "Babylon." Did they learn this from Peter? Eusebius wrote, "Peter ... in his former epistle, which also, they say that he composed at Rome itself, and that he means this when he calls the city in a figurative kind of way 'Babylon' ..." (*H.E.*, ii.15.2.).

[88] Traditions have Peter competing with Simon Magus. We first met Simon Magus in Samaria (Acts 8). According to tradition Simon Magus goes from city to city, and Peter follows right behind. Magus would work wonderful deeds by magic, and Peter would then put Magus to shame by miracles -- and people thus were converted to Christianity.

[89] Taking "she" as a reference to a congregation may be an important argument. It has been urged that "Babylon" must be taken literally since the context is literal. But note -- if "she" is a reference to a congregation, and "son" is a reference to a convert of Peter's, then the whole context is figurative, and we would expect "Babylon" to be figurative also.

Having examined the possible interpretations as to the place of writing, this commentator sees no reason to vary from the church's position of the first 16 centuries, that the letter was written from Rome, and that the term "Babylon" in 1 Peter 5:13 is to be understood figuratively.

VI. DATE OF WRITING

The actual date when 1 Peter was written cannot be fixed exactly. Peter, its author, was martyred in AD 68, so the letter is dated earlier than this.[90] But how much earlier? If the conclusion about the place of writing is correct, then the letter cannot be written at a time earlier than when Peter first comes to Rome.[91] In our study of the life of Peter, we have determined that AD 65 is about the earliest he can have arrived in Rome.

There are some corollary bits of evidence that 1 Peter was written in the mid-AD 60's. (1) It is just possible that the numerous points of correspondence[92] between several of Paul's letters and 1 Peter indicate Peter's letter is not written until after Paul's. If Peter is familiar with all of Paul's letters in which resemblances are found, then 1 Peter was not likely written prior to AD 65. (2) A time of persecution was pending (1 Peter 4:12-17, 5:8-10). It has been shown that Peter's description fits best with Nero's persecution, and this also would point to a date not earlier than AD 65.

The date this commentator assigns to 1 Peter is about AD 66 or 67. It is written before 2 Peter, which was also written from Rome, and before the apostle's death there.[93]

---

[90] Liberal theology has tried to date the letter not earlier than AD 100. Higher criticism has attempted to date Romans and Ephesians late (see E.J. Goodspeed, *Introduction to the New Testament* [Chicago: Univ. of Chicago, 1937], for example), and then since 1 Peter has resemblances to these letters, it too must be assigned a late date. Once the critics have rejected the Petrine authorship, then the persecution reflected in 1 Peter can be either that of Domitian (AD 81-96) or that of Trajan (AD 98-117). Pliny's Letter to Trajan (AD 115) is used to help date 1 Peter late.

[91] If the literal "Babylon" is the place of writing, you would have to date the writing of 1 Peter earlier, say AD 58-64.

[92] See the verses quoted in footnote #62. In addition, compare Colossians 3;8 with 1 Peter 2:1; compare Ephesians 5:22 with 3:1, and Ephesians 5:21 with 5:5; compare 1 Thessalonians 5:6 with 5:8; compare 1 Corinthians 16:20 with 5:14; compare Romans 8:18 with 5:1, and Romans 4:24 with 1:21; compare Romans 13:1-4 with 2:13,14; compare Romans 12:6,7 with 4:10; and compare 1 Timothy 2:9 with 3:3, and 1 Timothy 5:5 with 3:5. Paul's earliest letters were written about AD 51 or 52, while the last of these being compared comes from about AD 65. (Remember, 2 Peter was written after Peter had seen Paul's writings, 2 Peter 3:15).

[93] Peter arrives in Rome after 2 Timothy 4:11 was written. We have tentatively dated 2 Timothy about AD 67. Thus we are within a year or so of the deaths of Paul and Peter when 2 Timothy and 1 and 2 Peter are written.

VII. DESTINATION

A. The Place

The geographical area addressed is easily ascertained. "Pontus, Galatia, Cappadocia, Asia, and Bithynia" (1 Peter 1:1). The only question is whether the names are to be taken in a political or geographical sense. Roman political boundaries were different from Hellenistic geographical names. The Roman province of Galatia included considerably more land area than the old Hellenistic Galatia did. Pontus and Bithynia were merged into one Roman province in AD 65.[94] The Roman province of Asia included lands that in Hellenistic times were called Mysia and Caria and parts of Phrygia as well as Asia.

B. The Origin of the Churches in these areas

The book of Acts tells of Paul's missionary work in both Galatia and Asia. According to the South Galatia theory, Paul did not evangelize any of the towns in the northern part of the Roman province of Galatia. If Peter used "Galatia" in the old Hellenistic sense, then the Galatian churches he addressed in this letter were not founded by Paul. If he used Roman provincial titles, then Peter is addressing the churches at Antioch, Iconium, Lystra, and Derbe which were planted by Paul (Acts 13:14-14:13). Paul also was involved in the evangelism of the province of Asia (Acts 19:8-10).

We must turn to tradition and inference from Scripture to even suggest who might possibly have evangelized the other provinces. Local traditions in Pontus connect the apostles Andrew and Thaddeus with evangelistic labors in this region.[95] What seems more probable is that Peter himself preached the gospel in all these areas,[96] and he now writes to people he knows personally. In doing so, he was fulfilling part of his commission from Christ who commanded him to "shepherd my sheep" (John 21:15-17).

---

[94] A portion of the region called "Pontus" in Hellenistic times remained, after the Romans had captured this area and subjugated it, a separate kingdom under Polemon and his house from 36 BC to AD 63. See Wm. Ramsay, "Pontus" in *Hasting's Dictionary of the Bible* (New York: Scribners, 1909), Vol.4, p.5-19.

[95] Geo. E. White, "Pontus," in *International Standard Bible Encyclopedia*, edited by James Orr (Grand Rapids: Eerdmans, 1929), Vol.4, p.2419.

[96] Origen comments that Peter had visited the churches he addresses in his letter (Eusebius, *H.E.*, iii.1). But even if he did not, to have Peter writing to churches planted by other apostles, whether Paul or Andrew or Thaddeus, is not interfering in someone else's diocese. An apostle's sphere of authority was world-wide. Paul made it a matter of personal motivation not to preach where other apostles had been -- but he did not hesitate to write letters to churches he did not plant (cf. his letter to Colossae, and his letter to Rome), nor did he hesitate to begin his evangelistic work in any new place by going to the synagogue. The division of labor to which Paul, Barnabas, Titus, Peter, James, and John had agreed to at the Jerusalem Conference (Galatians 2:9) was general in scope. Peter should not be accused of violating those terms if he wrote letters to some areas whose churches were planted by Paul, and whose members were Gentile Christians.

C. The Ethnic Background of the Readers

Some language in the epistle has been interpreted to mean that Peter's intended readers were Jews who had been converted to Christianity. The principal argument used to prove this opinion is the terminology "dispersion" ("scattered as aliens, scattered" or "sojourners of the Dispersion," ASV) in 1:1 and what is said in 2:9 and 3:6, language it is alleged could be applied only to those of Hebrew extraction. The term "Dispersion" (see John 7:35, and perhaps James 1:1) was a name applied to Jews, after the Babylonian Captivity, who lived outside of Palestine and who maintained their religious faith while living among the Gentiles.[97] Since the term *diaspora* has no article here in 1:1, it has been a matter of debate whether it should be capitalized (making it a reference to ethnic Jews), or left in lower case (making it a figurative reference to the minority position of Christians living in alien lands). The ASV translators treated it one way, the NASB translators treated it the other.

Commentators have pointed to other verses which seem to imply that the intended readers were predominantly of Gentile background.

> The recipients are described as those who had been called "out of darkness into His marvelous light" (2:9), who once "were no people, but now are the people of God" (2:10). Their life before their conversion was described as "the time of your ignorance" (1:14), but as believers they had been redeemed from their "vain manner of life handed down from your fathers" (1:18). They were warned against heathen practices from which they had been delivered (4:3-4). If they had been Jews, their pagan neighbors would not have thought it "strange" that they no longer indulged in those pagan sins (4:4). The women are spoken of as having *become* daughters of Sarah (3:6) through conversion. Such statements clearly refer to Gentile Christians whom Peter considered strangers in an alien environment.[98]

A simple solution to this question of ethnic background is to agree with those writers

---

[97] God had warned the Jews through Moses that "dispersion" would be their lot if they departed from the Mosaic Law (Deuteronomy 4:27; 28:64-68). These prophecies began to be fulfilled in the two captivities, by Assyria and Babylonia, but there were other captivities by the rulers of Egypt and Syria, and by Pompey, which helped scatter the Jews. Further, since the time of Alexander the Great, many thousands of Jews emigrated for purposes of trade and commerce into the neighboring countries, particularly their chief cities. By the 1st century AD, the number of people living in the Diaspora greatly outnumbered the population of the Holy Land. Jews from Pontus were present at Pentecost (Acts 2:9) and Aquila came from here (Acts 18:2). Jews from Cappadocia likewise were present at Pentecost (Acts 2:9), and a letter in their favor from the Roman senate to Ariarathes, king of Cappadocia, about 139 BC, is mentioned in 1 Macc. 15:22. In the 3rd century after Christ, a great Jewish population in Caesarea is alluded to in the Talmud. Jews from Cappadocia and Bithynia are mentioned by Philo, *Legatio ad Gaium*, #36. (For information about Jewish people in Asia, see the articles on Cos, Laodicea, and Ephesus in *Hasting's Dictionary of the Bible*.) Since the New Testament (James 1:1; Acts 26:7) speaks of the "twelve tribes" long after the Babylonian Captivity, the legend of "ten lost tribes" who eventually migrate up the Danube river into northern Europe, and whose descendants are now known as the Aryan race, is a fiction. For a thorough refutation of "British Israelism," see chapter 2 in Roger Chambers, *The Plain Truth About Armstrongism* (Grand Rapids: Baker, 1972).

[98] D. E. Hiebert, *First Peter* (Chicago: Moody, 1984), p.16.

who believe the addressees were Christians – some converted from Judaism and some from heathenism. For those in the church, the middle wall of partition had been broken down, and Peter can address them all as members of the body of Christ. There is something in this epistle for each and all, whatever their ethnic and spiritual past had been.

VIII. THE PURPOSE OF WRITING

In some books of the New Testament the writer clearly states his purpose (e.g., John 20:30,31). In other books the purpose must be arrived at inductively by studying what the main ideas set down in the letter are. Most likely 1 Peter 5:12 is Peter's own statement of purpose.[99] "I have written to you briefly, exhorting and testifying that this is the true grace of God. Stand firm in it!"

Peter wants his readers to be confident that Christianity is the only genuine religion where the grace of God can be experienced. That being true, they are urged to be faithful to Christianity ("stand fast in it!", NIV), in spite of opposition and hatred and persecution they might encounter for the sake of the Gospel.[100]

Peter tells us he sought to accomplish his goal of ensuring his readers' faithfulness by two means – exhortation and testimony. His testimony is set forth in the doctrinal sections of the letter, where he extols the glories of our salvation, the exalted position of the church as the living temple of God, and the spiritual blessings that can accrue from sufferings, plus his numerous references to Jesus' own life, teaching, and example. After each of the doctrinal sections there is a hortatory section wherein the readers are encouraged to live a life in harmony with the exalted truths taught in Christianity.

IX. 20th CENTURY EMPHASES IN PETRINE STUDIES

During the early decades of the 20th century, scholars were emphasizing historical criticism. During the closing decades, there was a shift of emphasis to social science criticism. Each of these approaches lent a particular flavor to studies of Peter's letters.

---

99 Those who date the letter late and treat it as pseudonymous, of course, find a different purpose for it. B. H. Streeter ("First Peter" in *The Primitive Church* [London: Macmillan, 1929) and Bo Reicke ("The Epistles of James, Peter and Jude," *Anchor Bible Series* [Garden City, NY: Doubleday, 1964]) think that 1:3-4:11 originally was a baptismal sermon, and that 4:12-5:11 was a pastoral letter (written about AD 90 to strengthen people being persecuted). They have the two put together, written under the name of Peter, by Aristion of Smyrna (whom they affirm fits the description of 1 Peter 5:1 -- cf. Papias' statement about "Aristion the elder" whose preaching he still listens to).

100 Someone has said that 1 Peter is an epistle of hope in the midst of suffering. Whereas the main theme of Paul's writings is *faith*, and the main theme of John's writings is *love*, the main theme of Peter's epistle is *hope*. Faithfulness, patience under suffering, is the way to ultimately enjoying the hope that is set before the Christian.

A. Historical Criticism – till the early 1970's.

Two major topics occupied the minds of historical critics – attempting to identify the nature of the persecutions faced by the readers, and attempting to identify the literary form or structure of 1 Peter.

1. The Nature of the persecutions faced by the readers

In order to identify the persecution, it is necessary to exegete the relevant verses and then make a studied conclusion. (Detailed exegesis is given in the commentary; conclusions and opposing opinions are simply stated here). In 1:6,7, Peter speaks of "various trials" that will last for a "little while," and which will be "temptations" (KJV) which will "test the faith" (KJV) of the readers. The "little while" is thought to point to something temporary and local, rather than something that is the expected lot of Christians in all times and places. 2:12,13 speak about the Christian's day in and day out behavior being winsome, so that when Gentiles make an actual, personal study of what Christianity is, they may be led to glorify God "in the day of visitation." Part of this winsome behavior is to have a submissive attitude towards government officials who have a God-given responsibility to provide for an orderly society. 2:20 warns bondslaves they may be harshly treated (receive blows) from unsaved masters. 3:9 identifies evil actions, slander, and insults as being part of the harassment Christians will be facing. The verbs in 3:14 and 3:17 are optative mood, which makes it clear that the writer regards the suffering for Christ as no more than a possibility for at least some of those whom he is addressing. 3:15 speaks of giving a well thought out answer to those who ask the readers why they are Christians. In its primary sense, the answer is something given in a courtroom setting to government officials who are doing the interrogating. In 4:4 it is the Christians' unconverted neighbors and ex-associates who malign the Christians because of their radical change in lifestyles so as to no longer run round with the pagans in their dissipation. 4:7 calls for devout sobriety and sound judgment in light of the fact that "the end of all things is at hand."[101] 4:12 is the passage that speaks of a "fiery ordeal" the readers are about to face. In that ordeal they are going to "share the sufferings of Christ" (4:13). 4:14 speaks of the readers as being reviled for the name of Christ. 4:16 calls on the readers not to be ashamed to suffer as a Christian. In 4:17 this fiery ordeal is spoken of as being "judgment" that begins at the household of God. 4:19 is so worded that not every reader would so suffer, but some would. In 5:6, something is going to happen to the readers that can be called "the mighty hand of God" in action. 5:8 is the memorable passage about the devil prowling about as a "roaring lion" looking for someone to devour. Is this to be taken as figurative language describing something every Christian faces or taken literally describing something just the readers were facing? The devil's actions are to be resisted by the readers being deliberately firm in faith, partially for their own benefit, and partially because the readers are aware that their example will have a profound effect on others suffering similarly

[101] Interpreters will treat this clause so as to match their eschatology and their views of the thrust of the book. Is it the end of time Peter has in mind? Is it the end of the cruelty which the church was suffering about which Peter writes?

from the devil (5:9). 5:10 is a promise that the suffering caused by the "roaring lion" will be only "for a little while," and that God will fix and mend all that was harmed while the suffering was going on. 5:12 closes with a ringing exhortation to "stand firm" in the Christian faith no matter what!

Do these verses picture governmental persecutions? Bible students for many centuries since Peter's time certainly thought so. Especially the language of 4:12-16 and 5:8 has been thought to point to the Neronian persecution.[102] Though there was a time recently when some critics thought the name "Christian" required a post-AD 64 date for this letter, it no longer is fashionable to question Luke's statement that the "disciples were first called Christians in Antioch" (Acts 11:26). That was shortly before the year AD 44 (as Acts 12 indicates[103]). If followers of Jesus have been called "Christians" for 20 or more years, there is no reason to doubt that the term was currently in use in Rome before the Neronian persecution broke out. Perhaps the term "troublesome meddler" (4:15) fits nicely the time of persecution when Nero's government was trying to put down an alleged rebellion against its authority. To be involved in anti-government rhetoric or in a more overt form of rebellion (such as the zealots encouraged) was precisely the kind of evil behavior the Christians were to avoid. Certainly, the language about "fiery ordeal" and "lions prowling" fits what we know of the Neronian persecution.

Some 20th century commentators veered off in another direction as they have tried to identify the persecution the readers were facing. Instead of an official government policy or persecution, some contemporary writers present the idea that the persecution was the result of a local outburst of opposition and mob violence from an unconverted and hostile populace. Defenders of this view argue that there is nothing in 1 Peter that indicates an official state persecution is what Peter is warning his readers about. Paul and Barnabas had warned their converts that "through many tribulations we must enter the kingdom of God" (Acts 14:22), and it is such everyday tribulations that Peter's readers were facing, say the proponents of a mob violence interpretation. After reviewing and explaining the evidence in 1 Peter itself (e.g., no technical terms as *diogmos* for official persecution for religious reasons, and no statements of formal accusation such as *kategoria*), Kelly concluded that because "there is no evidence for any very extensive persecution [of Christians] initiated by the government in the first or second centuries AD," there is no reason to quarrel with "the impression which the letter as a whole conveys [which] is not of juridical prosecutions by the government (these seem ruled out by the references themselves,[104] by the statement that the ill-treatment is world-wide, and by the respect shown for the emperor), but of an atmosphere of suspicion,

[102] Earlier in these Introductory Studies we have addressed the issue of whether or not some other persecution (Trajan's or Domitian's) fits better the allusions in 1 Peter than does the Neronian. The conclusions reached there – that Peter references the Neronian persecution – are assumed in this discussion.

[103] The death of Herod Agrippa I, related in Acts 12, occurred in AD 44.

[104] Argument is made that the "proof (i.e., testing) of your faith" (1:7) is an echo of James 1:2ff, that "fiery ordeal" is too strong a translation for *purosis* at 4:12, and that "sufferings for Christ" is the lot of all Christians whenever they live (2 Corinthians 1:5, 4:10,17; Philippians 1:29; Romans 8:18). If these arguments are all true, what has become of any evidence for governmental persecutions?

hostility and brutality on the part of the local population which may easily land Christians in trouble with the police."[105] Elliott has appealed to the call for respect for the emperor and civil law (2:13-17), the positive outcome anticipated from the reader's good behavior (2:11-12, 3:13-17), the nature of the hostility encountered (namely, verbal abuse and reproach per 2:12, 3:16, 4:14), curiosity about the Christian hope (3:15),[106] and revenge over the severance of former social ties (4:4) as evidence that the theory of state-sponsored persecution is improbable, and he opts instead for sporadic local incidents of persecution and hostility directed against the Christians.[107] 1 Peter 5:9 is taken as a crucial endorsement of the notion that the "troubles" referred to in 4:12 are in no way exceptional, but have their counterpart in a great many places.

We have seen no compelling reasons to abandon the time-honored explanation that 1 Peter is persecution literature, and that the persecution was more official and government sponsored, rather than local and sporadic.

2. The Literary Structure -- Form, Genre -- of 1 Peter

Modern commentators, steeped in the worldview called humanism, love to speak of the literary genre of the different Bible books. Determining the genre is thought to be a helpful tool to assist the interpretation of the work being studied. In the case of 1 Peter, what is the genre?

Study in the middle part of the 20th century focused on the literary structure of the document as attempts were made to apply the discipline of form criticism to the epistles. Form critics assume non-original materials are imported and used by the "author" in ways he thinks best to meet the needs of his present audience. Any redactor could insert fragments of hymns, creeds, confessions, and even pieces of sermonic material, into a letter which was being written.[108] Applied to Peter, the intention of this discipline, according to its advocates, is to investigate the literary deposits (e.g., blessings, hymns, admonitions) assumed to be embedded in the letters in order to discover the religious and theological situations out of

---

105 J.N.D. Kelly, *A Commentary on the Epistles of Peter and Jude* in Harper New Testament Commentaries Series. New York: Harper and Row, 1969, p.10,22.

106 This is a curious explanation of 3:15. Surely it is an attempt to give the verse a plausible veneer of explanation that the whole thesis of a "hostile local populace" requires.

107 J. H. Elliott, "Peter, First Epistle of," in *Abingdon Bible Dictionary* (Garden City, NY: Doubleday, 1992), Vol.5, p. 274.

108 Form critics assume all the "authors" of the New Testament books did this -- whether they be "Matthew," or "Luke" or "Paul," or whomever. Gospel writers supposedly used Mark and Q; Paul allegedly used previously existing fragments, or early Christian hymns. For some strange reason, it is always the high Christological passages that are identified as being non-original fragments which were imported into the books and letters. Indeed!

which these pre-epistolary traditions emerged.[109]

Early on, when the method was new, sources such as the Gospel of John,[110] Isaiah 53,[111] or an early deposit of ethical teachings,[112] were tentatively identified as being imported into 1 Peter. Then it became popular to question the unity of the letter. It was asserted that there is an obvious break at 4:11.[113] Then what the critics tried to do was identify the form or genre of each separate part of the letter. Some of the 20th century attempts at identifying the materials allegedly imported are these: (a) *The epistle embodies hymnic materials.* Selwyn suggested that 1 Peter 2:4-8 is an early Christian hymn or rhythmical prayer common to both Peter and Paul (Romans 9:33).[114] Selwin had to argue that Peter's words "it is contained in writing" (2:6) means "it is contained in the hymn."[115] Windisch proposed that

---

[109] This corresponds to the *Sitz im Leben* in the study of the canonical Gospels.

[110] F.W. Beare (*op. cit.*, 2nd and 3rd eds., p.91) argued that the author of 1 Peter had read the Gospel of John, especially John 21.

[111] Since Paul made little use of Isaiah's Suffering Servant Poems, it is evident to the critics that Peter is not indebted to Paul for the use made of Isaiah 53 in 1 Peter 2:22-24 (and perhaps 1:19). Martin (*op. cit.*, p.810) urges that this material has been adopted from a sector of primitive Christianity. This is based on O. Culmann's *Peter: Disciple, Apostle, Martyr* (Philadelphia: Westminster, 1962), p.66-68, where it is argued that this title for Jesus was short-lived in the early church.

[112] Critics used to talk much about *haustafel*, a German name given to ancient moral codes that supposedly existed in many cultures alongside public law. Source critics have alleged for years that Christians had such a written code of ethical teachings, and that it is incorporated into Colossians, Ephesians, James, and 1 Peter.

[113] Various internal arguments were marshaled to show the break at 4:11. For example, Streeter (*op. cit.*) pointed out that there are two doxologies (4:11 and 5:11) each of which (he believed) would have been the ending of its own section. He argued that 4:12 serves as a new beginning because there is a change of verb tense at 4:12 -- the sufferings in 2:11-4:11 are viewed as future, whereas in 4:12-5:11 they are actually present. Joy in 1:6, 3:13-17 was a present reality, whereas in 4:12 it is in the future. The "amen" at 4:11 is unexpected. The connection between 4:11 and 4:12 is weak. The assumption that 1 Peter contains two separate parts can explain the "briefly" in 5:12, which would hardly be used of the whole document, some 1675 words.

In reply to these arguments -- doxologies in the middle of Romans (11:33-36) and Ephesians (3:20-21) are not treated as evidence against the unity of those letters. One can conclude a sublime train of thought with a doxology, just as much as he can conclude a whole letter with one. The argument about two different pictures of suffering overstates the evidence. In both alleged "parts" of the letter (compare 1:6 with 4:12), the picture of suffering and persecution are essentially the same -- for some readers it is only a threat, for others it is a reality. "The themes in the several parts are exactly the same (it is better to suffer for doing right than the reverse: 3:17, 4:15ff; brief tribulation to be followed by glory: 1:6ff, 5:10; rejoicing in suffering: 1:6,8, 4:13ff); and the same strongly eschatological note is present everywhere (1:20, 4:5,7, 17), the same threatening talk about those 'who disobey the gospel'." (W. Kelly, *The First Epistle of Peter* [London: Weston, 1904], p.20).

[114] E. G. Selwyn's (*The First Epistle of St. Peter*. 2 ed. [London: Macmillan, 1946], p.268-277) analysis produced a hymn of 7 lines, covering verses 6-8. Hans Windisch worked with the same materials and found a hymn of 4 strophes ("1 Peter," in *Die katholischen Briefe*. 3rd ed. rev. by H. Preisker [Tubingen: J.C. Mohr, 1951]).

[115] More than anything else he had to affirm in order to defend his "hymnic" hypothesis, what Selwyn was forced to do with "it is written" (which is unquestionably a recognized designation for Scripture) has led most scholars to reject his conclusions.

several other early hymns could be found in 1 Peter.[116] He described 1:3-12 as an *Eingangshymnus* (entrance hymn), and three other parts (1:18-21, 2:21-25, 3:18-22) of the letter as *Christuslieder* ("Christ- hymns").[117] Boismard tried to find in verses 1:20, 3:18,22, and 4:6 a connected seven-line Christ hymn which he then asserted was parallel in structure to 1 Timothy 3:16.[118] This alleged parallel to 1 Timothy 3 was developed by J.T. Sanders,[119] who saw in 1 Peter an early version of the same text allegedly used in 1 Timothy 3, with Timothy being a more refined or complete version.[120] (b) *The epistle embodied catechism instructions.* In the second century it became fashionable to have catechism classes for potential converts to Christianity.[121] 1 Peter 2:21-25 are alleged to be a pericope from a catechetical instruction based on Christ as a model. (c) *The epistle embodies a baptismal sermon.* Once a break had been discovered at 1 Peter 4:11, it was but a short step to suggest that the main part of the letter (1:3-4:11) was originally a sermon delivered to a group of newly baptized believers. The sermon was subsequently incorporated into a letter (by adding 1:1-2 and 4:12-5:14) intended as a message of consolation for those converts when the suffering anticipated in the sermon (future tense verbs) had become a reality (present tense verbs).[122] O.S. Brooks went further. He argued that our letter includes two baptismal homilies, one delivered before, and the other after the candidates were immersed.[123] (d) *The epistle embodies a baptismal liturgy.* Preisker developed this view as he edited and revised the commentary by Windisch. He suggested 1 Peter was not simply a baptismal sermon, but

---

[116] Windisch, *op. cit.*

[117] Windisch regarded 1 Peter 3:18-22 as a baptismal hymn, though he never explains whether it was a familiar hymn quoted by "Peter," or whether "Peter" was led by certain associations to break spontaneously into verse form himself. Bultmann ("Confessional and Hymnic Fragments in 1 Peter," *ContNT* 11 [1947], p.1-14) built on the foundation laid by Windisch. When Bultmann was finished reconstructing the original hymn it sounded suspiciously like the "Apostles' Creed." J. Jeremias (*ZNW* 42 [1949], p.194-201) an E. Lohse (*ZNW* 45 [1954], p.68-89) both found fault with Bultmann's handling. The price he paid to reconstruct his "original version" -- tearing asunder pieces of Peter's text, recasting the material, failure even after doctoring the text to produce a completely symmetrical arrangement, the inordinate length of v.22, his use of a gnostic redemption myth to explain v.20ff -- all is too much to swallow.

[118] *Quatre Hymnes baptismales dans la priemiere epitre de Pierre* (Paris: Cerf, 1961).

[119] J.T. Sanders, *New Testament Christological Hymns* (Cambridge: University Press, 1971).

[120] Frankly, we tire of reading all this speculation about early Christian hymns, whether we are studying Peter's or Paul's writings. We wonder why the "Bible" scholars are so intent on tearing down any possible foundation we might have for faith in Christ.

[121] *Epistle of Barnabas*, v.1-5 and 2 *Clement* i.2 are alleged to embody 2nd century examples of such catechetical instructions.

[122] R. Perdelwitz suggested this in 1911 (*Die Mysterienreligionen und das Problem des I Petrus-briefes* [Giessen: Topelmann, 1911]). It has since been adopted by B.H. Streeter (*op. cit.*), Windisch (*op. cit.*, p.82), Beare (*op. cit.*), Reicke (*op. cit.*) and J.N.D. Kelly (*Early Christian Creeds* [London: Longmans and Green, 1950], p.18).

[123] O. S. Brooks, "1 Peter 3:21 – The Clue to the Literary Structure of the Epistle," *Nov. Test.* 16 [1974], p.290-305.

was the transcript of an actual baptismal service, in progress at the time of writing. It is an eyewitness account of the rite in its several stages, and embodies the various contributions made to the service by those who took part. He has the actual baptism taking place between 1:21 and 1:22.[124] The new converts take a brief vow (1:22-25). The three-strophe hymn of 2:1-10 is sung by a Spirit-possessed individual. A new preacher stands up in the congregation at 2:11 and delivers the exhortation that culminates in a hymn to Christ (2:21-24).[125] Preisker continues on through our letter, identifying the characters who are speaking, and telling us what is going on as they speak. F.L. Cross offered a slight variation – he found 1 Peter 1:3-4:11 to be the celebrant's part in an Easter baptismal service.[126]

Evaluations of these composite theories: (1) The whole form-critical method is fraught with unacceptable presumptions, among which are a denial of the inspiration of the author and a copying and editing with no real interest in whether the result is true to the intent of the original.[127] (2) How did such documents (as baptismal sermons or liturgies, delivered or performed by some unknown person) get mixed up, without explanation, in a document that purports to be a letter sent by Peter to churches in Asia Minor? (3) What interest would Christians in Asia Minor have in a baptismal liturgy of the church at Rome, if such it was originally? Did Rome set the liturgical standards for the rest of the world? (4) If we are looking for the life situation, what situation in Asia Minor would have called out the need for such a liturgy, or what circumstances in Rome (assuming Rome to be the place of writing) would have led those folk to send it? (5) Where can the scholars point to any comparable contemporary example of Christian homilies or liturgies being embodied in letters? How can scholars talk about such a genre, when we have no criteria for distinguishing such a literary genre (baptismal homily, or Lord's Supper homily) either in apostolic times or at the end of the first century AD? (6) Why is there no manuscript evidence of 1 Peter in any other than its present form, if the composite theory is true? (7) In chapter 4, verses 11 and 12 mark not a sudden break from one letter to another, but rather a transition in the line of thought from doctrine to exhortation, precisely like the transition at 2:10,11. In summary, the attempt

---

124 Earlier commentators had the baptism actually taking place at 3:20. It is debated whether baptism is as prominent in 1 Peter as this hypothesis affirms. Baptism is specifically mentioned once (3:21); perhaps it is also alluded to at 1:2,3,23; 2:2,10,25. Even if we grant the allusions, that does not make this a "baptismal sermon." Peter is simply reflecting on the time and place of the change that resulted in the readers becoming God's "chosen" people, as a reason why they should "stand firm" in the faith they earlier embraced. Goodspeed has noted that "the address to servants, wives and husbands" (2:18ff), and especially to gifted speakers (4:11), "combined with a call to hospitality (4:9), hardly suits a group of new converts" (*An Introduction to the New Testament*, p.285).

125 Here Preisker (*op. cit.*) accepts without question Bultmann's conclusion that the author of 1 Peter took over a previously existing hymn.

126 F.L. Cross, *1 Peter, A Paschal Liturgy* (London: Mowbray, 1954). Cross confesses to an embarrassment when faced with trying to explain the remainder of the letter - 4:12-5:14. Any literary theory which is left with 4:12-5:14 on its hands, with no explanation, is under a cloud of suspicion.

127 When and if form criticism gives way to tradition criticism, will we have a whole new set of hypotheses about a wide stream of oral tradition of which the "writers" made use, each in his own time and each in his own way?

of some to strip off the "epistolary framework" of 1:1-2 and 5:12-14, and thus to treat our present work as being a composite, have met with little acceptance. There is no solid evidence for questioning the unity of the letter!

B. Social-Science Criticism -- since 1970.

While historical criticism was flourishing, scholars tried to determine the precise historical situation out of which or to which individual books of the Bible were written. Scholars wanted to know what is unique, datable, and historically and geographically fixed about the life setting of 1 Peter.[128] The emphasis in Biblical studies is now changing. No longer are historical studies of such an interest. Instead, social science criticism has begun to flourish. Social scientific theory looks at factors that are not unique to any one time and place, but at those which can be closely paralleled in other times, places, and different – sometimes very different – cultures.

Since the 1970s, studies of 1 Peter have been attempting to research and identify its social setting rather than its historical setting.[129] Social science is interested in such matters as the "haves" versus the "have nots," honor and shame, acculturation versus boundary markers, and social deprivation and ostracism. The works of J.H. Elliott and David Balch claim to have uncovered a tension in 1 Peter between "acculturation" (i.e., conforming where possible to dominant societal values) and "boundary maintenance" (i.e., the preservation of Christian distinctives in a hostile society). Virtually all the recent studies of the social world of the New Testament deal in some way with honor and shame. In no book of the New Testament is the contrast between honor and shame highlighted more than in 1 Peter, social science critics assert.[130] Numerous marks of ostracism are also observed in 1 Peter, such as

---

128 Such studies had not proven very satisfactory for 1 Peter. Peter may be persecution literature, but scholars could not quite identify the kind of persecution. It must have a literary genre, but they could not quite agree on the genre. There must have been sources used, but no agreement was forthcoming about the nature or length or even the wording of the alleged sources.

129 In particular, see the works of L. Goppelt (*Commentary on 1 Peter* [Grand Rapids: Eerdmans, 1993], originally published 1978), J.H. Elliott (*1 Peter: Estrangement and Community* [Chicago: Fransciscan Herald, 1979]), and D. Balch ("Hellenization/Acculturation in 1 Peter," in *Perspectives on First Peter*, ed. C.H. Talbot [Macon, GA: Mercer U. Press, 1986], p.79-102). Goppelt began the use of social science criticism as a tool to interpret 1 Peter. Goppelt identified the origin of the growing persecution as not the police or the state but popular slander (1 Peter 2:12; 3:16; 4:4,14). Goppelt was followed in this use of social science criticism by J. H. Elliott, *A Home for the Homeless: A Sociological Exegesis of 1 Peter, Its Situation and Strategy* (Minneapolis: Fortress, 1990).

130 Briefly, the ideas of honor and shame are explained in this way: for both those addressed in the letter and their enemies in Roman society, honor was a desirable goal, perhaps the supreme goal in life. Shame was something to be avoided at almost any cost. The difference between Christians and their unconverted contemporaries lay in what constituted honor and what constituted shame. In Roman society, honor and shame were determined by public opinion, or the emperor, or the Roman gods. It brought honor if a man or woman did some good deed either within the household or on behalf of the community, that brought honor to the family, the state, the emperor or the gods. In Christianity, what is honorable and what is shameful were determined by the God of Israel who had revealed Himself in the Lord Jesus Christ. Romans lived so as to be honored and esteemed by their fellow citizens. Christians lived so as to be honored and esteemed by their Lord, the Judge of the universe. When one is living as Jesus expects him to, social ostracism by his unconverted neighbors is no shame. What is

"sojourners and aliens," "Dispersion," and even "Babylon" (a place where Jews were in exile and alienated). The readers are certainly outsiders in the society among whom they lived. When faced with such pressures, groups struggling for their very existence usually have two interests: the social cohesion of their group; and determining how much social adaptation is permitted towards the society among whom they are living. Without the first, Christian identity would have been lost. Without the second, Christians would have had no social acceptability, which is also necessary for survival and outreach. Social science commentators find Peter addressing both these concerns in this letter. Balch sees Peter appealing to the church as God's household or family to pay particular attention to the needs of the socially deprived and ostracized groups – especially the needs of Christian women living in partially Christian households; and slaves living under unconverted masters.

An evaluation of the use of social science criticism to explain Bible books includes these objections: (1) Perhaps it is of some value when it comes to making *application* of the text to the present day, but hardly of value in understanding Peter's concerns when writing to his 1st century audience. (2) The emphasis is on what the reader gets out of the book rather than on the authorial intent. Without the authorial intent, we are likely to miss hearing God speak to us in these chapters of Scripture.

The text, as it stands, is an epistle. Historical-critical zeal to discern the supposed pre-history of a text often (if not always) leads the scholar to ignore the text as it stands (and as manuscript evidence shows it to have always stood) and also is a subversive, implicit denial of the work of the Holy Spirit in the process of inspiration behind the apostle's writing. We do not need a baptismal or Lord's Supper setting to make sense of Peter's exhortation and testimony to his readers who faced persecution.

The epistles of Peter are distinguished for great tenderness of manner and for bringing forward prominently the most consolatory parts of the gospel. There is great compactness and terseness of thought in his first letter. Each division of thought in Peter's letter will lend itself to an expository sermon in which the modern preacher finds he has less to leave out than he does on most any other part of the New Testament.[131] In the structure of his sections, Peter has this interesting method – he begins each section in such a manner that it refers to the principal word in the preceding section.

---

a shame is to live a lifestyle that is not winsome -- a lifestyle that would not make Jesus attractive to those unconverted observers. Loyalty to Christ and faithful endurance of "various trials" are what Christians will exchange for "praise, glory, and honor" at the future "revelation of Jesus Christ" (1 Pet. 1:6,7). The person who believes in Jesus will never be put to shame (2:6). There is real honor in suffering for doing good (2:20).

[131] There is almost nothing of local or merely temporary interest. There are no discussions pertaining to Jewish customs such as we see in Paul's writings. There is little that pertains particularly to one age of the world or country.

X. OUTLINE

What Peter has written seems to follow this outline:

EPISTOLARY OPENING: Signature, address, and greeting. 1:1,2

I. FIRST DOCTRINAL SECTION. 1:3-12.
The greatness of the salvation which belongs to the Christian. It is a salvation worth suffering for.

II. FIRST HORTATORY SECTION. 1:13-2:2
- A. Exhortation to Hope. v.13
- B. Exhortation to Holiness. v.14-16
- C. Exhortation to Reverence. v.17-21
- D. Exhortation to Love. 1:22-2:2

III. SECOND DOCTRINAL SECTION. 2:3-10
The church is the living temple of God.

IV. SECOND HORTATORY SECTION. 2:11-3:12
- A. Exhortation Concerning Conduct before Unbelievers. 2:11,12
- B. Exhortation Concerning Submission before Civil Rulers. 2:13-17
- C. Exhortation Concerning the Duties of Servants to Masters (enforced by the Example of Christ). 2:18-25
- D. Exhortation Concerning the Duties of Wives to Husbands. 3:1-6
- E. Exhortation Concerning the Duties of Husbands to Wives. 3:7
- F. Exhortation Concerning Duties of Christians to One Another. 3:8-12

V. THIRD DOCTRINAL SECTION. 3:13-4:6
The blessedness of suffering. It can open up whole new areas of service.

VI. THIRD HORTATORY SECTION. 4:7-5:9
- A. Exhortation to be Helpful to Suffering Brethren. 4:7-11
- B. Exhortation Concerning Inner Attitudes if you are Called on to Suffer. 4:12-19
- C. Exhortation to Elders. 5:1-4
- D. Exhortation to the Younger Members. 5:5a
- E. Final Exhortation to Humility, to Serene Submission to the Mighty Hand of God, and to Watchfulness. 5:5b-9

CONCLUSION
- A. Final Assurance of God's Help and their Ultimate Perfection after they have Suffered Awhile. 5:10,11
- B. Concluding Salutations. 5:12-14

1 PETER

SIGNATURE, ADDRESS, AND GREETING. 1:1,2

A. The Writer. 1:1a

1:1 -- ***Peter, an apostle of Jesus Christ, to those who reside as aliens, scattered throughout Pontus, Galatia, Cappadocia, Asia, and Bithynia, who are chosen***

Peter -- The opening words of first-century letters included three things: the name of the sender, the name of the addressee, and a word of greeting. The New Testament epistles follow the first-century form, save each point is expanded as the Christian perspective in each letter required. This signature says Peter was the writer of this letter.[1] "Peter" is the name which the Lord Himself had given to Simon Barjonah ("the son of John") on the occasion of their first meeting (John. 1:42).

An apostle of Jesus Christ -- The "Peter" who sends this letter carefully identifies himself. By designating himself as an "apostle of Jesus Christ," Peter called attention not to himself, but to his commission[2] and to the One who commissioned him.[3] "Jesus" is the name the Son of God bore in his humanity. It means "salvation (is) of Jehovah," and He was so-called because He came to save people from their sins (Matthew 1:21). "Christ" is the Greek translation of the Hebrew term "Messiah" which means anointed, something done to prophets, priests and kings. Jesus is the long-promised Messiah (John 1:41, Acts 2:36, 9:22), our prophet, priest and king. For Peter and the early church, the name "Jesus Christ" embodied their basic conviction that the incarnate Jesus was the promised Messiah, the bringer of Messianic redemption. An "apostle" was one sent on a mission with proper credentials, an envoy or ambassador who carried a special message. Peter was one of a dozen or more men who were "called and sent by Jesus Himself."[4] There is no proof offered of his apostleship

---

[1] In the Introductory Studies, we have examined in detail the whole question of authorship, and have found nothing that would cause us to doubt what this signature claims as far as the human authorship of this letter is concerned.

[2] If the readers will pause on the fact that Peter is an "APOSTLE" -- then what he writes in this letter has behind it the fact that he is acting as Christ's agent. This is what Jesus wants them to hear! This is how Jesus wants the readers of 1 Peter to act!

[3] The words and clauses of 1 Peter should be explained in the light of the author's stated purpose, 1 Peter 5:12. Peter knew well that Christian exhortation, to be vital and transforming, must be grounded in Christian doctrine. Therefore, as early as this opening of the letter, and as late as the closing words, we find rich doctrinal content. Get a grip on these, and one has a solid foundation for the urgent exhortations that constitute much of this letter.

[4] In the New Testament, one finds there are apostles of Christ, who are called and sent by Him (Luke 6:13-16), and apostles of churches, who are called and sent by a local congregation (2 Corinthians 8:23; Philippians 2:25).

since in Peter's case his authority had never been questioned (as Paul's was, on occasion).[5]

B. The Recipients of the Letter. 1:1b

To those who reside as aliens, scattered -- The recipients are identified at considerable length (1:1b-2a). Peter identifies them as Christians, gives their geographic location, and tells how they came to be Christians. The ASV reads "to the elect who are sojourners of the Dispersion." The translation "reside" may cause the English reader to miss the word picture included in the Greek word *parepidemois* used here. The Greek word speaks of one who comes from a foreign country into a city or land to reside there by the side of the natives; hence, stranger, or foreigner. In the New Testament it is used metaphorically with reference to heaven as the Christian's native country (Philippians 3:20), as compared to the earthly land in which he is temporarily living.[6] Peter's readers are reminded they are on a journey to a sacred or holy place as an act of devotion. That should positively influence how they live in their temporary home, and how they handle the ostracism and pending persecution they may be called on to endure at the hands of the natives. The NASB renders *diasporas* as "scattered," while the ASV used "Dispersion" with a capital "D." In the Introductory Studies it was explained that "Dispersion" was a technical term, used since the Babylonian Captivity to identify Jews who lived outside of Palestine. The translators of the ASV thought this letter was addressed especially to Christians who were ethnically Jewish. The translators of the NASB, on the other hand, think Peter has taken a word that originally applied only to the Jews, the "chosen" people, and broadened it to apply to all who have become Christians, whatever their ethnic background. In the Neronian persecution, a Christian's ethnic background would make no difference when it came to being targeted by the government or the mobs. All that mattered was whether or not you were a Christian.

Throughout Pontus, Galatia, Cappadocia, Asia, and Bithynia -- *Pontus* was a large province along the southeastern shore of the Black Sea (Pontus Euxinius) extending from Bithynia on the west to Armenia on the east. Before the Romans came, Mithradates was one of the famous rulers of this area. The Romans conquered this area in 65 BC and then redrew the provincial boundaries so that the western portion was united with Bithynia to form a new province, while the remaining eastern portion continued as a separate area. Before the Romans named this area "Pontus" it was known as the Kingdom of Polemon. *Galatia*, in Hellenistic times, was the name given to an area, in what we call north-central Turkey, which included the cities of Ancyra, Pessinus, and Tavium. The area was home to the old ethnic

---

[5] Some Protestant commentators have been ready to point out that Peter claims no authority over the rest of the apostles. He did not write "THE apostle of Jesus Christ."

[6] Thayer, *Lexicon*, p.488. The word occurs only three times in the New Testament, at Hebrews 11:13 (of Abraham, who confessed he was a traveler with a destination), here, and at 1 Peter 2:11.

Gauls, or Celtic tribes, who invaded this area about 280 BC, and in contemporary Bible studies is sometimes referred to as "Northern Galatia." In 25 BC, when the Romans converted this area into a province, they added parts of Phrygia, Lycaonia, Pisidia, and Isauria to it, to form the Roman province of Galatia, a province which covered the whole central area of the Turkish peninsula, and whose cities are Antioch, Iconium, Lystra, and Derbe, among others. *Cappadocia* was the wild mountainous region just to the east of Galatia (Lycaonia in Hellenistic times) and south of Pontus. It was bounded on the south by Cilicia. The name was apparently given to this region by the Persians, though its people were called "Syrians" by the Greeks. In AD 17 this province was incorporated into the Roman Empire and turned into a military defensive bastion. Roads were built through the "Cilician Gates" so that the region could be easily entered from the south. Jewish refugees and merchants took advantage of the roads to enter both Cappadocia and Pontus to the north. *Asia* was the name of the province that covered the whole western end of the land we call Turkey. When the Romans made this area into a province about 133 BC, it included the old Hellenistic lands of Mysia, Caria, Asia, and a portion of Phrygia. In New Testament times it was the most developed and most prosperous region of the five named here in 1 Peter 1:1. Its capital was moved from Pergamos to Ephesus in the time of Augustus. *Bithynia* was also located along the southwestern shore of the Black Sea, stretching from Constantinople southward and eastward. In 74 BC the last king of Bithynia bequeathed his kingdom to the Romans, and in 64 BC Pompey united it with the western portion of Pontus into a single Roman province. Provincial Bithynia now stretched along the Black Sea from Byzantium (Constantinople) and the Sea of Marmora (the Propontis) on the west to past Sinope on the east. It was while ruling this province that Pliny the Younger addressed his well-known letter to Trajan. Some of the chief cities of Bithynia were Nicomedia, Brusa, Nicea and Chalcedon. How there came to be churches in these areas (other than Asia and Galatia) may well be due to Peter's evangelistic work, though there were Jews present at Pentecost (Acts 2) from some of these areas. Just why these provinces were singled out to receive this letter from Peter is not clear. Perhaps not only does Peter know these people personally, but we might assume that the persecutions by the Roman authorities were most liable to occur in these provinces, some of which – like Asia – were very pro-Roman.

Who are chosen -- One of the outstanding things about the language we encounter in 1 Peter is that words and concepts that once were applied to the Jews are now applied to all, Jew or Gentile, who have become Christians. (For example, see 1 Peter 2:9, as well as "aliens" and "scattered" earlier here in verse 1.) "Chosen" or "elect" is another of these terms. The Greek word *eklektois* ("chosen") is a verbal adjective[7] and is passive voice, indicating that the readers

---

[7] A verbal adjective could function as an adjective modifying "aliens" (the word order in the Greek is "to chosen sojourners") or it can serve as a noun with the following phrases (verse 2) explaining how they came to be "chosen" (i.e., Christians) in the first place. This is how the NASB translators have treated the two words, separating them and moving "chosen" to the end of verse 1. If we put the terms together, the thrust of the passage is not *how* they became Christians in the past, but is a reference to *who* they are now -- and would call attention to what they need to do to remain "chosen" people. We tend to agree with the NASB translators that the phrases in verse 2 describe *how* they became Christians in the first place.

are objects of the electing action of God, who is the unnamed agent.[8] Throughout history, God has chosen, or elected,[9] certain men and nations to perform a special service for Him in this world.[10] By using this word, Peter reminds his readers that they are God's special people, and therefore have a challenge and responsibility. The doctrine of election is a "family truth" intended to foster the welfare of believers and encourage them in the face of the coming affliction. They aren't going to let the persecution cause them to fail to accomplish the special service for which God chose them, are they?

1:2 -- ***According to the foreknowledge of God the Father, by the sanctifying work of the Spirit, that you may obey Jesus Christ and be sprinkled with His blood: May grace and peace be yours in fullest measure.***

According to the foreknowledge of God the Father -- The three phrases in verse 2a probably should be connected with "chosen," just as they are in the NASB,[11] thereby reminding the readers how they have come to be Christians and thus the subjects of persecution in the first place. First of all, their selection (election) by God was in harmony with His

---

[8] For centuries, the religious world has been divided into two great warring groups -- Calvinistic and Arminian -- over the matter of election. Both have tended to focus on "election for salvation." One group teaches God's election to salvation or damnation is unconditional, having been made before the creation of the world. The other group teaches that God's election is conditional; He offers His salvation to those who choose to believe in Christ and accept the redemption offered in Him. In all this great controversy, often the real problem with election and free will is not in what the Bible says, but in what theologians have tried to make of one or the other of those doctrines, often teaching conclusions at variance with the Word of God! Scriptures that deal with "election" (e.g., 2 Thessalonians 2:13,14; Ephesians 1:3-14; Romans 9) show that God chooses *for service.* There is a work God wants done in His world and He chooses someone to do it. It is also true that God's eternal purpose (plan) includes not only the way of salvation (Jesus' death as an atoning sacrifice) but also the destiny to which both the forgiven and the unforgiven will be consigned. That destiny is conditioned on men's response to God's offer of forgiveness (Matthew 7:21; Luke 13:3; Acts 17:30; 2 Thessalonians 1:7-9; 1 John 2:4). That's the way God planned things would be before He ever created.

[9] The word "elect/chosen" can describe anything that is specially chosen. It can describe a specially chosen fruit, articles specially chosen because they are so outstandingly well made, picked troops specially chosen for some great duty or for some great exploit.

[10] There was a time when it was possible to speak of Israel as the "chosen" people of God, to the exclusion of other nations. They were chosen to keep monotheism alive in the world, and to be the channel through whom Messiah came into the world -- in this way they would bless their neighbors. However, the nation of Israel failed the purposes of God. Jesus warned them that the "vineyard" would be taken from them and given to others (Matthew 21:41-46). That is the basis of the great New Testament concept of the church being "Israel," the new Israel, spiritual Israel, the Israel of God (Galatians 6:16).

[11] The other option found in many of the ancient writers is to connect them with the term "apostle." When New Testament writers opened their letters with the three-fold epistolary form common in the 1st century, they expanded each point with a view to the needs of the readers. We see Peter expanding the point about who the addressees were. They were special in God's sight! They should never allow persecution to dull their sense of being special people.

"foreknowledge."[12] The word speaks of "approval ahead of time" and tells the readers they are actually important to God, chosen and preferred by Him whose favor was all important. They were important to God before He ever created, and they still are! If God is "Father," then the Christians are His children. If all our attention is concentrated on the hostility or indifference of our worldly neighbors, we Christians may well get discouraged. At such times, how comforting to remember that God is our *Father* and we are important to Him!

By the sanctifying work of the Spirit -- Here the readers are reminded that their position in Christ ("chosen") has been worked out by the influence or agency of the Holy Spirit.[13] We suppose the NASB translators were correct when they capitalized "Spirit," making it a reference to the Holy Spirit.[14] 2 Thessalonians 2:13 also speaks of "sanctification by the Spir-

---

[12] *Prognosis* has been interpreted four ways: (1) To "see beforehand," so as to know something before it happens. Acts 26:5 and 2 Peter 3:17 are examples of the word used with this meaning. Theologians have applied it to God to speak of His eternal pre-vision, His foresight of all that would come to pass. They then quickly enter into discussions of what God foresaw, and how He can "see" it without its also being programmed or absolutely predestined to occur. Calvinistic writers depend on the word to corroborate their doctrine of unconditional election. Arminian expositors understand it in an anti-predestinarian sense as the foresight of faith. Lutheran writers understand it to speak of the perseverance in the bestowed faith. Some theologians have even defended the idea that the faith which God foresees is the faith which He Himself creates (interpreting verses such as John 3:3-8, 6:44,45,65, and Ephesians 2:8,9 as though faith were so created, rather than coming by hearing the gospel as Romans 10:17 plainly affirms). (2) To "select" or "choose beforehand." This "choosing beforehand" differs from *eklego* ("chosen" or "elect") in that this word implies the "knowledge" is a loving, embracing knowledge. After all, *ginosko* ("know") sometimes means a knowing that places the knower in a personal relationship to the one known (Psalm 1:6; Hosea 13:5; Amos 5:2). "Foreknowledge" is then taken, as the dogmaticians define it, as "knowledge with affection and with a resultant effect." (3) To "determine beforehand." The RSV reads "destined by God" here at 1 Peter 1:2. Calvin argued that foreknowledge and predestination are the same things. To Calvin (1509-64) and Duns Scotus (1264-1308), "foreknowledge" is a way of saying that God knows the future because He determines all antecedent conditions; He foreordains and wills them. (The "openness of God" debate in the early 21st century is revisiting this whole key issue of Calvinism.) The Calvinist view of "foreknowledge" is that God from all eternity, of the mere good pleasure of His will, selected certain persons out of mankind to be the heirs of glory. (However, see this matter discussed at Romans 8:29, where both terms appear, and where, in this commentator's judgment, the terms "foreknowledge" and "predestination" are not synonymous.) (4) To "approve beforehand." The meaning of the phrase must be determined by the Biblical use of the word "know," which is very marked and clear (see Matthew 7:23; 1 Corinthians 8:3; Galatians 4;9; 2 Timothy 2:19; 1 John 3:1, in which the word "know" plainly is used with the sense of "approve"). In our study of God's eternal plan (Romans 8:28-30) we noted that back in eternity before creation, God made a plan in which He decided He would approve those who were "in Christ" (cp. Ephesians 1:4). Peter here reminds his readers that their "election" goes back to God's actions in eternity.

[13] Our comments reflect the decision made earlier that verse 2 is a reference to how the readers became Christians, not to the job an apostle was to do in the world. So as we explain "sanctifying" and "obey" and "sprinkled," we shall make reference to the time of conversion.

[14] The word *pneumatos* ("of the Spirit"), in the genitive case, may be interpreted two ways. It may be treated as a subjective genitive, meaning that the Spirit is the agent of the sanctifying. It is also possible to treat the genitive as an objective genitive, making the human spirit the object of the sanctifying work. Cook has suggested that Peter intentionally wrote an ambiguous expression to express the truth that "sanctification is the result of a complex work wrought by the Holy Spirit on the spirit of man" (F.C. Cook, "Hebrews" in the *Bible Commentary* [New York: Charles Scribners & Sons, 1909], p.174). It is man's spirit that must be "born again" (John 3:6), and it is man's spirit, dead because of trespasses and sins (Ephesians 2:1), that "becomes alive because of God's way of saving man" (Romans 8:10).

it." "Sanctify" means to "set apart," to "separate," to "dedicate to holy purposes."[15] Just as 1 Corinthians 12:13 tells how the Holy Spirit leads a man to want to be immersed into Christ, so we understand Peter here as affirming that the Holy Spirit, working through the Word, led the readers to obey Jesus Christ.

That you may obey Jesus Christ and be sprinkled with *His* blood -- The preposition *eis* (translated "that" or "unto") indicates the design and end of the sanctifying work of the Spirit – He leads men to obey Jesus and thus be covered by His blood. Thus "election" involves "obedience." God's choice of the readers has its origin in the foreknowledge of God, is worked out by the sanctifying influence of the Holy Spirit, and results in obedience to what Jesus Messiah commands.[16] If any of the items are missing, there is no assurance of being one of God's "chosen" people.[17] The phrase "and be sprinkled with His blood" also is governed by the preposition "unto." This is another of the results of the sanctifying work of the Spirit. He influences men to obey Jesus, and when they do, the blood of Jesus is applied to their sins. Christ's atoning sacrifice becomes effective for a man when he is obedient.[18] "Election" thus involves action on the part of the Godhead (i.e., sprinkling of the blood), just as it involves human action (i.e., obedience). "Sprinkled with the blood" reminds us of the event related in Exodus 24:8, "Moses took the blood and sprinkled it on the people, and said, Behold the blood of the covenant, which the Lord has made with you."[19] Compare with this Hebrews 9:18-23 where we learn that the new covenant was ratified by Christ's blood. Perhaps Peter's point is not only are our sins covered, but the Holy Spirit leads us into the new

---

[15] The word sanctification is used with several different senses in Scripture. One use of the word has reference to the time of our conversion (cp. 1 Corinthians 6:11), when we, by baptism, are set apart to God's service. Another use of the term has reference to the progressive growth of believers in Christlikeness (cp. Hebrews 12:14). Students should be careful at this place lest they think they have found a verse that supports the theory of a "second work of grace," the doctrine that at some time subsequent to salvation, the believer can expect another act by the Holy Spirit that will "sanctify" them and make them sinless perfect. The idea of a sanctification (which makes one sinless perfect, according to the theory) leading unto obedience (which is what Peter goes on to say), would be incongruous.

[16] The compound noun "obey" (*hupakoēn*) conveys the picture of listening and submitting to that which is heard. We are convinced, in this context, that it speaks more of initial obedience (in repentance and immersion) than about the obedience of the everyday life of the Christian.

[17] If any one, then, wishes to settle the question of whether he is among the elect or not, the way is plain. Let him be obedient (let him become a true Christian), and the whole matter is determined. Obedience is all the evidence which anyone needs that he is one of the Father's chosen children. We may not be able to go up to heaven and personally look upon the Lamb's Book of Life to see if our names are written there, but we have the assurance that if we are obedient to Christ's commands, our names are in fact written there.

[18] When does this sprinkling of Christ's blood take place? In the context, the reference is to the time when a man becomes a Christian, when he is obedient in baptism. *Wycliffe Bible Commentary* speaks of "cleansing from incidental defilement through the continuous sprinkling of the blood of Jesus Christ (Hebrews 12:24)," i.e., this "sprinkling" is something that follows conversion -- an every-day thing as we confess our sins (1 John 1:9).

[19] Notice that in the case of the ratification of the Old Covenant, there was ceremonial sanctification (Exodus 19:10), and the promise by the people of obedience to all that God had commanded, before the sprinkling of the blood.

covenant relationship with God, a covenant made possible by the shed blood of Messiah Jesus. "Jesus Christ" is in the genitive case in the Greek. Since the word order in the Greek is "unto obedience and sprinkling of the blood of Jesus Christ," interpreters disagree on whether "obey" and "be sprinkled" are both modified by the genitive. Our translators have so interpreted it by adding "His" to the second word, after putting "Jesus Christ" with "obey."[20] We now have had all three persons of the Godhead named in this verse. All three have been active in the readers becoming God's "chosen" people. Peter already is fortifying his readers with reasons why they should not be deterred from their Christian faith and position as God's children by any persecution they may have to face.

C. Peter's Greeting to The Recipients of the Letter. 1:2b

May grace and peace be yours in fullest measure -- Instead of a simple, perfunctory greeting such as many first-century letters contained, these words are actually a prayer offered by Peter that the readers may experience the distinctive Christian blessings of grace and peace. *Plethunthein* ("be multiplied") is an optative mood expressing a wish.[21] 'May it be conferred abundantly on you!' is Peter's prayer. The readers were already recipients of God's grace and peace. Peter's prayer is that they may have more! A multiplication of God's favor (grace) and peace (spiritual tranquility) is needed to match the growth of hostility with which the Christians addressed are about to be confronted.

I. FIRST DOCTRINAL SECTION. 1:3-12[22]

1:3 -- *Blessed* be *the God and Father of our Lord Jesus Christ, who according to His great mercy has caused us to be born again to a living hope through the resurrection of Jesus Christ from the dead,*

[20] Some scholars object to this wording since it involves the difficulty of simultaneously giving the genitive "of Jesus Christ" both an objective meaning with the first noun ("obedience TO Jesus Christ") and a subjective meaning with the second ("WITH His blood."). Yet the objection is not so great as to preclude numerous English versions from so translating it. On the other hand, William Kelley (*Epistles of Peter*, p.10) treated the genitive "of Jesus Christ" as subjective in both cases, "to obey AS Jesus Christ obeyed, and to be sprinkled with His precious blood." Another possibility is to accept "obey" as standing alone, as in 1 Peter 1:14, so the verse says the Holy Spirit led men to obey, and when they obeyed they were sprinkled with the blood of Jesus Christ.

[21] Peter's wording of his greeting differs from Paul's. Paul does not include a verb -- it must be supplied by the readers (and translators). Peter actually writes the verb, perhaps having learned it from examples in the Old Testament at Daniel 4:1 (3:31 LXX), and 6:25.

[22] In first-century letters the epistolary opening (signature, address, and greeting) was regularly followed by a thanksgiving. Some have outlined 1 Peter differently than we have chosen to -- on the belief that verses 3-12 are a paragraph of thanksgiving for the living hope Christians enjoy, and that the first major point of the body of the letter does not begin until 1:13.

Blessed *be* -- The Greek word here is *eulogetos*, which means "to speak well of another, to praise, to give thanks to." From it come the English words eulogize or eulogy. (This is not the word used in the Beatitudes, *makarios*.) When you are in the midst of persecution, may God be spoken well of, is the idea.[23] When God blesses men, He confers blessings on them, making them blessed. When men bless God, they declare that He, in is infinite excellence, is absolutely praiseworthy. What He does is to be celebrated!

The God and Father of our Lord Jesus Christ -- Sharp's rule of grammar[24] would indicate Peter is speaking of the One who is both the God and Father of Jesus.[25] Is there an implicit reminder that if God did not exempt Jesus, whom He loved dearly, from suffering, then Christians should not expect exemption either? That their "God and Father" so orders the lives of men on earth should be a matter of praise! It is not some remote, uncaring, or uninterested God with whom the Christian is dealing; rather, it is the same Being who watched over the life of His "only begotten Son," a "God" who is powerful enough to be in control, and a God who loves and cares for his children like a "Father." That "Jesus Christ is Lord" is the exultant confession of the redeemed. It acknowledges that the promised Messiah ("Christ") became incarnate ("Jesus") and also acknowledges Him as Master ("Lord"), the One to whom they gladly give their obedience.

Who according to His great mercy -- One of the characteristics of our "God and Father" is His great mercy. In the Greek language, there are two different words translated "mercy," both of which denote sympathy, fellow-feeling with hurting people, compassion. One is *oiktirmos*, which speaks of an inner feeling of compassion which abides in the heart, pity. The other, *eleos*, the word used here for "mercy," speaks of a sympathy manifesting itself in

---

[23] There is no verb in the Greek as evidenced by the italicized "be" in the ASV. Some form of the verb "to be" must be supplied. Some add an indicative form, a simple declaration, "God is praised ...." Others add a subjunctive form, making this a prayer wish, "May God be praised ...!" The same formula is found at 2 Corinthians 1:3 and Ephesians 1:3. Some writers argue Peter has borrowed the expression outright from Paul. Others suggest that the similarity of expression indicates Peter and Paul are in perfect harmony of feeling on this matter of God being spoken well of, whatever our earthly circumstances. Still others argue it is a time-honored Jewish formula that the early church took over with suitable adaptations.

[24] "When two nouns in the same case are connected by the Greek word 'and,' and the first noun is preceded by the article 'the,' and the second noun is not preceded by the article, the second noun refers to the same person or thing to which the first noun refers, and is a further description of it" (see Dana and Mantey, *A Manual Grammar of the Greek New Testament* [Toronto: Macmillan, 1927], p.147).

[25] While the incarnate Jesus was and is temporarily subordinate to the Father (John 14:28; 1 Corinthians 15:24-28), it is not a denial of Jesus' deity for Him to address the Father as "My God" as He did on the cross (Matthew 27:46) and during one of His post-resurrection appearances (John 20:17). Paul also speaks of God as being "the God of our Lord Jesus Christ" (Ephesians 1:17). To identify the Father as the "God" of Jesus Christ does not say that Jesus is not God, nor that Jesus is somehow *eternally* inferior to God. The Scriptures present Jesus as an eternal being (John 17:5, Hebrews 1:3), so "Father" does not imply that back in eternity God created or conceived Jesus. The doctrine of the eternal generation of Jesus (as stated in the Nicene Creed) is without foundation in the Scriptures. "Father" calls attention to the virgin birth, where the human body of Jesus was conceived of the Holy Spirit. We would not call Jesus "Son" if it were not for the incarnation.

actions rather than words.[26] God gets involved in His children's lives! He acts in harmony with His compassion and sympathy for them. Now there is a reason to speak well of Him!

Has caused us to be born again to a living hope -- Peter writes that because of God's mercy He "caused us to be born again to a living hope." (1) Some commentators interpret "us" to be a reference to both Peter and his readers; i.e., this is something true of all Christians. So explained, it is common to find long paragraphs about regeneration or the new birth at this place.[27] The hope which the born-again Christian has is called "living" because it is grounded on the promises of God, and is therefore not empty or deceptive; it is "living" because it is guaranteed by the living Christ. (2) Other commentators understand that "us" is a reference limited to apostles like Peter. So explained, this passage becomes a record of the renewal of hope in the hearts of the apostles when they saw the risen Lord! They had been discouraged and despondent when Christ was killed. "We thought that it was He who was going to redeem Israel," said those on the way to Emmaus, but those hopes had been dashed. But when Jesus rose from the dead, and appeared to them, their hopes and expectations rose to new heights. Because He lives, it is now obvious to all that the committal of our lives to Him and His service was not a waste of time, or a misguided lifestyle.

Through the resurrection of Jesus Christ from the dead -- Peter, who examined the empty tomb in which the dead body of Jesus had been laid, and to whom the risen Lord appeared, is speaking of His bodily resurrection.[28] If "us" in the previous phrase is Christians in general, then this passage says the new birth is made possible by Jesus' resurrection. Without His resurrection in the picture, there would be no way God could raise men to walk in newness of life either (cp. Ephesians 1:19,20 and Romans 6:4-11). If "us" in the previous phrase speaks of apostles in particular, then this passage says it was the resurrection that changed them from despair to hope and joy! Perhaps Peter refers to how Jesus' resurrection changes the way a man thinks, to strengthen and invigorate his readers to consider that there is more to life than what we experience in the here and now.

1:4 -- *To* obtain *an inheritance* which is *imperishable and undefiled and will not fade away, reserved in heaven for you,*

To *obtain* an inheritance -- The Greek construction (*eis*) exactly parallels what was written

[26] A criminal might ask for "mercy" from his judge; but hopeless suffering is the object of "pity."

[27] In second-century Christian literature, the verb "born again" was commonly used as synonymous with immersion into Christ. Some think the second-century church got the idea from how Peter uses the term here.

[28] By "resurrection" the Bible means that the dead body, which was laid in the tomb after Jesus' "spirit" had ceased to live in it, was re-animated by that spirit, and was gone from the tomb because it was no longer a dead body, but a living, glorified body. There is no such thing as a "spiritual resurrection" (meaning His spirit lives on, or His memory lives on). No one ever thought His spirit died!

earlier. "He caused us to be born again *TO* a living hope ... *TO* an inheritance." The word translated "inheritance" is *kleronomia*, a word with a great history. It is the word regularly used in the LXX for the inheritance of Canaan, the promised land (Deuteronomy 15:4, 19:10). To the Jew, that great inheritance, that land where he could settle down and be no more an alien or stranger, was the crown of his dreams and hope. Peter reminds his readers the Christian has an inheritance greater than the Holy Land on the eastern end of the Mediterranean Sea. Because of the resurrection of Jesus, the Christian may cherish a sure hope of one day settling down in his heavenly homeland.

***Which is* imperishable** -- In three different ways the heavenly inheritance differs from earthly treasures. One way is that the Christian's inheritance is "imperishable." Perhaps *aphthartos* means it is not subject to rust or decay or corrosion. Not a few are reminded of Jesus' timeless warning, "Do not lay up for yourselves treasures upon earth, where moth and rust destroy, and where thieves break in and steal; but lay up for yourselves treasures in heaven, where neither moth nor rust destroys, and where thieves do not break in or steal; for where your treasure is, there will your heart be also" (Matthew 6:19-21). Barclay has called attention to another meaning for the word, "unravaged by an invading army. Many and many a time the land of Palestine had been ravaged by the armies of aliens; it had been fought over and blasted and destroyed. But the promised land of the Christian has a peace, joy, safety, and serenity which no invading army can ravage or destroy."[29]

And undefiled -- The idea is that there is no spot or pollution. Expensive clothing can be lowered in value and estimation by just a spot of dirt. And many a time the land of Palestine had been defiled and polluted and rendered impure by the false worship of false gods (Leviticus 18:27,28; Jeremiah 2:7,23, 3:2; Ezekiel 20:43). But into the heavenly inheritance nothing that defiles will enter (Revelation 21:27). The promised land to which the Christian is journeying has a purity and holiness which never will be polluted by the worship of false gods.

And will not fade away -- Here in this age, the grass withers and the flower fades. But it is not so in the land that is very far off. Things there are not transient, like earthly inheritances. The heavenly inheritance never decays in its value, sweetness, or beauty, as do the enjoyments of this world (e.g., like the garlands of leaves or flowers, with which the ancient conquerors were wont to be crowned).

Reserved in heaven for you -- The verb here is a perfect passive participle. The perfect tense says the inheritance has been and is now being kept in heaven for the Christians.[30] The

---

[29] William Barclay, "The Letters of James and Peter" in *The Daily Study Bible Series* (Philadelphia: Westminster, 1960), p.204-205.

[30] Jesus spoke about "the kingdom prepared ... from the foundation of the world" (Matthew 25:34). Abraham, in his lifetime, had information about the city with the foundations whose builder and maker is God (Hebrews 11:10). (When Jesus spoke of going to prepare a place, John 14:2, it must speak of His preparing the way of entrance by means of Calvary, or perhaps it speaks of the cleansing of the heavenly things by means of his blood, Hebrews 9:23.)

passive voice implies God is the agent who keeps it safe. In Peter's day, the earthly property of Christians was sometimes confiscated by their persecutors. "Reserved" means that God is watching over and taking care of and guarding their heavenly inheritance. It is immune to the disasters that can befall earthly inheritances.

1:5 -- ***Who are protected by the power of God through faith for a salvation ready to be revealed in the last time.***

Who are protected -- Heaven is guarded and Christians are "guarded" (ASV). "Protected"[31] is a military term, indicating that the heirs of the heavenly inheritance need protection from their enemies. The participle is in the present tense indicating that God's protection and guarding and keeping of His "chosen ones" is an activity that He continually exercises. It does not promise the readers exemption from physical harm, but it does promise the pilgrims they will have His help on their way to their reward.

By the power of God -- Commentators have difficulty choosing between possible explanations of "power." (1) One order of angels is called "powers" (Colossians 1:16; Ephesians 1:21, 6:12), so some write about guardian angels sent to minister to Christians. Some appeal to Hebrews 1:14, some to Matthew 13:39, and some to Matthew 18:10, for verses that could have parallel ideas to what Peter here writes. (2) The Holy Spirit was a "power" the apostles received (Acts 1:7,8). (3) Others think Peter has in mind God's providential intervention in our lives (cp. Philippians 1:6, 2 Timothy 1:12, 4:18). With every temptation comes the way of escape (1 Corinthians 10:13).

Through faith -- Man's faithfulness is the condition on which God's protecting power is contingent.[32] The protection here promised by God's power does not supersede the Christian's care and endeavor for his own salvation. Compare Hebrews 10:38,39. Faithfulness is the condition. Persecuted believer, did you hear?

For a salvation ready to be revealed in the last time -- This clause begins with *eis* and so expresses the end or purpose, the aim or goal, of such protection as God's power affords in our final salvation. Such a salvation is ours now, in promise. It will be made fully manifest when Jesus returns. The "salvation"[33] here in verse 5 is roughly synonymous with the "inher-

---

[31] Compare 2 Corinthians 11:32, "the ethnarch under Aretas the king *guarded* the city of the Damascenes ...," and Psalm 34:7, "The angel of the Lord encamps around those who fear Him," that is, they are guarded.

[32] There is no hint in this passage of Calvinistic idea of unconditional eternal security. The condition for being "protected" is specifically stated -- it is faithfulness! God's power does not keep the person whose faith fails (1 Timothy 1:19; 2 Timothy 2:18; Hebrews 3:12; Colossians 1:23).

[33] The word "salvation" is used in several different senses in the New Testament: (1) deliverance from danger, Matthew 8:25; (2) deliverance from disease, Matthew 9:21; (3) deliverance from final condemnation by God, Matthew 10:22, 24:13; (4) deliverance from the power of sin, Matthew 1:21; and (5) to preserve in good condition (i.e., like one saves stamps), Luke 17:33. Therefore, each time we encounter this word we must determine from the context which of its meanings is intended.

itance" already described in verse 4.[34] Future salvation[35] is a many-sided thing. It surely includes redemption of the body, as well as deliverance from final condemnation. "Revealed" implies a specific act of uncovering or unveiling, and implies the previous existence of that which is unveiled. "There is a glorious day coming when God will draw back the veil that now hides our glorious salvation from mortal eyes. The unveiling is not deferred because the salvation is not ready but because the appropriate time in the eternal counsel of God has not yet come."[36] The phrase "in the last time" used by Peter is used nowhere else in the New Testament. It evidently has reference to what Jesus called "the last day," at which time the dead will be raised and judged, with the righteous being invited into the bliss and joy of the Father, while the wicked are sent to everlasting punishment.[37] The time referred to is the Lord's second coming, not the time of the individual believer's death. As this age (the last in the series of ages in God's dealings with men[38]) closes, Christ will come and take to heaven all those who have been "chosen" and "faithful."

1:6 -- ***In this you greatly rejoice, even though now for a little while, if necessary, you have been distressed by various trials,***

In this -- The intended antecedent of Peter's relative pronoun is uncertain. The Greek *en ho* can either be masculine or neuter; thus, the reference is not specifically to "salvation," which is feminine. If we take it as masculine, the one in whom we greatly rejoice is "the God and Father." Or perhaps the "last time" at the close of verse 5 may be the thing in which the Christian rejoices. If we regard it as neuter, the relative pronoun is a summary of the whole picture drawn in verses 3-5, of the Christian's present privileges and hopes, of his being guarded.

You greatly rejoice -- The Christian's joy is independent of earthly circumstances. That is why Paul and Silas could sing with lacerated backs (Acts 16:25). They were "guarded" (ASV) and they had a "salvation ready to be revealed." The assurance of redemption (1 Peter 1:18) and the hope of future glory (4:13) give the Christian a perspective that enables him to rejoice while undergoing suffering (Romans 5:3; 1 Thessalonians 1:6). The verb in the Greek

---

[34] The salvation here contemplated in 1 Peter 1:5 is not the same as that promised at Mark 16:15,16 -- the salvation from past sins granted when a man becomes a Christian. When you repent and obey, you are saved from your past sins. But that is not what is being spoken about here in verse 5 -- this "salvation" is something still future for people already Christians.

[35] We may say "I was saved" (from my past sins, when I was immersed), "I am being saved," and "I hope to be saved" (the salvation to be revealed). Salvation may be viewed as a past event (2 Timothy 1:9; Titus 3:5); a present happening (see the present passive verbs at 1 Corinthians 1:18, 15:2; 2 Corinthians 2:15); and as something yet future (cp. 1 Peter 1:9, 2:2; Romans 5:10, 13:11; 1 Corinthians 5:5; 1 Thessalonians 5:8; 2 Timothy 2:10; Titus 1:2; Hebrews 1:14, 9:28).

[36] D.E. Hiebert, *First Peter* (Chicago: Moody Press, 1984), p.53.

[37] John 6:39,40,54, 11:24, 12:48; 1 Peter 1:12; 2 Thessalonians 1:10; 2 Timothy 4:8.

[38] 1 John 2:8; Hebrews 1:2; Acts 2:17.

could be either indicative (i.e., a statement of what the Christians were already doing) or imperative (i.e., a command concerning what they were to do in the future). *Agalliasthe* is a strong expression, meaning to exult, or to leap for joy. It takes two English words to answer to the intense joy the Greek word speaks of.

We have an expression we use often when studying 1 Peter -- it is "Great Days with Jesus!" We use it when we come upon some expression or event in the letter that is reminiscent of Peter's personal experience with Jesus during His earthly ministry.[39] We very likely are looking at one here, for Jesus commanded His followers to rejoice and be exceeding glad (the same *agalliasthe* verb Peter uses) when they were persecuted for righteousness sake (Matthew 5:12). A person can endure suffering joyfully if he is convinced that the goal ahead is worthwhile and that the sufferings will help him reach the goal.

Even though now for a little while, if necessary, you have been distressed by various trials – The Greek phrase opens with *oligon*, meaning a "little [while]." It is descriptive of the duration of the suffering the saints were facing. The trials were but temporary, and better days were ahead. Next in the Greek word order is the adverb *arti*, which means just now, at this moment, even now. The "though" in the NASB probably represents an attempt to translate the circumstantial participle "distressed."[40] Since it is an aorist tense participle, we are probably to think of the "distress" as taking place before the "rejoicing."[41] "Various trials"[42] speak of something more than the ordinary vicissitudes of life. Included in the trials Peter has in mind would be their being accused by unbelievers of being evildoers (2:12), of being reviled and abused (3:16, 4:4), of facing "fiery trials" and the "devil as a roaring lion" stalking his prey (4:12, 5:8). *Lupeo*, translated "distressed", speaks not of the infliction of pain, but the inner feeling of distress or grief caused by outward circumstances. "If necessary"[43] reflects the uncertainty whether the persecution will reach all the readers. If it does, then when distressed, they will have opportunity to "greatly rejoice."

---

[39] We could have used this phrase already several times in our study. 1:1 -- Peter recalls his call to be an apostle of Jesus. 1:2 -- "Obey Jesus Christ" just might reflect what Jesus expects of those who love him -- namely "keep My commandments" (John 14:15). 1:3 -- "God and Father of our Lord" expresses the same idea expressed in Jesus' words to Peter, "My Father has revealed it to you" (Matthew 16:17). The "living hope through the resurrection of Jesus from the dead" was certainly a great and memorable day with Jesus!

[40] Numerous helping words are possible when translating circumstantial participles -- while, as, because, since, after, if, although, by means of -- and translators may use whichever one makes sense.

[41] An aorist tense participle usually indicates that the action of the participle preceded the action of the main verb, which is "rejoice" in this place.

[42] *Peirasmos* can be translated either "trial (test)" or "temptation (inducement to sin)." Compare notes at James 1:2-4 where we are told "trials" work endurance, so that we become perfect and entire, lacking nothing. When the Christians were persecuted, it was not only a test of their faith, but also it was a temptation to abandon Christianity. Christians can stand anything that comes, if they remember that every trial is, in fact, a test. Before gold is pure, it has to be tried and tested and purified by fire. The trials and persecutions which come to a man test his faith, and out of them faith can emerge stronger and clearer and firmer than it was before.

[43] It is consoling to know that God's people are never needlessly afflicted. Sometimes our loving father sees that discipline is necessary. "Whom the Lord loves he disciplines" (Hebrews 12:6). If you are placed in the world so as to have to face fiery and fierce temptations, face them! Pass the test victoriously!

1:7 -- ***That the proof of your faith,*** **being** ***more precious than gold which is perishable, even though tested by fire, may be found to result in praise and glory and honor at the revelation of Jesus Christ;***

That the proof of your faith -- With a *hina* clause Peter now gives the result of the "various trials" of which verse 6 spoke. The word translated "proof" is *dokimion,* which in classical Greek meant the means or instrument of testing. It was used for the crucible in which gold or silver is refined. Thus the trials through which Christians pass constituted the crucible in which their faith was tested to reveal its true character. "Your faith" in this context does not refer to the doctrinal content of the readers' faith (i.e., true versus false teaching), but to the genuineness of their personal response to the gospel.

Being **more precious than gold which is perishable, even though tested by fire** -- The verse is punctuated differently in the various versions as translators have struggled to smoothly express the idea of this verse in English. NIV has it, "These [trials] have come so that our faith – of greater worth than gold, which perishes even though refined by fire – may be proved genuine and may result in praise, glory and honor when Jesus Christ is revealed." The point apparently is not that their *faith* was more precious than gold, but that the *testing* of faith is of more value than the testing of gold.[44] Even pure gold, refined by fire, is a perishable thing. It will not endure forever. To hear "well done, good and faithful servant!" is far more precious than any amount of gold to the Christian. It is much more desirable to test one's religion than it is to test gold, for the religion is far more valuable.

May be found to result in praise and glory and honor at the revelation of Jesus Christ - - Here we come to the completion of the clause that began with "that" (*hina*). The NASB treats it as a "result" clause.[45] The "revelation of Jesus Christ" is Peter's way of describing the second coming.[46] Jesus is now hidden from human sight, but he will be "unveiled" or "uncovered." When Jesus comes to earth again, there will be a general judgment. That is when faithful people will be "found" (examined and judged) to be due praise, glory, and honor. "Praise" reminds us of the "Well done, good and faithful slave." It denotes the recognition or approval Christians will receive from the Judge. It is public commendation from the God of the universe. What is "glory"? It is hard to describe. Heaven immediately comes to mind. "Glory" may have some reference to the Christian's participation in

---

[44] The participle "tested by fire" agrees in gender with "gold" rather than with "faith." Some of our English translations are not clear on this.

[45] Some writers treat *hina* and the subjunctive, here, as a purpose clause, and speak of the purpose God has in mind when he allows the trials to happen to Christians.

[46] This commentator does not treat the words for Christ's return -- *apokalupsis* ("revelation"), *parousia* ("coming" or "presence"), *epiphaneia* ("appearance") -- as though they described different comings. This verse in Peter has Christians honored at the "revelation" of Jesus Christ. (This is different from modern premillennialism which distinguishes between Christ's parousia and revelation comings and has Christians honored at the parousia.) It is instructive to compare Peter's references to the second coming here in 1 Peter 1:5,7 with what he preached in the temple (Acts 3:20,21) and in his message to the house of Cornelius (Acts 10:42).

the radiance and glory of the heavenly city (Revelation 21:24-26; Luke 24:26; Romans 8:18; 1 Peter 5:1). Perhaps we should also think of the glorified body the redeemed receive, a body like the one Jesus now has (Romans 8: 21; Philippians 3:21). "Honor" calls to mind the distinctions granted to the faithful – the crown of righteousness, the white robe, the palm. If the Bible teaches degrees of reward, then "honor" denotes the positions of distinction to which Christ will promote his suffering servants (John 12:26), and the blessings they will enjoy. "The faith of Peter's readers, at the moment, was being rewarded with scoffing, rejection, and persecution; but when the Lord returns, the scene will be reversed (cf. 2 Thessalonians 1:6-10)."[47]

1:8 -- ***And though you have not seen Him, you love Him, and though you do not see Him now, but believe in Him, you greatly rejoice with joy inexpressible and full of glory.***

And though you have not seen Him, you love Him -- Peter is here drawing a contrast between himself and his readers. It had been his privilege to have seen the incarnate Jesus, and to have personally witnessed His earthly ministry. Peter even told the Lord to His face that he loved Him (John 21:15-17). Peter's readers had not seen Jesus during the days of His flesh, but that did not put them at a spiritual disadvantage (as compared with, say, Peter). By accepting the testimony of those who had seen Him, they had entered into a personal, loving relationship with Jesus. "Love" translates a present indicative form of *agapao*, an intelligent, purposeful love, a love that is a thing of the will, more than just a thing of the heart.

And though you do not see Him now, but believe in Him -- Peter's "now" implies that one day his readers will see Jesus (Revelation 1:7, 22:3,4). For "now," since He ascended, Jesus is in heaven, and to mortal eyes invisible, like the Father. Still Peter's readers "believe in Him." The prepositional phrase "in Him" following "believe" is the Greek language for an obedient faith, not just mental assent.[48] As Peter writes these words of contrast, how could he not remember the words of Jesus to Thomas, "Because you have seen me, have you believed? Blessed are they who did not see, and yet believed" (John 20:29). It is *not* tantamount to committing mental suicide to assert that Jesus is! Belief is based on testimony. A merchant will embark with perfect propriety in a commercial enterprise, on the supposition that there is such a place as London or Paris. He has never seen the city for himself, but he takes the word of others who have; and he goes on as if he had seen it himself, convinced by the evidence given by others. We may not have seen heaven, or the Savior, with our own eyes, but we can take the word of others who have! So we do what the Savior tells us. We act upon His word. That is what Peter's readers have done.

---

[47] Hiebert, *op. cit.*, p.59

[48] J.G. Machen, *New Testament Greek for Beginners* (Toronto: Macmillan, 1969), p.85. Also, Leon Morris, *The Gospel According to John* (Grand Rapids: Eerdmans, 1992), p.335-337.

You greatly rejoice with joy inexpressible and full of glory -- Because we love Jesus, and because we have obediently served him, we can rejoice[49] amid distress and persecution. These are relationships that will sustain us. Christian joy is difficult to put into words[50] because it is different from earth-born joys. Christian joy is full of "glory"[51] – there is joy even now (remember the joy you experienced as new converts); there is joy every day and hour, and there is the prospect of enjoying glory ever after. Verse 9 will explain it in more detail.

1:9 -- ***Obtaining as the outcome of your faith the salvation of your souls.***

Obtaining as the outcome of your faith -- The action of the participle "obtaining" or "receiving" is simultaneous with the rejoicing (verse 8). The participle likely should be taken as causal. You are rejoicing "because" you are receiving the salvation of your souls. "Faith" here likely speaks of a life of faithfulness to Jesus. "Outcome" (the Greek is *telos*, goal) says that this is what your faith is designed and adapted to secure. Concentration on the outcome of a life of faithfulness is a grand encouragement to be faithful whatever it may cost, be it persecution or martyrdom.

The salvation of your souls -- The opposite of salvation for a soul is eternal damnation. Peter seems to be talking to his saved readers about a salvation that is future.[52] But whose salvation? The marginal note indicates that "your" is omitted in some manuscripts. If it is, it may be their pagan neighbors whose souls are saved as a result of the readers' faithfulness (cp. 1 Peter 2:12). If it is included, the salvation is something that is very personal for the readers. If we opt to include "your," we suppose that Peter uses "souls" in this place to speak of the whole person – body, soul, and spirit.[53]

1:10 -- ***As to this salvation, the prophets who prophesied of the grace that*** **would come** ***to you made careful search and inquiry,***

---

[49] Just as in verse 6, this verb can be either present indicative (a statement of fact), or a present imperative (a command to be obeyed).

[50] The compound verb has two prepositions: up + out + to speak. You can't get it up out of your mouth.

[51] The verb form here is a perfect passive participle. The Christian's joy was filled with glory in the past, and it still is. (A perfect tense participle indicates a state simultaneous with the main verb, but which has resulted from an action prior to the action of the main verb.)

[52] In comments on "salvation" at verse 5, it was noted that in Scripture "salvation" can be either past, present, or future, depending on how we define the word.

[53] Sometimes "soul" is used in contrast with the body in which it is housed (as 1:22, 2:11,25, 3:20, 4:19; 2 Peter 2:8,14). Sometimes "soul" is used to speak of "persons" (as at Acts 27:37). Because context often helps define what is meant by "soul," some writers think "soul" is contrasted to the "body" here in 1 Peter 1:9. They think "glory" may speak of the future state with its resurrection body, while "salvation of your souls" speaks of what we have now.

As to this salvation -- In verses 10-12, Peter is assuring his readers that their faith and salvation, about which he has been writing, are worth suffering for. He highlights these reasons: it was the subject of prophecy; it was an object of study by the Old Testament prophets; it was the content of inspired preaching in their midst; it is a topic about which angels desire to learn more.

The prophets who prophesied of the grace that *would come* to you -- "Prophets" is anarthrous in the Greek. Since the verbs following are all aorists, the reference is to the Old Testament prophets.[54] They were God's mouthpieces, who spoke by inspiration as they predicted the Messianic age and all its benefits of salvation (here called "grace"[55]). It is doubtful that Peter is saying the Old Testament prophets predicted specifically the coming of the gospel to the regions addressed in this letter. But Old Testament prophets did foretell future deliverance for men of all nations, and had specifically foretold the inclusion of the Gentiles.[56]

Made careful search and inquiry -- Like a miner digs for precious ore, searching for something that is hidden, so the Old Testament prophets delved into their prophecies, scrutinizing them with care in order to understand the prediction they had just made by the inspiration of the Holy Spirit. What Peter here tells us about the Old Testament prophets' attempts to understand their own predictions reminds us of what Jesus said (Matthew 13:17; Luke 10: 23,24).

1:11 -- ***Seeking to know what person or time the Spirit of Christ within them was indicating as He predicted the sufferings of Christ and the glories to follow.***

Seeking to know -- The present participle "searching" (*eraunontes*) pictures the prophets as returning repeatedly to the problem their predictions created in their minds. Here is a remarkable glimpse into the consciousness of the Old Testament prophets. First, they were aware that the message they delivered was inspired by the Holy Spirit. Then when they had delivered the message, they examined their own predictions with care, struggling to under-

---

[54] Selwyn has argued Peter has New Testament prophets in mind, but his arguments have not convinced others. The language of this verse shows there was a time lapse between the time when the prophets prophesied and the time when salvation came to the readers of this letter. That time lapse points to Old Testament prophecies, in our opinion.

[55] This commentator believes that "salvation" and "grace" are synonymous in this context. Not all agree. Hiebert (*op. cit.*, p.64) thinks that "grace" in verse 10 is the same grace prayed for in verse 2. Still others argue that salvation is something that results from grace (and appeal to Ephesians 2:8). This commentator was long ago taught a definition for "grace" as being God's unmerited favor. He also has determined that man is not wholly passive in salvation, so there is no need to make "grace" synonymous with the convicting, converting work of the Holy Spirit, as though "saved by grace" means God (the Spirit) does it all to a wholly passive recipient. We have already seen in 1 Peter that there is faith, and obedience, and the work of the Holy Spirit involved in God's election. We should not offer comments on this verse that contradict what Peter has already clearly written.

[56] Hosea 1:10, 2:23; Isaiah 10:11, 52:15, 65:1; Psalm 18:49; Amos 9:11,12; cp. Luke 1:70 and 24:46,47.

stand who or when what they had predicted would appear.[57] The idea of salvation made available through a suffering Messiah was a mystery (Colossians 1:26,27)!

What person or time -- The ASV reads, "what *time* or what manner of time?" The problem the translator faces is whether the interrogative pronouns, *tina* and *poion*, are both neuter, modifying "time," or whether *tina* is to be disassociated from "time" and taken as a masculine, "who?" If the first view is correct, the prophets' question relates to the time and attendant circumstances of the Messiah's appearing. If the "or" is disjunctive, and a two-pronged search is indicated, it concerned both Messiah's identity *and* the time and setting of His coming. They knew they were speaking about the coming Messiah, but they had many questions in their minds about the Messiah that were unanswered.

The Spirit of Christ within them -- "Spirit of Christ" seems to be one of the numerous names found in Scripture for the Holy Spirit.[58] He likely is called "the Spirit of Christ" because it was the coming Messiah He was prompting the prophets to speak about.[59] "Within them" affirms the inspiration of the Old Testament prophets, just as 2 Peter 1:21 does. Those Old Testament prophecies about the coming Messiah were not of human origin, the dreams or imaginations of pious minds, but were communicated by the Holy Spirit – the same Spirit who in Peter's day spoke through him and the other apostles.

Was indicating -- The imperfect tense verb shows that all along, in prophet after prophet, the Holy Spirit was making these indications.

As He predicted the sufferings of Christ -- "Predicted" is a present participle. It is something the Holy Spirit kept doing,[60] beginning more than 700 years before Christ came.

---

[57] John the Baptist's question (Matthew 11:3) also shows a prophet struggling to understand a prediction he himself had made. The modern higher critics would say, "There is no predictive prophecy. No Old Testament prophet ever said anything he didn't understand." Of course, the critics never say that their pronouncements about prophecy are contrary to what Peter's epistle says.

[58] Compare the statements in Acts 16:6,7. Luke says in 16:6 that the Holy Spirit hindered them. Then in 16:7, he says that the "Spirit of Jesus" hindered them. These statements show that the two terms are but two different designations for the third person of the Godhead. Paul uses this same name for the Holy Spirit at Romans 8:9.

[59] Another way of explaining this genitive "of Christ" is to make it a subjective genitive, meaning that the Holy Spirit was sent "by Christ" upon the Old Testament prophets, just like in New Testament times He sent the Spirit (John 16:7; Acts 2:33). Such an interpretation requires a recognition that Jesus pre-existed from eternity, and would be in harmony with references that have the pre-existent Christ involved with the nation of Israel in Old Testament times (1 Corinthians 10:4; 2 Corinthians 3:17). This interpretation of "Spirit of Christ," which gives strong testimony to the pre-existence of Jesus was held by many in the early church.

[60] The Holy Spirit is a person, so the KJV rendering "as *it* testified beforehand" is improper. The "He" of the NASB is much better.

The Greek word speaks of a solemn declaration, made publicly. Perhaps Peter coined this Greek word as a way of reflecting the oft-repeated opening of prophetic messages, "Thus saith the Lord!" Peter lists two topics the prophets emphasized as they made these predictions. One was the "sufferings *unto* Christ" (the Greek *eis* denotes things directed toward Him, either by His enemies, or by divine foreordination). The plural "sufferings" causes us to contemplate all the painful experiences that were inflicted on Jesus during His earthly ministry.[61] Perhaps Peter worded it this way as a means of encouraging his readers. It was prophesied in Scripture that the Messiah would go through sufferings on the way to glory. That is the way Peter's readers are being asked to travel, too.

And the glories to follow -- This is the second point in Peter's two-point summary of Old Testament Messianic prophecies. First came the sufferings, then the glories.[62] Included in the glories would be Messiah's resurrection from the dead, His ascension and coronation (sitting at the right hand of the Majesty on high until His enemies be made the footstool of His feet), the coming of the Holy Spirit on Pentecost, the multitude of souls who accept Jesus as Savior from among all tongues, tribes, and nations, and the final day of glory, when Jesus returns on the clouds of heaven and presents the spotless bride to Himself (Ephesians 5:27).

1:12 -- ***It was revealed to them that they were not serving themselves, but you, in these things which now have been announced to you through those who preached the gospel to you by the Holy Spirit sent from heaven -- things into which angels long to look.***

It was revealed to them that they were not serving themselves -- As the prophets spoke their Messianic prophecies and then struggled to understand them,[63] this much was revealed to them: that the fulfillment would not be in their lifetimes ("they were not serving themselves"[64]). How it was "revealed to them" is not explained. Sometimes in the Old Testament, answers to questions come almost immediately (cf. Daniel 10:14). Perhaps as revelations were given later, as God revealed new details about His plans (Hebrews 1:1), the prophets began to understand the fulfillment was not in their lifetimes. The prophets, doubt-

---

[61] Some of the prophecies about Messiah's suffering which come to mind are the suffering servant poems of Isaiah 40-66, esp. 53; Psalm 2:1,2; Psalm 22 and 23; Psalm 26:8-11; and Daniel 9:2-27.

[62] The same verses that predicted a suffering Messiah also predicted the "glory" following. Earlier, in notes on verse 9, we debated whether "salvation" is present or future. "Glories to follow" certainly include the future.

[63] R.C. Foster, in class one day, tried to imagine the questions the prophets asked. "What time? What person? What things? What people? Suffering? Why is the Messiah to die? It is bad enough that the prophets had to die, but why the Messiah? How can He be a man and also God (Isaiah 7 and 9)? How do you harmonize Psalm 110 and Psalm 2? How can He be an eternal priest and also the Son of God. What does Daniel 9:24-27 point to? What is this 'coming on the clouds of heaven to rule'?"

[64] In a day when many are seeking some special measure of the Spirit for their own personal edification and benefit, it is well to note an important principle of inspiration, namely, that the gifts were given for the benefit of others.

less, like Abraham, rejoiced to see the day of Christ; they saw it by faith and were glad (John 8:56); but they saw it in the far distance; they desired to see and hear what the apostles saw and heard, but the time was not yet (Matthew 13:16,17).

But (they were serving) you -- "Serving" (ministered, cp. Acts 6:1-6) pictures the prophets' work as being like spreading a table so that others might afterward feed on the food laid on it. What the prophets were predicting about "salvation" (bound up with Messiah's sufferings and the glories that followed) has now come true in the lives of Peter's readers. The prophets predicted what, to them, was some unknown future time. Peter says that time they wanted to know about is now here!

In these things which now have been announced to you -- The Greek says "they ministered *the same things* which have now been preached to you." "Now" denotes a strong contrast between the time when the prophets lived and the time when the readers live. The things preached in the five provinces where the readers lived, the things believed by those who became Christians, were the very things predicted by the Old Testament prophets.[65]

Through those who preached the gospel to you by the Holy Spirit sent from heaven -- Who it was who preached the gospel to Peter's readers, Peter does not specify. He simply affirms that they were empowered in their preaching by the Holy Spirit who was "sent from heaven."[66] This leads us to think that the first preachers in the provinces addressed in this letter were apostles or prophets or teachers – men who were directed or helped by the baptism of the Holy Spirit, or by some supernatural spiritual gift, such as was received by the laying on of an apostle's hands. In any case, the preachers who preached the gospel were inspired by the same Spirit who spoke years before through the Old Testament prophets. No wonder the messages matched! Peter has now given his third reason why they should be impressed with a deep sense of the value of the gospel and the great privileges which they enjoyed as Christians. It was the subject of inspired preaching.

Things into which angels long to look -- Here is a fourth topic intended to increase his readers' appreciation for the gospel and the many blessings it had brought to them. Angels are created beings (Hebrews 1:7, Colossians 1:16), and superhuman (Hebrews 2:7), but they are not omniscient. So they too are anxious to learn the meaning of the predictions about Messiah's sufferings and the glories to follow. They learn much by watching what happens in and through the church (Ephesians 3:10).[67] The word picture in "long to look into" is of

---

[65] This is very contrary to modern dispensationalism, with its mystery-parenthesis theory, and its claim that the church age was not predicted in the Old Testament.

[66] Peter's statement about the Spirit's being sent from heaven reminds us of Jesus' promise to the apostles in John 16:13,14, and Acts 1:8 (fulfilled at 2:4). The aorist tense ("sent") denotes the historical event of the Spirit's coming as a thing of the past when 1 Peter is written.

[67] Bible students are likely to ponder this question, If angels are watching and learning, how about folk who have died, and whose souls have gone to heaven? Do they also watch what happens on earth? The answer is evidently, Yes! Hebrews 12:1-2 speaks of a great cloud of witnesses, made up, we believe, in part by the Old Tes-

one leaning sideways and craning the neck, in order to get a better view. How the angels must have looked on as Jesus suffered, went out to the cross, and all! Peter's implication is evidently this – angels (who stand outside the work of redemption) give special attention to the church, and to salvation. So why not by the men who really need them? How strange that our salvation is so wonderful as to be the object of interest to both prophets and angels, and yet is ignored or neglected by men for whom it was prepared. Peter's message is, such a great salvation is worth living for and worth suffering for!

II. FIRST HORTATORY SECTION. 1:13-2:2

A. Exhortation to Hope. 1:13

1:13 -- ***Therefore, gird your minds for action, keep sober*** **in spirit,** ***fix your hope completely on the grace to be brought to you at the revelation of Jesus Christ.***

Therefore -- This first group of four exhortations is based on what was written in the previous doctrinal section. The "chosen" who are participants of the "living hope" and the blessings, hopes, and privileges of the salvation offered in the gospel, have certain obligations arising therefrom.

Gird your minds for action -- Orientals wore long, loose, flowing robes. When they wished to run or fight or work, they had to bind up their garments with their belt, in order to work or move without hindrance. Figuratively, the term speaks of preparation for strenuous or vigorous activity,[68] and the middle voice verb in the Greek implies this is an action that one would perform for his own benefit or advantage. The word translated "minds" (*dianoias*) refers to what goes through the mind, one's thought processes. A man can control what goes through his mind, and Peter is commanding the Christians what things they should think about, if they are going to come off victorious from these pending persecutions. The first thing they must do is make up their minds (aorist tense) what topics they are going to concentrate on.

Keep sober *in spirit* -- Avoid anything that would result in loss of mental and spiritual self-control. The two participles – "gird [your minds]" and "keep sober" – designate mental ac-

---

tament heroes just named in chapter 11. Moses and Elijah on the Mount of Transfiguration knew what was happening on earth, and discussed with Messiah about His coming death. Revelation 6:9 speaks of souls (in heaven as it now is, the intermediate state) underneath the altar, watching what happens to Christians on earth, and asking God how long He is going to let such persecutions continue. (It is only after the second coming that "there will be no more tears and no more sorrow," Revelation 7:17, 21:4.) Just as angels in heaven are still looking down and watching (1 Corinthians 4:8,9; Luke 15:10), so apparently those who have gone on before are looking down and watching.

[68] Our equivalent phrase would be to "roll up your sleeves," or "take off your jacket," so as to be free to work unhindered. A determination to do something is what is pictured.

tivities that will support the imperative verb, "fix your hope ...." "Keep sober"[69] is a present tense participle, indicating habitual behavior. Without being sober, they will think about a host of things, or nothing at all, other than what Peter here directs them to think about. Christians are not to deaden their minds either with strong drink or with light, frivolous thoughts which would rob the mind of readiness to meet their fiery trials. A man can forget the important things he needs to think about while watching television, or listening to music, or watching a play or movie, or fishing or hunting. While none of these activities needs be abandoned by the Christian, the Christian must be careful lest those pursuits become his whole focus while eternal verities are ignored.

Fix your hope completely -- The imperative appeals to the will – such hope is not a matter of the emotions but of obedience! Hope can change a man's behavior. People have been known to alter their lifestyles because of hope for a new car, or a new home. Hope of home sustained Vietnamese prisoners of war through brutality and deplorable conditions. In a similar way, the hope of the future that the Christian cherishes[70] enables him to endure the trials of the present.

On the grace to be brought to you at the revelation of Jesus Christ -- The "revelation of Jesus Christ" is His second coming (as in verse 7[71]). In this context, the "grace"[72] that Christians will receive includes the resurrected and glorified body, the approbation of the Judge ("well done!"), glory and honor, the inheritance which is imperishable, the salvation of your souls. As God is moving history to its goal, that grace is already in the process of "being brought" to the Christian.

B. Exhortation to Holiness. 1:14-16

---

[69] Since the word "sober" can speak of absolute abstinence from wine, our translators have added "in spirit" to let us know there is something more than abstinence being talked about in this context.

[70] It is not easy to decide the relationship of the adverb *teleios* ("completely, perfectly") to the rest of the sentence. Some suppose it modifies "sober" ("be perfectly sober") since it follows the participle "be sober." It is usual for an adverb to follow the verb it qualifies. Others argue that word order for adverbs is not absolute, and *teleios* therefore should be taken with "hope." If we do that, does it mean "with finality," or does it mean "unreservedly," or "completely," or what? It is not a tentative or half-hearted setting of one's hope on the grace to come that Peter calls for.

[71] Because the Greek (both in verse 7 and here) reads *en apokalupsis Iesou Christou*, Lenski argues it is a mistake to translate it "at the revelation of Jesus Christ." He insists it is a reference, not the second coming, but to the incarnation and resurrection of Jesus, two stupendous events in which Jesus was revealed to be the unique Son of God. Furthermore, because the participle "is being brought" is a present tense form, Lenski also believes that "grace" is brought to us (*en*) in connection with this past "revelation" of Jesus. R.C.H. Lenski, *Interpretation of I and II Epistles of Peter, the three Epistles of John, and the Epistle of Jude* (Minneapolis: Augsburg Publishing House, 1966], p.53. However, "revelation of Jesus Christ" is regular language for the second advent and we see no real reason to depart from that meaning here.

[72] We have had "grace" at 1:2 and 1:10.

1:14 -- *As obedient children, do not be conformed to the former lusts* which were yours *in your ignorance,*

As obedient children -- The ASV rightly translates "as children of obedience." The Greek reflects a Hebraism – a Hebrew usage of the word "son" (or "child") followed by a word denoting a quality or characteristic that child exhibits. Peter's readers are God's "children," whose lives are characterized by obedience. There is an obedience that follows conversion[73] (cp. verse 3), and this obedience is the foundation for a call to holiness. The Heavenly Father has shown us His will ("be holy in all your behavior!"). He has taught us the kind of conduct that is expected and desired of us. The right kind of children, who are characterized by obedience, will honor the will of their Father.

Do not be conformed -- This participial phrase indicates one of the conditions that must be met before men can be holy in all their conduct. They will have to stop behaving like unconverted people behave. "Do not be conformed" seems to be an echo of Romans 12:2, "Be not fashioned according to this world" (ASV). "Not fashioned" equals "not modeling your life," not copying the outward form that is popular at the moment.

To the former lusts *which were yours* in your ignorance -- This language seems to indicate the readers came from a Gentile background (cp. Acts 17:30; Ephesians 4:18). Because they were without a written revelation such as the Jews had, and therefore dependent on oral tradition, as the generations passed the children and the children's children of the Gentiles came to know less and less of God's requirements, especially if their parents did not pass on to their children what they knew about God's will. As a result, the Gentiles came to be desire[74]-centered. They did things just because their desires led them to do them (cp. James 1:14). "Former" refers to the time before they became Christians. Barclay gives some illustrations of how desire-dominated first-century society was:

> As we read the records of the social history of the world into which Christianity came, we cannot but be astonished and appalled at the sheer fleshliness of life within it. It was a world in which there was desperate poverty at the lower end of the social scale; but at the top end of the scale we read of banquets which cost literally thousands of dollars, where peacocks' brains and nightingales' tongues were served, where the Emperor Vitellius set on the table at one banquet 2000 fish and 7000 birds. Chastity was forgotten. Martial speaks of a woman who had reached her 10th husband; Juvenal of a woman who had 8 husbands in 5 years; and Jerome tells us that in Rome there was one woman who was married to her 23rd husband, she herself being his 21st wife. And both in Greece and in Rome, homosexuality was so common that this unnatural vice had come

---

[73] In earlier verses, Peter has told his readers that they were "sanctified by the Spirit unto obedience" (1:2). Now he describes them as "children of obedience." Obedience is given great emphasis in the New Testament (cf. 1 Peter 1:22; Romans 1:5, 6:15-18, 16:26). After all, without it, a man's faith is not genuine.

[74] The word translated "lusts," *epithumiais*, is neutral in meaning; the "desires" can be either good or bad -- the context will tell. Here they are bad.

> to be looked on as natural. It was a world which was mastered by desire. Its aim was to find newer and wilder ways of gratifying its own lusts.[75]

Christians have to be very "sober," or they will find that their desires, just like their neighbors, have all been triggered by advertising from Madison Avenue.

1:15 -- ***But like the Holy One who called you, be holy yourselves also in all*** **your** ***behavior;***

But like the Holy One who called you -- The Holy God is the standard the Christian is to model when he fashions his behavior. The model to which Christians are to compare themselves is God! Men are called (invited) through the gospel to become Christians.[76] At the time of their conversion, God invited them to a life of holiness, called them to be saints. Refraining from undesirable conduct is only part of the Christian ethic. There is a positive command to be holy also involved. Jehovah is "the Holy One," that is, He is different[77] from the gods of men's creation. Men make gods in their own image and likeness and attribute to them all the unrighteous and lascivious deeds which men themselves do. Bacchus can be a drunkard and drive his chariot while drunk; gods and goddesses can seduce each other's mates. Moloch, Baal, and Dagon, the gods of the people surrounding Israel, were worshiped in rites which were abominable. But the God of the Bible is different. He is a holy God! He is called "the Holy One of Israel," indicating He is separate from all that is morally impure or evil.

Be holy yourselves also in all *your* behavior -- "Yourselves" is emphatic and implies a contrast. However others may live, you are to be holy![78] "All," used without an article, points to the multitude of occasions in the Christian's life when he may manifest holiness of conduct ("behavior"), be it "business or pleasure, labor or rest, joy or sorrow, easy or difficult situations" (Lenski, *op. cit.*, p.56). If our heavenly Father is holy, how can His children be anything but holy?

1:16 -- ***Because it is written,*** **"YOU SHALL BE HOLY, FOR I AM HOLY."**

Because it is written -- "Written" is a perfect passive verb form, implying something was written in the past and still stands true. Peter's call to holiness is nothing new. It is a clear

---

[75] William Barclay, *The Letters of James and Peter* (Philadelphia: Westminster, 1960), p.221.

[76] See 1 Thessalonians. 2:12, and compare 1 Peter 1:12 and 22. Such a "calling" (invitation to become a Christian) is part of God's eternal plan. "Whom He predestined, them he also called" (Romans 8:30).

[77] The root meaning of the word translated "holy" is "different" -- different from ordinary things, different because it is set apart for sacred service. The temple was "holy" because it was different from other buildings. The Sabbath was "holy" because it was different from other days. The Christian is "holy" because he is different from other men.

[78] The verb is an imperative. This is a command. The imperative is an aorist form of *ginomai*, which might be translated "become." On the other hand, *ginomai* may be used here because the verb *eimi* had no aorist forms. The aorist imperative says, "Settle it once and for all that you are going to be holy!"

part of God's recorded will for His people.[79] "It is written" is the regular way Old Testament passages are cited in New Testament writings. The verse about to be quoted is found several times in Leviticus (11:44-45; 19:2; 20:7,26), where God told His people He expected them to be different from the nations around them.

"YOU SHALL BE HOLY, FOR I AM HOLY" -- Translations vary at this place (e.g., the KJV has "Be ye holy!") because there is a manuscript difference. The Textus Receptus repeats the verb used in verse 15. The better attested text of verse 16 has a future indicative form, which is reflected in the NASB's "you shall be."[80] This probably does not mean that Christians are expected to be holy in the absolute, as God is, but this must be their aim and goal. Christians are to be "perfecting holiness" (2 Corinthians 7:1) in their lives, progressively attaining it as they grow more and more into the image of Christ.[81]

C. Exhortation to Reverence. 1:17-21

1:17 -- ***And if you address as Father the One who impartially judges according to each man's work, conduct yourselves in fear during the time of your stay*** **upon earth**;

And if you address as Father -- Verses 17-21 are one sentence in the Greek, and are best understood in the light of the governing imperative ("conduct yourselves in fear") in verse 17. The subordinate clauses give a number of reasons why a man should be reverent. One of those reasons is found in the word "Father." "If I am a Father, where is My honor?" (Malachi 1:6). Peter's readers were a praying people who followed Jesus' teaching on prayer. Jesus taught men, when praying, to say, "Our Father who art in heaven" (Matthew 6:9), and this is how Peter's readers invoked or addressed[82] God.

The One who impartially judges according to each man's work -- A number of passages

---

[79] The Old Testament was written for our admonition (1 Corinthians 10:11). See also Matthew 5:48.

[80] This may be one place where the Greek future tense has an imperative connotation, conveying a command. It would be similar to the LXX use of the future indicative in the Ten Commandments (Exodus 20:1-17).

[81] Christians are a people who are different (holy, saints). They are to lead lives separated from uncleanness and impurity, different from the way pagans live. Indeed, Christians, at the time of conversion, are sanctified, set apart, and are holy (1 Corinthians 1:2, 6:11). But they are to increase in holiness, and thus sanctification may be viewed as a continuous process (see the special study on "Sanctification" at the close of notes on Chapter 6 in the author's *Commentary on Romans*). Holiness is to be a growing thing, something to be pursued habitually (Hebrews 12:14). God does not connive at sin and unholy living -- let no one think he can remain a child of obedience while at the same time he tries to fashion his conduct according to the old lusts.

[82] *Epikaleo* (here translated "address") is one of the New Testament words for prayer (cf. Acts 7:59; 2 Timothy 2:22).

in the Bible call attention to God's impartiality[83]; it is an inherent aspect of His character. He does not show favoritism to the person being judged, while at the same time disregarding the evidence and the facts of the case. "Judges" is a present participle, and it is a judgment that God passes every day.[84] "He sees what you do, He hears what you say, My God is a-writing all the time!" And this is true for "each man." Let no one presume that because he is God's chosen, God's child, that he is exempt from his Father's examining and searching.[85] When we read in the Bible about God's judging according to "works," the word is usually plural. Here it is singular. It is not that God selects only one work, or a few that are either fair or faulty. The singular "work" here says that He takes into account the sum and substance of a man's life.

Conduct yourselves in fear during the time of your stay *upon earth* -- "Conduct yourselves" translates the same root word translated "behavior" in verse 15. The words "in fear" stand emphatically at the beginning of the clause in the Greek. "Fear" or reverence is a trembling anxiety lest we break any of God's commands. It is not a cringing fear, a terror, but a healthy respect for One who has omnipotent power. Reverence is the attitude of mind of the man who is always aware he is in the presence of God, who speaks every word, who performs every action, and who lives every moment conscious God is watching and passing judgment.[86] The idea in "your stay (sojourn) upon earth" (*paroikias*) is similar to the idea in the word "aliens" in verse 1. In fact, both words are used at 1 Peter 2:11 to describe the readers. That the readers are just temporary residents here is another reason for reverence. When we have safely reached our heavenly homeland, when the pilgrimage is over, then the exhortation to live "in fear" will no longer be needed.

1:18 -- *Knowing that you were not redeemed with perishable things like silver or gold from your futile way of life inherited from your forefathers,*

Knowing that you were ... redeemed -- The participle should be treated as causal, "because you know." Here is another reason for reverence, namely "you have been redeemed from your futile way of life." "Redeemed" is a word taken from the world of slavery. A man, captured and enslaved, could be ransomed or bought back out of slavery for a great sum of money. When Rome conquered foreign countries, all their citizens who had a useful trade

---

[83] Deuteronomy 10:17; Acts 10:34; Romans 2:11; Ephesians 6;9; Colossians 3:25.

[84] While it is true that there is a final judgment at the return of Christ, it is also true that God passes judgment on his children's behavior every day. Romans 4:5,24 and 1 Corinthians 4:4 show that "justification" is a daily thing. Hebrews 4:13 and perhaps Revelation 2:23 speak of His daily scrutiny of men's minds and actions.

[85] Lenski (*op. cit.*, p.59) wrote to the effect that God must not be thought of as an indulgent grandfather type, who shuts his eye to the sins of his children, who, like Eli of old, takes no stern measures with them when they disobey.

[86] "Would you have done your assignment differently if you had been handing it to Jesus for grading, rather than your teacher?" is a sobering question for a student to consider. Is the Christian who forgets God is watching, and then proceeds to live carelessly, not living in a false or presumptuous security?

were taken to Rome and forced into slavery. It was not uncommon for friends or relatives to trace the kidnapped and enslaved person to his new master, and buy his freedom. Well, the Christian should remember he has been freed from slavery to sin, and from the old pagan lifestyle; the price that was paid was not a great amount money, but the life blood of the Son of God.

Not with perishable things like silver or gold -- Alford noted that *argurio* and *chrusio* – the diminutives – usually stand for the coined or wrought metals. Silver and gold name two of the most highly treasured forms of currency in the ancient world, but there are not enough of these in the world to purchase redemption from sin or a futile way of life.

From your futile way of life inherited from your forefathers -- Probably this language reflects more how Gentiles lived than how Jews lived before their conversion to Christ.[87] "Futile" is a word sometimes used of idolatry,[88] and Peter seems to envision his readers as having spent their lives before their conversion in idolatrous worship with all its attendant vices. A "futile way of life" means a man has nothing for which to live, and nothing for which to die. Christianity gives a man a purpose for living, and a goal to be enjoyed at the end of a faithful life. Christ's redemption delivered the readers from (*ek*, "out of") the lifestyle in which they formerly lived. Their religion, before their conversion, had been a conventional, hand-me-down life, lived out by the sons as the fathers had lived it. Such sinners were in a rut from which, apart from God's help, they could not escape.[89]

1:19 -- *But with precious blood, as of a lamb unblemished and spotless,* the blood *of Christ.*

But with precious blood ... *the blood* of Christ. -- This clause finishes the contrast begun in verse 18. "But" (the strong adversative *alla*) points to the true means of redemption. Ransom prices are usually high, and man's redemption is no exception. According to Hebrews 10:11 the blood of bulls and goats could never take away sins. As much as we value life, even the life of an animal, we would hardly call animal blood "precious." But the blood of Christ is highly esteemed and held in honor. The universe has nothing more valuable to offer, of which we can conceive, than the blood of the Son of God. We think Peter has in mind the great saying of our Lord, "The Son of Man came ... to give His life a ransom for many" (Mark 10:45 KJV).

---

[87] Jews did have the "traditions of the elders" that had been handed down from one generation to another, but they also had the Law of Moses and the books of Scripture. Gentiles did not have anything like the Old Testament Scriptures.

[88] Cf. Leviticus 17:7; 2 Chronicles 11:15; Jeremiah 8:19, 10:15; Romans 1:21; Ephesians 4:17.

[89] Note that antiquity is no guarantee of correct beliefs or practice, and that we cannot safely argue that our conduct is morally right because it is sanctioned by long-standing custom and example. Perhaps our fathers acquired their ideas from their fathers, rather than from God.

As of a lamb unblemished and spotless -- This is what makes the blood of Jesus so precious – it accomplishes what silver and gold cannot. It effected man's redemption. It was possible for it to effect redemption because the life being sacrificed was sinless; it was without spot or blemish. "Unblemished" means without moral defect, no blemish, no character defect in himself. "Spotless" means without physical defect, without spot from the world, unstained by the evil around Him. The words "as of a lamb" apparently are intended to recall the typological significance of the Passover lamb.[90] The sinlessness of the Lamb and the vicarious nature of His suffering provide a basis for a new and heavenly scale of values. Surely what is bought with such a price must not be wasted on a sinful life!

1:20 -- ***For He was foreknown before the foundation of the world, but has appeared in these last times for the sake of you***

For He was foreknown before the foundation of the world – The nature of God's sinless Lamb is here in verse 20 presented under two aspects – His pre-existence and His incarnation. The death of Messiah was not the result of a change of purpose to meet unforeseen circumstances. It was a plan for the redemption of man approved in the eternal counsels of God before He ever began to create the world.[91] Revelation 13:8 likewise speaks of Jesus as being a "Lamb who has been slain from the foundation of the world." Involved in these counsels is the pre-existence of Jesus, and the fact that the creation of the earth (if man sinned) would make it necessary for God's agreed-on plan for redemption to be unveiled (cp. Acts 2:23).

But has appeared in these last times for the sake of you -- The aorist tense participle *phanerothentos* ("appeared, or manifested") marks the earthly life and death of Christ as the event Peter has in mind, something that both men and angels could see. God's eternal plan had to be put into action and it was made operational, something that could be seen (in contrast with Jesus in His pre-existent state), by the incarnation, passion, resurrection, and exaltation of Jesus. Bethlehem marks the point in time when Christ, previously hidden from human view, was "made visible" as He appeared as a man among men.[92] "The last of the times," so the Greek reads, says either that Jesus was made manifest at the end of the times between Adam and Messiah, or that when Jesus appeared it was the beginning of the Messianic age

---

[90] The two on the way to Emmaus were taught that Moses and the prophets had predicted that Messiah would suffer and die (Luke 24:25,26). Leviticus 22:20-24 and Malachi 1:8 tell about the required "without blemish or spot" necessary for sacrifices. 1 Corinthians 5:7 says that Christ our Passover has been sacrificed for us. Isaiah 53:7 pictures Messiah as being "like a lamb ... like a sheep."

[91] In verse 2, Peter has assured his readers that they were included in the redemptive foreknowledge of God. Now he tells them that the blood of Christ that purchased their redemption was also central to that foreknowledge. Calvinists have made efforts to change God's foreknowledge into an act of the will, a decree, a thing predestined or foreordained. Peter might have said that Christ was predestined, but he does not use such a term.

[92] John 1:14; Hebrews 9:26; 1 John 1:2.

(the Christian age) which is the last of the series of ages in God's management of human history. "For the sake of you" is a direct application of this teaching to the readers; he Greek reads "on account of you". When they see that the Heavenly Father planned in advance for their benefit, they will have even more reason to conduct themselves in reverence for Him.

1:21 -- ***Who through Him are believers in God, who raised Him from the dead and gave Him glory, so that your faith and hope are in God.***

Who through Him are believers in God -- After describing the Redeemer (verse 20), Peter now identifies some of the characteristics of his redeemed readers. They are believers in what God did, and will do. The RSV reads "Through Him you have confidence in God." We learn we can trust God[93] because of what God did in the life of Jesus.

Who raised Him from the dead and gave Him glory -- Here are the things we see God did in the life of Jesus. Note how important the death and resurrection of Jesus was to the early Christian writers.[94] Those mighty acts of God in Jesus' life were designed to give men a reason to believe. Peter's message is this: if the readers should be killed by their persecutors like Jesus was, they can expect their heavenly Father to do the same for them as He did for Jesus. This is certainly a strong incentive to reverence and trust.

So that your faith and hope are in God -- "So that" expresses result. The result of seeing that God raised and glorified Jesus is that we redeemed people may confidently expect the same to happen to us. Elsewhere Jesus' resurrection is called "first fruits," that is, there is more to come just like Him. Because God did what He did for Jesus, we can trust Him for our own resurrection and glorification. Christ has promised that where He is, there shall His servant be also. This is the third time Peter has spoken of hope in this chapter (see verses 3 and 13).[95] "God" stands last in the verse in the Greek for emphasis. Christians can rest on this assurance: GOD will do what He says He will do!

D. Exhortation to Brotherly Love. 1:22-2:2

1:22 -- ***Since you have in obedience to the truth purified your souls for a sincere love of the brethren, fervently love one another from the heart,***

---

[93] The word translated "believers" is difficult because a textual variant is involved. The Textus Receptus has a participle *pisteuontas*, while the Nestle-Aland text has a verbal adjective, *pistous*. Modern critical texts opt for the verbal adjective reading on the principle that the more difficult reading is more likely to be original. A verbal adjective ending in *–tos* expresses what may be done (i.e., capability or possibility).

[94] On the resurrection of Jesus, see notes at 1:3. Here Peter specifically says Jesus was raised *ek nekron*, "out of dead [bodies]" or "from among dead [bodies]." Other dead ones were left behind when Jesus was raised. For what the "glory" may mean, see notes at 1:11.

[95] Where do the eyes of the Christian turn at the season of the year the world calls "Easter"? What do we dominantly see? Is it the darkness that covered the earth from noon till three? Is it the pain and anguish Jesus suffered on the cross? Or is it the dazzling early-morning brightness that shone from the empty tomb? Indeed, the resurrection and glorification of Jesus form a firm basis for hope.

Since you have in obedience to the truth purified your souls -- Verses 22 and 23 form one sentence, and the imperative "Love one another" is the main verb. Before one can "love" with a sincere love, his soul will have to be purified.[96] "Obedience to the truth" surely points back to the time of baptism in the lives of the readers (cp. 1:2).[97] "Obedience to the truth" is the condition of purification. In this passage we have seen both God's part (redeemed with the precious blood of Christ) and man's part (obedience) in salvation. God provided the sacrifice and presented the truth; preachers preached by inspiration. Man is to respond by obedience to the truth if he wishes his soul to be pure.[98] Peter has a certain emphasis on the importance of the thing obeyed – the truth. Earlier he wrote "obey Jesus Christ" (1:2). In 2:8 he will write about those who are "disobedient to the word." He evidently regarded obedience to Christ, to the word, and to the "truth" as the same thing. The "truth" is God's truth, the gospel, the great system of truth respecting redemption and salvation.[99] Is Peter, in this verse, reflecting another moment with Jesus? Jesus had insisted that sanctification is "in the truth" and that men are "sanctified in truth" (John 17:17,19).

For a sincere love of the brethren -- The ASV has "unto unfeigned love of the brethren." Before a man becomes a Christian, he is very likely to be self-centered, and being selfish, his "love" may be only a hypocritical show of affection that lacks reality. Conversion makes a great difference; the heart is cleansed of evil thoughts and the behavior is greatly different. The Christian can "love" with genuine and heartfelt interest in that other person. "Love of the brethren" translates *philadelphian*, and there is every reason to believe that the term does not mean "brotherly love, but brother-love. Not 'love men *as though* they were your brothers,' but 'love men *because* they are our brothers'."[100] The "brothers" are "brothers" in the Christian faith (cp. Romans 12:10; 1 Thessalonians 4:9; Hebrews 13:1; 2 Peter 1:7). God's

---

[96] This commentator teaches man is made up of body, soul, and spirit (cf. 1 Thessalonians 5:23). When he commits his first sin, the spirit part ceases to function, and the Bible speaks of the spiritually dead man as being "fleshly" or "natural" (soulical, Grk.). The devil has the ability to stir up the desires of our bodies and to plant thoughts in our minds. Without the human spirit functioning to guide the man, his body and soul will be defiled with evil thoughts, sinful actions, and selfish love. When a person becomes a Christian, his spirit is alive again (see 1 Peter 1:23). He can practice self-control. He can resist the devil's overtures and enticements. The actions prompted by his soul can now be pure. His love can be directed toward others instead of only at his own selfish wishes and desires. In a spiritual sense, this phrase implies consecration to God's service, and an inward cleansing of the heart from all that defiles.

[97] The perfect participle points to a completed action in the past with lasting results. It is because they have been purified and now are in a purified state that they are able to love with a sincere love. "Obedience to the truth" is another way of expressing "faith." It involves a hearing of the Word, and a submission to that message (F.J.A. Hort, *The First Epistle of Peter* [Reprint. Minneapolis: Klock & Klock, 1980], p.88-89).

[98] Long-time Bible readers will have noted this verse has an extra phrase in the KJV. It reads "ye have purified your souls in obeying the truth through the Spirit ...." Those extra words "through the Spirit" appear in some later manuscripts, but are absent in the older Uncials and Papyri. If included, the words say the Holy Spirit has something to do with helping a man to become obedient to the truth (cp. John 16:8-10 and 1 Corinthians 12:13a).

[99] Oberst wrote correctly, "Souls are not purified when one submits to false teaching or deceitful doctrines." Bruce Oberst, *Letters from Peter* (Joplin, MO: College Press, 1962), *in loc.*

[100] J.H.B. Masterman, *The First Epistle of St. Peter* (London: Macmillan, 1990), p.89.

call leads us to become His children of obedience (verses 14,15). He is not only our Father, but we have a relationship to all His other obedient children.

Fervently love one another from the heart -- "Fervently" (*ektenos*) means to stretch out, intensely, with all your energies strained to the limit.[101] Other attempts at a translation include eager, constant, overflowing. "From the heart" stresses the source of Christian love; "fervently" expresses its intensity. "Love" is doing what is spiritually best for the other person. Such attitudes, given all our personality differences, don't just happen; they must be cultivated (Ephesians 4:1-3). The word he uses here for "love" is different than before – it is *agapao*, the same word used of love for Christ at verse 8. It is an intelligent, understanding, purposeful love, a love that can be commanded by an appeal to the will.[102]

1:23 -- *For you have been born again not of seed which is perishable but imperishable,* that is, *through the living and abiding word of God.*

For you have been born again -- The ASV reads "having been begotten again." [103] Having spoken of their "obedience to the truth" and their loving because they are brothers, Peter now shows how men are led to become God's children, members in God's family. The crucial importance of being "begotten again" is underscored by the expanded treatment Peter gives it (verses 23-25). In this context, the begetting "through the ... word" has some relationship to the obedience through which a man is purified. According to the tense of the participle, the "begetting" takes place before a man can "fervently love," before a man's soul is "purified."

Not of seed which is perishable but imperishable -- In physical conception and birth, the seed – the sperm – lives only a short while. So does the human being thereby conceived. But the seed – the Word of God – that brings about spiritual conception is not temporary at

---

[101] The only other place this word is used in the New Testament is Acts 12:5, of the prayer offered up for Peter himself. The word is used in the LXX of Jonah 3:8.

[102] "Our loving efforts are not always appreciated, are sometimes received with coldness or even rebuffs. Often, too, brethren are not very loveable, and while we ourselves have love in our heart we do not always manifest if fully. Many a child has loved father or mother, but when death calls one or the other away, it has regretted too late that it has not shown its love more fully while the parent was still alive. Peter is unlocking the floodgates so that the full stream may gush forth." Lenski, *op. cit.*, p.72.

[103] The Greek word *gennao* was used for both what we call "conception" and "birth." Every time we come across it in the Greek, we must decide which it is. In this writer's commentaries elsewhere (at John 3:1-5, at Acts 2 on the work of the Holy Spirit, at Matthew 19:28 on "regeneration," and at 1 Corinthians 4:15, and Titus 3:5) there are detailed studies on the new birth. A brief summary of what is there taught is as follows: When man commits his first sin, his spirit dies (ceases to function), and he becomes a slave to sin and lives in a body of sin. What is needed for his spirit is a "new birth" (John 3:6). When the man hears the gospel and believes it, he has been conceived (1 John 5:1, ASV). When he repents and is immersed (is obedient to the truth) the process of the new birth is completed. His spirit is alive (Romans 6:1-11, 8:10), and he can walk in newness of life because the old slavery to sin has been broken. He has been redeemed! If this summary is correct, then the ASV translation of 1 Peter 1:23 is to be preferred, because it is the "conception" (not the "birth") that is effected by hearing the Word.

all. It is imperishable.[104] It abides forever!

***That is,* through the living and abiding word of God** -- In this way Peter identifies the imperishable seed that brings about spiritual conception (belief). It "is living and abiding;"[105] that is, it will never lose its potency to bring about faith and it will always be available for men. This is Jesus' promise, "My words shall not pass away" (Matthew 24:35). God's Word will never be irrelevant or obsolete. It is intended for all periods of time, and will never be superseded in value or relevance by human philosophy.

1:24 -- *For,* "ALL FLESH IS LIKE GRASS, AND ALL ITS GLORY LIKE THE FLOWER OF GRASS. THE GRASS WITHERS, AND THE FLOWER FALLS OFF,

For -- The Greek is *dioti*, a word used elsewhere by Peter (1:16) to introduce a passage from the Old Testament. Here he quotes Isaiah 40:6-8 as a Biblical proof of his assertion that the Word of God abides forever. The quotation is from the LXX with enough variations to show that Peter was also acquainted with the Hebrew of this passage. James quoted the same passage (1:10,11).

"ALL FLESH IS LIKE GRASS – "Grass" is green vegetation in general. It grows and flourishes for a season, and then withers. "Flesh" speaks of every human creature. The connection here is this: Peter, in the previous verse, had been contrasting the seed by which men are physically begotten with the seed by which spiritual life is begotten – with emphasis on the imperishable nature of the latter. He now appeals to Scripture to corroborate his teaching.

AND ALL ITS GLORY LIKE THE FLOWER OF GRASS -- Most vegetation has a flower, but the flower is the shortest-lived part of the vegetation. Men ("flesh"), too, have a "glory." All that man takes prides in, his wealth, rank, talents, beauty, learning, splendor, apparel, is likened to the flower found on vegetation – it blooms quickly and is gone.

THE GRASS WITHERS, AND THE FLOWER FALLS OFF -- Grass soon dries up and shrivels. The petals and leaves fall off. This is parallel to saying that all men decay and die. That which is begotten of perishable seed perishes, too. "To Peter, who like James (1:11) was familiar with the drastic impact of the dry season on the Palestinian flora, the inevitable end of plant life was a standing lesson on the transitoriness of human existence."[106] How great the contrast between grass or human flesh and the Word of God!

---

[104] Peter had spoken of the inheritance of the saints as being "imperishable" (verse 4). Now the Word, the seed of the new birth, is so described.

[105] As far as the original is concerned, this phase may be connected either with God (who lives and abides) or with the Word (which lives and abides). The Vulgate, Calvin, Barnes, Hort, Rotherham, and others render it, "through means of the Word of a living and abiding God." Since Peter goes on to unfold the living and abiding nature of the Word by a quotation from the Old Testament, we too explain the phrase in this way.

[106] D. Edmond Hiebert, *First Peter* (Chicago: Moody, 1984), p.107.

1:25 -- BUT THE WORD OF THE LORD ABIDES FOREVER." ***And this is the word which was preached to you.***

BUT THE WORD OF THE LORD ABIDES FOREVER" -- "But" introduces the contrasting, abiding nature of the Word of God, as compared with human flesh and green vegetation. This is still part of the quotation of Isaiah 40:6-8. "Word" translates *hrema* (a spoken word, a message), not *logos* (as was used at verse 23).[107] The reading "word of the Lord (*kuriou*)" is a clear departure from the LXX reading "of our God (*theou*)." In the New Testament, the word "Lord" is a standard designation for Jesus Christ.[108] Peter's change to "the Lord" gives this quotation a Christian emphasis, and leads to his identification of the divine utterance with the gospel in his following phrase of explanation. Involved in the affirmation that the Word of the Lord "abides forever" are the ideas of divine preservation of His Word,[109] the providential control exercised over the transmission of the text, and its abiding ability to serve as a seed which will bring about spiritual conceptions in the hearts of those who hear it preached, until the end of the age ("forever").

And this is the word which was preached to you -- Peter is saying that the gospel which had been preached to his readers through Holy Spirit-inspired men (verse 12) is the selfsame "Word of the Lord" which "abides forever" about which Isaiah prophesied. Since Paul and his inspired helpers preached in some of the provinces addressed in this letter, what Peter here says is tantamount to affirming that the sermons and teachings of Paul and his companions were the "Word of the Lord." Furthermore, the claims of "modern revelations" to be the Word of the Lord run aground upon the affirmation that the word preached by the apostles is the complete and final codification of God's will for this last of the ages. "Preached" translates *euaggelisthen*, preached as good news. The gospel which the readers already had proclaimed to them, which had been instrumental in their regeneration (begetting), and in obedience to which they had purified their souls, was the Word which abides forever.

The obligation the readers now have to love the brethren is obvious. Peter follows in the opening verses of chapter 2 with some tests by which the readers can know if they are loving with a pure love.

---

[107] Both the Greek word used and the context are against the idea that "word" is a reference to Christ (as it is in John 1:1ff). We see the same transition from *logos* to *hrema* in Peter's sermon at Acts 10:36,37.

[108] *Kurios* (Lord) is the regular LXX word used to translate the four-letter sacred name of the covenant making and keeping God of Israel (Yahweh, Jehovah). That the New Testament uses *kurios* for Jesus is tantamount to saying Jesus is God.

[109] This promise of the preservation and the abiding nature of the Word of the Lord has considerable bearing on the matter of the inerrancy of Scripture. The evangelical view that Scripture is inerrant in its autographs, but not necessarily in the current critical text, must be modified to include this promise of preservation. While there are variant readings (such as we have already seen in 1 Peter), it still can be affirmed that the "Word" abides forever.

2:1 -- ***Therefore, putting aside all malice and all guile and hypocrisy and envy and all slander,***

Therefore -- The chapter divisions in our Bibles are not always exactly right. It would be better if the first two verses of what is chapter 2 were included as a part of chapter 1, for they continue and conclude the "exhortation to brotherly love" which began at 1:22. "Therefore" connects this section with the previous one. The sins listed here are primarily those which are destructive of brotherly love: since you are to fervently love one another, you will have to quit these sins.[1]

Putting aside -- This verb was commonly used for taking one's clothes off and putting them aside. Think of someone flinging off a badly stained or infected garment. The Christian should do the same thing with behavior that hinders him from loving with a sincere heart. The tense of the participle used here (aorist) indicates that the "putting aside" precedes the "desiring of the pure milk of the word." Perhaps it looks back to the time of their baptism.

All malice -- Note that the word "all" occurs three times in the remainder of this verse. Perhaps Peter designates three kinds of sin to be put away, wickedness, guile, and evil speaking. Guile is then shown to include the behavior designated by the terms "hypocrisy" and "envy." The repeated "all" leaves no room for exceptions in this demand for holiness. "Malice" is the desire to get even when someone hurts you or takes advantage of you.[2] A person cannot be "loving" and at the same time bent on getting even for every little hurt, real or imagined.

And all guile -- Guile is the conscious deception a man practices who deceives others to attain his own ends. There is deceit, cunning, and trickery involved, in order to get the better of someone. Think of "bait" for a fish, or of telling just the side of the story that makes you look good.

And hypocrisy -- A hypocrite is an "actor" who is playing a part to influence his audience, pretending to be something we are not, or "faking it" (an attempt to cover up the true identity with a false front). The hypocrite must conceal his real motives, and speak words which are very different from his real feelings.

And envy -- Envy is hatred, burning discontent, or unhappiness toward others on account of some excellency they have, or something they possess which we do not. It is very hard to be

---

[1] This interpretation has the "therefore" pointing back to the last few verses of chapter 1. Some interpreters try to make the "therefore" summarize all the points listed since 1:3. The idea would be in view of all the considerations alluded to (judgment, Christ's sacrifice, the greatness of salvation, the new birth), renounce all evil.

[2] The word *kakian*, depending on the context, can be a general word for all kinds of wickedness, or a special kind of evil, "malice." Our translators decided on the special meaning at this place. Those who choose the former often suggest that *wickedness* is the general term, and that the rest of the verse gives specific examples of wickedness. Either way, the list of sins outlines those character faults that hinder brotherly love.

envious of another, and to fervently love that person at the same time. Instead, envy is often the root of guile and hypocrisy and other sins. In fact, envy will destroy the possibility of brother love. Remember that the ten apostles were envious of James and John who had asked for chief places (Mark 10:41). The envy seethed underneath the surface, and at the last supper a week later the apostles were disputing who would occupy the seats of greatest honor (Luke 22:24). Not until Jesus washed their feet, and taught them a lesson in serving with humility, was any semblance of harmony restored among these brethren. See how brotherly love was vitiated by this sin!

And all slander -- This is speaking in such a way as to talk down or disparage or defame another. Detracting things are spoken about another in order to advance one's self. It usually takes place when the victim of it is not there to defend himself. (Have you ever been talking about someone who is absent, only to have that person enter the room, and see how quickly the talk stops? If so, you were guilty of "slander.") There are not many things a man can do which produces more trouble and heartbreak and which is so destructive of brotherly love and Christian unity as such backbiting speech.

2:2 -- ***Like newborn babes, long for the pure milk of the word, that by it you may grow in respect to salvation.***

Like newborn babes -- These words recall what was written at 1:23 about being "born again." We suppose Peter picked this term in order to illustrate how Christians are to long after the Word, like a hungry babe does for milk.[3] Anyone who has ever bottle fed a fawn, or a new calf, understands the "desire" that Peter is here alluding to. Hungry animals will almost pull the bottle from your hands, and suck so hard they will collapse the bottle.

Long for the pure milk of the word -- "Long for" is a strong word, indicating intense desire. It is used of a deer *panting* after water brooks (Psalm 42:1). "A healthy infant is a hungry infant. A spiritually healthy Christian is a hungry Christian."[4] This is the main verb in the sentence. Whether or not Peter's imperative contains a rebuke for lack of progress is disputed. Usually it is said they do not, but there certainly will be a rebuke if there is no desire for the word after they read this letter. "Pure milk of the word" is an effort to translate *to logikon adolon gala*. *Logikon* is a difficult word to translate because we have no synonymous English word. The same word is used at Romans 12:1, and our versions at that place vacillate between "spiritual" and "reasonable," but neither of those words makes much

---

[3] Some writers have supposed this word means the readers were all recent converts, but that is hardly true of the Galatians, for example, who have been Christians for years. Or again, those who view 1 Peter as originally a baptismal sermon appeal to this designation "newborn" as confirmation of their idea. The words are appropriate to the condition of converts who have just been immersed, it is asserted. Instead, we picture Peter as exhorting all his readers (however long ago they were converted) to desire spiritual food as newborn babes desire milk. Apparently, a keen appetite for the word is something that can be developed.

[4] Kenneth S. Wuest, *First Peter in the Greek New Testament* (Grand Rapids: Eerdmans, 1960), p.52.

sense in this passage.[5] The KJV and NASB translate *logikon* as "of the word," and that may be right.[6] In the preceding context, Peter has been talking about the "word of the Lord" that "abides forever" as being instrumental in their conversion. Now, perhaps, he indicates that it is that same "[inspired] word which was preached to you" which, if voraciously desired by the Christians, would be instrumental in their spiritual growth, so that they no longer exhibit the vices named in verse 1. The word the readers need is also described being "pure." The word *adolon* is an almost technical word to describe grain that is entirely free from any chaff or dust or useless, harmful matter. What Peter wants for them is God's Word, pure, unmixed with human traditions or falsehoods or with anything else which would destroy its purity. Contaminated milk can make a child sick and can even be fatal. So with a contaminated "Word."

That by it you may grow in respect to salvation -- There is emphasis on the fact that just as there is a food that goes to supply physical sustenance, so for Christians there is nourishment which sustains the inner man. The New Testament regularly shows that spiritual growth is expected of Christians, and Peter here makes their final salvation[7] (the Greek reads "unto [*eis*] salvation"[8]) conditional upon such growth. If we do not grow, it is implied we shall not have salvation. Peter's call for growth may be connected with all four exhortations in this first hortatory section. From a study of Scripture we can learn about the grace that will be brought to us at the revelation of Jesus Christ, and our hope will grow. From a study of the Word we learn about God's attributes that we should emulate, and as we do our holiness grows. From the Word we learn about God's commands and expectations, and when we see that our God is an awesome God we grow in our reverence for Him. And from the Word we learn how a man who loves his brother lives, and we deliberately work on eliminating the vices that would hinder such a love, and our love grows. Feeding our souls on the Word of God will surely keep us alive and growing unto salvation. Those who meditate upon the Word of God are like trees planted by the rivers of waters, whose leaf does not wither (Psalm 1:3).

---

[5] The "spiritual milk" of the ASV suggests that there is a nourishment for the spirit that governs a man's behavior. One then has go to the context, which has talked about the "word of the Lord," to find out what that spiritual nourishment might be.

[6] The root in *logikon* is *logos*, a word that can mean (1) a speaking, a saying, a word that expresses thought, (2) the thing spoken (doctrine, question, proverb, precept, rumor), (3) reason (used in the sense of something that rules or governs, hence, "spiritual"), (4) account or reckoning.

[7] Regarding "salvation" as something to be received in the future, see 1:5,9 and comments on those verses.

[8] The careful reader has noticed the KJV does not have this phrase as part of its text in verse 2. The omission, as Bruce Metzger (*A Textual Commentary on the Greek New Testament* [London: United Bible Societies, 1971], p. 689) suggests, was due either to "oversight in copying" or "because the idea of growing into salvation" was theologically unacceptable. The phrase is found in the better manuscripts, just as the NASB has it.

III. SECOND DOCTRINAL SECTION. 2:3-10[9]

2:3 -- *If you have tasted the kindness of the Lord,*

If you have tasted -- "Tasted" here is used in the sense of experienced. The condition is assumed, so we may translate it "since you have experienced," or "because you have tasted."[10] A number of expressions in chapters 1 and 2 have indicated the readers are Christians – "chosen," "obey Jesus," "obedience to the truth," "our Lord Jesus," "glory and honor at the revelation of Jesus Christ," "purified your souls," "newborn babes," and more. Peter no longer speaks much about the new birth in his letter. Now he builds on the fact of that life-changing event in the readers' past.

The kindness of the Lord -- "Lord" evidently has reference to Jesus.[11] *Chrestos* is the word translated "kindness." It means good [active goodness], useful, beneficial, gracious. The fact that the Lord Jesus is gracious and kind is not an excuse for us to do as we like and trust Him to overlook it; it involves an obligation to toil upward and onward out of gratitude for that graciousness and love which has been so kind to us. The "kindness of the Lord" is the greatest of all incentives to a positive response on the part of the recipients of that kindness.

2:4 -- And *coming to Him as to a living stone, rejected by men, but choice and precious in the sight of God,*

***And* coming to Him** -- Though the NASB has added it, there is no "and" in the Greek phrase, *pros hon proserchomenoi*; the ASV translated it "unto whom coming."[12] The NIV treats the circumstantial participle correctly by translating "As you come to him." Thus the sentence reads "because you have experienced the kindness of the Lord, as you are coming to him ...

---

[9] It seems reasonable at this writing to start the second doctrinal section with verse 3, finding the main verb in verse 5 ("built up"). More will be written concerning this matter as we begin comments on verse 4. The theme of this second doctrinal section is "the church is the living temple of God." We have a development of the idea that God's church today is the New Testament counterpart to Old Testament Israel as the people of God.

[10] Conditional sentences are made up of "if clauses" and "conclusion clauses." We are treating verse 3 as the "if" clause and the main verb in verse 5 as a part of the conclusion clause. Some have connected verse 3 to the preceding paragraph, thinking that "tasted" continues the figure of "milk." But "kindness" is not a word commonly applied to food, so that is one reason it appears to us that a new thought has begun with verse 3.

[11] It is not possible to be a witness for Jehovah and at the same time play down the deity of Jesus. Review the comments on "Lord" at 1:25. Thus, it can be affirmed that what was said of the Lord in Psalm 34:8 is here said of Jesus, "O taste and see that the Lord is good."

[12] The NASB recognizes the problem of trying to start a new paragraph with verse 4. In the Greek the verse begins with a relative clause. Since this is hardly the way to begin a sentence, the NASB has added "And." The RSV, treating the participle as though it were imperative rather than circumstantial, reads "Come to Him." This commentator has not been convinced that participles sometimes (e.g., when they are related grammatically to imperative verbs) have an imperative force. (See further on this at 2:18 and at 3:1.)

you are built up ...." "Coming" (present tense, continuous action) speaks of the voluntary, repeated, or habitual coming of believers to the Lord Jesus for sustenance and fellowship.[13] "Coming to Him" here speaks of drawing near to Jesus in worship, sacrifice (as Romans 12:1), or prayer. Peter here expresses his confidence that his readers will not let hard times or pending persecutions keep them from worshiping Jesus. Though their neighbors and government officials may scorn and ostracize them as a motley and negligible folk, Peter is going to assure them that they are a holy and glorious community, chosen and precious to God.

As to a living stone -- The "Him" in the previous clause and the "living stone" here both speak of Jesus. As the resurrected Lord, He is alive evermore, and is able to save to the uttermost those who come to God through Him (Hebrews 7:25).[14] But where did Peter get the idea of calling Jesus a living "stone"? Perhaps it was from Jesus' own use of the Old Testament prophecy; Jesus quoted Psalm 118:22 ("the stone which the builders rejected has become the head of the corner") to the religious leaders (Matthew 21:42), applying it to Himself.[15] Or perhaps Peter is applying the prophecy of Isaiah 28:16 to Jesus.[16] Or perhaps there is some reference to what Jesus said at Caesarea Philippi (Matthew 16:18), "On this rock I will build (future tense, continue to build) My church".[17]

Rejected by men -- "Rejected" means refused as unsuitable. Jesus was tested and found wanting, as though he lacked the proper qualifications. Peter attributes to men in general this rejection. Rejected first by the Jews, they killed Him. Now rejected by Gentiles, they refuse to serve Him, and persecute those who do.

---

[13] While eternal salvation is often represented as *coming* to Christ, it does not appear that the present participle here in verse 4 is a reference to this initial coming (i.e., the time one becomes a Christian). So Bigg's explanation of the present participle as picturing people all through the church age as "coming one after another" (Charles Bigg [*A Critical and Exegetical Commentary on the Epistles of St. Peter and Jude* [Edinburgh: T&T Clark, 1901], p.128) to become Christians is not quite the point. The present tense better expresses the continuing experience of each individual believer.

[14] At 1:3, we had "living" hope -- a hope that motivates men to action. At 1:23 we had "living" Word -- a word that cuts to the heart and motivates to action. So "living" stone also pictures Jesus as motivating believers to action.

[15] Peter will allude to this passage in a moment as he writes verses 7 and 8. Jesus' use of Psalm 118 surely made an impression on Peter for he quoted it (Acts 4:11) when talking to the same religious leaders to whom Jesus had quoted it.

[16] Peter quotes this prophecy when he writes verse 6.

[17] While Peter in this place talks about the church being continuously built up, it should also be noted that Peter's word for "stone" (*lithos*) in this verse and Jesus' word for "rock" (*petra*) at Matthew 16:18 are not the same words. *Petra* is a solid native rock, the bedrock, a huge ledge of unhewn stone on which a temple is built. *LIthos* indicates a stone shaped and wrought, e.g., of the kind suitable for a chief cornerstone.

But choice and precious in the sight of God -- Two diametrically opposite evaluations of Jesus are indicated by the Greek particles *men* and *de*. "Men" and "God" stand first in each of their clauses. Men think of Jesus one way; God thinks of Him in exactly the opposite. Since Christians are to reflect their heavenly Father, then Peter's readers should value Jesus as highly as God does. Jesus is the one chosen or elected[18] by God as the suitable foundation on which to raise His church. "Precious," highly esteemed, has been explained at 1:7,19 – there is nothing more valuable in the world. Believers who value Jesus as God does will have plenty of reason to keep "coming to Him."

2:5 -- ***You also, as living stones, are being built up as a spiritual house for a holy priesthood, to offer up spiritual sacrifices acceptable to God through Jesus Christ.***

As living stones -- Christ's spiritual house is not built of inanimate rocks like the cathedrals built by men. Christ's house is made up of living Christians (called "living stones" because, since conversion, they share an identity of nature with Christ[19]). The church is not the building; the church is people, and they are alive spiritually (cp. Romans. 6:1-11).

You also ... are being built up -- This present tense main verb can be either indicative or imperative in mood, and either middle or passive in voice.[20] The NASB reflects a decision to treat it as indicative passive. The agent doing the building is implied. We are reminded of Jesus' own promise that He would build His church. Into that grand spiritual house the readers already have been incorporated. "Since you have tasted that the Lord is gracious, as you keep coming to Him ... you are being built up as a spiritual house," is how we would translate verses 3-5.

As a spiritual house -- Peter doesn't use *hieron* or *naos* (both are translated "temple"), both of which might have had wrong connotations. God's "house" (*oikos*) now is no longer a temple of stones localized upon a mountain in Jerusalem. There is a clear contrast with the Old Testament system. Israel's temple was made of inanimate, perishable material. Living Christians are themselves the material out of which God builds His spiritual house.[21] Thus

---

18 See notes at 1 Peter 1:1 on "chosen (elect)."

19 "Because I live, you shall live also," promised Jesus (John 14:19).

20 Modern translations have tried almost every possible combination of options as they attempt to translate this verse. Some treat it as imperative middle, "build yourselves up ...." Some treat it as indicative middle, "build up yourselves for your own benefit." Some treat it as imperative passive, "Be built up ... (allow God to do with you as He sees fit)!" Those who treat the current paragraph as doctrinal, rather than hortatory, object to treating the main verb as hortatory (imperative).

21 Paul used a similar figure when he wrote that Christians are "a holy temple in the Lord ... into a dwelling of God in the Spirit" (Ephesians 2:22). That Peter calls the "stones" out of which God's house is being built "spiritual" may reflect the fact that it is not a literal building, or that the Spirit has been and is at work in these people's lives, or that the congregation of believers form a "house" (temple) in which the Spirit dwells (1 Corinthians 3:16).

the church transcends the glory of the Jewish temple.[22] Hiebert (*op. cit.*, p.121) has written,

> "The Scriptures know nothing of an individual piety that is out of touch with the living body of God's people" (Cranfield). Furthermore, a house is not a jumbled pile of stones. The image implies the orderly and purposeful arrangement of the individual stones, each one shaped and placed to fulfill its assigned task (cf. Paul's image of the members of the body in 1 Corinthians 12:12-31).

The church as a spiritual house, capable of indefinite growth, is Peter's way of expressing the same idea found in Paul's image of the church as the body of Christ.[23]

For a holy priesthood -- The Greek preposition is *eis*, "into," or (ASV) "to be a holy priesthood."[24] Peter's living stones are both, constituting both the house *and* the priests who serve in it.[25] The noun translated "priesthood" occurs only in 1 Peter 2:5 and 9 in the New Testament, and only twice in the LXX (Exodus 29:6, 23:22) from which Peter likely got the term. It may be understood either as an abstract noun, or (more likely in this context) as a collective singular that denotes the body of persons who function as priests. Lightfoot has written, "The kingdom of Christ ... has no sacred days or seasons, no special sanctuaries, because every time and every place alike are holy. Above all, it has no sacerdotal system. It interposes no sacrificial tribe or class between God and man."[26] Barclay has enumerated several great characteristics of a priest: (1) he is a man who himself has direct access to God; (2) he is a go-between for others and God (a bridge-builder for others to come to God); (3) he brings offerings to God. So it is with Christian priests.[27]

---

[22] *Wycliffe Bible Commentary* (Chicago: Moody, 1962), p.1446, suggests that "the argument in this part of the chapter, to 1 Peter 2:10, may indicate that the indignities and pressures being experienced by the [readers] were at the instigation of the Jews." There is a possibility that behind Nero's idea of throwing the blame for the burning of Rome onto the Christians, thus starting the persecution the readers were now facing, was none other than a suggestion by Poppea, Nero's wife, who favored the Jews.

[23] Romans 12:5; 1 Corinthians 10:17, 12:12-27; Ephesians 1:23, 2:16.

[24] The NASB translation "for a holy priesthood" might give the wrong idea, namely, that the spiritual house is a place where priests (who are separate and distinct from the house) live. This is not it, at all!

[25] All Christians are priests (Revelation 1:6, 5:10, 20:6). Jesus is the great high priest of our religion (Hebrews 5:6, 7:1-17, 8:1-5, 9:11). Luther, in his Reformation, tried to restore the New Testament emphasis of the priesthood of all believers. While Luther was right, it has been a concept slow to catch on in the minds of believers. In fact, less than half a century ago, William Robinson wrote a book entitled *The Unfinished Reformation* in which he lamented that most contemporary believers do not think of themselves as "priests" and as a result don't function as priests, either.

[26] J.B. Lightfoot, "The Christian Ministry" in *St. Paul's Epistle to the Philippians* (Grand Rapids: Zondervan, 1953), p.181.

[27] Barclay, *op. cit.*, p.232. Some references to help focus our thinking are Larry Beaverson, *The Private Life of an Ordinary Priest* (Traverse City, MI: Jonah Publishers, 1976), Cyril Eastwood, *The Priesthood of All Believers* (Minneapolis: Augsburg, 1962), and W. Carl Ketcherside, *The Royal Priesthood* (St. Louis, MO: Mission Messenger, 1956).

To offer up spiritual sacrifices – The sacrifices which Christian priests offer are spiritual; they are not bloody offerings like bulls and lambs. Scriptures elsewhere specify some of these spiritual sacrifices: (1) prayer and praise, Hebrews 13:15; (2) our bodies as living sacrifices, Romans 12:1; (3) love to the brother and deeds of charity, 1 John 3:16, Philippians 4:1; (4) Gentiles won to Christ were offered up by Paul, Romans 15:16; (5) material possessions used in God's service, Hebrews 13:16. These are "carried up to the altar" and presented to God.[28] Jesus Christ has opened the way into the heavenly Holy of Holies for all believers, and Christian priests may now make acceptable offerings to a Holy God.

Acceptable to God through Jesus Christ -- The compound adjective *euprosdektous* ("acceptable") literally means to receive to one's self with pleasure. Peter assures his readers this is God's response to all the sacrifices the spiritual priests offer. "Through Jesus Christ" may be connected either with the verb "offer" or the word "acceptable." It may be the sacrifices are offered through Jesus Christ who serves as our great mediator (high priest). It may be the sacrifices are acceptable because of what Jesus did for us.[29]

2:6 -- *For* this *is contained in Scripture:* "BEHOLD I LAY IN ZION A CHOICE STONE, A PRECIOUS CORNERSTONE, AND HE WHO BELIEVES IN HIM SHALL NOT BE DISAPPOINTED."

For *this* is contained in Scripture -- As before (1:16,24), *dioti* introduces a passage from the Old Testament. Some believe the verses about to be quoted are intended to give Scriptural proof that Jesus may be called a "living stone." Others believe Peter is offering Scriptural evidence why the offerings of the Christian priests are acceptable. We see no reason why both ideas cannot be included. The idea about Jesus being a living stone was clearly stated in the Old Testament (verses 6-8), while the idea about the priesthood of believers was implied (verses 9-10). "Scripture" in the oldest manuscripts is anarthrous.[30] To the ancient Jews, the only thing worth recording, and keeping, and being called "writings" (i.e., Scripture) was the Word of God. The passage about to be quoted is taken from Isaiah 28:16,[31] a recognized Messianic passage.[32]

---

[28] Christians have an altar, Hebrews 13:10 (perhaps the altar of burnt offering in heaven, Revelation 6:9, 8:4 cp. with Hebrews 8:5), and "offer up" (*anaphero*) is the regular word for "carrying [your gift] up to the altar."

[29] Christ is man's only means of approach to God, and God accepts only those sacrifices from man which are made in connection with Christ (Acts 4:11; 1 Timothy 2:5; Colossians 3:17; Hebrews 7:25).

[30] "Anarthrous" means there is no "the" (an article) in the Greek. Because the Textus Receptus has an article, the KJV reads "in the scripture."

[31] Peter's wording is neither exactly as in the LXX nor the Hebrew. Some think he is quoting from memory; some think there was another text of the Old Testament (in addition to the LXX and Masoretic) available in the first-century world, and that the readings in the New Testament that differ from the LXX and Masoretic texts reflect this alternative text.

[32] Isaiah 28 had received a Messianic interpretation in pre-Christian Judaism. Both Peter and Paul (who also quotes it, Romans 9:32,33, 10:11) understood the stone in Isaiah 28:16 to be a direct reference to the Messiah. It

"BEHOLD I LAY IN ZION A CHOICE STONE -- "Behold" may say that it is an astounding thing God is going to do. It may also call attention to the importance of the divine announcement made through Isaiah. "I laying (I am laying)" says that no matter what men might do, God was going to set up Jesus Christ as the chief cornerstone. "Zion" is both a name for earthly Jerusalem (since the western of the two hills on which the city was built was named Zion, Isaiah 40:9; Micah 3:12) and for heavenly Jerusalem (Psalm 48:2; Hebrews 12:22). Peter may have reference to what God did for Jesus at earthly Jerusalem or he may have reference to the heavenly significance of Jesus' redemption. "Choice" (see at 1:1) says that it was not just some ordinary stone God was going to use but one that was the specific object of His selection and approval.

A PRECIOUS CORNERSTONE -- The stone God has chosen is identified as a "precious cornerstone." Now the word Peter uses (*akrogoniaion*) can be translated as cornerstone, capstone or keystone. The keystone was important to hold an archway in place; the capstone gave beauty to the structure; the cornerstone was the first stone laid, and it was the stone from which all the rest of the building was framed and squared. Its location governed where the building would be, and in what directions its walls would extend. In this place it is appropriate to think of Jesus as the "cornerstone," whose death and resurrection and Great Commission gave impetus to the building of God's spiritual house. "Precious" says this "stone" is very valuable in God's sight (see "precious" at 2:4).

AND HE WHO BELIEVES IN HIM SHALL NOT BE DISAPPOINTED" -- "Him" is Christ, the precious cornerstone. "Believes" is a present participle indicating continuing action. "Believes in Him," we learned at 1:8, is an obedient faith. Christians who are being persecuted need to hear this encouragement to continue on in their belief in Him because it is precisely such who will never be "disappointed" in their hopes or put to shame.[33] The Stone will never fail them, leaving them to eternal shame and disgrace. He is living and present and will help them to come out of the persecution victoriously (cp. 1:7). In Isaiah 28:16, God Himself assured the believers of the beneficial impact this "stone" would have for them.

2:7 -- ***This precious value, then, is for you who believe. But for those who disbelieve,*** **"THE STONE WHICH THE BUILDERS REJECTED, THIS BECAME THE VERY CORNERSTONE,"**

This precious value, then, is for you who believe -- Here in verse 7 Peter applies the Scripture quoted in verse 6 to his readers. Human reactions to the stone divide mankind into

---

is only in later rabbinical writers that we find attempts to dull the telling point Christians made of this prophecy by affirming it referred (not to Messiah, but) to Hezekiah.

[33] The Hebrew reads "shall not be in haste." Peter follows the wording of the LXX here, using a word that means to flee in panic or flee like a coward. Peter is not promising exemption from persecution, or promising them they will never become refugees fleeing the persecution, but he is promising that the one who keeps believing in Jesus will never need be ashamed he is a Christian.

two classes: the believing and the unbelieving. For believers, there is a promise of no shame. Translators and commentators have struggled with how to treat *he time* ("the honor"). The KJV and RSV read "He is precious," meaning that Christ is precious in the eyes of believers. The problem with this is that *he time* is feminine.[34] The ASV offered "For you ... is the preciousness," meaning that God places a precious value on the believer. The problem with this is that the words *he time* stand in direct connection with, and antithesis to, "shall not be disappointed" (in the previous verse). We think Peter here is talking about the same "precious value"[35] that he spoke of in 1:7. At the revelation of Jesus Christ the believer will find he is the one whom God delights to honor.

But for those who disbelieve -- There is a manuscript variation here, some reading *apeithousin*, "disobedient" (as the KJV reads), while others read *apistousin* ("disbelieve" as the NASB reads). The former word carries the connotation of a stubborn refusal to be persuaded. Actually, there is little difference in meaning between the two different Greek words when it comes to how a man lives.[36] Peter quotes Scripture in the rest of this verse and in the beginning of the next to show what will happen to the unbeliever. The "cornerstone," a "stone of stumbling," and a "rock of offense" is what unbelievers will find Christ to be, much to their sorrow in this life and the next.

"THE STONE WHICH THE BUILDERS REJECTED, THIS BECAME THE VERY CORNERSTONE" -- As one very familiar with the LXX, Peter weaves quotations from it into the sentence he is writing. This quotation comes from Psalm 118:22. The only way the rejected Jesus can be the cornerstone is if he is *living* after his rejection and crucifixion. As was explained in comments above on verse 5, "rejected" brings to mind the picture of a group of builders rejecting a certain stone which they think is not suitable for the building they are attempting to erect. Jesus did not meet the specifications of the Jewish religious leaders for a Messiah, so they rejected Him. They wanted a political house and continued secular domination. That is not the kind of spiritual house Jesus came to build. God repudiated what the religious leaders did to Jesus by raising Him from the dead, and exalting Him to His own right hand in the heavens. God's building includes Jesus in the very important "cornerstone" position; so should any spiritual house men attempt to erect! Unbelievers are lumped together with the builders who rejected Jesus.

2:8 -- *And,* "A STONE OF STUMBLING AND A ROCK OF OFFENSE"; *for they stumble because they are disobedient to the word, and to this* doom *they were also appointed.*

And -- The quotation from the Old Testament which follows is another passage which shows what happens to unbelievers. The words are a combination of Isaiah 8:14 and 28:16.

---

[34] The NIV's "the stone is precious" is open to the same objection.

[35] This treats the article in the Greek before "precious" (*timē*, honor) as the article of previous reference.

[36] In fact, in verse 8 Peter uses "disobedient" as though it were synonymous with "disbelieve."

"A STONE OF STUMBLING AND A ROCK OF OFFENSE" -- Jesus is a stone over which unbelievers stumble.[37] Stumbling is more serious than simply stubbing the toe. Men choose of their own free will whether to be a believer or an unbeliever. If they choose to be an unbeliever, their rejection of the Savior becomes the cause of their ruin. "Offense" translates *skandalou*, a word regularly used of the trigger that springs on a trap. It is an unusual expression used of Jesus. How is it to be explained? He is a snare, a trap. Strange, but true! Men do not let this "rock" alone by simply walking past or by wholly ignoring Jesus. Unbelievers will attack and bad-mouth Jesus in a way they do for no other religious leader in history. It is almost as though they feel compelled to take a shot at Jesus in passing. Thinking about these two solemn truths will help the readers understand what motivates their persecutors.

For they stumble because they are disobedient to the word -- Peter here shows how the words quoted from Isaiah apply to the unbelieving. They've heard the "word"[38] but they deliberately refused[39] to submit to the invitation of the Holy One offered in the "word."[40] In his application, Peter makes stumbling at the "word" tantamount to stumbling over Christ. Men come into contact with Jesus by means of the "word." They stumble against Christ by rejecting and disobeying the "word."[41]

And to this *doom* they were also appointed -- All the Greek says is "to which they were appointed." The NASB translators, perhaps, have thrust a bit of Calvinistic theology at us with their addition of "doom" in italics.[42] J.B. Phillips translated the verse so that it is obvious that "stumbling" is what a man is appointed to do who disbelieves. A man's eternal

---

[37] The NIV's handling of these quotations ("A stone that causes men to stumble, and a rock that makes them fall") is not quite suitable, for it reflects a Calvinistic bias, as does their translation of the remainder of the verse.

[38] A number of synonymous expressions in 1 Peter explain what the "word" is. It is the "the truth" of 1:22; it is the imperishable "seed" and the "living and abiding word" of 1:23; it is the "good news which was preached" of 1:25.

[39] As has been indicated earlier, "disobedient" is a stubborn refusal to be persuaded.

[40] In this present passage, "believe" is contrasted with "disobedient." This is only possible if "belief" (the faith that saves) includes obedience. Much has been said about obedience already in 1 Peter.

[41] There is a technical problem involved in translating the Greek at this place. The Greek word order is "they stumble to the word being disobedient." The problem is this: shall we take "to (at, KJV) the word" with the word "stumble" or with the word "disobey"? If, as with the NASB, we translate the phrase as "because they are disobedient to the word," the phrase means the unbelievers stumble precisely because of their willful disobedience to the word. Henry Alford, *The Greek Testament* [London: Rivingtons, 1871], Vol.4, p.348) pointed to 3:1 and 4:17 in support of this way of translating the Greek because, in his opinion, it gives proper prominence to the Word as the means of Christian growth, the very Word that is being rejected willfully by the unbelievers.

[42] Calvinism often teaches double predestination -- predestination to salvation, and predestination to damnation. It certainly could be argued that this verse is made to teach the latter by the addition of "doom." On the other hand, one might recall that Mark 16:16 says "He who disbelieves shall be condemned." It could be affirmed that all the addition of "doom" does is to reflect the fact that God has so ordained that those who choose to disbelieve will be lost.

destiny is not determined by chance or accident. God has set certain laws into motion, and man's destiny is determined by that arrangement.[43] God's eternal plan, which has one destiny ("praise and glory and honor" in 1:7) for those whom He approves (remember what was said about "chosen according to the foreknowledge of God" in 1:2), has sadly ordained the disobedient to the only alternative.

2:9 -- *But you are* A CHOSEN RACE, A ROYAL PRIESTHOOD, A HOLY NATION, A PEOPLE FOR *God's* OWN POSSESSION, *that you may proclaim the excellencies of Him who has called you out of darkness into His marvelous light;*

But you are -- Peter is finished with his unfolding of relevant Scripture that presented Jesus as a "living stone." Now he is launching into the topic of "holy priesthood" which he introduced in verse 5. He calls attention to two passages from the Old Testament to make his point. All the words in verse 9 are taken from Exodus 19:5,6, a passage in which there are a series of collective nouns, all of which are in the singular and which were used in Old Testament times to describe Israel. Peter is evidently thinking of the church as spiritual Israel, the new Israel of God (Galatians 6:16). "You" is emphatic and draws a contrast between the believing and the unbelieving. It is the believing who are now the "chosen race."

A CHOSEN RACE -- You church members, chosen by God,[44] are special people! You have been chosen for service. Thus their priestly functions are implied. "Chosen race"[45] is very reminiscent of Christ's own teaching. Christ's reference to the rejected cornerstone was in connection with His parable to the rebellious vinedressers who had slain the son of the owner of the vineyard. At the same time and along with His reference to the rejected stone, He said to the Jewish leaders, "The kingdom of God will be taken away from you, and be given to a nation (Gentiles) producing fruit of it" (Matthew 21:43). Peter is now writing to this nation, whose evident royalty and worth at once marks them as the King's children and reflects credit upon Him who called them from the world's darkness into His marvelous light.

A ROYAL PRIESTHOOD -- The priesthood of all believers has been developed in notes on verse 5. The word translated "royal" can be either a noun or an adjective. Some take it as a noun and make it a fifth title (i.e., kingly or regal, like the king's palace [Esther 1:9 LXX, Luke 7:25]) applied to the church. Others take it as an adjective modifying “priesthood" and

---

[43] Observe the effect of sunlight on different materials. The same sun melts wax and hardens clay. And so it may be said, in the light of the above, that those who reject Christ are appointed to stumbling and falling. That is part of God's general arrangement. The gospel is so constituted by Him that to reject it hardens a man, and God deals with hardened sinners accordingly.

[44] This is the fourth and last time the word "chosen" (elect) is used in 1 Peter. It was applied to individuals in 1:1. It was applied to Jesus in 2:4,6. Here it is applied collectively to the people of God.

[45] *Genos* can denote offspring, nation, stock or race, kind or species, or family. Perhaps there is allusion to being born into the family of God.

then explain that Christians are both kings and priests (Revelation 1:6), or they see some reference to the fact that Christians sit with God and reign with him (Revelation 5:10). Peter's implied exhortation is that Christians must learn to think of themselves as highly as Peter and John do, namely as kings and priests.

A HOLY NATION -- As was true of the previous phrases, this, too, is a reminiscence of Exodus 19:6. "Holy" means set apart, sanctified, different (see notes at 1:15), separated from other the nations and consecrated to the Word of God. "Nation" conceives of the church as a "people" or a national body. Although "aliens (foreigners) and strangers" and "scattered" among the many nations, in a special sense Christians nevertheless constitute the Lord's special nation.

A PEOPLE FOR *God's* OWN POSSESSION -- Christians are described in the language reminiscent of Exodus 19:5 as God's special property.[46] As previously, a term that used to be applied to Israel is now applied to the church. Believers are a special people, the private, special, treasured possession of God.[47] One other point to be noted is the Greek simply reads "a people unto possession." Some have supposed Peter is writing something like we can read in Hebrews 10:39, where the same Greek word is translated "preserving" (or in some versions, "the saving of the soul"), and contrasts there with "perdition" or "destruction." Maybe Peter is using this term to remind the faithful of their eternal destiny. In any case, each of the terms has wrapped up within it the implication that Christians are priests; they have a job to do for God.

That you may proclaim the excellencies of Him who has called you -- Peter here states the purpose ("that" translates *hopos*) why his readers are what they are. God's special people are saved to serve! That's what a priest does! He doesn't just sit down and quietly contemplate who he is while doing nothing for his Master. "Proclaim" translates *exaggello*, a word that denotes to publish abroad, make widely known. Church members, the new covenant priests, have an evangelistic function to perform. "Him who has called" them is God (1:15). *Aretas* is not an easy word to translate.[48] KJV and NIV have "praises." NEB has "triumphs." RSV and NEB have "wonderful deeds." If we use "virtues" we are emphasizing that God always desires to do what is right. "Excellencies" (NASB) points to God's pre-eminent qualities, His superiorities to any other gods, that Jehovah is unique in His inherent nature as well in His self-manifesting deeds. In any case, it is the job of royal priests, not to center their message on their own experience, but to publish abroad the uniquenesses of the God in

---

[46] Others appeal to Deuteronomy 7:6, 14:2, 26:18; Isaiah 43:21; and Malachi 3:17.

[47] "A very ordinary thing acquires a new value, if it has been possessed by some famous person. In any museum we will find quite ordinary things -- clothes, a walking-stick, a pen, books, pieces of furniture -- which are of value because they were once used and possessed by some famous person. It is so with the Christian. He may be a very ordinary person, but he acquires new value and dignity and greatness -- because he belongs to God." Barclay, *op. cit.*, p.236.

[48] It occurs but four times in the New Testament, Philippians 4:8 (where it means "a desire to do right"), 1 Peter 2:9, 2 Peter 1:3,5.

whose service they are employed.

Out of darkness into His marvelous light -- The time when the Christian priests were so "called" was their conversion (see comments at 1:15). "Darkness" is often used metaphorically to stand for the dominion of Satan and "light" for the dominion of God (Acts 26:18). Before conversion a man is under the power of slavery to sin and the Devil. Animistic concepts fill him with fear and superstitious behavior. He guesses and gropes his way along. "Darkness" aptly describes the state of sin and spiritual ignorance and the consequent wretchedness of the unsaved, in this life and the world to come.[49] When men turn to Jesus they find the power of sin is broken; they are free indeed, and are part of the kingdom of God. They are walking in the Light of His Word.[50] This difference – being able to see the way to live and walk – is as different as night and day. His light[51] is marvelous, wonderful, extraordinary, causing amazement.[52]

2:10 -- ***For you once were*** **NOT A PEOPLE,** ***but now you are*** **THE PEOPLE OF GOD;** ***you had*** **NOT RECEIVED MERCY,** ***but now you have*** **RECEIVED MERCY.**

For -- Peter is still calling attention to Old Testament passages where the priesthood of all believers was intimated. In this verse he weaves in words found in Hosea 1:6-10 and 2:1,23. In a chapter dealing with God's predestination of His chosen vessels to service, Paul (Romans 9:25,26), just as Peter does, uses this same passage from Hosea with reference to the calling of the Gentiles.

You once were NOT A PEOPLE, but now you are THE PEOPLE OF GOD -- What a difference conversion makes. "Once," before conversion, they were not "a people."[53] "Now," after conversion, they are "the people of God." "Before conversion they had no distinct existence as a community of people who were of any usefulness in God's program. They were just a heterogeneous mass of Gentiles, aliens from God and separated from each other by race, language, customs, and religion."[54] Now they are not just "a people," but "the people of God," a community of priests with a job to do for God.[55]

---

[49] Matthew 6:23b, 22:13, 25:30; John 3:19; 2 Corinthians 6:14; 1 John 1:5,6.

[50] God's word is light, Psalm 19:8, 119:130; Proverbs 6:23.

[51] "Light" may speak of more than the blessedness and joy and the purity and holiness of salvation. "His" may include that "unapproachable light" in which He dwells (1 Timothy 6:16). When the redeemed reach heaven, they will behold the "glory" of God and the "glory" of Christ (John 17:24).

[52] For other uses of *thaumastos* see Matthew 21:42; Mark 12:11; Revelation 15:1,3.

[53] Very likely there is a reference to the Gentile ancestry of Peter's readers.

[54] Hiebert, *op, cit.*, p.137

[55] Careful students of the Old Testament have observed two things: (1) there is a difference between "people"

You had NOT RECEIVED MERCY, but now you have RECEIVED MERCY -- Peter is still weaving in words found in Hosea. Once his readers had not enjoyed the forgiveness of sins; now they do. When the meaning of "having received mercy" is unfolded, Peter has found another implication that redeemed people (a royal priesthood) have a function to perform. A man who has received mercy certainly should show it (Matthew 18:23-35).

With these words from Hosea the second doctrinal section comes to an end. Peter has reminded the readers of their exalted status in God's sight; they are living stones in God's spiritual house and a royal priesthood to offer up spiritual sacrifices. With these truths in view, we are ready for some exhortations. A people so mightily blessed should not hesitate to respond to these admonitions.

IV. SECOND HORTATORY SECTION. 2:11-3:12

A. Exhortations Concerning Conduct Before Unbelievers. 2:11,12

2:11 -- ***Beloved, I urge you as aliens and strangers to abstain from fleshly lusts, which wage war against the soul.***

Beloved -- While the word is often explained of Peter's own warm affection for his readers, one wonders, given what has been already written, whether Peter isn't using the word with the meaning "divinely loved ones."

I urge you as aliens and strangers -- It is from *parakalo*, "I am pleading with you, I beg you, I implore you," that we get the title for this section of the letter. As he begins this new section, Peter addresses them once again as "aliens and strangers." As explained in notes at 1:17, an "alien" or "sojourner" (*paroikous*) is a foreign settler,[56] temporarily dwelling in a strange *house,* and as explained in notes at 1:1, a "stranger" or "pilgrim" or "alien" (*parepidemous*) is a visitor who tarries for a time in a foreign *country* but who shortly will be traveling on to his homeland destination. It is precisely because they are "strangers and pilgrims" (KJV) that they should "abstain." The standards of life in their native land are far

---

and "peoples." The singular term refers to Israel, a community of people useful to God. "Peoples" (plural) is a reference to all nations (sometimes including Israel, and sometimes not). (2) The names of Hosea's children enshrine a prophecy of the inclusion of Gentiles among God's people. Hosea's children originally were named Loammi (*lo* = "not" and *ammi* = "My people") and Lo-ruhamah (*lo* = "not" and *ruhamah* = "pity, mercy"). Later the names were changed to Ammi and Ruhamah, that is, "My people" and "Mercy." This change of names is treated in the New Testament as a prediction of the admission of the Gentiles into God's favor. Before Christ came, the Gentiles were not the people of God, and had not been recipients of His mercy. But because of His coming, now they are, through faith.

[56] Often an "alien" lives with restrictions which give him less rights than citizens of the land have. So the Christian has less rights, because God so decrees it, not because the laws of the land he is visiting require it.

superior to those of the pagan culture in which they find themselves at the present time.

To abstain from fleshly lusts -- "Fleshly lusts" are the desires (see 1:14) that motivate unsaved men.[57] These desires are planted in the "flesh" by the promptings of the devil.[58] Peter's readers, scattered throughout the provinces of Asia Minor, lived in cities which were pagan and characterized by gross immorality. Many of the converts used to live the same way their unsaved neighbors still do (2 Peter 2:18-20). The temptations the devil used to use to entice these people will still be tried, for after all, the devil thinks, if they worked once, perhaps they will work again. The Christian will have to watch his thoughts and desires, and make a conscious effort to "abstain" (i.e., to hold himself off or keep a distance) from what these fleshly desires are prompting him to do.[59] Rather than seeing how close to evil they can come, Peter urges his readers to see how far away from sin they can get. Christians must avoid the immoral customs and wicked practices of the pagan lands in which they temporarily reside and through which they are travelling.

Which wage war against the soul -- The present tense verb *strateuontai* speaks not of hand-to-hand fighting but of a planned expedition against a military objective. The desires stirred up in our bodies by the devil are part of his carefully planned effort to thwart what God is trying to do with His chosen people.[60] We might liken it to Delilah's cool exploitation of Samson's appetites for his destruction. "Soul" means here what it did in 1:9 but with this difference: there it was saved; here it is blasted and ruined by the devil's warfare.

2:12 -- ***Keep your behavior excellent among the Gentiles, so that in the thing in which they slander***

---

[57] To us "fleshly lusts" often connote sexual sin, but in Bible times the word had a much broader meaning. See Galatians 5:19-21.

[58] Since the NIV reads "sinful desires" it seems appropriate, here, to be careful lest our comments and explanations border on the idea that the Christian has an old sinful nature still residing in his "flesh" even after baptism. In the author's *Commentary on Romans* is a Special Study documenting the fact that the idea of an inherited sinful nature is something brought into the church from Greek philosophy (spirit is good, matter is evil), not something originally taught in Scripture. However, once it was determined to be a church dogma, theologians went searching for verses that might support the idea of hereditary total depravity and an inherited sinful nature. (See how some handle Romans 7:13-25, as though there is an evil problem that the Christian has -- rather than there is a problem the pre-converted man has.) While repudiating the idea of an inherited sinful nature, it is recognized that Galatians 5:19ff and Romans 6:11,12 do indicate that even the Christian still has temptations (from the devil) over which he will have to practice self-control or he will find himself continuing to sin. The devil is the real source of the "desires of the flesh" rather than an inherent, hereditary nature derived from Adam.

[59] "Abstain" means the Christian is not to permit his mind to show any hospitality when such desires seek a place to stay (Ephesians 2:3; Colossians 3:5; 1 Thessalonians 4:3; Titus 2:12).

[60] James (1:14, 4:1) speaks of bodily desires which become the source of temptations, and which fight against men's souls. The fulfilling of those fleshly desires, without restraint, results in habits which destroy the body (Galatians 6:8) and result in slavery to their demands (Romans 6:16; 2 Peter 2:19).

you as evil-doers, they may on account of your good deeds, as they observe* them, *glorify God in the day of visitation.

Keep your behavior excellent among the Gentiles -- When we come to verse 12, we have come to a third reason Peter gives for his exhortation concerning their conduct. First, they were "aliens and strangers;" second, "fleshly desires" do the soul no good; now he emphasizes the influence for good they can have on their Gentile neighbors. Steadily they are to hold up an attractive lifestyle.[61] The Greek has several synonyms for "good." *Agathos* emphasizes good in quality. *Kalos*, the word used here, denotes not only good, but lovely, fine, attractive, winsome. Peter is exhorting his readers to make their way of life so lovely, so fair, so good to look upon, that it will positively attract admiration.[62] "Excellent behavior among the Gentiles" embodies a timeless truth. The best argument for Christianity is a real Christian; therefore, whether we like it or not, every Christian is an advertisement for Christianity. By his life and words he either commends Christianity to others, or he makes others think less of Christianity. It is part of our "priestly job."

In the thing in which they slander you as evil doers -- A smoother translation of the circumstantial participle might be, "while they speak against you as evil doers."[63] An "evil doer" is a bad actor, one who does evil in such a way as to be liable to punishment from the magistrates. Among the unconverted populace there were charges commonly whispered against the Christians. They met secretly at night (Acts 20:7). They are cannibals (in the Lord's Supper they eat the body and blood). They practice incest ("brothers" and "sisters" live together). They damage trade and business (Acts 18:21-31, 16:16, 19:23ff). They turn slaves against their masters. They are disloyal to Caesar. Wherever they go they disturb the peace (Acts 24:5). They are irreligious (they refuse to bow down to the images of the gods). Remember, it was the general acceptance of such vicious charges against the Christians in Rome that enabled Nero to make the Christians the scapegoats as he tried to shift the blame for the burning of Rome from himself to some one else.[64]

So that ... on account of your good deeds, as they observe *them* -- If and when the day ever comes, when instead of listening to vicious rumors your Gentile neighbors actually "observe"

---

[61] The participle "keep" is present tense, continuous action. The participle here (following the infinitive of the previous verse) seems to teach that any possible interest we may have in influencing other people for good is dependent on the safety of our own souls. "Behavior" is the same word we've already had at 1:15. It is a favorite word with Peter. He will use it again at 3:1,2,16 and 2 Peter 2:7,18. In the 17th century, the KJV's "conversation" included a man's whole conduct, his whole way of life, not just his "speaking."

[62] The same word was used by Jesus in Matthew 5:16, of which Peter's present passage is strongly reminiscent. "Great Days with Jesus!"

[63] Think of how a little group of foreigners who settle in a neighborhood are accused of all kinds of vile actions and crimes by people of prejudice.

[64] Tacitus, *Annals*, 15:44; Suetonius, *Lives of the Twelve Caesars*, p.250.

(carefully scrutinize) your actions, they will see that your actions are "good."[65] They are to see that your behavior is such that there can be no possible truth to the rumors.

They may ... glorify God in the day of visitation – In the previous phrase, "so that" introduces the purpose behind Peter's exhortation of his readers to winsome living. It is so that those observing the behavior of the Christians may "glorify God." It is likely that "glorify God" means to honor, adore, praise Him (cp. the centurion at the crucifixion, Luke 23:47), and this would best be done (not just by a change in attitude towards Christians while these ex-detractors remain pagans, but) by their conversion so they worship the true God (1 Timothy 1:17). That their conversion is evidently in Peter's mind follows from the evangelistic note he wrote in 2:9, and from the obvious reference to Jesus' words "Let your light shine ... that they may ... glorify your Father who is in heaven." Explanations offered for "day of visitation" have followed one of two lines of thought, neither of which has proven to be wholly without question. One is that it is a day God visits the Gentiles, the other is that it is a day when the Gentiles visit the church. The first one might be acceptable as long as we carefully define our terms,[66] so that God's visit is similar to the visit Jesus made to Jerusalem (Luke 19:44). As Jesus the Messiah rode into the city at His Triumphal Entry, we recall that He lamented the fact that Israel was blind to her time of visitation (a day when God was visiting them to offer salvation). He was referring to Himself, and He was brokenhearted because He foresaw that by their own deliberate choice they were going to reject Him and His offer of grace and blessing, and that rejection would result in their suffering and ruination. If we accept this explanation, what shall we do with "day"? Was there to be one particular day when God would come to visit the Gentiles (among whom Peter's readers lived) with His offer of salvation? The second option, that it is a day when the Gentiles personally investigate (observe or inspect[67]) the lives of the Christians firsthand, also raises some difficult questions. Precisely when and how this visit is envisioned to occur is not easy. Some write about a day of trial, a magisterial investigation connected with the persecution. But are we to think that in such a heated atmosphere the potential persecutors are actually converted as a result of the testimony and good works of the Christians? Others treat "day" as being no particular individual day, but rather as any time the door of grace is opened (such as in "now is the day of salvation" 2 Corinthians 6:2). Kelcy writes about "a time of the spread of the Gospel among the Gentiles" as he tries to explain "day of visitation."[68]

---

[65] It is the same word for "good" used previously (and translated "excellent" in the NASB).

[66] So the NIV which reads, "glorify God on the day he visits us." This visit is then explained as resulting in the conversion of the Gentiles (as though God, by fiat, converts them). Lenski words it, "when God looks on them in mercy and brings them to conversion." (In comments on 1 Peter 1:18-22, we have rejected the dogma that man is wholly passive in salvation, so that salvation is something that God does to man.)

[67] The word translated "visitation" is *episkopes*, the same root that sometimes means "oversee" and sometimes "overseer."

[68] Raymond Kelcy, *The Letters of Peter and Jude* (Austin, TX: R. B. Sweet Co., 1972), p.54.

B. Exhortation Concerning Submission to Civil Rulers. 2:13-17

2:13 -- ***Submit yourselves for the Lord's sake to every human institution: whether to a king as the one in authority,***

Submit yourselves ... to every human institution -- "Submit yourselves" denotes a voluntary acceptance of or obedience to superior authority. The middle voice implies this is something the Christian does for his own benefit. "Every human creation" (so the Greek reads) is that to which the Christian is exhorted to submit. Macknight observes that what we call the "appointment" of magistrates and rulers, the Greeks and Romans called the "creation" of them. So it is not so much the ordinances and laws these rulers make, as it is the rulers themselves (as the following phrases in this verse show) who are identified as "every human institution." Jesus taught His followers to "render to Caesar the things that are Caesar's" (Matthew 22:21). Of course there is no contradiction in "human" to Paul's affirmation that the "powers that be are ordained by God" (Romans 13:1 KJV), nor does "every" contradict the limitation everywhere implied in Scripture that God's people obey only those laws and rulers which are not contrary to God's laws (as Peter himself taught, Acts 4:19, 5:29). The reason for submission is that it just is not possible for a "royal priest" to function effectively and be constantly in conflict with government officials. After all, if Christians are not generally submissive, will they not find themselves lumped together in the same category with the zealots (who, in Palestine, at the time Peter wrote, were revolting and triggering the war that would lead to the destruction of the city of Jerusalem)? And will they not be treated the same way?

For the Lord's sake -- Peter here supplies the Christian motive for civil obedience. It is because Jesus our Lord requires it (Matthew 17:24-27). When we are submissive to civil rulers we are obeying the command of Jesus.[69]

Whether to a king as the one in authority -- With "whether ... or" Peter indicated two classes of such "human institutions" to which Christians are to be submissive. "King" refers to the Roman emperor. Nero (ruled AD 54-68), the very ruler who had started the persecution he writes to warn about, was the emperor when Peter wrote. The personal worthiness of the office holder does not cancel the duty of submission to the office. He was supreme or in authority over all the subordinate officers in the empire, whatever their title. Herod the Great, for example, may be called a "king," but he was still answerable to Caesar.

2:14 -- ***Or to governors, as sent by him for the punishment of evil-doers and the praise of those who do right.***

---

[69] Other (less satisfactory, in this commentator's opinion) explanations of "for the Lord's sake" include: (1) So as not to bring dishonor on the name of Christ. Obedient conduct will bring honor to the Lord. (2) "Lord" is a reference to God the Father. Christians should obey civil authorities because such authorities find their source in God. While both these ideas are true, we are not convinced they are the point Peter has in mind as he writes "for the Lord's sake."

Or to governors, as sent by him -- "Sent by him" is best taken to refer to the emperor ("king"), rather than to the Lord.[70] "Governors" (Latin title, procurators) were appointed by the emperor to be the chief administrator of a given Roman province.[71] Pilate, Felix, and Festus, are examples of "governors" in the pages of the New Testament. The present participle "sent" pictures the governors being commissioned one after another, over a period of time.

For the punishment of evil-doers -- Peter here gives the purpose behind the "institution" and sending of these government officials. Such officials have one responsibility toward criminals and another responsibility towards law-abiding people.[72] In the case of criminals (habitual "evil-doers," a present participle indicating continuous action) they[73] are to see that such are punished. Ulpian, the celebrated Roman lawyer, described the power of the governors in Roman provinces in these words:

> It is the duty of a good and vigilant president to see to it that his province be peaceable and quiet. And that he ought to make diligent search after sacrilegious persons, robbers, man-stealers, and thieves, and to punish every one according to their guilt. They who govern the provinces have the power of sending to the mines.

And the praise of those who do right -- "Praise" here stands opposed to "punishment" in the preceding clause, and so means "commendation, applause, reward." Just as "evil-doers" pictures a continuous action, so "those who do right" is a continual doing of the right. Praise to such could be done by protecting persons and property, by defending men's rights, and by publicly lauding those who do citizenly acts. Of course, neither Peter nor Paul implies that what God intended for civil government will always be carried out in our world. But even bad rulers make some efforts to preserve law and order, and when they do this, they are kind of rulers Christians can submit to gladly.

2:15 -- *For such is the will of God that by doing right you may silence the ignorance of foolish men.*

For such is the will of God -- That is, this is the thing that God wills, or this is the way God wills that ignorant men be silenced – not by violence or retaliation or passive resistance or riot or rebellion.

---

70 "King" is the nearer antecedent, and the preposition used here, *dia*, speaks of the intermediate agent. If the Lord were the sender we would expect the preposition to be *hupo*, the direct agent.

71 The chief administrators in provinces that were peaceful, with no need of an army to keep law and order, were called "proconsuls" and they were appointed by the Roman senate.

72 Paul's corresponding statement is that the government official is an "avenger of wrath on those who do evil" but a "minister of God for good to those who do good" (Romans 13:3,4).

73 It would appear correct (from this passage and Romans 13:4) that Christians are not to take the law into their own hands. Civil officials, not the citizens, punish evil doers.

That by doing right you may silence the ignorance of foolish men -- The charges voiced against the believers by "foolish men" were based, for the most part, on ignorance of the real life and calling of the Christians. Men can behave in a foolish ("senseless, lack of reason") way. Think of the senseless attitude and unreasoning behavior of the cattlemen toward the sheepherders on the western lands of the United States a generation or two ago. How easy it was (and is) for a group of people, in ignorance of facts and unfairly jumping to conclusions, to arrive at their attitudes about another group simply because the second group is different in some of the ways they do things. How often these ill-formed attitudes are all wrong. The opponents of Peter's readers have been doing a lot of talking, spreading a lot of false and prejudicial information. The way to "silence"[74] them is by "doing right" to them. Did not Jesus teach, "Love your enemies" (Luke 6:27)? Do not the Scriptures say, "If your enemy is hungry, feed him; if he is thirsty, give him a drink" (Proverbs 25:21; Romans 12:20)? There seems to be a connection between verses 14 and 15 in the repetition of the words "doing right." Peter seems to be saying Christians are to pre-empt possible government attacks by being pro-active, doing good to the very officials who might later be asked by Caesar to arrest and punish those arsonists. Did he not just write that government officials have a duty to "praise" (not persecute) those who "do right"?

2:16 -- Act ***as free men, and do not use your freedom as a covering for evil, but*** **use it** ***as bondslaves of God***

Act **as free men**[75] -- The "aliens and strangers" are constantly reminded that they are citizens of the heavenly country. As Jesus Himself taught (Matthew 17:24-27), when one is a citizen of another country, he is technically exempt from the laws of the land in which he temporarily lives, but he voluntarily lives by those laws, lest he give offense. Peter here reflects another of his "Great Days with Jesus."

And do not use your freedom as a covering for evil -- In most every land, natives are familiar with how foreigners with diplomatic immunity often flout local laws. Well, Christians are sons of the King and therefore exempt from local laws (one could say they have diplomatic immunity), but they are not use that immunity as an excuse to live above the law.[76] Precisely because they are free they can choose to be "doers of winsome deeds".

---

[74] The Greek word means "to muzzle," i.e., to tie the mouth shut, as one might do to a vicious dog to stop it from attacking. Applied metaphorically, the verb means the mouth of the objector is stopped so that he is unable to say anything further.

[75] The connection of this verse to the context is disputed. Some take it with what follows. By the punctuation of our version, our translators took it as part of the exhortation begun in verse 13, and so shall we in our comments.

[76] The word here translated "evil" in the NASB is the same word translated "malice" in 2:1. In this place it seems to have its general significance, all sorts of wickedness and evil, a flaunting of local laws. Some commentaries launch into a discussion of "Christian liberty" (cp. Galatians. 2:4, 5:1,13) but the "freedom" Peter here speaks of does not seem to be exactly synonymous with "Christian liberty" which has reference to freedom from the Law of Moses, rather than freedom from the laws of the land in which the strangers and aliens were temporarily living.

But *use it* as bondslaves of God -- Christians may be "free men" but they are not free from all restraint. The fact they are "bondslaves" of God carries with it the implication a slave had better please his Master. Since this is true, Christians are not to use their freedom as an excuse to ignore the rulers and rules of the lands in which they live. Rather, they keep in mind that they have allegiance to a higher ruler (God), and they submit to their human rulers because that is precisely how they should live as God's bondslaves. Being a bond-servant of God is a wonderful privilege and a high concept. His service is not galling or brutal or degrading. So, as they live to please Him, Christians make the best of all citizens in all areas of service not contrary to the spirit and letter of His Word.

2:17 -- *Honor all men; love the brotherhood, fear God, honor the king.*

Honor all men -- With four ringing imperatives Peter summarizes his presentation of exhortations concerning submission to civil rulers.[77] One of Peter's emphases has been "doing right." When it comes to "doing right" the object of our good will (is it "all men" or the "brotherhood"?) may have some bearing on the intensity ("honor" or "love") with which we go about "doing right." Christians "do good to all men, and especially to those who are of the household of the faith" (Galatians 6:10). "All men" seems to be in contrast with Christian "brothers."[78] If so, it speaks of the unsaved. "Honor" is related to the word "precious" and Peter commands his readers to hold all men, especially the unconverted, as precious. Despise none of them; hold no prejudices.[79] Peter has written about having "excellent (winsome) behavior" among the Gentiles. Since God loves the lost and seeks to save them at infinite cost to Himself, Peter urges his saved readers to have an attitude toward the lost in keeping with their heavenly Father's.

Love the brotherhood -- Between those who are brothers in Christ, this "honor for all men" burns to something warmer and closer. It turns to love. *Adelphotes*, "brotherhood," may be Peter's term for the church, for he does not use the word "church" in his letters. It suggests

---

[77] Commentators have differed on whether there is any special order in these commands. The NASB puts a semicolon after the first, and groups the last three together with commas between. This may be an attempt to reflect the fact that the first imperative is an aorist tense, while the last three are present tense. Others, including this commentator, feel that the change in tense, while puzzling, is not to be stressed, and that the four imperatives are to be grouped into two pairs, one pair being "all and brotherhood," the other "emperor and God."

[78] The adjective *pantas* ("all") is masculine plural, so "men" is the likely noun to supply.

[79] If the citizenry of Rome and the empire had no prejudices, there would have been no fertile seed bed in which the slanders about the Christians being evil-doers (2:12) could take root. Well, Christians are not to be seed beds in which prejudices can grow and people be injured. Barclay has a long note about the 60 million people who were slaves in the Roman Empire at the time Peter wrote. Slaves were treated as things, who did not even possess the elementary rights of a person, and for whom justice did not exist. There was an attitude of prejudice towards them -- they were not even second-class citizens. "Honor all men" would require of Christians that they treat slaves differently than the average Roman citizen treated them, precisely because they were "men" (human beings), not "things."

the aggregate of Christian brothers, the community or body of believers.[80] A time of persecution such as existed when Peter wrote, when brothers in other cities and regions are suffering, is an especially opportune time to show love, and "do right" for those family members (cp. Hebrews 13:3).

Fear God -- "The fear of the Lord is the beginning of wisdom" (Psalm 111:10). This is the first duty and priority of the Christian. "Honor ... Love ... Fear ...." Here is expressed self-abnegation and a willingness to give each his due. The reverence that is here commanded is a reiteration of what was said in 1:17. The present tense verb says to keep on fearing God!

Honor the king -- The "king" (emperor) was Nero, and Peter commands his readers to keep paying honor to the king! Of the four injunctions in this verse, this is the most amazing, for Nero was persecuting Christians, having falsely accused them of burning Rome. "*Fear* God" – yes. Reverential awe is the proper attitude toward God. But "*Honor* the king." The proper attitude toward the king is honor. The wise Christian will know the degree of awe to be given to God and the degree of honor to be given to Caesar. "What can even ignorant men say against us if we follow these injunctions? What charge can they bring against us before any magistrate if we live thus; honoring all men, in particular loving our brethren, fearing God in holy reverence, and honoring the king?"[81]

C. Exhortations Concerning the Duties of Servants to Masters (Enforced by the Example of Christ). 2:18-25

2:18 -- ***Servants, be submissive to your masters with all respect, not only to those who are good and gentle, but also to those who are unreasonable.***

Servants -- The word here is not "slaves" (*douloi*) but "household servants, domestics" (*hoi oiketai*), the same word used at Acts 10:7 and Romans 14:4. As the etymology of the term indicates, it means a slave as a member of a household, not emphasizing the servile idea, but rather the relation which would tend to mitigate the severity of his condition.[82] The frequency with which slaves are addressed in the New Testament (here, Ephesians 6:5-8, Colossians 3:22, 1 Timothy 6:1,2) indicates that a large number of converts belonged to that class. Though he is a slave, the Christian slave is still a "royal priest" and can function in his God-given priestly tasks. Peter has commanded in verse 17 to "honor all [unsaved] men!"

---

[80] While the New Testament church polity involves the local autonomy for each congregation, membership in local congregations does not prevent closeness and fellowship and cooperation between congregations. Early Christians moved freely from place to place (Acts 18:27) and carried letters of recommendation introducing them to congregations in neighboring towns (Romans 16:1ff). Congregations joined together to "do good" -- think of the congregations that participated together in the offering for Jerusalem during Paul's third missionary tour (1 Corinthians 16:1-4; 2 Corinthians 8:23, Acts 20:4). Local churches should not put so much emphasis on congregational independence that we become isolationist, a behavior that is contrary to what is revealed of the feeling and working of "brotherhood" in the pages of the New Testament.

[81] Lenski, *op. cit.*, p.114.

[82] George R. Berry, *New Testament Synonyms* (Chicago: Wilcox and Follett, 1948), §45.

He now specifies how "the servants"[82] can put such "honor" into concrete action.

Be submissive to your masters with all respect -- Habitual, voluntary submission (see the meaning of the verb explained at 2:13) is the way servants honor their masters. *Despotes* is the word that denotes a person who is head of family. It also implies absolute ownership and unlimited control over the things and persons in the household. The NASB translators supposed the object of "respect" was the master. Another writes, "not fear of punishment, but fear of neglecting duty." However, since the Greek word is the same used for "fear God" (verse 17), not a few English versions read "with all fear." In other words, a slave's submission is not absolute. There is still fear of God that takes precedence over fear of human masters. The Christian slaves are to carry out their role in such a way that their primary allegiance to God is not compromised.

Not only to those who are good and gentle, but also to those who are unreasonable -- Unsaved masters come in all classes and kinds. Some are *agathos* (good, kind, reasonable) and *epieikes* (mild, fair, easily forgiving). Others are *skolios* (cruel, unfair, impossible to please, belligerent, overbearing, harsh). Honoring the latter, submitting to them, would be difficult, but a Spirit-filled man is enabled to meet demands which are unreasonable, perhaps even quite impossible on any other basis. Both classes of masters need the ministrations of a "royal priest." The Christian slave who remembers who he is can serve unsaved masters well,[83] for he will not make the character of his master a criterion for honor or submission.

2:19 -- ***For this* finds *favor, if for the sake of conscience toward God a man bears up under sorrows when suffering unjustly.***

For this *finds* favor -- Literally, "This is grace (*charis*)." This honor, this submission, especially to the harsh master, is lovely beyond what could ordinarily be expected. This pleases God. God favors such actions.

If for the sake of conscience toward God -- "Conscience toward God" in this context means an awareness of God's presence.[84] Remember what was written in 1:17 and compare what Peter says as he talks about Jesus' awareness of God's presence while He was suffering wrongfully (2:23). The Christian servant, aware that God is watching and that His approval

---

[82] This comment treats "the servants" as nominative, rather than vocative, and it treats the circumstantial participle as giving the means by which such honor can be shown, namely "by submission." In this commentator's opinion, this is better than treating the participle as if it had an imperative force.

[83] In our society, we might speak of employers and employees (rather than masters and servants), but the principles that guide a Christian worker's behavior are still applicable even when the employer is a non-Christian.

[84] In some verses, "conscience" is used of the innate faculty in man that prompts him to do what his mind thinks is right, and criticizes him when he does what his mind thinks is wrong. In other passages, it is used of what we call awareness -- awareness that we are living in His presence, and that he watches and judges our thoughts and actions.

is what really counts, can "bear up" ("endure") when the unreasonable master mistreats him.

A man bears up under sorrows when suffering unjustly -- "Sorrows" (*lupas*) indicates actions that produce grief or sorrow. Think of the abuse, pain, and even torture that unreasonable masters, at times, inflicted on their servants. "Unjustly" says the servant had done nothing to deserve the harsh treatment. Every Christian who is wronged has a wonderful opportunity to show a spirit which will honor the gospel.

2:20 -- ***For what credit is there if, when you sin and are harshly treated, you endure it with patience? But if when you do what is right and suffer* for it *you patiently endure it, this* finds *favor with God.***

For what credit is there -- Peter explains what he meant in the statement just made about enduring griefs while suffering wrongfully. His rhetorical question implies there is nothing especially commendable[85] about enduring punishment if one deserves such punishment for his wrongdoing.

If, when you sin and are harshly treated, you endure it with patience? -- Both the sinning and the buffeting (harsh treatment[86]) are present participles, picturing continuous or repeated actions. Receiving blows – being struck by the master's fist, or beaten with rods – was a common occurrence in the life of servants. "Patience" here might be an uncomplaining spirit, or a lack of chaffing and rebellion and restlessness, because, after all, he was caught in some sin and is being deservedly punished for it. Patiently enduring the punishment earns him no extra credit with God. He is simply getting his just due.

But if when you do what is right and suffer *for it* you patiently endure it -- It might be that these servants were buffeted for no other reason than for being a Christian, or for no other reason than the "cruel" master got joy out of such treatment of those in his power. They have been "doing what is right" but have been falsely accused and undeservedly punished. Christian servants show "honor" to their unfair and unsaved masters by patiently enduring the punishment, not by flashing anger in their eyes and clenching their fists as though they would like to strike back.

This *finds* favor with God -- Peter here uses the same expression he used in the opening of verse 19. God is pleased with such submissive conduct, especially when the suffering is undeserved. To suffer patiently when one deserves better treatment is to manifest an attitude which will bring God's approval.

---

[85] The KJV reads "glory" where the NASB has "credit." The Greek word is *kleos*, "glory" or "praise."

[86] This word is found at Mark 14:65 in connection with the cruel treatment received by Jesus when He was being mocked during His trials just prior to His crucifixion.

2:21 -- ***For you have been called for this purpose, since Christ also suffered for you, leaving you an example for you to follow in His steps,***

For you have been called for this purpose -- "This" points back to what Peter has been saying, "to do what is right and even possibly to patiently suffer for doing it." "Called" refers back to the reader's conversion (see notes at 1:15). "All who desire to live godly in Christ Jesus will be persecuted" (2 Timothy 3:12).

Since Christ also suffered for you -- Here Peter begins the enforcement of the special duties of servants to their masters by appealing to the example of Christ.[87] Christians are not the only ones who suffer while doing good. Jesus did! He did it for others' benefit.[88] The Christian servant does it, hoping to benefit his unsaved master by winning him to Christ.

Leaving you an example for you -- "Example" (*hupogrammos*) comes from the way in which children were taught to write in the ancient world. Sometimes parents and teachers used an outline sketch which the learner had to fill up and fill in. Sometimes there was a writing exercise on the top of the page which the child had to reproduce in the lines underneath. Today's children can even put a blank page on top of a printed one, and trace what is on the printed page. Jesus is the example or pattern to be imitated by those who would be true disciples of His.[89]

To follow in His steps -- Paul would say, 'Follow me as I lead the way to Christ.' Peter words it, 'Follow in Christ's steps, one by one, as closely as you can.' Place your feet exactly where His were. He suffered undeserved insult and injury with uncomplaining steadfastness and unfailing love. He suffered that he might bring men to God. Christians are to do likewise.

2:22 -- WHO COMMITTED NO SIN, NOR WAS ANY DECEIT FOUND IN HIS MOUTH;

WHO COMMITTED NO SIN -- This is the first of four relative clauses describing Christ's sinlessness. He was doing good, not evil, when He suffered. The words Peter uses in this verse are from the LXX of Isaiah 53:9.[90] Not even one act of sin was committed by Jesus.[91] Hence, all the punishment and indignity He received was undeserved.

---

[87] Peter will paint a detailed picture of Christ's exemplary and redemptive sufferings in verses 22-25.

[88] "For you" is *huper humon*. The preposition indicates that Christ's suffering and death were vicarious. It was a substitutionary atonement. Peter will elaborate more on this at 2:24 and 3:18.

[89] Of course, this is not the only reason why Christ suffered, but it is one reason. See 2:24 for another reason for Christ's death.

[90] Isaiah's "suffering servant" (Isaiah 40-66) was a messianic prediction. Both Peter and Philip the evangelist (Acts 8:32,33) apply Isaiah 53 to Jesus.

[91] On the sinlessness of Jesus, see 1 Peter 1:19; Matthew 26:59,60; Luke 23:41; John 8:46, 18:38b; John

NOR WAS ANY DECEIT FOUND IN HIS MOUTH -- "Deceit" (guile) was explained at 2:1. Jesus' enemies searched rigorously and carefully, looking for any lack of sincerity, any craftiness, any attempt to take advantage of others by stealth or trickery. "In his mouth" indicates not only were there no sinful acts (per the previous phrase from Isaiah 53), but there was no sinful speech ever to come out of Jesus' mouth. "The Gospel records substantiate what Peter says. Jesus stands forth as the sinless One. In all His clashes with his cunning enemies, no trace of evasion, guile, deceit, or trickery is found; nothing but the pure, holy truth; with that alone He discomfited them"[92] Christians will have to work at their "holiness" (1:15, 2:9) if they are ever to come close to walking in Jesus' steps.

2:23 -- ***And while being reviled, He did not revile in return; while suffering, He uttered no threats, but kept entrusting*** **Himself** ***to Him who judges righteously;***

And while being reviled, He did not revile in return -- Jesus' sinlessness in action and word did not come from a lack of opportunity to sin. In fact, there were plenty of opportunities, as the present tense verbs ("reviled," "suffering") in this verse indicate. Plenty of opportunities, but no sin! In addition to what the mockers said as He hung on the cross, some of the examples of abuse heaped on Jesus include the times He was called a Samaritan, a glutton, a wine-bibber, a blasphemer, a demoniac, one in league with Beelzebub, a perverter of the nation, and a deceiver of the people.[93] There were times Jesus spoke to His detractors, but what He said was never just an outburst of personal hatred or an attempt at retaliation.[94]

While suffering, He uttered no threats -- Jesus suffered much. He was struck in His face, crowned with thorns, beaten with a reed, scourged, and nailed to a tree. Yet through it all, He never threatened retaliation on His tormentors, nor did He call down the wrath of heaven. Instead, over and over again, Jesus kept on saying, "Father, forgive them ...." Peter's language here in verse 23 is reminiscent of Isaiah 53:7, and may reflect what Peter himself saw as he witnessed the trials and the crucifixion of Jesus – a memorable day with Jesus! Jesus' example while suffering has proven to be a difficult one for his followers to imitate. Some early martyrs could not resist the natural urge to threaten their executioners with divine punishment, but when they did, they were not following the example of Jesus.

But kept entrusting *Himself* to Him who judges righteously -- The word "entrusting" has no object in the original. We might supply "Himself," or His cause or His sufferings or those who inflicted them. Perhaps Peter is saying Jesus committed His tormentors to God when He

19:4,6; 2 Corinthians 5:21; Hebrews 4:15.

[92] Lenski, *op. cit.*, p.120-121.

[93] See Matthew 26:61-63, 66-68, 27:12-14, 28-31, 39-44.

[94] The Lord again and again denounced hypocrisy and unbelief when he found it, especially in the Pharisees (Matthew 23). He bade Caiaphas to remember the coming judgment. But when He spoke, it was the language of prophetic warning and the sternness of love. He did not return abuse for abuse.

prayed "Father, forgive them" – to His mercy, if it might be; to His judgment, if it must be. Or perhaps Peter reflects Jesus' saying later on the cross, "Father, into Thy hands I commit My spirit" (Luke 23:46), though the imperfect tense "kept entrusting" points to something Jesus did more than once. "Him who judges righteously" is God.[95] In Jesus we see a perfect fulfillment of the principle seen in Romans 12:19,20, "Vengeance is Mine ... says the Lord." God doesn't make mistakes when He administers justice in conformity with His truth and holiness. Jesus could, with full assurance, entrust His vindication into God's hands. The application of this passage to the conduct of slaves unfairly suffering abuse and hurt is at once apparent.

2:24 -- ***And He Himself bore our sins in His body on the cross that we might die to sin and live to righteousness; for by His wounds you were healed.***

And He Himself bore our sins in His body on the cross -- In the Greek, this is the third of the relative clauses (see notes at verse 22) Peter uses to show that Christ was doing good and not evil when He suffered. It was "our sins," not His own, He was dealing with. "Himself" is emphatic and shows there is a contrast between Jesus' sufferings and ours. There is a sense in which we cannot suffer like Christ suffered. Our sufferings will not bring about redemption for other people's sins like His did. In "bore our sins" there is evidently an allusion to Isaiah 53:12. Like Old Testament priests carried sacrifices for sins up the incline[96] to the altar where they were to be offered, Jesus offered His own body[97] as the sacrificial victim. Both here and at Acts 5:30, when referring to the "cross," Peter uses the Greek word *xulon*, "tree," to describe the instrument on which Jesus was crucified. The cross was evidently not made of smooth boards; rather, it was just two rough logs fastened together. Is Peter here vividly recalling the scene he himself witnessed on Calvary's hill, down to the details of the "tree" itself?

That we might die to sin and live to righteousness -- Peter here states what Jesus had in mind for us when He died vicariously. He wanted it to be possible for us to "die to sins" and to "live to righteousness." All who are Christians have died to sin (Romans 6:1-11; Colossians 3:3), and the aorist tense participle indicates that the dying precedes the living.

---

[95] The Latin Vulgate has a negative adverb here. It reads "to him who judged Him unjustly." According to this reading, which has no Greek MSS evidence to support it, Peter is speaking of Jesus entrusting his fate to Pilate.

[96] See comments on "offer up" at 2:5. The same verb is used here for what Jesus did. Selwyn, *The First Epistle of St. Peter* (London: Macmillan, 1961), p.95, thinks the figure behind Peter's language is the "scapegoat" on which the priest laid hands, figuratively transferring the people's sins to the goat. Selwyn calls attention to three different Old Testament figures used by Peter to explain why Jesus died: (1) the paschal lamb -- without blemish or spot (1:19); (2) the suffering servant of Isaiah 53, "by His stripes we were healed"; and (3) the scapegoat "who his own self bore our sins in His own body."

[97] What Peter here writes flatly contradicts what Docetists would later teach, namely that Jesus only "seemed" to have a body.

"Die to sins"[98] suggests folk who utter threats and retaliate do so because they have listened to one of the desires of the flesh stirred up by the devil. Instead, they should listen to the stimuli from God, who wants to use them as instruments of righteousness (cp. Romans 6:13). If they do this – if they die to sin and do what is right – they will live "unto justification,"[99] i.e., being counted as just because of Christ's atoning work.

For by His wounds you were healed -- This fourth relative clause (see verse 22 notes) is another allusion to Isaiah 53, verse 5 this time. We are more familiar with the KJV reading, "By his stripes we were healed." A "stripe" is the mark or welt left on a man's body where the scourge struck. The servants to whom Peter is writing may suffer undeserved scourgings, and to encourage them to bear up he urges them to remember the beating Jesus received. Wuest gives a vivid description of the terribleness of the beating:

> The word "stripes" in the Greek presents a picture of our Lord's lacerated back after the scourging He endured at the hands of the Roman soldiers. The Romans used a scourge of cords or thongs to which latter were attached pieces of lead or brass, or small, sharp-pointed bones. Criminals condemned to crucifixion were ordinarily scourged before been executed. The victim was stripped to the waist and bound in a stooping position ... [sometimes they may have been suspended above the floor by the wrists] to a post or pillar. The suffering under the lash was intense. The body was frightfully lacerated. The Christian martyrs at Smyrna about AD 155 were so torn by the scourges that their veins were laid bare, and the inner muscles and sinews and even bowels exposed. ... The [Greek] word here [in 1 Peter] is singular, not plural. Peter remembered the body of our Lord after the scourging, the flesh so dreadfully mangled that the disfigured form appeared in his eyes as one single bruise.[100]

"Healed" is used metaphorically, meaning to bring about one's salvation.[101]

---

[98] Peter writes the plural "the sins" as the NASB margin indicates. Some commentators have tried to affirm that when the word "sin" (in the singular) appears, the reference is to an hereditary sinful nature, and that when "sins" (plural) occurs, it is a reference to "acts of personal sin." A study of pertinent passages (such as Romans 5:12, 6:1-14 and 1 John 1:8,9) fails to bear out this proposed explanation for the singular "sin" and the plural "sins." Rather than a hereditary sinful nature, "the sin" in Romans 5 and 6 talks about the dominion of sin, or is a personification (read "the devil"). See this explained in the author's *Commentary on Romans, in loc.*

[99] *Dikaiosune*, if translated "righteousness" speaks of right living, doing our God-given duty towards our fellow man. If it is translated "justification," then it speaks of God thinking or reckoning the person as "forgiven." In comments on 1 Peter 1:17 (and footnote #81) we've observed that God watches and judges every day, and that "justification" is something that God counts to faithful men on a regular basis.

[100] Kenneth Wuest, *First Peter in the Greek New Testament* (Grand Rapids: Eerdmans, 1942), p.68,69.

[101] The context indicates Peter is not writing about healing of physical sickness or disease. It was our sins Christ bore on the tree. (The Pentecostal emphasis on "healing in the atonement" has this truth in it -- Christ died for body as well as soul. However, it is not until the second coming that the Christian will get his incorruptible body. Then, all sickness will be a thing of the past. In the meantime, even Christians who have the Holy Spirit will groan and suffer as they await their adoption, to wit, the redemption of their bodies [see Romans 8:23].)

2:25 -- ***For you were continually straying like sheep, but now you have returned to the Shepherd and Guardian of your souls.***

For -- Peter here seems to be unfolding the reason why Christ suffered and bore our sins. He was doing good for others. The language is reminiscent of Isaiah 53:6.

You were continually straying like sheep -- "Straying like sheep" is a way of saying they were lost in sin. The comparison of sinners to straying sheep is a common Biblical figure. It is not a complimentary picture. A lost sheep soon finds itself in a wretched position, and so do unforgiven sinners.

But now you have returned to the Shepherd and Guardian of your souls -- With "but now" Peter proceeds to describe the condition of his readers since their conversion. This return was made possible all because Jesus suffered while doing good. They are no longer like lost sheep without a shepherd. They now have Jesus as the shepherd of their souls. The figure suggests the guidance and loving care which Jesus provides for His people.[102] Barclay helps us get the feel for what a first-century reader might hear:

> It may be difficult for those of us who live in towns and in an industrial civilization to grasp the greatness of this picture; but in the East the picture would be very vivid and very precious. In Judea there is a narrow central tableland and plateau. On either side there is danger. On the west there lie the wastes of the Shephelah; and on the East the precipices with their jagged cliffs and crags which precipitate themselves more than a thousand feet downwards to the Dead Sea. It is in this narrow tableland that the sheep graze. Grass is sparse; there are no protecting walls [fences]; the sheep wander. The shepherd, therefore, has to be ceaselessly and sleeplessly on the watch lest harm should come to his flock. In *The Historical Geography of the Holy Land,* G. A. Smith describes the shepherd of Judea. "With us, sheep are often left to themselves; but I do not remember ever to have seen in the East a flock of sheep without a shepherd. In such a landscape as Judea, where a day's pasture is thinly scattered over an unfenced track of country, covered with delusive paths, still frequented by wild beasts, and rolling off into the desert, the man and his character are indispensable. On some high moor, across which at night the hyenas howl, when you meet him, sleepless, far-sighted, weather-beaten, armed, leaning upon his staff, and looking out over his scattered sheep, everyone of them on his heart, you understand why the shepherd of Judea sprang to the front in his people's history; why they gave his name to their king, and made him the symbol of providence; why Christ took him as the type of self-sacrifice."[103]

"Guardian" ("bishop" or "overseer") is another very descriptive term for Jesus. It is difficult to find an English equivalent for *episkopos*. Barclay tells us that it is a Greek word with a great history.

---

[102] Think of how farmers care for their live stock -- on a daily basis making sure of their welfare. That is how Jesus cares for us Christians. See Mark 14:27, John 10:2-5,11-18, Hebrews 13:20, Revelation 7:17.

[103] *Op. cit.*, p.256.

> In Homer's *Iliad* Hector, the great champion of the Trojans, is called the *episkopos*, who during his lifetime **guarded** the city of Troy and kept safe its noble wives and infant little ones. The word *episkopos* is used of the gods who are **guardians** of the treaties which men make and of the agreements to which men come, and who are the **protectors** of house and home. Justice, for example, is the *episkopos*, the **over-seer**, who sees to it that a man shall pay the price for the wrong that he has done. In Plato's *Laws*, the **Guardians** of the state are those whose duty it is to oversee the games, the feeding and the education of the children that "they may be sound of hand and food, and may in no wise, if possible, get their natures warped by their habits." The people whom Plato calls market-stewards are the *episkopoi* who "supervise personal conduct, keeping an eye on temperate and outrageous behavior, so as to punish him who needs punishment." In Athenian law and administration, the *episkopoi* were rulers and governors and **administrators** and inspectors sent out to subject states to see that law and order and loyalty are observed. In Rhodes the main magistrates were five *episkopoi* who presided over the good government and the law and order of the state. The word *episkopos* is, therefore, a many-sided but always noble word. It means the protector of public safety; the guardian of honor and truth and honesty; the overseer of right education and of public morals; the administrator of public law and order.[104]

So, to call Jesus the *episkopos* of souls[105] is to call Him our guardian, our protector, our guide, our director. Knowing who Jesus is, servants can be submissive to their human masters, and even endure suffering when they don't deserve to suffer, because their Shepherd and guide will be there to help. They must permit Him to do as He sees best for them – even if that be to permit persecution and suffering.

---

[104] *Op. cit.*, p.257-258.

[105] On "soul" see notes at 1:9.

D. Exhortations Concerning the Duties of Wives to Husbands. 3:1-6

3:1 -- ***In the same way, you wives, be submissive to your own husbands so that even if any*** **of them** ***are disobedient to the word they may be won without a word by the behavior of their wives,***

In the same way, you wives -- "In the same way" takes us back to 2:12ff.[1] In the beginning of this second hortatory section, Peter appealed to the Christians to have a winsome behavior that would attract unbelievers to Christianity. Elements of that winsome behavior include submission to recognized authorities, and honor being extended to all men. He then launches into some concrete examples of such honor. Christian slaves (2:18-25) are shown how to honor their unsaved masters. Now (3:1), Christian wives are shown how to honor their unsaved husbands.[2] Some modern readers have expressed surprise that Peter's exhortation to wives is six times as long as his exhortation to husbands (verse 7), but if those readers will recall how things were in the first-century world, their surprise will turn to understanding and then to appreciation of what Peter here does. Just as the breakdown of the family is viewed in our time as symptomatic of a society being in trouble, so a breakdown in lines of family authority was viewed as symptomatic of trouble and something to be vigorously resisted in the Roman society. The emperor was *pater familias*, the head (father) of the household (the state). His subordinates and functionaries derived their authority from his position. Likewise, in each family, the father had *patria potestas*, the absolute right to do anything he wished as head of the family. Everyone in the family – wife, children, slaves – was under his power. Anything, be it rebellion or religion, that might tend to undermine the father's power was viewed as dangerous to the fabric of society and would hardly be tolerated. Now we begin to appreciate the position new converts to Christianity were in. If the wife were converted and the husband was not, her problem was far more difficult than that of her husband. If the husband became a Christian, he would automatically extend his "father power" and expect his wife (and his slaves) to join him in his new religion. If they followed him, there would be no problem, no suspicion that this was a surreptitious attack on his "leadership power." But if a wife became a Christian while her husband had not, she had taken a step which in the ancient world was viewed as dangerous, and which could produce the acutest problems. The attitude of the Roman world was that no woman dared make any decision without her husband's permission. What, then, must have been the problems of the wife who became a Christian while her husband remained faithful to the ancestral gods?

---

[1] It is wholly incorrect to interpret the "in the same way" as though it implies that submission of wives to their husbands is comparable to submission of slaves to their masters.

[2] Just as we treated "servants" in 2:18 as a nominative rather than a vocative, and the circumstantial participle as expressing means, so in 3:1 we are treating "wives" as a nominative case and the circumstantial participle "submitting yourselves" the same way. Wives "honor" their husbands by submitting. (While the Greek text reads "the servants" at 2:18, and "the husbands" at 3:7, there are a few manuscripts [Aleph, A, B] that omit "the" before "wives" here at 3:1. Vocative cases usually do not have an article, nominative cases well may.)

Be submissive to your own husbands -- Peter is not teaching the general subjection of women to men. But, in the marriage relationship, submission[3] to one's own husband is legitimate and Biblical. The New Testament gives emphasis to the fact that the husband is head of the wife.[4] We suppose the case envisioned is one where the couple has been married and the wife becomes a convert while the husband does not. What was the Christian's responsibility in such a mixed marriage? Peter's directives are the same as Paul's in 1 Corinthians 7:12-16. If the unbeliever is content to continue the marriage, the Christian is not to start divorce proceedings. In fact, the Christian does what can be done to try to win the unconverted mate.

So that even if any *of them* are disobedient to the word -- This purpose clause ("so that") indicates that when a Christian wife finds herself in a mixed marriage, her submission assumes an evangelistic function. "Even if" shows that not all Christian wives will face this distressing situation, but many of them will. The husbands talked about are described as "disobedient to the Word." They were not just unbelievers, but they have explicitly refused to be persuaded by the Christian message preached to them.[5] The Holy Spirit works through the Word in conversion (cf. 1:23ff). These husbands have been resisting the Spirit's attempts to lead them to Christ.

They may be won without a word by the behavior of their wives -- "Won" (be gained) means in this context won to Christ.[6] The future tense ("will be won") portrays the anticipated result in relation to the time when the wife adopts the recommended strategy. In view of the husband's persistent rejection of the gospel, the wife stops nagging him about it[7] and instead lives a Christ-like life before him. The husband will be influenced toward Christ not by words but by the winsome behavior of holy living.

3:2 -- ***As they observe your chaste and respectful behavior.***

As they observe -- The tense of the participle indicates that close observation precedes the winning of the husband. How carefully the unsaved watch Christians.

---

[3] See notes at 2:18 on the force of this present middle participle. It is voluntary submission that is habitual.

[4] 1 Corinthians 11:3-12, especially verse 7; Ephesians 5:22-33; Colossians 3:18,19; Titus 2:4,5. Submission to a Christian husband is a joy and not a burdensome duty. But Peter is writing about situations where the husband has not converted. Marabel Morgan's book, *The Total Woman* (Old Tappan, NJ: Revell, 1973), shows Christian women how to do this and how fulfilling it can be.

[5] See how the verb "disbelieve" was explained at 2:7,8.

[6] The same word is used in 1 Corinthians 9:19-21 and Matthew 18:15 of winning converts to Christ.

[7] "Without a word" does not say the husbands will be won without hearing the gospel. The gospel is always the instrument of conversion (1 Peter 1:22; James 1:18; John 3:8). "Without a word" must therefore mean the wife is not to be constantly talking about the husband going to church with her, or letting the preacher talk to him, or reading Scripture verses to him with the intent of letting him know how unhappy she is with his refusal to submit to the Lord.

Your chaste and respectful behavior -- "Chaste" comes from the root which means holy. The wife's behavior is pure in all phases of life, not just in fidelity to the marriage relation. "Respectful" translates a phrase which the margin renders "with fear." Her behavior is pure because it moves in the fear of God.[8] At this place we learn that the wife's submission to the unsaved husband does not include obedience when the thing commanded by the husband is contrary to the Word of God. The Christian's ultimate allegiance is to God, and when God and husband contradict, the wife obeys God!

3:3 -- ***And let not your adornment be*** **merely** ***external -- braiding the hair, and wearing gold jewelry, and putting on dresses;***

And let not your adornment be *merely* external -- *Kosmos* here means decoration, ornament, adornment, and speaks of ways women "decorate" their bodies by jewels or clothing or hair arrangements. Peter's present tense prohibition forbids Christian wives from attempting to depend simply on their outward appearance in their effort at winning their unsaved husbands to the Lord.[9] Perhaps these women were thinking mistakenly that if they dressed as the world dresses, they would have a better chance of pleasing and impressing their unsaved husbands. Peter is not prohibiting the wives from giving any thought to making themselves attractive to their husbands, nor is he saying they can be careless in their dress and appearance. Peter's instructions are that Christian wives are to depend on the "hidden person of the heart" for their attractiveness more than they depend on outward appearance. Peter now lists some specific types or examples of external adornment.

Braiding the hair -- "Braiding" (*emploke*) does not denote, as with us, the weaving of three strands of hair together but instead the gathering of hair into elaborate knots to attract attention. Some first-century women spent ten hours once per week at the hair dressers to get their hair waved, dyed, wound, pinned, and bejeweled, into an artificial and ostentatious shape, some extending a foot or more above the top of the woman's head.

And wearing gold jewelry -- English translations often sound like an absolute prohibition of wearing any jewelry, but it is not so in the Greek. "Wearing" represents a verb that means putting on around and pictures a person wrapping her body – neck, ankles, arms, fingers, ears – with a lavish, conspicuous, glittering display of gold chains, rings, and bracelets. Rebekah wore jewelry (Genesis 24:53), and godly women today may wear Rebekah's jewelry if they have Rebekah's modesty.

---

[8] It is probably best to think of the wife as the one who does the "fearing" rather than the unsaved husband. Also, there is some question about who is the object of the fear. Some think it is the reverence for the husband the wife feels. Others think it is reverence for God the wife feels. Compare 1 Peter 1:17, 2:17. Such reverence is an essential ingredient of a holy life -- it offers strength and motivation for daily conduct.

[9] The prohibition is no more an absolute prohibition of "adornment" than is the prohibition of John 6:27 an absolute prohibition of eating food. ("Do not work for the food which perishes but for the food which endures to eternal life.") What it does require is a proper perspective, or priority. The inner person is more important than the outward adornment. Compared to Christian graces, the use of ornaments is nearly worthless when it comes to winning men to the Lord.

And putting on dresses -- *Himation* is the common Greek word referring to outer garments.[10] Peter is certainly not forbidding the wearing of all clothing, but he is warning against wearing the kind of clothing the world wore: immodest, gaudy, conspicuous. Such garments worn by a Christian wife would tend to hide the Lord Jesus Christ from the husband's view.[11] If a wife depends only on how she looks on the outside to attract her husband, she will find it won't be long until someone prettier (in his eyes) comes along, and then what will happen to his attentions and affections?

3:4 -- *But* let it be *the hidden person of the heart, with the imperishable quality of a gentle and quiet spirit, which is precious in the sight of God.*

But *let it be* the hidden person of the heart -- Verse 3 gave the negative side of Peter's command to Christian wives. Now he gives the positive side as he states the principle that women should follow as they try to win their unsaved husbands. The Christian wife should be dependent on the beautiful qualities which flow from one's inner spiritual being.[12] These qualities are usually "hidden" or concealed, secret, not readily obvious to the physical eye as are conspicuous ornaments and clothing deliberately chosen to attract physical attention. Peter will specifically identify the quality he has in mind in the phrase that follows.

With the imperishable quality of a gentle and quiet spirit -- Since Peter is talking about a person's "heart," this is likely one passage where "spirit" refers to attitude, rather than to one of the immaterial parts of the inner nature of man.[13] The attitude he wants Christian wives to model is a "gentle" and "quiet" one. "Gentle" describes her bearing as meek, considerate, and unassuming in its relations to others. She conducts herself in full awareness that she is not always right. "Quiet" pictures a calm, tranquil, serene bearing, which bears disturbances caused by others, and doesn't flash into anger when others speak harshly or behave with lack of consideration. She does not deliberately create disturbances, and she spreads peace around when she can. Such an attitude, Peter says, has an "imperishable quality." "Imperish-

---

[10] Though the Greek word is the common word for clothing, some English translations have used the word "apparel" here, since "apparel" is the synonym for clothing that adorns or displays personal vanity, whereas clothing has the connotation of practical dress that protects the body. Perhaps those translators have picked the right word to catch Peter's point of emphasis.

[11] Similar commands about how Christians "adorn" themselves are found in 1 Timothy 2:9 and Titus 2:10. If the inner being is right, the outward "adornment" will be right. Perhaps if Peter were to write to 21st century believers, he would have to remind us that it is possible to be guilty of wearing too-little rather than wearing too much. Appropriate Christian dress should be a reflection of our inner spiritual life. We dress in such a way as not to attract notice to ourselves.

[12] "Heart" here refers to the inner man, the inner self, the personal thoughts. See Paul's discussion of the "real Jew" (Romans 2:28,29). See also Romans 7:22 and 2 Corinthians 4:16 where we read of an "inner man" and an "outer man."

[13] The use of "spirit" to designate one of the three parts that make up a man (body, soul, and spirit) has been explained in notes at 1 Peter 1:9,23.

able" has been used to describe the Christian's future inheritance (1:4) and the seed of the new birth (1:23). As contrasted with outward adornment (jewels, apparel), there is nothing temporary about such a quiet attitude. Nothing will blast, ravage or destroy or outshine this kind of appeal.

Which is precious in the sight of God -- This statement is intended to give comforting assurance to tested wives. If they are ever tempted to think no one appreciates what they are doing, they should think again. God appreciates it! It may be the gentle and quiet spirit, or the whole preceding strategy for winning the unsaved husband, that is described as precious[14] in God's sight. The way for a Christian wife to display a winsome behavior (cp. 2:12) is by relying on her inner spiritual beauty rather than outward appearance (as non-Christians might do).

3:5 -- ***For in this way in former times the holy women also, who hoped in God, used to adorn themselves, being submissive to their own husbands.***

For -- Here we have a reason for something just said. Perhaps it is Scriptural evidence about God's approval of feminine reliance on their inner spiritual qualities.

In this way -- Namely, in a gentle and quiet spirit, submissive to their husbands.

In former times -- In Old Testament days. When Peter wrote, the Christian church had hardly been in existence long enough to furnish examples like Peter needs.

The holy women also -- Saintly[15] wives in Old Testament times did exactly what Peter is asking Christian wives to do. The Old Testament was written for our example.

Who hoped in God -- Abraham looked for the heavenly city which has "the foundations" (Hebrews 11:10). He said he was a stranger and a pilgrim at the time of Sarah's death (Genesis 23:4; Hebrews 11:13). Men hoped in God in Old Testament times. So did the women.[16] They were looking for the heavenly city and were anxious to have God's approval, both while they lived here and in the world to come. In chapter 1, Peter has already written about how hope could change a person's behavior. Such a living hope would enable wives to be submissive under difficult and trying circumstances.

---

[14] "Precious" translates *poluteles*, the same word used to describe the ointment as "costly" at Mark 14:3, and the garments at 1 Timothy 2:9.

[15] "Holy" has been explained in comments on 1:15,16, and 2:9. The word means set apart, consecrated, dedicated, sanctified. These ladies were not some unique class of individuals, but common, ordinary women who had been forgiven of their sins, and were consequently living so as to please the One who forgave them.

[16] The present participle indicates that this hoping by Godly wives was a continuous thing over an extended period of time.

Used to adorn themselves -- Saintly wives in Old Testament times made it a practice to "adorn themselves" with that gentle and quiet spirit that Peter is advocating. This is one way those wives sought the approval of their husbands.

Being submissive to their own husbands -- This is another way wives in Old Testament times sought the approval of their husbands. Scripture everywhere teaches the voluntary submission of wives to their own husbands.[17] Such submission is expected even in mixed marriages, where the wife is a Christian and the husband is as yet unconverted.

3:6 -- *Thus Sarah obeyed Abraham, calling him lord, and you have become her children if you do what is right without being frightened by any fear.*

Thus Sarah obeyed Abraham -- From among the holy wives whose lives are recorded in the Old Testament Scriptures, Peter singles out one example, Sarah. If Abraham were the father of the chosen people, then it would be proper to speak of Sarah as the mother of the chosen people. Sarah habitually obeyed her husband.[18]

Calling him lord -- Sarah habitually called (present participle) Abraham "lord"[19] (sir, mister, master), acknowledging by her respectful language that she recognized him as her superior, and that as husband he had a right to rule in his own house, to direct the affairs of the household, and that he was head of the family.

And you have become her children -- If Abraham is the "father of the faithful," then his wife Sarah is the mother of the obedient wives. They became her "daughters" (KJV[20]) at the time of their conversion.[21]

---

[17] See what has been written about "submission" at 2:13,18, and 3:1.

[18] There is a manuscript variation at this place, some manuscripts reading an aorist tense and some reading it as an imperfect tense. If we adopt the aorist reading, it speaks of her action as going on over a long period of time, but looking at it in one single view. Either way, the whole tenor of Sarah's life was one of obedience (submission) to Abraham. Certainly, she wasn't subject 100% of the time – look at the case of Hagar. But the tenor of her life was right.

(Perhaps 1 Peter 3:5,6 should be referred to by those who are pushing egalitarian agendas. Let it be observed that in verse 6 Peter uses "obey" where earlier he had written "submissive." Scripture certainly does recognize a hierarchy of authority -- God, Christ, husband, wife -- 1 Corinthians 11:3.)

[19] Peter may have reference to Genesis 18:12 where the LXX has "lord."

[20] The Greek is the neuter plural noun, *tekna*, "children," but in this place two feminine participles follow, showing that female children are intended.

[21] Some have argued that the wives being instructed by Peter were former Gentiles. But even a Jew becomes a faithful child of Abraham only by conversion (cp. Luke 19:9 where Zacchaeus, after his repentance, is designated as a "son of Abraham").

If you do what is right -- Since they have "become" Sarah's children, habitually doing what is right[22] is one of the results expected in their lives,[23] just as it was in Sarah's.

Without being frightened by any fear -- This second participle turns attention from the wife's conduct to her inner feelings. Christian wives are not to live in terror or panic worrying what their unsaved husbands may do. While a few wives may experience cruel treatment from the unbelieving husband from time to time, the wife whose behavior reflects a submissive spirit, a gentle and quiet spirit, will face few outbursts of anger or wrath even from an unsaved husband. As long as the believing wives are doing good, they need not be afraid that their unbelieving husbands may terrorize them. The Christian wife should not allow possible threats of what an unbelieving husband might do scare her out of her Christian faith.

E. Exhortations Concerning the Duties of Husbands to Wives. 3:7

3:7 -- ***You husbands likewise, live with your wives in an understanding way, as with a weaker vessel, since she is a woman; and grant her honor as a fellow-heir of the grace of life, so that you prayers may not be hindered.***

You husbands likewise -- Since 2:12 encouraged Christians to exhibit winsome behavior toward the lost, this is the third group of Christians to whom Peter gives specific instructions about such behavior. First he wrote about how Christian slaves should behave toward their unsaved masters, then how Christian wives should behave so as to win their unsaved husbands. Now he writes about how Christian husbands should live in order to win their unsaved wives.

Live with your wives in an understanding way -- Again it is observed that Peter's instructions about mixed marriages are the same as those written by Paul in 1 Corinthians 7:12-16. The Christian makes every effort to continue the marriage with their non-Christian mate. If the unbeliever departs, there is not much the Christian can do. But the Christian does not start the divorce proceedings. The Christian looks for ways to keep the marriage together. They live together as a married couple. The husband, being a Christian, has a view

---

[22] The participle here translated "do what is right" is the same one translated "do what is right" in 2:20, and its repetition here recalls the example of Jesus who suffered while doing what is right.

[23] The circumstantial participle could well be rendered "if you do what is good." Since this translation makes the doing of good a condition on which their good standing with God depends (after all, they argue, a man is saved by faith only, not by works), not a few commentaries have rejected the means of constructing the sentence followed in these notes. Some (see the ASV marginal reading) have argued that the two participles at the close of this verse are parallel to the participle "being in submission" with which verse 5 began, and all three participles then relate to the subject of the verb "adorned themselves." This requires us to take all of verse 6 down to these participles as a parenthesis. Such a lengthy parenthesis is doubtful, for it leaves "you have become her children" alone and isolated.

of marriage learned from Jesus, and acts toward his wife in harmony with this knowledge.[24] Christians have God's revelation regarding marriage and are supposed to demonstrate that knowledge in their everyday relationships with their mates.[25]

As with a weaker vessel, since she is a woman -- Here is one area where his knowledge of God's revelation shows itself in the husband's attitudes and actions. Commentators have struggled as they try to explain in what sense woman is a "weaker vessel."[26] How is she weaker? Spiritually? No! Mentally? No! Morally? No! Physically? Perhaps in brute strength, but not in stamina. How many a sick husband and family have been nursed by a wife who works around the clock to minister to the sick one while the husband is too weak to get out of bed to help? Perhaps the area where woman is "weaker" is in their emotional makeup. She is more easily crushed than a man, and Peter tells the Christian husbands to be careful lest they crush the deeper, inner emotional nature of their wives. Barclay offers a slightly different explanation. He says the idea is that the husband is to be chivalrous, to treat the woman with perfect courtesy. "In the ancient world chivalry to women was well-nigh unknown. It was, and still is, no uncommon sight in the East to see a man riding on a heavily-laden donkey while the woman trudges by his side. It was Christianity which introduced chivalry into the relationships between men and women."[27] Susan Foh has suggested another attractive alternative explanation of the word "weaker." "The wife may be considered weak because of her role as wife. She, by marrying, has accepted a position where she submits herself to her husband. Such a position is vulnerable, open to exploitation. The husband is commanded not to take advantage of his wife's vows of submission."[28]

And grant her honor -- We have a translation problem here. Shall we take this participle with the words that precede (as the ASV does, "giving honor unto the woman, as unto the weaker vessel") or with the words that follow (as the NASB does)? Either way, since the participle means "assign to, portion off," the husband is instructed to be deliberate and purposeful in his channeling of honor to his wife. "Honor" may refer to maintenance and support (the husband is to provide material needs for his wife), or it may have reference to her

---

[24] The Greek behind "in an understanding way" literally is according to knowledge. We suppose there is an obvious reference to the special knowledge (Biblical knowledge) of the relation of husband and wife, as contrasted with non-Christian views of such relationships.

[25] We are treating "live with" as a global reference to all aspects of a shared home life, and not as a mere euphemism for sexual relations. Sexual relations are of course included, and the Christian does not behave as a brute beast, but as an intelligent being in this as well as all relationships with his mate. It goes without saying that cohabitation, as God intended it, is limited to your own wife, whether the man is a Christian or not.

[26] The figure of speech "vessel" (dish, tool, instrument, utensil) is applied to human beings in Romans 9:21-23 and 1 Thessalonians 4:4. A container that is fragile is often marked "Handle with Care!" The husband is here instructed to handle his wife with gentleness and care.

[27] Barclay, *op. cit.*, p.264-265.

[28] Susan Foh, *Women and the Word of God: A Response to Biblical Feminism* (Nutley, NJ: Presbyterian And Reformed, 1980), p.133.

spiritual needs (if she is not a Christian, she needs to be won, and his continual "honor" for her will go a long way towards influencing her positively for Christ).[29]

As a fellow-heir of the grace of life -- Christ died for women as well as for men. There is neither male nor female when it comes to eligibility to hear and obey the gospel and benefit from its blessings.[30] As far as salvation is concerned, woman is in every way equal to man. She is entitled to all the hopes and promises which Christianity imparts. She is redeemed just the same as man is. She is addressed in the same tender language of invitation. She will be elevated to the same rank and privileges in heaven. The Christian husband is to keep this fact in mind, and so order his thoughts and behavior toward her that he puts no stumbling block in the path of his unsaved wife.[31]

So that your prayers may not be hindered -- "Your prayers" is a reference to the personal prayer life[32] of the Christian husbands addressed in this verse. Prayer is a normal feature of the Christian life, and Peter assumed that the Christian husbands to whom he was writing were men of prayer. Domestic relations can have a profound impact on spiritual fellowship with God. Did you ever try to pray for someone toward whom you had less than a good attitude? If the husband did not have a special place in his heart for his wife and her salvation, how would he ever pray for her? Did you ever try to have a prayer time just after you and your wife have had a fight? Why, you'd just as soon not pray! Your prayers are hindered.[33] Here is a great truth – our relationships with God can never be right when our relationships with our fellow men are wrong.

---

[29] Some writers have observed that one of the positive ways Christianity has influenced society is in the raising of the status of women. Before Christianity, woman was regarded as worthy of little honor and respect. She was considered as a slave or a mere instrument to gratify the passions of man. But having learned from Jesus how to treat a lady, His genuine followers have treated women with respect and honor.

[30] "Grace of life" could be a genitive of apposition, the grace that consists of [eternal] life. It could be treated as an objective genitive, the grace that bestows life. It is the rising to walk in newness of life (cp. Romans 6:4) that Peter is writing about, and so we speak of salvation in our comments at this place.

[31] In previous years, this commentator explained verse 7 as though both the husband and wife were Christians, and his comments and exhortations reflected that point of view. Now, even with a slight change of emphasis (recognizing these instructions are to the husband in a mixed marriage), he does not suggest that where both mates are Christians, the Christian husband is free from having to "honor" his wife as a weaker vessel and as an heir of the grace of life. The only difference in the Christian husband's assignment of honor to his wife will be the way that honor is demonstrated in everyday life. In one case, it is to win the wife to Christ; in the other it is to help her stay true to Christ.

[32] Some writers, not recognizing this is a mixed marriage, explain "prayer" to be a reference to family worship, where the wife and children join the husband.

[33] There is a manuscript variation here. Some manuscripts have *egkoptesthai* while others read *ekkoptesthai*. The word picture of the first comes from the military world, where impediments and obstacles are thrown in the road to make normal movement difficult or impossible. The second word means "to cut off," and suggests that the husband's failure to maintain right relations with his unsaved wife will cut off his practice of prayer. He will hardly pray at all. Bigg (*in loc.*) thought the object of the prayers is for blessings on the marriage. But all prayers are hindered when there are harsh words or feelings.

F. Exhortations Concerning the Duties of Christians to One Another. 3:8-12

3:8 -- ***To sum up, let all be harmonious, sympathetic, brotherly, kindhearted, and humble in spirit;***

To sum up -- Perhaps "the goal" would be a better way to translate than "finally" (ASV) or "to sum up" (NASB).[34] In the title we've assigned to this paragraph, we've spoken about the duties of Christians one to another. That is a deduction based in part on some of the words he uses, such as "harmonious" and "brotherly" or loving as brothers.

Let all be harmonious -- In the previous paragraphs he has been speaking to individual groups of Christians about their winsome behavior. Now he turns to ("all") the whole congregation. If as a whole they behave positively and beautifully toward each other, Christianity will be more attractive to the outsiders. *Homophrones* occurs only here in the New Testament and may be translated as like-minded, concordant, or harmonious. Each of the members of a congregation are part of a team, and it hurts when one or more of the church members is not consistent in his witness, for if one of the team lets down, the whole team suffers.

Sympathetic -- A contemporary expression of the same idea is to get involved in the other person's life, as opposed to being aloof and indifferent. It speaks of entering into each other's feelings and showing regard and concern for each other's welfare. Think of a dog with a thorn in its paw. The whole body works in an effort to help the hurt member. So with the members of the body of Christ.

Brotherly -- Peter has used *philadelphia* before at 1:22 and 2:17. Because Christians have been born again, and God is our father, we are brothers, members of God's family, and we are to have a special love for other members of the family. Such love is a sign that we have passed from death into life (1 John 3:14, 4:20), and a badge of true Christian discipleship (John 13:35).

Kindhearted -- The word can also be translated compassionate or pity. It is not saying Christians should be the kind of persons who arouse pity; rather we are to be full of pity, acutely sensitive to the burdens others are bearing, easily touched and moved to action by the needs of his brothers and sisters in Christ. This is a Christ-like attitude, for do we not read in the Gospels that Jesus was often "moved with compassion" to act to help men?

---

[34] The construction is somewhat like we find in 1 Timothy 1:5 which gives the "goal" of Paul's instructions to Christians. Paul (e.g., 2 Corinthians 13:11) used a different word for "finally" at the close of his letters, so, if we may take Paul's example of the word Greeks used at the close of letters, it is doubtful that we should treat 1 Peter 3:8 as the close of the letter (though some have tried to use this as a key to the outline of the first half of two separate fragments allegedly put together by some editor). "To sum up" might be defended if verses 8-12 are treated as the conclusion of Peter's second section of exhortations, but the words he uses hardly summarize what he has been saying since 2:12 about winsome behavior toward the unconverted.

And humble in spirit -- In the KJV we read "be courteous" because the word occurring in the Textus Receptus is *philophrones*, a word that means to be "friendly, kind, courteous." Modern Greek texts read *tapeinophrones*, a word not used elsewhere in the New Testament, though there are places where "mind" and "lowly things" (a verb and a noun) appear. It depicts an inner attitude of voluntary submissiveness to authority. It is the opposite of haughty and high-mindedness.

3:9 -- ***Not returning evil for evil, or insult for insult, but giving a blessing instead; for you were called for the very purpose that you might inherit a blessing.***

Not returning evil for evil -- This is the very response to hostility which Jesus taught his followers (Matthew 5:38-48). His followers are not to give back evil in exchange for evil received. Retaliation, returning evil for evil, does nothing to stop the evil, it only increases it. A very difficult question to answer is whether the hostility is thought of as coming from an outsider, or from a brother. If we have outlined this paragraph correctly, Peter is dealing with relationships between Christian brothers. When a brother, in spite of all Jesus taught to the contrary, mistreats you, do not respond in kind. It would appear that in two different places, Jesus' apostles tried to help Christians understand and properly apply Jesus' teaching about not returning evil for evil.[35] In both places (here and 1 Corinthians 6:7) the apostles apply Jesus' words to instances where Christians have injured fellow Christians. Among brethren there is a spiritual kinship, a family give and take, that ought to make lawsuits (1 Corinthians 6) or getting even (1 Peter 3) needless.

Or insult for insult -- Retaliation can occur in word as well as deed. "Insults" or "railing" (KJV) speaks of harsh, abusive language toward those with whom we are at odds. This is something that happens very commonly in disputes about small and unimportant matters. The Christian has a responsibility to control his language when he faces hostility. It is not only suffering slaves who are not to insult their oppressors (2:23), but it is a behavior expected of every Christian not to use insolent and abusive language against another who has injured him. Just as Jesus was giving a principle and His followers were to judge when and how to

[35] As Jesus delivered His Sermon on the Mount, he referred to the Old Testament rule intended to guide the decisions of judges when sentencing evil doers, "an eye for an eye, and a tooth for a tooth and burning for burning" (Exodus 21:24,25; Leviticus 24:20; Deuteronomy 19:21). Instead of limiting it to magistrates, the Jews had tried to extend this rule to private conduct, and made it a rule by which to take revenge. They considered themselves justified by this rule to inflict the same injury on others that they themselves had received. It is against this idea of "revenge" that Jesus objected. In His Sermon (Matthew 5:38-42), Jesus was teaching His disciples how to behave towards each other (at least that is how Jesus' apostles later taught it). He did not intend His directives ("I say unto you") to be applied to every situation. He never intended that we are to sit by and see our families murdered, or be murdered ourselves, with no resistance or attempts at self-defense. In the very context where Jesus stated His expectations, He also gave examples of what He meant by it. As He explained the principle, He confined Himself to small matters, to things of comparatively trivial interest -- smitten on the cheek, a coat taken, carrying a burden a mile. (If it should be a non-Christian demanding a trivial thing, the Christian, by his actions, may open a door of opportunity to explain to the man who makes the demands why a Christian's actions and attitudes are different from the resentment and rebellion the non-Christian would usually encounters when such demands are made.)

apply His teaching as best they could, so Peter is giving a rule about submission to evil if it will accomplish a spiritual victory. Absolute non-resistance (pacifism) may encourage crime and become a sin.

But giving a blessing instead -- The Christian has not done all that is expected of him when he merely refrains from retaliation when he is the recipient of hostile treatment. There is also a positive side to the Christian's conduct – he is to constantly be blessing the one mistreating him. Peter here likely reflects another of his Great Days with Jesus – the day when Jesus taught his disciples to "bless those who curse you" (Luke 6:28). "Bless" means to speak well of, to call down God's blessings on them, and to actively do appropriate deeds to minister to them.

For you were called for the very purpose -- Now that Peter has outlined the appropriate Christian response to hostility, he here comes to the motive for the Christian's positive behavior. "The very purpose" seems to point back[36] to the command to "bless those who curse you." "Called" looks back to the time of their conversion (see notes at 1:15, 2:9,21) and suggests that part of the teaching a potential convert received included instructions about how Christ's followers are to handle hostile treatment.

That you might inherit a blessing -- Peter now calls attention to the result[37] that accrues to the Christian who blesses those who curse him. He will inherit from the Lord the blessings about to be enumerated in the following verses from Scripture.

3:10 -- *For* "LET HIM WHO MEANS TO LOVE LIFE AND SEE GOOD DAYS REFRAIN HIS TONGUE FROM EVIL AND HIS LIPS FROM SPEAKING GUILE.

For -- Verses 10-12 are taken, with but slight variation, from Psalm 34:12-16 (33:12-16, LXX) and are intended to be an explanation of the "blessing" the Christian receives from living the kind of life God approves. Psalm 34 has been called an ancient recipe for a happy life.

LET HIM WHO MEANS TO LOVE LIFE AND SEE GOOD DAYS -- A life you can love is one of the blessings accruing to the Christian. Instead of boredom and frustration, it is a life that is meaningful and delightful. Though some will face persecution, Peter is not wholly pessimistic about this earthly life. He thinks God can and will make life sweet and enjoyable. The expression "good days" describes another of the blessings. The Psalmist was confident

---

[36] The word translated "the" is *houtos*. *Houtos* and *ode* both mean "this." Though the distinction is not always followed in the New Testament, *houtos* usually refers to something already mentioned ("this, the aforesaid"), while *ode* refers to something yet to follow ("this, the following").

[37] It is a *hina* clause, and such clauses can express either purpose or result. To take this as a purpose clause, making it say the Christian blesses others in order that he may receive a blessing, seems like an unworthy purpose. But to say that such a life results in blessings to the Christian is perfectly in harmony with the high ethics taught by Christianity.

God would eventually bestow His blessings on those who were righteous. Peter would have Christians share this belief. These blessings are not to be thought of merely in terms of outward prosperity, but more with emphasis on the favor of God, days of spiritual triumph. With God in control, even a day of persecution can be a "good day" – a day when the sufferer triumphs spiritually and sees the delight on the face of his heavenly Father, who is watching.

REFRAIN HIS TONGUE FROM EVIL AND HIS LIPS FROM SPEAKING GUILE -- Now the Psalmist describes the path wherein one must walk if he desired the blessing from God. First there are some demands concerning speech. He controls his tongue so that he does not return evil for evil.[38] He controls the words that pass his lips so there is no deceit, lies, or treachery.[39]

3:11 -- AND LET HIM TURN AWAY FROM EVIL AND DO GOOD; LET HIM SEEK PEACE AND PURSUE IT

AND LET HIM TURN AWAY FROM EVIL AND DO GOOD -- Peter continues his quotation from Psalm 34 describing the course of living which results in receiving a blessing from God. Not only does the Psalm cover the area of speech, it also presents demands in the realm of conduct and action. The KJV reads "Let him eschew evil." "Eschew" is a Norman word meaning to shun, avoid. The Greek is *ekklinato*, "to lean away from." It pictures getting as far away from doing evil as you can. Take evasive action because of a holy aversion to doing evil. Note again, it is not enough that a man merely avoids the evil. He must actively do the right, good, brave thing.[40]

LET HIM SEEK PEACE AND PURSUE IT -- Is this a peaceful spirit in the Christian (a serene, calm, equal temper), or is it peace with the other man (the one who has demonstrated hostility towards the Christian), or is it that man's peace with God, that the Christian is to pursue? That such peacemaking is a positive endeavor which requires great effort is emphasized in the admonition to "pursue it." Think of the effort men exert to find a hidden treasure, or to bring up from the ocean floor millions in gold bullion from sunken galleys. There is an intensity to the pursuit. That is precisely the intensity expected of Christian peacemakers.

3:12 -- FOR THE EYES OF THE LORD ARE UPON THE RIGHTEOUS, AND HIS EARS ATTEND TO THEIR PRAYER, BUT THE FACE OF THE LORD IS AGAINST THOSE WHO DO EVIL."

---

[38] To retaliate against someone who does evil to you by calling down a curse from God upon him or her is hardly refraining the tongue from evil.

[39] We've had "guile" explained at 2:1. Guile is the evil of saying one thing and meaning something else, so worded as to lead another astray as to your real meaning.

[40] Compare Galatians 6:10, "Do good to all men, especially to those who are of the household of the faith."

FOR THE EYES OF THE LORD ARE UPON THE RIGHTEOUS -- Peter continues his quotation of Psalm 34 which he began in verse 10. Here are more blessings from the Lord promised to the one who habitually does what is right. Not only will the practicing Christian have a life he can love, and see good days, but another reason for pursuing the course prescribed in verses 10 and 11 is that it will bring the approval of the Lord. We wonder if, as Peter writes, he recalls the night the Lord once turned and looked at him (Luke 22:61). The righteous men whom the Lord approves are those who have been justified, and who as a consequence live uprightly as the Spirit leads, doing positive deeds of goodness as just enumerated in the Psalm.

AND HIS EARS ATTEND TO THEIR PRAYER -- The Greek says His ears are "into" their prayers. What a picture of the Lord bending down so as to better hear the prayers of His children, earnestly listening to their petitions, eager to answer them and come to the aid of those who pray. Here is another of the blessings from the Lord that makes the Christian life a life you can love, and the days good days.

BUT THE FACE OF THE LORD IS AGAINST THOSE WHO DO EVIL -- That the Lord "turns his face away" is a vivid picture of His disapproval of what He sees. What He sees that He disapproves of and punishes is habitual evil.[41] It is not certain who is thought of as doing the evil. Perhaps it is the Christian who has disobeyed and has returned evil for evil (verse 9) who finds the Lord's blessings are withheld. Perhaps the first part of verse 12 assures Peter's readers that the Lord watches those who are being persecuted, while the last part of the verse assures them that their persecutors (those who are doing evil) will find they are in deep trouble with the Lord. All along the Lord is angry with the wicked (Psalm 7:11), and you can see it in His face.

V. THIRD DOCTRINAL SECTION. 3:13-4:6

A. The Blessedness of Suffering While Doing Good. 3:13-22

3:13 -- ***And who is there to harm you if you prove zealous for what is good?***

And who is there to harm you -- The implied answer is "few." Peter here begins his third doctrinal section. The gist of what he writes in the rest of chapter 3 is this – suffering while doing good may open up whole new areas of service. It did for Jesus; it can for the Christian. Peter is now giving the doctrinal basis for what he writes to these people as he prepares them for the suffering that may come because of governmental persecution of Christians since they were falsely accused of burning Rome. "Harm" occurs elsewhere in the New Testament only in Acts, where it is used of what the Egyptians did to the Israelites (Acts 7:6,19), and of antagonism toward the church, expressed either in active persecution (Acts 12:1, 18:10) or in

[41] The present participle "doing evil things" pictures continuous, habitual, customary, repeated action.

bitter or vicious attitudes toward believers (Acts 14:2).[42]

If you prove zealous for what is good? -- The verb here is a form of *ginomai*, "to be, or become." The noun is *zēlōtai*, "zealots."[43] What Peter is saying is, "Love doing good with the same passionate intensity with which the most fanatical patriot loves his country." "Good" is *agathos*, the same word found in the quotation from Psalm 34 in the phrase "let him ... do good."[44] It is not just an occasional good deed that Peter expects, but a lifestyle that just loves to do the morally good thing even when the object of the good deed has been hostile to the Christian.

3:14 -- ***But even if you should suffer for the sake of righteousness,*** **you are** ***blessed.*** **AND DO NOT FEAR THEIR INTIMIDATION, AND DO NOT BE TROUBLED,**

But even if you should suffer for the sake of righteousness -- Verses 13 and 14a go together and show that sometimes people do suffer[45] even while doing good, or simply because they are Christians.[46] Aggressive well-doing will not disarm a determined persecutor, and this is especially true when the persecutors (as was true in Nero's persecution) are after men simply because they are Christians.

You are **blessed** -- The adjective "blessed" has no verb in the Greek, giving it the force of an exclamation. *Makarioi* ("blessed") is not the same word used at 1 Peter 1:3. It is the same word Jesus used in the "Beatitudes"[47] and means spiritually prosperous. Peter is not promising them they will find positive enjoyment when being persecuted, but they were to regard it as something that would be favorable to their spiritual growth and salvation.

---

[42] The Greek form here is a rather unusual future tense participle. We do not find many of these forms in the New Testament. Such a tense implies that the action of the participle follows the action of the main verb.

[43] The KJV word "followers" translates a different reading, *mimetai*, "imitators." "Zealots" is the better supported reading. The zealots were fanatical Jewish patriots, who were pledged and sworn to liberate their native land by every possible means. They were men who were prepared to take their lives in their hands, to sacrifice ease and comfort, home and loved ones, in this passionate love for country.

[44] The genitive form used in verse 13 can be either masculine or neuter. Some have defended the idea it is masculine here, "him that is good" and they make it a reference to Jesus. Probably, in light of the Psalm just quoted, the neuter in this place is correct, "that which is good."

[45] The Greek form (*ei* with the optative mood, this being one of the few instances in the New Testament of the optative mood in conditional sentences) implies that it would be a rare thing, but possible, that one would suffer for righteousness' sake.

[46] It is not easy to decide whether "righteousness" here means "treating one's fellow man aright" as God teaches they should be treated (the word often does refer to our relationships with our fellow man), or whether it is synonymous with Christianity (God's way of saving man, God's way of making men right with Himself).

[47] Peter here likely is reflecting another of his Great Days with Jesus. Compare what Jesus said, as recorded in Matthew 5:11,12.

AND DO NOT FEAR THEIR INTIMIDATION, AND DO NOT BE TROUBLED -- Peter cites God's words to Isaiah (8:12,13) as he begins to give some practical directives (verses 14b-16) to his readers who are about to be persecuted for being Christians. Do not let the fear which they strive to instill in your hearts[48] affect your faithfulness. Do not let them agitate you or disturb[49] you so that you become silent when you have opportunity to witness about your faith.

3:15 -- ***But* SANCTIFY *Christ as Lord in your hearts, always* being *ready to make a defense to everyone who asks you to give an account for the hope that is in you, yet with gentleness and reverence***

But SANCTIFY Christ as Lord in your hearts -- Peter is still reflecting Isaiah 8:12,13. That passage reads (KJV), "Neither fear ye their fear, nor be afraid. Sanctify the Lord of Hosts Himself; and let Him be your fear, and let Him be your dread." Peter's directive brings to mind Christ's own warning as to whom to fear (Matthew 10:28). Peter commands his readers to fear Christ[50] more than they fear any human persecutor, lest they deny Him and sin against Him. "Lord" (see notes at 1:3,25, 2:3,13) is an important term in Scriptures. When applied to the Father or to the Son, it implies deity! Remember who Jesus is, when men begin to persecute you. He is God! Unless Christ is sanctified "as Lord[51] in your hearts," i.e., enthroned and worshiped as sovereign, acknowledged in the inner part of the mind ("heart") as supreme, feared more than any human persecutor is feared, there was a real danger of defection in the face of persecution and violent death.[52] The antidote to defection is to give Jesus the special place in your hearts and thoughts that He deserves.

---

[48] The genitive "their fear" can be either objective or subjective. If taken as subjective, Peter tells his readers not to feel the terror which their persecutors feel. So reads the NIV, "Do not fear what they fear." Christians should not fear the things their non-Christian opponents fear. We agree with the NASB translators who took it as objective, do not be affected by the fear they try to inspire in your heart.

[49] The same verb "troubled" is used of the troubling of the waters at the pool of Bethesda (John 5:4, KJV) and in a figurative sense of Christ's troubled soul (John 12:27). Put a lid on a glass of water and shake it a vigorously; the water is troubled or agitated. That's what persecutors try to produce in the minds of their victims.

[50] Peter substitutes Messiah's name where the Old Testament reads "the Lord of Hosts, Jehovah Sabaoth." That such a substitution can be made is a strong affirmation of the deity of Jesus Messiah. Lenski insists Peter's language here reflects the LXX *kurios ho theos*, "the Lord God," which is exactly who Jesus is. To acknowledge Jesus as "Lord" and "Christ" involves the incarnate fulfillment of Old Testament Messianic prophecies.

[51] The concept of Christ as "Lord" is an important one in the New Testament. Peter in his sermon on Pentecost quoted Psalm 110:1 and went on to apply it to Christ (Acts 2:34-36). Paul summarized his preaching by saying, "We preach Christ Jesus as Lord" (2 Corinthians 4:5), and he also taught the necessity of a corresponding confession on the part of man (Philippians 2:9ff; Romans 10:9). Jesus Himself had said, "Whosoever confesses Me before men, him will I confess before My Father." A failure to confess Jesus as Lord when on trial for being a Christian would have eternal consequences for Peter's readers.

[52] A generation after Peter wrote, Pliny described how curtly the alternative was given to Christians to curse Christ or die, and how not a few Christians turned away from the faith, rather than suffer torture and death.

Always *being* ready to make a defense to everyone -- Instead of being intimidated and silenced, be ready to give convincing reasons why you Christians believe and live as you do! Plan and prepare ahead of time[53] what you will say when you are on trial for being a Christian. "Defense" (*apologian*) is the regular word for an answer before a magistrate.[54] It is a reasonable and intelligent statement of one's position.[55] "Always ... ready" means never unprepared, never unwilling, never too timid to respond to those who question them.

Who asks you to give an account for the hope that is in you -- The things the Christian hopes for have been enumerated in 1 Peter 1:3,13,22 (as well as Romans 8:23,24). The KJV has the Christian being asked for a reason for his hope. The Greek word denotes a rational account, an answer, given in response to such an inquiry. The Christian ought to be able to explain why he himself cherishes a hope of heaven.[56]

---

[53] *Hetoimoi* ("ready") carries the idea not only of being ready or anxious to take advantage of some opportunity given you, but also speaks of making the necessary preparations. It is instructive to note that Peter gives a bit different instruction than did Jesus. Jesus, speaking of the years between His ascension and the destruction of Jerusalem, said, "When they arrest you and deliver you up, do not be anxious beforehand about what you are to say, but say whatever is given you in that hour; for it is not you who speak, but it is the Holy Spirit" (Mark 13:11). And in harmony with this promise of miraculous leading of the Spirit, recall the unanswerable apologetics of Stephen (Acts 6:10-15) and Paul (Acts 24;25, 26:24-28). Instead of taking no thought (Mark 13:11 KJV) what to say, Peter instructs his Christian readers to give some thought to what they will say, to prepare ahead of time the answer they will give. When it is taken into account that the spiritual gifts were only temporary (1 Corinthians 13:8-10), it becomes a rather easy thing to explain why Peter's instructions differed from Jesus'. Peter's readers were living in a time when the spiritual gifts received by the laying on of an apostle's hands already were passing, and the "words" to say were no longer just "given to you in that hour." Christians had to prepare ahead of time the defense they would give.

[54] Cp. Acts 22:1, 25:16, 2 Timothy 4:16. The word is used in 2 Corinthians 7:11 ("what vindication of yourselves") of a defense of one's Christian commitment when called on to discipline an erring member. In this instance it was not before a magistrate, but in the sight of any who was watching the Corinthians' behavior. In the post-apostolic age, there were certain Christian men (like Justin Martyr, c. AD 100-165) called "apologists" who wrote formal treatises in defense of Christianity.

[55] Since Peter writes "to everyone" (not just magistrates), and since he uses the informal term "asks," this verse has become a favorite with contemporary apologetics teachers as giving a Scriptural reason for having a course where Christians learn to defend their faith. Christians will be confronted by officious neighbors and by officials, and should plan ahead of time what they will say if asked a reason for their hope. How many Christians today are able to give a clear explanation of what they believe, and why (including Scriptural references) they believe? John Calvin, pondering this verse, wrote, "Hence we learn how all those abuse the name of Christians who understand nothing respecting their faith; and have nothing to give as an answer for it." (Quoted in John Owen, *Commentary on the Catholic Epistles* [Grand Rapids: Eerdmans, 1948], p.109.) Verse 15 is a challenge to every preacher. As James Smart has written, "The battle front between belief and unbelief is manned by laymen, not by seminary-trained ministers. The minister's task is to train the laymen to give a good account of themselves in the battle ... What chance has the church of Jesus Christ if its frontline soldiers are untrained, vague, and confused in their understanding of the Christian faith and unable to speak coherently on its behalf?"

[56] Why do you think there is life after death? Heaven? Hell? Who is Jesus? Why do you think you are saved? On what grounds do you regard the Christian religion as true, as furnishing a ground of hope for mankind that other religions do not? These are some questions to which every Christian ought to be able to give an answer.

Yet with gentleness and reverence -- "Yet" is the strong adversative. Give a reason, yes! *BUT*, be careful of your attitude. The Christian must give heed to the manner of his defense, as well as to the substance of it. Peter has already warned against responding to hostility with a retaliatory spirit. Christians must practice self-control when answering those who have attacked them, for it is possible to speak in such a tone of voice that we injure ourselves and the one with whom we are speaking. To keep any injury from occurring, we need a gentle attitude, courtesy, consideration[57] for the questioner so that we may present Christianity with winsomeness and with love; we need a trembling anxiety to think and say only what is acceptable to the Lord.[58]

3:16 -- ***And keep a good conscience so that in the thing in which you are slandered, those who revile your good behavior in Christ may be put to shame.***

And keep a good conscience -- The "conscience" is that innate faculty which urges us to do what our mind thinks is right, and criticizes us when we do what our mind thinks is wrong. A clear conscience is one that doesn't bother us, or criticize us concerning our behavior. What is the connection of this command with the context? Perhaps it is connected with what goes before. A good conscience is one of the reasons for the hope of heaven we have. Perhaps it is connected with what follows. When we are accused of wrong, our conscience does not accuse us of having done the wrong of which we are accused. The Christian makes his defense knowing he is not guilty of any of the crimes he is charged with perpetrating. Perhaps it is connected with both. Before and after we make our "defense," we keep a good conscience. And we do that only if we sanctify the Lord in our hearts, and give a reason for our hope, and do it with meekness and fear, and know we are not guilty of any of the crimes of which we are falsely accused.

So that in the thing in which you are slandered -- "So that" introduces the expected result of the Christian's self-defense in the spirit indicated. Peter envisions the accusers as "speaking against" the Christians, falsely accusing them of being enemies of the state, of participating in monstrous crimes. Many of the unbelievers little understood many of the doctrines and practices of Christians, and jumped to false conclusions about what they did see and hear.

---

[57] *Prautetos*, meekness or gentleness, is a difficult attitude to practice. It is not present when people state their beliefs with a kind of arrogant belligerence. It is not present when people give an impression of haughty superiority toward their ignorant opponents. It is not present when people try to ram their beliefs down other people's throats. Anyone who has lovingly and patiently spoon-fed a baby has shown "gentleness." All you are interested in is that the little one is fed and nourished and grows and lives.

[58] While it is Biblical for Christians to respect civil authority, we think "reverence" in this place is fear of the Lord, rather than fear of men. See the notes on "reverence" earlier in this epistle (e.g., 1:17, 2:17). Speak to the magistrate (or to the non-Christian questioner) as though you were speaking to Jesus! Then your answer will not be in a wrong tone of voice, or made with a wrong attitude.

Those who revile your good behavior in Christ may be put to shame -- "Put to shame" means that they will be proven to be maliciously misrepresenting[59] the Christians in public, and this will be humiliating to them. Of what was it they had mistakenly accused the Christians? Why, the accusations about their lifestyle[60] and their complicity in the crimes of which the Neronian government was accusing them. One is reminded of how Stephen's opponents were not able to withstand the wisdom and the Spirit by which he spoke (Acts 6:10). Peter is confident that if his Christian readers make a clear and transparent defense (backed up by a lifestyle of doing good), it would result in their accusers being put to shame. Honest observers of the proceedings in the trial would go home convinced that the charges against the Christians were false. It would be the officials, not the Christians, who would be shown to be in the wrong.[61]

3:17 -- ***For it is better, if God should will it so, that you suffer for doing what is right rather than for doing what is wrong.***

For it is better -- "For" shows this verse is intended to be a reason for something just said. Perhaps it is a reason for this call for a good conscience (verse 16). Or perhaps it is a reason for continuing to do good (verse 13). Peter is meeting the common objection that suffering could be borne more easily if it were deserved. His argument is that suffering for doing good is "better" – *kreitton*, meaning "more useful, more powerful." "Better" contrasts two conditions of suffering. Neither kind mentioned in this verse is pleasant, but their results differ greatly.

If God should will it so -- The Greek words (*ei* plus the optative mood) do not present a probability, but only a possibility. The suffering of God's people for well-doing is not His usual will for them, but God's will does sometimes allow suffering for Christians. Sometimes He sees it is necessary, for our own good, that we should suffer.[62]

That you suffer for doing what is right rather than for doing what is wrong -- This participial construction suggests that not only would they suffer *while* they were doing good, but *because* they were doing good. Peter is thus assuring the Christians that God has some

---

[59] "Revile" means to spitefully use, to insult, to traduce, to ridicule, to sneer at. There is a certain viciousness of attitude implied by Peter's use of the word *epereadzontes* (rather than the *katalaleo* used just before). In Luke 6:28 (KJV) this word is translated "despitefully use you."

[60] The word translated "behavior" has been used by Peter before at 2:12 and 3:2. "Behavior in Christ" is another way of designating one's conduct as a Christian, conduct that has Christ at the center and circumference of all one's thoughts and words and deeds.

[61] There is a similarity between this exhortation and the one in 2:12. However, a difference is seen in that 2:12 envisions the conversion of the adversaries, whereas here Peter thinks of them as being "put to shame" but not necessarily converted.

[62] Concerning the problem of suffering, see the sermon titled "The Uses of Misfortune" in R.C. Foster's *The Everlasting Gospel* (Cincinnati: Standard, 1929).

purpose in mind ("it is better") when He permits His people to suffer and be hurt for doing right. Let it be noted, too, that men do suffer for doing evil, and that at the hand of God in this life, as well as the next. But it is better to suffer at God's hand for doing well, than for doing evil! Verse 17 is a sort of transition verse, summarizing verses 13-16 and preparing for verses 18-22. The same function was served in chapter 2 by verse 20, which expresses a very similar sentiment.

3:18 -- ***For Christ also died for sins once for all,*** **the** ***just for*** **the** ***unjust, in order that He might bring us to God, having been put to death in the flesh, but made alive in the spirit;***

For -- In verses 18-22, by calling attention to the blessings that flowed from the sufferings of Christ, Peter is going to show that "it is better" to suffer for doing good. When Jesus suffered, He was innocent. It wasn't for any wrong doing on His part that He suffered. He was helping others. His suffering opened up a whole new world of service for Him. Likewise, Christians suffering for righteousness' sake may find a wonderful new world of opportunities for service opening up for them.

This paragraph (verses18-22) is notoriously obscure and difficult to interpret, one of the most difficult not only in Peter, but in the whole New Testament.[63] The difficulty arises in the central part of the paragraph, where every word and phrase is the subject of controversy, and when a decision is made about the possible meaning for one word or phrase, it immediately affects the interpretation of all the rest of the passage. But while the middle part may be ambiguous, the first part is not. The language in verse 18 has been characterized as "one of the shortest and simplest, and yet one of the richest, summaries given in the New Testament of the meaning of the cross of Jesus."[64]

Christ also died for sins once for all -- "Christ" is not a proper name. Peter says "Messiah" is the One who died.[65] "Once for all" says He has no need to suffer and die again. His was a perfect sacrifice for sins that need not be repeated.[66] "For sins" is the regular phrase in the LXX for a "sin offering" (cf. Leviticus 5:7, 6:30). This gives emphasis to the atoning nature of Messiah's death. He died as a sin offering.

---

[63] The reader who wishes to go more into depth than the purpose of this commentary permits may wish to study J.P. Lange's "Excursus on the Descensus Ad Inferos" in *Lange's Commentary* on 1 Peter (Grand Rapids: Zondervan, 1950), p. 67-71; Bo Reicke, *The Disobedient Spirits and Christian Baptism* (Copenhagen: Ejnar Munkstgaard, 1946); or W.J. Dalton, *Christ's Proclamation to the Spirits* (Rome: Pontifical Biblical Institute, 1965).

[64] J.M.E. Ross, *The First Epistle of Peter. A Devotional Commentary* (London: Religious Tract Society, nd), p.151-152.

[65] Some of the older versions read "Christ suffered once for sins." There is a manuscript variation, some reading "suffered" and some reading "died." "Died" is the stronger attested reading, but "suffered" better fits the context. Even if we read "died," we sadly recall that much suffering attended the final hours of his earthly life and ministry.

[66] On the completed nature of the sacrificial death of Christ (as compared to the need of constant repetition of animal sacrifice under the Mosaic covenant), see Romans 6:10; Hebrews 7:27, 9:28, 10:10,12.

***The* just for *the* unjust** -- Peter here answers any possible question concerning whose sins. Jesus was sinless. He was not suffering on account of His own wrong doing.[67] He was suffering for unrighteous men,[68] a just person in character dying in behalf of[69] persons unjust in character. Messiah's death was vicarious. Jesus Messiah may be thought of as "righteous" in the sense that He lived in perfect harmony with the will of the Father. In fact, He was known as "the Righteous One" (Acts 3:14, 7:52, 22:14). His sinlessness qualified Him to act in behalf of others who were not. Several important truths are emphasized by Peter in this passage concerning the death of Jesus Messiah: there was suffering and death involved; it was "for sins"; it was "once for all"; it was vicarious ("the just for the unjust"); and the aim He had in mind when He died – "that He might bring us to God."[70] Peter's language may well reflect Isaiah 53. "It was the expressed mission of the Messiah voluntarily 'to give his life a ransom for many' (Mark 10:45), a message that lies at the very heart of the Christian gospel of forgiveness and salvation (Romans 8:3,4; 2 Corinthians 5:21; Galatians 3:13,14; 1 John 2:2)."[71]

In order that He might bring us to God -- Christ (suffered) died in order that sinners might be reconciled to God and have access to Him.[72] Unforgiven sin interrupts the relationship

---

[67] Peter has previously referred to the sinlessness of Christ (see 1:19, 2:22).

[68] Unrighteous men include all above the age of accountability, for "all have sinned and fall short of the glory of God." Potentially, Messiah's death could be a "sin offering" for all who have sinned. Whether or not it becomes so is conditioned on men's positive response to the gospel.

[69] The preposition "for" is *huper*, in behalf of, in the stead of, in place of. In harmony with other Scripture, Peter teaches the substitutionary, vicarious atonement.

[70] How sad that source criticism has robbed this passage of any real assurance for us. Source critics attempt to isolate the "sources" of the sayings found in the pages of the New Testament, after any supernatural source is rejected. In this place, not a few interpreters have hypothesized that Peter is quoting some early Christian hymn or creed. (E. Gordon Selwyn, in *The First Epistle of Peter* [London: Macmillan, 1949], p.17-18, argues that Peter simply copied or adopted the creedal hymn quoted at 1 Timothy 3:16. Some have argued the stanzas of the early hymn Peter used included 1:20, 3:18,19,22. Others have argued that parts of 1:20, 3:18b, 3:22, 4:6a made up the stanzas of the hymn. The latest edition of the Nestle Greek text even prints 3:18-19 in poetic format to reflect this speculation.) Of course, in the source critic's mind, the hymn or creed may or may not have been right in its content. Ever since liberal theologians have begun to identify all the high Christological passages in the New Testament as hymns, this commentator has been suspicious and skeptical. It impinges on the doctrine of apostolic inspiration to say Peter simply copied some uninspired source, and most attempts at identifying the actual words of the hymn or creed require unwarranted and unrestrained alterations and reconstructions of the text.

[71] Hiebert, *op. cit.*, p.223.

[72] "Bring" translates *prosagage*, the word used of "access" in Romans 5:2, Ephesians 2:8, 3:12. "In Greek this word had a special meaning. At the court of kings there was an official called a *prosagogeus*, the 'introducer,' the 'giver of access,' and it was his function to decide who should be admitted to the king's presence, and who should be kept out. He, as it were, held the keys of access. That is to say, it is Jesus Christ, through what He did, who brings men into the presence of God, who gives them access to God, who opens the way to God" (Barclay, *op. cit.*, p.278). The source critics have sought Peter's source for this language in the Greek mystery religions where the initiate was "brought into the presence" of the god. Machen, *The Origin of Paul's Religion* (Grand Rapids: Eerdmans, 1925) long ago thoroughly answered all these attempts to find the sources of Christianity (whether Paul's or Peter's) in the mystery religions.

which should exist between God and men. The whole object of Messiah's death was to restore that lost relationship.[73] Following His death, Jesus' whole new world of service not only benefits Old Testament saints, but also New Testament saints.

Having been put to death in the flesh, but made alive in the spirit -- We have come to the phrases that are so notoriously difficult to interpret. If we are to grasp what it means, we will have to follow Peter's own advice and gird up the loins of our mind to study it!

We propose that the general thrust of the passage is this: just as Christ's suffering and death opened up a whole new world of service for Him, so the implication for the Christian is that if he suffers, and even if he is martyred, that doesn't end all. There may be for him a ministry in the unseen world, too.

Now, let's pay attention to the details in these verses. The Greek words are *thanatōtheis men sarki zōopoiētheis de pneumati.*[74] We notice the absence of any article or preposition, and the exact balance and correspondence of the two clauses. The use of *men* and *de* – "on the one hand ... on the other" – marks an antithesis, where there is a contrast between verbs as well as nouns. The two words "flesh" and "spirit" are both in the dative case, and may be either a dative of sphere or a dative of means. Since there is a balance in the two phrases, we would expect both to be taken in the same sense.[75] If both are taken as a dative of means, it says Christ was put to death by means of "flesh" (i.e., by men), and made alive (probably speaking of His resurrection) by means of the Holy Spirit.[76] If both are taken as a dative of sphere, then the verse says Christ's flesh was put to death (i.e., He was put to death in the sphere of flesh), but His spirit continued to live on (i.e., He was energized in the sphere of spirit).[77] "Flesh" has reference to Jesus' physical body.[78] It was His fleshly body that died. Soul and spirit do not die. It is the body, not the soul or spirit, that is put to death.

---

[73] Hebrews 10:22 also suggests the nearness to God that salvation makes possible for the redeemed, a direct personal relationship, a personal closeness and fellowship.

[74] Some more recent manuscripts have *to pneumati*, but the best reading is anarthrous in both phrases.

[75] The KJV translators regarded one as a dative of sphere and the other as a dative of means. We think this is not proper and would not therefore attempt to defend the KJV's rendering "put to death in the (sphere of) flesh, but quickened by (means of) the Spirit." Making *pneumati* a reference to the Holy Spirit would destroy the balance in the verse, "flesh ... spirit."

[76] Lenski (*op. cit.*, p.159-160) argues for small "s" – "by means of *spirit*," which he explains means Jesus' spirit returned to His body. This does not quite preserve the contrast, in this commentator's opinion.

[77] Most English translations (cp. ASV, RSV, NASB) take it as a dative of sphere, and also use a small "s" on spirit, showing their beliefs that it does not speak of the Holy Spirit.

[78] Jesus had a body just like other human beings. He was no docetic phantom who only appeared to have a body. Jesus assumed a human body at the incarnation. He was incarnate deity. John 1:14, 1 Timothy 3:16.

Is "made alive" a reference to Jesus' resurrection, as a number of writers believe? Apparently not. His resurrection, it appears, is not mentioned until verse 21. Thayer translates "quickened as respects the spirit," endued with new and greater powers of life.[79] Energized would catch the idea. When the Lord said, "Father, into thy hands I commend My spirit," when He bowed His head and gave up the spirit, His spirit passed from this life to the next. Jesus resumed the spiritual nature He had before He became incarnate. Jesus' spirit was delivered from the limitations of the suffering flesh which He had graciously taken for our salvation. Far from terminating his existence or destroying His influence, the death of His physical body merely enabled Him, with new energies, to enter into the spiritual realm and engage in new and blessed activities in that world.

3:19 -- ***In which also He went and made proclamation to the spirits* now *in prison,***

In which -- Verses 19 and 20 are evidence that Jesus was energized in spirit; thus, the reading "in which" is to be preferred over the alternate reading "in whom." There are nine words in the Greek original of verse 19, and each one has been differently understood. Seven questions will help us to focus on the major explanations that have been proposed for the meaning of these 9 words.

(1) *Who went to make the proclamation?* (a) Some of our English translations read that it was the Messiah who went. This is the position advocated in these comments. (b) Some of our English versions read in such a way that it was the Holy Spirit[80] who went and inspired some man to preach. (i) Moffatt, Lake, and Goodspeed have made a conjectural emendation of the text at this place on the supposition that the word Peter originally wrote was ἐνώχ (Enoch) rather than ἐν ῷ ("in which"). They make the passage read "Enoch went and preached ...." They also understood that the "spirits" referred to fallen angels who were disobedient in the days of Noah. The evidence they offer for such an emendation is the pseudepigraphical *Book of Enoch.* In that work it is said Enoch was sent down from heaven to announce to the wicked angels their final doom (Enoch 12:1) and that he proclaimed to them that for them, because of their sin, there was neither peace nor forgiveness forever (Enoch 12,13). Several objections have been raised against this emendation. There had been consensus among interpreters that the "sons of God" in Genesis 6:1 (see notes at Jude 6 and 2 Peter 2:4) are not fallen angels but rather human beings in the family line of Seth. Moreover, Genesis 5 shows Enoch was translated 69 years before Noah was born and 569 years before Noah began his ministry for God. Yet Moffatt, Lake, and Goodspeed would have Enoch preaching to fallen angels who are living on earth, married to the daughters of

---

[79] See Henry Thayer, *Thayer's Greek-English Lexicon of the New Testament* (New York: American Book Co., 1889), p.294. It is true that the verb *zōopoieō* is used to refer to bodily resurrection in John 5:21, Romans 8:11 (where the resurrection of Jesus is attributed to the Holy Spirit), and 1 Corinthians 15:22. But the KJV's rendering "quickened" notwithstanding, that does not seem to be the meaning here. In passing, if (instead of waiting till verse 21 to introduce it) this verse does speak of the bodily resurrection, it does not impinge on the main thrust of the passage, namely, that the death of Jesus did not end His service. It just opened up a whole new area of activities for Him.

[80] Recall that the KJV has "quickened by The Spirit, by which also he went ...."

men, in the days of Noah! What would be the value of introducing Enoch in this place where the illustration calls for something Messiah did? To this commentator's knowledge, there is not one manuscript of the book of Peter that reads ἐνώχ at this place. What Peter wrote is this: "The spiritually vibrant Messiah, having died in flesh but not in spirit, went and preached." (ii) It was actually Noah whom the Holy Spirit inspired to preach to his contemporaries. Noah was the instrument but the Spirit of Christ was using his vocal chords.[81] It may be objected to this proposed interpretation that it is out of sequence (to what purpose would Noah's preaching several millennia earlier be brought into a discussion of what Jesus did between His death and resurrection?), "in prison" doesn't fit such an interpretation, and "spirits" seems to refer not to living men but to departed spirits. (iii) A third variation on the theme that it was the Holy Spirit who did the preaching through some man is the one which has the Spirit of Christ inspiring the apostles of Jesus after Pentecost to preach to men bound in the prison of the body, or the prison (bondage) of sin. This view does not fit the sequence in these verses, nor does it do justice to "prison," nor to "in spirit," nor to the verb "went."

(2) *When did He go?* At least three answers are offered to this question. (a) During His pre-existent state, Christ preached to Noah's contemporaries,[82] warning them of the coming flood and urging them to repent. The New Testament does speak of Jesus' pre-existent activities on earth (cf. John 1:3; 1 Corinthians 10:4; 1 Peter 1:10,11), but that is hardly the emphasis of this passage. The participle "going" ("went") can hardly refer to something Christ did in Old Testament times. What is needed here is something after Messiah's death that can serve as an assurance for Peter's persecuted and threatened readers. (b) Between His death and resurrection. If verse 18 speaks of Messiah's death and verse 21 is the first mention of His resurrection, then His going and preaching took place during the days his dead body was in the tomb. This is the view advocated in these comments because it seems there is a sequence in these verses – *death, energized, went, preached, raised, ascended.* (c) After His resurrection and ascension. If "quickened by the Spirit" (verse 18) were a reference to Jesus' resurrection (a view we have rejected, see above), then His going and preaching took place after His resurrection.[83] It might also be argued that verse 22 indicates that His "going and preaching" occurred after Jesus had ascended and sat down at the right hand of God.

(3) *Who were the spirits?* Answers to this question have been many. (a) They were

---

[81] We may believe that the Holy Spirit inspired Noah's preaching of repentance as the ark was being built, but we would not appeal to 1 Peter 3:19,20 to prove it, if for no other reason than that it contradicts verse 18's balance "put to death in flesh, made alive (energized) in spirit."

[82] Augustine taught this view, and it became the dominant one in the Western church for centuries. Some Protestants accept it so as to avoid any possible implication this passage might give of sinners receiving an opportunity for salvation after death.

[83] If this explanation is adopted, then we must admit we have no other verses that tell of this trip the glorified Christ made. While we would have no reason to doubt He could have made such a trip, we have no other information about this trip than what we can read in 1 Peter.

contemporaries of Noah who were dead and in Hades at the time Christ went and preached to them. This seems to be the opinion of the NASB translators who added "now" to what the Greek says, so that it reads "spirits *now* in prison."[84] This is the view advocated in these comments. (b) They were contemporaries of Noah who were alive when the pre-existent Christ came to earth and preached to them, or sent His Spirit to inspire Noah to preach to them. (c) They are fallen angels.[85] However, if we opt for "spirits" being fallen angels, how shall we explain that they sinned ("were disobedient") in the days of Noah? We can't appeal to Genesis 6 for that activity occurred in the era before the flood. (d) The spirits are contemporaries of the apostles. Christ, through the Spirit-inspired agency of the apostles, preached to men who were in the prison-house of bondage and sin, and it happened after Pentecost. The men to whom the apostles preached were sinners just like the men of Noah's day. Ephesians 2:17 and Acts 26:23 are appealed to corroborate this proposed interpretation for this passage in 1 Peter. By way of objection, it is an unusual and highly figurative use of "prison," and it makes the main clause and the subordinate one apply to different sets of persons.

(4) *Where or what is the prison?* The answer to this question is interwoven with the answer to the previous one. (a) When the angels sinned,[86] the fallen angels were "cast into Tartarus, and committed to pits of darkness" (2 Peter 2:4), "kept in eternal bonds under darkness for the judgment of the great day" (Jude 6). If we let the New Testament guide us,[87] Tartarus would be the prison if fallen angels made up Jesus' audience. (b) If the spirits are the spirits of wicked dead men, then Hades would be the prison. This is the view advocated in these comments. (c) The idea that the "prison" is figurative for the "bondage of sin" is rather difficult to accept, being a sort of Sputnik hurled into orbit by peculiar answers to the questions "Who preached?" and "Who were the spirits?"

(5) *Which direction did the preacher go?* (a) He came down to earth if it is the pre-existent Christ who preached in Noah's time. (b) He descended to Hades if the reference is to something Christ did between His death and resurrection. This is the view adopted in these

---

[84] The word "spirits" is used in our Bible with a number of connotations. It can refer to the spirits of dead people (Hebrews 12:23). That is evidently the meaning, too, when we are told that the Pharisees believed in "spirits" but the Sadducees didn't (Acts 23:8). "Spirits" can also refer to demons, as in the phrase "unclean spirits" (Matthew 10:17).

[85] Such passages as 2 Peter 2:4; Jude 6; Hebrews 1:7,14; Matthew 8:16; and Luke 10:17,20 are urged as evidence that the word "spirits" sometimes speaks of angels.

[86] This commentator understands that Revelation 12:7-9 describes the origin of Satan and his demons, and that the "war in heaven" took place sometime before the devil came to tempt Adam in the garden of Eden.

[87] Jewish apocryphal and pseudepigraphical literature have the fallen angels bound in the depths of the earth (Jubilees 5:6,10), in darkness (1 Enoch 10:4ff), in the valleys of the earth (1 Enoch 10:12), in the abyss (1 Enoch 21:1-7), in prison at the end of heaven and earth (1 Enoch 18:12-14), or in the second heaven (2 Enoch 7:1-3; Testament of Levi 3:2). We find the canonical Scriptures to be a more trustworthy guide in this whole matter of where fallen angels are imprisoned as they await the final judgment and their sentence to eternal fire.

comments.[88] (c) He ascended into heaven[89] and then sent the Spirit to the apostles who preached to their contemporaries.

(6) *What was the content of His preaching?* (a) Christ ascended to heaven after His resurrection and proclaimed His victory over the fallen angels as He subjected them to Himself (verse 22). Compare Colossians 2:15. This view requires verse 18 ("quickened by the Spirit" KJV) to be a reference to Jesus' resurrection, and the preaching that comes after that cannot be in Hades since He ascended to heaven following His resurrection. It is rightly raised as an objection to this view that the attributive position of the prepositional phrase "in prison" (literally, "the in-prison spirits") most naturally implies they were in prison (not heaven) at the time Christ spoke to them. (b) Christ went to Hades and preached good news to the spirits there in order to convert those who were not saved. Some have appealed to the fact that obedience to Christ is a condition of salvation, so all the Old Testament people would (they assert) have to hear a sermon from Christ if they were to have any opportunity to be obedient to Him.[90] (c) Christ went to Hades and made a proclamation to the spirits imprisoned there.[91] The word used in 3:19 is *kerusso*, a word that means to make an announcement of some kind, like a herald crying out.[92] Perhaps He announced to the wicked

---

[88] All Peter says is Jesus "went" or "journeyed." What He did was move in whatever direction the "prison" was. Some object to the use of the expression "descended to Hades" since it tends to leave the reader with the mistaken impression that the Bible describes a "three-storied universe" in which we live -- with heaven above, earth in the middle, and hell beneath the earth.

[89] Dalton insists that since the same participle ("having gone") in verse 22 refers to the ascension, it must also refer to the ascension here in verse 19. We believe the term itself is neutral and does not determine the direction of the movement. It is the words "into heaven" in verse 22 that determine the direction of the movement in that passage.

[90] While the Bible clearly states that the death of Christ covers the sins of faithful men in Old Testament times as well as New (Romans 3:25; Hebrews 9:15), the Bible nowhere makes obedience to a gospel sermon a pre-requisite to salvation. All that God expected was faithfulness to the revelation men had, and for those who were faithful but not sinless perfect, Calvary covers it all.

[91] Just before He died, Jesus promised the penitent thief that the two of them would be together in Paradise yet that day (Luke 23:43). In the author's *Commentary on Acts*, in the Special Study entitled "Hades and the Intermediate State of the Dead," it is shown that before Jesus' resurrection Hades was made up of two compartments, one for the righteous (Paradise, Abraham's bosom), and one for the wicked. Thus, when He died, Jesus' spirit could journey to Paradise, from which an announcement could be made (1 Peter 3:19) that would be heard even by the wicked across the great gulf (Luke 16:23-26). Or we might say that Jesus visited both compartments -- He went to Paradise where he was joined by the penitent thief, and He went to the prison where he made this proclamation Peter calls attention to. Other verses that tell about Christ's whereabouts while His body was in the tomb are Acts 2:25-28 (Hades) and perhaps Ephesians 4:9 (He descended to the lower parts of the earth).

[92] When *kerusso* (the word here translated "made proclamation") means "preach the gospel," we regularly find a word for "gospel" in the same context. See for example *keruxate* at Mark 16:15, where *to euaggelion* denotes the content of the thing preached.

their doom was sealed now that He had died.[93] Perhaps He also told the Old Testament saints their redemption was complete (or about to be completed when He rose from the dead and ascended to present His blood in the antitypical Holy of Holies, Hebrews 9:11-14).[94] This is the view advocated in this commentary.

(7) *What is the relationship of 3:19 to 4:6?* As before, answers are varied. (a) Both refer to the same time and the same audience. That is, the "spirits now in prison" (3:19) and the "dead" (4:6) are the same beings. This explanation would be favored by those who would defend the idea that Jesus is offering salvation to the imprisoned spirits. (b) They refer to the same time, the descent into Hades, but to different audiences; that is, 3:19 is fallen angels and 4:6 is dead people. (c) They are not related at all. That is, 4:1-6 is a different topic altogether than what is written in 3:18-22. This is the view presented in this commentary.

Also -- This word can be inserted in two places when we make an English translation, either with what goes before or what follows. If the latter, it would be translated "in which he went and *also* preached." It would affirm that just as Christ ministered to men on earth before His death, He also ministered (in spirit) after His death. The NASB adopts the former with its translation "in which *also* he went and preached." The effect is to limit his "preaching" (proclamation) to the time between His death and resurrection.

He went -- The word *poreuomai* is regularly used of one traveling, going on a journey, making a change of place. The same verb is used in verse 22 in the phrase "gone into heaven." Good hermeneutics would require the word, when used in the same context, to be given a similar meaning in both places. In verse 22 it asserts a change in locality; we should understand it indicates a change in locality here in verse 19. If in verse 22 it indicates Messiah changed locations (ascended from earth to heaven), it can hardly mean (here in 19) that without any such change of place, Christ preached to the spirits in prison. While His body was lying in Joseph's tomb, we should picture His spirit as traveling from Paradise to the prison in order to make this proclamation.

---

[93] Lutheran theology for several centuries argued that Christ between His death and resurrection had proclaimed judgment in Hades on the wicked such as Noah's contemporaries, whose spirits had been imprisoned there since their deaths on earth. The "Harrowing of Hell" was a medieval term for the doctrine that after the resurrection Christ descended into hell to free its captive souls and defy its powers. The name was given a 13th century English poem on that subject, and the idea was popular in medieval drama.

[94] The passage about the rich man and Lazarus (Luke 16:19-31) is pointed to as an analogy. Those in different places in the intermediate state were able to communicate across the great gulf fixed between "Abraham's bosom" and "torment." We know that Christ went to Paradise at His death (as He told the thief he too would do). It is asserted that He could have spoken to those in Paradise, and those in the prison across the gulf in the place of torment could have heard. Is there any indication that Jesus ever talked with those in Paradise about redemption? Well, Moses and Elijah did talk with Jesus before His death about it at the transfiguration. R.C. Foster felt they would certainly have talked about it again when Jesus entered Paradise after His death. All in the prison could hear, but the antediluvians (1 Peter 3:20) are singled out as an example to introduce the figure of baptism which Peter wishes to weave into his argument.

And made proclamation -- *Kerusso* is the word used in secular Greek of an official announcement, a proclamation made by a representative of a government.[95] The word itself does not indicate the content of the message being proclaimed.

To the spirits -- The next verse identifies these "spirits" as being ungodly men, such as once were disobedient to God. They once were human beings living on earth, but have left their bodies behind at death, and are living in the intermediate world (state). We picture dead men as being disembodied spirits while they are in the intermediate state.[96]

***Now* in prison** -- The reference is apparently to that part of Hades in which the souls of the ungodly are held unto the Day of Judgment.[97]

So, if we have made proper choices on all the key words, verse 19 tells us that Messiah (in His pre-incarnate nature), between the time His body died on the cross and when He arose from the dead, went to the prison (Hades) and there made a proclamation to the spirits held there (some of which are further identified in the following verse).

3:20 -- *Who once were disobedient, when the patience of God kept waiting in the days of Noah, during the construction of the ark, in which a few, that is, eight persons, were brought safely through* the *water.*

Who once were disobedient -- The participle with which this verse opens has no article, and Lenski urged that it thus does not say that *only* those disobedient in Noah's time were heralded to.[98] It rather says those spirits in prison were *such as* the ones who had been disobedient.

---

[95] Peter does use the Greek word *euaggelidzomai* that of itself means "preach the gospel" at 1:12 and 4:6. Here he uses a different word. No doubt Peter was acquainted with the fact that in the LXX the verb *kerusso* is used with the bringing of bad news as well as good (cf. Jonah 1:2, 3:2,4).

[96] The word "spirits" is used in Hebrews 12:23 to refer to the disembodied state of human beings, there it speaks of "the spirits of righteous men made perfect." See also Luke 24:37 and Revelation 22:6. Even Revelation 6:9 seems to picture the dead souls as being disembodied.

[97] In footnote #91, speaking of conditions as they were before Jesus' resurrection, we have called attention to the two compartments of Hades -- one holding the souls of the righteous and one holding the souls of the wicked. The devil is "in prison" during the "thousand years" (Revelation 20:1-3,7). Likewise, the fallen angels are "in bonds" (2 Peter 2:4; Jude 6). So it would not be surprising to learn the spirits of wicked men likewise are "in prison" in Hades awaiting Judgment and condemnation to the lake of fire (Revelation 20:14).

The Apostles' Creed (as it now reads, though originally it did not contain the phrase) speaks of Christ "descending into Hell" between His death and His resurrection on the third day. Portions of the Creed may be traced to the middle of the 2nd century, and its present form dates from the 16th century. "Hell" and "Hades" are two different places, but 400 years ago (the KJV is an example) the word "Hell" was used for both. Nowhere in the Bible are we told that Jesus went to "Hell." Acts 2:31 states He went to "Hades" (ASV), but "Hades" is not "Hell." (Calvin and his followers have taught that after Christ's death on the cross, He was further humiliated, making a descent to Hell to suffer there for other's sins until resurrection morning. We reject this reconstruction of events, insisting John 19:30 means that Jesus' sufferings were finished before He died. The idea expressed in the Apostles' Creed seems to us to represent what Peter here tells us about Jesus between His death and resurrection, but we would not use the word "Hell" to describe the place where Jesus was.

[98] Lenski, *op. cit.*, p.163.

Christ's proclamation in Hades (prison) dealt with others than just the antediluvians who perished in the flood.[99] "Once" ("aforetime," ASV) indicates that their disobedience took place prior to their imprisonment and prior to Christ's proclamation to them. The next phrase in this verse shows the disobedience took place during the days of Noah. That the antediluvians were disobedient is stated in Genesis 6:5. Man's sinfulness "was great on the earth" prior to God's announcement of the approaching flood. This disobedience even continued all the while righteous Noah was building the ark.

When the patience of God kept waiting in the days of Noah -- God's "patience" is seen in the long postponement of punishment and judgment, and waiting for the antediluvians to amend their lives. He held His wrath in check, even when He was being heavily provoked by men's wickedness. But the day finally came when disaster came upon the "disobedient" as compared with salvation for the few who entered the ark. Surely Peter intends this illustration as an assurance to his readers that the wicked will not prosper forever.

During the construction of the ark -- The present tense participle translated "construction" (or "being prepared") implies a long period of time. Compare Hebrews 11:7, 2 Peter 2:5 (which says Noah preached), and Genesis 6:3 (perhaps for all 120 years). It is probable Noah and his sons were in the process of building the ark all those 120 years. Noah's ark was a wooden vessel built to float.

> The ark was made of gopher wood, a kind of timber, which both for its lightness and its durability was employed by the Phoenicians in building their vessels. After the boards of the ark were fastened, each was to be protected by a coating of pitch, which was to be placed on both the inside and outside of the ark. In effect, the ark became waterproof. The ark was to consist of a number of small compartments for the convenient distribution of the different animals and their food. These compartments were to be arranged in three tiers, one above another. God likewise instructed Noah concerning the provision of a window in the ark. Nothing is said concerning the shape of the ark, but its dimensions are given. It was 300 cubits in length, 50 in breadth, and 30 in height. Assuming twenty-one inches to be the measure of the cubit, the ark would have been 525 feet in length, 87.5 feet in breadth, and 52.5 feet in height.[100]

In which a few, that is, eight persons, were brought safely through *the* water -- "In which" refers to the ark. When it comes to the relative number of believers and unbelievers, eight

---

[99] Perhaps the reason for singling out this generation that was swept away with the flood is because it allows Peter to bring in the point he wishes to about baptism. We remember that Peter's point is that there is activity after death. Death didn't end Messiah's opportunities for service. And death (if his readers should be martyred) won't end the Christian's opportunities for service. All this was prefigured in their baptism into Christ -- that death, burial, and resurrection were followed by activity, the activity of the new life in Christ.

[100] Virtus Gideon, article on "Noah," in *The New Smith's Bible Dictionary*, revised by Reuel G. Lemmons (Garden City, NY: Doubleday, 1966), p.262.

is a "few." Noah, his wife, his three sons, and their wives made up the "eight persons" (Genesis 7:13).[101] "Brought safely through" translates *diasozo*, for which Thayer offers "to preserve through [danger], to keep safe, to keep from perishing, to rescue." The beings inside were carried safely through the water that bore up the ark. Perhaps reference is made to the small number of those saved to encourage the little flock in Asia to whom Peter was writing. Peter's readers may be few compared to the numbers of men who were unbelieving in the world around them. Look at all the unbelievers who perished in the flood, whose spirits are now with all the other damned in Hades. The message is clear. The unbelievers ultimately perish but the believers are saved, even if they do have to suffer for a while at the hands of the unbelievers of this world.

3:21 -- ***And corresponding to that, baptism now saves you – not the removal of dirt from the flesh, but an appeal to God for a good conscience – through the resurrection of Jesus Christ,***

And corresponding to that -- The Greek words which are thus translated are *hŏ kai antitupon*. The first word (*hŏ*) is a neuter singular relative pronoun, and it is difficult to construe. Thus there is an abundance of variations in the manuscripts at this place.[102] *Antitupon* is also neuter and can be translated "antitype, figure, picture, representation." The KJV offered this translation, "the like figure whereunto even baptism doth also now save us." ASV reads "which also after a true likeness ..." Does the "figure" refer back to "ark" or "water"? The relative pronoun is neuter. *Antitupon* is neuter. "Ark" is feminine. "Water" is neuter. The question seems settled. The water of the flood and the water of baptism correspond as type and antitype.[103]

Baptism now saves you -- "Now" probably means in this dispensation as contrasted to what happened to the "few" back in Noah's day. As the waters of the flood lifted Noah and his family out of the sinful world and brought them safely to a cleansed earth, so baptism in wa-

---

[101] The Greek reads "eight souls" (and the KJV and ASV did likewise). There are times that the word "soul" is used to stand for the whole person (cf. Acts 2:41, 27:37; Romans 13:1).

[102] Erasmus adopted a dative singular (*hō*) on the basis of some cursive manuscripts, and this forms the basis of the reading in the Textus Receptus. On the basis of textual evidence Westcott-Hort text retained the *hō*, but Hort regarded it as a "primitive error" by some copyist. The apparatus in UBS[2] shows some manuscripts omit the pronoun, some read *hōs*, and one reads *hŏs*, in addition to those which read as our current critical text has it.

[103] Great care should be exercised as comments are made at this place. Peter does _not_ say baptism is only a symbol – the "outward symbol of an inward grace" as it is sometimes worded by those who do not accept what Peter here flatly says about the importance and place of baptism. The reader is cautioned to make sure he or she is listening to what is being said. This commentator is not teaching baptismal regeneration (that the mere act of dipping in water causes the new birth to occur), nor is he saying that material water washes away sin. He is saying that, in God's mind, it is at the moment of immersion that one's sins are forgiven and he is a new person, living a new life. Of course, the prerequisites of faith, repentance, and confession, are understood, or immersion in water will not be of any effect. Remember that Peter has written that when one obeys Jesus, he is forgiven (sprinkled with the blood), 1 Peter 1:2.

ter[104] is the line of demarcation between the kingdom of darkness and the kingdom of light. Before one is immersed, he is outside of Christ; after a penitent believer is immersed, he is in Christ (Romans 6:3; Galatians 3:27) and rises to walk a new life.

Just as walking a new life after baptism presents the Christian a whole new area of service, so the new life after a Christian's death opens to the Christian a whole new area of service. This is the point Peter is making: that what happens when a Christian dies was prefigured in what happened at his baptism. Pagan societies have often permitted inquirers to study Christianity all they wish with little or no opposition. However, it is when they allow themselves to be immersed that their unsaved friends and relatives consider them to have actually changed religions and become a Christian. Then opposition begins in earnest. If Peter's readers hadn't been immersed, they would not be facing persecution. Were some of them thinking, "Maybe it would have been better if I had avoided baptism, for then I wouldn't be in danger of being persecuted"? Peter stops that thought cold by reminding them of all the blessings from God that are connected to their immersion.[105] "Baptism now saves you!" he reminds them.[106]

Not the removal of dirt from the flesh, but an appeal to God for a good conscience -- Peter is still reminding his readers of what is involved in the "baptism (that) now saves." More was involved than, for example, in Jewish ceremonial washings (a clean body),[107] for the baptism that saves has something to do with the conscience. When a penitent believer is immersed, he is by that act making (in the words of the NASB) "an appeal to God for a good conscience." The Greek words are *suneideseos agathes eperotema eis theon.* They have been translated various ways, with the KJV's "the answer of a good conscience toward God"

---

[104] Baptism in water is clearly in Peter's mind, not the baptism of the Holy Spirit. It was water that had something to do with the safety of the few in Noah's time, and it is water that has something to do with salvation in this Christian age.

[105] The specific form of the word for "dip" that Peter uses (*baptisma*) does not occur in pagan or Jewish literature before the time of the New Testament. Jews did use another derivative of "dip" (*baptismos*) for their ceremonial washings (cp. Hebrews 6:2, 9:10; Mark 7:4). *Baptisma* always occurs in the singular and is the distinctive New Testament designation for John's baptism (cf. Matthew 3:7; Acts 1:22) and for the baptism commanded in the Great Commission (Ephesians 4:5; Colossians 2:12). With the *-ma* ending, the thing emphasized is not so much the act of dipping but its true resulting significance. Beasley-Murray suggests that the New Testament writers adopted this term "to express their consciousness that Christian baptism was a new thing in the world, differing from all Jewish and pagan purificatory rites." ("Baptism, Wash," *NIDNTT*, 1:150).

[106] The KJV reads "us" (*hemas*). But this reading, which has fair textual support, is probably an error for the original "you" (*humas*). The few in Noah's day were saved through water. You also are saved through water. You pass through the water of baptism into safety as Noah passed through into safety. R.C. Foster said, "With an impressive sweep of logical discussion, the apostle Peter presents the death, burial, resurrection and ascension of Jesus (with a parenthesis to introduce baptism -- which also beautifully sets forth death, burial, and resurrection)."

[107] The word translated "dirt" is *hrupou*, whose root means "dirt, filth, defilement (by sin), soil." That Peter compares baptism with a bath strongly implies that baptism in New Testament times was done by immersion, for Peter's language would be meaningless if baptism were no more than sprinkling a few drops of water on the head. Compare Hebrews 10:22.

being very familiar to us. The problems facing the translator are these: are the words "good conscience,"[108] which are in the genitive case, to be treated as an objective or a subjective genitive?[109] And what English word is a good equivalent for *eperotema*? Translators have tried "answer," "appeal," and "pledge," among others. Perhaps Peter was saying baptism is the *answer* of a good conscience. God asks the sinner, "Where are you?" In vivid contrast to guilty Adam who tried to hide from God, only if he responds in obedience to the command of baptism can the penitent sinner have a good conscience and answer "here!"[110] Perhaps Peter was saying that baptism was the way a sinner *appeals* to God for a good conscience. Known sins which are unforgiven keep us from having a clear conscience. Since the age of accountability, the sinner's conscience has been bothering him. How is he to get a clear conscience? Peter's answer is that this wonderful thing happens when the man is immersed.[111] Perhaps Peter is saying that baptism was a *pledge* that made a contract valid. *Eperotema* was almost a technical business or legal word in the first century. The Latin equivalent for the same process is *stipulatio* (stipulation). In every legal contract there was a definite question and answer (a stipulation, a pledge) which made the contract legal and binding. The question was, "Do you accept the terms of this contract and bind yourself to observe them?" And the answer before witnesses was "Yes!" Peter is, in effect, saying that in baptism God and the sinner who is coming to God make a binding contract. God asked, "Do you accept the terms of my service? Do you accept its privileges and promises, and do you undertake its responsibilities and its demands?" And in the act of being baptized in the presence of witnesses, the penitent sinner is answering "Yes!" The result of such an immersion is a "good conscience" because the person has done what his mind has been taught is the right thing to do. The delightful thing about these possible meanings is that they are all true!

Through the resurrection of Jesus Christ -- The challenge facing interpreters here is what is accomplished by the resurrection?[112] Is it the "good conscience"? Is it "salvation" (baptism now saves you)? If we opt for the former, then Peter is saying that the reason our conscience no longer accuses us is because we are united with Jesus in His resurrection. Instead of habitual sinning, we are walking in newness of life! If we opt for the latter, we are

---

[108] As explained at 3:16, the conscience is an innate faculty that prompts the person to do what his mind thinks is right, and criticizes or accuses when the person does what his mind thinks is wrong. Thus, a "good conscience" is one that has no need to accuse its owner of having done wrong, or having failed to do the right. A person's conscience is evil or guilty when the person fails to do what the mind thinks is right.

[109] If "conscience" is an objective genitive, then we might translate "a pledge to God to maintain a good conscience." If "conscience" is a subjective genitive, then we might translate "the answer to God that a good conscience makes."

[110] This treats "good conscience" as a subjective genitive.

[111] This treats "clear conscience" as an objective genitive.

[112] That "resurrection" means Jesus' bodily resurrection from the tomb, has been documented in our notes at 1 Peter 1:3.

told that baptism derives its saving power from the resurrection. Without the resurrection of Jesus from the dead, baptism would be an empty form, having no more value than the washing of dirt off the body. Either way we construe it, we have another illustration of Peter's point; namely, how suffering opened up a whole new world of service, both in Jesus' case and in the Christian's.

3:22 -- ***Who is at the right hand of God, having gone into heaven, after angels and authorities and powers had been subjected to Him.***

Who is at the right hand of God -- Now follows a further consequence of the sufferings of Christ – His ascension, His exaltation, His further opportunities for service. The relative pronoun "Who" refers to Jesus Christ. To say, "Jesus is now at God's right hand" signifies His position of honor and sovereignty.[113] He has been crowned king and His reign from His royal throne is under way.[114] He is there to rule until all enemies have been put under His feet, the last such enemy being death itself (1 Corinthians 15:25,26). His rule at the right hand of God precedes his *parousia* (coming) and the resurrection of the dead.

Having gone into heaven -- Here is another reminiscence by Peter of one of those "Great Days with Jesus." Over thirty years before writing this letter, Peter had been an eyewitness of Christ's ascension, an unforgettable event (Acts 1:9-11).[115] Jesus' ascension occurred before His coronation, and His session at God's right hand.

After angels and authorities and powers had been subjected to Him -- "Angels", "authorities," and "powers" seem to be three different ranks of angelic spirit beings in the unseen world.[116] These angels were "subjected" to Jesus before He sat down at the right hand of God. Since the three ranks are found both among good and evil angels, we can't tell whether Peter has in mind good angels or evil angels or both when he here speaks of how they have been subjected to Christ. Hebrews 1 tells how the good angels are now, since His glorification,[117] His servants, subject to His beck and call, and are often sent on missions by Him to minister to the redeemed. Evil angels are also subject to Jesus, since Colossians 2:15 tells how He "triumphed over them through [the cross]." Would not both these truths be

---

[113] Cf. Psalm 110:1; Romans 8:34; Hebrews 1:3, 12:2.

[114] Acts 2:33,36, 5:31; Ephesians 1:20-22.

[115] "Gone" is the same verb used in 1:19 (q.v.).

[116] See notes at Romans 8:38; 1 Corinthians 15:24; Ephesians 6:12; Philippians 2:10; Colossians 1:16, 2:15; and 2 Peter 2:11.

[117] There was a time, during His incarnate days here on earth, when Christ (in order to become a man and to suffer death) was made a little lower than the angels (Hebrews 2:9), but He no longer is lower than the angels. He is "much better than the angels" (Hebrews 1:4) and has been "anointed with the oil of gladness above His [angelic] companions" (Hebrews 1:9).

helpful to Peter's suffering readers? Christ can send good angels to minister to them. He can limit and control what the evil angels – including the devil – are able to prompt evil men to do to the Christians.

Peter speaks of the work of Christ in terms of complete triumph and victory. There is no created being in heaven or earth outside the empire and power of the glorified Messiah. Furthermore, Jesus had promised His disciples that where He was, there they would be also. The reason why Peter here adverts to the fact the Lord Jesus is exalted to the right hand of God and is so honored in heaven seems to have been to encourage those to whom he wrote to persevere in the service of God, even though they should be persecuted. They too will be honored. As Noah, who had been faithful and steadfast when surrounded by a scoffing world, was at last preserved by his faith from ruin; and as the Redeemer, though persecuted and put to death, was at last exalted to the right hand of God, so the Christian will be exalted if he but bear his trials patiently and not faint or fail in the persecutions which he might be called on to suffer.

B. Suffering While Doing Good Has a Purifying Effect. 4:1-6

4:1 -- ***Therefore, since Christ has suffered in the flesh, arm yourselves also with the same purpose, because he who has suffered in the flesh has ceased from sin,***

Therefore -- The third doctrinal section begun at 3:13 continues with an application based on what has been said so far.

Since Christ has suffered in the flesh -- Earlier in this doctrinal section, Peter has been calling attention to Jesus' suffering and death. "Suffered"[1] is an aorist tense. It recalls Calvary. Jesus' suffering is a thing of the past when Peter writes. "In the flesh" reminds us that Messiah was for a while incarnate. His suffering was only during the time He was in the flesh.

Arm yourselves also with the same purpose -- Just as servants were exhorted earlier (2:18-25) to take Jesus as an example of suffering, so if any Christians are called on to suffer for righteousness' sake, they ought to follow the example of their Savior. They should equip and arm themselves with the same holy resolve, or purpose,[2] that motivated Him. Christ resolved to do the will of the Father, and to finish the work He came to do (cp. John 4:34, 17:4). The word picture in "arm yourselves" is of a heavily armed Greek soldier putting on his armor and taking up his weapons, ready to fight. Peter is saying that the state of mind when we are *ready* to meet with persecution and trial, and when we are ready to die, if necessary, for our faith, will answer the same purpose (i.e., maximum protection, opportunity to win the fight) that heavy armor served when put on by the soldier before the fight. The verb is an aorist tense, middle voice. Do it once and for all, and do it for your own benefit, is the implication. You have a personal responsibility and a personal interest in developing such a holy resolve as motivated Jesus. The Christian, when facing persecution, must arm himself with the same great thought, the same holy resolve that filled the mind of Christ. That thought is this: it is better to suffer even while doing right than to fail to please God the Father.

Because he who has suffered in the flesh has ceased from sin -- The first word in the Greek is *hoti,* a word that can be translated either "that" (giving the content of what we are to think when we have the same mind as Christ) or "because" (giving a reason why Christians should arm themselves in the way Peter admonishes). It has become rather common for translators to adopt the view that *hoti* here is causal. With the proper arming having been done, there is a value to be derived from suffering ("ceased from sin"). Commentators have differed when it comes to answering the question, "Who is the 'he'?" Some think it speaks of Christ, others

---

[1] Some manuscripts read "died." There is considerable manuscript support for the addition of "for us" (KJV) or "for you," but the shorter reading has strong early support, and best explains the other readings as probably scribal additions that express the teaching of 2:21 and 3:18.

[2] The ASV and KJV translated *ennoia* as "mind." It can also mean "thought, intention, resolve, purpose." Philippians 2:5 uses a different Greek word in "Have this attitude" but the thought is very similar. The way Christ thought is a good way for Christians to think!

that it speaks of the Christian. "Suffered in the flesh" is viewed as already in the past, but how is this to be understood? Perhaps the sufferer has died, and has passed into the next world. Perhaps the suffering is over, and the sufferer is still living in this world. "In the flesh" denotes something that is a physical experience, something that happens during this earthly existence. The verb form "has ceased" may be either middle or passive in voice. Some commentators take it as passive voice. Comparison is made with Romans 6:7, "he who has died is freed (*dedikaiotai*) from sin." In Romans, Paul is speaking about dying to sin in baptism. So it is suggested that Peter writes something similar to what Paul wrote. Peter would be saying the Christian in baptism (1 Peter 3:21) is freed from the power of sin, just as in death Christ was freed from the power of sin.[3] Some interpreters take it as a middle voice, denoting something the subject does for his own benefit, or does to himself. If we take it as middle, Peter is holding up the suffering of Christ as an example (2:21, 3:18) for the Christian to follow, and gives his readers further encouragement by stating that the one who suffers is aided by the suffering to quit a lot of his sinning (i.e., suffering has a purifying effect).[4]

What Peter may mean by "has ceased from sin"[5] has been given at least three different explanations. One idea is that, after baptism (in which one dies, "suffers"), the Christian lives by a different set of values (the will of God rather than the lusts of the flesh, as the next verse specifies). A second idea is suffering in this life has a purifying effect – it destroys the power of sin. People who have endured great sufferings are not as attracted by temptations as they once were. They have a different set of values (Psalm 119:47). A Christian who has been so strong in his conviction that he patiently endures persecution for it, though not sinless-perfect, will no longer yield to many of the temptations he used to. After all, it would be foolish to suffer for the faith rather than to yield to coercion only to voluntarily yield to temptations to join the pagans in their wicked ways. Who wants to give up voluntarily what they have had to fight for? A third idea is that, after death, the sufferer is beyond temptation and sin.[6] When the soul of the Christian is with the Lord in heaven (Philippians 1:23), the devil can't tempt him or hurt him anymore. The Christian can equip himself with the idea (*ennoia*) suffering will only happen while he is in the flesh. When this life is over, so will be the suffering.[7]

---

[3] This interpretation regards 4:1a as a reference to Christ's physical death, and regards "suffered in the flesh" in 4:1b as metaphorical (dying with Christ in baptism).

[4] This solution obviously requires 4:1b to be taken as a reason for what was said in 4:1a, for we could not understand Peter to be saying Christ had to think about ceasing from sin. He was sinless! (1 Peter 1:19, 2:22).

[5] Some manuscripts have a genitive singular, *hamartias*, "from sin," and this is the reading adopted by the UBS. Others have a dative plural, *hamartiais*, "to sins," and this is the reading adopted by Westcott-Hort.

[6] Interpreters who think "he" (in "he who has suffered") refers to Christ observe that only while Jesus was on earth was He subject to temptations from the devil. God cannot be tempted, and when Jesus has been glorified and coronated, He is beyond anything the devil can do to Him.

[7] A person can put up with great pain if they know it is only going to be temporary. It is when it is obvious there will be no end to it that people give in to hopelessness and despair. One of the bad things about Hell is that there is no end in sight to the torment.

4:2 -- ***So as to live the rest of the time in the flesh no longer for the lusts of men, but for the will of God.***

So as to live the rest of the time in the flesh -- "So as to live" translates *eis* and an articular infinitive, a construction that ordinarily expresses purpose. It would be connected with "arm yourselves."[8] Not only does the Christian have the same holy resolve Jesus did when He was willing to suffer while doing what is right, but the Christian also adds another weapon to his armor. That weapon is the determination that he will no longer live his earthly life in the sphere of the lusts of men, but he is going to live in the sphere of doing the will of God. "Rest of the time" implies that the length of their earthly pilgrimage, the length of their time of probation on earth, will not be long.

No longer for the lusts of men -- "No longer" says there was a time before the suffering, before they received this letter, when the readers were living too much merely by the physical drives and desires by which unconverted men of the world live. "The lusts of men" remind us of what was written at 1:14, "the former lusts ... in your ignorance."

But for the will of God -- That which God wants a man to do – "the will of God" – is the rule by which the Christian orders his life. What Peter writes reminds us of similar language in Romans 6:12ff, where Christians are exhorted to stop responding to the old stimuli and instead to present the members of their bodies to God as instruments for His service. Once a man has become a Christian, doing what God wants a man to do is a matter of personal determination.

4:3 -- ***For the time already past is sufficient* for you *to have carried out the desire of the Gentiles, having pursued a course of sensuality, lusts, drunkenness, carousals, drinking parties and abominable idolatries.***

For the time already past is sufficient -- This seems to be irony. Surely you have lived "in the flesh" long enough. "For" shows this is a reason why the Christian determines to no longer serve sin.[9] The "time already past" is the time before they became Christians (or the time before they received this letter). The old way of life should be closed and done. The old habits, associates, practices, places, amusements, everything of the old life which is not in accord with the will and Word of God should be closed and done with. It is the life described in 1 Peter 1:18 as "futile" – handed down from their forefathers. "Sufficient" says enough time has been spent in vice, indulging themselves![10]

---

[8] There is no subject expressed in the Greek for the infinitive phrase, so it must be implied from the context. Our versions are divided in how they translate, some using "you," some using "we," and some using "he." We follow the view that the "you" in the imperative is the implied subject of this infinitive phrase.

[9] Hiebert (*op. cit.*, p.240) observes that Peter gives three reasons to motivate his readers to arm themselves. This motivation is drawn from the past (verse 3), from the present (verse 4), and the future (verses 5,6).

[10] The Textus Receptus and KJV read "sufficient to us," but "us" (*hemin*) lacks manuscript support and is best omitted. Peter, who grew up Jewish, did not identify himself with the evils of the Gentile world.

***For you* to have carried out the desire of the Gentiles** -- "Gentiles" equals unconverted, pagans. Many of Peter's readers are former Gentiles.[11] In a moment will follow a listing of the kinds of things Peter has in mind when he speaks of "the desire"[12] of the Gentiles.

Having pursued a course of sensuality -- The ASV read, "and to have walked in lasciviousness." "Pursued a course" is a good translation for the perfect tense participle;[13] it speaks of a course of regular conduct, a past way of living.[14] "Sensuality" (*aselgeiais*) refers to wanton words, lustful and sexually suggestive bodily movements, actions that excite disgust and shock public decency.

Lusts -- *Epithumiais* indicates hidden sins of unclean thought, hidden sins of voluptuousness, inward unchastity and lewdness, where the power to indulge the acts is wanting. This verse is one of the reasons to stay away from pornographic materials, for the lusts and desires stirred up by such are here proscribed for the Christian.

Drunkenness -- Perhaps the word *oinophlugiais* (literally, to bubble up, or overflow, with wine) describes habitual drunkenness.[15] "Wine swillings" is the translation offered by Lenski.[16]

Carousals -- *Komois* often alluded to drunken youths parading the streets, or festal processions and dancing in honor of Bacchus. Think of the New Orleans Mardi Gras, or some Ger-

---

[11] The NASB adds "for you" in italics at the beginning of this clause. This follows from the decision made earlier concerning the implied subject of the articular infinitive ("so as to live") in verse 2.

[12] Some writers have commented at length on the perceived difference between "will" (*thelema*) used of God in verse 2, and "desire" (*boulema*) here used of men. Some of the comments are colored by a predilection to the doctrine of inherited total depravity, and so "desire" is explained as being inclination, whereas "will" speaks of choice and purpose. We are not convinced the alleged distinction between the synonyms holds all the way through the Scriptures. See G.R. Berry, *New Testament Synonyms* (Chicago: Wilcox and Follett, 1948), section #32.

[13] By using the verb *poreuomai* Peter compares life to a journey, and it vividly pictures the eagerness to go from sin to sin that often characterizes the unsaved.

[14] The KJV reads "we walked in" – and the commentaries are quick to excuse Peter from the list of vices by suggesting that this is an editorial "we" – not necessarily meaning that Peter himself had been addicted to these vices. All this is unnecessary. There is no "we" in the Greek, and so such an apology for Peter is not needed. He is simply listing vices that are generally committed by pagans/Gentiles – and sometimes, sadly, by Jews also. (Technically, the Greek construction is an accusative absolute. The accusative participle has no expressed antecedent. It relates to an implied accusative of general reference with the infinitive "to have carried out.")

[15] The KJV read "excess of wine," a translation sometimes improperly used to infer that some wine is OK, but that "excess" is improper. This is squeezing more out of the word than the Greek allows. Whether *any* use of intoxicants, by Christians or other persons, is wise or advisable, is another question. This commentator is a total abstainer, and thinks others should be, too.

[16] Lenski, *op. cit.*, p.182.

man festivals (Ocktoberfest), or the near drunken riots following world championship sport contests, or at times some of the tail-gate parties prior to athletic contests, and you will have examples of "carousals."

Drinking parties -- The thing forbidden is an assembling together for the purpose of drinking. Euphemistically, some of these are today called happy hour. Christians, thus, determine they will not attend those celebrations in which drinking alcohol or drinking toasts are understood to be an essential part of the festivities.[17]

And abominable idolatries -- "Abominable" is a good choice to translate *athemitois*, a word found elsewhere in the New Testament only at Acts 10:28, where it is translated "unlawful." This Greek adjective denotes things opposed to law as laid down by instinctive convictions with regard to what is right rather than opposed to law as set forth in statute.[18] If practices at idol feasts were bad enough that even unconverted men think them not right, they had to be pretty bad, and "abominable" catches the idea. Idol worship encouraged as part of its regular ceremony both drunkenness and sexual vice and laxity. The worship of the gods degenerated into debauchery and destroyed the dignity of their participants.

4:4 -- ***And in* all *this, they are surprised that you do not run with* them *into the same excess of dissipation, and they malign* you;**

And in *all* this -- The Greek reads simply *en ho*. It might be translated "in which," and refer back to "sufficient": they think it strange that the past is sufficient. It might be translated "wherein" and refer back to "having pursued": while they are enjoying all these desires of the flesh, they are surprised the Christian avoids them. The thing that the unconverted struggle with is that the Christians once lived like the Gentiles, but now are wholly changed.

They are surprised -- The word picture is that of being astonished at some strange sight. The unconverted are surprised at the change in the Christian's lifestyle. The change is something the Christian's old accomplices and partners in vice just don't understand.

That you do not run with *them* into the same excess of dissipation -- Each of the key words produces a vivid mental image. "Run with them" calls to mind a picture of a euphoric stampede of pleasure seekers. It means to "run in company with others" or to "troop with others." It expresses the blind haste of the wicked man who rushes headlong into opportunities to sin. "Like a pack of animals they move from one bar to another, from one

---

[17] The KJV reads "banquetings." There is nothing in the Greek word that refers to eating as the KJV term now commonly connotes.

[18] "Unlawful" (Acts 10:28) means something other than contrary to Roman law, or to the Mosaic law, or to Christ's law. The word there means "not customary." That unconverted men would have certain standards which they accept as right and wrong, ultimately, reflects the rules that God gave when He first created, rules which have been passed down from generation to generation by word of mouth.

'key club' to another, seemingly rejoicing on their way to hell, and taking solace in knowing they are not going alone."[19] "Excess" is a meaningful word picture. Think of the trash along the sea shore after high tide. Think of the waste when sewers back up and overflow. Well, the sinners were swimming in such garbage and effluent as they ran around together. "Dissipation" translates *asotias*, literally, "no salvation." The same word was used of the prodigal son (Luke 15:13), who spent his substance in "riotous" living (it likely included prostitution, just as the elder brother accused him of doing). It describes a dissolute life of recklessness in which there is no restraint. The Gentiles worried none about reputation, earthly position, or their immortal souls. All they wanted was more and more of such a dissipated life, and they were astonished that Christians would refrain from such a life.

And they malign *you* -- The fact the Christians won't join them condemns their wickedness, and they try to get back at the Christian. They use harsh and reproachful words in speaking against those[20] who no longer run with them in this riot. How tempting it must have been for Peter's readers to succumb under such pressure, and to conform to their former ways of living. It is very hard to face contempt, slander, ridicule, and outright violent persecution, and still keep the faith.

4:5 -- *But they shall give account to Him who is ready to judge the living and the dead.*

But they shall give account -- The NASB is likely correct in translating in such a way that we English readers get the idea it is the maligners who will have to answer to the Judge.[21] Peter is promising the harassed Christians that the Judge is taking note of all the evil men do, and that those evil men will be called to give an account of their actions in the Great Judgment Day. Is this not another of Peter's reminiscences of "Great Days with Jesus"? Peter has just portrayed the evil words spoken by the unconverted detractors of the way Christians choose to live. This vividly recalls the time when Jesus spoke concerning how men would give an account for their words (Matthew 12:36,37).

To Him who is ready to judge the living and the dead -- "To Him" can refer either to the Father or the Son. It seems probable that Peter refers to Christ as the judge in this present

---

[19] Harold Fickett, Jr., *Peter's Principles* (Ventura, CA: Regal Books, 1981), p.107.

[20] It will be observed that there is no object in the Greek for the verb "malign." Perhaps it was the Christians, or the Christian religion, or Christ Himself, who was maligned by the pagans.

[21] Verse 5 begins with a relative pronoun in the nominative plural. Its antecedent might be the saved ("you") of verse 4, and if so, Peter is warning his readers that Christians will stand in the judgment and answer for their lives, so they had better make sure they spend the rest of their time doing the will of God. Now the Bible everywhere has all men judged, the righteous as well as the wicked, so there is nothing unscriptural about taking the relative as pointing to the saved. However, the subject of verse 4 ("they") is continued by a nominative plural participle ("maligning") and, we believe, is continued on by the relative pronoun and the third person plural verb "they shall give account" with which verse 5 begin.

passage,[22] and that at the final judgment the Father executes judgment through the Son.[23] "Ready" means holding Himself in readiness. The meaning is not that He was *about* to do it, or that Peter mistakenly supposed the judgment day was near at hand when he wrote, but that Christ was *prepared* for it. All the arrangements were made with reference to it. There was nothing to hinder it. "Judge" certainly alludes to the final judgment. It is a time, as particularly emphasized in the Psalms, when the righteous are vindicated. "Living (men)" and "dead (men)"[24] will both be called into judgment. Some writers take these words in a physical sense. There are some who will be living on earth when Jesus returns, and many who will have died. Whatever their state, they will be judged! Some writers take these words in a spiritual sense. Both the saved (the living) and the unsaved (those dead in trespasses and sins) shall be judged.[25] Unsaved men may call you to give an account now (1 Peter 3:15), but they themselves must give their account to the Judge. What we do with verse 6 will probably determine how we will explain the words living and dead here in verse 5.

4:6 -- ***For the gospel has for this purpose been preached even to those who are dead, that though they are judged in the flesh as men, they may live in the spirit according to*** **the will of** ***God.***

For -- Verse 6 is another of Peter's verses which has proven to be a challenge to interpreters. One writer, Mastermann, thought that for him this was the "most difficult text in the Bible."[26] Over a dozen interpretations have been proposed, so again we must gird up our minds as we slowly and carefully work our way through what Peter says.

The gospel has for this purpose been preached -- "For this" indicates that verse 6 is tied to something in the previous verse or verses. Perhaps it is tied to what was said in verse 5: because Christ is going to judge the living and the dead (verse 5), the gospel was preached ... (verse 6). It was preached because God really wants people to "live"! It was preached because there is going to be a judgment, and God does all He can to be absolutely fair and impartial. Perhaps it is tied to what was said in verse 3, so that verse 6 then would give a

---

[22] Cp. Matthew 25:31; Romans 14:10; 2 Corinthians 5:10.

[23] Cp. John 5:22,27; Acts 17:31; Romans 2:16.

[24] There is no article in the Greek with either word, so both "living" and "dead" are qualitative, the two words comprehending the two great divisions of all human beings.

[25] Several popular contemporary systems of eschatology exempt the righteous from ever being judged (at least, in the view of these systems' proponents, at the Great White Throne judgment). This commentator's studies of last things does not include a multiplicity of future judgments (e.g., Sheep and Goat as one judgment, the Judgment Seat of Christ as another, and the Great White Throne as yet a third). He explains these different depictions of the final judgment as being illustrations the readers could identify with from their own everyday experiences. Verses that have Christians at the final judgment and which identify some of the things for which they will have to give answer to the Judge include Matthew 16:27, 25:31-46; Hebrews 13:17; 2 John 8; 1 John 2:28, 4:17; 1 Corinthians 3:12-15, 4:5; Revelation 22:12; 2 Corinthians 5:10; James 3:1; 1 Timothy. 3:6, 5:12; Colossians 3:25, and Romans 14-15. Even Revelation 20:11-15 have the righteous being judged, for the "sea" that gave up the dead in it is the sea of glass on which the souls of the redeemed were located (Revelation 15:1,2).

[26] Mastermann, *op. cit.*, p.138.

reason why Christians no longer need walk according to the desires of the Gentiles. They are alive unto God! "Preached" (*euaggelisthe*, an aorist tense) directs our thoughts to some definite occasion in the past. The verb form is passive, and the agent is only implied. Was it Christian missionaries who did the preaching? Or is there some connection to 3:19, so that it is Christ who did the preaching?

Even to those who are dead -- Literally, "even to dead (ones)." In this commentator's opinion, certain principles of interpretation should be followed. One, it would seem probable the "dead" of verse 6 and the "dead" of verse 5 refer to the same "dead ones." If one is physically dead, so is the other. If one is spiritually dead, so is the other. Two, it would seem they were "dead" (whatever that means) at the same time the gospel was preached to them. With these principles in mind, let us study the leading interpretations that have been offered for this verse.

(1) The "dead" are people who died physically before the church age began. They had the gospel preached to them (while they were living[27]) so that they would not be in an unfavorable position in the final judgment. The "gospel" was preached to Abraham (Galatians 3:8), and the wilderness wanderers (Hebrews 4:2), and by parity of reasoning to others also.
(2) The "dead" are the spiritually dead.[28] Since Pentecost, and even in the provinces of Pontus, Galatia, Cappadocia, Asia, and Bithynia, the gospel has been preached so people could become spiritually alive (even though this means they may be criticized by their old cronies with whom they used to run). This interpretation is the one this commentator prefers, though it is not totally free from difficulties.[29] If this explanation is accepted for 4:6, then there is no reference at all in 4:6 to what was written in 1 Peter 3:18,19.
(3) The "dead" are people who have died physically since they became Christians. They were already dead when Peter wrote, but they were living on earth when the gospel was preached to them. The remainder of verse 6 is explained to mean that because they had become Christians they were judged by men (and often put to death), but (even though persecuted and killed) they lived (in the spirit) eternally with God. This is the interpretation espoused by Kelcy and Lenski and the NIV, which reads "the gospel was

[27] Defenders of a post-mortem opportunity for lost people to respond to a gospel invitation treat this verse differently. They think that the "dead" ones have died physically, that their souls were in the intermediate state, and that in the intermediate place the gospel was preached to them there. (Their appeal for proof of all this is found in a possible interpretation of 1 Peter 3:18,19.)

[28] This interpretation, which has long been accepted by some in the church, can appeal to Ephesians 2:1 and Colossians 2:13 for the meaning of "dead."

[29] Especially difficult is the phrase translated "that though they are judged in the flesh as men." Other objections raised have included the allegation that Peter does not use "dead" elsewhere to refer to the spiritually dead, that such an interpretation calls for a present tense ("is being preached") rather than an aorist, and those who view Christians as being exempt from any final judgment are scandalized by what this interpretation makes Peter say.

preached to those who are now dead."[30] It is doubtful that the tenses of the Greek verbs in this verse will allow this rendering,[31] for it requires "dead" to be given a different meaning in verse 5 than we give it in verse 6,[32] and it requires that we take "judged" differently in verse 5 (something Christ does) than we explain it in verse 6 (something wicked men do). If this explanation could be accepted for 4:6, then there is no reference at all to what was written in 1 Peter 3:18,19.

(4) The "dead" are the same people spoken of in 3:18,19, "the spirits *now* in prison." While 3:18,19 might seem as though Christ preached only to the "disobedient," 4:6 would tell us that He preached to all the dead – to the wicked (chapter 3) and to the saved (chapter 4). What is objectionable about this interpretation is that, first, it involves a (second) chance after death to be saved, an idea that seems everywhere else in Scripture to be denied. Second, how do we explain "preached the gospel"[33] if the audience already is "saved"? Third, how could souls in Hades (disembodied souls) be judged "according to men in the flesh"?[34]

That though they are judged in the flesh as men -- Possible meanings assigned to this phrase are dependent on how the previous phrase was interpreted.

(1) If we opt for the gospel being preached to those who died before the dawn of the gospel age, this phrase says the gospel was preached in order that those Patriarchal and Mosaic Age people could be judged by the same standards as men who live on this side of the cross. They will be judged just as all men are judged, but they live in the spirit (and their spirit will be saved in the day of the Lord). Such a twist would seem to contradict Romans 2:12-16 which says men shall be judged impartially on the basis of their available light.

(2) If we opt for the meaning that the gospel was preached to those who were spiritually dead, the last part of verse 6 says "although they receive in the body the sentence common to men, they might in the spirit be alive with the life of God" (NEB). The sentence common to men is physical death.[35] All men die bodily because Adam sinned (Romans 5:12-21;

---

[30] Some interpreters have argued for a close parallel between Peter's writing and Paul's at 1 Thessalonians 4:13-18. Both, it is asserted, were dealing with Christians who were concerned about whether or not Christians who had died would have a share in the triumph of the day of the Lord. Both, it is asserted, were assuring their readers that death (as Greek beliefs had it) was not the end of men's existence.

[31] If *kai nekrois euaggelisthe* may mean the gospel was preached to some during their lifetime who are now dead, exegesis no longer has any fixed rule, and Scripture may be made to prove anything. This is exactly the kind of interpretation to which we objected in 3:19, which some try to make say Christ preached to some [in the days of Noah] who are now in prison.

[32] "Dead (ones)" at the end of verse 5 clearly mean all who are dead, as opposed to all who are alive. How then do we give the words "to dead (ones)" in verse 6 a restricted meaning of the Christian dead as this proposed interpretation would require us to do?

[33] Remember the word used here in verse 6 is *euaggelisthe*, the regular word that means preach the gospel.

[34] "In the flesh" is the same phrase used of Jesus' suffering "in the flesh" (verse 1). A very good reason should be offered for giving it a different meaning here in verse 6 from what it was given in verse 1.

[35] This option treats "judged" the same way (something God does) in both verses 5 and 6.

1 Corinthians 15:22-28). While He has not revoked the sentence of physical death, God really does want men to live spiritually.[36] Once they have obeyed the gospel their spirits are alive again (Romans 8:10). Yes, they will still stand in the judgment, but their sentence will be far different from that pronounced upon their pagan antagonists.

(3) If we opt for the gospel being preached to men who became Christians and then died physically before Peter wrote, then "judged in the flesh as men" means as far as the treatment the Christians received from other men, it was often unfair criticism and condemnation and railing and blasphemy. But even though persecuted and killed, they are living eternally with God. By men they were condemned in the flesh. By God they were made to live in the spiritual world. Man's verdict (death) was not the final verdict. They are still living with God.

(4) If we opt for the fourth view, we have flowing from Peter's pen the doctrine of a postmortem opportunity for wicked men to hear, repent, and be saved. The last part of verse 6 would say they died in the flesh, but Christ offered the gospel of salvation to them, and many of them accepted the offer and so live in the spirit. This idea of a second chance after death is everywhere opposed elsewhere in Scriptures, so we doubt it is correct here.

They may live in the spirit according to *the will of* God -- Accepting the second option in the previous two clauses as correct, this phrase says that the new-born Christians may live as God wants them to live because their spirits are alive. They are no longer dead in trespasses and sins (Ephesians 2:1).[37] If we are correct in treating 4:1-6 as a paragraph which shows that suffering while doing good can have a purifying effect, then the "living" is something the Christian does in this life (recall what Peter wrote in 4:2,3 about living the rest of your time for the will of God).

VI. THIRD HORTATORY SECTION. 4:7-5:9

A. Exhortation to Be Helpful to Suffering Brethren. 4:7-11

---

[36] We might even recall another one of Peter's "Great Days with Jesus." At the raising of Lazarus, Jesus said to Martha, "He who believes in Me shall live even if he dies, and everyone who lives and believes in Me shall never die" (John 11:25,26). The verb tenses Jesus used speak of the present time, not the future. They continue to live, even if they die (physically)!

[37] Some writers think there is a future emphasis here, rather than something done in this present life. They observe that "flesh" and "spirit" in 4:6 exactly parallels what was said of Jesus in 3:18. Their comments then follow this line: Christ's suffering and being put to death in the flesh ended His earthly life. The same thing may well happen to Peter's readers. However, Christ's "spirit" continued alive, and in the spirit realm he continued to minister. The same thing will happen to his readers, Peter implies. If a person is a Christian, physical death does not end his or her existence. He or she will live right on through death and share fully in the life bought by their Savior. He or she will live with Him now in the spiritual world, and will share with Him in the blissful vindication when He returns in glory. (While all of this may be true, the only question is are they appropriate comments for this passage in 1 Peter?)

4:7 -- *The end of all things is at hand; therefore, be of sound judgment and sober* spirit *for the purpose of prayer.*

The end of all things is at hand -- The doctrinal section just finished serves as the basis for the exhortations that follow. Since suffering can open up whole new worlds of service and can have a purifying effect, Peter's readers are given some specific ways they can serve and some Christian attitudes they can develop. The NASB and NIV leave untranslated the *de* that occurs at the beginning of this clause, while the KJV/ASV both begin verse 7 with "but," and Marshall's interlinear begins the verse with "now." *Eggiken* (a perfect tense, emphasizing past completed action with present continuing results) can be rendered "has drawn near," "has come near," "is at hand." How "all things"[38] is explained will depend greatly on how the other words in the phrase are treated. *Telos* can be translated either "goal" or "end." If we read "goal," we are reminded that God, ever since He created, has been moving history toward a goal, and Christians are living in the last of the series of dispensations[39] God planned for history. If we read "end," we may think of the time when the judgment (verse 5) occurs as having come closer than it was before Jesus appeared in the flesh and died as a sin offering (3:18).[40]

---

[38] Commentators speak variously of persecutions, persecutors, sufferings, sin, earthly probation, the end of the world, the destruction of Jerusalem (AD 70), as they offer comments on this word.

[39] Acts 2:16,17; 1 Corinthians 10:11; 1 Peter 1:20.

[40] As we offer possible explanations of Peter's words, we are attempting to avoid being drawn into a contemporary theological battleground. The topic being bitterly contested is whether or not the New Testament writers, like Peter, were mistaken in their views as to when the second coming would occur. Through the pages of the New Testament one finds the theme of the near approach of the end (cf. passages in 1 and 2 Thessalonians; Romans 13:12; Philippians 4:5 (?); James 5:8; 1 John 2:18; Revelation 1:3, 22:20). It is rather common to read comments to the effect that in the earliest books to be written, the writers were looking for an imminent return. As time passed, it is asserted, the later books show a change of emphasis: now there is going to be a delay of some time before Christ returns. The "scientific higher critics" even date some books early or late, depending on the view of the time of Christ's return presented in the books! Some critics do not hesitate to say flatly that the New Testament writers were mistaken. They looked for His return in their own generation, but they were wrong. Clearly, this approach impinges on inspiration and the trustworthiness of the narratives.

In his second letter (2 Peter 3:4-7), Peter will allude to the fact that each day that passed with no return of Christ did provide scoffers with an argument that no second advent should be looked for. But that Peter or any of the apostles changed their theology, or attempted to sweep away any disappointment over an unexpected delay in His coming, is a figment of the imagination of the critics. To change theology would be a tacit admission that what they had received by revelation and spoken by inspiration was only at best provisional or at worst flat erroneous. There is no need for such drastic measures. No dates for Christ's return were revealed to the apostles (Matthew 24:36), so we should not expect to find any "dates" identified or espoused in any of the apostles' writings.

Nevertheless, modern theologians have produced volumes of hypotheses and corroborating arguments and evidence as they have tried to explain for modern readers what Jesus and the apostles actually predicted. C.H. Dodd has given us "realized eschatology." Tillich and Niebuhr have given us "symbolic eschatology." Paul Althaus gave us "teleological eschatology." Then there is "futuristic eschatology." A mediating view between futuristic and realized eschatology is "inaugurated eschatology." And so the debate continues. Some dismiss all these eschatologies by simply affirming that God does not count time as men count time, so for Him (with Whom a thousand years is like a day) the "end of all things is at hand." While to men it has been nearly 2000 years since Peter wrote these words by inspiration, to God it has been only a couple of days. Others have proposed taking the verses about the nearness of the end in an individual sense (for each of us, we don't have much time until we are at the end of our time of probation here on earth). Still others have supposed that the Hebrew way of looking

Therefore, be of sound judgment -- "Therefore" indicates the imperatives[41] that follow are vitally related to what was just said about the very real possibility of suffering for righteousness, the need to live the rest of our days doing the will of God, and the end of all things being at hand. When Peter wrote "be of sound judgment," he was commanding his readers to think before they acted, to keep their heads, to be aware of the consequences of their actions in time and in eternity. When, in the middle of an emergency or under pressure, a person does things that are out of character, we say "He lost his head." In effect, Peter is saying, "When you are faced with persecution for righteousness sake, be careful that you don't do anything stupid! Think carefully what you are about to do!"

And sober *spirit* for the purpose of prayer -- At 1:13 Peter has already spoken about the need to be "sober", to make sure nothing dulls your mind so that you fail to concentrate on doing important spiritual things. In the Greek the two imperatives are connected by "and," which raises the question of whether only the latter or whether both imperatives are conditions of prayer.[42] We think two distinct duties are set forth. First is a command to not lose your heads when under pressure. Second is a command to be fully alert in your thinking so as to not forget to pray. "Prayer" is plural in the Greek; it is not just one prayer the Christian offers, but many. Peter does not specify for what the Christians will be praying, but certainly included is for the Christian to say in all things, "Thy will be done!" It could also include requests to God for help to faithfully carry out the commands about to be given in the following verses.

4:8 -- ***Above all, keep fervent in your love for one another, because love covers a multitude of sins.***

Above all -- Before all things in order of importance. It is likely Peter means when you have finished[43] your prayers, when you have strengthened your relationship with the Lord, then give top priority to being fervent in your love for one another.

Keep fervent in your love for one another -- "For one another" (literally, "to yourselves") is one of the expressions in this paragraph that causes us to give it the title we did ("exhortation to be helpful to suffering *brethren"*). The KJV rendering of *agape* as "charity," i.e., alleviat-

---

at "judgment" should influence our explanation of Peter's language. The Hebrew looked at all calamities and catastrophes as the "day of the Lord" or "the end" (cf. Amos 8:2, 5:18; Ezekiel 7:2,3), while at the same time recognizing that those that occur from time to time are but precursors to the great and final day of the Lord (the final judgment). See more on this at 2 Peter 3:10.

[41] Codex Sinaiticus has only one imperative ("be of sound judgment"), but other ancient exemplars for the text have two imperatives.

[42] KJV and ASV put a comma between them, thus making only the second imperative a condition of prayer. NASB and NIV have no comma between them, so both imperatives are made a condition of prayer. If both verbs are connected with "unto prayer" (i.e., "for the purpose of prayer") the importance of that activity is emphasized.

[43] Some suppose Peter means even before you pray, make sure you love.

ing the other person's needs,[44] likely catches the idea Peter had in mind when he wrote this. The word translated "fervent" calls to mind the strenuous effort of a horse at full gallop, or the sustained effort of an athlete to win. Loving one another is not always easy. It demands everything a man has of mental and spiritual nerve and muscle and sinew. Why? There will be occasions when sins on the part of the brethren may tend to slacken our love for them. There will be times when the love is not returned, but spurned. Getting involved in others' lives when they are being persecuted may very well draw the attention of the persecutors to the benefactors. With such dire consequences connected with loving, brethren will be tempted to avoid opportunities to be helpful. The word translated "keep" is a nominative plural participle, very likely dependent on "be of sound judgment" (verse 7). A Christian who is thinking clearly and who hasn't lost his head will keep right on extending his love to other Christians.

Because love covers a multitude of sins -- This is the reason why Christians are strenuous in their love for each other. The same statement also occurs in James 5:20.[45] "Covers" represents the Greek word *kalupto*, which means "to cover up, to hide, to veil, to hinder the knowledge of a thing" (Thayer). Perhaps the "multitude of sins" that are covered are the sins of the one extending his or her love. The idea would be that when we love others God forgives our own sins.[46] Perhaps the "multitude of sins" that are covered are the sins[47] of the one who is the object of the Christian's love. Love doesn't magnify or publicize the sins of others into an excuse to quit showing love. The person who wants to love (extend acts of help and kindness) can do so in spite of the sins observed in the life of the one being helped. It is not that love is blind, but it is that love loves a person just as he is, faults and all. Genuine love not only extends a hand to a brother who is hurting, but when there is habitual, unforgiven

---

[44] Charity now has the connotation of alleviating the needs of the poor, so that word may no longer be a good one to use for translating the Greek word "love." Two of the Greek synonyms for "love" were explained in notes at 1 Peter 1:22. *Agape* is the way God acted in Jesus Christ toward us who hated and despised God and refused to serve Him. It is not a romantic, sentimental thing; it does not even necessarily mean affection. But it does do good to another, even an enemy, when that person has a need. It is the love of intelligence and purpose that desires the welfare of the one loved.

[45] The source of this saying is often given as Proverbs 10:12 ("love covers all transgressions"), but if so it is taken either from the Hebrew text, or from a Greek text other than the LXX (the wording of which is very different from the wording used in the New Testament) known to both James and Peter. Contemporary scholars are researching the possibility that there was another version besides the LXX of the Greek Scriptures current in the first-century world, and often used for quotations by Christian writers and preachers. As C.E.B. Cranfield, *I and II Peter and Jude* (London: SCM, 1960), p.114, discusses the source of this saying, he quotes a third-century writer who attributed it to the Lord Himself. If so, Peter is here reflecting another of those "Great Days with Jesus."

[46] Protestant commentators have generally shied away from this interpretation of the saying in Peter and John. They are objecting to the idea that acts of charity can earn indulgences. While men don't earn forgiveness, there are certain conditions God has laid down which He expects men to meet before He forgives. Jesus did teach one of these conditions when He explained that men will be forgiven our trespasses as we forgive others their trespasses.

[47] The word Peter uses for "sins" is *hamartia*, the most comprehensive term for sin in the New Testament. It denotes all that "misses the mark" or "falls short" of God's standards of right. It can be failures in our relationship to God and/or failures in our relationship to men.

sin, there is another teaching of Jesus (Matthew 18:15-18) that guides the Christian's behavior.

4:9 -- *Be hospitable to one another without complaint.*

Be hospitable to one another -- The verb form in this verse is a participle, which suggests this is another way one expresses the "sound judgment" that was exhorted in verse 7. "Hospitable" translates *philoxenoi*, literally "friendly to strangers." Christians traveling from one place to another, traveling missionaries spreading the Good News, and refugees from persecution needed to find comfort and lodging in the homes of fellow Christians, since the inns of the day were impossibly filthy and notoriously immoral. Congregations of believers needed a large room in which to meet. For those whose homes had such spacious rooms, here was another avenue for the practice of hospitality. The traveling or fleeing Christian may need information and help to become located, to transact his business, to find work, to expedite him on his journey. The duty of hospitality is pressed upon Christians in a number of places in the New Testament.[48]

Without complaint -- This is a frank recognition that it takes extra work and time and expense on the part of the host to extend hospitality. There are times when showing hospitality can be inconvenient, and times when it can be attended with danger (if the persecutors should catch the fleeing refugees in your home). The spirit[49] in which Christians extended hospitality is very important. A good deed can be vitiated by a complaining attitude on the part of the one performing it (1 Corinthians 13:3).

4:10 -- *As each one has received a* special *gift, employ it in serving each other, as good stewards of the manifold grace of God.*

As each one has received a *special* gift -- "Sound judgment" (verse 7) has been the theme for several verses now. Here is another way such sound judgment can be shown, this time in mutual ministry. "As" (*kathos*, "according as", ASV) indicates that the kinds of ministry a man might perform to help his brother are governed by the nature of the gift received. "Each one" should not be pressed to prove that every individual Christian is specially gifted. "According as" indicates that not all were gifted, though some were. "*Special* gift" lets the English reader know that the Greek word for "gift" is not the usual word *doron*, but *charisma*, the word often used of the supernatural spiritual gifts received by the laying on of an apostle's

---

[48] Matthew 25:35,43; Romans 12:13; 1 Timothy 3:2, 5:10; Hebrews 13:2; Titus 1:8; 2 John 6-8. Sometimes traveling Christians would have letters of commendation or introduction (as mentioned by Paul, 2 Corinthians 3:1) which would serve to introduce them to Christians in another community, but those brethren who were fleeing persecution would hardly have such in their possession.

[49] The Greek term "murmuring" can denote a muttering or mumbling under one's breath because of an attitude of disgust. Murmuring is an attitude opposite to cheerfulness. An uncheerful attitude can also be expressed by a look on the face that shows the guest the host is irritated and unhappy about this extra burden.

hands.[50] Our study of spiritual gifts has led us to the conclusion that there were two kinds of gifts of the Spirit in the early church: (1) The supernatural, miraculous gifts received by the apostles when they were baptized with the Holy Spirit, or received by church members through the laying on of an apostle's hands. These were temporary for the infancy of the church. (2) Non-miraculous ones received when a man becomes a Christian, which are available all through the church age.

Employ it in serving one another -- The gifts were for the benefit of the whole congregation (1 Corinthians 12:7), so "sound judgment" would require Christians to exercise their gifts so their brethren could be edified (cp. 1 Corinthians 14:3-19). Christians minister[51] to each other with their gifts.

As good stewards of the manifold grace of God -- Stewards were managers or superintendents of someone else's property. Often, like Joseph in the Old Testament, they were slaves who were entrusted with a solemn responsibility to manage another's household. The expression "manifold grace" refers to the great variety of God's gracious gifts which He has bestowed on Christians.[52] When Christians are engaged in ministering to one another, they do it not as though they were conferring a personal favor or as distributing bounty out of their own personal largess, but in the consciousness that when they are giving or distributing it is simply part and parcel of managing what they have first received from God. It is required of stewards that a man be found faithful (1 Corinthians 4:2). The best way to continue to enjoy God's grace is to share it.

4:11 -- *Whoever speaks,* let him speak, *as it were, the utterances of God; whoever serves,* let him do so *as by the strength which God supplies; so that in all things God may be glorified through Jesus Christ, to whom belongs the glory and dominion forever and ever. Amen.*

Whoever speaks, *let him speak,* as it were, the utterances of God -- Peter is now giving examples of the proper use of gracious gifts which Christians received. "Speaking" is one example. "Serving" is another. As Christians serve one another, they may help in word or in deed. Whether or not the speaking is inspired speaking depends much on the place where the speaking took place, and it is difficult to decide whether Peter had speaking in an assembly in view (as Paul did in 1 Corinthians 14:26-36) or whether it is speaking outside the assembly,

---

50 The proper use of the supernatural spiritual gifts is the topic of 1 Corinthians 12-14. A Special Study entitled "Gifts of the Spirit" is included at the close of comments on chapter 4. It supplements what is included in a Special Study in the author's *Commentary on Acts* on "The Person and Work of the Holy Spirit."

51 The root word in *diakonountes* is often translated "deacon" or "minister," but the reference here is broader than just to the function of deacons. "Serving" (or "ministering," ASV) pictures the proper attitude and action when Christians exercise their gifts. The proper attitude is that this gift was not given to me for my benefit; rather, it is for your benefit, and I will serve you as best I can.

52 Cp. "grace" at 1 Peter 1:2,10,13.

in private conversation or perhaps even in ministering to the sick.[53] "Utterances" (*logia*) is a word with a kind of divine connotation when used in religious contexts. Gentiles used it for the oracles which came to them from their gods. Christians used it for the words of Scripture.[54] If a Christian opens his mouth to speak, to impart a helpful word, he should be speaking "as the utterances of God" – sharing God's word, governed by the pertinent things that God has said.

Whoever serves, *let him do so* as by the strength which God supplies -- As indicated in earlier notes, this is a second example of the proper use of any "special gift" which the Christian has received. "Serves", the same word used in verse 10, speaks of practical deeds of Christian service, mutual ministry. This is a timely reminder that Christian service is to be rendered in a spirit of humility and an awareness of divine enablement. The one serving must avoid any conceit that the strength and ability to perform the service are his own. "God" is put at the end of the clause for emphasis. *God* is the One who has supplied the needed strength and means to do the service (cp. Philippians 2:13). How foolish to forget or ignore His lavish generosity![55]

So that in all things God may be glorified through Jesus Christ -- Now Peter is talking about the goal of our sound judgment, our loving, and our good stewardship of God's gifts in speaking and serving. That goal is that God will be glorified. "Glorified" might speak of praise being offered to Him. It might mean He is well thought of, that His value grows in people's estimation. Whether it is the person who is doing the service or the person who benefits from it who gives God glory is not easy to decide. *En pasin* could be "in all of you" (masculine) or "in all things" (neuter). Our translators have taken it as neuter and as catching up all that has been written in this paragraph, whether speaking or ministering or showing hospitality or extending your love. "Through Jesus Christ" may be intended as a reminder that only folk who remain faithful to Jesus Christ will bring glory to God.[56] A new grace and glory would enter the church if Jesus' people ceased doing things just for themselves, and did them instead so that God would be glorified.

To whom belongs the glory and dominion forever and ever. Amen. -- Commentators are divided when it comes to identifying the antecedent of "to whom." Jesus Christ is the nearer

---

[53] If speaking in an assembly, then it might be inspired speaking. If it is private conversation, then it is doubtful such speaking would be inspired. When not even all the words that came from an apostle's mouth were inspired, we would hardly think that any private conversation (by ordinary Christians) was inspired.

[54] In Acts 7:38 it is used of the Law given through Moses. In Romans 3:2 it refers to the Hebrew scriptures, and in Hebrews 5:12 to the word of God. Some English versions use "oracles" – a message from a deity, a divine utterance – to capture the flavor of the Greek word.

[55] The word translated "supplies" (*choregei*) was used in classical Greek of supplying the expenses of a chorus at a Greek drama. It took a grand donation, lavish generosity, to cover such the expenses. So the word came to have the connotation of liberal giving in general. God gives liberally!

[56] Cp. 1 Peter 1:21, 2:5, 3:18.

antecedent. God, the subject of this whole sentence, is the farther antecedent. Therefore, either may be the One whom Peter is describing. Perhaps he is reminding us of Jesus' exalted position to show how glory can redound to God through Him.[57] Perhaps Peter is giving a reason why God should be glorified in all things. "The glory[58] and the dominion"[59] – there is a definite article before both nouns in the Greek – are separate and distinct prerogatives that rightly belong to God. Since these prerogatives belong to Him "forever and ever,"[60] men, as they attempt to serve Him, should not usurp them. "Amen" is a transliteration of a Hebrew word that means "So let it be!" Peter is expressing his own approval on what the Spirit has just prompted him to write.[61]

B. An Exhortation Concerning Inner Attitudes If You Are Called on to Suffer. 4:12-19

4:12 -- ***Beloved, do not be surprised at the fiery ordeal among you, which comes upon you for your testing, as though some strange thing were happening to you;***

Beloved -- This is the second time Peter has used this word (see 2:11). We think it calls attention to the fact that God loves them, as much as it calls attention to the fact that Peter loves them. With this word ringing in their ears, they should never be tempted to think that the fiery ordeal they are experiencing was evidence God no longer loved them. This paragraph instructs Christians concerning their inner attitudes and thoughts as they are called on to suffer for righteousness' sake. While Jewish people for years had experienced persecution for their religion, for Peter's readers, who grew up as Gentiles, facing persecution for religion was a new experience. Peter will try to help them keep from "losing their heads"

---

57 Some interpreters have a low view of Jesus, and bristle at the idea Peter might be ascribing divine glory to Christ. Yet the Bible plainly shows Jesus is God (Hebrews 1:1-3; Romans 9:5), equal with the Father ("Jehovah" is used both of Father and Son), and divine glory is ascribed to Jesus (Hebrews 13:20,21; 2 Peter 3:18; Revelation 1:6). Thus there would be nothing incongruous if here in verse 11 Peter also ascribes divine glory to Christ.

58 "Glory" here may be the right to receive praise and words of appreciation and blessing.

59 The right to be held in highest esteem, the right to exercise sovereign rule over all.

60 Literally, "unto the ages of the ages." This expanded form of "forever" occurs 21 times in the New Testament and is the strongest way to express the thought of "eternity." It pictures eternity as a series of ages flowing on endlessly.

61 In passages that are doxologies (a word of praise to God), the "amen" was a signal for the Christians to respond at these places when the Scriptures were read out loud in the public assemblies. We hesitate to call this phrase at the close of verse 11 a doxology since doxologies are usually prayers urging that praise be given. In most doxologies (e.g., Romans 11:36, 16:27) the verb is not stated but only implied. In this case the verb (*estin*, "is," or "belongs" as per NASB) is stated and is indicative (a statement of fact) rather than subjunctive (a prayer or a wish) in mood.

(verse 7) by emphasizing certain great principles to keep in mind when one is being persecuted for his faith.

Do not be surprised at the fiery ordeal among you -- The present imperative with *me* prohibits the continuance of an action already going on. "Stop being surprised (astonished)!" is what Peter commands.[62] Persecution is not something strange or unusual for a Christian. This is Principle #1. Christianity does not provide immunity from a "fiery ordeal." *Purosis* is used in Proverbs 27:21 of a smelting furnace where gold is refined. The only other place in the New Testament where this word appears is Revelation 18:9,18, where it refers to the burning of Babylon. We think it very likely that Peter refers to what happened to Christians in the Neronian persecutions after the burning of Rome in AD 64. Christians were nightly burned as torches in the emperor's gardens. Peter, in Rome, warns his readers that this violence is spreading to the provinces in which they live and may involve them. "Among you" says some of them (but not everyone) may well experience the pain caused by exposure to literal fire as they are persecuted for their faith.

Which comes upon you for your testing -- *Peirasmos* can be translated either test or tempt.[63] Here we learn two more principles about facing persecution. Principle #2: Persecution may be a source of testing, acting like a refiner's fire to see if a man's faith is genuine. A man's devotion to any cause or belief can be measured by his willingness to suffer and to sacrifice for it. Principle #3: Persecution may be a source of temptation. The devil will use the persecution as an occasion to tempt the Christian to quit Christ.

As though some strange thing were happening to you -- The compound verb, made up of *sun + baino*, pictures the fiery ordeal as an undesired companion on their journey. So Peter provides Principle #4: Persecution and suffering didn't just happen. A loving heavenly Father permits them for our good. God works all things together for the spiritual good of those who love Him (Romans 8:28), and Jesus Christ as Lord is also actively ruling and overruling the Christian's experiences. Unless they understand it as a purifying process going on in their lives, they may well regard persecution as foreign to their acceptance of salvation in Christ.

4:13 -- ***But to the degree that you share the sufferings of Christ, keep on rejoicing; so that also at the revelation of His glory, you may rejoice with exultation.***

But ... keep on rejoicing -- Instead of thinking some strange thing is happening, rejoice! Peter insists that instead of letting persecution cause bewilderment, the proper response is an attitude of rejoicing. Peter is speaking from experience (Acts 5:41), and he is repeating what Jesus taught (Matthew 5:11,12).

---

[62] We've had the word "surprised" at 1 Peter 4:4. It means something thought to be foreign and therefore the unexpected has happened.

[63] The translator of James 1:12 faces a difficult decision whether to translate *peirasmos* at that place as "test (trial)" or "temptation."

To the degree that you share the sufferings of Christ -- The idea apparently, as it was in 2:19-25, is that the readers as followers of Christ may suffer in some of the same ways Jesus did.[64] If they are despised and ridiculed, they can remember that so was Christ (recall the crown of thorns, the purple robe, the cruel jests). If they are crucified for their faith, they are bearing a cross like Jesus bore. *Katho* is an adverb of degree suggesting that degrees will vary as far as the fiery ordeal among them is concerned. Some will be struck fully, fearfully; others will be affected less.

So that also at the revelation of His glory -- "Revelation" here is likely a reference to the second coming of Christ. When Jesus returns His glorified body will be glowing and shining like it did for a few moments at the transfiguration and like it does now since His resurrection. He will be surrounded by a brilliant sphere of light – the Shekinah – as He returns on the clouds of heaven. A better resurrection was in prospect for those who, when persecuted, are faithful unto death. But for those who prove to be unfaithful, the day of the revelation of Christ will be a day of terror.

You may rejoice with exultation -- *Agalliaō* means leaping for joy, jubilating, skipping and bubbling over with shouts of delight.[65] The Greek word is onomatopoetic. It is not a single isolated response, but a continuous activity. Perhaps it speaks of the joy Christians feel when they see their Savior and King returning on the clouds of heaven. Perhaps it speaks of the time of judgment and the joy that the man will feel when in the presence of assembled multitudes he hears the words, "Well done! You are a good servant! How pleased your Lord is with you!" This is Principle #5: The way of the cross leads home! If we suffer with Him, we will be glorified with Him (Romans 8:17). If we suffer with Him, we shall reign with Him (2 Timothy 3:11).

4:14 -- *If you are reviled for the name of Christ, you are blessed, because the Spirit of glory and of God rests upon you.*

If you are reviled for the name of Christ -- Having pictured the shouts of delight from the redeemed when Christ returns, Peter now offers guidance for the painful present. "If you are reviled" says not everyone will be so reviled, but most will be. "Reviled" means that one has verbal insults heaped upon him, rather than physical. Verbal abuse, slander, defamation of character, ridicule, all may be hurled against the readers continuously. Why? Simply because they confess the name of Christ in word and deed.

You are blessed -- *Makarioi*, the same word Jesus used at Matthew 5:11,12, means more than happy; it means spiritually prosperous. There is a state of bliss already existing, though it cannot be seen with the naked eye.

---

[64] It has also been explained that the hatred shown to Christians is in reality directed toward Jesus.

[65] Peter has used the word before at 1:6,8.

Because the Spirit of glory and of God rests upon you -- There is a manuscript variation here,[66] and translators are challenged even after they tentatively decide on one reading over against another. The text upon which the NASB is based reads *hoti to tes doxes kai to tou theou pneuma eph' humas anapauetai.*[67] It can be seen that each genitive modifier has a neuter article in front of it, and that the two genitives "of glory" and "of God" are in the attributive position between the article "the" and the noun "Spirit." By writing in this order, and by repeating the article before each genitive, what Peter is doing is highlighting two distinct characteristics of the Holy Spirit – namely, He has something to do with glory, and He functions as God the Father wishes! Peter seems to be describing one of the functions of the indwelling gift of the Holy Spirit. We speak of "Holy Spirit" because "Spirit of God" is a common designation for the third person of the Godhead. Perhaps He is called "Spirit of glory" because He is an earnest of the glory yet to be revealed to the Christians (cp. Ephesians 1:13,14); think also of the glory the redeemed bask in (Revelation 21 and 22). Perhaps He is called "Spirit of glory" because when Christians are falsely accused by authorities, something happens to their visage similar to what happened to Stephen (Acts 6:15). Could that angelic glow be the work of the Spirit of glory? "Rests upon you" is a word from the world of agriculture.[68] The farmer rested his land by sowing light crops, by rotating his crops, giving the land a chance to recuperate. When Peter says the Holy Spirit "rests upon you," he is promising that they would not be forsaken when they were being reviled. You can expect the Holy Spirit to abide with you and help you recuperate from your verbal abuse.

4:15 -- ***By no means let any of you suffer as a murderer, or thief, or evil-doer, or a troublesome meddler;***

By no means let any of you suffer -- Christians may be reviled for the name of Christ; they may share the sufferings of Christ when they have committed no crime. In such cases they were blessed, and had exuberant joy awaiting them. But there was no blessing inherent in suffering punishment when they had committed a crime. "Let not any one of you" makes this prohibition individual. Each person is responsible to make sure he or she commits no crimes.

---

[66] The variations are well represented in our English translations. The RSV has "because the spirit of glory and of power and of God rests on you." Phillips has "for you can be sure that God's Spirit of Glory is resting on you." NEB offers, "Because then that glorious Spirit which is the Spirit of God is resting on you." ASV has "because the *Spirit* of glory and the Spirit of God resteth upon you." (As the italics in the ASV show, the word "Spirit" occurs only once in the Nestle Greek text, and the word "glory" is in the genitive case.)

[67] Some manuscripts, as the KJV shows, add another clause to this verse. It reads "On their part He is evil spoken of, but on your part He is glorified." Most modern textual critics reject these added words as being a gloss since they do not appear in the best Greek exemplars. Pulpit Commentary finds that what is included in the gloss is true, even if the words are not part of Peter's original text. Among the men of the world, the Holy Spirit is evil spoken of. Those who revile the Christians are really blaspheming the Holy Spirit by whom the Christians were guided and strengthened. The Holy Spirit was glorified by the honor done to Him in the patience the Christians displayed in their trials.

[68] Jesus used the word when He offered His great invitation, "Come unto me, all who are weary heavy-laden, and I will give you rest" (Matthew 11:28). Literally, it reads, 'I will rest upon you.'

As a murderer -- Peter now lists four crimes the state regularly punished. The first one he specifies is premeditated murder, with malice aforethought. Premeditated murder is here proscribed in terms as specific as thundered from Mt. Sinai ("You shall not commit murder!")

Or thief -- Such things as shoplifting, embezzlement, pilfering tools and supplies from one's place of work, stealing clothes and money from the locker rooms at the gym, would be included in this prohibition. "Stealing" is as wrong under the New Covenant as it was under the Old.

Or evil-doer -- The Greek word, *kakopoios*, is sometimes translated malefactor, or revolutionary, or terrorist. Bad actor ("a doer of what is base," *kakos*) covers many other crimes besides insurrection.[69]

Or a troublesome meddler -- *Allotriepiskopos* is evidently a word coined by Peter since it has not been found in writings before Peter's time but has been found in writings after Peter's time. It is a compound of *allotrios* ("belonging to another, alien or foreign to oneself, not of one's own family") and *episkopos* ("overseer, superintendent"). Some suppose the crime alluded to was that of being an unfaithful guardian of goods committed to them by others for safekeeping, i.e., being covetous enough to appropriate those goods for personal use. Another writer offers the suggestion that what is prohibited is the Christian's entering into illegal money-making and money-laundering schemes. A third suggestion is that the term is Peter's designation of political agitators. At the very time Peter wrote, the zealots were very active trying to overthrow the established Roman government. Peter here cautions his readers against getting involved in political opposition movements that would subject them to efforts by the authorities to squelch them. Make sure you are not doing what Nero has falsely accused the Christians of doing against Rome.

4:16 -- ***But if*** **anyone suffers** ***as a Christian, let him not feel ashamed, but in that name let him glorify God.***

But if ***anyone suffers*** **as a Christian** -- To "suffer" for being a criminal (verse 15) meant to be punished by the government. To "suffer" for being a Christian likewise means to be punished by the government. Peter is talking about his readers being persecuted because of their religion, because they belong to Christ.[70] In Peter's time, his readers were not suffering

---

[69] See notes on "evil-doer" at 2:12,14 (and 3:16 in some manuscripts and versions).

[70] Wuest (*op. cit.*, p.121) offers this interesting explanation of word formation. "The word for Caesar is *Kaisar.* Those who worshiped the *Kaisar* were called *Kaisarianos*. The word for Christ is *Christos.* He who worshiped Christ is called *Christianios*." In English "-ian" added to a noun shows possession. Compare Flag of Canada and the Canadian Flag. In the author's *Commentary on Acts*, it shown that the name "Christian" was divinely given to Christ's disciples by Paul and Barnabas (Acts 11:26). If it was a name given by inspiration, and if Peter used the name "Christian" with approval, how can some say that it was only a nick-name (originally given in derision by enemies of the church) until the time of Ignatius?

just for the name itself (as was true a generation later in Trajan's persecution[71]) but for believing and living as Jesus Christ Himself taught His disciples to do.

Let him not feel ashamed -- Did Peter recall the night he was ashamed of Jesus? A man should be ashamed only of the wrong he has done. One who suffers as a murderer or as an evil-doer should feel shame, but there is no cause for shame in suffering because one is a follower of Christ. Peter urges the brethren not to be ashamed of their religion so as to refuse to suffer for it.

But in that name let him glorify God -- "Glorify God" here, as in 1 Corinthians 10:31-33, is done by a thoughtful, edifying, winning approach to our neighbor. Instead of letting a feeling of shame silence him or paralyze him into inaction, the Christian has an opportunity to bring honor to God while he is being persecuted for being a follower of Jesus.[72] Peter says, Do it! Seize the opportunity!

4:17 -- ***For*** **it is** ***time for judgment to begin with the household of God; and if*** **it begins** ***with us first, what*** **will be** ***the outcome for those who do not obey the gospel of God?***

For *it is* time for judgment to begin with the household of God -- Peter fortifies his exhortation by giving a reason why his readers should glorify God while they are being persecuted. These persecutions are a divinely permitted purging of the believers. The italicized words at the beginning of this verse in the NASB indicate there is no verb in the Greek. All Peter wrote is "time ... to begin." That is, this is now to be expected. There is reason to believe it will begin shortly. It is the season for it. "Judgment" here seems to refer to the persecution the readers are being warned about. *Krima* ("judgment") is used of the decision passed on the faults or crimes of another, and in a forensic sense it is used of the sentence passed by a judge. It is often used of a sentence passed by God as the judge, and in that light we speak of the persecutions being divinely permitted. This preliminary judgment through which the readers are passing is a preview of how things will be at the final judgment. God's judgments begin with the church ("the household of God"[73]) and from the church spread to the unsaved.

And if *it begins* with us first -- Peter expected Christians ("us," he writes) to be judged before God finally judges the wicked. Even the Old Testament taught that the sanctuary was the proper place for God's judgment to begin.

---

[71] Pliny, writing later, speaks of a punishment because of "the name itself" (i.e., "Are you a Christian?"). Peter has been giving instructions (see the hortatory sections of this letter) about how his readers were to live, day in and day out, not just the name they wore. They were to go about living consistent Christian lives without being intimidated by the threat of possible persecution.

[72] Some manuscripts read "in this behalf" or "on this part" and the KJV follows this reading. The NASB follows the better reading, "in that name," i.e., the name "Christian."

[73] The "household of God" is not the temple nor the Jewish nation. This expression is explained in the next clause to mean the church, "us" Christians.

What *will be* the outcome for those who do not obey the gospel of God? -- The fiery ordeal through which believers were going was terrible, but the "end" that awaits unbelievers is beyond imagination. If God permits such trials upon us who have obeyed the gospel of God,[74] what will be the punishment of those who have not obeyed[75] and whose sins have never been forgiven? The temporal judgments which God permits upon His own people make it certain the wicked will be punished. The punishment of the wicked is merely delayed.

4:18 -- AND IF IT IS WITH DIFFICULTY THAT THE RIGHTEOUS IS SAVED, WHAT WILL BECOME OF THE GODLESS MAN AND THE SINNER?

AND IF IT IS WITH DIFFICULTY THAT THE RIGHTEOUS IS SAVED -- Using the language of the LXX of Proverbs 11:31,[76] Peter continues unfolding the reason his readers as they are called on to suffer for being a Christian should glorify God (verse 16). In Peter's application of Proverbs, his Christian readers would be "the righteous," i.e., living in harmony with the laws of God.[77] In what sense can we say that people already identified as "righteous" are "saved" by the suffering they endure? Only in that it proves their faith, strengthens them, and makes them pure.[78] Where the NASB reads "with difficulty," the KJV has "scarcely." The same Greek word, *molis*, occurs in Acts 14:18 where Paul and Barnabas "with difficulty" restrained the people from offering sacrifice to them as gods. Christians are saved "with difficulty" in the sense that it was necessary for God to purify the lives of the saints by drastic actions, namely, persecution and suffering.

WHAT WILL BECOME OF THE GODLESS MAN AND THE SINNER? -- If the righteous require these judgments, how much more do the unrighteous receive punitive judgments from God? A "godless man" is one who is devoid of reverence for Him, impious in attitude and conduct. The "sinner" is one who regularly violates the standards in God's law, and has never had his sins covered by the blood of Christ. Instead of "what will become of" the ASV reads "where shall [he] appear?" If the righteous man must be disciplined to fit him for heaven, how could an unrighteous man who has never been disciplined be fitted? When the unrighteous stand in the final judgment, what hope of salvation do they have? None

---

[74] "Of God" is in the attributive position in the Greek, and this stresses that the good news is by its very nature *God's*, sent by Him as His authoritative message of salvation to mankind. It is *God* with whom these people are at cross-purposes!

[75] There has been a pronounced emphasis on "obedience" in 1 Peter (e.g., 1 Peter 1:2,14). Everywhere in the New Testament, including Romans, we learn that the "faith" which is a condition of salvation is an obedient faith!

[76] The LXX reads considerably different from the Hebrew, which is accurately represented by the KJV, "Behold, the righteous shall be recompensed in the earth; much more the wicked and the sinner." The righteous shall be requited in the earth; that is, chastened for their transgressions.

[77] See the word "righteous" at 1 Peter 3:12.

[78] Remember what was written in 4:1-6 about the purifying effect of suffering.

at all! So, using a passage from Proverbs, Peter has explained in Biblical language what God is trying to accomplish in the lives of his readers. Certainly they are not going to frustrate the kindness and goodness of God by refusing to glorify Him when they have a chance, are they?

4:19 -- *Therefore, let those also who suffer according to the will of God entrust their souls to a faithful Creator in doing what is right.*

Therefore -- The word is *hoste*, "as a result." Peter closes this exhortation by making a specific application of all that has been said. If God, in His providence, sees we need the purifying benefits that can accrue from enduring persecution and suffering, then let us commit the keeping of our souls to Him! If the sufferings of Christians as Christians are a sign of God's favor, if He is trying to help them lest they perish with the ungodly world, then they have every reason to trust Him, and to continue in their well-doing.

Let those also who suffer according to the will of God -- "Suffer" is a present participle, meaning to continue to suffer, to suffer at any time, be it now or in the future. The precise connection of "also" is somewhat uncertain. It may be related to the imperative, "Let those entrust ...." Peter earlier admonished his readers to "glorify God" when they suffer (verse 16). Now ("also") he adds the thought they are to trust God while suffering. It may be that "also" is related to "those who suffer." Lenski thinks Peter meant that not all will suffer, but those who do suffer should do this further thing, "entrust their souls ...."[79] "According to the will of God" emphasizes once more the idea that things don't just happen in our world. God in His providence[80] is still in control.

Entrust their souls to a faithful Creator -- If these persecutions are allowed by God in His providence to come to the towns and provinces where the readers live, if they are designed to help purify and save the readers (and that is what the Bible says), then the Christians have every reason to trust their souls[81] to Him. "Entrust," or "commit," (*paratithesthosan*) is a banking term, used of depositing money with a trusted friend for safekeeping. It is the term used by Jesus on the cross when He said "Father, into Thy hands I *commit* My spirit" (Luke 23:46). Peter recalls one of those "Great Days with Jesus" as he commends the example of Jesus to his readers. They can trust the Father just like Jesus did (1 Peter 2:23), and with the same positive outcome in the end. God is characterized as a "faithful Creator." He didn't create us with the intent that we always be miserable and hurting. So, if we commit our souls to Him and do His will, He who made us will faithfully take care of us (cp. Romans 8:28).

---

[79] Lenski, *op. cit.*, p.213.

[80] Providence has been defined as "the care, preservation, and government that God exercises over His creation so that it accomplishes the purposes for which He made it."

[81] See notes at 1:9 on "souls."

In doing what is right -- Peter probably means they should trust God while at the same time continuing to do what is right. The Christian's business was always to do what God had said was right.[82] The result was then to be left with God. Surrendering to the will of God is joined, not by careless indolence, but with the active practice of good. Trusting God and doing well must be indissolubly united.

---

[82] See what Peter has already written about continuing to do right, 2:14,15,20; 3:13,14,17; and 4:2,8-11, 16. This phrase about "doing what is right" should not be understood to mean that the "depositing" was done *by* our well-doing (the Roman Catholic interpretation).

Special Study #1

GIFTS OF THE SPIRIT[1]

INTRODUCTION

A. Why preach a message on this topic?
   1. It is part of the series of messages on 1 Corinthians being preached to this men's fellowship.
   2. Why me? Perhaps our host preacher looked around for someone who had studied this material, and who was also not smart enough to know you can't cover all about this topic in one 30-minute sermon. And he found one!

B. Let me set the stage for this message by showing the relevance of the topic.
   1. We are hearing much more about the "gifts of the Spirit" than we used to.
      a. "Gift theology" (C. Peter Wagner's term) is exploding in the market place. Before 1965, little was written on the "gifts of the Spirit." In fact, 80% of all the books on the subject have been written since 1970. The publishers' have found a topic that will sell books, and every publisher (it seems) has rushed a book to the market. People read them and it fuels the interest in "gifts."
      b. Perhaps we hear more about "gifts of the Spirit" than we used to because of the pervasive influence of the Charismatic Movement. They get a lot of attention when they talk about the "gifts of the Spirit," while no one comes to hear me preach (I feel). Maybe I need to use the topic of "gifts" to get people's attention and allegiance.
      c. Whatever the reason, the topic is one people are talking more about.

   2. The Charismatic Movement did not invent the expression "gifts of the Spirit." It was in the Bible all the time.
      a. But when we non-Charismatics and non-Pentecostals came to these verses, we just skipped over them because we supposed they could not be understood.
      b. Along came the Charismatic Movement, with their anecdotes based on peculiar definitions and explanations of the "gifts" (some of which were just not right), and with their amazing numerical growth.
      c. When our people went to the Charismatics out of curiosity (or because we had not been meeting their needs), and came back to us for an explanation of what they had seen and heard, we were at a loss to give them any Biblical directions.
      d. Without Biblical directions to guide them, folk just assumed what they were seeing and hearing from the charismatics must be true.

   3. There is also a non-theology, which reads the Scriptures but deems an experience of the "gifts" as more important, that has arisen in our time.
      a. Experience of the gifts is deemed of more importance than Scripture – yet the non-theologians still want to use the Biblical language and will try to tie their experience to

---

[1] This study was first prepared and delivered as a sermon to an area men's fellowship held at Knob Noster, MO, October 26, 1984. The footnotes included in this study were not part of the original sermon.

Scripture to give the facade that the experience is Biblical. As a result we are bombarded with doubletalk.

At the "Jesus '79" program, a Protestant speaker compared the Charismatic Movement with the older ecumenical movement. The older ecumenical movement pushed aside Biblical doctrines in an effort to create unity, she affirmed. In the Charismatic Movement, by contrast, she insisted, the "unity" based on a shared experience (of baptism in the Holy Spirit) has "a more solid Scriptural basis." On the same program was Leon Joseph Cardinal Suenens, a Roman Catholic charged by the Vatican to oversee the charismatic renewal movement in the Catholic Church. He was present to make sure there would be no pushing aside of cherished Catholic dogmas for the sake of unity among those Catholics who had "experienced the gifts of the Spirit." (*Christianity Today*, June 29, 1979, p. 43)

b. Does the Scripture have nothing to say to such doctrinally divergent participants? Is the experience all that matters?

4. So the topic surely is relevant, and you are to be commended for showing the mental discipline to want to understand this matter better.

C. A word of caution. My homiletics teacher said, "A good sermon ought not to leave questions in the hearer's mind that were not there before the message began!"

1. Well, this is a topic that could do just that if we don't roll up the sleeves of our minds and prepare for some serious meditation and study of the Word of God.
2. Someone may ask, "Won't you just create confusion in the minds of your hearers? Wouldn't it be better not to discuss this at all?"
3. My answer is "No! It is not better to fail to discuss it!" For these reasons:
   a. If the Holy Spirit saw fit to speak about these gifts in such detail that it takes over 4 chapters in the New Testament to tell about them, they must be important!
   b. Since these gifts were given to the church, if I (as a member of the Restoration Movement) want the church to be like the church I read about in the Bible, what the New Testament says about the gifts is important.
   c. Where there is so much erroneous "gift theology" and "non-theology" going around, I must know how to correct folk in error. Aquila and Priscilla's correction of Apollos in Acts 19 is my model.
4. Indeed, it is true that this topic is one church people did not talk about when I was growing up.
   a. Did not the churches get along without the "gifts," or talking about them, then? Can't we still get along without talking about them?
   b. Or, did folk have them and we called them by another name?
   c. Or, maybe the churches limped along – with many of us members inert – while a few tried to make up for the lack of involvement in body life by the rest of us!

I remember back in the early years of my ministry, we tried to get every convert involved somewhere in congregational life, so we wouldn't lose them. We preachers spent much of our time trying to "give them a job to do." (The Disciples of Christ even came up with the idea of "junior board members" to give the new converts a taste of what it was to run a church. Immediately after being immersed they were asked to sit in on church board meetings, and often had a voice as influential as the voice of the long-time elders. It didn't always work!) Maybe we were trying to give people jobs they weren't suited for. Maybe we were trying to force square pegs into round holes.

d. Is it possible that our attention was not directed to the verses we needed in those years gone by (verses we'd been ignoring) to help solve a problem?

D. This is not an easy topic.
1. Many verses and ideas must be collected, collated, and explained.
2. It is my customary way, as I attempt to understand what the Bible says on any subject, to put together all the verses on the subject, and see what they teach. Whatever all the verses teach becomes my belief and practice. That is what we have tried to do on this topic.
3. We may be a little longer on this message than 30 minutes, but we hope to be helpful, and not leave you asking more questions when we are finished than you were asking before we started.
4. Some of what we say may be "new" to many of us, but, if it is, we hope at least to stimulate further study on your part.

E. *SCRIPTURE MUST BE ELEVATED ABOVE EXPERIENCE!* This is absolutely fundamental!
1. We learn this guideline from Peter, who treated Scripture as a more sure proof of who Jesus was than his own personal experience on the Mount of Transfiguration (2 Peter 1:19).
2. This message is a call back to the Word of God as the foundation and building material for all our beliefs and practice.

   Scripture – all the verses on the topic – must be the basis for our beliefs. We must be absolutely sure that what we teach and believe about the "gifts of the Spirit" is what results from a study of all the pertinent verses.

3. There is so much being written, believed, and taught about the "gifts of the Spirit" these days that is based on experience rather than on the Word. It is subjectivism – teaching and belief founded on personal experience.
   a. So much of what is written is based on *experience* that we now find many teachers and preachers suggesting we can get along quite well without any real contact with the Scripture.

      C. Peter Wagner, Fuller Theological Seminary, as he presents his version of "gift theology," downgrades objective understanding of the Scripture, making the Bible second to one's own personal experiences! He tells churches not to be concerned about their position on the "gifts." He tells them not to worry about examining in the light of Scripture what is happening in their church.

   b. If the Bible does not have absolute authority in our belief and practice, then absolute authority is placed in man.

      One young man said, "You can't deny my experience!" I was not trying to deny his experience, but I was denying that it was Scriptural! Not all have seen the difference.

4. If my experience (subjectivism) closes the door to a search of the Scriptures (objectivism), then I have denied the authority of God's Word in my life! That is a serious denial, with eternal repercussions!

5. If we are to stand with those who historically lived and died for the Word of God, we must choose the objective approach to faith and practice, and found our beliefs on Scripture.
   a. Acts 17:11 – to study the Word to examine if something is true is a noble thing.
   b. 1 Thessalonians 5:19-21 – to test and prove what claims to be from the Spirit is proper.
6. The test of what is or is not of God is Scripture, not our experiences!

PROPOSITION: We shall try as succinctly as possible to summarize what the Bible says about "Gifts of the Spirit" and to make application to our own lives. To accomplish this we shall:

1) Define terms, so we all understand the scope and nature of the topic we are covering;
2) Learn Biblical attitudes about "gifts of the Spirit" and compare our own attitudes to see if they are Biblical;
3) Get acquainted with the temporary gifts of the Spirit; and
4) Encourage development and use of the permanent gifts of the Spirit.

I. DEFINITION OF TERMS

A. We must distinguish between the "Gift" and the "Gifts."

1. The "gift of the Holy Spirit" is something every Christian receives at baptism (Acts 2:38).

   The resulting indwelling Spirit helps Christians to live the Christian life – practice self-control, quench temptations, helps in answered prayer, etc. (Romans 8)

2. The "gifts of the Spirit" – sometimes called "spiritual gifts" – were abilities or tasks or "tools" given to Christians to help others in the congregation. (1 Corinthians 12-14)

   The "gift" is related to helping the Christian himself. The "gifts" are related to helping other members of the body of Christ.

B. Where do we read about the gifts (or gifted men)?

1. 1 Corinthians 12:8-12
   a. the word of wisdom
   b. the word of knowledge
   c. faith
   d. gifts of healing
   e. effecting of miracles
   f. prophecy
   g. distinguishing of spirits
   h. tongues
   i. interpretation of tongues

2. 1 Corinthians 12:28
   a. apostles
   b. prophets
   c. teachers
   d. miracles
   e. healings
   f. helps
   g. governments
   h. tongues
   i. interpretation of tongues

3. Ephesians 4:11
   a. apostles
   b. prophets
   c. evangelists
   d. pastoring teachers

4. Romans 12:6-8
   a. prophecy
   b. ministry
   c. teaching
   d. exhorting
   e. giving
   f. ruling
   g. showing mercy

5. 1 Peter 4:10, 11
   a. speaking
   b. serving

(The listings somewhat overlap -- and can be reduced to about 20 different "gifts.")

C. Categories from which these 20 gifts may be viewed.

1 J. Oswald Sanders wrote of gifts that have to do with the ministry of the Word, and gifts that equip their possessors to render service of a practical nature.

> The gifts of the Spirit may be classified roughly as follows: (a) Gifts which qualify their possessors for the ministry of the Word: apostleship, prophecy, teaching, shepherding, evangelism, knowledge and wisdom, kinds of tongues, interpretation of tongues, discerning of spirits. (b) Gifts which equip their possessors to render services of a practical nature: miracles, healing, administration, ruling, helps. (*Holy Spirit and His Gifts*, p.110)

2. J. Dwight Pentecost wrote of temporary and permanent gifts.

> The Word of God recognized two kinds of gifts: permanent and temporary. Some gifts were designed to operate as long as the church has its existence upon the earth; others were designed to be temporary in duration. If one puts emphasis upon that which was divinely designed to be temporary, and seeks to make those temporary gifts the norm for spirituality in a day when they do not operate, he will be led into disillusionment and to some fleshly excess which manifests a pseudo-spirituality (*The Divine Comforter*, p.166).

3 Standard Pentecostal/Charismatic doctrine is that all gifts were intended to be permanent for the whole church age. But the Bible distinctly shows some were intended to be but temporary! There may be a difference of opinion as to how long the "temporary" was, but that some were temporary cannot be gainsaid!

D. When are the gifts received, and how?

1. It is the thesis of this message that the temporary gifts of the Spirit were by the apostles through the baptism of the Holy Spirit, and after that were received by some church members by the laying on of an apostle's hands.

2. It is also my (hesitatingly held) conviction that the permanent gifts of the Spirit are received at baptism. 1 Corinthians 12:13 says "all were made to drink of one Spirit" at the time of their baptism. The gifts may not show up immediately after conversion, but they are latent within us, as are natural talents and gifts at our physical birth.

3. If these theses are correct, then several things follow:
   a. The spiritual gifts differ from natural talents (the abilities men are born with) – musical, or non-musical, for example.
   b. The spiritual gifts differ from the fruit of the spirit. The list in Galatians 5:22, 23 – love, joy, peace, etc. – does not match the listings of "spiritual gifts" given earlier in this message. Furthermore, much can be said that "spirit" in Galatians 5:22 is the human spirit that is alive as a result of God's way of saving man (Romans 8: 10), not the Holy Spirit (though "Spirit" is capitalized in many of our English versions at Galatians 5:22).
   c. Likely each Christian (usually) receives but one of the permanent gifts. Had you lived in the days of the apostles, and had hands laid on you, you might have had two or more gifts – one temporary and one permanent.
   d. If some gifts were temporary (because they were received through the laying on of an apostle's hands), then any class on "discovering your spiritual gifts" that would cause a contemporary Christian to seek one of the temporary gifts would be totally out of place.
   e. To have one of the spiritual gifts would not necessarily prove that a man was "spiritual." The Corinthians came behind no other congregation in the matter of spiritual gifts (1 Corinthians 1:7), yet Paul writes (1 Corinthians 3:1-3) that he could not talk to them as "spiritual." Instead he had to treat them as carnal. The gifts were many at Corinth, but they did not guarantee "spiritual" lives.

II. WHAT THE BIBLE SAYS ABOUT OUR ATTITUDES TOWARD GIFTS OF THE SPIRIT.

A. An Attitude of **Superiority** is to be Eschewed!

1. The gifts are God-given – not something *I* have achieved by my own efforts!

   1 Corinthians 12:11, the Holy Spirit divides to each man as He wills.
   1 Corinthians 12:18, God has set the members in the body as it pleased Him.
   1 Corinthians 12:28, God has set some in the church ... apostles, prophets ...
   1 Corinthians 12:4-6, all the gifts radiate from the Spirit, God.

   > Spiritual gifts are not to be sought by men. A man does not receive a spiritual gift because he prayed for it, because he sought it, coveted it, trained for it. Spiritual gifts are a sovereign bestowal apart from the will or the inclination of the individual. The recognition of that fact immediately dispels a great deal of the excess and abuse attached to false teaching on spiritual gifts. (Pentecost, *op. cit.,* p. 169)

2. There is no room for spiritual pride -- either in the Charismatic Movement, or on our parts!
   a. There obviously is a gradation of gifts -- some more important than others. But all are necessary to the body!

      Ronald E. Baxter, *Gifts of the Spirit* (Chicago: Kregel, 1983) has written (p.58-59):

"Notice how Paul reasons in 1 Corinthians 12:14-17:

> For the body is not one member, but many. If the foot shall say, Because I am not the hand, I am not of the body; is it therefore not of the body? And if the ear shall say, Because I am not the eye, I am not of the body; is it therefore not of the body? If the whole body were an eye, where were the hearing? If the whole were hearing, where would be the sense of smell?

"For the body to function properly, each part needs to fulfill its function. Envy and pride would argue for a ridiculous 'body' -- the whole 'an eye,' or the entire system 'an ear.' "And if they were all one member, where were the body?" (1 Corinthians 12:19). Such bodies would be caricatures of the real thing.

"Thus Paul continues by stressing the necessity of each 'member,' each 'part' of the body of Christ, the local church at Corinth. In 1 Corinthians 12:20-23 he wrote:

> But now are they many members, yet but one body. Again, the eye cannot say to the hand, I have no need of you; nor again the head to the feet, I have no need of you. Nay, much more those members of the body, which seem to be more feeble, are necessary. And those members of the body, which we think to be less honorable, upon these we bestow more abundant honor; and our uncomely parts have more abundant comeliness.

"United they stand, divided they fall. None is an island unto himself, for each is a part -- and that a necessary part -- of every other member.

"Therefore, though the body has 'many members,' none can survive without the rest. Hear Paul's concluding argument (1 Corinthians 12:24-26):

> For our comely parts have no need, but God hath tempered the body together, having given more abundant honor to that part which lacked, that there should be no schism in the body; but that the members should have the same care one for another. And whether one member suffers, all the members suffer with it; or one member be honored, all the members rejoice with it.

"Did you catch it? Because the body is one regardless of the different functional gifts given, "the members should have the same care one for another." The honor of one is the honor of all. The dishonoring of one dishonors "all the members."

"So, when the Spirit chooses (i.e., wills) to give any believer a certain gift, he should be humbled rather than exalted by it. Paul wrote of the need for this humility in 1 Corinthians 4:7, "For who maketh thee to differ from one another, and what has thou that thou didst not receive? Now if you didst receive it, why do you boast as if you had not received it?"

3. Baxter is teaching that we should be humbled by the reception of whatever spiritual gift we have received.

4. An attitude of superiority because of some gift we possess is clearly out of place!

B. An Attitude of **Inferiority** is also out of place.

1. We've already read 1 Corinthians 12:14-17, where it is the one feeling "inferior" that is moping around because it is not what it considers a better member of the body.

   Romans 12:3, which does speak about thinking soberly of ourselves "as God has allotted a measure of faith to each man," clearly prohibits feelings of inferiority about gifts (cf. following verses) as well as pride.

   1 Peter 4:10, "As each one has received a special gift, employ it in serving one another, as good stewards of the manifold grace of God," shows that God cannot be glorified by one who is moping about the "inferior" gift he has received. How incongruous to feel inferior about something God has given us! An inferiority complex about our gifts is the devil's tool to destroy our effectiveness for God.

2. The current emphasis (craze) on DISCOVERING YOUR GIFT plays on this inferiority feeling.

   One example would be Gothard's clinics where hesitant church members are taught to discern their gifts. Another example is C. Peter Wagner, *Your Spiritual Gifts Can Help Your Church to Grow.*

   Gene Getz' earlier work (*Sharpening the Focus of the Church*) taught Christians to seek to discover their gifts. Now he has totally reversed that position (*Building Up One Another*), and rejects gift-seeking because of the confusion caused among Christians; because of the rationalizations made from gift theology for not fulfilling normal, biblical role-functions, and because of the self-deception by which people think they have spiritual gifts, which they do not possess.

   Many of these books are simply interjecting modern psychology into the church by dressing up personality profiles in spiritual gifts clothing.

3. At the same time, without completing any of the "Discover Your Gift" workbooks that have proliferated on the market, you can find out where your gift fits into the local body (the congregation).

   a. Know the Scriptures. Study what gifted persons did, and compare your interests.
   b. Pray about it. "Lord, what do you want me to do for you today?"
   c. Expect confirmation from others. When a number of church folk suggest a task for you to do, do it!!

4. Quoting from Ronald Baxter again (p.66),

   "Recognizing our spiritual gifts, and putting them to work, can make service for God a real blessing instead of a burden. A fable suggested by Charles Swindoll helps us to see this:

   > A group of animals decided to improve their general welfare by starting a school. The curriculum includes swimming, running, climbing and flying. The duck, an excellent swimmer, was deficient in other areas, so he majored in climbing, running, and flying, much to the detriment of his swimming. The rabbit, a superior runner, was forced to spend so much of his time in other classes that he soon lost much of his famed speed. The squirrel,

who had been rated "A" as a climber dropped to a "C" because his instructors spent hours trying to teach him to swim and fly. And the eagle was disciplined for soaring to the treetop when he had been told to learn how to climb, even though flying was most natural for him.

What's the point? It is simple. God has endowed us with certain gifts. All gifts are not the same. They do not even fit us all to do the same work (1 Corinthians 12:17), but they are all necessary within the church (1 Corinthians 12:20-23). When each of us exercises his particular gifts within the local church the way God intends, then the body moves forward with the precision, vitality and efficiency of a trained athlete. But, when we ignore our personal gifts and try to be what we are not, then our total service quotient drops."

5. Learn what your gift is, use it to the glory of God, and you'll never feel inferior again.

C. An Attitude of **Understanding** is what is specially needed.

1. The gifts are not given to produce a "spiritual high" -- that's a 20th century false idea! Why are the gifts given? That old stalwart John Owen put it well:

   "By his work of saving grace ... he makes all the elect living stones; and by his communication of spiritual gifts, he fashions and builds those stones into a temple for the living God to dwell in." (*The Holy Spirit*, p.832)

   Discounting his Calvinistic language, Owen has shown that the gifts are the equipment to enable us (each one of us) to be spiritual builders for Christ.

2. And how do we go about this work of temple building?

   a. We use the gifts we are given to glorify Christ!

   That's in harmony with John 16:14, "The Spirit will glorify Christ."

   Stover wrote, "Gifts are never to be employed to magnify the one who possesses them. The Holy Spirit is not in the business of building great reputations for men; His ministry is to reveal and glorify Jesus Christ." (*The Power for Christian Living*, p.46)

   In the same spirit, William Carey, the great missionary to India, said, "Speak not of Dr. Carey, but of Dr. Carey's Savior!"

   Such will be the heartcry of all endued with the gifts of the Holy Spirit of God.

   b. Use the gifts to edify others!

   Read 1 Corinthians 14. See how many times "edify others" is emphasized.
   Read 1 Corinthians 13. Use the gifts in a loving way (to help others), or their possession and use is worthless.

   c. Use the gifts to equip the church.

   Eph. 4:11-12 -- "for the equipping of the saints so they may do the work of ministry."

   James. Bryant has written,

"Spiritual gifts are not to be considered from an egocentric point of view, i.e., in terms of what they do for the individual. Rather they are to be considered from an ecclesiological point of view, i.e., in terms of what they do for the Church, the body of Christ." (*The Doctrine of the Holy Spirit in the New Testament*, p. 66)

God help us to be looking for ways to be helping the other members of our church by the use of our spiritual gift. That's a right understanding of the gift.

III. THE TEMPORARY GIFTS OF THE SPIRIT

A. We probably must take a moment to show that some gifts of the Spirit were temporary in nature.

"As surely as there were gifts which were permanently needed in the church, there were also gifts which were temporary in nature. These gifts were as necessary to the founding of Christianity as the others are to its continuance. Yet, as we shall discover from an understanding of what these gifts really were, they have fulfilled their purpose and have been withdrawn." (Baxter, *op. cit.,* p. 83)

1. The gift lists keep getting shorter.

It is interesting to notice in this respect, that the lists themselves indicate the temporary nature of some gifts. If we take Paul's order of recording the gifts to be 1 Corinthians, Romans, and Ephesians (this is the order in which the books were written), then we begin to uncover evidence that certain gifts were temporary.

For example, in Romans there is no mention of healings, miracles, tongues or interpretation. Indeed, in Ephesians, there are but four gifts mentioned (4:11), indicating that by AD 63 a number of authenticating gifts earlier alluded to (1 Corinthians) were passing away.

Indeed, some have pressed this thought one step further. They refer to 1 Peter 4:10-11, written perhaps 4 years after Ephesians, and note only two gifts are specifically mentioned. "The list is striking in its brevity compared to the lists in 1 Corinthians. While an apostle is writing the letter (so that gift is still functioning in the church), there is nothing said about prophets, healing, or speaking in tongues. Yet Peter can write 'as each one has received a special gift ...'." (Adopted from Pickford, "Baptists and the Charismatic Movement," *Evangelical Baptist,* December 1969, p.7)

2. At least five passages of the New Testament indicate the temporary nature of some gifts.

1 Corinthians 13:8-10 – when the "complete" is come, i.e., when the New Testament revelation is completed, the "gifts" will cease, says Paul.

Mark 16:16-20 – by the time (AD 68) Mark writes verse 20, the promised "signs" were past. See the past tense verb used in verse 20.

Ephesians 2:20 – the "foundation" of apostles and prophets. This verse is nearly universally acknowledged as teaching the temporary nature of these two offices.

Hebrews 2:1-4 – the verb tenses used indicate that the distributions of the Spirit intended to corroborate the "great salvation" were a thing of the past when Hebrews was written.

1 Peter 3:15 compared with Matthew 10:17-23 – The instructions given are contradictory, unless the gifts are passing by the time Peter writes. (See notes on 1 Peter 3:15.)

3. Some gifts were temporary because they were limited to the apostles of Jesus or to those on whom the apostles had laid hands to pass the gifts on. Cp. Acts 8:17, 2 Timothy 1:6.

B. Now it is time to make a brief study of the temporary gifts themselves.

C. Some of the temporary gifts of the Spirit might be called **servant gifts**.

1. Apostles (of Jesus)

a. The meaning of the word "apostle" – is one sent on a mission, one commissioned to deliver a message.

b. The making of an apostle. Acts 1:21-23.

Certain qualifications had to be met -- i.e., travel with Jesus during His earthly ministry; be a personal witness of one of His post-resurrection appearances; and a call from the Lord Himself to office. (John Owen, *The Holy Spirit*, p. 851)

1. An extraordinary call unto an office, such as none other has or can have, by virtue of any law, order, or constitution whatever.
2. An extraordinary power communicated unto persons so called, enabling them to act what they are so called unto, wherein the essence of any office doth consist.
3. Extraordinary gifts for the exercise and discharge of that power.
4. Extraordinary employment as to its extent and measure, requiring extraordinary labor, travail, zeal, and self-denial.

All these do and must concur in that office and unto those offices which we call extraordinary.

c. The ministry of an apostle.

- Laying the foundation of the church, Ephesians 2:20
- Confirming the message, Hebrews 2:3,4
- Oversight of the church, Acts 8:14, 15:1-29.
- They wrote inspired letters to the churches, now included in the New Testament canon.

d. The miracles of an apostle. The miracles performed by Paul authenticated both him as an apostle and the message he preached as being from God.

- 2 Corinthians 12:11,12, "the signs of a true apostle were performed among you."
- Romans 15:18,19, "I will not presume to speak of anything except what Christ has accomplished through me, resulting in the obedience of the Gentiles by word and deed, in the power of the Spirit ...."

e. The idea there are still apostles in the flesh today is a MIRAGE! It is a pretentious claim!

You don't, in the pages of the New Testament, find successors to the apostles, save in the case of Judas (Acts 1:16-26). When James was martyred, no one was chosen to replace him (Acts 12). No one today can meet the qualifications (Acts 1:21,22).

f. To be an apostle of Jesus was a temporary gift to the church, but their work has left a foundation for us to build on for the whole church age.

2. Prophets

a. A "prophet" was one who spoke by inspiration, no matter the content of the message. It might be prediction, like Agabus (Acts 11). It might be edification, exhortation, or comfort (1 Corinthians 14:3).

b. Some of the New Testament prophets wrote some of the books of the New Testament: Luke, Jude, Mark, and perhaps Silas (as penman for 1 Peter).

c. The FINALITY OF SCRIPTURE. Books written by apostles and prophets are the only books that are God's inspired message to men in this new covenant age.

No other religious books are recognized as authoritative. Not Joseph Smith's. Not Ellen White's. Not Mary Baker Eddy's. Not the writings of the "Kansas City prophets." Just the books of the New Testament apostles and prophets.

D. Some of the temporary gifts of the Spirit might be called **service gifts**.

1. Word of wisdom

We are dealing here with an immediate grasp of the secret plans and purposes of God in their totality. This information also became Scripture.

1 Corinthians 2:7,8 (KJV), "We speak the wisdom of God in a mystery, even the hidden wisdom, which God ordained before the world unto our glory; which none of the princes of the world knew." It is a direct intuition into otherwise unknowable mysteries of God. (A "mystery" was something not clearly revealed in Old Testament times, but now is.)

This gift was temporary because it dealt with revelation and was therefore foundational to the church.

2. Word of knowledge

The ability to know things beyond what is ordinary or natural. Examples include:

– Peter's "knowledge" of what Ananias and Sapphira were secretly trying to do (Acts 5).
– Elisha's telling the king of Israel all that went on in the Syrian camp, to the degree the king of Syria thought he had a traitorous informer in the camp (2 Kings 6:11,12).
– Paul on the voyage to Rome, his prescience of the shipwreck but with no loss of life (Acts 27:21-24).

This gift was temporary. 1 Corinthians 13:8 says so.

3. Discerning of spirits

The ability to judge whether a teacher is speaking the truth or not, just by looking at him.

Examples:

– Paul and Elymas (Acts 13:6-11).
– Judge what the prophets say (1 Corinthians 14:29).

This gift was temporary. Now we judge by comparing the message with Scripture.

4. Faith to move mountains

In 1 Corinthians 12:9,10, "faith" is a miraculous ability, somewhat distinguished from healings, miracles, and the like. 1 Corinthians 13:2 and Matthew 17:20 refer to this service gift.

> Care must be taken as we discuss this gift. It is not the same thing as "saving faith," for that faith comes by hearing the Word of God (Romans 10:17). It is not the same "faith" as referred to as a "fruit of the spirit" (Galatians 5:22). While in this day we hear some religious leaders speak of "faith healing" and "miracles of faith," the "faith" in those cases is resident in the patient, not the healer. The faith to move mountains is in the gifted person, not in the recipient.

New Testament examples of this gift have not been satisfactorily identified even by Pentecostal/Charismatic interpreters, though some appeal to James 5:15 (the prayer of faith will save the sick) as a possible example.[2]

The only argument for this gift being temporary is its placement in 1 Corinthians 12:9.[3]

E. A third kind of temporary spiritual gift might be called **sign gifts**.

1. Gifts of healings

Different kinds of sicknesses (sick in body, sick in mind, sick in soul) call for different kinds of healings.

Pentecostal/Charismatic mistakes about the gift of healing:

a) The claim that there is "healing in the atonement" based on Isaiah 53:5 and Matthew 8:17. See Romans 8:22-23 where it is affirmed that Christians, even with the Holy Spirit, are still going to get sick.
b) The claim that all sickness is the result of personal sin is a view mistakenly deduced from the fact that in some of Jesus' miracles people got well when He said "your sins are forgiven." But Scripture gives other reasons for sickness, including a penalty on the race for Adam's sin, a result of satanic activity (Luke 13:11-13), and some sickness is for the glory of God (John 9:1-3).

---

[2] Because no clear examples are found, some treat "faith" as a "family name" for the second group of gifts, namely, healings, miracles, prophecy, and discerning of spirits. However, since there are no "family names" for the other three groups of gifts sometimes identified in 1 Corinthians 12:8-11, it would not be expected that "faith" serves as such a name.

[3] Romans 12:3-6 might point to the need to place it in the list of permanent gifts, since some of the gifts in that list are permanent. Baxter places this gift among the permanent ones, but he struggles to explain what it is. He thinks Abraham had this gift (appealing to Hebrews 11:17-19), evidently forgetting that the Spirit is not given till after Jesus is glorified. He also thinks Elijah had this gift to enable him to believe that God would extend the meager supply of meal and oil for the widow of Zarephath and her son over the period of three years of the drought God sent upon the land (1 Kings 17:15,16). He also appeals to Stephen as a man "full of faith and the Holy Spirit" (Acts 6:5), but this was before the hands of the apostles were laid on him. He speaks of this "faith" as being the great confidence that some people exhibit that God will intervene in routine life situations. Some would appeal to Francke of Germany, Mueller of Bristol, and Hudson Taylor of China as modern examples of men who had the "gift of faith." Does this mean that not everyone will have prayers answered as those men did?

c) The claim that "Jesus wants you well," that it is not God's will that any of His children should ever be sick. So, if any person doesn't get healed it is because there is something spiritually wrong in his heart or life. That this doctrine is wrong is clear from the fact that during Jesus' ministry, even when there was a "great multitude of sick," He didn't heal them all, but only one (John 5:1-9). God didn't heal Timothy (1 Timothy 5:23), or Trophimus (2 Timothy 4:20), or Paul (2 Corinthians 12:7-10). Will anyone say there was something spiritually wrong in those men's lives that precluded a healing?

Not all healing related in the Bible is an example of the "gift of healing" in operation.

There obviously is a difference between healings in general and the miraculous healings done by those who had the "gifts of healings" as mentioned in 1 Corinthians 12:28. If this were not so there would have been no healings before the Spirit bestowed the gifts. There would be no healings apart from those individuals who received the special gift. But, such plainly is not the case.

Long before there were miraculous healings done by the apostles, or by spiritually gifted people, we read in Exodus 15:26 of Jehovah Rapha, "the Lord who heals." In those days, God healed independently of any gifts of healing bestowed on any intermediary (see Genesis 20:7, Numbers 12:14, Isaiah 38:1-5).

Acts 10:38 tells how God anointed Jesus "with the Holy Spirit and power," and as a result Jesus "went about doing good, and healing all who were oppressed by the devil, for God was with Him."

All of this is different from those "gifts of healing" about which we read in 1 Corinthians 12:9,28,30.

God does heal in answer to prayer (James 5:15, a "prayer offered in faith").

We sometimes mistakenly identify healing in answer to prayer with the miracles of healing. We may mistakenly assume that if healings occur in answer to prayer, it must be the gift of healing in operation.

Answered prayer is not miracle; it is the providence of God.

The miraculous "gifts of healing" were a sign (Mark 16:17,18) to authenticate the truth of the gospel, to authenticate the claims about Jesus. They were temporary.[4]

---

[4] Some argue gifts of healing still occur. If "healers" have real power over organic (not just psychosomatic) sicknesses, why don't the healers simply walk into hospitals and empty the wards? Why must patients come to tent meetings and auditoriums and pass through screening lines before the "healer" will work with them? Two carefully researched works of attempts to find one case of genuine miracle over an organic malady came up empty. See Carrol Stegall, Jr., *The Modern Tongues and Healing Movement* (Published by the author: Shalimar, FL, 196?) and Wm. A. Nolen, *Healing: A Doctor in Search for a Miracle* (NY: Random House, 1974).

2. Working of miracles is another of the temporary "sign gifts."

"Miracle" is a loosely defined term in our language, but not in Scripture. In Scripture, a "miracle" was an extraordinary, awe-inspiring, supernatural act of God wrought to credential a message or a messenger.

The same event can be a "miracle" (emphasis on the power it took to perform it), a "sign" (it points to something God wants known), and a "wonder" (it produces awe in the person who sees it). Acts 2:22.

A "miracle" is not the *suspension* of the pattern to which events conform but the *feeding of something new* into the pattern. (C.S. Lewis, *Miracles*, p. 72)

Miracles didn't happen every day in the Bible. After creation, there are only 3 or 4 periods of time when miracles are recorded in Bible history -- the flood, the time of Moses and Joshua, the time of Elijah and Elisha, and the introduction of Christianity into the world.

Miracles were temporary, to credential the message (Mark 16:20; Hebrews 2:4).[5]

3. Divers kinds of tongues

"Tongues" are foreign languages (Acts 2; Mark 16; 1 Corinthians 14:21).

Not everyone spoke in tongues (1 Corinthians 12:30). The question Paul asks expects a negative answer. Pentecostal doctrine, that tongues are for all, is in error.

Much is written in the New Testament to regulate the use of tongues (foreign languages):

a) They were to be used to edify. 1 Corinthians 14:6
b) They were a sign for unbelievers. 1 Corinthians 14:21,22
c) Decency and order in the public service were not to be disturbed by the way tongues were used. 1 Corinthians 14:40
d) An interpreter (translator) was to be present, or the language was not to be spoken. 1 Corinthians 14:28
e) It may be that 1 Corinthians 14:34-35 prohibits the use of tongues by ladies in the public assembly.
f) In the age when this gift was available, its use in the public assembly was not to be totally forbidden. 1 Corinthians 14:39
g) No potential tongues' speaker should relax all conscious control of his vocal organs, or dispense with the use of his mind or reason. 1 Corinthians 14:15

---

[5] Some appeal to Hebrews 13:8 ("Jesus Christ is the same yesterday and today, yes and forever") to argue that if He granted miracles when the church began, He would do the same today. To apply Hebrews 13:8 to the argument about whether or not miracles have ceased is to drag the passage out of its context. Further, if the argument is true, why did the apostles have to wait until Jesus was glorified before they were empowered by the Spirit? We have shown that apostles and prophets were temporary -- a fact that could not be if the argument about "Jesus being the same ..." were a legitimate argument.

h) The proper use of tongues was in an evangelistic situation, when an unbeliever (with a foreign language as his native tongue) came into the services. 1 Corinthians 14:22

This gift is specifically named as one of the temporary ones (1 Corinthians 13:8).

4. Interpretation of Tongues

This is the translation from one language into another. Compare 1 Corinthians 12:10, 14:26-27, and all the familiar verses in Mark's Gospel which read "which being interpreted means." Mark is translating the foreign word into the language of his readers.

This gift, being tied to the gift of tongues, was temporary. When they ceased, the need for the gift of interpretation did too.

F. There was a compelling need for these temporary gifts of the Spirit – received by the laying on of an apostle's hands. Baxter, *op. cit.,* p. 85-86 explains it this way:

"It is hard for us in our smug twentieth century existence to imagine a world without Christianity. Yet that was the very case with the early church. Behind this new religion were no traditions, so it was not readily accepted in the communities where groups of believers gathered. The fact is, Paul could say of the situation, 'We are made as the filth of the world, and are the off-scouring of all things unto this day' (1 Corinthians 4:13).

"Now how does one get acceptance for his ministry under such circumstances? The answer is found in the 'signs following' of Mark 16:17,18. These were authenticating signs from God, signaling to the world that the fledgling church and its new gospel were real. What God promised to do in these signs He fulfilled; for we read clearly, 'And they went forth, and preached everywhere, the Lord working with them, and confirming the word with signs following' (Mark 16:20).

"These signs that followed the inroads of the gospel in the apostolic age were very important. They were the stamp of God's approval upon this strange new religion. As 'Jesus of Nazareth' was 'a man approved of God -- by miracles and wonders and signs' done in the midst of the people, so the early church (including the apostles, prophets, and others) was approved. Moreover, the message of redemption through the resurrected Christ was 'approved' also."

IV. THE PERMANENT GIFTS OF THE SPIRIT

A. These gifts, received from the Spirit at conversion (rather than post-conversion by the laying on of an apostle's hands) are important to the body, all through the church age.

"While there were gifts which were by their very nature and purpose temporary gifts to the church, it is very obvious that there were also a number of permanent gifts. These latter are those gifts which do not have an authenticating ministry but a settled ministry. They are the gifts which are needed within the churches for the continuance of the ministry until Jesus comes again.

"BODY LIFE IS IMPORTANT. In 1 Corinthians 12, Paul argues for the importance of every member of the body. He states the unity of that body, though there may be 'many members' in it (verses 12-14). The body of which he speaks is identified as the Corinthian church (verse 27). We are told that the members of this church were not placed there haphazardly (verse 18), but sovereignly by God for 'God hath set' them 'in the church ...' (verse 28). Further our attention is drawn to the fact that to each member has been given 'the manifestation of the Spirit' (verse 7) and that these gifts are divided 'to every man severally' as the sovereign Spirit wills (verse 11).

"Thus the gifts of the Spirit make each member important to the functioning of the church. Each one has need of every other one (verses 15-17) and there is room for neither jealousy, nor scorn (verse 21). Whether the gift be a servant gift for public ministry, or a service gift for enablement in some office, or a serving gift to function humbly in a way we may carnally consider "less honorable" (verse 23), all are necessary to the spiritual welfare of the total church ...

"When we comprehend the importance of the gifts of the Spirit to the body life of the local assembly, we are not surprised to discover that there are fulfilling gifts for the ministry of the church today. Indeed, without these our churches could not function as God intends. They can be divided into three basic categories for the purpose of understanding their place and function within the body of Christ." (Baxter, *op. cit.,* p. 169-171)

B. One kind of permanent gifts we might call **servant gifts**.

1. Christ gave some to be EVANGELISTS.

Their job is similar to that of the modern preacher. Share the good news, plant churches, strengthen churches.

"Laymen" can become evangelists. Philip was a deacon (Acts 6:5) who became an evangelist (Acts 21:8). (Cp. 1 Timothy 3:13 – "those who have served well as deacons obtain for themselves a high standing and great confidence in the faith that is in Christ Jesus.")

Where evangelists work –

a) Evangelists may work in a city.

Philip went down to the city of Samaria (Acts 8:5). Many people with one accord gave heed to the things Philip spoke. Later on, he will be located in the city of Caesarea (Acts 21:8).

b) Evangelists may work one-on-one.

Philip is one-on-one with the Ethiopian treasurer, a good example of personal soul winning (Acts 8:26-31).

c) Evangelists may work with an established congregation.

Timothy is working with the church at Ephesus (2 Timothy 4:5), a congregation that had elders (Acts 20:17ff; 1 Timothy 5:19ff).

Maybe you can do this job!

2. Christ gave some to be PASTORING-TEACHERS

This is likely a reference to elders, who are called by different names in the New Testament.

a) "Pastor" – a shepherd who feeds and cares for the flock.
b) "Bishop" – an overseer, superintendent. He looks over and watches over a local congregation. He safeguards the church from error (wolves), he sees that things are done decently and in an orderly fashion.
c) "Elder" – says the man is older. It speaks of dignity. (According to Acts 20:17-28 and Titus 1:5-7, "elder" and "bishop" are interchangeable names for the same office.)

This is an important gift to the church – so important that qualifications of those who would be chosen to serve are carefully given in 1 Timothy 3, Titus 1, and 1 Peter 5.

a) Some qualifications deal with the man's Christian character.
b) Some qualifications deal with the man's Christian experience.

Maybe you can do this job!

C. Another kind of permanent gifts of the Spirit might be called **service gifts**.

1. Gift of governments (KJV), "Administrations" (NASB)

1 Corinthians 12:28 -- the Greek term for guide or pilot who steers a ship, a governor who directs or governs the course the ship takes.

In early Christian literature, when a crisis came up the church had to face, Ignatius wrote to Polycarp and said to him, "the occasion demands thee, as pilots (*kubernetai*) the winds." Polycarp was the one who had a gift that would enable him to guide the church through all the fortunes and vicissitudes of daily life, maintaining order and holding the congregation to its heavenly assignment.

The modern term might be "administration," organizing, overseeing, helping folk do their part so the whole functions, dealing with details and generally making sure the church runs smoothly.

Maybe you can do this job!

2. Gift of ruling

   The Greek word, *proistamenos*, means to take the lead in something, to be up front.

   1 Timothy 5:17, "Let the elders who rule well be considered worthy of double honor, especially those who work hard at their preaching and teaching." The "ruler's" real job is to take the lead in showing the rest of us how to serve. Elders do that, but the gift of ruling is not necessarily limited to elders.

   Maybe you can do this job!

3. Gift of ministry (serving)

   Romans 12:7, "if service, in his serving."
   Acts 6, meeting the physical needs of the poor and hungry and elderly.

   Maybe you can do this!

4. Gift of speaking

   1 Peter 4:11, "Whoever speaks, let him speak, as it were the utterances ("oracles," KJV) of God."

   It is hard to know just the word from Scripture a hurting brother needs to hear. To have just the word from God the person needs to hear is a gift that can be developed (study, work at knowing what is in your Bible).

   A native from a village 200 miles away kept coming to a missionary in Mexico. "Send us a missionary!" he kept begging. The missionary had to say, "I'm sorry, I can't come now and there is no one I know whom I can send." Finally, the native arrived at the mission station and said, "Give me God's message for our village for this week. I will carry it home."

   Maybe you can do that!

D. Finally, another kind of permanent "gifts" of the Spirit might be called **serving gifts**.

1. The gift of exhortation

   Romans 12:6-8a

   Barnabas, the "son of exhortation" may be the perfect example of this gift in action. Through his ministry both Mark and Paul were rescued. Just the right word of comfort and help to rescue the discouraged. Comfort, encouragement, consolation, assistance.

   Maybe you can do this!

2. The gift of helps

   1 Corinthians 12:28

   In a world where we strive after the illusion of self-sufficiency, we all come to the place where we need someone to help. What a blessing to a congregation to have such a gifted person, who is there, ready to move in alongside, and support us, just when we need that support. In this place we are not talking about officers of the church, but instead these are people who have tender hearts and quick eyes and listening ears.

An example might be the household of Stephanas, who "devoted themselves for ministry to the saints" (1 Corinthians 16:15,16). They saw a job and volunteered to do it. They didn't wait to be asked.

Maybe you can be a helper.

3. The gift of mercy

Romans 12:8, "he who shows mercy, *let him do it* with cheerfulness."

This person feels sympathy with the needs of others who are hurting. "Cheerfulness" suggests the attitude of mind – joyfulness and cheerfulness at the opportunity to express sympathy.

It might picture the ability to walk into a sick room and immediately sense the needs of the person on the bed, and minister to them.

It might picture ministries to the deaf, blind, the educable slows, the skid row transients, ghetto children, physically handicapped, refugees, migrant workers.

Maybe you can do this!

4. The gift of giving

Romans 12:8, "He who gives, with liberality (simplicity, KJV)."

God enables some members of the body of Christ to contribute their material resources to the work of the Lord with liberality and cheerfulness.

John Wesley lived in voluntary poverty. When he died, he left an estate of 2 silver spoons and a well-worn frock coat. However, during his lifetime, he gave $150,000 to the work of the Lord.

To R. G. LeTourneau, it was not "how much of my money I give to God, but rather how much of God's money dare I keep." In answer to this, LeTourneau gave 90% of his business to the Lord by way of a Christian foundation, and then gave 90% of the part he kept for himself to Christian causes.

Maybe you can do this!

E. These permanent gifts of the Spirit may not be showy, but they are important.

Serving gifts: the gifts of exhortation, of helps, of mercy, and of giving. In general, they represent the unassuming *charismata* of the Holy Spirit. While they are found modestly at work behind the scenes, they are of utmost importance to the work of the Lord. Of none of them can the church say,

"I have no need of you" (1 Corinthians 12:21). Rather, unless each member possessing them exercises these gifts to their fullest extent, the whole church suffers loss. "Having then gifts differing according to the grace that is given us" (Romans 12:6), let us use them to God's glory, the church's good, and our own spiritual fulfillment. (Baxter, *op. cit.*, p. 230)

CONCLUSION

A. Summary

We've defined our terms, so we all understand the scope and extent of the topic.
We've learned the Biblical attitudes about these "gifts of the Spirit."
We've gotten acquainted with the nature and utility of the temporary Spiritual gifts.
We've encouraged the development and use of the permanent gifts of the Spirit.

B. Exhortation

You are parts of the body (the local church, where you live).

Each one has a contribution to make.
We received a "gift" -- a special task or function we can do -- when we became a Christian.

For many of us, perhaps we've unwittingly made the church suffer along without the ability God gave us to use in the body.

What should I have been supplying to the body?
What permanent gift do I have? Where do I fit? What is expected of me?

Resolve to take the responsibility to exercise our "gift" -- beginning tonight!

C. Help Me Find My Place

There's a place for every worker in the vineyard of the Lord,
Where with all our powers united, we can toil with one accord;
There are needy hearts now waiting for the help which we can give,
Let us guide them safely onward, Let us show them how to live.

There's a place for every teacher in the Bible training school,
Where our natures are made sweeter as we teach the Golden Rule;
There's a call for loyal service, where we all may work and pray;
Let us then be up and doing, teaching men the Savior's way.

There's a place for every Christian in the church which we would serve,
Where we may uphold her standards, and from duty never swerve;
There are burdens to be lifted, there are hearts in pain and grief,
Let us help the heavy laden, bringing comfort and relief.

There's a place, oh, may I find it, where my mission I can fill,
Be it humble, or exalted, may I hold it with a will;
Help to serve my generation with a heart of love and grace,
Help me Lord, from this time onward, find and occupy my place!

-- Neal A. McAulay

C. Exhortation to Elders. 5:1-4

5:1 -- ***Therefore, I exhort the elders among you, as*** **your** ***fellow-elder and witness of the sufferings of Christ, and a partaker also of the glory that is to be revealed,***

Therefore -- "Therefore" indicates a logical thought connection between the previous hortatory section and this one which follows. Knowing that faithfulness of church people (such as has just been encouraged in 4:12-19) will depend to a large extent upon their leaders, Peter now admonishes the elders among his readers.

I exhort the elders among you -- The instructions given to these "elders" in verses 2 and 3 seem to indicate the word is used in its official sense, not just in its original sense of one who is older. The New Testament consistently pictures a plurality of elders in each local congregation,[1] and we suppose Peter is speaking to the elders of each congregation where this letter was received and read out loud in the public assembly.[2]

As *your* fellow-elder -- Peter here introduces several reasons why he has a right to exhort the elders as he is about to do. Reason number one is "I am the co-elder" or "the fellow-elder."[3] Various conjectures have been offered to answer the question "Why did Peter designate himself 'co-elder'?" Some suppose Peter had been selected as an elder in some local congre-

---

[1] Acts 11:30, 14:23, 20:17-28; Philippians 1:1; 1 Thessalonians 5:12; James 5:14. Since it is "elders" (plural) in each church (singular), we would treat 1 Peter 5 as reflecting the same form of church polity. With 1 Peter written before AD 70 (see Introductory Studies), it very likely would be a mistake at such an early date to suppose that an elder (singular) might be presiding over several congregations in any of the given provinces to which 1 Peter is addressed. Such "bishoprics" did not begin until early in the second century AD, and then it likely was an evangelist (not an elder) who presumed to preside over the churches in any given geographical area. The absence of any distinction between "bishop" and "elder" is an argument for the early date of 1 Peter. In post-New Testament times the two words were not synonymous, but while the apostles were still alive the terms "bishop" and "elder" were synonymous (Acts 20:17,28; Titus 1:5,7).

[2] Actually, each commentator on 1 Peter tends to write about what "elders" were in the light of the polity of the religious group of which he is a member. In some, "elders" and "priests" are interchangeable terms. In some "elders" and "preachers" (or "pastors") are viewed as being the same office. In some "elders" are subordinate to "bishops." In some "elders" are subordinate to "evangelists," while in others "evangelists" and "deacons" are subordinate to "elders." Attempting to avoid any self-serving comments, we do note that in the New Testament three different words are used for "elder" -- *presbuteros*, "elder, older" [Greeks did not consider a man as "older" until he was in the 40 to 50 year old range], a word that speaks of the dignity of the leadership task, one worthy of respect; *episkopos*, "overseer, bishop," a word that emphasizes one of the chief tasks of the elder; and *poimen*, "shepherd, pastor," another word that emphasizes the work the elder does. The reader who wishes to pursue the topic in depth will find helpful comments and Special Studies in the author's *Commentary on 1 & 2 Timothy and Titus.*

[3] The words *ho sumpresbuteros* are in the nominative case, and the article "the" is present. It is not just "a fellow-elder." At times the article can serve as a pronoun, so the NASB has translated it "your fellow-elder."

gation.[4] Some suppose Peter is saying that he understands from his own long experience shepherding congregations[5] just what he is asking of the local elders. As he appeals to (not commands) the elders, Peter sympathetically is saying that from experience he personally knows what he is asking them to shoulder, the weight of the responsibilities, the very real dangers, and the multitude of difficulties encountered when one tries to shepherd a flock. Or again, some suppose that Peter is using the term here in its unofficial sense, 'I, Peter, the old man who deserves some respect, am encouraging you elders.'

And witness of the sufferings of Christ -- This is reason number two why Peter can exhort the elders. It is not easy to decide if "witness" means Peter bears testimony concerning the sufferings of Christ or whether it means he was a personal eyewitness of those sufferings.[6] Either way, if some elder should be tempted to decline the responsibility of shepherding the flock because it may involve him in personal suffering, he is called on to include in his thinking the terrible sufferings of Christ[7] for him. What the elder was being asked to do paled into insignificance compared with what Christ went through for the elder.

And a partaker also of the glory that is to be revealed -- Here is reason number three why the elders should heed Peter's exhortations. It is the way to glory, both for them (see verse 4) and for Jesus. The reference is not so much to the glories of the intermediate state entered

---

[4] Peter's language here has been used as a Biblical precedent by some modern preachers to get themselves appointed "elder" in the congregation to which they preach. If the evangelist meets the qualifications of elder (1 Timothy 3; Titus 1), there might be no objection to the evangelist also serving as a local elder. But if the evangelist's entire motivation for wanting to be an elder is so he can have more voice in the control over the congregation (after all, elders do oversee the congregation!), then the preacher's motivation is wrong! The Biblical way is for leaders to take the lead in showing the members how to live and serve. It is perfectly pagan when the leader wants the office simply so he can rule and boss (Luke 22:24-26).

[5] John the apostle likewise called himself "the elder" (2 John 1; 3 John 1), and Papias (writing about AD 120) used the term of John as well as the other apostles (*H.E.*, 3.39). Instead of saying that apostles (like Peter) were automatically also elders, it would be better to suppose that the higher office (apostle) included many of the functions that the lower office (elder) would be expected to do. Just like elders had to feed and shepherd the congregation (singular) that ordained them, so the apostles had to feed and shepherd the congregations (plural) they planted and ministered to. "What the elders were for the individual congregations, that is what the apostles were for the whole church" (Huther, *op. cit.*, p.328-329).

[6] As far as the Gospel record is concerned, the last we see of Peter is about 3 AM in the morning, when after the rooster crowed, Peter left the court room where Jesus was being tried and went out and wept bitterly at his denial of Jesus (Matthew 26:75). The next mention of Peter in the four Gospels is on Sunday morning when he and John race to the empty tomb (John 20:2ff). Yet in 1 Peter 4:19 Peter uses the exact word Jesus used on the cross ("commend," cf. Luke 23:46). Peter also recalled Jesus' lacerated body after His scourging (1 Peter 2:24). Two other lines of argument support the personal eyewitness experience meaning here: the following description of himself as a "partaker of the glory" and his use of the term in the sense of a personal eye-witness in Acts 2:32, 3:15, 5:32, 10:39. Like John who had seen with his own eyes (John 19:34,35) we think Peter is also declaring that he had seen Jesus' sufferings with his own eyes. Peter is saying he was there at Calvary and saw it all.

[7] On Christ's sufferings, see notes at 1:11, 2:21, 3:18, and 4:1.

at death but to the unveiling of Christ's glories at His return to earth. Peter had been promised he would share with Christ in His glory (John 13:36), and Peter here has another reminiscence of those "Great Days with Jesus." In Jesus' high-priestly prayer He prayed that His followers might one day join Him and behold His glory (John 17:24). This is why Peter can promise "glory" to the faithful elders he is now addressing.

5:2 -- ***Shepherd the flock of God among you, exercising oversight not under compulsion, but voluntarily, according to*** **the will of** ***God; and not for sordid gain, but with eagerness;***

Shepherd the flock of God among you -- Peter may well be echoing the words of Jesus, "Shepherd My sheep!" (John 21:16), remembering another of those "Great Days with Jesus." The "flock of God" reminds the elders that the flock belongs to God, not to the shepherds. The use of the shepherd and sheep for the elders and the church members is a metaphor which occurs also at Acts 20:17,28 when Paul reminds the Ephesian elders of their duties. "Among you" is plural in the Greek. This harmonizes with the consistent New Testament picture wherein each congregation had a plurality of elders whose duties were confined to that particular congregation which had selected them as elders. "Flock" is diminutive, literally "little flock," and may express the idea that each local elder's flock was not nearly as large as the one Peter (the apostle and co-elder) was commissioned to shepherd. "Shepherd" or "tend" conveys the idea of the verb *poimanate* better than did "feed" used in the KJV.[8] Think of the personal care farmers give their livestock (it is more than just seeing the animals have food and water) and we have a good model of how functioning elders conscientiously treat the members of the congregation (flock) they have been selected to shepherd. Livestock management includes helping as needed as little ones are born, in some cases feeding the young with a bottle, setting goals for growth, guarding against disease, protecting from predatory animals, doctoring the sick, providing shelter when needed especially in times of storm, and knowing each animal's habits and quirks and individual needs.[9]

Exercising oversight, not under compulsion, but voluntarily, according to *the will of* God -- Peter now writes three contrasting pairs of descriptive terms in order to make plain to the

---

[8] Based on the KJV reading has come an idea productive of much discord in the modern history of the churches, because it led some Bible students to suppose that elders must do all the "teaching" (feeding) in the congregation. While church members should voluntarily ask their elders for guidance, and habitually and voluntarily keep their spiritual leaders informed about what is being taught, and who is being asked to teach, it hardly means the elders alone are qualified teachers of the congregation.

[9] There is another word in this verse in the KJV and ASV, "taking the oversight" or "exercising the oversight," but the Greek word *episkopountes* is not included in Vaticanus or Sinaiticus (in the first hand), though it is included in P^{72} and Sinaiticus in the third hand and in Alexandrinus. Textual critics debate whether it is an explanatory expansion of "shepherd" made by some scribe in accordance with 2:25, or whether it was deliberately omitted by copyists after Peter had dictated it. Whether or not the word is treated as original at this place, the idea is not diminished that elders have an "oversight" responsibility, for such a superintending function is included in the synonymous term "bishop" often used of elders. They were to look after, oversee, watch with great care. Lenski (*op. cit.*, p.218) is probably right when he insists there is no material difference between being a shepherd and "oversight" (we are not to think of the one as preaching and teaching and the other as practical management).

elders the attitude, the motive, and the feelings they should hold as they go about their shepherding work. The first contrasting pair (stated both negatively and positively) relates to the elder's personal attitude towards his assignment. They shepherd the flock not because they feel they *have* to, but because they *want* to. "Compulsion" or constraint is a feeling that drives a reluctant draftee who is doing an irksome task because he feels he cannot escape it. Well, one of the qualifications to become an elder is to desire the task (1 Timothy 3:1), and one of the ongoing job requirements is "voluntarily," i.e., he continues to be delighted to do the work. His attitude is not "Wish I didn't have to," but "I get to!" "According to God"[10] says the elder does his shepherding the same way God shepherds His flock. God's example is the model the elder tries to emulate. The idea is best illustrated in the way the Chief Shepherd Himself went about His work saying, "My food is to do the will of Him who sent me, and to accomplish His work" (John 4:34).

And not for sordid gain, but with eagerness -- With these two contrasting terms Peter highlights possible motives behind the shepherding. The eldership was apparently a paid position in the early church (1 Timothy 5:17),[11] and some might continue functioning as an elder simply because of the money they received for doing the work. What is condemned is not the financial support functioning elders received but the motive of being more interested in the money[12] than in doing the elder's work. In stark contrast to "What do I get?", "eagerness" pictures zeal and enthusiasm for the job, an inward delight and zeal in the salvation and guidance and care of souls, a heart-felt pleasure in being able to give rather than simply to get.

5:3 -- ***Nor yet as lording it over those allotted to your charge, but proving to be examples to the flock.***

Nor yet as lording it over those allotted to your charge -- With a third pair of contrasting adverbial phrases, Peter calls attention to the manner in which an elder should go about his

---

[10] These words are not in the Textus Receptus or the KJV. The phrase is not found in some uncials and in some minuscules, but it does appear in various early Greek manuscripts and different ancient versions, so recent textual editors generally accept the words as authentic. Our comments on the words are based on the omission of "the will of" found in the NASB.

[11] If elders were paid a living wage by the congregation, being freed from any worries about how to feed and clothe and house their own families, they could give 24 hours a day, 7 days a week to the important ministry they have been called to do, namely shepherding the flock. It is very possible that the qualification "free from the love of money" (1 Timothy 3:3) reflects the likelihood that some might initially seek the office just for the money, and this was to be guarded against carefully. Perhaps our churches would do well to put some elders on salary for full service lest they be so engrossed in making a living that they feel they have little time for their work as elders. If we should do this, we might have less temptation to make a "pastor" out of the preacher!

[12] Barclay (*op. cit.*, p.315) calls attention to Theophrastus' character sketch of a man who is "eager for base gain." He gives himself a bigger serving of food than he gives his guests. He waters the wine. He goes to the theater only when he gets a free ticket. He always borrows money from his fellow travelers to pay the fare. The sides and bottoms of bushel measures are dented so that the container doesn't hold a full bushel, but he charges for a full bushel. Rather than give a wedding present, he will go away from home when a wedding is coming. Barclay calls desire for sordid gain an "ugly fault."

shepherding duties, a manner which would put actions on one or the other of hidden personal attitudes toward the members of the flock. J. B. Phillips offers "Don't be little tin gods" as his translation of "not lording it over those." The Greek word pictures a high-handed autocratic rule, acting like a petty tyrant, domineering over those who are (as far as you are concerned) obviously beneath you. Most likely Peter is reflecting another of the "Great Days with Jesus," for Jesus Himself on two separate occasions carefully explained how He expected leaders in the church to act (Matthew 20:25-26 and Luke 22:24-27). On both occasions He indicated that leaders in the church are not to attempt to domineer over their people as pagan leaders do. While elders are not to lord it over the flock, they do have certain ruling and leading and overseeing responsibilities (1 Thessalonians 5:12; 1 Timothy 5:17).[13]

Calling the church members whom the elders shepherd "charges" (the word is plural in the Greek) has provoked numerous comments. One suggestion is that "charges" refers to "tasks." In light of the difficulty explaining just what "lording it over" any of these tasks might mean, it is difficult to see how anyone could suppose the "charges" were different tasks individual elders might be called upon to perform in behalf of the flock. Another suggestion offered is that Peter's expression implies a college of elders, each one over a separate charge (a house church). This however flies in the face of the uniform presentation in Scripture that each congregation (singular) had a plurality of elders. Since the Greek word is *kleros*, some commentators take in the modern sense of clergy, finding this command of Peter to mean "Don't lord it over the clergy!" (as if Peter were commanding the bishops not to tyrannize over the inferior clergy). Such an interpretation is an anachronism, for such a distinction between bishops and lower clergy is a post-apostolic development.[14] Furthermore, it is erroneous to explain *kleros* as denoting orders of clergy (i.e., leaders) when it answers to "flock" in verse 2. Since *kleros* originally spoke of a lot or a portion assigned by casting lots (Matthew 27:35; Acts 1:26), and then the possessions of the tribes of Israel (Deuteronomy 9:29; Joshua 19), and then an inheritance allotted to someone (Colossians 1:12), some suppose Peter's use of the word reflects the fact that each individual elder had a certain number of members of the congregation assigned to his particular care – a kind of 1st century "pastoral shepherding" program.[15] Still others speak of how God was the One who allotted to each el-

---

[13] In this commentator's view, there are several dangers in the churches today. One is a growing concept that the elders are a sort of board of directors (like one would find in a large business) who think they have authority from God to act according to their combined judgment without any accountability to the church. This borders dangerously and uncomfortably close to the very lording it over the flock which Peter prohibits. Another danger is seen on the mega-church scene where the congregations are staff-run rather than elder-run. In these, the senior minister (is that a Biblical title?) and/or his staff make the everyday decisions and the elders are simply informed of the decisions already made. Where is the "oversight" by the elders in such an arrangement?

[14] It is interesting to note that our word "cleric" comes from this Greek word, and the latter was contracted to "clerk," which in ecclesiastical writings referred to the preacher. This passage hardly can be made a proof text that, in Peter's view, elders are overseers of (i.e, lords, in a position superior to or over) preachers (evangelists).

[15] Years ago Wayne Smith devised a *Membership Shepherding Plan* (Cincinnati, OH: Standard, 1960). It was intended to acquaint new members with every phase of the congregation's life and to shepherd members -- old and new -- so that they will continue to be faithful. Jay Sheffield reviewed some of its methods in the June 26,

der the people who were to be his responsibility to shepherd. If God assigned the tasks, then the elders were not to think they could do with their allotted portions as they pleased.

But proving to be examples to the flock -- The elder leads and shepherds by example, not by highhanded ordering. They were to be models whom their people could imitate.[16] As spiritual shepherds, they were to lead, not drive. In chapter 4:7-11, Peter has spoken of love, hospitality, speaking, and practical service. In these areas, as well as others, the elders take the lead in setting the example of how Christians live. They show the Christians how to do it.

5:4 -- ***And when the Chief Shepherd appears, you will receive the unfading crown of glory.***

And when the Chief Shepherd appears -- As in 2:25, when Peter speaks here of Jesus as being the Chief Shepherd, many a thought and memory must have been in his mind.[17] There is this difference between the elders and Jesus – He is the Chief Shepherd over them, they are under-shepherds whose work will be evaluated and rewarded by Him. When Peter writes "appears," he has reference to the visible return of Christ, the second coming (Colossians 3:4, 1 John 2:28). Peter has already used this word (which means to become visible to human eyes) of the first coming of Christ (1:20). Here, as is done by other New Testament writers, Peter uses it of Christ's second coming. A quality in an elder that will make for a good "shepherd" is a desire to please Christ alone, recognizing that a great reward is in store (at His second coming) for those who have served Him faithfully.

You will receive an unfading crown of glory -- Instead of sordid gain, and the empty honor of ruling as a tin god, Peter shows to them noble gain and a true crown of honor. "Receive" is the same word used in 1:9 where Peter assured the readers that they would obtain the salvation of their souls. The crown is a festal garland (*stephanos*) of victory or celebration, not a kingly crown (*diadema*). Garlands made of flowers, herbs, ivy, laurel leaves, or olive branches were given to victors in Greek athletic games, or to bestow honor for military victories, or for festive dress at marriage feasts. After a few days, like pretty flowers pressed in a dictionary, these cut flowers or branches would wither and fade and turn brown. The crown the Chief Shepherd gives to the shepherd elders is not made of some material that will

---

1960 issue of *The Lookout*. This commentator is of the persuasion that present-day elders should have some similar pastoral shepherding program up and working so none of the sheep stray or become lost.

[16] Whether the verb Peter uses (*ginomai*, not *eimi*) implies the elders have not yet been the examples, but are to "become" such quickly, is not certain. Perhaps it does.

[17] He may have recalled some of the "Great Days with Jesus," when Jesus described Himself as "the good shepherd" (John 10:1-18), and how Jesus likened Himself to the shepherd who sought at the peril of his life for the sheep which had gone lost (Matthew 18:12-14; Luke 15:4-7), and the day when Jesus sent out His disciples to gather in the lost sheep of the house of Israel (Matthew 10:6).

fade and die and lose its beautiful quality.[18] The "glory" is everlasting. It doesn't fade away, or wither, or shrivel up.[19]

D. Exhortation to the Younger Members. 5:5a

5:5a -- *You younger men, likewise, be subject to your elders.*

Likewise -- This word (as it did in 3:1,7) marks a transition to a new series of exhortations. "In like manner" suggests that just as the leaders should have a proper attitude (verses 1-4), the members of the flock whom the elders are shepherding should maintain a proper attitude also.

You younger men -- *Neoteroi* (a masculine plural noun) has been assigned a number of different meanings. One view is the word has an official meaning, like those who in Acts 5:6 were called "young men," and whom the author of *Pulpit Commentary* calls "deacons." Another view, reflected in the NASB, is Peter speaks of masculine members younger than the elders. A third view is Peter speaks of all the members in general, all those who are not "elders," who are "younger ones," whether male or female, all those earlier described as "charges."

Be subject to your elders -- "Be subject" translates the same verb rendered "submit yourselves" at 2:13. Submission has been explained in notes at 2:13,18 and 3:1,5. It is something a born-again Christian can will to do as he practices self-control. When the spirit of the elders[20] is loving and exemplary, it is natural and proper and expected that the "charges" will loyally follow their shepherds' lead. What foolish and hurtful things sheep get into when they wander off, ignoring or rebelling against their shepherds. The same is true of the flock of God. When they need help the most, and when the shepherd could give the very help needed, off they go on their own, making havoc of their Christian lives and faltering and quitting Christ at the first outbreak of any persecution, all because they find it difficult to make it on their own.

---

[18] The word in its noun form was the name of a flower that did not wither or fade and which, when picked, revived in water. The adjective form, used here and translated "unfading," ends in *-inos*. In Greek word formation, words ending in *-inos* point to the material from which something is made. For this crown of glory, it is not so much the unfading quality as the non-deteriorating material of which it is made that is emphasized.

[19] Scripture speaks of several types of crowns. There is a "crown of righteousness" (2 Timothy 4:8), a "crown of glory," a "crown of life" (James 1:12; Revelation 2:10), and sometimes simply of a "crown" (1 Corinthians 9:25; Revelation 3:11). Scripture also speaks of a "prize" (1 Corinthians 9:24; Philippians 3:14). Whether there is any difference in these crowns and/or prizes will be disclosed in eternity.

[20] This commentator tends to agree with those writers who take "elder" in its same official sense it had in verse 1. Of course, it is wise for those young in the faith to listen to those who are spiritually older, but we are not convinced that "elders" is used here in verse 5 in an unofficial sense of those who are older, let alone those who are older in the faith. Instead, this commentator sees this verse as one of several which teach that members of the congregation are to obey and submit to the eldership when the elders are imitating Christ.

E. Final Exhortation to Humility, to Serene Submission to the Mighty Hand of God, and to Watchfulness. 5:5b-9

5:5b -- ***And all of you, clothe yourselves with humility toward one another, for*** **GOD IS OPPOSED TO THE PROUD, BUT GIVES GRACE TO THE HUMBLE.**

And all of you -- We have chosen to outline the paragraph differently than it is done in the NASB, where the new paragraph begins with verse 6.[21] Verse 5b, we think, begins a new series of appeals to all the readers, elders and church members alike. 5b is an appeal to humility; verses 6 and 7 follow with an appeal to serene submissiveness to the hand of God; and verses 8 and 9 are an appeal to watchfulness.

Clothe yourselves with humility toward one another -- Here again it may be that Peter's memories of "Great Days with Jesus" are reflected. The word he uses for "to clothe yourselves" is a very unusual word, *egkombosasthe*, which comes from *kombos*, which describes anything tied with a knot. An *egkomboma* was the apron worn by slaves, tied around them while they worked. When you saw a man with an apron on you knew he was a servant. There was a time when Jesus had put upon Himself just such a garment. As they arrived in the upper room on the night when the Lord's Supper was instituted, Jesus took a towel and "girded" himself – He tied it around his waist – and took water and began to wash His disciples' feet (John 13:4,5). He was teaching a lesson on humility. Humility is a disposition that does not mind serving others or serving under others.[22] A humble person does not think of himself as being too good to perform the needed service which will benefit the other person. Whether in times of persecution or not, humility is an expected attitude for any Christian. He is glad to serve others whenever he can. He does not lurk back in the shadows and let the leaders do all the helping.

For GOD IS OPPOSED TO THE PROUD, BUT GIVES GRACE TO THE HUMBLE - - With a quotation from Proverbs 3:34, Peter clinches his argument about their need for humility.[23] God has plainly revealed how He responds to both humility and pride in men. In the light of this clear passage of Scripture on the subject, a man should learn the need of working on his humility lest he find himself fighting against God! Pride, the very opposite of "humility," is something that God opposes. *Antitassetai* ("opposes") is a military term used of an army drawn up for battle. Pride calls out God's armies. God sets Himself in array against the proud person. Their plans for self-show and self-advancement will be strongly

---

[21] If verse 5b is included in the previous paragraph, then perhaps the NASB's rendering of *neoteroi* in verse 5a as "younger men" is correct, since it would be contrasted with "all of you" in this part of the verse. There is a *de* at the beginning of this clause which the KJV/ASV render "yea" and which the NIV leaves untranslated. The KJV reads "Yea, all of you be subject one to another, and be clothed with humility ...." However, this second "be subject" is omitted from the better manuscripts. The ASV reads, "Yea, all of you gird yourselves with humility to serve one another."

[22] On "humility," see Matthew 18:1-6, 20:25-28; Philippians 2:1-11; Colossians 3:12.

[23] James 4:6 also quotes this verse from Proverbs.

resisted and thwarted by God. Pride and humility are antonyms; placing them side by side helps us understand what humility is. The proud man has a swollen estimate of himself; he thinks of himself as too proud to stoop to serve and help others, and the result is that he finds he receives no help from God. In bold contrast to this, the man who delights in serving others, especially when they are in need, is the very one who himself receives help from God.[24] God's good pleasure rests upon him, and He gives proof of it. Unless a man has been wearing his apron of humility, serving others when they are in need, he should not expect to receive many blessings from God when he himself is in need.

5:6 -- ***Humble yourselves, therefore, under the mighty hand of God, that He may exalt you at the proper time,***

Humble yourselves, therefore, under the mighty hand of God -- "Therefore" shows that this plea is based on what was just written in verse 5. "Humble yourselves" is actually a passive voice verb in the Greek, "permit yourselves to be humbled." The process God was using ("the mighty hand of God"[25]) was the persecution and suffering through which Peter's readers were passing. If the proud are to be resisted and the humble are to be given grace, we ought to allow ourselves to be humbled. We have suggested "serene submission to the mighty hand of God" as a summary for verses 6 and 7. In the confidence that our Father in Heaven knows what He is doing, we take advantage of the opportunities for service which He permits to come our way that require us to humble ourselves before we can and will act.

That He may exalt you at the proper time -- *Hina* ("that") can introduce either a purpose or a result clause. Some think it is the purpose the Christian holds in view as he humbles himself. He is anticipating the time when he will be exalted by God. Others suppose Peter is simply holding out the result that is sure to follow when Christians permit themselves to be humbled. Peter could not only appeal to the Old Testament (Proverbs 3:34) but he could also appeal to the promise Jesus made, "whosoever shall humble himself shall be exalted" (Matthew 23:12; Luke 14:11, 18:14).[26] The Christian's hope for the future should make its impact on how he lives in the present. The fulfillment of this promise of exaltation may come in this life; its fulfillment may await the second coming. God in His matchless wisdom will determine in each individual's case just the right time to comfort and help and honor so as to promote His glory and the real welfare of His humble servants.

---

[24] "Grace" has been used before in 1 Peter with several different meanings, depending on the context. See 1:2,10,13, 2:19,20, 3:7, and 4:10.

[25] This phrase was common in the Old Testament, especially when Moses led Israel out of Egypt "by the mighty hand of God" (Exodus 23:9; Deuteronomy 3:24, 9:26). The idea is that God's mighty hand was controlling the destiny of His people, and if they humbly and faithfully accept His guidance, all will be well.

[26] Is this another of Peter's reminiscences of his "Great Days with Jesus"?

5:7 -- ***Casting all your anxiety upon Him, because He cares for you.***

Casting all your anxiety upon Him -- Peter is still unfolding his appeal to serene submissiveness.[27] Perhaps verse 7 is a quotation from the LXX of Psalm 55:22.[28] "Anxiety" (*merimna* is from *meridzo*, to divide, to separate) is the feeling when the heart's attention is drawn in different directions.[29] During persecution there could well be conflicting circumstances tugging in opposite directions resulting in excessive care and worries which one does not know quite how to handle.[30] When your mind is full of anxiety,[31] that is precisely the time to remember that there is a heavenly Father to whom one can turn for help and consolation. *Epiripsantes* ("casting") means to roll a burden over onto, to pass over to another, to deposit with. When the burdens press and the cares distress, it helps a man to be serene if he just turns the problems over to the Lord.

Because He cares for you -- The reason Christians can be serenely submissive in God's hand is because it is certain that He cares for us. Since "it matters to Him about you!" we can be certain that He is not out to break us but to make us. He'll cause all things to work together for good to them who love Him (Romans 8:28). Jesus taught us to "consider the lilies" and the "birds of the air" (Matthew 6:26-28 KJV) as He drove home the lesson that God knows and cares. Our very hairs are numbered (Luke 12:7). For a man to roll his anxieties onto God is not a misplaced confidence. God will make a personal response because He is concerned about His children.

5:8 -- ***Be of sober* spirit, *be on the alert. Your adversary, the devil, prowls about like a roaring lion, seeking someone to devour.***

Be of sober *spirit*, be on the alert -- This is the same way Peter began the first hortatory part of this letter (1:13). Times were perilous. Christians needed to think clearly rather than losing their heads and doing something harmful or foolish. After they cast their anxieties upon God, there was need to be vigilant lest their freedom from care degenerate into apathy

---

[27] *Epiripsantes* is a participle, dependent on "permit yourselves to be humbled under the mighty hand of God." Some of our English versions translate the participle as if it were a separate imperative, making this "casting" a separate, independent duty. This blurs the connection with verse 6 that is obvious in the Greek. While they are being "humbled," they were to cast all their cares on Him.

[28] Compare also what Jesus said in Matthew 6:25-34 about "do not be anxious!"

[29] It is the word used of Martha's attitude when she wanted to sit and listen to Jesus at the same time she wanted to be a good hostess (Luke 10:40,41).

[30] For example, if I get involved helping others when they are hurting, what will happen to my own family and loved ones when the persecution begins? Don't I have a responsibility to my own that plausibly precludes me from having to get involved with others?

[31] "All your anxiety" stands emphatically first in the clause. *Pasan* may be translated "all" or "every." Whether it be "every" individual anxiety, or "all" the individual reader's concerns and cares wrapped into one bundle, the Lord is a good place to deposit such a burden.

and inactivity.[32] We have summarized verses 8 and 9 as an exhortation to watchfulness lest the devil's temptations result in disobedience to God and denial of Christ.[33]

Your adversary, the devil -- "Adversary" translates *antidikos*, a compound word made up of *dike*, "justice" and *anti*, "against." What was happening as Christians were persecuted was unjust, but what else might be expected from an "adversary" like the devil? He is against all that is right and proper. "Devil" translates *diabolos*, a word meaning slanderer or false accuser. In Classical Greek it meant to defame, accuse, calumniate. "Accuser" calls to mind the devil's activities in the case of Job where he made accusation before God and was permitted to intervene in Job's life. He still habitually does something very similar against Christians, for we read he "accuses the brethren" before God's throne day and night (Revelation 12:10). Even in Peter's case, the devil had asked permission to sift Peter like wheat (Luke 22:31,32). We are convinced Peter is reminding his readers that bad things happen to good people because in the unseen world the devil has been at work and has been given permission (up to a point) to get involved in the lives of the Christians.

Prowls about like a roaring lion -- This is very likely a veiled reference to Nero's use of hungry lions against the Christians in the Circus Maximus. Peter's words vividly portray the restless energy of the hungry lion as it walks to and fro searching for food, and the terrifying roar as it finally pounces.[34] Peter is saying, "See behind this method of persecution the activities of a personal devil.[35] He is the one who gave Nero the idea. He planted the idea in Nero's mind to see if he could get you to renounce Christ."

Seeking someone to devour -- "Devour" translates a word that literally means "to drink down." It is used in 1 Corinthians 15:54 of death being "swallowed." The hungry lion is gulping down his food, swallowing it whole. "Someone"[36] implies the devil can't swallow everyone, but only those who are not vigilant and sober, those who (next verse) are not steadfast in their faith.

---

[32] Is there a reflection of another of Peter's experiences with Jesus? Peter knew how hard vigilance was, for he must have remembered how in Gethsemane he and his fellow-disciples had slept when they should have been watching and praying as Christ had commanded them (Matthew 26:36-46; Luke 22:39-46).

[33] C.S. Lovett has suggested in his book *Dealing With the Devil* (Baldwin Park, CA: Personal Christianity, 1967) that in order to obey this command given by Peter, Christians must watch their thoughts, to catch those that have been planted by the evil one.

[34] When a hungry lion has its prey cornered, with no way to escape, as the lion pounces, it roars, freezing the prey in the spot in petrifying fear. It should be noted that the devil does not always roar; at times he comes disguised as an angel of light (2 Corinthians 11:14).

[35] In Job 1:7 and 2:2 we are told the devil goes roaming "about on the earth and walking around on it."

[36] Depending on the accent used, the Greek word may be either an indefinite pronoun "someone" (*tiná*) or an interrogative pronoun "whom" (*tína*). Either reading is possible. The NASB represents the former, the KJV/ASV translate it as an interrogative.

5:9 -- *But resist him, firm in* your *faith, knowing that the same experiences of suffering are being accomplished by your brethren who are in the world.*

But resist him -- As the margin shows, the Greek reads simply "whom resist ...." Perhaps Peter's language here indicates his knowledge of the epistle of James (cp. James 4:7, "Resist the devil and he will flee from you"[37]). By refusing to deny Christ even under threat of death, Peter's readers would resist what the devil is trying to do.

Firm in *your* faith -- The Greek reads "the faith" and we are required to decide whether "faith" is to be taken objectively (a body of doctrine, a Christian teaching[38]) or subjectively (your own personal faithfulness to Jesus). Because they are determined to be "firm"[39] they do not waver in their faithfulness to Christ simply out of fear of a martyr's death. They must resist the allurement of freedom if only they will curse Christ or if only they will worship the emperor.

Knowing that the same experiences of suffering are being accomplished by your brethren who are in the world -- Is this a way to resist, or is it a reason to be firm in their faith? Some take it in the former way, saying there are two ways to resist the devil: in firm faith and in the thought your suffering is not peculiar or unique, but is something that is the universal lot of all Christians. Others opt for the latter, suggesting Peter is telling his readers their faithfulness can be contagious. Their example may well encourage other Christians[40] who are suffering similar persecution to be faithful also and thus help them to resist the devil. Peter uses two expressions that cause us to pause and reflect. One is "accomplished" and the other is "in the world." *Epiteleo* ("accomplished") was a business word used of the payment and discharge of taxes and debts or of the discharge and completion of some business contract. It also has the idea of bringing something to its goal. It also can mean to appoint to or to impose upon. Perhaps the ideas may be combined. These sufferings are being endured by your brethren with a view to their completion, i.e., their perfecting, by the appointment of God (recall what was written in 4:19 and 5:6). "In this world" may be a reminder that Christians live in an imperfect world, among transitory things, and amidst children of unbelief.

---

[37] James speaks of standing against temptations to commit some particular sin, a bit different from the problem faced (a temptation to defect from Christianity) by Peter's readers. Whatever the thing they were being tempted to do, resistance to the temptation results in victory over the devil.

[38] We recall that Jesus used Scripture to counter and resist the devil's temptations (Luke 44-11). Some think this is what Peter has in mind here. Hiebert (*op. cit.*, p.397) thinks that the objective sense of "the faith" is essential to the meaning of this passage. Victory, he states, is not assured by the individual tenacity with which we cling to our personal beliefs. Victory lies in adhering to the work of Christ on the cross, where He defeated the devil. "Victory over Satan lies in faith, because faith unites us to Christ, the victor." Gerhard, quoted in G.F.C. Fronmüller, "1 Peter" in *Commentary on the Holy Scriptures,* by John Peter Lange (Grand Rapids: Zondervan, nd), p.91.

[39] *Stereos* means solid, hard, rigid, firm, immovable.

[40] *Adelphoteti* is a collective term, brotherhood, brethren, fellow Christians. The whole body is affected when any of its members are faithful to death. The whole body may be affected when any of its members are unfaithful. See notes on "brotherhood" at 2:17.

"In this world" may be a reminder that for Christians this life is the only place men will suffer. How different will be the lot of those who are devoured by the devil. Did not Jesus Himself warn, "Do not fear those who are able to kill the body, but are unable to kill the soul; but rather fear Him who is able to destroy both soul and body in hell" (Matthew 10:28; Luke 12:5)?

CONCLUSION. 5:10-14

A. Final Assurance of God's Help and of Their Ultimate Perfection After They Have Suffered a While. 5:10,11

5:10 -- ***And after you have suffered for a little while, the God of all grace, who called you to His eternal glory in Christ, will Himself perfect, confirm, strengthen*** **and** ***establish you.***

And after you have suffered for a little while -- Peter has finished his exhortations; he has told his readers what they must do. He now offers them a very precious promise that God is not finished with them yet. The day will come when He who so faithfully helped them in the past will mend all their hurts and set them in a place where they can never again be shaken by any adversary. "Suffer" is another reference to the impending persecutions the readers were facing. The NASB translators have understood the Greek *oligon* ("a little") as describing not the degree, but the duration of their sufferings at the hands of their persecutors.

The God of all grace -- This description of God occurs only here in the New Testament[41] and describes Him as the source of whatever grace a man may need in his life.[42] God has proven Himself rich in His bestowal of grace in the past; Christians may be assured that He will continue to supply all their needs.

Who called you to His eternal glory in Christ -- Not only was God's grace visible when Jesus went to Calvary, it also resulted in an invitation being extended to the readers. Peter is thinking back to the time of the conversion of his readers, the time when God called them through the gospel (1:15, 2:9,21, 3:9; 2 Thessalonians 2:14). That invitation ultimately embraces their participation in "His eternal glory." This phrase evidently tells of God's purpose in calling them – that they might share in His "glory." "Eternal glory" reminds us of all Peter has written about heaven (1:4,12, 4:13, 5:1,4,6). In that world to come Christians will be honored, and they will bring glory to God. It is "eternal" because, unlike this present transitory scene, it belongs to the coming age which has no end. "In Christ" likely empha-

---

[41] Compare 2 Corinthians 1:3 where we read the "God of all comfort."

[42] See notes on grace at 1 Peter 5:5 and the verses cited there. There is a great variety of gracious help from God for every need and occasion.

sizes that only those who are one with Christ,[43] and who remain faithful to Him, will participate in that eternal glory. Indeed, Peter has written of what is in store in the future for those who disobey (2:8, 3:19,20, 4:5,17,18).

Will Himself perfect, confirm, strengthen *and* establish you -- Peter is making some great promises here to his suffering readers, assuring them of what God Himself, the very One who is the God of all grace, will yet do for them. It seems most probable the perfecting, confirming, and strengthening[44] are things that will take place in heaven – at the same time as they share in the "eternal glory."[45] We are reminded that the sufferings of this present time are not to be compared with the glory that follows (Romans 8:18). "Perfect" translates *kataridzo*, not *teleioō*.[46] The word here is the word used at the calling of the four fishermen, when they were "mending" their nets (Mark 1:19). It is a surgical term for setting a broken bone. Peter is promising the persecuted readers God will repair whatever injuries their bodies may have sustained. Their new, glorified bodies will be whole and complete, no parts missing. It might even include the idea that God will have adjusted them so as to be fit for the heavenly world (cp. 1 Corinthians 15:50-54).[47] "Confirm" translates *sterixei*, a word that means "to give firm support to what is tottering, to ground upon a solid foundation."[48] Bengel's comment on this word is, "Shall stablish you that nothing will cause you to waver."[49] "Strengthen" represents *sthevosei*, a word that means "fill with strength, to be steadfast." In

---

[43] Peter has emphasized how his readers obeyed Jesus Christ (1:2), how they "believe in Him" (1:8), how they are "living stones" and offer "sacrifices acceptable to God through Jesus Christ" (2:5), how the one "who believes in Him will not be disappointed" (2:6), how they have returned to the Shepherd and Guardian of their souls (2:25), how they are to fear Christ above all else (3:15), how they "share the sufferings of Christ" (4:13), how they belong to him ("Christian") (4:16), how they are the "household of God" (4:17), how they are members of the flock over whom Jesus is Chief Shepherd (5:1-4).

[44] The marginal note in the NASB indicates that the fourth word "and establish you" is not found in some of the better manuscripts. It does appear in Sinaiticus, but it is omitted in Vaticanus and Alexandrinus and in the Vulgate version, and probably does not enjoy integrity. Those who include it and comment on it speak of being "established on a firm foundation," a comment that differs little from those offered for "confirm" earlier in the verse.

[45] Some minuscules have the verbs in the optative mood. Those that have them as future tense indicative forms are more likely correct.

[46] *Teleioō* is sometimes translated "perfect" in the sense of full-grown, mature, spiritually complete. While the redeemed in heaven will be no longer tempted and will be (it might be said) "sinless perfect," it would be a mistake to use "perfect" here in 5:10 as a proof text, since the word Peter uses is not *teleioō*.

[47] It is from this passage that the words of the song "Let Him Have His Way With Thee" are derived. The song takes Peter's promise as something that will happen in this life after their suffering is through, rather than in the life to come. Thus the lyrics are "Would you live for Jesus, and be always pure and good? Would you walk with Him within the narrow road? Would you have Him bear your burden, carry all your load? Let Him have His way with thee. His power can make you what you ought to be; His blood can cleanse your heart and make you free; His love can fill your soul, and you will see 'twas best for Him to have His way with thee." The phrase in the chorus about His power making you what you ought to be reflects Peter's "perfect ... you" found here in verse 10.

[48] Christ once told Peter, "When you have turned again, *strengthen* your brothers" (Luke 22:32).

[49] John Albert Bengel, *Gnomon of the New Testament* (Edinburgh: T & T Clark, 1860), Vol.5, p.83.

Revelation 3:12, Jesus promises the faithful that He will make them a "pillar in the temple of My God" in the intermediate state, and then make them citizens of the New Jerusalem which comes down out of heaven.

5:11 -- *To Him* be *dominion forever and ever. Amen.*

To Him *be* dominion forever and ever -- The Greek behind "forever and ever" literally is unto the ages of the ages. Eternity is pictured as an unending series of ages, one following another. "Dominion" translates *kratos*, a word that speaks of "might, rule, authority, power."[50] There is no verb in the Greek, so we must supply one.[51] If we supply an indicative form of "is" then it reads "The dominion *is* His." Peter would be saying "God can do what He says in verse 10, for His 'dominion' lasts forever." If we supply a subjunctive form of "is" then it reads "*Let* the dominion *be* to Him forever." Peter would be praying that his readers will allow God to have His way in their lives, both now and hereafter. Whatever God's mighty hand and providence sees is needed, let it be serenely and gladly submitted to, is Peter's prayer for his readers.

Amen -- Since there is no manuscript evidence for the omission of this "Amen," we presume it originated with Peter and was included in the autograph copy of this letter. "Amen" is a Hebrew word transliterated into Greek. It means "So be it!" It was a way for a man to express hearty agreement with what has just been said.[52] Up to this place the writer has been carried along by the Holy Spirit's inspiration (cp. 2 Peter 1:21). As he finishes with the statement about God's dominion, he expresses his own agreement with what he has just been led to write.[53] When the letter was read out loud in the public assembly, such an "amen" en-

---

50 Thayer explains the difference between the synonyms for "power" or "might." He says that *bia*, "force," often speaks of oppressive power, exhibiting itself in single deeds of violence. *Dunamis*, "power," is natural ability, general and inherent. *Energeia*, "working," is power in exercise, operative power. *Exousia* primarily means liberty of action; then, "authority" as delegated power or as unrestrained, arbitrary power. *Ischus*, "strength," is power (especially physical strength as an endowment). *Kratos*, "might," is relative or manifested power. (*Lexicon*, p.159-160.)

51 Compare the similar expression in 4:11 which does have the verb written out. At this place the KJV reads "To him *be* glory and dominion ...," but the better manuscripts here omit the word "glory."

52 The same word was often used by Jesus, and in the Gospels is often translated "verily, verily" (KJV), and "truly, truly" in the NASB. See Matthew 5:18,26, 6:2,5,16. See notes on "Amen" at 1 Peter 4:11.

53 Care must be taken at this place lest our comments be thought to impinge on the inspiration of this word of agreement, or on the personal message which follows. In no way should the rest of 1 Peter be thought of as somehow less inspired than the earlier chapters and verses. From our study of 2 Peter 1:21 and 1 Corinthians 2:12,13, which explain how inspiration worked, we learn that the Spirit (as He moved men to speak or write) did not just overwhelm the human penman or mouthpiece. God's mouthpieces knew when the Spirit had come upon them to inspire them to speak God's thoughts after Him, and they searched their vocabularies for just the right word to express what they had learned by revelation (or sometimes by diligent research, Luke 1:1-4). As long as they used the right word to express the truth God wanted taught, the Spirit allowed his human voices to speak or write those words. If they were going to pick a wrong word, the Spirit hindered the writing or speaking, till they searched their vocabularies and picked just the right word. Thus, Peter can write "Amen" as well as the personal greetings in verses 12-14, and we may still affirm they are the result of the Spirit's inspiration just as what was written before was under the influence of the Spirit's inspiration. Worded another way, we are expressing our confidence in the verbal, plenary inspiration of the books of Holy Scripture.

abled the hearers (and us) to express their own personal agreement with the sentiments expressed.

B. Concluding Salutations. 5:12-14

5:12 -- ***Through Silvanus, our faithful brother (for so I regard*** **him*****), I have written to you briefly, exhorting and testifying that this is the true grace of God. Stand firm in it!***

Through Silvanus ... I have written to you briefly -- Verses 12-14 (and perhaps the "amen" at the close of verse 11) were probably a postscript in Peter's own handwriting.[54] It was customary to employ a scribe to write the body of a letter, and the person actually sending it then took the pen in hand and wrote a few words as a means of showing the letter was genuine and what it claimed to be.[55] "Silvanus" is the Latin spelling of Silas. That Silas (the name we are familiar with from Acts 15:22,40) is the same man as the "Silvanus" of the Pauline letters (2 Corinthians 1:19; 1 Thessalonians 1:1; 2 Thessalonians 1:1) is established by a comparison of 2 Corinthians 1:19 with the Acts narrative.[56] "Through Silvanus" has been interpreted in three different ways: (a) Silvanus was the bearer of the letter to the churches;[57] (b) Silvanus served as Peter's amanuensis as Peter dictated the letter; (c) Silvanus composed the letter under Peter's instructions.[58] Of course, the first could be combined with either the second or third view, and in the light of similar language at Acts 15:23 we see no reason Silas could not have carried this letter which he had a chief part in writing. He would have been known to many of the churches addressed in this letter, since on an earlier occasion he had delivered the letter from the Jerusalem Conference to some of the same churches. "I have written" is an epistolary aorist (the reference is to this letter, the writing of which was in the

---

[54] The letter is from Peter, as 1 Peter 1:1 shows.

[55] Compare Paul's statement at the close of 1 Corinthians (16:21). An example of the professional lettering by a scribe, and the scrawled writing of the sender at the close of the letter, can be seen in a papyrus document from the first century pictured with the letter to Philemon in *The Good News*, an illustrated New Testament published by the American Bible Society (New York, 1955).

[56] In the Introductory Studies, we have gathered up the references to Silas (Silvanus), and noted that he was a "prophet" (a New Testament prophet) and one of the leaders of the early church. In Acts, we found both Silas and Mark working with Paul. Now (1 Peter 5:12,13) we have Silas and Mark working with Peter. This certainly calls into question Baur's theory that Peter and Paul were hostile to each other.

[57] In many of the subscriptions found in the KJV, the words "through (someone) ..." mean that that person was the one who carried the letter to its destination. There was no postal system for common citizens in the first century world. Anyone who wanted a letter delivered had to find someone trustworthy who was going to the place to which the letter was addressed and who could be prevailed upon to see the letter was delivered.

[58] Behind the scenes lies the controversy concerning the authorship of 1 Peter, especially the claim that Peter could not have written the "good Greek" of this letter. If "through Silvanus" refers to his mission, and not to his part in the composition of the letter, another explanation for the "good Greek" will have to be found. See the Introductory Studies for more details on this matter.

past when it is publicly read to the readers).[59] What Peter has written is brief – literally, "a few words" – when you consider of the magnitude of the theme and all that he might have said to strengthen and encourage and sustain the readers in their persecutions and sufferings.

Our faithful brother -- Peter praises Silas as being faithful to Jesus and to His church.[60] Is there a subtle hint that such "faithfulness" is exactly what is expected of the readers?

(For so I regard *him*) -- "So (As) I regard" can be explained several different ways. (1) Perhaps it means "I am fully convinced concerning his *faithfulness*." This is the way the ASV/NASB treat it, putting "him" in italics. (2) Perhaps it means, "I suppose I have written *briefly*." (3) Perhaps it means, "I suppose *Silas will carry this letter* to you." Since the letter was intended to pass through the hands of several congregations, Peter recognizes the possibility that someone else might finish the journey that Silas started.

Exhorting and testifying -- These two words are a characterization by Peter of the contents of this letter. In some parts, which we have called the "Doctrinal" sections, Peter is testifying, bearing witness to the facts and truths of Christianity.[61] In the other parts, which we have called the "Hortatory" sections, Peter is exhorting, earnestly and persuasively appealing to their wills in an attempt to brace them for the trials they will have to face.

That this is the true grace of God -- What is the "true grace of God"? Why, the religion to which they are called on to be true till death, the message of salvation presented in this letter, all the promises of what God will do for them to help them in this life and the next. Christianity – not Judaism or paganism – is the only valid, genuine religion in the world, the only avenue through which grace from God (see notes at 5:10) is available to men.

Stand firm in it! -- This is the final imperative[62] in Peter's letter of encouragement. Given the probability of the persecution and opposition they are to face, Peter's ringing cry is "Stand fast!" No wavering, no quitting, no denial of Jesus! In the strength that God supplies, be brave and courageous for Jesus!

---

[59] There is no reference to 2 Peter, or to a lost letter, as some have thought, after treating the aorist tense verb "I wrote" as though it were an historical aorist. An "epistolary aorist" was perfectly proper Greek. In English we prefer to use either the present or the perfect tense to express the same idea.

[60] Paul, likewise, often spoke a similar word of praise for his assistants who were being sent on a mission.

[61] The Greek for "testifying" is *epimarturon*. Some try to make the *epi-* mean that Peter is "adding" his testimony to that of Paul and others who had gone before through these areas evangelizing. Peter is testifying to the same truths those original preachers taught. (Again, contrary to Baur, Peter and Paul agree in their teaching.)

[62] There is a manuscript variation here. Some (followed by the KJV) read it as perfect indicative "in which you [having entered in the past] are standing." The imperative is the better attested reading.

5:13 -- ***She who is in Babylon, chosen together with you, sends you greetings, and*** **so does** ***my son, Mark.***

She ... chosen together with you – Literally, the Greek reads "the co-elect (something feminine) in Babylon sends greetings." "Chosen" (or elect) reminds us of 1:1, where we learned that Christians are God's New Testament "chosen" people. The KJV and NASB margin read "the *church* in Babylon ...." The feminine word "church" is found in no extant papyrus or uncial manuscript with the remarkable exception of Sinaiticus. It is also found in the Latin Vulgate and Peshitto Syriac versions. If we don't supply the noun "church," what feminine noun could we supply? Some have thought Peter has reference to his wife who accompanied him on his missionary journeys (1 Corinthians 9:5) and who would therefore have been known to Peter's readers. If this is Peter's meaning, then verse 13 includes greetings from two individuals, Peter's wife and Mark. This commentator has concluded Peter probably has reference to the congregation in the place where he is when he writes this letter. Since 1 Peter is addressed to numerous congregations, it is likely the *sun-* in *suneklekte* points to the co-elect ("chosen together") as being a congregation also, rather than an individual. It seems unlikely that an individual, even Peter's wife, would be described as co-chosen.

Who is in Babylon -- In the Introductory Studies, we have noted that there generally are four different interpretations given to this word – Babylon in Egypt, or the one on the Euphrates, or taken figuratively it might refer to Jerusalem or Rome. In those same studies we opted for the choice of Rome. We believe this letter was written from Rome.

Sends you greetings -- This is another subtle encouragement to the readers to stand firm in the faith. The church in the town where Peter is when he writes is aware he is writing this letter. The church there is being persecuted and continues to stand firm for Christ. The implication is that we expect you readers to do the same as we are doing in the face of Nero's persecution.

And ***so does*** **my son, Mark** -- Mark, too, sends you his greetings. This is the well-known John Mark whom we meet in Acts 12:25. He has made good after his failure during Paul's first missionary journey (Acts 13:13), likely because of the help and encouragement he received from Barnabas (Acts 15:36-40). Peter's calling Mark "my son" is reminiscent of Paul's description of Timothy (1 Timothy 1:2,18; 2 Timothy 1:2, 2:1). It indicates more than a close existing personal relationship between the men. In both cases "son" seems to point to a spiritual relationship, Timothy being Paul's convert and Mark being Peter's convert. We can even conjecture when Mark was led to Christ by Peter. One congregation in Jerusalem, after Pentecost, met in Mark's mother's home (Acts 12:12). We can see Peter as the one who often preached to the Christians assembled here, and at one of those meetings (if not already at Pentecost), Mark responded to the invitation offered by Peter to become a Christian. As suggested in the Introductory Studies, Mark is included in sending greetings because he is with Peter at the time the letter is written.[63] So then, gathering up the conclusions reached in this verse, we have suggested that a congregation at Rome and Mark, the companion of Peter, are included in this word of greeting being sent to the readers of this letter.

5:14 -- *Greet one another with a kiss of love. Peace be to you all who are in Christ.*

Greet one another with a kiss of love -- In obedience to this command, at this point as this letter was being read to the congregation, each person present would bestow a "kiss of love"[64] on the cheek of every other member.[65] It was to be a warm greeting prompted by love and was to be an expression of genuine Christian love for that person. Of course, after one has in such a loving fashion greeted a brother, how could there be any thought of hiding or failing to get involved when those same brothers needed help because they were suffering persecution?

Peace be to you all who are in Christ -- Peter closes his letter with a prayer like he often heard from Jesus' own lips. True peace (like that mentioned in 1:2) can be enjoyed only by those who are "in Christ."[66] The peace of God is greater than all the troubles and distresses that the world can bring!

Amen -- The manuscript evidence is against this "Amen" (which appears in the KJV, but not the NASB) being in Peter's autograph.[67] This one may have been added by a later copyist as

---

[63] In footnote #57 in the Introductory Studies, we have quoted Papias' statement about Mark and Peter being together in Rome. In the same way, Irenaeus (AD 180) says that after the death of Peter and Paul at Rome, "Mark, the disciple and interpreter of Peter, also handed down to us in writing what had been preached by Peter." *Adv. Haer.* 3.1.1.

[64] Some manuscripts read "with a holy kiss," but "kiss of love" is the better supported reading in the manuscripts.

[65] "Greet one another" is an aorist imperative. Peter expects his readers to do it once. A kiss on the cheek was a common form of Oriental greeting among friends (cp. Luke 7:45). It was as common among orientals as shaking hands is in Western culture. At some point in early church practice it became a custom for the brethren to welcome each other with a "holy kiss." In some congregations this happened after the prayers. In some congregations it occurred just before the Lord's Supper. In some it was at the close of the service. As the years passed, the custom began to be abused, so the practice was regulated, men kissing only men, and women only women; and in due time the custom gradually dwindled and fell into disuse. See further comments concerning the "holy kiss" in the author's commentaries on 1 Corinthians 16:20; 2 Corinthians 13:12; 1 Thessalonians 5:26; and Romans 16:16. "The obligation of brotherly love," says MacDonald, "is a standing order for the church, though the manner of expressing it may vary in cultures and times." William MacDonald, *1 Peter: Faith Tested, Future Triumphant* (Wheaton, IL: Shaw, 1972), p.109.

[66] The KJV reads "all that are in Christ Jesus," but the better manuscripts omit "Jesus."

[67] It is possible that this "Amen" is authentic as were the ones in 4:11 and 5:11. However, the fact that the scribes of a number of Greek manuscripts, as well as the Coptic and Ethiopic versions, resisted the strong liturgical temptation to add it casts doubt on its presence in Peter's autograph copy of this letter.

a signal for the congregation to respond with a vocal "Amen" at the conclusion of the reading of this letter in the public assembly.

Someone has summarized what Peter has written under the title "Something to Hold Onto." Ideas presented are these: 1) As Peter went from shifting sand to solid rock, so may we. 2) Our great salvation provides a hope that sustains us. 3) Be holy! 4) Christians are God's special people. 5) Each Christian has a job as a priest, a bridge builder. 6) There is an attitude toward life to be embraced – to live in purity, to live with the end in view, to live for others. 7) Wear the name "Christian" with honor. 8) Right relationships are important – right relationships with God and right relationships with our fellow men. Both must be stressed. 9) Be true to Jesus! Christianity is the only valid religion in the world.

Commentary On

2 Peter

2 PETER

INTRODUCTORY STUDIES

Preliminaries

2 Peter is a much neglected book, one of the most neglected of the New Testament. It appears to have been neglected in the decades after it first was written. It is neglected still today. It is a book which very few modern people will claim to have read, still less to have studied in detail. Sadly, some modern critical studies are likely to result in the book being neglected still more.

Should this book be in our Bible? The evidence that any particular book belongs in the Bible is sometimes stronger, and sometimes weaker, than for other books in the Canon. Now it is true that the external evidence for 2 Peter is weaker than for any other book of the New Testament. The first annotated reference to 2 Peter comes from the third century AD. Because of this, some scholars have suggested it was not written until the second century, and not by Peter but by someone who forged Peter's name to the work. There is such a similarity between chapter two of 2 Peter and the Epistle of Jude that some scholars have questioned who copied from whom. (This is an especially important question, for if 2 Peter is a copy of Jude, it cannot have been written by the apostle Peter. If 2 Peter is not apostolic, then there is doubt as to its inspiration, and consequently doubt as to its rightful place in the New Testament canon.)

Because so many scholars today reject this letter as being a genuine work of the apostle Peter, and because of the multitude of what sound like plausible reasons given for so treating it, this Introductory Study will be longer and more technical as an attempt is made to arrive at a true appraisal of all the evidence.

I. GENUINENESS OF 2 PETER

A. **Genuineness has to do with authorship.** 2 Peter is genuine if Peter wrote it. Objections to the genuineness of 2 Peter are more serious than those objections raised against any other book in the New Testament canon.

B. **External Evidence.**[1] *(It is weaker than the external evidence for any other New Testament book.)*

There are no annotated quotations of this epistle in early Christian writings for at least

[1] In our New Testament Introduction studies, we have learned there are four kinds of external evidence: (1) allusions; (2) quotations; (3) annotated quotations; and (4) canonical listings.

a century after it was written. There are, however, some *scattered allusions*[2] to 2 Peter from those years before AD 210. Typical of such allusions are these:

> Clement of Rome, AD 96,[3] wrote, "Noah preached repentance, and those who obeyed him were saved" (I Cl. 7.6; cp. 2 Peter 2:5). "On account of his hospitality and piety, Lot was saved out of Sodom when all the surrounding region was condemned by fire and brimstone. God made it appear that He does not forsake those who trust in Him; but on the other hand, those who turn aside He appoints to punishment and torment" (I Cl. 11; cp. 2 Peter 2:6-9). "These things we have heard even in the time of our fathers; and behold, we are grown old, and none of these things have happened to us" (I Cl. 23; cp. 2 Peter 3:4). Two distinctive and rare phrases are peculiar only to 2 Peter and 1 Clement. One is "the Majestic Glory" (1 Cl. 9:2; cp. 2 Peter 1:17); the other is where the Christian life is called "the way of truth" (1 Cl. 35:5; cp. 2 Peter 2:2).[4]

An interesting piece of evidence for the use of 2 Peter is found in the *Apocalypse of Peter*,[5] which Harnack dated as probably AD 120-140. It contains some striking allusions to 2 Peter. It speaks of the Mount of Transfiguration as a "holy mountain" (cp. 2 Peter 1:18). In the Akhmim Fragment of that work: verse 1, "Many of them shall be false prophets and shall teach ways and diverse doctrines of perdition" (cp. 2 Peter 2:1); verse 21, "another place ... very gloomy" (cp. 2 Peter 1:19); verses 22,28, "blaspheming the way of righteousness" (cp. 2 Peter 2:2,21). Bigg and Strachan concluded the *Apocalypse* is dependent on 2 Peter, rather than vice versa.[6]

---

[2] It should be remembered that an "allusion" is not as word-for-word exact as would be a "quotation." F.H. Chase ("Peter, Second Epistle of," *Hasting's Dictionary of the Bible* [New York: Scribners, 1908], V.3, p.799ff) examines the allusions we are about to reference (and many more in addition), but because he finds no evidence of "literary dependence" he argues that none of the references prove anything about the existence of 2 Peter. His term "literary dependence" matches our term "quotation." He may not find any "quotations" but he never discusses what we call "allusions" (until [p.814] he wants to make a case for 2 Peter being a copy of the *Apocalypse of Peter* -- then he can, with hearty approval, give a whole page of examples of such "a remarkable series of coincidences"). All an "allusion" does is show the writer was aware a certain work existed because he gives the gist of some passage or passages found in that work.

[3] If Clement alludes to 2 Peter, that is strong evidence that 2 Peter was written before AD 150, the date many modern critics assign to the letter on internal grounds.

[4] See Robert E. Picirilli, "Allusions to 2 Peter in the Apostolic Fathers," *JSNT* 33 (1988), p.59-60.

[5] After New Testament times, when the Gnostic heresy was flourishing in the Mediterranean world, a whole body of literature was produced with the intent to give written justification of the heresy. These apocryphal and pseudepigraphical writings were made to look like they were written by famous men who had lived years earlier than when the writings were actually produced. Peter's name, as well as that of Thomas, James, Matthias, Mary, Bartholomew, and others, can be found affixed to these fictitious writings.

[6] Charles Bigg, "2 Peter" in the *ICC* (Edinburgh: T&T Clark, 1901), p.207-209. R.H. Strachan, "The Second Epistle General of Peter," *The Expositor's Greek Testament* (Grand Rapids: Eerdmans, 1967), p.88-89. Bauckham considers this evidence good enough to rule out a date later than the *Apocalypse* for 2 Peter ("Jude, 2 Peter," *Word Biblical Commentary* [Waco, TX: Word, 1983], p.162.)

2 Clement, c. AD 120-140, speaks of the destruction of the earth by fire. (2 Cl. xvi.3; cp. 2 Peter 3:10.)

The Shepherd of Hermas, AD 140, alludes to 2 Peter 2:15. "They are such as have believed, but through their doubting have forsaken the true way" (*Vision* iii.7; cp. 2 Peter 2:15).

The *Gospel of Truth*, c. AD 150, a Gnostic document, written to try to prove by appealing to Biblical writings that Gnosticism is not a heresy, may have allusions to 2 Peter 1:17 and 2:2.[7]

Justin Martyr, AD 150, may allude to 2 Peter 3:8, "A day with the Lord is as a thousand years" (*Dial.* ch.81). Some doubt this is a reference to 2 Peter, thinking it comes from Psalm 90:4 instead.[8] Most likely *Dial.* ch.82.1 is a reminiscence of 2 Peter 1:21 and 2:1 with its use of "false teachers" and "false prophets" in the same sentence. "But as there were false prophets (*pseudoprophetai*) in the time of the holy prophets who arose among you, so also in the present day there are many false teachers (*pseudodidaskaloi*) also, of whom our Lord forewarned us to beware."[9]

Melito of Sardis, AD 170, may allude to 2 Peter 3:5-7 in his *Apology* addressed to Antoninus. He speaks of a "flood of fire" and the "earth being burnt up."

The *Epistle of the Churches of Vienne and Lyon*, AD 177, may have two striking resemblances to 2 Peter, which seem to demand that the author was acquainted with 2 Peter. One is "not wasted nor unfruitful," (quoted in Eusebius, *H.E.*, v.1.45; cp. 2 Peter 1:8). The other is the use of *exodos* of death (Eusebius, *H.E.*, v.1,35,66; 2:3; cp. 2 Peter 1:15).

Irenaeus, AD 180, has a reminiscence of 2 Peter 3:5-7. "A day with the Lord is as a thousand years" (*Adv. Haer.* 5.23.2., *Adv. Haer.* 5.28.3; cp. 2 Peter 3:8).[10]

---

[7] W.C. van Unnik, "The 'Gospel of Truth' and the New Testament," in *The Jung Codex*, edited by F.L. Cross (London: Mowbray, 1955), p.116. The codex was discovered at Nag Hammadi in 1945. The copies found at Nag Hammadi are believed to be copies of documents that originally were made about the middle of the second century at Rome and then taken to Egypt.

[8] F.H. Chase (*Hasting's Dictionary of the Bible*, Vol.3, p.796ff) has subjected all these allusions in the primitive writings to a very keen and searching criticism. His criticism requires that defenders of any supposed allusion to 2 Peter must be careful lest they overstate the evidence. (See also comments in footnote #2, above.)

[9] The word *pseudodiskaloi* occurs only in 2 Peter before the time of Justin.

[10] Michael J. Kruger, "The Authenticity of 2 Peter," *JETS* 42/4 (Dec. 1999), p.653 shows convincingly that Irenaeus' language is a reminiscence of 2 Peter 3:8, rather than Psalm 90:4. Part of his argument is that both Irenaeus' and Peter's quotations vary widely from the LXX but are virtually identical with each other. He also calls attention to a statement by Methodius (c.260-312) who in his *De Resurrectione* says this quotation is from "the apostle Peter."

Theophilus of Antioch, late 2nd century, perhaps has an allusion to 2 Peter 1:20-21. "Men of God filled with the Holy Spirit, and becoming prophets, inspired by God Himself, and being enlightened, were taught of God" (*Ad Autolycus* II.9).

Clement of Alexandria, AD 190, wrote expositions (i.e., commentaries), not only on the canonical Scriptures, but also on the disputed books, as the Epistle of Jude and "the remaining Catholic Epistles," so Eusebius tells us (*H.E.*, vi.14). This actually tells us little concerning 2 Peter, saving that it may imply that it was in existence.[11]

After AD 200, there are some clear *annotated quotations* of 2 Peter.

Origen, AD 210, wrote, "Peter speaks aloud through the two trumpets of his epistles ..." in his 7th *Homily on Joshua*. **This is the first annotated reference to 2 Peter in early Christian literature.**[12] Many reviews of external evidence include a statement like "The epistle was not certainly known until Origen's time." The way that statement is worded ignores the allusions and instead leaves the impression that the authenticity of 2 Peter is immediately suspect. This is a misleading implication to convey!

Origen also wrote, "Peter ... has left one epistle universally acknowledged. And let it be granted likewise that he wrote a second, for this is disputed" (*Commentary on John*, 5.3). Origen recognized that some had doubts about 2 Peter, but he himself certainly did not.[13]

Hippolytus of Portus (a suburb of Rome), AD 220, has a passage which seems to be an expansion of 2 Peter 1:20,21. "These fathers were furnished with the Spirit and largely honored by the Word Himself ... and when moved by Him the prophets announced what God willed. For they spake not of their own power, neither did they declare what pleased themselves ..." (*De Antichristo*, ch.2). In Hippolytus' *Refutation of All Heresies* (9.7.3) he has language that is most likely an allusion to 2 Peter 2:20 ("a sow, after washing, returns to wallowing in the mire"), since both writers use the second half of the proverb as a reference to heretics.

Firmilian, bishop of Cappadocian Caesarea, AD 270, in his epistle to Cyprian, speaks

---

[11] Michael J. Kruger, *op. cit.*, p.652 gives a succinct summary of the value of Clement's evidence. He cites references used by those who would deny 2 Peter's existence and references by those who defend the genuineness of 2 Peter. He concludes it is probable Clement did possess, use, and comment upon 2 Peter.

[12] To some, these testimonies from Origen are suspicious since they are found only in the Latin translation made by Rufinus – whom many claim took the liberty of adding to Origen's words, especially in his Homilies. In none of Origen's authentic Greek works is 2 Peter quoted or attributed to the apostle Peter, though 1 Peter is. See this discussed in Chase (*Hasting's Dictionary of the Bible*, Vol.3, p.803b).

[13] See below, footnote #135.

"of Peter and Paul, the blessed apostles ... who execrated heretics in their epistles, and warned us to avoid them."[14] Peter says nothing of "heretics" in his first letter; therefore, the reference must be to 2 Peter.

Methodius, bishop of Tyre, who died c. AD 305 (apparently, he was martyred during the persecutions of Diocletian's reign), speaks of the conflagration that shall purify and renew the earth. (*Ad. Epiphan. Haeres.*, LXIV.31; cp. 2 Peter 3:5-7).

The Bodmer VIII Papyrus from the "early 200's"[15] (see picture next page) is one of the most exciting of the recent papyrus discoveries. The papyrus manuscripts are, for the most part, the oldest copies of the New Testament books we have. Bodmer VIII is a copy of 2 Peter, and it is very early. Just when critics have been attacking the genuineness of 2 Peter, may we suggest God has allowed the archaeologists to uncover just the kind of evidence needed to reassure us of the validity of the sources on which our faith is based![16]

The two great Egyptian versions of the third century, the Bohairic Coptic, probably originating in the first half of the century, and the Sahidic Coptic, apparently going back to the very beginning of the century,[17] both included 2 Peter.

Canonical Listings begin to occur in early Christian literature when the church was revisiting the question of the canon, after heresies had begun to challenge the accepted books.

Eusebius, AD 325, classified the writings that came to him into three groups: 1) *Homologoumena* – All men everywhere accept them as Scripture (because their authorship is accepted). 2) *Antilegomena* – Some people in some places doubted their

---

[14] This reference is in *Epistle 74* (in the collection of Cyprian's Epistles, *Ante-Nicene Fathers*, Amer. ed., Vol. V, p. 391). It is *Epistle 75* in the Oxford edition.

[15] This is the date given by R. Laird Harris in his article on "Canonicity" in *Zondervan Pictorial Dictionary of the Bible* (Grand Rapids, MI: Zondervan, 1963), p.145. The UBS^2 apparatus gives the date as the third or fourth centuries.

[16] P^{72} (Bodmer VII-IX) contains 1 and 2 Peter and Jude (all copied by the same scribal hand) along with Psalm 33 and 34, and a seemingly miscellaneous collection of non-canonical works. Some call attention to these non-canonical works (the Nativity of Mary, the apocryphal correspondence of Paul to the Corinthians, the Apology of Phileas, etc.) in an attempt to minimize the testimony of P^{72} to 2 Peter. P^{72} contains 1 Peter and Jude as well as 2 Peter. At the end of each Scripture manuscript there is a blessing on the readers more elaborate than for the non-canonical works. (See Edwin A. Blum, "2 Peter," in *Expositor's Bible Commentary*, Vol.12, ed. Frank E. Gaebelein [Grand Rapids: Zondervan, 1981], p.257.) It may be argued how much P^{72} helps us with the question of what books were included in the canon, but it is not debatable that it does help us with the existence and value attributed to the book in Alexandria. It helps explain how Clement of Alexandria and Origen were familiar with 2 Peter. It may also help explain why 2 Peter and Jude were both included in the 3rd century Coptic versions.

[17] Henry C. Thiessen, *Introduction to the New Testament* (Grand Rapids: Eerdmans, 1943), p.56,57.

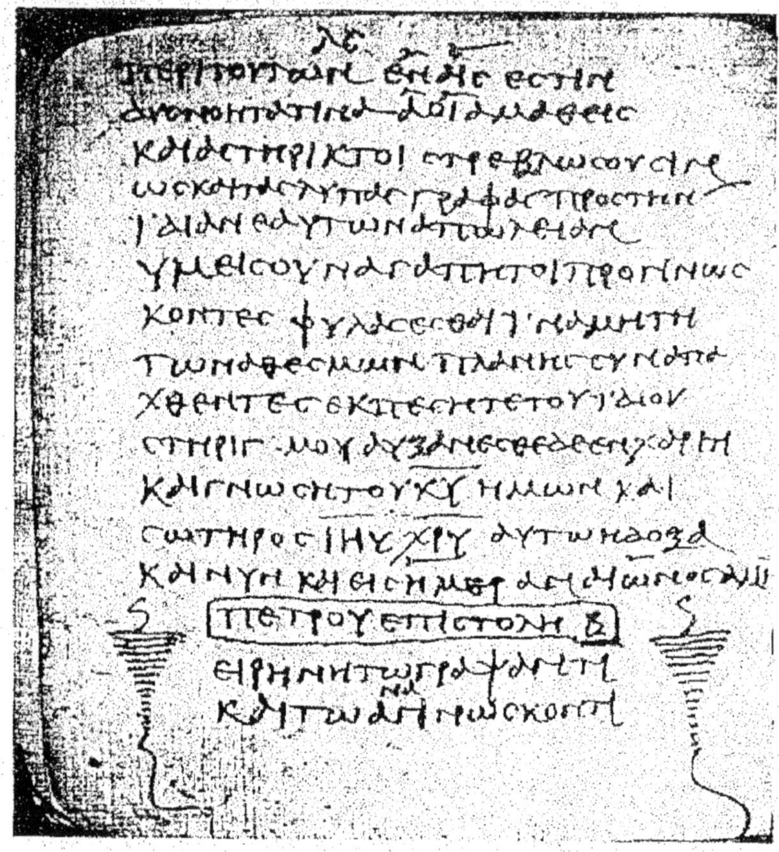

P^{72} -- Bodmer VIII, a 3rd century manuscript. This leaf shows 2 Peter 3:16-18, followed by the "title" (ΠΕΤΡΟΥ ΕΠΙΣΤΟΛΗ Β, "Second Epistle of Peter"), and ending with the scribe's prayer for himself and for the reader "Peace to the one who has written, and to the one who reads [out loud]."

---

authorship, and spoke against them. 3) *"Spurious" or Rejected* – Certain books were rejected altogether.[18] Eusebius placed 2 Peter in the *Antilegomena*, not the "spurious."

> "Of Peter, one Epistle, which is called his former Epistle, is acknowledged by all; of this the ancient presbyters have made frequent use in their writings as indisputably genuine; but that called his second epistle, we have been informed, has not been received into the New Testa-

---

[18] "Spurious" books and "pseudepigrapha" are two terms for the same thing. Thus those who attempt to insist that a document can both be a *known* forgery and still be included in the canon are tragically out of step with the early church fathers.

> ment but as it appeared to be useful to many, it has been diligently studied with the other Scripture." (*HE.*, iii.3)
>
> "Among the disputed writings (*Antilegomena*), which are nevertheless recognized by many, are extant the so-called Epistle of James, and that of Jude, also the second Epistle of Peter, and those that are called the second and third of John ...." (*H.E.,* iii.25)

After the time of Eusebius, the epistle we call 2 Peter appears to have been generally recognized as canonical.[19] 2 Peter was recognized as canonical by the Councils of Laodicea (366),[20] Hippo (393), and Carthage (397). It is not in the Muratorian Canon as the fragment presently reads,[21] or the Peshitto Syriac version (c.AD 425),[22] but Ephraem Syrus received seven Catholic Epistles,[23] as did the Philoxenian Syriac (a new Syriac version produced about AD 508).

Jerome, c.AD 347-420, spoke of two epistles as written by Peter. "Peter wrote two epis-

---

[19] It is included in Codex Sinaiticus and Codex Vaticanus. It has been argued on the evidence of the "capitulations" in Vaticanus that an earlier ancestor possibly did not have 2 Peter in it. "Capitulations" are section titles, and this manuscript apparently has two systems of division into sections, one older than the other, with the older one missing 2 Peter.

[20] The Council requested that only the "canonical" books be read in the churches. The 60th canon gives a list of the accepted New Testament books, but there are some who insist the 60th canon is not authentic. (Cf. B.F. Westcott, *A General Survey of the History of the Canon of the New Testament* [London: Macmillan, 1870], p.400-407.)

[21] What is to be made of this circumstance must be weighed against the fact that 1 Peter, which was universally accepted, was also omitted, yet the *Apocalypse of Peter*, which was universally rejected, is included in the canon. The Muratorian Canon is a poor Latin translation of a listing of New Testament books evidently originally written in Greek. The present text is incomplete. Zahn made an ingenious attempt to emend the Latin text to include a reference to both epistles of Peter in place of the *Apocalypse of Peter* (*Geschichte des neutestamentlichen Kanons* [Leipzig: Deichert, 1904], p.96, n.4). Westcott also has discovered indications of breaks in the present copy which he believes imply a lost clause due to careless copying, and that the Greek original did indeed contain the New Testament books (James, 1 and 2 Peter, Hebrews) which are missing in the Latin copy. (B.F. Westcott, *op. cit.*, p.198,199.)

The date of the Muratorian canon is still disputed. It has been rather customary to give it a second-century AD date. However, A.C. Sundburg, Jr., argued for a fourth-century date in "Canon Muratori: A Fourth Century List," *HTR* 66 (1973), p.1-41.

[22] The Peshitto Syriac contained all the New Testament books except 2 Peter, 2 and 3 John, Jude, and Revelation. They were omitted because at the time this version was produced the Syrian Church did not recognize any of those books as canonical.

[23] Ephraem the Syrian (c.AD 308-373), working at Edessa, Syria, wrote many commentaries, homilies, and hymns. His Bible was the "Old Syriac" (of which only two fragmentary copies of the Gospels are extant -- the Sinaitic Syriac and the Curetonian Syriac), a translation first produced before AD 200. The Peshitto (which means "standard") Syriac replaced the Old Syriac version as the standard Bible for the Syrian churches, holding a place among the Syrian churches comparable to the Vulgate in the Roman Church, or the KJV in the English churches. (Until the Sinaitic and Curetonian Syriac manuscripts were discovered in the late 1800's, scholars presumed the Peshitto was the oldest Syriac version, and many of the older commentaries treat the Peshitto as though it were the same as the Old Syriac.) Ephraem's evidence shows the Syrian church wavered about including these books in the canon -- first they did, then they did not, then they did again.

tles which are called catholic, the second of which most persons deny to be his, on account of its disagreement in style with the first" (*De Scriptor. Ecclesiast.* ch.1). In another place, he explains the difference of language and style by the fact that Peter employed a different "interpreter" (*hermeneutes*) in the case of the second epistle.

> Paul therefore had Titus for his interpreter, as Peter also had Mark, whose gospel was composed by Peter narrating and the other writing. Finally, also, the two epistles which are called Peter's differ from each other in style and character and structure of words. Whence we understand that he used different interpreters, according to the necessity of the case.[24]

Augustine accepted it as did Epiphanius. By the time of the Reformation, Luther seems to have had no doubt of its genuineness though he questioned 2 Peter 2:9,15. Erasmus regarded 2 Peter either as spurious or written by Silvanus on Peter's direction.[25] Calvin, in the preface to his commentary on 2 Peter, felt 2 Peter must have been written by a disciple at Peter's direction because of the "discrepancies between it and the First." Then came the critics in the 19th and 20th centuries[26] – who concluded 2 Peter is not an apostolic document, was not written by Peter, and was not written in the first century of our era, but about the middle of the second century.[27]

> "If this [critical] view is accepted, we must pronounce the epistle a forgery, pseudonymous and pseudepigraphic, with no more right to be in the NT than has the Apocalypse of Peter or the romance of the Shepherd of Hermas."[28]

When compared with allusions, annotated quotations, and canonical listings found in Christian literature for other New Testament books, what we find for 2 Peter is sparse.[29] When

---

[24] *Epist. cxx ad Hedibia, Quaest.*11.

[25] 2 Peter itself gives no support whatever to the idea that an amanuensis helped in its writing. Compare 1 Peter 5:12.

[26] Modern critical doubts can be traced as far back as Grotius who dated the Epistle to Trajan's time. J.S. Semler in 1784 characterized the epistle as a forgery. Eichhorn (1814) rejected it because he thought 2 Peter was dependent on Jude.

[27] When J.N.D. Kelly wrote his *Commentary on the Epistles of Peter and Jude* (London: Black, 1969), p.235, his observation was "scarcely anyone nowadays doubts that 2 Peter is pseudonymous." Since then, a well-written defense of the Petrine authorship of 2 Peter has been produced by Michael J. Kruger, "The Authenticity of 2 Peter," *JETS* 42/4 (Dec. 1999), p.645-671.

[28] Wm. G. Moorehead, "Peter, the Second Epistle of," *International Standard Bible Encyclopedia,* edited by James Orr (Grand Rapids, MI: Eerdmans, 1949), Vol.4, p.2355. More will be said about pseudonymity later in these Introductory Studies.

[29] 2 Peter has significantly more support for its inclusion in the canon than the best of those books which have been rejected. Kruger (*op. cit.*, p.652) asks, "Is it possible that we only consider 2 Peter's evidence to be meager and inadequate when we compare it to the overabundance of evidence that is available for the primary books of the New Testament? Perhaps when 2 Peter is compared with what is necessary to authenticate any other early writings of the [same] time period, [the external evidence] will prove to be quite sufficient." He then calls attention to Warfield's list of examples, how other writings with as much (or less) external evidence as 2 Peter has are never

in the history of the church it became necessary to "guard the books[30] of the canon," 2 Peter was very slowly acknowledged as Scripture.

A little meditation on the matter will produce several possible reasons for this hesitancy. (1) The letter is not definitely addressed. When copies circulated, their source could not be promptly traced. It would not be easy to go to the original destination(s) in order to verify the fact that Peter wrote this letter to that place. (2) At the time the canon was being guarded there was a whole body of pseudo-Petrine literature circulating which the church had to judge as being genuine or not. Gnostic groups were using Peter's name to drive home their own peculiar tenets. Was 2 Peter just another of these fakes? The church would have to take care not to give an imprimatur to any spurious "Petrine" letter. The fact 2 Peter ultimately was accepted in spite of the pseudo-Petrine literature is evidence favorable to its authenticity and its contents.[31] If the evidence for the existence, use, and acceptance of 2 Peter as an apostolic work is really as unconvincing as modern critics assert, it is remarkable the letter has survived.[32]

The external evidence is small and weak, yet it testifies to a wide circulation of the epistle. If all the allusions are real, then in the far separated districts of Alexandria, Palestine, Cappadocia, Proconsular Asia, Italy, and Carthage were Christians into whose hands the epistle had come. The authorship was doubted by some but rejected by none. There is no evidence from any geographic area of the early Church that 2 Peter was ever rejected as "spurious."[33] Rather, the evidence was sufficient to convince the church in spite of the fact some spoke against it. Jerome noted the difference in style, yet it was the great respect in which his scholarship was held that overcame the doubt about 2 Peter in the Greek and Latin churches as we come to the close of the period of the guarding of the canon.

---

questioned. "Herodotus is quoted once in the century which followed its composition, but once in the next, not at all in the next, only twice in the next, and not until its fifth century is anything like as fully witnessed to as 2 Peter is in its second. Again, Thucydides is not distinctly quoted until quite two centuries after its composition; while Tacitus is first cited by Tertullian. Yet no one thinks of disputing the genuineness of Herodotus, Thucydides or Tacitus." B.B. Warfield, "The Canonicity of Second Peter," in *Selected Shorter writings of Benjamin B. Warfield*, vol. 2 edited by John E. Meeter (New Jersey: Presbyterian and Reformed, 1973), p.65.

[30] A brief overview of the growth of the New Testament canon is given in notes below.

[31] R.C.H. Lenski (*The Interpretation of I and II Epistles of Peter, the Three Epistles of John, and the Epistle of Jude* [Minneapolis: Augsburg, 1966], p.238) conjectured that 2 Peter was written from a now unknown place during one of Peter's missionary journeys (before his visit to Rome late in his life). He thinks this would cause further problems to those trying to verify the authenticity of this letter since they would have trouble going to the place where it was written to ascertain if folk there knew Peter wrote it. (Not many have followed Lenski in his conclusions about the "place of writing" of 2 Peter. More will have to be said on this topic in a moment.)

[32] 2 Peter 3:1 says this is "the second letter" being written to the readers. Lenski argues the "first one" is not our 1 Peter but was a letter now lost. That makes the survival of our "2 Peter" even more remarkable. We'll have more to say on this matter later in this Introduction.

[33] This is significant, for if 20th century scholarship is correct – that 2 Peter is a pseudonymous writing – and if the early church knew it, they would have classified it as "spurious," not "antilegomena."

C. Internal Evidence. *(It is stronger than the internal evidence for any other New Testament Book.)*

The personal allusions found throughout the letter point to Peter as the author. Examples of such allusions include: (1) 1:1 – "Simon Peter, an apostle of Jesus" signed the letter. (2) 1:3 may well be a reference to the Lord's call of the twelve apostles, as well as an allusion to their empowerment on Pentecost. (3) 1:14 – "The laying aside of my earthly dwelling is imminent, as also our Lord Jesus has made clear to me." Cp. John 21:18,19, where it is recorded Jesus signified "by what death [Peter] should glorify God." (4) 1:16-18 – The writer claims to be an eyewitness of the transfiguration of Jesus. That limits the writer to one of the three men, Peter, James, and John, who were with Jesus at the transfiguration. (5) 3:1 – "This is ... the second letter I am writing" fits Peter, for we have another epistle written by Peter. (6) 3:15 – He places himself on a level with the apostle Paul, and claims acquaintance with Paul. Paul was an acquaintance of Peter. Compare Acts 15 and Galatians 2 to see evidence of this. And Paul was not one whit beneath Peter when it came to apostolic authority (Galatians 2:6-12).

The writer claims to be Peter. Either Peter wrote this letter, or the writer is a liar. Plagiarism (or forgery, or pseudonymous writing) was not an accepted practice of that time as some modern Bible critics assert. The modern contention that the ancients had no conscience about forgery is false. A man from a church in Corinth was excommunicated for forgery of a letter, exactly what the liberals claim someone did for 2 Peter.[34] For the same reason (i.e., that it was pseudepigraphic) Serapion rejected the *Gospel of Peter*.[35] The spurious epistles to the Laodiceans and to the Alexandrines were listed for that same reason among the rejected works in the Muratorian Fragment.[36]

---

[34] The author of the *Acts of Paul and Thecla* was removed from his position as elder for trying to pass off something he wrote as being written by Paul. (See Tertullian, *On Baptism*, 17). Some defenders of pseudonymity have attempted to minimize this testimony that such was not an accepted practice by affirming the author was not disciplined for using Paul's name, but for passing off false doctrine (e.g., allowing women to baptize). However, in the passage from Tertullian, it specifically says that the *Acts of Paul and Thecla* are "writings that *wrongly* go under Paul's name," and that the pseudepigrapher was disciplined for attempting to "augment Paul's fame from his own store."

[35] When Serapion had examined the writing and found Peter did not write it, he said, "We receive both Peter and the other apostles as Christ, but the writings which falsely bear their names (*pseudepigrapha*) we reject" (Eusebius, *H.E.*, vi.12.1). Defenders of pseudonymity try to dull the force of this statement by asserting that it was false doctrine, not authorship, that was the main issue that prompted Serapion. William R. Farmer contended that Serapion at first allowed the *Gospel of Peter* to be read in the church before he found out it was heretical, and argues on this basis that it was doctrine that was the issue. However, Farmer fails to make a distinction between apostolic writings that were deemed *authoritative*, and those writings which were *used* because they were highly valued. J.A.T. Robinson commented, "Though the *motive* of [Serapion's] condemnation of [the *Gospel of Peter*] was the docetic heresy that he heard it was spreading, the *criterion* of his judgment, to which he brought the expertise in these matters that he claimed, was its genuineness as the work of the apostle." *Redating the New Testament* (Philadelphia: Westminster, 1976), p.188, (emphasis GLR).

[36] Those letters, though claiming to be written by the apostle Paul, were rejected as "forgeries." That term is hardly compatible with the modern idea that pseudonymous works were accepted by people in the early church.

In opposition to the internal evidence that appears strong at face value, negative critics have marshaled numerous arguments from internal evidence against the Petrine authorship of this letter. Some of their assertions require examination.

(1) The writer "**tries too hard to make himself look like Peter**" in a manner that is forced and unnatural, some have claimed. (a) Several assertions are offered to support this claim: The writer uses a double name "Symeon Peter" (1:1); the reference to the Lord's prophecy of Peter's death (1:14); a supposed poorly camouflaged attempt by the writer to claim credit for Mark's Gospel (1:15), thereby giving himself more credibility; there is a reference to the transfiguration (1:18); an attempt to identify himself with the author of 1 Peter (3:1); the writer reasserts his apostleship (3:2); and another attempt to appear as an apostle (3:15). (b) *Refutation:* (i) If there is little or no evidence of the authorship, the liberal critics say "We have too little evidence of the authorship for ... to have written it." If there is strong evidence for the authorship, the liberals say, "There is too much evidence for the authorship – some forger must have written it." It begins to become obvious that it is not the presence or absence of internal evidence that is the determining factor, but some preconceived notion that must be defended. (ii) The personal notes in 2 Peter are just what we would expect if Peter wrote it. We would expect him to sign the letter, and even to use both names (since both names occur together in the Gospels, Matthew 16:16, John 1:42), and even to use his Hebrew name if there were some reason to do so.[37] If he were involved in the production of Mark's Gospel, we would expect him to say so. We would expect him to mention the fact he had been with Jesus. We would expect him to allude to the earlier epistle. A forger wouldn't have restrained himself from saying that when Jesus predicted Peter's death He was referring to crucifixion. The apostles often asserted their apostolic authority when writing, at times more than once in the same book, especially when there were enemies of the cross to be confronted. (iii) Would not a forger have reproduced Peter's signature exactly as it is in 1 Peter ("Peter, an apostle of Jesus Christ") rather than using his Hebrew name and adding the appellation "bond-servant"? (iv) There is no Christian document *of value* written by a forger who uses an apostle's name, though there are numerous heretical pseudepigraphical and apocryphal books with forged signatures among the literature from the second and third centuries AD. In all this literature there are no close parallels to 2 Peter if this epistle is pseudepigraphic.

(2) The "**approving reference to Paul**" in 3:15,16 is not such as might be expected from Peter, nor is the citation of Paul's letters under the title of "**Scripture**" something to be expected from Peter, is a second internal argument raised against the Petrine authorship of 2

---

[37] M.R. James who disputed the apostolic authorship of 2 Peter admitted that the use of "Symeon" was one of the strongest arguments for the genuineness of the epistle. (*The Second Epistle of St. Peter and the General Epistle of St. Jude* [Cambridge: University Press, 1912], p.9.)

Peter. (a) *Evidence:* (i) Since F.C. Baur's time, with his philosophical theory of Petrine vs. Pauline factions in the church, the liberals claim that there was a great controversy, both personal and theological, between Peter and Paul. (ii) It is claimed one apostle would not be likely to give his imprimatur to another's writings. (iii) One prominent reason the liberals deny the genuineness of 2 Peter is because these verses picture Paul's epistles as being collected and used and considered to be Scripture while both Peter and Paul were still alive. This is very contrary to the liberals' picture of the time of the collection of the epistles, and therefore Peter could not have written something like this.[38] (b) *Refutation:* (i) There is no evidence of a split or antagonism between Peter and Paul such as Baur had postulated (as he tried to make the Bible match Hegel's philosophy).[39] In fact, 1 Peter is full of references to Paul's epistles, though Paul is not mentioned by name.[40] The reserve with which Paul is named ("our beloved brother") hardly matches the gushing and fawning language used of Paul in the second century.[41] The warm language of 2 Peter is how we would expect Peter to speak of his brother apostle in the first century. (ii) Why wouldn't Peter mention Paul's letters? Paul's writings were important. Old Testament writings were called "Scripture" because they were Holy Spirit-inspired. Paul was Holy Spirit-inspired. Far from being incongruous for Peter to call Paul's letters Scripture, it is just as expected as to have Paul call Luke's Gospel "Scripture" (1 Timothy 5:18). Further, in the first epistle there is an allusion to Paul as Peter speaks of "those who have preached the gospel to you" (1 Peter 1:12). (iii) Why not make our reconstructions of how and when the New Testament books were collected fit the evidence rather than twisting the evidence to make it fit our theories? The only fair inference to be drawn from Peter's citation of Paul's epistles is that some of his writings have been collected and are used in the churches to whom Peter writes this second letter. They were used because the Christians rightly understood them to have Scriptural authority.

(3) "**A striking difference in style and vocabulary**" is a third line of internal evidence enlisted to deny the Petrine authorship of 2 Peter.[42] (a) *Evidence:* (i) As far back as Jerome, this difference in style was noticed. Jerome felt the difference in style was because of a difference in secretaries (amanuenses). (ii) There are 369 words which occur in 1 Peter which do not occur in 2 Peter. There are 230 words which occur in 2 Peter that do not occur

---

[38] See below for details pro and con on this matter of when collections of New Testament Scriptures began to be made.

[39] See the Introductory Studies in the author's *New Testament History: Acts*, where this "eirenikon" theory is explained and rejected.

[40] See page xv in the Introductory Studies to 1 Peter in this volume for documentation.

[41] Compare "the blessed and glorious Paul" (Polycarp, *Ad Phil.* iii); "the blessed Paul" (*1 Clement*, xlvii.1; Polycarp, *Ad Phil.* xi); "the sanctified Paul .. right blessed" (Ignatius, *Ad Eph.* xii.2).

[42] Those who deny that Peter wrote 1 Peter certainly cannot appeal to stylistic differences with 2 Peter as evidence for 2 Peter's pseudonymity!

in 1 Peter.[43] The vocabulary common to both epistles is 153 words, the differences totaling 599. (iii) Elaborate papers have been written pointing out the different linguistic character between the two letters.[44] (iv) The vocabulary used in 2 Peter includes a number of Greek religious and philosophic terms[45] that critics think seem unlikely to have come from a Galilean fisherman like Peter. Critics argue that such terminology is more easily attributed to some Christian of Diaspora Jewish or Gentile origin.[46] (v) The effect of the few bold, hurried strokes makes 2 Peter a more hasty composition than 1 Peter, which is seen as a calmly and deliberately written epistle.

---

[43] Bigg, *op. cit.*, p.225. Of the words used in 1 and 2 Peter, 71% of the words used in 1 Peter are found only in that book; 61% of the words in 2 Peter are peculiar to that book. These percentages compare favorably with similar statistics gathered for 1 and 2 Corinthians. When it comes to the Corinthian correspondence, no one uses the slight difference in percentages to prove that Paul did not write one of those two letters. Why should such statistics be thought significant of different authorship in the Petrine letters?

[44] Samuel Davidson, *An Introduction to the New Testament* (London: Bagster, 1848), Vol.3, p.430ff, lists the following particulars: in the two epistles the appellations applied to God the Father and to Christ differ; different expressions are used of Christ's second coming; there is no use of the particle *hos* in the second after it frequently occurred in the first; the attributes and phrases by which the Christian religion are designated differ in the two letters; there is a great difference in the frequency in which the Old Testament is quoted; the second epistle is distinguished by a poverty of language and by drawling repetitions, which are entirely absent from the first. W. White, Jr., "Peter, Second Epistle of," in *Zondervan Pictorial Encyclopedia of the Bible* (Grand Rapids, MI: Zondervan, 1975), Vol.4, p.730, draws attention to the peculiar features in Greek grammar in 2 Peter. Richard Bauckham (*op. cit.*) also has a section on "Language" in his introduction to 2 Peter on, p. 135-138. F.H. Chase (*Hasting's Dictionary of the Bible*, Vol.3, p.808) characterized the vocabulary of the writer as "ambitious" and yet considered its extraordinary list of repetitions as stamping it as "poor and inadequate."

[45] It is 2 Peter 1:3-11 ("in your faith supply virtue ... knowledge ... self-control ..." KJV) the critics have in mind when they speak of "Hellenistic religious language." It is argued that the terms are drawn from Hellenistic moral philosophy, famous for its Virtue and Vice lists. So. it is claimed, are the ideas in 2 Peter 1:4 ("escaped the corruption" and "partaking of the divine nature"). "Divine power" (1:3), "godliness" (1:3,6,7), "knowledge" (1:2,3,8, 2:20), "eye-witnesses" (1:16), and "brotherly kindness" (1:7) are allegedly further examples of an apparent use of terms found in Hellenistic religions. The alleged post-apostolic fictional author of 2 Peter supposedly gives these terms a Christian definition, and is making a deliberate attempt to appeal to people in a pagan cultural context by using their language, while at the same time trying to defend the gospel against excessive Hellenization.

[46] John H. Elliott ("Peter, Second Epistle of," *Abingdon Bible Dictionary* [New York: Doubleday, 1992], Vol.5, p.284) is an example of a writer who places great emphasis on this "Hellenistic" hue to deny the Petrine authorship. He writes, "In 2 Peter there is a taste for obscure and grandiose language in a style marked by excess rather than economy of expression. Many passages in the Greek contain verbal repetitions and recurrent sounds (1:3-4, 5-7, 12-15, 17-18, 19-21; 2:1-3, 7-8, 12; 3:6,9,16), pairs of synonyms (1:7,10; 2:13; 3:14), and graceful rhythmic formulations (1:16,17,19-21; 2:4-9, 3:13) ... Much of the content has a pronounced Hellenistic hue: the conventional Greek virtues encouraged in 1:5-7; the notion of death as a 'putting off the bodily tent' (1:13-14); identification of the realm of the [wicked angels] as 'Tartarus' (2:4); dispute about myths (1:16-18); prophecy (1:20,21), and involvement of the gods in human history and final judgment (3:3-7); interest in knowledge as a means of access to God (1:2,3,6,8,18; 2:20,21; 3:3,17,18); salvation conceived as godliness (1:3), escape from corruption (1:4; 2:20), and participation in divine being (1:4); and the conception of God and/or Jesus Christ as benefactor and Savior (1:1,11; 2:20; 3:2,18)." T. Fornberg (*An Early Church in a Pluralistic Society. A Study of 2 Peter* [Lund: Gleerup, 1977], p.111-148) argued all these features indicate an author and audience at home in a pluralistic Hellenistic society.

(b) *Refutation:* (i) We do recognize a different style as we read the letters in the Greek. In 2 Peter there may be a more rugged style and more rare words. We meet here and there an anacolutha[47] and strange participial connections. There is a tendency to repeat a word 3 or 4 times in the space of a sentence or two. This difference in style, such as it is, may well be traced to the difference in penman.[48] (ii) Arguments based on alleged differences in style can, in this commentator's opinion, be easily overdrawn. The style of both Petrine epistles is nervous and energetic. In both there is an abundance of unusual words and an obvious fondness for striking and picturesque expressions.[49] If linguistic differences are recognizable,[50] it can be asserted they may be accounted for without denying the Petrine authorship of one of the letters. Subject matter influences style and vocabulary. 1 Peter offers encouragement and hope to those being persecuted; 2 Peter warns about false teachers who could ruin the church.[51] A passage of time between when two letters are written could account for some differences in style.[52] The needs of the readers often account for some differences in style. (iii) Such short writings as these two epistles actually furnish us with insufficient data to deal authoritatively with the question of style. This is illustrated by the way the critics contradict one another on many of the examples of alleged differences in style. For example, some say 1 Peter is better Greek than 2 Peter. Others say 2 Peter is more class-

---

[47] The sentence is broken, the second thought does "not follow" the first. "If you don't reform – well what can you expect?" is an example of an anacolutha.

[48] In the Introductory Studies to 1 Peter we documented the very likely possibility that the good Greek of 1 Peter is to be traced to Silas (Peter's amanuensis) while 2 Peter reflects more Peter's own style. If 1 Peter were written by Silas, then any stylistic comparisons with 2 Peter are irrelevant. Chase (*Hasting's Dictionary of the Bible*, p.183) criticized this solution to the stylistic differences on the grounds that in his mind it involves giving up the real Petrine authorship of 1 Peter in order to defend the Petrine authorship of 2 Peter.

[49] The truly remarkable thing about vocabulary is 1 and 2 Peter have a host of words in common that are different from the rest of the New Testament. Homer K. Ebright, *The Petrine Epistles, A Critical Study of Authorship* (Cincinnati: Methodist Book Concern, 1917), p.121. Peter uses pairs of synonyms, near-synonyms, words that are onomatopoetic; he repeats words in the same text, and occasionally there is a deliberate echo or word-play, all of this in the style of an orator who knows how to use words to get his message across.

[50] A.Q. Morton's computer analysis (*Authorship and Integrity of the New Testament* [London: SPCK, 1965], chap.3) showed that 1 and 2 Peter are linguistically indistinguishable, but that 2 Peter is distinct from any book that is longer. J.B. Mayor (*The Epistle of St. Jude and the Second Epistle of St. Peter* [reprint Grand Rapids: Baker Book House, 1965], p.civ) said "there is not that chasm [in grammar and style] between 1 and 2 Peter which some try to make out."

[51] "The same author tends to use an entirely different vocabulary and tone when he discusses different subject matter. This is readily demonstrable for all the great authors of world literature who have written on different themes and in different genres. For example, Milton's prose essays bear little resemblance to his pastoral poems ... and those in turn present a notable contrast to his epic poetry like *Paradise Lost*. Yet these contrasts, which could be supported by long lists of words found in the one composition but not in another, would hardly suffice to prove a difference of authorship. Everybody knows that Milton wrote them all." Gleason Archer, *The Encyclopedia of Bible Difficulties* (Grand Rapids: Zondervan, 1982, p.426.

[52] The passage of time between 1 and 2 Peter is not more than one or two years at most. Were the interval between letters greater, we might expect even greater differences in style and vocabulary.

ical and is better Greek than 1 Peter.[53] (iv) The use of Hellenistic religious language and ideas by a Palestinian Jew should no longer be regarded as incredible. If a man is going to expose a heresy to his audience, he must somehow let the people know who he is talking about. Either he will have to name the heretics by name, or he will have to use some of the terminology they use, terminology his audience will immediately recognize and identify. (v) Rather than emphasize the differences, why not emphasize the points of resemblance between the two epistles? Both contain *hapax legomena*; there are 63 in the first, 58 in the second.[54] Words and phrases of 2 Peter can be found in 1 Peter and in the speeches of Peter as recorded in Acts, and often are not used by any other New Testament writer.[55] This seems to be evidence of nothing more than that Peter had a large working vocabulary.

(4) The "**topics covered**" in 2 Peter are not what we would expect from the Apostle Peter, say the modern critics, since (they allege) they exhibit the "early Catholicism" characteristic of the late first and early second centuries.[56] (a) *Evidence:* (i) The concept allegedly held by

---

[53] "Peter's style is difficult to determine because we have so little written by him. Can we really assume the 543 different vocabulary words of his first epistle really capture the fullness, breadth and potential of Peter's style? Thus it seems many of the stylistic arguments against 2 Peter engage in circular reasoning at this point: 1 Peter's style is only able to provide an absolute standard for what is constituted 'Petrine' (thus not allowing any other document with stylistic divergence) if we already assume from the outset that 1 Peter is the only authentic work that we possess." Kruger, *op. cit.*, p.658,659.

[54] Mayor (*op. cit.*, p.lxxii and lxiv) gives the figure as 59 in 1 Peter, 56 in 2 Peter. The numbers differ a bit, depending on which Greek text of 2 Peter is being studied. See B.C. Caffin, "2 Peter" in *Pulpit Commentary* (Grand Rapids, MI: Eerdmans, 1962), p.vii,viii, for a listing of the *hapax legomena*. Bauckham and Elliott find 57 or 58 *hapax legomena* in 2 Peter, or over 14% of the 402-word vocabulary (a total of 1,105 words) used in the letter, the highest proportion for any book of the New Testament. (The 63 *hapax legomena* in 1 Peter comprise 12% of his vocabulary.) Thirteen of the *hapax legomena* found in 2 Peter are very rare, not yet noted as occurring anywhere outside of 2 Peter. Mayor (p.lxii) suggested that several of 2 Peter's rare forms were deliberately used in preference to commoner terms for the sake of euphony and rhythm.

"The number of words in a book can be computed in three different ways: (1) The total number of words, even counting the repetition of certain words. This total is 1680 for 1 Peter and 1098 for 2 Peter. (J. Arthur Baird and J. David Thompson, *A Critical Concordance to 1 and 2 Peter* [Montgomery, AL: Biblical Research Associates, 1989.) (2) The total number of *different* words, counting the same vocabulary words with different endings; e.g., it would count both αὐτήν and αὐτῆς, but not the repetition of either. This total is 817 for 1 Peter and 605 for 2 Peter. (Baird and Thompson) (3) The total number of different *vocabulary* words. So both αὐτήν and αὐτῆς would count as only one word since they both come from the same vocabulary word. This is likely the method used by Green (*op. cit.*) who came up with 543 words for 1 Peter and 399 for 2 Peter." Kruger, *op. cit.*, p.656.

[55] See H. Alford, *Alford's Greek Testament* (London: Rivingtons, 1871), Vol.4, p.57, for details about these Petrine words and phrases. See also B.C. Caffin, *op. cit.*, p.viii, ix.

[56] In fact, critics such as E. Kasemann (who dubbed 2 Peter an "early catholic" work) affirm that 2 Peter's testimony to "early Catholicism" is one of the values of this work as a piece of history. (See his "An Apologia for Primitive Christian Eschatology," pp.169-195 in *Essays on New Testament Themes* [London: SCM, 1964].) See also Ralph Martin, "Early Catholicism" in *Dictionary of the Later New Testament and Its Developments* (Downers Grove, IL: InterVarsity, 1997), p.310-313. The Neo-liberal scholars treat the so-called Deutero-Pauline letters, as well as Luke-Acts, as reflecting a "distinctive voice, offering variations and emphases not apparent in Paul's situational and contingently driven theology." The non-Pauline parts of the New Testament, asserted Kasemann,

the writer of the letter that apostleship was a thing of the past (3:2). (ii) The reference to "all [the] letters" of Paul (3:16), as if there were a collected body of works ranked as "Scripture,"[57] is typical of "early Catholicism." (iii) The lively contest the early church engaged in when trying to decide what books would be admitted to the canon is allegedly illustrated by the long debate over 2 Peter and Jude.[58] That too, it is affirmed, was a special interest in the period when "early Catholicism" flourished. (iv) The idea that the Mount of Transfiguration was a "holy mountain" is an indication the epistle was written late. (v) The prediction of Peter's approaching death (1:14) looks very much like a reference to Jesus' prophecies recorded in John 21:18,19. The fourth Gospel was not written until about AD 85-90 (AD 100 says Barclay). If the Gospel of John is the source of the writer's information, that makes it impossible for Peter to have written 2 Peter, for Peter was dead before John is written. (vi) Clearly, much time has passed before 2 Peter is written. Proof of this is discovered in the fact that men have begun "to abandon hope" of the second coming altogether (3:4)[59] and in the fact that "the fathers" (defined as being a first generation of Christians) have already died. (vii) The picture of the false teachers (identified as Gnostics) condemned in the epistle points to a later date for the writing of 2 Peter. (b) *Refutation:* (i) Rather than the apostleship being a thing of the past when 2 Peter is written, the writer claims to be an apostle (1:1), writing a letter to "all the churches" – which is something an apostle could do because of the "concern for all the churches" (2 Corinthians 11:28) that was part of an apostle's commission. Folk in the second century were quite aware there were no such authoritative figures still living among the churches. (ii) First, as we respond to this argument, we must comment on "Scrip-

---

not only express their message in idioms and ideas that have no counter-part in Paul; instead, they are in conflict with Paul and they promote a version of Christianity at odds with Paul. "The church as an institution [with an organized, regulated, and structured life] with an organized ministry and sacraments has begun to replace the Word as the means of salvation." Martin also had an article on "early Catholicism" in the *Dictionary of Paul and His Letters* (Downers Grove, IL: InterVarsity, 1993), p.223-225.

57 James Moffatt wrote, "This allusion [3:15,16] to a collection of Pauline epistles is an anachronism which forms an indubitable water-mark of the second century." (*An Introduction to the Literature of the New Testament* (Edinburgh: T&T Clark, 1949 reprint), p.363-364. Wm. Barclay (*Daily Study Bible* [Philadelphia: Westminster, 1960, p.340) says that it was not until at least AD 90 that Paul's letters were collected and published, and that it was many years after that before they acquired the position of "Scripture." Barclay concludes, "It is well-nigh impossible for anyone to write like this [2 Peter 3:16] until midway through the second century."

58 A series of articles has appeared in the *Bible Review* broaching the view that there were numerous divergent schools or strands of Christianity in the first and second centuries. When one finally became dominant, the books favored by that sect were the only ones accepted into the canon, the theory goes. See Robert J. Miller, "The Gospels that Didn't Make the Cut," August 1993; Charles Hedrick, "The 34 Gospels: Diversity and Division Among the Earliest Christians," June, 2002, both in the *Bible Review*.

59 2 Peter is the only book in the New Testament where we find the idea of a *parousia* (Christ's second coming) being deliberately rejected. There were erroneous teachings about the *parousia* refuted in other books, but not any heretical views that it would not even occur. Critics have argued that it was not until the second century that the Gnostics rejected any idea of the return of Christ. Therefore, critics argue, this letter must come from a time much later than Peter's own lifetime.

ture." In a previous paragraph we have shown that "Scripture" (*graphai*) in New Testament writings is a technical term regularly used to refer to the inspired books of the Old Testament canon. But it also was used of inspired books written by New Testament apostles and prophets. Instead of the New Testament writings just being accorded "Scriptural" status in the mid-second century, the growth of second-century pseudepigraphic apostolic literature presupposes an already existing body of authoritative apostolic writings. Second, we must speak about "all his letters." "All his letters" leaves some room for debate as to how many were known and accepted. Perhaps it means all those known to Peter. How many was that? Well, if we date 2 Peter after Paul wrote 2 Timothy, Peter could know about all of Paul's letters.[60] Perhaps it means all those known to Peter's readers. How many was that? There is no reason to exclude any that bear Paul's name save perhaps those to Timothy and Titus. Paul's letters were circulated almost as quickly as they were written, as suggested, for example, by Colossians 4:16. There is evidence from Egypt of the early collection of Paul's letters. The Chester Beatty Papyrus II (P^{46} – a codex containing all of Paul's letters) has been dated on paleographical evidence to the mid-AD 80's, before the reign of Domitian, by Y.K. Kim.[61] If this date is correct there should be no more claims that Paul's letters were not collected until c.AD 150! Peter speaks of Paul's letters being misinterpreted. It didn't take long for that to happen. Some of Paul's letters were misinterpreted almost immediately. For example, 2 Thessalonians corrects a misinterpretation of 1 Thessalonians. See also 1 Corinthians 5:9-11, where Paul worries the very letter he was then writing will be misconstrued. And see Paul's regular practice of taking the pen in hand and signing his own name as a sign of authenticity (1 Corinthians 16:21). In the light of these examples, who says we must wait till the second century (like the defenders of pseudonymity for 2 Peter 3:16 claim) to find malicious and ignorant distortions of Paul's letters? (iii) A brief note of explanation is surely needed concerning the whole concept of the development of the New Testament canon. We treat the canon's development under these headings:

- The Making and Accepting of the New Testament Books (AD 45-96).
- The Collecting of the New Testament Books (AD 60 [?]-140).
- The Guarding of the Books of the New Testament (AD 140-400).[62]

This third period is *not* the first time the canon was decided. During this third period, because the Gnostics wrote and used apocryphal sources, churches rejected books if they even looked as if they had quotations from apocryphal sources. Antipathy to apocryphal materials, and the belief that the *Assumption of Moses* was quoted in them, caused some churches to reject

---

[60] Peter's apparent knowledge of many of Paul's letters as implied by the similarities to Paul found in 1 Peter, surely indicates a collection of Paul's letters was available in Rome at the time 1 Peter was written.

[61] Y.K. Kim, "Paleographical Dating of P^{46} to the Later First Century," *Biblica* 69 (2, 1988) p.248-257.

[62] See the author's notes on the "canon" in his *General Introduction to the New Testament* Syllabus, published Moberly, MO: Scripture Exposition Books, 1998. See chapter 16, "Development and History of the New Testament Canon" in Norman L. Geisler and Wm. E. Nix, *A General Introduction to the Bible* (Chicago: Moody Press, 1986), p. 277ff.

Jude and 2 Peter, for the moment, from their canons.[63] If the principle of divine inspiration in their authorship and providence in the preservation and collection of the Biblical books is rejected, then the canonization of any specific writing becomes a matter of fallible human judgments where the majority eventually wins. If, on the other hand, a belief in inspiration and divine preservation is held, the development of the New Testament canon becomes something the church accepts rather than invents, and accepts because of the evidence of God's hand in the matter. (iv) Peter's calling the Mount of Transfiguration a "holy mountain" does not indicate he is venerating this place. A person familiar with the Old Testament account of God's appearance to Moses and His command to Moses to take off his shoes because the place where he stood was "holy ground," would have no difficulty calling the place where it was so obvious Jesus was God ("He received honor and glory," 1:17) a "holy mountain." (v) Peter, to whom Christ made His prediction (as recorded in John 13 and 21), did not have to wait for John's gospel to be published in order to know about Jesus' prediction. (vi) That hope of Christ's *parousia* has been abandoned is false wording. Far from being an idea they abandoned, the scoffers never did believe it. It is scoffers, not church members, who are saying "Where is His promised coming?" The Apostolic Fathers do not betray any concern over the alleged delay in the *parousia*.[64] Why should an imaginary contemporary pseudonymist then express such a concern in this letter he is inventing? That "the fathers" have fallen asleep (died) does not prove the writer of 2 Peter is a second or third generation Christian. 1 Thessalonians 4:13ff, written some 15 years before Peter's death, already makes reference to church members who have died. And what is to keep us from seeing in "the fathers" a reference to the Jewish patriarchs as they appeal to the uniformity of nature as arguing against any second coming. (vii) It is a mistake, as we shall see in notes below, to assume 2 Peter presupposes the full-blown Gnosticism of the second century. Instead, it reflects incipient Gnosticism of the same kind that already existed in some places when Paul wrote to the Colossians, Timothy, and Titus. Bigg confidently has stated that "every feature in the description [in 2 Peter] of the false teachers and mockers is to be found in the apostolic age."[65] There is no evidence here demanding a post-apostolic date for 2 Peter.

(5) As negative critics continue their arguments against the Petrine authorship of this epistle, it is asserted **2 Peter is a copy of the epistle of Jude**. (a) *Evidence:* (i) Compare 2

---

[63] The Jewish Gnostics utilized apocalyptic Jewish writings and apocryphal writings to substantiate their teachings. Does this explain the Syrian church's reluctance to include 2 Peter and Jude in their Peshitto Syriac version? "It is precisely in Syria, where the extravagance of Jewish angelology was most notorious, that one would naturally expect the most violent reaction against anything that might be adduced in their support." E.M.B. Green, *2 Peter Reconsidered* (London: Tyndale, 1961), p.7ff. In fact, we suppose that Jerome had reference to the Syrian tradition of rejection when he noted that "most" denied that 2 Peter should be in the canon.

[64] See Donald Guthrie, *New Testament Introduction* (Downers Grove, IL: InterVarsity, 1970), Vol.3, p.160.

[65] Bigg, *op. cit.*, p.239.

Peter 2:1-16 and Jude 4-11:

2 Peter 2	Jude
1-3	4
4	6
6	7
11	9
12	10
15	11

(ii) There is a high degree of similarity in subject matter, choice of vocabulary, and even order of ideas. The same Old Testament allusions are used in exactly the same way in both letters.[66] 19 of the 25 verses in Jude have parallels in whole or in part in 2 Peter. Of Jude's 460 word vocabulary almost one-quarter (111) are found in 2 Peter. (iii) The date assigned to the writing of Jude by the vast majority of conservative scholars is AD 75-80. Since Peter was martyred c. AD 68, there is no way Peter wrote 2 Peter if there is literary dependence on Jude.

(b) *Refutation:* The problem is how to explain the likenesses between 2 Peter 2 and Jude. Four possible answers have been put forward:

(i) *Perhaps both writers were copying a common source.*[67] The references to apostolic tra-

---

[66] J.W. Roberts, "An Introduction to the Epistles of 2 Peter and Jude," in *1 and 2 Peter and Jude* (Austin, TX: Sweet, 1964), p.63ff, has outlined "the problem of the common material in Jude and 2 Peter 2" in this manner:

The common subject. Both Jude and 2 Peter are concerned with the problem posed to the church by a group of false teachers. Peter says, in 2 Peter 2:1, "There shall be false teachers, who shall privily bring in destructive heresies," and Jude 4 has it, "For there are certain men crept in privily, even they who were of old written of beforehand unto the condemnation, ungodly men ...." The same general identifications are given in the detailed denunciation of these teachers. The difference is that Peter gives the denunciation as a prophecy that the false teachers would come, whereas Jude treats the situation as having already developed.
Common warnings of Judgment. In denouncing these teachers, both Jude and Peter make clear by a series of examples drawn from the Old Testament that God "knows how" to bring swift and sure punishment upon such sinners. Peter uses the angels who sinned, the world of Noah, Sodom and Gomorrah, and Balaam, in that order. Jude uses ancient Israelites destroyed in the wilderness, the angels, Sodom and Gomorrah, Cain, Balaam, and Korah, in that order. Thus we see there are differences but the same subject and general outline.
Common denunciation. In the denunciations the false teachers are labeled with the same sins and practices. Such descriptions as "rail at dignities," "spots," "blemishes" at feasts, "wells (clouds) without water," "creatures without reason," and "mists driven by storm (winds)," show a common list of faults and descriptions.
Common language in Greek. The most telling evidence to scholars cannot be set forth in English because it concerns the use of the same words and phrases in the original language. Several times rare words, used nowhere else in the New Testament, are used by both Peter and Jude. Too, the same verbs, prepositional phrases, and other constructions are used, even where a choice would have been available. Often there is a subtle change in tense, or a reversal of words, or a slight change of wording when using the same statement.

[67] This has shades of the "Q" theory that colors studies of the Gospels. Scholars postulate that a common source, labeled "Q," just must have existed, else how does one explain the similarities between Mark and the Gospels of Matthew and Luke. Etta Linnemann (*Is There a Synoptic Problem: Rethinking the Literary Dependence of the First Three Gospels* [Grand Rapids: Baker, 1992]) has forcefully questioned the scientific character of most historical-critical methodology as far as a study of the Synoptic Problem is concerned. Just abandon the idea of "literary dependence" and there is no need to hurl a sputnik called "Q" into orbit! In the same way, we think claims of "literary dependence" between 2 Peter and Jude should be abandoned.

dition in Jude 17ff and 2 Peter 3:2 suggest to some critics the possibility the two epistles may have used as their common source some anti-heresy tract (or tracts) attributed to the apostles.[68] But if there were such a source, the parallels are unfortunately not close enough to permit its reconstruction. Another critic has argued both writers made use of common oral tradition,[69] but not many scholars have followed this suggestion. A third variation on this theme is that both works were composites, and each redactor made use of a "prophetic source."[70] If either or both can be shown to have merely copied, then the value of either is greatly reduced.

(ii) *Some argue the writer of 2 Peter copied Jude.*[71] Of course, it is hard to believe Peter the apostle would have to rely on Jude for his message, but a second century forger might! One alleged evidence that 2 Peter is later than Jude is the claim that the writer (as he copied) suppressed Jude's two references to non-canonical literature (*1 Enoch* in Jude 14, and the *Assumption of Moses* in Jude 9). But this reasoning is precarious. First, it has never been shown that Jude is indeed copying non-canonical literature.[72] Second, if 2 Peter avoids apocryphal material, that practice stands squarely with the rest of the New Testament rather

---

[68] It is significant that few critics appeal to Holy Spirit inspiration as a possible explanation of the similarities between the two letters. Could not the Holy Spirit have inspired both men to say the same thing? A similar need, dealt with from the standpoint of the Gospels, would explain their similarities. We also appeal to oral tradition to help explain the same matter of similarities in the so-called Synoptic Problem. Might not that explanation help here? As the apostles and prophets preached, common expressions and Scripture illustrations became part of the common Christian vocabulary. It is very evident that the "copying" solution to the similarities should not be resorted to as quickly as some critics habitually do.

[69] Bo Reicke, *The Epistles of James, Peter, and Jude* in the Anchor Bible Series (Garden City, NY: Doubleday, 1964), p.90.

[70] E. Iliff Robson, *Studies in the Second Epistle of St. Peter* (Cambridge: University Press, 1915).

[71] It is the general consensus of current scholarship on Peter and Jude that the longer letter is a revision and expansion of the shorter one. See Mayor (*op. cit.*), Bauckham (*WBC*), T. Fornberg (*op. cit.*), and J.H. Elliott (*op. cit.*, p.284) for details defending this view. (Instead of the author of Peter copying Jude, several writers have offered the hypothesis that the same author wrote both books, one even suggesting that Jude wrote both. Bauckham [*WBC*, p.141] argues that common authorship is implausible.) J.H. Neyrey ("2 Peter and Jude," *Anchor Bible* 37c [New York: Doubleday, 1993], p.122) argues that those who suggest the priority of Jude "have by no means proven it."

What is happening recently among the scholars (Fornberg, Neyrey, Bauckham) is that the methods of redaction criticism are being applied to Jude and 2 Peter. Redaction criticism studies parallel passages in order to determine what each redactor was trying to say as he deliberately omitted or added material to the common source. Neyrey, Fornberg, and Bauckham assume the priority of Jude as a working hypothesis, and their redaction criticism therefore consists in explaining 2 Peter's redactional treatment of Jude. These writers also assume that the two letters derive from different situations, oppose different adversaries, and that each redactor made appropriate changes to the material they have in common.

[72] If we recall (1 Corinthians 2:10ff) that inspired writers came to know what they spoke or wrote by revelation, why can we not on the basis of such a revelation have Jude quoting Enoch himself (not the *Book of Enoch*)? By the same means we presume Jude learned of Michael's dispute with the devil over the body of Moses.

than with what folk were doing in the second century. Selwyn, arguing for the priority of Jude, argued 2 Peter starts out as a prophecy. The copyist intended to cast the entire chapter he is copying from Jude as a prophecy or prediction in order to make it look like it had been written before Jude. Thus he used the future tense in the early part of the chapter. But, it is argued by Selwyn, the writer unconsciously slips into the use of the present tense (2 Peter 2:3b-22, 3:1-10,16b-17), thus betraying to us the fact that it was copied.[73] Selwyn uses what he calls "the lack of any solid external evidence till the second century" to prove 2 Peter was not actually composed until long after Jude wrote (i.e., long after AD 75). So confident is Adeney that 2 Peter is a copy of Jude and that Peter didn't write it that he can say, "in defending the genuineness of 2 Peter we accuse the great apostle Peter of plagiarizing in a remarkable way."[74] Scholars holding the priority of Jude have struggled to explain why so much of Jude had to be copied into 2 Peter. Had the little tract of Jude failed to gain a hearing because of its lack of an impressive name? Has Peter recently seen a copy of Jude, realized the seriousness of the dangers mentioned, and being thus prompted wrote this letter (2 Peter) to the same folk to whom he wrote 1 Peter, knowing Jude was not addressed to them? Is the pseudepigrapher trying to send a clear message that Jude is the source of much that is included in the letter? The whole idea 2 Peter copied Jude depends on two presuppositions – the priority of Jude, and indisputable evidence of literary dependence – neither of which has ever been demonstrated beyond a shadow of a doubt. Further, there are a large number of rare words in Jude. If the pseudepigrapher of 2 Peter is really copying, why is it only a few of these rare words (perhaps no more than four) are copied?

(iii) *Some argue Jude copied 2 Peter.*[75] One alleged evidence for the priority of 2 Peter is the argument that since 2 Peter is more elaborate and wordy, and Jude is more coherently and compactly written, Jude is a copy of Peter.[76] Sometimes obscure verses in 2 Peter are clarified by their parallels in Jude (e.g., 2:11 v. Jude 9).[77] A second evidence for the priority

---

[73] The answer to the argument based on the future and present tense verbs is rather easy to imagine. First, Peter does not mean that the menace is wholly future. Paul and others had already warned against this same coming heresy. But the full manifestation was yet to come. (This is easier to believe than that the present tenses are intended to depict the future with vividness, as though present.)

[74] W.H. Bennett and Walter F. Adeney, *A Biblical Introduction* (London: Methuen, 1919), p.449.

[75] Theodor Zahn, *Introduction to the New Testament* (Grand Rapids, MI: Kregel, 1953), Vol.2, p.238ff, argues strongly that Peter is older and that Jude cites from it. Bigg, Luther, and Spitta also held that Jude copied Peter.

[76] This again gets us into the area of redaction criticism. Would a reviser be more likely to expand his source or to abridge it? Those who embrace the "assured conclusions" of redaction criticism insist examples of both abridgement and expansion can be cited (e.g., Matthew has expanded Mark's Gospel with material of his own, they allege, yet in many individual pericopes he has abridged the [alleged] earlier Gospel for the sake of conciseness and emphasis on one main point). Redaction critics, after some seeming success with the Gospels, are struggling to apply their methods to the epistles.

[77] If clarification is a legitimate argument for priority, since Jude 11 is clarified by 2 Peter 2:15ff, could it not be just as plausibly argued that Jude copied Peter? It begins to appear that proponents of the priority of one or the other of these letters are sometimes "cooking" the evidence to fit their theories.

of 2 Peter is the fact that what Peter predicts (the coming of false teachers), Jude speaks of as having occurred.[78] This indicates 2 Peter was written first. (Once priority is established, then the critics launch into all the evidences of actual literary dependence.) Even if we grant copying, is it not an acknowledged and acceptable practice for Scripture writers to quote inspired works? If the apostle Peter wrote 2 Peter and it is inspired (as chapter 1 indicates), what would be wrong with Jude quoting it. New Testament writers often quote other Holy Spirit-inspired work – e.g., constantly quoting the Old Testament – often without giving notice that they are so quoting. Why can't Jude so quote the apostle Peter? In spite of this, we are not convinced there is any literary dependence between the two letters.

(iv) *The real connection between 2 Peter and Jude is that of* ***prophecy*** *and* ***fulfillment.***

> Let us suppose, then, that some time had passed after the death of Peter. Jude, a brother of James, who is acquainted with the Christians to whom Peter wrote, writes to them on the subject of "the common salvation." He gives additional warning against the errorists. And what better way is there to do this than to appropriate the warning given earlier by the apostle Peter!
>
> Further, it just may be Jude does acknowledge that he is alluding to an earlier prophecy. Note carefully Jude 17,18. After he has set forth the warning in virtually the same outline and in many of the very words of Peter, he writes, "But ye, beloved, remember the words which have been spoken before by the apostles of our Lord Jesus Christ; that they said to you, 'In the last times there shall be mockers ....'" Jude calls attention to the words of the apostles which the readers already knew. And the words he reminds them of come from 2 Peter 3:2.[79]

The idea of prophecy and fulfillment explains the similarities between 2 Peter and Jude without any appeal to copying. In fact, both 2 Peter and Jude have all the earmarks of being two independent and truthful accounts. In any eye-witnesses' truthful testimony to an event, we expect some similarities and some differences. That is precisely what we have in 2 Peter 2 and Jude. The similarities, expected because the subject matter is the same – i.e., heretics – have already been documented. As far as differences, there is a difference in the illustrations used about impending judgment. There are striking differences in vocabulary, even where the subject matter is the same. These are just the differences expected from two different witnesses telling the truth about an event that both personally were involved in.

---

[78] Peter's principal verbs are future tense (2:1,2,3,12,13). Jude, throughout his short letter, speaks of the false teachers as having already come.

[79] These paragraphs are adapted from Roberts, *op. cit.*, p.64. In a context where we have been discussing the evidence for the existence of a letter, and for the circulation and collection of New Testament books, it should not escape our notice that Jude's appeal to 2 Peter implies that 2 Peter has already (by AD 75, the date we give to Jude) been circulated and accepted among Jude's readers. It matters little whether Jude was addressed to Asia Minor, or was a circular letter sent to Palestinian Christians, it still speaks of the early acceptance and use of 2 Peter!

(6) One final internal argument used by the negative critics against the Petrine authorship needs to be examined. Resemblances between 2 Peter and Josephus' *Antiquities* (AD 94) are said to indicate that **the author of 2 Peter had read Josephus' works**. Therefore, the "author" of the epistle called 2 Peter cannot be the apostle Peter, who died in AD 68. (a) *Evidence:* Examples of this coincidence of language:

> Dr. Abbott has called attention, in the *Expositor [2/3, 1882, p.49-63]*, to some verbal coincidences between 2 Peter and the writings of Josephus, especially two passages in the 'Antiquities.' In the fourth section of the Preface, Josephus says that Moses deemed it exceedingly necessary to consider the *Divine nature*; that "other legislators *followed fables*, and by their discourses transferred the most reproachful of human sins unto the gods;" but that Moses demonstrated that "God was possessed of perfect *virtue*;" and that there is nothing in his writings "disagreeable to the *majesty* (*megaleiotes*) of God." (We note resemblances to 2 Peter 1:4,16,3.) ... Again in bk.IV.vii.2, where Josephus is relating the last address of Moses, he uses seven or eight words which are found in 2 Peter; such as "departure" in the sense of death, "the present truth," etc. ... Dr. Abbott also pointed out several other scattered parallels, besides those contained in the two passages referred to, as well as some remarkable coincidences with the writings of Philo.[80]

(b) *Refutation:* The possible explanations of this similarity of language include these options: (i) Josephus could have copied Peter.[81] However, Josephus, though he records a bare-bones account of the death and resurrection of Jesus, shows no acquaintance with any other writings of the New Testament. Scholars who have looked for every possible allusion to 2 Peter in ancient writings have not appealed to these coincidences in language as being evidence that Josephus is alluding to 2 Peter. (ii) Both 2 Peter and Josephus could have copied a common source. Some have tried to make a case that both the author of 2 Peter and Josephus copied Philo. To show Peter might have copied Philo, appeal is made to the legend that Philo visited Rome in the reign of Caligula and met with Peter.[82] To show Josephus might have copied Philo, it is affirmed that Philo's works were known to educated Jews such as Josephus. (iii) The alleged 2nd century writer of 2 Peter copied Josephus. Are we to believe that this imaginary Christian writer reproduced the words and phrases of Josephus when he was trying to palm off his production as a writing by the apostle Peter? People acquainted with Josephus' writings would have caught the plagiarism immediately and would have therefore rejected the alleged Petrine authorship. (iv) It is quite possible these resemblances are accidental. The words cited are common expressions any educated person would have in their vocabularies. We must remember that "virtue" (*arete*) is ascribed to God in 1 Peter 2:9 (KJV); that "fables" (*muthos*) occurs four times in Paul's letters to Timothy and

---

[80] Caffin, *op. cit.*, p. xii. Salmon, *Introduction to the New Testament* (New York: E. and J.B. Young, 1889), p.548-53, has convincingly refuted Abbott.

[81] F.W. Farrar, *Expositor*, II/3 (1882), p.401-423, proposed that Josephus had read 2 Peter. If this could be documented, we would have another external evidence for the early existence of 2 Peter.

[82] This legend is recorded in Eusebius, *H.E.*, ii.17. Romans 15:20 (written in AD 58), that Paul goes where no other apostle has been, seems to say that Peter was not in Rome as early as Caligula's reign (AD 37-41).

Titus; and that "divine nature" (*theios*) is not uncommon in the LXX.

Using the same kind of reasoning the critics do, what can be said in favor of Petrine authorship from the internal evidence? (1) In general it can be affirmed 2 Peter contains none of the legendary and apocalyptic details that characterize the apocryphal Petrine literature (e.g., the *Gospel of Peter*, the *Apocalypse of Peter*, the *Preaching of Peter*, and the *Acts of Peter*) produced in the second century AD. (Remember, modern higher critics want to date the writing of 2 Peter in the second century.) Being free of these wild imaginary features, 2 Peter is more like 1 Peter than like any other writing to which Peter's name has been affixed by some forger. (2) If it were a testament,[83] forged in the second century, would not the theme of martyrdom be more emphasized?

> Christian writings of this period tended more and more to glorify the martyrs. Their heroism and faithfulness to Christ in the face of threats and torture served as an example to Christians everywhere. Before AD 100, Clement of Rome could write specifically of Peter's martyrdom: "Let us set before our eyes the good apostles: Peter, who because of unrighteous jealousy suffered not one or two but many trials, and having thus borne witness as a martyr went to the glorious place which was his due ..." (1 Cl. 5:3ff). It is remarkable that a second-century tract pretending to be Peter's testament would omit any reference to his glorious martyrdom. The reticence we see in 2 Peter about Peter's death is precisely what we would expect if Peter wrote it before he died, and before people were glorifying martyrdom.[84]

(3) If 2 Peter were written in the second century, and it deals with certain heresies confronting the church, would we not read about Peter's arch-heretical rival, Simon Magus?

> Simon Magus is mentioned but once in the New Testament (Acts 8:9-24), but the 2nd and 3rd century literature is replete with tales about their rivalry and confrontations. In the *Acts of Peter* and the pseudo-Clementine *Recognitions* and *Homilies*, Simon Magus becomes Peter's constant foe in philosophical debate and in contests of miraculous power. Is it not strange that an anti-heretical tract in Peter's name allegedly from the second century would have missed an opportunity to make reference to Simon Magus. But there are none of these legendary features in 2 Peter.[85]

(4) Not much that is written in 1 Peter is referred to in 2 Peter. If 2 Peter is an example of second-century writers of apostolic pseudepigrapha, why doesn't it echo Biblical writings as those pseudonymous productions did?

---

[83] More will be said on this hypothesis below.

[84] J.R. Michaels, "Peter, Second Epistle of," *International Standard Bible Encyclopedia*, edited by G.W. Bromiley (Grand Rapids: Eerdmans, 1986), Vol.3, p.817.

[85] *ibid.*

> In cases where writings attributed to their pseudonyms were extant, these [2nd century pseudepigraphers] usually echo such writings in their own pseudonymous productions. The pseudo-Pauline *Laodiceans* is nothing but a patchwork of Pauline phrases; *"3 Corinthians"* is full of Pauline terminology and ideas; though less-pervasive, there are clear echoes of Paul in the *Prayer of the Apostle Paul*, in the *Apocalypse of Paul*, in the Speeches of Paul in the *Acts of Paul*, and even in the apocryphal correspondence between Paul and Seneca. In the case of the Petrine pseudepigrapha, the *Apocalypse of Peter* and the speeches of Peter in the *Acts of Peter* certainly echo 2 Peter, and the *Acts of Peter* probably echoes 1 Peter, too.[86]

Bauckham thinks this lack of correspondence to second-century pseudepigrapha indicates 2 Peter did not come from as late as the second century. With this conclusion we agree!

D. Summary of the discussion on authorship

To Bible students accustomed to the abundant evidence for books Eusebius classified as *Homologoumena*, the external evidence for 2 Peter is weak, while the internal evidence is strong. None of the objections to Peter's authorship based on internal evidence is so conclusive as to silence those who would defend his authorship. The internal evidence should be taken at face value.

The writer of this epistle asserts himself to be the apostle Peter. There are reminiscences and allusions that only the apostle Peter could have known. The author's familiarity with Paul continues what was seen in 1 Peter where there are numerous parallels to Paul's writings. Late in Paul's life, he was concerned with Jewish Gnosticism making inroads into the church; he writes Colossians and 2 Timothy (among others) to warn about this danger. Is it not what we would expect if, about the same time on the calendar that Paul wrote his warnings, Peter also wrote this letter we call "2 Peter" to warn against the same very dangerous heresy?

There are no anachronisms in 2 Peter. If this is a forgery of the second century, why is there no reference to the more developed heresies of the second century? Peter is dealing with false teaching, yet there is no reference to Gnosticism as it was developed in the second century. (The false teachers warned about may be incipient Gnosticism, but not the developed heresy.) If this is a forgery written after AD 70, why is there no mention of the destruction of Jerusalem? The writer is writing about the tremendous catastrophes of the day of the Lord. Jerusalem's destruction would have furnished a prime and contemporary example, had it already occurred.

---

[86] Bauckham, "2 Peter" (*WBC*), p.146,147.

Pseudonymity, the only alternative to Peter's authorship of 2 Peter, **is unbelievable**! (1) What was the purpose of the supposed forger? We have seen before there is no antagonism between Peter and Paul such as the Tubingen school hypothesized. Therefore, this book cannot be an attempt to show that these two apostles had reconciled. There wasn't any dispute to reconcile! If Peter wrote it, then everything fits. If not, then we have an insoluble psychological riddle. No one knows who wrote it, or when, or why it was written. (2) What peculiar doctrine was being promoted? All the pseudepigrapha have an "axe to grind," some view that needed to be promoted as apostolic, or otherwise it would not be accepted in the church. It might be docetic Christology, or a peculiar view about the future life, or a Gnostic worldview. The doctrine in 2 Peter promotes none of these things. It is not heretical. On the hypothesis it is pseudonymous, what is its real reason for existence? (3) What are we to think of the "spin" put on pseudonymity that "posthumous publication in Peter's name does not necessarily imply any intent to deceive"? Michaels has several sentences typical of what one reads where an attempt is made to show there is no "deception" involved in pseudonymity:

> If the tradition behind 2 Peter was genuinely Petrine (or even if it was thought to be), then the only kind of compiler of the material who might be guilty of fraud would be one who presumptuously signed *his own* name to the apostle's teaching. ... The relation of 2 Peter to the historical Peter would then be somewhat analogous to the relation of the Gospel writers to Jesus as they preserved His teaching while adapting it to their own needs ... There are clues in the Epistle itself that this compendium theory may have some merits. [That 2 Peter is a compendium of materials traceable to Peter accounts for the double time perspective in chapter 2. In some of the quotations Peter was making a prediction. In others, he was speaking of the present. The redactor did not change verb tenses when he included the material in this "letter" or "testament."] [The words of 2 Peter 3:1 are made to mean "second" or "secondary epistle," not in its relation to 1 Peter but in its relation] to the traditional teachings of Peter out of which this "letter" has been built. In accord with Peter's expressed wishes (2 Peter 1:15), the second-century compiler is attempting to bring Peter's teaching and personality to bear on the increasingly complex problems faced in the second century.[87]

If we have to change the meaning of "second" and if the material in 2 Peter is adapted, isn't this deception? It certainly could not be categorized as a straightforward presentation of what Peter actually said or wrote!

---

[87] Michaels, *op. cit.*, p.818. (The words included in brackets are this author's abbreviation of what Michaels actually wrote.) Redaction criticism is evident in the language Michaels uses. Redaction criticism has claimed to find three levels of material in our New Testaments: 1) what Jesus actually said and did, of which we know very little; 2) what the apostles said as they took Jesus' teaching and adapted it to their contemporary situation; 3) what the early church taught as they took the words of the apostles and edited and adapted them to their then current situation. Our New Testament is actually (the redaction critics affirm) mostly what the early church taught, not what Jesus or the apostles taught.

"If we ask what is the evidence for orthodox epistles being composed in the name of the apostles within a generation or two of their lifetime, and for this being an acceptable literary convention within the church, the answer is nil."[88]

Several more points render the hypothesis of pseudonymity quite doubtful. (a) The writer of the letter is distinctly a Christian; in the wording of the KJV, he is a participant in the "like precious faith" based on the "righteousness of Jesus Christ;" he is a sharer in the "great and precious promises;" he has escaped the corruption that is in the world; he anticipates becoming a partaker of the divine nature. Is it at all probable that one with such a faith and such expectations would deliberately forge the name of "Simeon Peter, apostle of Jesus Christ"? (b) The writer is unsparing in his denunciation of false teachers, corrupters of others, and perverters of the truth. He rehearses the fall of the angels, the destruction of Sodom, and the rebuke of Balaam as examples of the doom of those who know the truth and yet live in shameful sin and crime. Would a Christian and servant of Jesus Christ be at all likely to commit in the most flagrant manner the things he so vehemently condemns? If the writer of 2 Peter was not the apostle Peter, he was a false teacher, a corrupter of others, and a hypocrite. Pseudonymity in this case is not just an innocent literary device. (c) To claim to speak by inspiration and then tell a lie are incompatible ideas. There is a quality to inspired writings that can be felt when they are read. That quality is present when we read 2 Peter; it is not present when we read apocryphal and pseudepigraphical works. The difference is not traceable to the skill of the pseudonymist; it is a matter of inspiration. (d) Defenders of pseudonymity have had difficulty finding a suitable occasion which might have prompted this writing or a believable reason why Peter's name was assigned to it, and they have not been able to explain the problem to their theory caused by its ultimate acceptance into the canon. Did the Church eventually forget it was pseudepigraphical? (e) The actual examples of pseudonymous works still extant were written by heretics who put the names of famous Biblical characters on their works. Can we believe Barclay, who supposes that since the heretics were the ones who issued misleading and pernicious books under the names of the great apostles, that "the church retaliated in kind – issuing books in which men set down for their own generation the things they were quite sure the apostles would have said had they been facing this new situation"?[89] The church did not have to make up books to present the truth or defend the faith. They had Holy Spirit-inspired writings to do that very thing. It was the non-Christians who had no compunctions about resorting to forgery. Who has ever shown the Christians did?

---

[88] Robinson, *op. cit.*, p.87.

[89] Barclay, *op. cit.*, p.341. Does not Barclay's argument tend to destroy any confidence we might have in 2 Peter, bringing it down, instead, to the level of heretical writings? Furthermore, many of Barclay's assumptions are based on doubtful evidence, and doubtful dating of the books. Here is an interesting fact -- after using certain verses in 2 Peter to build a case in his introductory studies for the late date of 2 Peter, Barclay apparently forgot what he wrote in the introduction as he later commented on the verses, or else he did not find it possible to consistently comment on the verses and still hold the conclusions set forth in the introductory remarks, and so abandoned some of them as he actually commented on the verses in question.

"We may lay down as a general principle that, when biblical books specify their own authorship, the affirmation of their canonicity involves a denial of their pseudonymity. Pseudonymity and canonicity are mutually exclusive."[90]

We find nothing in the internal evidence that is conclusive against the idea that the Apostle Peter wrote 2 Peter, just as the book itself claims, and we find the external evidence as in the case of Bodmer VIII gradually becoming stronger, though it already was greatly superior to the evidence for any of the books that were omitted from the canon. We accept the conclusion that Peter was the author of this letter.

II. INTEGRITY OF THE TEXT[91]

Source criticism went through our Bible books with a fine-tooth comb, looking for sources that were copied.

Some source critics have questioned the integrity of 2 Peter because they have found what they construe to be interpolations, i.e., material added later. Some theories are based on the notion that portions of Jude have been interpolated by the writer of 2 Peter. Some see chapter 2 as an interpolation from Jude; others extend the interpolation to include 1:20-3:3, or 2:1-3:7. Other theories are based on the notion that 2 Peter is a compilation of a number of different sources. For example, one holds that only chapter 1 was written by Peter; another says that only 1:1-12 and the doxology are Peter's; another holds that chapter 3 was once a letter separate from chapters 1 and 2. Yet another theory is that each of the three chapters was once a separate letter. Robson presented the theory that there are four fragments which he thought were of apostolic origin (1:5b-11, 1:12-18, 1:20b-2:19, and 3:3b-13); the remainder of 2 Peter was interpolated.

Refutations of these alleged interpolations and evidence for the integrity of the text include these points: (1) There is no evidence from the manuscripts or versions in favor of the interpolation theory. The text appears in these in substantially the form we have it. (2) The lack of agreement as to the alleged interpolations is a strong argument against the attempts to disintegrate the epistle. One looks in vain for evidence of any sutures which might be evidence of the patching together of different sources. (3) In the last two verses (3:17,18), the writer sums up the substance of his teaching:

[90] James I. Packer, *Fundamentalism and the Word of God* (Grand Rapids: Eerdmans, 1985), p.184.

[91] "Integrity" is a technical term. It has to do with the wholesome preservation of the text in substantially the same form as it issued from the pen of the original author. Specifically, 2 Peter enjoys integrity if the words in our Bibles are substantially the same as those Peter wrote. In this commentator's judgment, they are.

> "You therefore, beloved, knowing this beforehand, be on your guard lest, being carried away by the error of unprincipled men, you fall from your own steadfastness, but grow in the grace and knowledge of our Lord and Savior Jesus Christ."

This is exactly what the whole of 2 Peter talks about. Elliott summarizes his discussion of integrity this way: "A coherent development of themes and line of argumentation and a consistency of terminology and style mark the integrity of the document as a whole."[92]

There is no reason to suppose there has been displacement of any large parts of the text. One scholar tried to rearrange the letter so that 3:1-16 stood after 2:3a. He did this to smooth out the apparent awkwardness of the sequence of verb tenses in chapter 2 and the apparent digression in the same chapter. Moffatt, who thinks we must rearrange John 14-17 for essentially the same reasons, criticized this handling of the Petrine text as being unnecessary in order to explain the interchange of verb tenses.

> "The Greek text and syntax of the letter is uncertain at several places and its meaning obscure. The many textual variants reflect early attempts to make sense of these obscurities (1:4,10,15; 2;1,4,6,12-18,21-22; 3:5,7-12)."[93]

III. DESTINATION[94]

Three or four verses are involved in any discussion of the destination of 2 Peter: 1:1, 3:1, and 3:15,16.

- No town, country, or church is specifically named in 1:1. Peter addresses his letter generally to "those who have obtained like precious faith as we," i.e., Christians who were ethnically Gentiles, as our comments on verse 1 will show. There must have been some reason for Peter to use his Jewish name, "Symeon," and some reason why he referred to the readers as having the "same precious faith as we." Gnosticism took root among Jewish folk first. Is Peter implying, "I'm Jewish and I've not been duped; you Gentiles should not be duped by a Jewish heresy either"?

- 3:1 identifies the readers of the second epistle as being those to whom a first letter was addressed. If this first letter is our 1 Peter, then the destination of 2 Peter is "Pontus, Galatia, Cappadocia, Asia, and Bithynia."[95]

---

[92] Elliott, *op. cit.*, p.285.

[93] Elliott, *op. cit.*, p.284.

[94] If the Petrine authorship is rejected, then no certain destination can be proven. Such places as Palestine, Egypt, Rome, or Asia Minor have been proposed, but all these proposals are guesses. Zahn suggested the destination as being Palestine and the adjoining regions (*ibid.*, p.206ff). Falconer (*Expos.* VI/6 (1902), p.47ff, 117f, 218f) suggested 2 Peter was a circular to the churches in Samaria.

[95] Zahn, Roberts, Lenski, and others argue 2 Peter 3:1 is a reference to a letter now lost, not a reference to

- According to 3:15,16, the addressees knew Paul or at least some of his letters. Paul did write letters to some of the same geographical areas identified in 1 Peter 1:1 (cf. Galatians, Ephesians, Colossians, Philemon, 1 Timothy, and 2 Timothy). One of the concerns in these letters from Paul was the same as the concerns of 2 Peter – heretical teachers.

IV. PLACE AND TIME OF WRITING

As to the *place* where this letter originated, no certain intimation is given in the epistle itself. If Peter wrote it,[96] it is probable that 2 Peter was written from the same place as 1 Peter, namely Rome.[97] If it were not written from the same place, we may presume that there would have been some reference to the fact that he had changed his residence, or some local allusion which would have enabled us to determine the fact. The writer was looking forward to the "laying aside of [his] earthly dwelling" (2 Peter 1:13,14). Tradition tells us that Peter was martyred in Rome. This makes it most probable that Peter was in Rome when he wrote this letter. (Notably, Clement of Rome alludes to 2 Peter, and he does so 50 years before other early Christian writers.[98]) Evidently, the writer had received news of a disturbing nature between the writing of his first and second epistles, so he writes the second letter with these new dangers uppermost in his mind.

---

what we call 1 Peter. The argument goes like this: 3:1 implies that both this letter and the previous one were on the same subject. Of course, it is argued, this does not fit 1 Peter because that letter deals with persecution and says nothing about false teachers. If these men's argument holds, then we do not know for sure to whom 2 Peter is addressed since we do not know the destination of the lost previous letter, though a good guess might be Asia Minor. (Zahn thought the readers were predominantly Jewish. Lenski thought they were predominantly Gentiles.) And if their arguments hold, we do not know the date of writing of the letter we call 2 Peter. It could come from the AD 60s, before Peter's arrival in Rome, and even before the writing of what we call 1 Peter – any time after the Jewish Gnostics began to appear on the scene.

[96] Of course, if the Petrine authorship is rejected, then no certain place can be designated as the place of writing. J.W.C. Wand suggested the pseudonymist lived in Egypt (*The General Epistles of St. Peter and St. Jude*, 1934, p.144). So did Chase (*Hasting's Dictionary of the Bible*, Vol.3, p.816). Bauckham (*WBC*, p.146) has him living in Rome.

[97] See the discussion concerning the place of writing of 1 Peter in the Introductory Studies to that letter. "Those who hold to Babylon as the place from which 1 Peter was written generally hold that this second epistle was written on the way to Rome or even in Rome." D. Edmond Hiebert, *An Introduction to the Non-Pauline Epistles* (Chicago: Moody Press, 1962), p.169.

[98] Lenski has 2 Peter written from Peter's missionary journeys, somewhere other than from Rome, and he also dates it before the writing of the letter we call 1 Peter. We reject Lenski's theory that "2 Peter" antedated "1 Peter." We do agree with his view that the books in our Bibles are arranged according to length, not according to when they were written, but we disagree with several of his other views. (1) We do not see any reason to posit a "lost letter" written by Peter. There is no reason 2 Peter 3:1 cannot be a reference to our 1 Peter. (2) 1 Peter deals with impending persecution, says Lenski, whereas 2 Peter says nothing about such. Therefore, Lenski believes, 3:1 has reference to a lost letter that was written before the persecution broke out. But why could not 2 Peter also have been written after the first wave of Neronian persecution died down? (3) Lenski also notes there is no warning about false teachers in 1 Peter, so how can 2 Peter be the "second" warning. 3:1 must refer to some letter other than our 1 Peter, Lenski affirms. But read it carefully. Does 2 Peter 3:1 say that the "first letter" contained such a warning? Read 2 Peter 3:1-2 again!

As to *time* of writing, any time after the writing of 1 Peter, any time after it became obvious that a new heresy had moved in to threaten the churches, and probably not long before the apostle's martyrdom, will satisfy the evidence. The letter was composed when Peter was looking forward to the speedy release from the tabernacle of his body (1:14). The apostle suffered martyrdom in the spring of AD 68, the 14th year of Nero's reign.[99] It was probably not long before this when this epistle was written. **Thus, we will date it c. AD 67.**

We reject the late date hypothesized by the negative higher critics[100] because we have rejected the internal arguments and the allegations of literary dependence they advance favoring a late date.[101]

V. PURPOSE OF WRITING

Sometimes New Testament writers tell us, in one verse or another, why they wrote. Sometimes we must discern the purpose by calling attention to the major themes or issues emphasized in the letter.

Perhaps in 1:13 and 3:17 Peter tells us his purpose. He says it was to **warn, encourage, and instruct the faithful concerning the approach of certain false teachers**. Peter indicates many false teachers will shortly make their appearance among the readers, corrupting and contradicting the truth as preached by the apostles and evangelists. Forewarned is forearmed. Peter writes this warning to prevent the nefarious teachings from getting a foothold within the churches. He uses denunciation and apologetic argument in defense of apostolic teaching.

Who were the false teachers about whom Peter warns? It is difficult to draw a picture of the false teachers to whom the epistle refers because the traits listed are few and not clearly defined or marked. We suppose the false teachers described in Jude are the same as those

---

[99] See this date documented in footnote #41 in the Introductory Studies to 1 Peter.

[100] Those who deny the Petrine authorship generally assign a mid-second century date for the writing of 2 Peter. Bleek dated it from AD 100 to 150. Meyerhoff dated 2 Peter about AD 150. Semler dated 2 Peter at about AD 170. Harnack, in his *Lehre der Zwolf Apostle*, p.15 and 159, dated 2 Peter as late as the time of Clement of Alexandria, and assigned its place of composition as being Egypt. Barclay dates it in the second century. Bauckham (*WBC*, p.158) dates 2 Peter at c.AD 80-90. Elliott (*ABD*, p.287) dates it to "sometime in the first quarter of the second century." So does Chase (*Hasting's Dictionary of the Bible*, p.817).

[101] "The evidence which really rules out composition *during Peter's lifetime* is that of literary genre and that of date." Bauckham, *WBC*, p.159.

described in 2 Peter.[102] We suppose the "false teachers" of chapter 2:1 and the "mockers" of chapter 3:3 speak of the same group of people.[103] Peter seems to indicate several objectionable emphases in the doctrines and practices taught by the false teachers. According to 2:1, they deny the Master who bought them[104] and "introduce destructive heresies." From 1:16a, their claim that the apostles had cleverly invented the story of the first coming of Christ[105] must be denied. From 1:20, their claim that the Messianic prophecies of the Old Testament were not inspired, but simply the prophets own mistaken attempts to interpret their dreams and visions, must be answered. From 2:3b and 19a, their claim that Paul's teaching about freedom supported their libertine views and immoral lifestyle must be repudiated.[106] From 2:10b, their laughter at the supposed power of the devil and his angels must be countered. From 3:4, their denial of any second coming at all must be answered. From 3:16, their twisting of Scripture[107] must be made plain to all. And from the many times Peter uses "know," "knowledge," or "full knowledge" (1:2,3,5,6,8; 2:20,21; 3:3,17, 18), it appears he is countering the false teacher's emphasis on their own brand of superior "knowledge."

The view taken herein is that the false teachers and mockers were the forerunners of the antinomian Gnostic heretics of the second century.[108] That Jewish Gnostic[109] ideas were al-

---

[102] This conclusion rests on the fact that Jude claims to be speaking about the same false teachers Peter predicts. The conclusion will be rejected by those who identify the false teachers of Jude as being different from those in 2 Peter.

[103] This identification will be documented in the comments offered on the pertinent verses.

[104] Gnostic doctrine taught auto-salvation, rather than a redemption wrought by Jesus on Calvary.

[105] Gnosticism eventually asserted the historical Jesus was only a phantom. Because matter is evil He could not have had a material body. It just looked like He did, they would affirm.

[106] As Peter insists that the Christian is a man who has escaped the corruption of the world (1:4,9), he objects to their libertine lifestyle (2 Peter 2:10b-22). In contrast, "holy living" is expected of Peter's readers (3:11-16). There are some thought-provoking questions to consider as one studies this letter. Does the libertine lifestyle espoused by the false teachers reflect the societal breakdown that followed the post-Augustan era? There was a breakdown of external political control, and with it came a decline and dissolution in public morals. Magic and astrology were prevalent. Society members are at times sadly influenced by the culture in which they live. Did these antinomian libertines attempt to sell the idea that their immorality was simply an alternative way to practice "Christian liberty"?

[107] Irenaeus frequently charges the Gnostics of his day with dishonesty in their handling of Scripture (*Adv. Haer.* i.3.6, 8.1, 9.1). They argued that the living voice was more authoritative than Scripture, and by living voice they meant their own secret traditions which led them to deny the validity of orthodox apostolic writings and to substitute their own esoteric writings.

[108] Kasemann (*op. cit.*, p.272) maintains the false teachers were Gnostic, but he comes to the subject already convinced that 2 Peter is a second-century document.

[109] That Gnosticism began first as a Jewish heresy and then later came into the church, only to become a Christian heresy, is documented in "history of the development of the Gnostic heresy" in the author's *New Testament Epistles: Timothy and Titus* (Moberly, MO: Scripture Exposition Books, 1999), p.lvix-lxiv.

ready, in the mid-first century, beginning to infiltrate the churches is evident from Paul's writings; remember, 2 Peter 3:12-18 is a reference to Paul's epistles. That it would be a continuing and growing problem is evident from the later writings of John.[110] The heresy Peter had in view was incipient Gnosticism.[111] Many a Gnostic also taught a libertine lifestyle,[112] exactly what Peter opposes.

What are we to think of the idea presented in many contemporary commentaries, namely that 2 Peter is an example of the genre[113] of ancient literature known as a "**testament**"? Typical is Elliott's summary of 2 Peter as "a composition of the post-apostolic period that claims to be the testament of the apostle Peter dispatched as a letter."[114] A "testament" was a "farewell speech" of one who is about to die. Among the Old Testament pseudepigrapha are the *Testament of Abraham, Testament of Moses, Testament of Job,* and the *Testaments of the Twelve Patriarchs.* The common elements in these Jewish apocryphal testaments are: (1) Some famous Bible figure is fictitiously presented as giving a final message to his people, containing: (2) A prediction of the writer's imminent death; (3) Reminiscences of the past; (4) "Predictions" of what is to come, often with special emphasis on hard times or apostasy (whatever is the current issue the writer wishes to address); (5) Exhortations to the hearers (i.e., the readers) to be faithful through all these things; (6) Some kind of positive disclosure of final victory or vindication. (7) The most common element in these Jewish testaments is that they were all fiction.[115] The whole speech – i.e., words these famous Bible figures might have been expected to say in farewell speeches – was made up and put in the mouths of these long dead men whose names were affixed to the speech. The pseudepigrapher wrote in this fashion to secure for his teaching and position the authority antiquity confers.

---

110 The pertinent Pauline and Johannine epistles that are anti-Gnostic are cited above (pp.xv-xviii) under "topics covered" in the paragraphs on the genuineness of 2 Peter.

111 The indefiniteness of description of the false teachers, this commentator believes, is a strong argument in favor of an early date for this epistle. A writer in the second century, with the full-blown Gnosticism of Basilides, Carpocrates, Valentinus, and Marcion around him, could scarcely have divested himself of his experience and given us, not the details of what he saw and heard, but the germs of what would develop into these after a half a century of growth.

112 Gnostics included Greek philosophical ideas in their worldview. Greek philosophy with its dualism (spirit is good, matter is evil) led some to argue that it does not matter what a man does with his body. Is that where the false teachers got their idea that we may glut and sate its appetites, yet have it make no difference to our spirit?

113 Identifying "genre" is of special interest to contemporary humanistic literary criticism.

114 John H. Elliott (*ABD*, Vol.5), p.282. Kasemann also suggested 2 Peter 1:15 was included by the pseudepigrapher to give 2 Peter the character of a testament from Peter.

115 Of course, a testament could be a genuine product of a man's last days or years summing up the most vital concerns of his life. But these Jewish testaments were not genuine.

Proponents of the "testament" idea have been hard pressed to find examples of such fiction written by Christian authors. Almost in desperation, it seems, they appeal to the farewells spoken by Jesus (Matthew 24,25; John 14-16) and Paul (Acts 20:17-38; 2 Timothy),[116] and to the apocryphal "Acts" (which according to Findlay were of Gnostic tendency and use[117]) which contain "farewell speeches," among them the *Acts of Peter* 36-39, the *Acts of John* 106-107, and the *Acts of Thomas* 159-160.

Trying to convince themselves and their readers that they have correctly identified the genre of 2 Peter, these modern scholars confidently tell us all the usual testamental elements are present in 2 Peter. The writer cites as his reason for writing the fact that he is soon to die, just as Jesus had told him (1:12-14). He warns against false teachers who will come to destroy the church with their heresies (2:1-11, 3:3-7). He exhorts his readers to guard themselves against this threat and to build lives of faithfulness and virtue (e.g., 1:1-12, 3:11-18), knowing that in the end God will triumph (1:4,11, 3:8-13). All along the way, however, the pseudepigrapher gave little hints (e.g., the accidental or deliberate change in verb tenses in chapter 2[118] and 3:16, where the wresting of Scriptures is not a prediction for the future but a present reality) which let the readers know this "testamental" presentation was really transparent fiction.

What the defenders of the "testament" idea fail to tell us is that there is a great difference between 2 Peter and Jewish apocalyptic books in testamentary form,[119] that difference being that those books all have a discourse addressed to the immediate descendants, but which is really destined for future generations. 2 Peter is addressed to fellow Christians, not immediate descendants.

Classifying 2 Peter as a "testament" certainly discredits the letter's authenticity and value.[120] Why did the pseudepigrapher choose to write in Peter's name? "That the fictional writer chose to write Peter's 'testament' is probably best explained if the writer lived in Rome,

---

[116] These men may be saying farewell, but with the exception of 2 Timothy, they are not separate letters. Nor are they made up speeches imported into another document like is claimed for 2 Peter.

[117] A.F. Findlay, "Apocryphal Acts," *International Standard Bible Encyclopedia*, edited by James Orr (Grand Rapids, MI : Eerdmans, 1929), Vol.1, p.183-195.

[118] The use of present tense verbs (2 Peter 2:3b-22, 3:1-10, 16b-17) certainly leaves the impression the false teachers are contemporaries of the author, rather than figures who will appear in the distant future.

[119] "That pseudonymous apocalypses were widespread is demonstrable; that pseudonymous letters were widespread is entirely unsupported by the evidence." (Carson, Moo, and Morris, *An Introduction to the New Testament* [Grand Rapids, Zondervan, 1992], p.495. How can scholars speak of a genre of apocalyptic *letters* to which they can then compare 2 Peter?

[120] "These considerations of literary genre are probably the most important elements in the scholarly consensus that 2 Peter is pseudepigraphical, [a consensus] from which only a few recent discussions of the work still dissent." (Bauckham, "2 Peter" in *Dictionary of the Later New Testament and its Developments*, [Downers Grove, IL: InterVarsity, 1997]. p.924.)

which had counted Peter as one of its most prestigious leaders in the previous generation."[121] It leaves the initial impression that 2 Peter can continue to be safely ignored, because if it is a work of fiction by some unknown lover of Peter, it is not an inspired word from God! When one gets finished reading the long defenses of the testamentary genre and pseudonymity of 2 Peter, it begins to become painfully obvious that this fiction would have had little impact on the heretics it was supposed to overturn. It has been robbed of any value as a warning against something false. Furthermore, it probably should not even be included in the Bible; after all, other apocryphal and pseudepigraphical books were rejected precisely because they were fictional in authorship and destitute of real Biblical content.

The early church identified the form as an **epistle**. When they added titles to the Greek manuscripts, they named it the "Epistle of Peter B." The epistolary opening (1:1-2) and reference to its being a "second letter" (3:1) show that 2 Peter was dispatched as a "letter." Though it lacks a specific epistolary conclusion or any final personal allusions, as did most first century letters, it does close with a doxology (3:18b).[122] We too will call it an epistle, rather than a testament, lest we leave our listeners with a greatly degraded and diminished feeling about this work we call 2 Peter. 2 Peter can be easily understood without recourse to the testamentary hypothesis, something that certainly could not be said of the Jewish farewell discourses.

2 Peter is an appeal for loyalty to Christ in the face of subtle heresy. The readers will have to grow in grace and in full knowledge to safeguard against this vicious error. Such growth will require careful attention to the Old Testament Scriptures and the words of the apostles.

VI. ABOUT THE KJV TRANSLATION OF 2 PETER

It is well known that the translators of the King James Version, while on the whole making an enormous advance on previous English versions, sometimes went backwards. In some instances, the changes they made, when compared to the translations already made into English, were the reverse of improvements.

Perhaps no portion of the New Testament is more full of cases of this kind than 2 Peter. In a substantial number of such cases, it will be found that the earlier versions which are superior to the KJV are Wycliffe's and the Rhemish, and that not infrequently the version which led the KJV translators astray was the Genevan.

[121] So says Bauckham (*DLNTD*, p.925). The same writer (*WBC*, p.160,161) finally and hesitantly names either Linus (2 Timothy 4:21), listed by Hegesippus as bishop of Rome after Peter, or Anecletus, whom the same lists name as Linus' successor and Clement's predecessor, as being the pseudepigrapher.

[122] There is an absence of personal messages and greetings in Galatians. The omission of such concluding words in circular letters is to be expected.

None of these three versions were among those which the translators were instructed to use. Of Wycliffe's, they probably made very little use. Of the other two, they made a great deal of use. Wycliffe's and the Rhemish were made from the Latin Vulgate, not from the Greek, so we have what at first sight seems to be a startling fact – that versions made from a Latin translation are often superior to the KJV, which was made from the Textus Receptus. But the explanation is simple. The Vulgate is a good Latin translation of excellent Greek texts; our KJV is a good English translation of very defective Greek texts.[123]

VII. THEOLOGY

Few documents in the theological literature contain so much overview of the Christian message and its ramifications for history as 2 Peter.

> It covers creation, prophecy, law, imprecation, judgment, cosmology, atonement, and all points of the classical *ordo salutis*. It is of special value for its attestation of the objectivity of the apostolic witness in 1:16. Because of this, 2 Peter is of prime importance in the understanding of inspiration, revelation, and inerrancy. The terminology of the book is made up of two clear sources: the Old Testament [a large part of his vocabulary is drawn directly from the LXX] and its interpretation in the Gospels and epistles. Peter mixed and combined both strands as no other author did. The ethical application of the principle of the Parousia is carried throughout the book. Peter was not allegorizing the Second Coming, but he was demonstrating the important concern that each age has a response and a duty to perform until Christ's coming. The book adds to the New Testament the all-encompassing interpretation that is provided by the Old Testament prophetic visions. The basic motive of the Christian religion – that of creation-fall-redemption-restoration – is repeated several times with differing emphases in each case. Peter defined false teaching as false teaching about the Scriptures. For Peter, the Old Testament and the Apostolic writings were truth – any divergence, falsification, or perversion of this truth is error ... The Church would be dependent on the written descriptions of the truth in Christ that the apostles had left. Peter fully realized this and provided the Church with a compendium of the Christian faith in the face of unbelief. [The portrayal of Christ in 2 Peter is central.] In the first verse, Peter is an apostle of Jesus Christ ... In the succeeding verses Christ is presented as Lord, Gr. *kurios*, as authority of truth, as deliverer of the believers, as the escape for Christians from worldly pollutions, as the coming and eternal King. The authority of Peter and the apostles to warn and teach is derived from their functions as apostles, servants of the Lord Jesus Christ. One of the themes developed in the book is the Old Testament concept that ethical and religious commitments determine empirical situations. The historical judgment upon Sodom and Gomorrah took the form of a physical calamity, thus the apostle illustrates God's providence. The surety of the resurrection and final triumph of the believer is rooted in this same providential care. The passage in 3:8 indicates clearly the idea of God's eternity and of the created nature and structure of time. The Parousia is related directly to this, to remove it from mere humanistic theory.[124]

---

[123] This comment presupposes that the theory behind the Westcott-Hort and Nestle-Aland texts is correct, and that the textual theory behind the Textus Receptus is faulty. See comments on these matters in the author's notes on "New Testament Criticism -- Canon, Text, Inspiration, and Principal Versions."

[124] White, *op. cit.*, p.732.

Chapter 1 of 2 Peter develops the key idea of "True Knowledge." In the outline we have provided below, Peter speaks of the basis of saving knowledge – it rests on divine power that has granted everything pertaining to life and godliness and includes precious and magnificent promises. Peter speaks of a growth in this knowledge that is expected from those who would enter heaven. And Peter speaks of the inerrant sources of this true knowledge that are available to the readers.

In 3:5-13, Peter speaks of "three ages," three enormous epochs in earth's history. Using the Flood and the second coming of Christ as dividing points, he breaks history into three clearly defined periods and mentions some characteristic features of each. First, there was the *old* world, the world that "was" before the flood (3:6). Noah was a "preacher of righteousness" during this period (2:5). Second, there is the *present* world (3:7), "the heavens and earth that now are" since the flood. This is stored up for fire (or with fire), and all that delays that conflagration at the second advent of Christ is God's patient waiting for men to repent. Third, the *future* world that follows Christ's return is "the new heavens and new earth in which righteousness dwells" (3:13). The accomplishment of Peter's predictions will involve a fundamental change in the constitution of our universe.

Ernst Kasemann's critical views of the theology of 2 Peter need to be addressed since his scholarship has tended to influence a whole generation of his students. (1) Does 2 Peter betray a degenerate Christology, as Kasemann thought? Kasemann claimed the "manward-oriented eschatology of 2 Peter pushes the lordship and pre-eminence of Christ into the background.[125] However, a fair assessment of the evidence would not support such a contention. The titles applied to Jesus are "Christ" (8 times), "Savior" (5 times), "Lord" (14 times) and "Master" (1 time). The great emphasis on His Lordship presupposes the resurrection and ascension, since without these such a doctrine could not be defended. Henry Alford[126] maintained that the lordship of Christ is prominent in 2 Peter because of the writer's purpose to warn the readers and caution them against the rebellion encouraged by the false teachers. The honor and glory ascribed to Jesus at the transfiguration declares Him to be God's own incarnate Son. He is central to the whole thinking of the believer (2:20, 1:2,8). To Him is ascribed eternal glory (3:18). (2) Does 2 Peter betray a defective soteriology, as Kasemann maintained? Kasemann argued that in 2 Peter Christ is no longer regarded as a redeemer.[127] The allegation is that references to the cross, the resurrection, and the atoning work of Christ common in 1 Peter are missing from 2 Peter. Like Kasemann, Chase long ago argued there is no reference to the resurrection.[128] However, redemption *is* present in 2 Peter. 1:9 speaks of "purification from ... former sins." That cannot happen without the cross. 2:1 speaks of the "Master who bought them." Man's salvation was purchased by the blood of Jesus at Calvary (cp. 1 Peter

---

[125] Kasemann, *op. cit.*, p.182

[126] Alford, *op. cit.*, p. 155.

[127] *Essays on New Testament Themes* (London, SCM, 1971), p.183-84.

[128] *Hasting's Dictionary of the Bible*, Vol.3, p.810.

1;18,19). Further, the expression "the way" (2:2, "way of truth"; 2:15, "right way"; 2:21, "way of righteousness") likely reflects the theme that the cross of Christ with its power for changed lives is "the way of salvation."[129] (3) Does 2 Peter betray a sub-Christian eschatology, as Kasemann thought? Kasemann interpreted "becoming partakers of the divine nature" (1:4) as something that happens wholly in this life, thus eliminating any future eschatological emphasis on the *parousia*.[130] He argued that in the case of the earthly Jesus, the transfiguration has been substituted for the resurrection, as an example of what awaits us in this life.[131] Kasemann's presentation of 2 Peter's eschatology, however, is not exactly fair. The "divine nature" is more than a reference to a Christian's sanctification in this present life. The escaping of the corruption in the world (1:4) precedes the becoming "partakers of the divine nature." Involved in that latter phrase is not only a change of the spiritual man on the inside but also includes the resurrection body received at the *parousia*.[132] The hope of the *parousia* with its practical outcome in providing a motive for holy living (2 Peter 3:10-12) is fully in accord with the eschatology of the rest of the New Testament (cp. 1 John 2:28, 3:3). As Kasemann tried to make his case for "sub-Christian eschatology," he completely ignored what chapter 3 says about the "day of the Lord" with its accompanying destruction of the heavens and earth by fire[133] and the final judgment.[134] Peter did speak of the "restoration of all things" in Acts 3:21, so finding a similar idea in 2 Peter 3:13 should not be thought surprising.[135]

---

[129] C.G. Berkouwer, *Studies in Dogmatics: Faith and Justification* (Grand Rapids: Eerdmans, 1954), p.35.

[130] Kasemann, *op. cit.*, p.179.

[131] *Op. cit.*, p.187.

[132] The different terms used in 1 and 2 Peter to refer to the second coming (*apokalupsis* and its cognates in 1 Peter 1:13, 1:7 and 5:1 versus *parousia, hemera kuriou, hemera kriseos* in 2 Peter) have been noted, but little weight may be put on this. Both words (*apokalupsis* and *parousia*) are used by Paul of the second advent in Romans 2:5, 8:18, and 2 Thessalonians 1:7, so why could not Peter have used both?

[133] The idea of the renovation of the universe by fire is not a novel idea with Peter. It also occurs in Paul when he writes about the judgment saying, "for the day shall declare it, because it is revealed in fire" (1 Corinthians 3:13 ASV). 2 Thessalonians 1:7 talks about "flaming fire" at the *parousia* of Jesus.

[134] The description of the *eschaton* ("end"), although dramatic with its accompanying destruction of the heavens and earth by fire, is seen to be extraordinarily restrained when compared, for instance, with the *Apocalypse of Peter*. Defenders of pseudonymity will have to explain this extraordinary restraint. There is an absence in 2 Peter of any second-century Chiliastic interpretation of Psalm 90:4, in spite of the fact this passage is alluded to in 2 Peter 3:8. Would a second-century pseudonymist have avoided this possible pitfall?

[135] According to Irenaeus (*Adv. Haer.* i.7.1), second-century Gnostics held ideas about a "fire which lies hidden in the world" that "would blaze forth and burn" ... "destroying all matter ... so that it has no further existence" after men's souls had entered into the Pleroma. In other words, the Gnostics taught annihilation of matter. 2 Peter is not speaking of annihilation but renovation. One wonders, however, if what Peter wrote about renovation was confused with annihilation, thus leading some second-century people to regard 2 Peter with suspicion, as noted by Origen when he observed that some "disputed" 2 Peter (*Commentary on John*, 5.3).

There is not any substantial difference in doctrine when this Epistle is compared with other New Testament books. If there had been, in the period when the canon was being guarded, those substantial differences would have kept it out of the canon altogether.

VIII. SUGGESTED OUTLINE OF SECOND PETER

Signature, Address, and Greeting. 1:1,2

I. THE FULL KNOWLEDGE OF CHRIST. 1:3-21
  A. The Completeness of This Knowledge. v.3,4
  B. Qualities of Life to Complement What Christ Has Done. v.5-11
  C. The Inerrant Sources of Full Knowledge about Jesus Christ. v.12-21
    1. The truth already present with them. v.12
    2. The apostle Peter's testimony -- both oral and written. v.13-18
    3. The Old Testament prophecies. v.19-21

II. CONCERNING FALSE TEACHERS. 2:1-22
  A. Prophetic Warning Portraying Coming False Teachers. v.1-3
  B. Historical Proofs that God's Judgment is Not Idle. v.4-10a
    1. Angels who sinned were punished. v.4
    2. Ungodly people in Noah's time were punished. v.5
    3. The ungodly in Sodom and Gomorrah were punished. v.6-8
    4. Peter's conclusion drawn from the three examples. v.9,10a
  C. Further Description of the False Teachers. v.10b-19
    1. Their negative attitude toward "glories." v.10b,11
    2. Like mad animals, they will be destroyed for the harm they do. v.12-13a
    3. Their vices and sins. v.13b-16
    4. The worthlessness, emptiness, and unprofitability of their teaching. v.17-19
  D. The Condition of Those who Listen to These False Teachers. v.20-22

III. CONCERNING CHRIST'S SECOND COMING. 3:1-16
  A. The Certainty of Christ's Second Coming in Spite of Mockers. v.1-10
    1. A call to remember the Word of God. v.1,2
    2. A prophecy about mockers who will deny Christ's second coming. v.3,4
    3. Refutation of the mocker's arguments. v.5-9
    4. Emphatic affirmation that the day of the Lord will come! v.10
  B. Exhortations with Reference to the Approaching Day of the Lord. v.11-16
    1. A call to holy living. v.11
    2. A call for an attitude of expectation. v.12,13
    3. A call for diligence. v.14
    4. A call to make proper use of the Lord's patience. v.15,16

Concluding Exhortations and Doxology. 3:17,18
  A. Exhortation to Guard Against the Error of the Wicked. v.17
  B. Exhortation to Grow in Grace and Knowledge. v.18a
  C. Doxology to Jesus. v.18b

2 PETER

SIGNATURE, ADDRESS, AND GREETING. 1:1,2

The first chapter of 2 Peter is a great chapter! It has the wonderful passage about God's generous provision for man's life and godliness, on partaking of the divine nature, the growth of Christian qualities of life, Peter's recollection of the glory of Jesus observed at the transfiguration, the more sure word of prophecy, and the passage about the Scriptures being inspired.

A. The Writer. 1:1a

1:1 -- ***Simon Peter, a bond-servant and apostle of Jesus Christ, to those who have received a faith of the same kind as ours, by the righteousness of our God and Savior, Jesus Christ:***

Simon Peter -- The author signs his name "Simon Peter," or perhaps he wrote "Symeon Peter." The manuscript evidence is about equally divided.[1] "Simon" was the Greek spelling, "Symeon" the Hebrew, and the forms were at times nearly interchangeable.[2] Bible students have naturally inquired why he used two names, and why (perhaps) his old Hebrew name, a spelling of his name that occurs nowhere else in the New Testament save at Acts 15:14 in a speech in a meeting where there was a strong Jewish setting, by the strongly Jewish James, the Lord's brother. How natural to picture Peter, now an old man, reminiscing about the important change in his life that Jesus had wrought. "Symeon" was his old name, and recalls his life during his youth and during those years he was a Galilean fisherman. "Peter," the name given to him by Jesus the first day he met Jesus (John 1:40-42), pictures the profound change Jesus made in his life. "Cephas" is the Greek transliteration of an Aramaic word for stone, and "Peter" is its Greek translation. Oscar Cullmann has suggested that if we repro-

---

[1] Sinaiticus, A, K, P, and the Byzantine text reads *Symeon*. P^{72}, Vaticanus, the Old Latin, the Vulgate, and the Palestinian Syriac read *Simon*. If the Greek spelling were original, it is difficult to decide why some scribe would have corrected it to the older Hebrew form. But we can picture a scribe correcting the Hebrew spelling. Certainly, we may imagine, a pseudonymist in the second century would have signed his forgery the same way 1 Peter was signed.

[2] In 1 Maccabees 2:3 and 2:65 we find both forms applied to one of the sons of Mattathias. Used of someone other than Peter, the Hebrew form "Symeon" occurs several in our Bibles. See Revelation 7:7 (where Simeon identifies one of the sons of the patriarch Jacob), Luke 3:30 (a Simeon was an ancestor of Jesus), Luke 2:25,34 (a devout old man who spoke glowingly of the baby Jesus when He was presented in the Temple at 40 days of age), and Acts 13:1 ("Simeon called Niger").

duced his name as "Simon Rock" we would catch its impact.[3] It has often been observed that the opening words of New Testament letters often strike many of the emphases that will be unfolded in the body of the letter. This may be happening here, too. Peter is solid in his commitment to Jesus, and by implication, his readers should be too. No more of the old life for him or them!

A bond-servant and apostle of Jesus Christ -- To further identify himself, Peter uses two nouns to describe his relationship with Jesus Christ. His authority for writing flows from Jesus Christ. As explained at 1 Peter 1:1, when Peter and the early church use the name "Jesus" and the title "Christ (Messiah)" together, it expressed their conviction that Jesus of Nazareth was the long-promised Messiah.[4] This is something Peter's readers must have clear in their minds or they will be vulnerable to the false teachers about whom Peter is warning. "Apostle" was explained in comments on 1 Peter 1:1. It recalls his call to be an apostle and it also serves to remind his readers of his divinely-given mission. Peter adds "bond-servant"[5] in this letter. We immediately begin to wonder why the addition. Does it reflect some of Peter's interests as he writes this letter? In the Old Testament, the prophets (God's special mouthpieces) were called "my servants, the prophets."[6] Is Peter reminding his readers that Christ does have mouthpieces, and the Gnostics who think a man can safely ignore what these prophets say are in error? Or perhaps Peter is using "bond-servant" in the sense that all Christians have been purchased at a great price, by the precious blood of Jesus[7], and therefore have an obligation to their Master. Peter could be setting the stage for making this telling point: Christ's servants live lives qualitatively different than one sees the false teachers (who are stigmatized as being "slaves of corruption" [2:19]) living.

B. The Recipients of the Letter. 1:1b

To those who have received a faith of the same kind as ours -- The recipients are described in general terms. If the conclusions reached in the Introductory Studies are valid, the readers

---

[3] *TDNT*, 6:101. "Peter" originally was a descriptive title rather than a proper name.

[4] This conviction arose from their study of the prophetic Scriptures and their learning experiences with Him during His earthly ministry (cp. John 1:41; Matthew 16:16), and it received unshakable and unmistakable verification when He rose from the dead (Acts 2:32-36).

[5] The Greek word is *doulos*, which means "slave" or "bond-servant." Because "slave" can arouse images of forced and cruel servitude our versions try to choose a word to translate it that will portray a spiritual and voluntary servanthood of someone totally devoted to his loving Lord Jesus Christ.

[6] Amos 3:7; Isaiah 20:3. God's special mouthpieces in New Testament times also appropriated this title for themselves. See Romans 1:1 (Paul), James 1:1, and Jude 1:1.

[7] 1 Peter 1:18,19; 1 Corinthians 6:19,20.

are Christians who lived in the provinces of Asia Minor.[8] Each of the words Peter uses to describe the readers has become the subject of theological debate. "Received" translates *lachousin*, the verb that means "to obtain by lot."[9] It says God somehow had a hand in these people's faith. Faith, we learn in Romans 10:17 comes by hearing the Word of God.[10] We recall on Paul's second missionary journey (Acts 16:6-9) how the Spirit led the missionaries. We suppose something similar is here claimed for the readers of 2 Peter. God had a hand in sending to them the first missionaries who preached to them. "Faith" has been taken objectively (i.e., denoting a body of apostolic doctrine, like Jude 3) by some, subjectively (i.e., each man's obedient response to the gospel, as in 2 Peter 1:5) by others.[11] *Isotimon*, which occurs only here in the New Testament, comes from two words: *isos* ("equal in quantity or quality") + *timos* ("held as of great price, honor, privilege").[12] "Like precious" or "equally precious" would be better a better translation than "same kind." Observe too that the word stands emphatically forward in the sentence, emphasizing the truth. Does "with us" ("as ours," NASB) mean "us Jews" or "us apostles" or both? Many suppose this letter is addressed to readers who were mostly from Gentile backgrounds. The same precious faith that Jewish Christians held is precisely what had been taught to and accepted by the Gentiles.[13] Others suppose Peter says the apostles did not change any of the truths as they began evangelizing Gentiles; the same truths the apostles originally received are precisely what they

---

[8] In the Introductory Studies, we have called attention to other clues in the letter that may help identify the readers. 1:12 indicates Peter has a personal acquaintance with the readers. 3:1 says this is the second letter written to them. (1 Peter is likely the first one, we believe.) 3:15 says Paul also wrote letters to some of them. 2:1 shows an awareness of the insidious influence of certain false teachers who have tried to infiltrate the churches to whom this letter is addressed.

[9] Compare Luke 1:9; John 19:24; and Acts 1:17 where the same word occurs in a speech by Peter.

[10] Certain denominational writers, who are confident that saving faith is a gift given directly by God to each of the elect, are anxious to find corroboration of that questionable dogma here in 2 Peter. Several writers say, "It implies that faith is a gift of God." We think this handling of "received" borders closely on what Peter condemns men of doing in his day to the Scriptures, namely, "wresting them" (2 Peter 3:16 ASV)

[11] Some appeal to the absence of the Greek word "the" before "faith" as evidence it must be intended to be subjective in this place. We admit that very often when objective faith is meant, the Greek reads "*the* faith" (cp. Acts 6:7, 13:8; Galatians 1:23); however, we also affirm that the article is not always present when "faith" is intended to be objective (cp. Ephesians 4:5).

[12] The word *isotimos* was particularly used in connection with strangers and foreigners who were given equal citizenship in a city where they were strangers and aliens. Josephus, for instance, writing of Antioch, says that in Antioch the Jews were given all the rights of citizenship, and were made *isotimos*, equal in honor and privilege, with the Macedonians and the Greeks who lived there. (Wm. Barclay, "The Letters of James and Peter," in *Daily Study Bible* [Philadelphia: Westminster, 1960], p.343.)

[13] This "like precious" is thought to explain the Jewish emphasis implied in Peter's use of his Jewish name "Symeon." Peter would be saying, there was no need for Gentile Christians to think they had received an inferior brand of faith, a deficiency which the Gnostics said could be quickly remedied if those Gentile believers would just accept the "knowledge" the Gnostics had to offer.

had shared with the Gentiles.[14] Summarizing, it seems that "faith" should be taken objectively, and Peter is affirming that the truth already taught to the readers by the apostles – the truth that had been sent to them by God – is the whole truth and nothing but the truth, and that the Gnostics have nothing additional to offer.

By the righteousness of our God and Savior, Jesus Christ -- That anyone, Jew or Gentile, has an opportunity to obtain "a like precious faith" is because of "the righteousness of our God and Savior." Precisely what this means is debated; in fact, the meaning of every word in this phrase has been disputed. The preposition *en* may introduce either a dative of means or a dative of sphere.[15] "Righteousness" may be the means or basis upon which God could offer the "like precious faith" (KJV); or, "righteousness" may be the sphere in connection with which the offer could be made by God. In our study of Romans we learned that "righteousness" sometimes is an attribute of God, sometimes it is God's way of saving man, and sometimes it refers to right living. All three ideas have been proposed in an attempt to explain what Peter means, and all three could be seen to express a view contrary to what the false teachers were promoting.

- Perhaps it means that because our God and Savior is just, or fair, He has shown no partiality. Gentiles as well as Jews have received the same offer of faith. All obtain the "like precious faith" because Jesus does right in His dealings with men.
- Perhaps it means that an offer was made to Jew and Gentile alike because that is how God's way of saving man works. Men are justified by faith; the righteous shall live by faith. If faithfulness is the condition on which justification is imputed, then, of course, our God and Savior would give men an opportunity to hear the gospel and believe.
- Perhaps it means that men of faith, whatever their ethnic background, are to live right – both in their relations to God and in their relations to their fellow men.

The series of words in the genitive case that are translated "our God and Savior, Jesus Christ" raises a well-known problem. Is Peter speaking of two persons (our God, and Savior Jesus) or one person (our God and Savior, Jesus)? Because in verse two both the first and second persons of the Godhead are distinguished, some have supposed the same is true of verse 1. However, strict grammar would incline us to make "God" and "Savior" both apply to Jesus,[16] just as is done in the NASB. Peter's calling Jesus "God" is in perfect harmony with

---

[14] There is something to be said for "ours" (in this verse) and "us" (in verses 3 and 4) being a reference to Peter and the other apostles. If we are correct, then this verse speaks negative volumes on the modern critical dogma that the apostles edited and molded and redacted the message they heard as they went from place to place and audience to audience.

[15] The suggestion that "righteousness" is the object of faith -- "to them that have obtained a like precious faith ... in the righteousness ..." (ASV) -- seems a less likely option.

[16] There is a rule of Greek grammar called "Sharp's Rule of Grammar." "When two words in the same case are connected by 'and,' and the first noun is preceded by the article 'the,' and the second noun is not preceded by the article, the second noun refers to the same person or thing to which the first noun refers, and is a further description of it." (H.E. Dana and Julius R. Mantey, *A Manual Grammar of the Greek New Testament* [New York: Macmillan, 1954), p.147.)

his own good confession (Matthew 16:16), with Titus 2:13, Hebrews 1:1-10, Romans 9:5, John 1:1, 20:28, and with the words of Jesus Himself (John 5:19-29, 13:13).[17] Since the deity of Jesus was a point the false teachers were denying, Peter here highlights standard Christian doctrine to counteract their denials. The addition of the name "Savior" to Jesus is frequent in 2 Peter (1:11, 2:20, 3:2,18; see also Peter's calling Jesus "Savior" in Acts 4:12, 5:31) and reflects another place where Peter's Christian teaching and the doctrines of the false teachers were at odds. The vicarious, atoning death of Jesus does provide a ransom from sin, freedom from slavery to sin in this life, and safety from perdition at last. Men do not save themselves, in spite of what the false teachers insisted. Hiebert thinks "the 'our' is confessional; Peter and his readers gladly confess that Jesus Christ is both 'God and Savior'."[18] This reminder of their confession would reinforce their resistance to any contrary teaching the false teachers might offer.

C. Peter's Greeting to the Recipients of the Letter. 1:2

1:2 -- ***Grace and peace be multiplied to you in the knowledge of God and of Jesus our Lord***;

Grace and peace be multiplied to you -- These words of greeting – actually a prayer Peter offers to God – are identical with 1 Peter 1:2b, even to the use of a verb.[19] As before, Peter's readers were already recipients of God's grace and favor. Peter's prayer is that they may have more! But there is a sphere within which the readers must stay if they would experience that for which Peter prays. That sphere is indicated in the next phrase.

In the knowledge of God and of Jesus our Lord -- This is a significant addition, and clearly is a preview of Peter's counterattack against what the false teachers might claim for their false knowledge.[20] It is in the sphere of the "knowledge of God ..." that grace and peace will be multiplied, not in the knowledge taught by the false teachers. "Knowledge" translates *epignosis*, and it is not quite a strong enough translation. The compound word implies a fuller, riper, more intimate and personal knowledge than does the uncompounded form *gnosis*.

---

[17] In light of all the verses where Jesus is called "God," contemporary commentators like J.N.D. Kelly, *A Commentary on the Epistles of Peter and Jude* (New York: Harper and Row, 1969), p.298, are mistaken when they urge that this claim that Jesus is "God and Savior" is confirmation that 2 Peter was written in the second century.

[18] D. Edmond Hiebert, *Second Peter and Jude* (Greenville, SC: Unusual Publications, 1989), p.37.

[19] In most of the New Testament greetings, the verb must be supplied. Only in the letters of Peter and Jude is the verb actually written. The verb "be multiplied" is in the optative mood, expressing a wish.

[20] "Knowledge" has been called the key word in 2 Peter. *Epignosis* appears at 1:3,8, 2:20. The related verb *epignosko* occurs twice in 2:21. *Gnosis* occurs at 1:5,6, 3:18. The related verb *ginosko* occurs at 1:20 and 3:3. That is a total of eleven times in this short letter that some form of the word "knowledge" appears.

Peter emphasizes that his readers already have "full knowledge"[21] – there are no additional truths that need to be learned from the false teachers.[22] Of course the readers can grow (2 Peter 3:18) in their understanding of the "full knowledge" that has already been delivered to them by the apostles and prophets, but there are no truths that have been hidden from them. As a result, there is no need to be initiated into the Gnostic circles in order to be better informed. The genitives "of God" and "of Jesus our Lord" are likely objective genitives: it is "full knowledge" about God and about Jesus our Lord that has already been taught to the readers by their apostles and prophets. Of course, genuine knowledge about God the Father is inseparably linked with His self-revelation in Jesus Christ (John 14:6-17, 17:3; 1 John 5:20). Peter, we believe, deliberately added "Jesus our Lord" because the false teachers were denying "the Lord that bought them" (2:1). The knowledge they offered was diametrically opposed to the "full knowledge" that had already been preached to and accepted by the readers of this letter.

Peter has done several things in these few words of signature, address, and greeting. He identified himself along with his credentials, indicated the readers whom he is addressing, and wishes the blessings of grace and peace upon them. But he also establishes the base from which the epistle is written. That base is the establishment of a faith which is equal to, or like that of, the apostles. Throughout the book he certifies the content of that faith over and against the uncertainties of the false teachers.

---

[21] The word *epignosis* (translated "true knowledge" in the NASB) is used again in verse 3, and in fact verse 3 begins with *hos*, as though Peter were explaining exactly how he is using "full knowledge" here in his prayer of greeting.

[22] The word "full knowledge" (*epignosis*) begins to appear with greater frequency in Paul's later letters, which were anti-Gnostic in thrust (cp. 1 Timothy 6:20; Colossians 1:9,10, 2:2, 3:10). This fact, coupled with its appearance here, agrees well with the suggestion that it is incipient Gnosticism that Peter is combating in this letter as he attacks the "false teachers and mockers." In earlier years, Paul had fought long and hard with the Judaizers, who sought to fasten Pharisaic Judaism onto Christianity. We see the story of this conflict in Acts 15, 1 and 2 Corinthians, Galatians, and Romans (and perhaps echoes of the struggle in Philippians and the Pastoral Epistles). In the late AD 50's or early 60's, in Colossae, we see the beginnings of a heresy of a different kind. It should be noted that Paul was not opposing the fully developed Gnosticism of the second century, but incipient Gnosticism of the kind that led directly to the complicated system known to Irenaeus and Ignatius. The ideas behind this heresy came mainly from Persian and Babylonian mythology, and found a welcome first among Jewish peoples. To it they added some ideas from Jewish apocalypticism and some ideas from the Greek mystery religions. The early Gnostics sought salvation by *gnosis* ("knowledge") as well as by the mysteries. Gnostics claimed to have a richer and fuller revelation than the Christians. Major doctrines held by the Gnostics included: (1) God is an impersonal force; (2) Jesus was a created being, lesser than God (and "Jesus" and "Christ" are different -- we all can become "Christs"); (3) dualism (spirit is good, matter is evil); (4) auto-salvation; and (5) reincarnation. In light of their doctrines, later Gnostics interpreted Jesus Christ in two different ways. (a) the Docetic Gnostics denied the actual humanity of Jesus. He was only a phantom (see this answered in John 1:1,14; 1 John 1:1,3 and 2 John 7). (b) Cerinthianism held that the Christ came on Jesus at His baptism, and left Him at the cross just before Jesus exclaimed "My Power, my power, why did you leave me?" (*Gospel of Philip*) (See this answered in Colossians.) In light of their dualism, Gnosticism took a double turn on ethical problems. (a) One wing argued for asceticism as the real escape from sin and sensuous things (i.e., forbid certain kinds of food, marriage, etc.). (b) The other wing took the extreme of antinomian license. The Nicolaitans and Ophites may be cited as later examples of those who held that the way to overcome sensuality was to indulge it to excess, even to exhaustion. It is this latter wing Peter confronts here in 2 Peter.

I. THE FULL KNOWLEDGE OF JESUS CHRIST. 1:3-21

A. The Completeness of This Knowledge. 1:3,4

1:3 -- ***Seeing that His divine power has granted to us everything pertaining to life and godliness, through the true knowledge of Him who called us by His own glory and excellence.***

Seeing that -- The whole first part of verse 3 is a genitive absolute in the Greek,[23] and there is no agreement whether it is to be connected with what precedes or with what follows. Our NASB has done the former, using a colon at the close of verse 2 and placing a period at the close of verse 4.[24] In verses 3 and 4 Peter reminds his readers where the "true (full) knowledge of God and Jesus" can be found. It is certainly not in Gnosticism! Rather, it is in what has been granted by Jesus to the apostles. The RSV, NEB, NIV all have a period at the close of verse 2, and begin a new sentence with verse 3,[25] which makes all of verses 3-7 one long sentence in the Greek, the main verb of which occurs in verse 5. Christ's provision for full knowledge (verses 3-4) forms a perfect basis for the exhortation that begins in verse 5. Since Peter's grammar is not clear, in our comments we will combine both ideas.

His divine power has granted to us -- The nearest antecedent to "His" (*autou*) is "Jesus our Lord." It is Jesus our Lord who has granted[26] "divine power." We are persuaded the "us" in verses 3 and 4 – as contrasted with the "you" Christians of verse 4 – refers to the apostles of Jesus.[27] The word for "divine" (*theios*) occurs in only two other places (Acts 17:29; Romans 1:20) and it is an attribute of God the Father. Here it modifies "power" (*dunamis*)

---

23 A "genitive absolute" is to Greek what a dangling participle is to English. The person or thing acting in the participle is different from the person or thing acting in the main verb.

24 The Greek texts of Westcott-Hort, and Souter, as well as the KJV, ERV, ASV, Rotherham, have either a comma or a semi-colon after verse 2.

25 The Greek texts of Scrivener, United Bible Society, Nestle-Aland, and the Textus Receptus, all have a period at the close of verse 2. Those English translations made from one of these texts (20th Century New Testament, Moffatt, Goodspeed, New Berkeley, Jerusalem Bible, and others) more commonly than not use a period at the close of verse 2.

26 The verb translated "granted" (*doreomai*) is not the ordinary word for "give" (*didomi*). *Doreomai*, which occurs only in this epistle and in Mark 15:45, is a stronger word than *didomi*, and means "to grant or bestow." It is middle voice -- Jesus did it for His own benefit, or in His own interest. It is a perfect tense participle which speaks of past completed action with present continuing results. The apostles were still (when Peter writes) in possession of the divine power which had been bestowed upon them.

27 In verse 1, we treated "ours" as being a reference to the apostles. We have studied those comments which propose to make "us" refer to Christians in general (rather than to the apostles in particular), and while some make a pretty good case for the idea that Peter refers to the power of the indwelling Spirit in the lives of those Christians, we have difficulty tying such a thought to the topic Peter is writing about (the Gnostics can add nothing to the content of their "full knowledge"). Furthermore, it requires a totally different explanation of "glory and virtue" in the close of verse 3.

that was granted to the apostles ("us"). Is this "divine power", a power that belongs to deity, a reference to the Holy Spirit, described as "power from on high" (Luke 24:49; Acts 1:5,8; Colossians 1:29), who specially empowered the apostles to speak and who confirmed their message as being truth via the miracles He wrought? We think so! Go to the Holy Spirit-empowered apostles of Jesus, not to the Gnostics, if you want real, true, full knowledge from God.[28]

Everything pertaining to life and godliness -- The Gnostics have nothing they can add to the "true (full) knowledge" already delivered by the apostles. The apostles provided "everything"; what can the Gnostics add? We are reminded of Jesus' promise to the apostles that the Holy Spirit would guide them into "all the truth" (John 16:13) and would bring to their remembrance "all" that Jesus had said to them (John 14:26). Peter talks about the same complete knowledge when he writes about "the commandment of the Lord and Savior spoken by your apostles" (3:2). Life is not *bios* ("the necessities of life, food, clothing, shelter"), but *zoe*, the new, spiritual life which believers experience in Christ. Where once men's spirits were dead in trespasses and sins, now they are alive again, once the new birth has resulted in their being immersed and rising to walk in newness of life. "Godliness" translates *eusebeian*, a Greek word that appears in Acts 3:12 in a speech of Peter's, four times in this letter, and in Timothy and Titus. It denotes a reverence toward God that is anxious to be well-pleasing to Him. It also speaks of correctly serving one's fellowman, giving to all men their due. It is introduced here, we think, in deliberate opposition to the godlessness and licentiousness being promoted by the false teachers. It is Peter's reminder that Christians do not live in the manner the false teachers promulgate. Even Peter's word order may be significant. One is not going to be godly where "life" is absent. First comes "life" then comes "godliness."

So far, 2 Peter 1:3 has emphasized the same truth found in Jude 3 ("the faith which was once for all delivered to the saints"). Peter is affirming that the Holy Spirit (Christ's "divine power") has provided the Apostles with a complete system of faith ("full knowledge," "everything pertaining to life and godliness").[29]

Through the true knowledge of Him who called us -- The grant of "everything" was not something the apostles[30] received unconsciously. It was mediated through or related to (the construction is *dia* plus the genitive) their knowledge of Christ who called them to be apostles

---

[28] The only other live possibility for "power" is to suppose Peter has something in mind similar to what Paul wrote in Romans 1:16 (ASV) about the "gospel" being the "power (*dunamis*) of God unto salvation."

[29] We need no esoteric knowledge from the Gnostics, we need no tradition, no voice of the living church (a pope or a council), no modern-day revelation to give us more. Anything more is superfluous if not presumptuous.

[30] We are still treating "us" as a reference to the apostles, rather than all Christians. Those who think "us" is all Christians will write notes at this place explaining how men are called (invited) to become Christians through the Gospel (2 Thessalonians 2:14). That is true, but we think it is not the point at this place. Because they take it as a call to become a Christian, scholars even debate who is thought of here in 2 Peter as doing the calling -- whether it is the Father (as in 1 Peter 1:15, 2:9) or Jesus. If it is a call to become an apostle, it is Jesus who did the calling.

(Luke 6:12-16). Peter claims for the apostles "full knowledge" (*epignosis*) of Jesus the Christ.[31] The implication is the apostles, we who were there and who carefully examined Him (1 John 1:1ff), can tell you better about who Jesus is than any Gnostic can.

By His own glory and excellence -- If we are correct that Peter alludes to the calling of the twelve, then "glory and excellence" describe certain unique things these men witnessed as they accompanied the incarnate Christ during His earthly ministry.[32] There were times they beheld his glory, glory as of the only begotten from the Father (John 1:14). At those moments they plainly saw that He was God in the flesh! *Arete* (here translated "excellence") is a word for which it is not easy to find an expressive English equivalent. Our versions use "virtue" and "excellence."[33] We have suggested that *arete* indicates a desire to do always what is right in God's sight. As the apostles carefully watched Jesus, they saw in Him an inner moral excellence that attracted them and convinced them He must be the Messiah He claimed to be. If we read *idios*, then Peter is speaking about Jesus' own private, unique, peculiar possession of glory and excellence.[34] It was Jesus' "glory (who He was in His being) and virtue (how He acted)" that caused the apostles to leave all and follow Him.

1:4 -- ***For by these He has granted to us His precious and magnificent promises, in order that by them you might become partakers of*** **the** ***divine nature, having escaped the corruption that is in the world through lust.***

For by these – "By these" (*di' hōn*) is plural in the Greek. Commentators are not in agreement what "things" in the previous context are alluded to. Some suppose all the ideas preceding (divine power, knowledge, called, glory, excellence) are gathered up in this plural. Others point to the plural "all things which pertain to life and godliness." Still others think the plural refers to the "glory and excellence" of Christ just spoken of. We suppose Peter is still alluding to what Jesus has done for the apostles, and here tells us it was because of Jesus' "glory and excellence" that certain promises were granted to the apostles so they could in turn benefit others.

---

[31] This note reflects a conscious decision to treat "Him" as a reference to Jesus, rather than to the Father. It also treats the genitive "of Him" as though it were an objective genitive, "knowledge about Christ."

[32] This comment reflects the view that though the manuscript evidence is about evenly divided between *dia doxes kali aretes* and *idia doxe kai arete*, neither can mean "to glory and virtue" (KJV). That would require *eis* and the accusative (see Bruce M. Metzger, *A Textual Commentary on the Greek New Testament* [London: United Bible Society, 1971], p.699). Because of the KJV, it is not unusual at this place to read comments to the effect that, instead of the licentiousness promoted by the false teachers, "glory and virtue" are what the Christian aims for in his life (though some have trouble explaining exactly what "glory" is). If we read *dia* plus the genitive, "through" would be the translation. If we read *idia* in the dative, "by" would be a good translation.

[33] *Arete* appears in 1 Peter 2:9 where it is rendered "excellencies." That verse is strikingly parallel to this one.

[34] It was not something added to Jesus for a few years between his baptism and crucifixion. It was His, day in and day out.

He has granted to us His precious and magnificent promises -- "He" is Christ. "Granted" is the same verb (*dedoretai*) used in the previous verse and in the same perfect tense. "Us" is the same "us" about which verse 3 spoke. The promises were granted to the apostles in the past, and are still in their possession. They were not and have not been granted to the false teachers. The article before *epaggelmata* ("promises") may have a possessive force (see "His ... promises" in the NASB) or it may point to the well-known promises voiced in the gospel.[35] Peter characterizes these promises as being "precious" and "magnificent."[36] They are precious, "of great worth, because of the spiritual riches involved."[37] Like the pearl of great price for which a man would sell everything to obtain (Matthew 13:46), they are something to be dearly prized and held on to, not carelessly given up in an effort to follow the false teachers. The promises are the greatest![38] If apostolic Christianity is the greatest, the Gnostics have nothing better to offer!

In order that by them you might become partakers of *the* divine nature -- Peter here indicates why divine power and precious promises were granted to the apostles.[39] It was "so that" others might "become partakers of the divine nature." Here Peter shows the readers of this letter[40] that what Christ granted to the apostles has application to them. Hear it! It is by involvement with what the apostles teach that one becomes a partaker of the divine nature – not by involvement with the false teachers!

"Partakers of the divine nature" is an expression that occurs nowhere else in the New Testament. What does it suggest? In the beginning, man was made in the image of God. When man sinned, that image was marred. His spirit ceases being able to direct his behavior and his physical body is dying. That is far from the "image of God" which Adam bore before

---

[35] The termination *-ma* on *epaggelma* (a word which occurs elsewhere only at 2 Peter 3:13) shows that the thing promised, not the act of promising, is what is in Peter's mind. Commentators struggle trying to identify exactly which promises Peter may have in mind. Some point to the promises of Christ's second coming. Some point to "partakers of the divine nature." Some point to "life and godliness." Some emphasize the having "escaped from the corruption that is in the world by lust."

[36] The NASB follows a Greek text that has a different word order than the Textus Receptus and the KJV (which read, "exceeding great and precious").

[37] Hiebert, *op. cit.*, p.47.

[38] The Greek adjective here is superlative in degree.

[39] "Through these" (ASV, "by them," NASB) we think points back to what (i.e., the power and promises) Christ has granted to the apostles. This is better (in this commentator's opinion) than thinking that "these" point back to Christ's "glory and excellence."

[40] The change from "us" of the earlier verses to "you" (plural) in this verse is significant. In this verse, "you" refers to the readers in contrast to "us" the apostles.

he sinned. Now, Peter says that his readers may once again become partakers of that image.[41] When a man becomes a Christian, he is restored to the image of God on the inside. When he gets his resurrection body, he will be restored to the image of God on the outside.[42]

Having escaped the corruption that is in the world by lust -- "Escaped" is an aorist participle.[43] Thus the action ("escaped") of the participle precedes the action of the main verb ("become partakers"). Are you listening? If Peter's readers choose to live corrupt lives such as were encouraged by the false teachers, the chances of partaking of the divine nature decline to zero. Christians are supposed to have escaped from such a lifestyle. "Escape" is *apopheugetai*, "escape by flight," and occurs only here in the New Testament. Peter's readers are to run away from the corruption which is in the world.[44] "Corruption" (*phthoras*) probably refers to moral deterioration, as it does in 2:12,19.[45] The root idea in the word is that of decomposition; one immediately can picture in their minds the bloated bodies and smell the putrid odor of decaying organisms. Peter has aptly and vividly described how licentious men live. And why do they live like that? They are doing what their lusts suggest to them. An *epithumia* is a strong desire or craving. The word itself is neutral – human desire may be either good (Luke 22:15; Philippians 1:23; 1 Thessalonians 2:17) or bad, depending on the thing desired. Here what the false teachers desired was bad, so "lust" is a good rendering of the word. Peter had to tear away the camouflage and make obvious to all the real reason the false teachers were living as they did. The Gnostics were simply thrilled to sin. They wanted to sin. They desired the temporary satisfaction that can accompany certain sins. Jesus can help a person get rid of his fascination for things of the world.

---

[41] The verb "become" (*genesthe*) here is an aorist tense. It does not so much express what might happen in the future as it expresses what is happening right now. Compare John 12:36, "believe in the light, in order that you may become (*hina genesthe*) children of light." As Alford says, the aorist seems to imply "that the aim was not the procedure, but the completion, of that indicated; not the *ginesthai*, the carrying on the process, but the *genesthai*, its accomplishment." (*Alford's Greek Testament*, Vol.4, p.391.)

[42] "Divine nature" is language Peter's readers knew well. Even pagans talked about sharing the "divine nature," but there was a difference. The pagan believed that in every man there was a spark of the Divine Nature. Every man was regarded as essentially divine, as he was, all by himself. All man had to do was to live in accordance with the divine nature which was already in him. (The whole trouble with this is that all of life contradicts such a theory. We see bitterness, hatred, lust, crime, moral failure.) What Christianity says is that man can again share in the "divine nature" as he responds to the gospel preached through the apostles. (In his use of the words "divine" [*theios*], "excellence" [*arete*], and "divine nature" [*theias phuseos*], Peter should not be accused of using second-century Hellenistic words. He was using words that were familiar to people living in the Mediterranean world in the first century AD, but he is giving them a peculiarly Christian definition.)

[43] It is a circumstantial participle, and in this place "if" might be a good helper to translate it. "If you have escaped the corruption ...."

[44] "World" here probably stands for the kingdom of darkness. Cp. 1 John 2:15-17; Colossians 1:13. It is the sphere where men alienated from God live.

[45] The "corruption" from which creation shall be delivered (Romans 8:20,21), defined in that passage as "decay" and "futility," is not quite synonymous with the "corruption" Peter here talks about.

B. Qualities of Life to Complement What Christ Has Done.[46] 1:5-11

1:5 -- ***Now for this very reason also, applying all diligence, in your faith supply moral excellence, and in*** **your** ***moral excellence, knowledge;***

Now for this very reason also – *Kai auto touto* is frequently used in classical Greek. It sums up what has been said in the previous verses.[47] Christ's gracious gifts and precious promises have as a necessary corollary a certain expected response from men. Because Christ has done His part, men are expected to do their part. Those men who would participate in the life and godliness He has provided are to work at developing certain qualities in their lives.

Applying all diligence -- "Applying," *pareisenegkantes*, a word that occurs only here in the New Testament, means "bring alongside," "contribute besides."[48] Christians are to contribute something alongside what Christ has done. "Diligence" (*spouden*) is placed first in the clause for emphasis. It means to make haste, to be eager, to do one's best, to exert one's self, to make every effort. What the word asks for is quick movement (get to it right away!) and zeal and seriousness and effort to get it done. Peter is asking his readers for an intense effort to add certain qualities to their lifestyle.

In your faith supply moral excellence -- "Supply" is the verb that describes what is to be diligently and energetically performed. The verb is an aorist imperative; what Peter writes here is a command, an urgent preemptory command. There is a word picture behind the verb *epichoregeo*. In ancient Greek, the word was used of a rich patron who lavishly provided all the expenses for the training, equipping, and staging of a Greek drama in the theater at some public celebration. It was not unusual for the expenses to equal 3000 days' wages for a working man, yet there were rich men who bore these expenses voluntarily out of love for their city. In time it came to mean to provide or supply, with the thought of a chorus being dropped. So Peter urges his readers to equip their lives with seven qualities, and that equipping is not to be a provision of a kind of necessary minimum, but a lavish and generous supply. He does not tell his readers they are to supply faith, or faithfulness. Being Christians, they already have that (verse 1). "Your faith" here is personal faith, yet it clearly

---

[46] It is difficult to write a satisfactory title for this paragraph. Those this commentator has tried include, "Growth according to full knowledge," "The necessity of godly living," "Qualities needed to participate in the divine nature," "Qualities of life demanded by full knowledge," "The necessity of escaping the corruption in the world," "Character qualities that respond to what Christ has done." None has as yet quite caught the heart of what Peter here has written, it would seem. Others have offered "The necessary growth in the new life," "The duty of man," "Growth in true knowledge," "The duty and hope of diligence."

[47] In the Greek text, Peter began verse 3 with "as", which warns us to look for a "so" to complete the thought. Here in verse 5 we find it in the strong expression *kai auto touto* translated "now" in the NASB.

[48] Hiebert (*op. cit.*, p.51) observes that the word sometimes has the meaning of smuggling, or bringing in goods by means of byways and side roads. Perhaps the implication is that they must apply this diligence "quietly and without ostentatious display."

has objective content.[49] The Greek exhorts us to develop one quality in the exercise of another. Each new quality springs out of the attempting and perfecting of the former.[50] "Moral excellence" represents the same word used of Christ ("excellence", *arete*) in verse 3. Moffatt translates it "resolution," i.e., the desire to always do what God says is right. Such resolution is something the Christian can deliberately will, each moment of his life!

And in *your* moral excellence, knowledge -- In the Greek, it reads "the moral excellence," "the knowledge," etc. While the Greek article "the" might be translated as a possessive pronoun, it seems more likely that the article is intended to make each new trait specific; they may not be substituted for. If a man is going to do the right, he will have to know what is right. That's where "knowledge" is needed. "Knowledge" here is *gnosis*, the simple word, not the compound used in verses 2 and 3. This is a knowledge that may grow. There is always knowledge to be added. Of course, Peter is warning his readers not to go to the Gnostics, supposing they can get such knowledge there.[51] It is only in the words of the apostles and prophets of Christ that one learns what God says is right and wrong. Diligent Bible study is the key to this kind of knowledge.

1:6 -- *And in* your *knowledge, self-control, and in* your *self-control, perseverance, and in* your *perseverance, godliness,*

And in *your* knowledge, self-control -- *Egkrateia* is "controlled power, restrained power."[52] The Christian controls his passions rather than letting his passions control him.[53] There is a point in "self-control" being placed as the next quality after "knowledge." The false teachers would insist that knowledge led to liberty, which to them meant emancipation from all con-

---

[49] There may even be a hint of exhortation in the use of this word. Faithfulness to Christ is what Peter longs for in their lives -- as opposed to deviation into the ways suggested by the false teachers.

[50] Readers of the KJV ("add *to* your faith ...") are likely to miss the connection. The Greek says "*in* your faith supply ...." M.R. Vincent, *Word Studies in the New Testament* (Wilmington, DE: Associated Publishers and Authors, 1972), p.324.

[51] "'*The* knowledge' stands over against the spurious 'knowledge' of the false teachers." Hiebert, *op. cit.,* p.53.

[52] Barclay (*op. cit.*, p.357) calls attention the to four states possible in a man's life as described by Aristotle. The four states are "perfect temperance," "self-control," "incontinence," and "unbridled lust." He wrote, "There is *sophrosune*, in which passion has been entirely subjugated to reason; the fight is won, and reason reigns supreme; we might call it *perfect temperance*. There is *akolasia*, which is the precise opposite; it is the state in which reason is entirely subjugated to passion; the fight is lost, and passion reigns supreme; we might call it *unbridled lust*. In between these two states there is *akrasia*, in which reason fights but passion prevails; the battle is still on, but at the moment it is a losing battle; we might call it *incontinence*. There is *egkrateia*, in which reason fights against passion and prevails; the battle is still on, but it is a winning battle; we might call it *self-control* or *self-mastery*."

[53] The words *egkrateia psuches* are the heading of a section in the Greek of Ecclus. 17:30, and are followed immediately by the maxim, "Go not after thy lusts, but refrain thyself from thine appetites." B.C. Caffin, "2 Peter" in *Pulpit Commentary* (Grand Rapids: Eerdmans, 1962), p.4.

trol whatever. Peter contradicts that view. To him, knowledge leads to self-control, and that leads to that perfect freedom which consists in true service to God and man. Of course, as we learn from Romans 6 and 8, it is fruitless to talk to a non-Christian about self-control, for until they are justified they are slaves to sin; consistent self-control is difficult if not unattainable. What we see are almost uncontrollable addictions. But a man who has been freed from his old slavery can be expected to put to death the deeds of the flesh (Romans 8:13) and to stop letting sin reign in his mortal body (Romans 6:12). Self-mastery does not come automatically. It, too, is something a Christian must work on diligently.[54]

And in *your* self-control, perseverance -- Self-control is not something one does just once in a while. First there is the resolve to do right. From the Scriptures we learn what is right. Then we begin to control our bodies so we do what is right. The next quality is "perseverance" or persistence in practicing self-control. *Hupomone* almost implies it won't be easy to habitually practice self-control. At times it will almost seem like a burden to be borne. But the Christian keeps on, whatever the pressures and temptations to give in.[55]

And in *your* perseverance, godliness – This is how the "godliness"[56] Peter spoke of (verse 3) is produced in the Christian's life. From his study of Scripture the believer learns what is right and wrong, both in his relationship to God and his relationship to man. He begins to practice self-control so that his life displays the right and avoids the wrong. He reverently seeks to please God in all things. He does this day in and day out, persistently. Little by little, then, his life begins to reflect what God is like. The Christian consciously and deliberately submits his human will to the holy will of God. This quality would be an obvious contrast to how the ungodly false teachers were behaving (2:5-22, 3:7).

1:7 -- *And in* your *godliness, brotherly kindness, and in* your *brotherly kindness,* Christian *love.*

And in *your* godliness, brotherly kindness -- In 1 Peter 1:22 and 3:8, the same Greek word here translated "brotherly kindness" was translated "love of the brethren" and "brotherly." 1 John 5:1 reminds us "whoever loves the Father loves the child born of Him." Christians, who are members of the same great family, God's adopted children, are to give diligence to

[54] The use of the term "self-control" elsewhere in the New Testament is instructive. Paul uses it of the unmarried -- if they cannot control themselves, they should marry (1 Corinthians 7:9). Preaching to Felix and Drusilla, Paul reasoned concerning "self-control" (Acts 24:25). Paul speaks of his own practice of self-control for the sake of the gospel (1 Corinthians 9:25). It is one of the fruit of the spirit (Galatians 5:23).

[55] Some suppose the mockers have provided some of the pressures. They were saying, "What's the use of consistent self-control? Jesus' return hasn't happened, and isn't going to happen (3:3,4)." Their enticements to the flesh were certainly tempting.

[56] Barclay (*op. cit.*, p.359) calls attention to the fact that the Latin word for "godliness" is *pietas*. He writes, "Warde Fowler describes the Roman idea of a man who possesses that quality: 'He is superior to the enticements of individual passion and self ease; [*pietas* is] a sense of duty which never left a man, of duty first to the gods, then to father and to family, to son and to daughter, to his people and to his nation'."

expressing a warm affection toward each other who are spiritual relatives. They deliberately look for ways to help fellow Christians in times of need. They work at cultivating their relationships so that nothing is allowed to drive a wedge between them. How then can there be any relationship with the false teachers who are bringing in attitudes and actions that are "divisive" and will destroy any brotherly relationship (2:1)? Another anti-Gnostic writing, 1 John 4:7-20, also speaks of the need of love for the brethren, so it is evident one of the dastardly things those false teachers did was to destroy brotherhood.

And in *your* brotherly kindness, *Christian* love -- We have defined "love" (*agape*) as deliberately and thoughtfully doing what is spiritually best for the other person.[57] The circle of their affection widens. Their love is not restricted to fellow believers, but reaches out to all men. Christians not only express love for their brothers, they look for ways to spiritually benefit those who are not yet their brothers in Christ, and willingly make self-sacrifices to accomplish what love asks them to do. Like the other qualities in Peter's list, this one too is a contrast to the false teachers whose behavior was characterized by selfishness.

1:8 -- *For if these* qualities *are yours and are increasing, they render you neither useless nor unfruitful in the true knowledge of our Lord Jesus Christ.*

For if these *qualities* are yours and are increasing -- Since each new quality[58] springs out of the exercise of the previous one, not all Christians will be equally developed. However, each Christian is expected to be working on the next quality needed in his or her own life. Both verses 8 and 9 begin with "for," giving some reasons or incentives why Christians will want to be applying all diligence to develop the next quality, until all are present in their lives. "Are yours" translates *huparchonta*, a word that speaks of actual possession,[59] a rightful part of their character, as opposed to a fleeting manifestation. "Increasing" is a present tense participle indicating a continuing process. By daily practice these qualities grow and increase until they are present in abundance. Moffatt has commented that the Christian life is not "an initial spasm followed by a chronic inertia."[60]

---

[57] C.S. Lewis, in his book *Four Loves* (New York: Harcourt, Brace, and World, 1960) has shown the difference between *philadelphia* ("love for the brother"), which springs from warmth and affection and the desirability of the object loved, and *apage* ("love"), which springs from intelligence and good will and purposefully seeks the welfare of the one loved, even though outwardly there is nothing especially attractive in the object being loved.

[58] The Greek reads simply "these things." Some writers prefer to call them "graces," some prefer "virtues," and others call them "qualities." We've used "qualities" because that is how our NASB has done it.

[59] The word can be used of property which is owned and can be disposed of as one wishes (Luke 8:3, 12:15; Acts 4:32,37).

[60] James Moffatt, *The General Epistles, James, Peter, and Judas* (London: Hodder and Stoughton, 1947), p.181. Caffin (*op. cit.*, p.4) has written, "Out of faith, the root, spring the seven fair fruits of holiness, of which holy love is the fairest and sweetest (cp. Ignatius, *'Ad Ephes.'* xiv, *Arete men pistis, telos de agape*)."

They render you neither useless nor unfruitful -- It is obvious that if the qualities are not being diligently added, the Christian is useless and unfruitful. The present tense indicates an ongoing process. "Useless" translates *argous* (from *ergon*, work, with an alpha-privative, thus "no work, idle"). Many Christians do nothing (they are idle, complacent) because they make no attempt to grow in these seven qualities Peter has identified. "Unfruitful" (*akarpous*) gives the word picture of a fruit tree that produces no fruit even under the most favorable conditions. Perhaps there is not a great difference between "unfruitful Christians" and the false teachers described in chapter 2. They weren't producing any good spiritual fruit either. Christians want to do something valuable in the world for time and eternity; they want to produce fruit that will last. Thus they apply all diligence to develop the proper qualities that are expected to be laid alongside what Christ has done to save us.

In the true knowledge of our Lord Jesus Christ -- In the Greek this phrase begins with the preposition *eis*. Some treat it as meaning "in respect to," that is, the person growing in the seven qualities will be living in respect to the full knowledge of Jesus as he is expected to. Others give the preposition its usual meaning of "to" or "toward;" that is, there is a goal toward which their growth looks. The various qualities, realized in the heart, will lead us on toward a fuller knowledge of Jesus Christ. "Full knowledge" translates the same *epignosis* used in verses 2 and 3. Here it seems to speak of an intimate and growing knowledge of One whom they already know. As Peter told us earlier, such knowledge has something to do with escaping the corruption that is in the world and partaking of the divine nature. One cannot claim he knows Jesus as "Lord" and at the same time display a lazy indifference towards developing the seven qualities named in verses 5-7.

1:9 -- *For he who lacks these* qualities *is blind* or *short-sighted, having forgotten* his *purification from his former sins.*

For he who lacks these *qualities* -- Just as verse 8 began with "for," so does verse 9. We are still in the midst of the reasons or incentives for developing the seven qualities. By using the third person ("he who") rather than the second person ("you"), Peter is making the thought of the verse abstract. Each reader will apply it to his own situation to see whether he is lacking,[61] but Peter is not accusing them of lack. He is simply delineating of what lack of growth in these seven qualities[62] is indicative.

Is blind *or* short-sighted -- "Blind" is likely used here in a metaphorical sense to describe one's spiritual condition, as it is in John 9:39-41. The person isn't able to see clearly the nature and requirements of Christianity. It is surprising to have "short-sighted" (*muopazon*, compare the English "myopic") follow "blind" in the Greek. In fact, the NIV, which reads "nearsighted and blind," simply reverses the order. The NASB puts "or" in italics between

[61] "Lacks" translates *me parestin*. It means "not present," which is a sharp contrast to "yours and ... increasing" (verse 8).

[62] As in verse 8, the Greek simply reads "these things."

the words. This reflects the possibility that *muopazon* could be a causal participle. If so, this verse says the person is spiritually blind because he is so nearsighted.[63] A nearsighted person partially shuts his eyes when he tries to see distant objects, and squints when in the full light of day. The spiritually nearsighted person can only see things which lie close around him – earth and earthly things – and he shuts the eyes of his spirit against the light whenever it is disagreeable with him. It is almost as though spiritual qualities – like virtue, knowledge, self-control, etc. from verses 5-7 – are beyond the scope of his earthbound vision. "Is blind" and "short-sighted" are both present tense verb forms, marking an ongoing condition. As long as there is no diligence being applied to develop these seven qualities, you can say the person is blind and short-sighted. What an indictment!

Having forgotten *his* purification from his former sins -- The forgetfulness (or spiritual amnesia) is not something that accidentally happened, but as *lethen labon* shows, it is something that was willingly received. It was something that is the inevitable result of neglecting to cultivate the Christian qualities named in verses 5-7. He purposefully forgets the obligation which he owes to Christ for the redemption that Christ purchased with His own blood. When Peter says "purification" (Greek, *katharismos*, "cleansing"), we have no doubt but that he is alluding to the fact that when his readers were baptized for the remission of sins,[64] their former (old) sins (the ones they committed before they were cleansed in baptism) were removed, because Christ had purchased their redemption. Every penitent believer who has been immersed can recall the joy and elation they felt as they came up out of the water because they knew all was well between them and God. How sad to forget the sense of freedom and well-being they could continue to enjoy by growing and increasing in the seven qualities. How ungrateful to forget the implications of Calvary in their lives.[65]

---

[63] A. Plummer ("2 Peter," in *The Layman's Handy Commentary on the Bible*, ed. by Charles John Ellicott [Grand Rapids: Zondervan, 1957], p.140) explains, "The Greek word means literally 'closing the eyes' -- and the point seems to be, not the willful shutting of the eyes (those who *won't* see), but involuntary and partial closing, as in the case of short-sighted people; in a spiritual sense, those who have only a very hazy apprehension of the objects of belief and of the bearing which their beliefs should have on their conduct." The word "short-sighted" occurs only here in the New Testament.

[64] Compare Acts 22:16 ("arise, and be baptized and wash away your sins"), 2:38 (where Peter himself had said in his first recorded sermon "Repent, and let each one of you be baptized in the name of Jesus Christ for the forgiveness of your sins"), Ephesians 5:26; 1 Peter 1:2,22, 3:20,21; and Romans 6:1-7. In Paul's words, when a person is immersed, he rises to walk in newness of life. That newness involves "stop letting sin reign in [his] mortal body" (Romans 6:12), or in Peter's words, it involves growth in the qualities of virtue, knowledge, self-control, etc.

[65] Calvinism teaches that once a person is saved, he is always saved. It is called "perseverance of the saints." Writers approaching this passage from a Calvinistic standpoint struggle with what Peter here writes. They want to know, "Is this a picture of a man who has lost his salvation?" This commentator sees no way around the inevitable conclusion that a Christian who fails to develop the Christian qualities named by Peter will not be given an "entrance into the eternal kingdom" (verse 11) nor will his calling and election be guaranteed (verse 10). Both those happy eventualities are conditioned on growth, are they not?

1:10 -- ***Therefore, brethren, be all the more diligent to make certain about His calling and choosing you; for as long as you practice these things, you will never stumble.***

Therefore, brethren -- *Dio* (here translated "therefore") means "for this reason. " It is hard to decide whether the reason involves only what immediately precedes (verses 8 and 9) or the whole paragraph since 1:3. If the former, then Peter is saying, 'If you want to avoid being idle and unfruitful and blind and nearsighted, here is what to do.' If the latter, Peter is saying, 'Because all the things pertaining to life and godliness have been granted, yea, in order that you may be partakers of the divine nature, here is what true knowledge requires you to do.' Either way, with the term "brethren," Peter resumes his exhortation with more earnestness.[66]

Be all the more diligent to make certain about His calling and choosing you -- "Be diligent" translates the same root word used in verse 5, save here it is an imperative verb. With the word *mallon* Peter is calling for more effort on their part to add those seven qualities.[67] The word "to make" (*poieisthai*) is middle voice, implying something done for one's self, or for one's own benefit. "Calling and election" (choosing, NASB) are viewed as one thing.[68] Their calling (invitation) to become a Christian came through the Gospel (2 Thessalonians 2:14). They became God's chosen people when they responded to the invitation.[69] This "calling-election" is what Peter wants his readers to guarantee or make certain. "The word (*bebaian*, 'certain') has a legal sense. It is the legal guarantee obtained by the buyer from the seller, to be gone back upon should a third party claim the thing. Here the readers are called upon to produce a guarantee of their calling and election. This may be done by cultivation of the Christian graces."[70] Do you want to guarantee your salvation?

---

[66] This is the only time in his letters that Peter addresses his readers as "brethren," but it is a term we are familiar with as we have heard his sermons as recorded in Acts (cf. Acts 1:16, 2:29, 3:17, 15:7).

[67] Two ancient manuscripts, Sinaiticus and Alexandrinus, read "give diligence through your good works to make your calling and election sure." (One reads *dia ton kalon ergon*, the other *dia ton kalon humon ergon*.) Neither reading is well supported. Because the word "diligent" is repeated in the Greek, it is better to derive what they are to be diligent about from verse 5 ("in your faith add virtue," etc.) than to add the word found in the two ancient manuscripts.

[68] In an earlier footnote (see footnote #16 above), Sharp's rule of grammar was explained. That rule comes into play here since the Greek is *ten klesin kai eklogen*.

[69] See Matthew 22:14 and 20:16 (KJV) where we are told "many are called, but few are chosen." Compare what was said at 1 Peter 1:2 and 2:9,21 on "calling" and "chosen." Calvinistic theologians are anxious at this place to remind us that in God's counsels "election" precedes the "call" (Romans 8:28-30). It is true that back in eternity, as He was making His plans for creation (Romans 8:28 calls it His "eternal purpose"), God determined that those who of their own free will and choice would be in Christ should ultimately be glorified. In order for these plans to be carried out, God planned to call, justify, and then glorify those folk. Those folk who are "in Christ" are the ones who are the chosen or the elect. The reason Calvinistic theologians are quick to point all this out is because what Peter here (1:10) writes seems to contradict one of their major dogmas, so what Peter here writes must be explained in such a way as to protect that cherished dogma.

[70] R.H. Strachan, "The Second Epistle General of Peter," in *The Expositor's Greek Testament* (Grand Rapids: Eerdmans, 1967), p.128. Calvinistic writers are greatly bothered by this explanation, for they doubt that Christians have to validate God's election. As a result, their comments on this passage will read like this: "He is concerned

Then diligently and habitually see to it that the Christian qualities "are yours and are increasing."

For as long as you practice these things, you will never stumble -- "These things," just as *tauta* did in verses 8 and 9, refer to the seven qualities named in verses 5-7. The present participle translated "practice" (literally, "are doing") shows that adding these qualities is not just done once or occasionally but is to be done continuously. It is a circumstantial participle, and so could be rendered "if" or "as long as." It certainly shows the security of the believer is conditional (cp. Colossians 1:23). In "you will never stumble" there is a double negative in the Greek. It is very emphatic. You absolutely will not! But is it stumbling into sin or stumbling into perdition?[71] Probably the former is intended here.[72] There is a difference between stumbling (*ptaio*) and falling (*pipto*), Romans 11:11. A horse that doesn't stumble over rough and rocky terrain is called surefooted (*ou ptaio*). A near-sighted person (one not making any effort to supply the qualities of verses 5-7) could be expected to stumble over the temptations placed in his way.[73]

1:11 -- ***For in this way the entrance into the eternal kingdom of our Lord and Savior Jesus Christ will be abundantly supplied to you.***

For in this way -- "For" says that verse 11 is either a reason for something just said or an explanation of something just said. If we think it is an explanation, then it probably explains "never stumble," and "stumbling into perdition" would be the right explanation for verse 10. If we think it is a reason, then it probably is another reason (verses 8 and 9 also begin with "for") why Christians should be diligent to supply the needed qualities. "This way" translates an adverb (*houtos*) which means "thus," and it seems to pick up everything that has been said since verse 5. When Christ's part in salvation has been matched by man's proper response, this is the way to the eternal kingdom of our Lord.

---

about their personal assurance that they are the called and chosen of God. We base that personal assurance on the appropriate evidence (namely the qualities just listed) in our own lives." Or, "Peter is speaking of election in a corporate sense, not an individual sense." The NASB surely reflects a Calvinistic bias when it offers "to make certain about His calling and choosing you" as a translation for this clause. In spite of these efforts to the contrary, there is certainly the implication in this passage that one's call and election may be nullified by apostasy on the part of Christians (see 2:20-22).

[71] *BAGD* (p.734) says that "stumble" involves the "loss of salvation." Some writers appeal to the aorist tense used for the verb stumble, arguing that it points to a stumbling that is final, a stumble from which there is no arising.

[72] Of course, if a person lives in sin long enough, perdition will be his destiny. Romans 6:23, written to Christians, warns that the wages of habitual sin is death!

[73] Peter is not saying that a zealous, growing Christian will never sin. He is saying that in exact proportion to how one works on adding the qualities, in that exact proportion he will find that he stumbles less when tempted. The less we work on the qualities, the more we will find ourselves sinning.

The entrance ... will be abundantly supplied to you -- "The entrance" points to the specific hope believers entertain of being invited to "enter into the joy of their Lord" (Matthew 25:21, 23) and share with Father, Son, and Holy Spirit a future life in the realm where righteousness is at home (2 Peter 3:13). "Supplied" is the same verb (*epichoregeo*) used in verse 5, where it was explained that there is a lavishness involved in this verb. It is a passive verb here, and the implied agent is God.[74] "Abundantly" translates the adverb *plousios*, which means richly. "Abundantly supplied" is Peter's way of saying that God's response is lavishly generous to the man whom He finds faithful. We cannot decide whether this language pictures a warm welcome being given to the souls who enter,[75] or whether richly is intended to remind the readers that there are degrees of reward hereafter,[76] proportioned to their faithfulness in developing and adding the qualities named in verses 5-7.

Into the eternal kingdom of our Lord and Savior Jesus Christ -- Christians are already citizens of Christ's kingdom on earth; they enter this kingdom at the time of conversion (Colossians 1:13; Hebrews 12:29; Revelation 1:6,9). The "eternal kingdom"[77] into which they will enter at the time of Christ's second coming is that which Peter has in mind in this present passage (Matthew 25:34; Acts 14:22; 2 Timothy 4:18). We suppose "eternal tabernacles" (Luke 16:9) and "a house not made with hands, eternal, in the heavens" (2 Corinthians 5:1) speak of the same thing Peter here calls "the eternal kingdom."[78] According to Acts 2:30-33, Christ is now sitting on David's throne. He is sitting at the Father's right hand (Colossians 3:1; Hebrews 1:3, 8:1). Christ's reign precedes His *parousia*. He will con-

---

[74] Some suppose the agent is Jesus Christ. The Greek word translated "entrance" is *eisodos*. John 14:6 has Jesus saying, "I am the way" (*hodos*). Hebrews 10:19,20 says, "having therefore, brethren, boldness to enter the holiest by the blood of Jesus, by a new (i.e., freshly-slain) and living way (*hodos*)."

[75] In *Pilgrim's Progress*, John Bunyan pictures what it will be like to be welcomed into heaven. "[The gates of glory were thrown wide open]. Now I saw in my dream that these two godly men went in at the gate [of heaven], and lo, as they entered, they were transfigured [they received their glorious resurrection bodies]; and they had raiment put on them that shone like gold. There were also those that met them with harps and crowns ... all the bells in the city rang again for joy, and ... it was said to them, 'Enter ye into the joy of your Lord'." What a glorious welcome home!

[76] Caffin (*op. cit.*, p.6) wrote, "Peter here seems to imply there will be degrees of glory hereafter proportioned to our faithfulness in the use of God's gifts here." (Cp. 1 Corinthians 3:12-15, Matthew 5:12.)

[77] Although "eternal" and "kingdom" are both common terms in the New Testament, their combination into "eternal kingdom" occurs nowhere else in the New Testament or Apostolic Fathers. The combination does occur in Aristides' *Apology* xvi, written about AD 129. This is an allusion that is a witness to the early existence of 2 Peter.

[78] A man's ideas about the "kingdom" will affect his comments on this passage, and a man's eschatology (a millennial kingdom yet to come?) will also color his comments here. In this commentator's syllabus on "The Climax of Jesus' Earthly Ministry" is a study of "kingdom," "kingdom of heaven," and "kingdom of God." Because they occur in parallel passages in the Gospels, the latter two terms are interchangeable. It is then observed that the Greek word translated "kingdom" can have three connotations: (1) the area ruled, (2) the people ruled, or (3) the idea of the rule or sway being exercised. Westerners automatically think of one of the first two when we hear the word "kingdom;" an Oriental thought of the third. If we would think like an Oriental as we read Scripture, many of the passages that have proven problematic to theologians would no longer be problems. God's rule, or Christ's rule, is something both present (in the church) *and* future (in the new heavens and earth).

tinue to reign until all enemies have been put under His feet (1 Corinthians 15:25). The last enemy that shall be destroyed is physical death, and that is destroyed when the dead are raised at His second coming. Jesus will relinquish His mediatorial reign to the God, even (Greek, *kai*) the Father (1 Corinthians 15:24), but His rule will continue on forever, for "the kingdom of the world has become the kingdom of our Lord and of His Christ, and He will reign forever and ever" (Revelation 11:15). The ruler in that future eternal kingdom is the same Lord and Savior Christians now acclaim,[79] the same Master the false teachers disown (2:1). A Biblical eschatology does provide a motivation for Christian ethics.

We have concluded the first two paragraphs of this letter. They present the completeness of the knowledge of Jesus Christ that is contained in the apostolic message such as Peter presented, and to which the Gnostics have nothing to add. They also set the tone for the holy living that is the exact opposite to what the false teachers were encouraging. Hiebert has a beautiful summary of the Christology of these two paragraphs:

> These first eleven verses of the epistle reveal the centrality of Jesus Christ in the thinking of Peter. As the "servant and apostle of Jesus Christ" (verse 1) he acknowledges Him as "our God and Savior" (verse 1), "Jesus our Lord" (verse 2), "our Lord Jesus Christ" (verse 8), and "our Lord and Savior" (verse 11); he speaks of "the righteousness of our God and Savior" (verse 1), "the knowledge of God and of Jesus our Lord" (verse 2), "the knowledge of our Lord Jesus Christ" (verse 8), and "the eternal kingdom of our Lord and Savior Jesus Christ" (verse 11). This exaltation of Jesus Christ offers support for the view that "our God" (verse 1), "His divine power" (verse 3), and "Him that called us" (verse 3) are further references to Him. Peter's faith is indeed Christocentric.[80]

C. The Inerrant Sources of Full Knowledge about Jesus Christ. 1:12-21

1. The truth already present with them. 1:12

1:12 -- *Therefore, I shall always be ready to remind you of these things, even though you* already *know* them, *and have been established in the truth which is present with* you.

Therefore -- As it did in verse 10, the opening *dio* gathers up all that has been said thus far in the letter about the full knowledge of our Lord Jesus Christ. But what if the Gnostics dispute Peter's claims? Where can the readers turn in order to know the truth, beyond any shadow of a doubt? Peter will point them to three inerrant sources of full (true) knowledge.

---

[79] We learned about Jesus as "Savior" at verse 1. We learned about Jesus as "Lord" in verse 2. Notice the exact correspondence of the Greek words here, *tou Kuriou hemon kai Soteros Iesou Christou*, with those in verse 1, *tou Theou hemon kai Soteros Iesou Christou*, as a strong argument in favor of the translation "Our God and Savior Jesus Christ," in that verse. (Caffin, *ibid.*)

[80] Hiebert, *op. cit.*, p.62.

I shall always be ready to remind you of these things -- Peter seems to be saying that, 'As long as I am here in this world, I will remind you where to find the truth.' We say "seems to be" because the meaning of several of the expressions in this clause is debated. For example, shall we read as the NASB, "I shall always be ready," or as the KJV, "I will not be negligent"?[81] The present tense of the verb itself means "be ready." To find the verb "be ready" in the future tense as we do here is unusual in our New Testaments.[82] Perhaps using the future tense was a way of expressing certainty about some intended action. "To remind you" is a present infinitive in the Greek. It is a compound verb, *hupomimnesko*, and it means "to cause to remember, to undergird what they have been told before" (the prefix *hupo* shows this). It is something Peter is ready to do repeatedly, as often as necessary.[83] "These things" are the truths, especially the anti-Gnostic ones, already spoken about in verses 1-11. He will remind his readers of the truths and duties which he has been describing because that is the only way they will get to heaven.

Even though you *already* know *them* -- These words imply Peter was well acquainted with the readers to whom he was writing. They were not ignorant of the gospel. Peter is aware that the preachers who evangelized them were divinely guided to work among them (1:1). Some of them had heard the preaching of Paul or one of his helpers. Peter himself has ministered in some of their cities. They had read Peter's first letter (3:1).

And have been established in the truth which is present with *you* -- The word translated "established" (*steridzo*) is the same root used on the solemn occasion when Jesus said, "Once you have turned again, *strengthen* your brothers" (Luke 22:31,32). The verb here in 2 Peter is a perfect tense, indicating past completed action with present continuing results. The Gospel truth[84] had come to them, they had embraced it, and on subsequent occasions their knowledge of it had been reinforced. In 1 Peter 5:12, Peter had written, "This is the true grace of God. Stand firm in it!" Peter here indicates he is aware his readers have been doing just that. "The truth" implies a coherent and fixed body of doctrine (cp. Jude 3) which the apostles and prophets proclaimed (Acts 2:42), and which the early church accepted. It was present with them long before Peter writes this present letter to remind them of and undergird

---

[81] It was not until the eighth or ninth centuries that manuscripts started having this reading, so the reading found in the Textus Receptus (and so also in the KJV) is most likely a scribal change deliberately made in an effort to smooth out what seemed like a difficult reading. After they have read the future tense "I shall ... be ready," commentators find it difficult to explain just what Peter may have had in mind, so it is guessed the scribes stepped in and tried to help out.

[82] The future tense occurs only here in 2 Peter 1:12 and in Matthew 24:6.

[83] One of the "preacher's" tasks is very often reminding a man of what he already knows.

[84] "Truth" is another word for the "true (full) knowledge of our Lord Jesus Christ" about which Peter is writing. It is not only moral truth or truth in the abstract, but the historical and doctrinal truth in contrast to the fables (cleverly devised tales) of verse 16. (Charles Bigg, "A Critical and Exegetical Commentary on the Epistles of St. Peter and St. Jude" in *The International Critical Commentary* [Edinburgh: T&T Clark, 1902], p.263.)

what they already know.[85] That the readers were "established in the truth" does not make unnecessary either reminders of what is included in that truth, warnings about spiritual pitfalls, or exhortations to continue in the truth, as is obvious from this very letter.

2. The apostle Peter's testimony – both oral and written. 1:13-18

1:13 -- ***And I consider it right, as long as I am in this*** **earthly** ***dwelling, to stir you up by way of reminder,***

And I consider it right -- Perhaps the *de* with which this verse begins contrasts with *kaiper* ("even though") in the middle of the previous verse. We would translate it "but" or "though I concede you already are established in the faith, nevertheless I feel an obligation to remind you. It is the right thing for me, as an apostle of Jesus, to do." Peter now discusses the second inerrant source of true (full) knowledge about Jesus Christ.

As long as I am in this *earthly* dwelling -- "Dwelling," literally "tabernacle" (ASV), is an apt metaphor for the human body.[86] Just as a tabernacle or tent was but a temporary dwelling – sometimes erected only for the night, sometimes erected for a longer time by people who were strangers and pilgrims on a journey – Peter's figure of speech introduces the idea that his stay in his present human body is but a temporary thing. Men's physical bodies are but temporary dwelling places for their souls.[87] "As long as I am in this tabernacle" means as long as I am alive here on this earth, and it is contrasted with "laying aside of my earthly dwelling (tabernacle, ASV)" that appears in the next verse.

To stir you up by way of remembrance -- "To stir you up" is a present tense infinitive of a compound verb. Peter understands his apostolic commission includes the obligation to keep arousing them thoroughly or, we might say, to keep nudging them in order to keep them spiritually awake. Whenever he sees folk tending to become spiritually drowsy, it is his task to shake them and alert them of potential danger. This stirring up will be done by a reminder, i.e., he will refresh their memory of the facts they already knew about gospel history and the solemn responsibilities which that knowledge involves.

---

[85] The notion, held by some who advocate "early Catholicism", that Christian doctrine grew by evolutionary increments until in the second century it became a fixed body of doctrine, is just wrong! The gospel message had a definite doctrinal content from the very first, because the message came from the Lord Jesus Christ and was correctly spoken by His Holy Spirit-inspired mouthpieces.

[86] Peter's words remind us that the same metaphor (with a slightly different but cognate word for "tent") was used by Paul (2 Corinthians 5:1-4). Perhaps the figure of speech was suggested to both writers by the Old Testament record of the patriarchs who dwelt in tents (tabernacles).

[87] The earthly bodies that men have are but "tents" in which to dwell during our earthly pilgrimage. These bodies are not our permanent dwellings. Plato called the body a "prison, the grave of the soul." Bible writers have a different attitude towards the physical body.

1:14 -- ***Knowing that the laying aside of my*** **earthly** ***dwelling is imminent, as also our Lord Jesus Christ has made clear to me.***

Knowing that the laying aside of my *earthly* dwelling is imminent -- In verse 13 Peter wrote, "as long as I am in this earthly dwelling." Now he indicates he is aware his temporary residence in his mortal body may not last much longer. Like one lays aside a tent after it has served its purpose, so Peter will lay aside his earthly body.[88] The Greek word here translated "imminent" is translated "swift" in 2 Peter 2:1. The adverb *tachine* may indicate Peter's awareness that the time of his death was approaching speedily, or it may describe the manner of his death when it did come, i.e., it would be swift, violent. Whichever, Peter is confident that physical death does not end it all. "Peter moves out of his earthly tent, but he lives on."[89]

As also our Lord Jesus Christ has made clear to me -- Is it the imminence, or the death itself, that Jesus signified ("made clear") to Peter? Some interpreters, basing their comments on the KJV ("as our Lord Jesus hath showed me"), suppose Peter is telling his readers he has just recently had a special revelation from Jesus about his death being imminent.[90] Others suppose Peter is referring to what the risen Jesus predicted concerning Peter's death, as recorded in John 21:18,19.[91] If he understood Jesus' words, Peter went all through the rest of his life knowing one day he would be crucified. In Rome during the Neronian persecutions, and knowing there was a warrant out for the arrest of apostles like himself, Peter did not need any recent revelation to be able to figure out his days on earth were numbered.[92] Because he knew his days were numbered, it was important to Peter to issue this reminder to

---

[88] It is possible that we have a mixture of metaphors here. "Laying aside" is regularly used of putting off a piece of clothing. Whether or not it is a mixed metaphor, it demonstrates that death holds no terrors for the Christian. It is like putting off old clothes, or a departure or an exit (*exodos*, verse 15), or taking down a tent when a journey is over and the temporary housing is no longer needed. Paul's explanation (Philippians 1:23) helps us understand. He says that to be absent from the body (i.e., to die physically) is to be present with the Lord. Peter's words in 1 Peter 1:4 show why the temporary dwelling is not needed anymore -- he is going to a permanent place.

[89] J. Nieboer, *Practical Exposition of II Peter Verse by Verse* (Erie, PA: Our Daily Walk Publishers, 1952), p.80. H.A. Ironside added this keen observation, "He had no thought of going to sleep in his tabernacle ... Scripture leaves no room whatever for the doctrine of the sleep of the soul." *Expository Notes on the Epistles of Peter* (New York: Loizeaux Brothers, 1947), p.73.

[90] J.B. Mayor, *The Epistle of St. Jude and the Second Epistle of St. Peter* (reprint, Grand Rapids: Baker, 1965), p.102; M.R. James, "The Second General Epistle of Peter and the General Epistle of Jude" in *Cambridge Greek Testament for Schools and Colleges* (Cambridge: University Press, 1912), p.15; and *TNDT*, 2:61-62.

[91] In a class he was conducting on 2 Peter, R.C. Foster wondered how old a man Peter was at this time. He asked, "How old was Peter when Jesus called him to be an apostle?" Students answered "perhaps about 30, or a bit older." Prof. Foster concluded, "If that is so, Peter would be somewhere in his late 60's or early 70's when he wrote this letter." Christ's prophecy to Peter indicated his death would occur in his old age.

[92] Some suppose Peter has already been arrested, tried, and sentenced to death, and that he writes this letter while he awaits his execution day.

them now about the truth.[93] Peter's allusion to Jesus' prediction implies that Peter's readers were aware of it.[94] John's Gospel has not been written yet when Peter writes. How would the readers know what Jesus had said? Peter was there when Jesus made the prediction. In the years before he wrote this letter, Peter has preached in many of the lands where his readers live. We suppose they knew about it because Peter told them while he was preaching to them!

1:15 -- ***And I will also be diligent that at any time after my departure you may be able to call these things to mind.***

And I will also be diligent -- Having urged diligence on his readers (verses 5,10), Peter now promises diligence on his part so they will have an inerrant source of knowledge about Jesus Christ. He opens this promise with two particles (*de kai*). Perhaps *de* connects this verse with verse 13, and *kai* reflects an additional resolve.[95] 'Not only will I refresh your memory while I am alive, but I will be diligent to make sure you have something to help you remember even after I am dead.'

That at any time after my departure -- The adverb of time, *ekastote* ("at every time, whenever there may be need"), occurs only here in the New Testament. "Departure" translates *exodos*, "the road out, departure, exit from this life."[96] The same term was used on the Mount of Transfiguration to refer to Christ's "departure (death)" at Luke 9:31.[97] Peter is thinking of the time after his death and of their need then to be reminded from time to time of the truths of which he is speaking.

---

[93] What Peter writes is not a "testament" in the pseudepigraphic sense of "testament" (a "made-up speech" put in the mouth of someone long dead, cp. Introductory Studies). Just as knowledge of his approaching death led Paul to write some of the things he did in 2 Timothy, personal considerations by Peter about his own situation are certainly in the background of what he writes here, and may even have been one of the reasons that prompted this letter.

[94] In the Introductory Studies, it has been pointed out that this allusion to what is related in John 21:18,19 has been used as an argument that whoever wrote 2 Peter was copying John's Gospel at this place. If that is true, it is fatal to the Petrine authorship of our letter. All this negative criticism has been answered in the Introductory Studies. 2 Peter carries the earmarks of being written by an eyewitness.

[95] The NASB's translation "I will also be diligent" reflects this understanding of the particles. A slightly different meaning results if we connect "also" to the infinitive ("you may also call these things to mind").

[96] "Exodus" is the name given in the LXX to the second book of the Old Testament. Hebrews 11:22 applies it to the "exodus (departure)" of the Israelites from Egypt at the close of the Egyptian captivity. The Greek term "denotes a transfer, not a termination" (Hiebert, *op. cit.*, p.68). Physical death is not the end of a man's existence, just the transfer to another realm.

[97] In two consecutive verses, Peter has used two words ("dwelling [tabernacle]" and "departure") which remind us of the transfiguration. Only an eyewitness is likely to have known that Moses and Elijah were talking to Jesus about His "departure" which would be accomplished in a few months at Jerusalem. "The simple unconscious occurrence of these [two words] is a strong proof of the genuineness of our Epistle; it is inconceivable that an imitator of the second century should have shown this delicate skill in adapting his production to the circumstances of the supposed writer." Caffin, *op. cit.*, p.7.

You may be able to call these things to mind -- Peter is promising that he will furnish them with an authentic and lasting written record of the truths of Christianity.[98] When it comes to identifying that lasting record, scholars have been provoked into much discussion. Some are certain Peter has reference to this very letter he is now writing, which they could read whenever they liked. But would he have to tell them he was going to endeavor ("I will also be diligent," future tense) to write a letter which he is already actually writing? Because this seems unlikely, some suppose Peter's point is that he will endeavor to have copies of this letter made so it will have wider distribution. Others have suggested Peter plans to commission "faithful men" to teach these things, or even establish a succession of teachers to keep the truth alive.[99] The simplest and most believable explanation is that we have a tacit reference to the book we know as the Gospel of Mark. Indeed, such an identification would match the traditional statement of the origin of Mark's Gospel. Early Christian literature says that Mark's Gospel contains what Peter used to preach,[100] and that Mark's Gospel was produced just about the time Peter died.

1:16 -- ***For we did not follow cleverly devised tales when we made known to you the power and coming of our Lord Jesus Christ, but we were eyewitnesses of His majesty.***

For -- "For" shows that Peter is giving a reason why he is going to leave a lasting record of the life of the Lord Jesus Christ. Such a record will be "truth." It will not be cleverly devised myths, but objective historical facts that can be established and corroborated by eyewitnesses.

We did not follow cleverly devised tales -- "Tale" is *muthos*: myth, legend, fable, fictitious stories as contrasted with true historical accounts.[101] Some people in the first century used the word "myth" of the legendary accounts about the descent of pagan gods to earth. Perhaps Peter is saying that the incarnation and earthly life of the Lord Jesus is not such a legend, it is historic fact. "Myth" was also used in Jewish circles of the rabbinical embellishment of the Old Testament record (e.g., Talmudic fables, Cabalistic lore, and the *Book of Jubilees*). Peter

---

[98] Bigg (*op. cit.*, p.265) may be correct when he surmises that the writers of the later pseudonymous Petrine literature used this passage as an excuse to affix "Peter's" name to their forgeries.

[99] The doctrine of apostolic succession to guarantee the truth is hardly more believable than the explanation given by some Roman Catholic commentators, who suppose this passage contains a promise that Peter would, after his death, continue to remember the needs of the church on earth, and help them by his intercession. One can only say that the dogmatic theologians (who were searching the Scriptures for Biblical proof of their already held doctrines) were desperate to find proof of the intercession of the saints if the best they could do was to latch on to this passage in 2 Peter.

[100] Papias, quoted by Eusebius, *H.E.*, iii.39.15; Irenaeus, *Adv. Haer.* III.1.1; Clement of Alexandria, quoted by Eusebius, *H.E.*, ii.15.2; Origen, quoted by Eusebius, *H.E.*, vi.25.5, and Eusebius himself, *H.E.*, ii.15.

[101] This word is found elsewhere in the New Testament only in the Pastoral Epistles in which Paul was attacking incipient Gnosticism and the wild tales on which it was based.

would be saying the content of gospel preaching did not include any such embellish-ment.[102] Perhaps by his use of the word "myth," Peter is attacking the Gnostic teachers on their own ground. *Muthos* (myth) was used "to refer to the Gnostic speculations about aeons or emanations which arose from the eternal abyss, the source of all spiritual existence, and were named *Mind, Wisdom, Power, Truth.*"[103] The Gnostics, in stark contrast to Christianity, certainly had some cleverly devised tales! "Cleverly devised" or "cunningly devised" (KJV) are attempts to convey the meaning of *sesophismenois*. That word can have either a good[104] or bad sense[105] depending on the context. Here its bad sense is intended. It would seem the apostles have been charged by the false teachers of cleverly spinning out yarns and passing them off as fact, and of doing this because they were motivated by selfish interests. Peter flatly asserts these accusations are false.

When we made known to you the power and coming of our Lord Jesus Christ -- It is difficult to determine precisely when this making known took place. Perhaps it is a reference to Peter's first epistle. More likely Peter's "we" includes himself and other apostles who, on a missionary tour, had been through the regions where the readers lived.[106] "Power" and "coming" are so constructed in the Greek (Sharp's rule of grammar) as to form almost one idea – "the powerful coming" we might render it. Because 2 Peter 3 talks about a denial of Christ's second coming by the scoffers, and because the word translated "coming" (*parousia*) in this verse is used in 3:4 of His second coming, not a few commentators think the second coming is Peter's topic here. We are not convinced.[107] In verses 16-18 we think Peter is talking about Christ's *first* coming to earth. *Parousia* was a technical term, occurring fre-

102 R.C. Foster, in 2 Peter class, observed that this passage contradicts one of the emphases of Neo-liberalism. On the supposition that our Gospels contain "embellishment," the Neo-liberal believes it is the job of the interpreter to "demythologize" the accounts so we are left with just the kernel of truth. Peter says there was no "myth" to begin with.

103 Vincent, *op. cit.*, p.326. Plummer, *op. cit.*, p.144, expresses his conviction the false teaching was incipient Gnosticism, and that the false teachers were Jewish Gnostics. He states his conviction that Peter is dealing with errors similar to those condemned by Paul (1 Timothy 1:4, 4:7; 2 Timothy 4:4; Titus 1:14 -- the only other passages in which the word "fables" [tales] occur) and later by Jude in his epistle.

104 In the good sense it means "to make wise, to teach" as at 2 Timothy 3:15.

105 "Subtly and slyly concocted" by human wisdom, told in such a deceptive way as to hide the teller's self-interest.

106 Remember that the word "obtained" (received) at 1 Peter 1:1 implied a divine hand in the evangelization of the readers. Furthermore, the verb "make known" is used in the New Testament of preaching the gospel (Romans 16:26) and of telling or explaining the "mystery" of God's counsel (Luke 2:17; John 15:15, 17:26; Ephesians 1:9, 6:19; Colossians 1:27).

107 This interpretation would have Peter basing his proof of the second coming on the transfiguration (verses 17-18). Wouldn't the resurrection have been a stronger, more believable argument for the second coming?

quently in the papyri for the visit of a king.[108] Instead of being in some faraway capital city, he was actually present right here in our town! At the first coming of Jesus, the King was present on earth![109] He made a personal appearance, and there was "power" involved with it. Not only was there a virgin birth, a transfiguration, an empty tomb, and an ascension, but there were some awesome miracles witnessed by Peter and the others. It took power to still the storm, to raise the dead, to heal the sick, and to cast out demons. In addition to this, "all authority in heaven and earth" was invested in Him before His incarnation at Bethlehem.[110]

But we were eyewitnesses of His majesty -- Rather than make up fables about Christ's powerful first coming, we apostles saw with our own eyes! "Eyewitnesses" (*epoptai*) means to watch and observe.[111] Peter and the others carefully observed and understood the implications of what they saw. At Jesus' transfiguration what they saw was "majesty." "Splendor, sublimity, greatness" (*megaleiotes*) is a quality that God possesses or displays (cp. Luke 9:43). In reference to Jesus' first coming, Peter says in this verse, 'I know from experience that what the Gnostic doctrine teaches about Jesus and Christ being different is not true!' As He was transfigured, His physical appearance was altered so that the observers saw His face shining like the sun, and His garments become a dazzling white light flashing

[108] *Parousia* is a compound word made up of *para*, "alongside" and *ousia*, "to be." Thus the word means to be alongside, to be present, to make a personal appearance.

[109] One way of reading Luke 17:21 is that Jesus was telling the Pharisees that the "kingdom ... was in their midst" in the sense that the King was already present.

[110] Matthew 28:18 sometimes is mistakenly supposed to say that only since the resurrection does Jesus have "all power" or "all authority." However, long before the resurrection, He claimed this authority as part of His incarnation mandate. See Mark 2:10 and John 3:35, 5:27, 13:3. Jesus was exercising a delegated authority (1 Corinthians 15:28).

[111] This word occurs nowhere else in the New Testament. A kindred verb, "to be an eyewitness", occurs in 1 Peter 2:12, 3:2, and nowhere else. This is a coincidence worth noting, said Plummer (*op. cit.*, p.145). Ever since source criticism began to try to find sources of Biblical ideas in the Greek mystery religions (see J.G. Machen, *The Origin of Paul's Religion* [Grand Rapids: Eerdmans, 1925]) it has been customary for commentators to note that "eyewitness" was a technical term used in the mystery religions to designate those who were initiated into the highest grade of the mysteries. In the mystery religions -- sort of passion plays -- there was a drama which acted out the life of the god. It was only after a long course of instruction and preparation that the worshiper was finally allowed to be present at the passion play and thus personally experience "union" with the god. When he reached the state of being allowed to attend the actual drama, he was an initiate, and the technical word to describe him was in fact "eyewitness"; he was a prepared and privileged eyewitness of the experiences of the god. (Adapted from Barclay, *op. cit.*, p.367). Michael Green ("The Second Epistle General of Peter and the General Epistle of Jude" in *The Tyndale New Testament Commentaries* [Grand Rapids: Eerdmans, 1979], p.83), believes that Peter was using the false teacher's own vocabulary against them. The thrust of Peter's argument here, he suggests, is that the false teachers were outside the circle of initiates to which Peter and the apostles belong, so the false teachers have nothing they can tell about the experiences of Jesus.

like lightning (Matthew 17:2; Mark 9:2,3; Luke 9:29). What they were seeing was the glory of God, because Jesus was God in the flesh.[112]

1:17 -- ***For when He received honor and glory from God the Father, such an utterance as this was made to Him by the Majestic Glory, "This is My beloved Son with whom I am well pleased," --***

For -- Peter here (verses 17 and 18) explains how and when he was an eyewitness of the majesty of Jesus Christ. It was at His transfiguration. The Greek sentence is broken as the dash at the close of the verse in the NASB indicates. The sentence begins with two participles, but there is no verb for them to lean upon to complete their meaning.[113] Nevertheless, the sense of what Peter writes is clear.

When He received honor and glory from God the Father -- "God the Father" is a familiar designation for the First Person of the Godhead,[114] and serves to distinguish Him from the Son. Jesus was honored by the Father's public acknowledgment of His Sonship, and "glory" (or "praise") may refer to the Father's words of delight in the Son.[115]

Such an utterance as this was made to Him by the Majestic Glory -- "Such as (this)" (*toiasde*), a classical Greek demonstrative found nowhere else in the New Testament, shows there was something unique about the voice.[116] "Was made" is the same verb used in Acts 2:2 of "the *rushing* mighty wind." "Made" (*enechtheises*) comes from the verb *phero*, "to bear, to carry," literally "there was borne along." It is repeated in the next verse. It seems

---

[112] John 1:14 asserts that all the apostles saw in Jesus the glory of God while He was here on earth among them. James and John on the occasion of the transfiguration saw that glory, for they were there along with Peter. When the others saw glimpses of His glory we are not told in the Gospels. Perhaps it was during some of His post-resurrection appearances when He appeared in His glorified body. In any case, Peter gives the only extant account of the transfiguration by one of the eyewitnesses. While Matthew, Mark, and Luke tell about the transfiguration in their Gospels, they were not personally present for it.

[113] For a similar broken sentence ("anacoluthon") see 2 Corinthians 5:6.

[114] See Galatians 1:3; Ephesians 6:23; Philippians 2:11; 1 Thessalonians 1:1; 2 Timothy 1:2; Titus 1:4; 1 Peter 1:2, etc.

[115] The way the NASB reads, both "honor" and "glory" refer to what the voice from heaven said. Commentators working with the KJV tend to treat "honor" as referring to the testimony of the voice and "glory" as referring to the splendor of the Lord's transfigured person. We've already spoken of the glorious splendor of His appearance under the word "majesty." It is doubtful Peter makes a second reference to it in "glory" at this place. "'Glory' here does not refer to the bodily brilliance of Jesus that the disciples saw, since the Synoptics picture His transfiguration as taking place before the voice came. The Gospels present His radiance as bursting forth from within, [followed by] God's expression of approval [that] brought 'honor and glory'" (Hiebert, *op. cit.*, p.74).

[116] Wm. F. Arndt and F.W. Gingrich, *A Greek-English Lexicon of the New Testament and Other Early Christian Literature* (Chicago: University of Chicago Press, 1957), p.828.

intended to assert emphatically the real objective character of the voice. It was not a vision, not a dream. The voice was real. This is not a myth or a figment of the imagination. The ASV reads "from the Majestic Glory," as though the voice came out of the cloud.[117] That is not what Peter wrote. He used the preposition *hupo* with the genitive case, a construction called genitive of agent. It should be translated "by" as the NASB does, and "Majestic Glory" must be understood as a periphrasis for God.[118] God was there and He spoke!

"This is My beloved Son with whom I am well pleased – " -- Our translation makes these words correspond exactly with the quotation given in Matthew 17:5 (except that "Listen to Him!" is added there). However, in the Greek there are some slight variations. In Peter's quote there is a second *mou* after "beloved" that does not occur in Matthew, and Peter uses a different prepositional phrase, *eis hon*, than the one (*en ho*) which occurs in Matthew.[119] "My ... Son" points to Jesus' unique relationship to the Father.[120] "My beloved" marks the Son as the special object of His love. "With whom" (*eis hon*, "toward whom") says that God's pleasure, God's approval, has been directed[121] towards the Son from before creation of the world[122] and God's good pleasure is still directed toward Him because of what He sees in Jesus. "I" is emphatic. What a contrast between God's attitude toward Jesus and that of the false teachers who were denying him (2:1)!

1:18 -- ***And we ourselves heard this utterance made from heaven when we were with Him on the holy mountain.***

And we ourselves heard this utterance made from heaven -- Without ever finishing the sentence he started in verse 17, Peter plunges in anew to underline the presence of not only

---

[117] Indeed, Matthew 17:5 and Mark 9:7 say the voice came out of the bright cloud that overshadowed them. There is no doubt that that cloud was the Shekinah, the visible manifestation of the presence of God, which had appeared in ancient times on Mount Sinai, led the children of Israel through the wilderness, and rested over the tabernacle and temple above the mercy seat.

[118] For "majestic" used to refer to God the Father, compare the LXX of Deuteronomy 33:26, "the Majestic One of the firmament." (The KJV gives a more exact translation of the Hebrew, "in his excellency in the sky.") Clement of Rome (ch.ix) uses "majestic glory," doubtless one of his allusions to 2 Peter.

[119] We would expect a forger to follow Matthew exactly. The slight differences may be an argument for the genuineness of 2 Peter.

[120] We call Jesus the "Son" because of the virgin birth. It is the incarnate Jesus that God claims as His Son.

[121] The verb "well pleased" is an aorist tense in the Greek. The aorist tense usually indicates completed action in the past time. If we take it as an historical aorist, it expresses the Father's delight in Jesus before the incarnation, when He committed Himself to the work of men's redemption. Our versions treat the aorist as a timeless aorist when they translate it as "I *am* well pleased."

[122] Compare Isaiah 42:1-4 (quoted at Matthew 12:18-21) about God's soul being pleased with Jesus.

eyewitnesses but of earwitnesses on the Mount of Transfiguration. With eyewitnesses and earwitnesses to testify, no one can say this is a cunningly devised myth or vision or hallucination. "We ourselves" (Peter, James, and John) is emphatic in the Greek. All had the same objective personal experience. They actually heard the "utterance"[123] that was borne[124] out of heaven.[125]

When we were with Him on the holy mountain -- An ordinary mountain[126] was transformed into a holy place by the presence of God there – both God the Father and God the Son. This description of the Mount of Transfiguration supposes that Peter's readers already had a knowledge of the history of that event.[127] The first coming of Jesus in the flesh, no matter what the false teachers say, was an historical fact; Peter and the other eyewitnesses can personally testify to it! Their oral and written testimony is an inerrant source of full knowledge about Jesus Christ.

3. The Old Testament prophecies. 1:19-21

1:19 -- ***And*** **so** ***we have the prophetic word*** **made** ***more sure, to which you do well to pay attention as to a lamp shining in a dark place, until the day dawns and the morning star arises in your hearts.***

And ***so*** **we have the prophetic word** ***made*** **more sure** -- "And" coordinates this verse with what has already been said. We suppose it gives a third inerrant source of full knowledge about Jesus Christ. That third source is the "prophetic word." This expression means the whole Old Testament body of prophecy respecting the subject at hand – who Christ is. That

---

123 The Greek word in both verses 17 and 18 is *phone* and can be translated either "sound" or "voice." Since actual words were spoken by God, the choice of "utterance" by the NASB is felicitous.

124 Peter repeats for emphasis the remarkable word *enechtheisan* ("made") he used in verse 17.

125 Whereas the Synoptics have the voice coming "out of the cloud," Peter here words it as "out of heaven," another slight variation that is perfectly acceptable from a genuine witness who can afford to take his own line because he knows he is on firm ground.

126 Which mountain should be identified as the site of the transfiguration has been debated. In the time of the Crusades, Mount Tabor on the plain of Jezreel was identified as the place, and modern tourists are still shown a chapel on its top commemorating the transfiguration. Since Jesus is close to Caesarea Philippi at the time of the transfiguration, many would choose Mount Hermon as the place.

127 As indicated in the Introductory Studies, the designation "holy mountain" gives no support to a theory of a post-apostolic date for our letter. It is a view that is centuries older than the apostles that wherever God had specially manifested Himself was "holy ground" -- Exodus 3:5; Joshua 5:15; Genesis 28:16,17; Exodus 19:12; Acts 7:33.

the reference is to the Old Testament is shown by verses 20 and 21.[128] *Bebaioteron* ("more sure, more reliable") is a comparative adjective, but Bible students have trouble agreeing when it comes to trying to decide what is more reliable than what. Several alternatives have been suggested that to this commentator do not seem quite right. (1) Old Testament prophecy is more reliable than the testimony of the apostles referred to in verses 13-18, or more reliable than what the voice on the Mount said.[129] (2) "*Made* more sure" means what was seen and heard at the transfiguration increases our perception of the reliability of the Old Testament prophets.[130] (3) We are sure of the meaning of the words of Old Testament prophecy when we see their fulfillment like we did on the Mount.[131] (4) What we saw on the Mount of Transfiguration makes it even more certain that what is foretold in the prophets about Christ's second coming must be true.[132] Interpretations that to this commentator seem more likely are: (1) Old Testament prophecy is more reliable than the fables referred to in verse 16.[133] (2) As far as the readers are concerned, Old Testament prophecy would be a better source of information about Christ's first coming than Peter's personal experience. After all, they cannot duplicate his experience, but they can search the Scriptures.[134] We would translate it, "We have the more reliable prophetic word ...."[135]

To which you do well to pay attention – Peter's wording shows that he assumes the thing

---

[128] Does such an appeal, as we understand the verses to be, mean that 2 Peter is written early -- before the anti-Gnostic Johannine books were written? We think so. If those Johannine books had been in existence, Peter could have appealed to them.

[129] Why these views ever saw the light of day is hard to imagine. Does anyone suppose the inspired apostles were less reliable in their pronouncements than were the Old Testament prophets? And who would believe that the prophets were more reliable than the voice of God?

[130] The ASV/NASB translators who added "made" have let us know that this was their understanding of this disputed passage. We are not sure we should add the words "so" and "made." The NIV's translation, "We also have the prophetic message as something completely reliable," is to be preferred.

[131] Peter's words actually say that the prophetic word itself is more sure -- not that his or our understanding is made more sure.

[132] Barclay wrote, "The glory of Jesus on the Mount of Transfiguration is the strongest guarantee that the prophets were right when they foretold the Second Coming of the Lord" (*op. cit.*, p.368). In our opinion, those writers who think 2 Peter 1 deals with the *second* coming of Christ are in error. 2 Peter 1 deals with Christ's *first* coming.

[133] This would require us to understand that Peter by his use of the word "myth" is attacking the Gnostic teachers on their own ground. Peter is saying Scripture is better than anything the Gnostics have to offer.

[134] To Jewish Christians, the evidence of the prophets of the Old Testament was of supreme importance. See the 41 Messianic prophecies quoted in the Gospel of Matthew. Nathanael, the "Israelite indeed" was drawn to the Lord by the assurance that "We have found Him of whom Moses in the Law, and the prophets, wrote" (John 1:45). Jesus thrilled men's hearts when He opened the scriptures and explained to them all the things written therein about Himself (Luke 24:27,32).

[135] When Peter says "we" in this place he includes both himself and his readers.

being urged is already being done, and he praises them for doing well. Peter's argument is not drawn out, but his point is that the readers would do better paying attention to the prophecies than to the false teachers. Christian apologists have always found in fulfilled prophecy one of the strongest arguments for the truth of the Christian religion. That such a minute and detailed record could be written hundreds of years beforehand is inexplicable unless the hand of God is in it.

As to a lamp shining in a dark place -- Ancient lamps gave about the same light as a candle, since both were burning wicks. The light was meager but it was better than no light at all. "Dark place" is *auchmeros*,[136] literally "a dry place, a desert." We suppose that "dark place" and "in your hearts" have a similar meaning.[137] As we understand it, Peter is saying, 'If you want to keep your head screwed on right, pay attention to Scripture.' The Old Testament prophecies serve a very similar beneficial purpose that a lamp does on an obscure road at night. It keeps one from going utterly astray, until sunrise frees one from difficulty. God's word is a lamp unto our feet, and a light unto our path (Psalm 119:105). The Old Testament prophecies will give us correct guidance to Christ. From them we'll get a right idea about who He is.

Until the day dawns and the morning star arises in your hearts -- "In your hearts" seems to say that the subject Peter is driving home is still "What is the best source of informed and correct thinking about who Jesus the Messiah is?"[138] Instead of heeding the misrepresentations made by the false teachers, Christians are to study and ponder and meditate on the Old Testament prophecies until the day dawns and the morning star arises. Apparently two different things are talked about in the words "day dawns" and "morning star arises." The word picture in "day dawns"[139] is this – in the half-hour or so before sunrise, the eastern sky begins to get brighter as the first rays of light dispel the darkness. That glow in the sky is better light than what you have simply with a lamp. This, we believe, is a poetic and figurative way of describing a new and deeper knowledge and faith, an advanced state of un-

---

[136] The word occurs only here in the New Testament.

[137] Unless "dark place" in this clause is explained by "in your hearts" at the end of the verse, it can be said that Peter does not explain what the "dark place" is. Commentators then rush in to supply the deficiency. J.A. Bengel (*Gnomon of the New Testament* [Edinburgh: T&T Clark, 1860], Vol.5, p.93) thought the reference is to the dimness of the Old Testament revelation in contrast to the bright sunlight of the New Testament age. Many suggest the "dark place" is this present world which is characterized by "darkness" (John 1:5; Ephesians 6:12; 1 Thessalonians 5:4-6). But are not the "dark place" and Peter's Christian readers somehow related? If so, this "present world of darkness" seems to be an extraneous comment.

[138] It is uncertain with which words the phrase "in your hearts" is to be connected. Perhaps Peter meant "pay attention in your hearts." Perhaps he meant "know this first in your hearts." Perhaps he meant "arises in your hearts" (see how the KJV puts a comma after "dawn" so that "in your hearts" goes with morning star "arises"). Perhaps he meant "dawns and arises in your hearts." Our comments follow this last option, since the Greek word order seems to point to it as being correct.

[139] The verb "dawns" (*diaugase*) is a compound form that occurs only here in the New Testament (unless a variant reading at 2 Corinthians 4:4 is accepted as genuine).

derstanding just who Messiah was predicted to be.[140] Study the Old Testament prophecies until you see the light, i.e., arrive at a full conviction and strong faith that those prophecies predicted that Messiah would be "God in the flesh." Then the low Christology of the false teachers will no longer be attractive. The word for "morning star" (*phosphoros*) is found no other place in the New Testament, but the word "star" (*astron*) is used for the Messiah in Numbers 24:17 and Jesus is called the "bright morning star" (*aster*) in Revelation 2:28, 22:16. At certain times in the year, a very bright star shows on the eastern horizon just before the sun comes up. That "morning star" (usually the planet Venus, though sometimes another of the visible planets) reflects the light of the sun which is still below the horizon and heralds the coming day. This, too, we believe, is a poetic way of picturing the growing conviction of who Messiah is as one studies the Old Testament prophecies.[141]

1:20 -- *But know this first of all, that no prophecy of Scripture is* a matter *of one's own interpretation,*

But know this first of all -- There is no "but" in the Greek; instead, we have a nominative

---

[140] Because different decisions were made about the meaning of earlier phrases in this paragraph, commentators have proposed a variety of explanations for "day dawns." (1) It has been taken as a reference to the second coming by those who think verse 16 ("power and coming") alluded to the second coming. *Objections* to finding this meaning in verse 19 include: (a) against this interpretation (that it is "the day of the Lord") is the absence of the article before "day"; (b) it would make the time of the Christian's walk here on earth a time of walking in darkness; (c) the last words ("in your hearts") would mean that the second coming is not an actual happening, but only something subjective in the mind. Wouldn't the false teachers who are denying any second coming in history (3:4) like to hear that? (2) "Day dawn" has been explained as a reference to the time of conversion. *Objections*: (a) the readers are already Christians, so their conversion is already past; (b) Peter's argument is, "Pay attention ... till the day dawns." Do we give up the prophecies and quit studying when we become Christians? (3) Some see a reference to the completed canon. The idea is that you have to listen to the Old Testament prophecies until you have all the New Testament books at hand. *Objections*: (a) they already have a number of New Testament books at hand (3:16); (b) even after Christians have New Testament books at hand, there is still a value in studying the Old Testament Scripture (2 Timothy 3:16). (4) A fourth suggestion is that "day dawns" is a reference to their attainment of the gift of prophecy. Such gifts were given by the laying on of an apostle's hands, so Peter is telling them to study the Old Testament until some apostle comes and confers on one of their members the gift of prophecy which will give them fuller information about the coming of Christ. *Objections*: (a) apostles have already been among the readers (3:2); (b) the false teachers could nay-say any New Testament prophet who was teaching straight-line Christian doctrine by asking, "What else would you expect him to say?" Thus, an appeal to the Old Testament would have more weight with the false teachers than an appeal to a New Testament prophet's message.

[141] Less believable are the ideas of R.C.H. Lenski (*The Interpretation of the Epistles of St. Peter, St. John and St. Jude* [Minneapolis, MN: Augsburg Press, 1966], p.295) who thinks Peter refers to the "signs of the times" which immediately precede the *parousia*. In this commentator's view, Lenski has misinterpreted Jesus' Olivet Discourse. While there are signs (Matthew 24:3-28) of the approaching destruction of Jerusalem (AD 70), there are no signs of the near approach of the second advent (Matthew 24:29ff). Albert E. Barnett ("The Second Epistle of Peter," in *The Interpreter's Bible* [New York: Abingdon, 1957], Vol.12, p.185) supposes there is a covert reference to the indwelling Holy Spirit. Ray Summers ("2 Peter" in *The Broadman Bible Commentary* [Nashville: Broadman Press, 1972], Vol.12, p.179) decides the reference is to the rapture of the redeemed at the *parousia*. (But isn't that an objective event, rather than something that simply happens "in your hearts"?)

plural participle that connects grammatically with "you do well" (verse 19). In other words, while you study the Old Testament prophecies, here is something to keep uppermost in mind all the time. "First of all" says this demands your special attention.

That no prophecy of Scripture is *a matter* of one's own interpretation -- This phrase (*hoti pasa propheteia graphes idias epiluseos ou ginetai*) expresses what the students of Old Testament prophecy are to keep in mind. A literal rendering would be "all prophecy of Scripture of private loosing is not." In the Greek it is the verb that is negated. However, a number of writers suggest this is a common Hebraism for "NONE ... arises of private ...."[142] "Prophecy of Scripture" seems to refer to the Old Testament Messianic prophecies, just as "prophetic word" (verse 19) did.[143] The verb translated "is" is not *esti* but *ginetai*, "arises, becomes, comes into being." Those Old Testament prophecies did not arise or come into existence "by private loosing" is the idea. But what does *idias epiluseos* mean? The word for "private" is *idias*, "special, one's own, personal (as opposed to what belongs to someone else)." The noun *epiluseos* occurs nowhere else in the New Testament, though the verb form of the same word occurs at Mark 4:34 ("explained") and Acts 19:39 ("determined" or "settled"). The long and well-known argument[144] over the meaning of *epiluseos* could have been avoided, we believe, if scholars had just paid attention to what is said in the next verse. Verse 21 begins with "for," so is explaining in what sense Peter is using *epiluseos*.[145] What that verse says is that we do not look for the *origin* of the prophecy in the prophet's own mind.[146] We think this is a rather plain rebuke of the false teacher's fables. Their myths did arise in their own minds. There was no Holy Spirit prompting them!

1:21 -- *For no prophecy was ever made by an act of human will, but men moved by the Holy Spirit spoke from God.*

---

142 "It is a firm denial concerning all that belongs to the subject negated." Hiebert, *op. cit.*, p.81.

143 The KJV in the next verse has "no prophecy came *in old time* by the will of man" -- showing that they believed "prophecy of Scripture" to be a reference to the Old Testament.

144 The argument is this: Is it to us, or to the original human writers of the prophecies, that no prophecy was of private *epiluseos*? Because of the context, this commentator opts for the latter.

145 What will be unfolded in verse 21 shows the following interpretations (while some are true by themselves) to be beside the point: (1) Men are not to make individual verses mean anything they want to. The interpretation placed on Scripture by Christ and the apostles must be the norm of understanding. (2) Scripture must be interpreted by Scripture. Analogy of Scripture will keep us from error as we work through any individual passage. (3) The prophecies, besides having a literal interpretation, also have a hidden and mystical sense. No prophecy has just one interpretation, is what "private interpretation" (KJV) is alleged to mean. (4) In the Roman Catholic church, individual members are not allowed to interpret Scripture. Instead, the church (or the curia) gives the official interpretation, lest any Scripture be of "private interpretation." (5) The original prophets did not understand what they wrote (just as 1 Peter 1:10-12 affirmed). (6) One must not interpret a prophecy in isolation. Its unfolding fulfillment must be taken into account to avoid a "private interpretation."

146 Grammatically we are treating the genitive "private loosing" as a genitive of source.

For -- Verse 21 is intended to be an explanation of *idias epiluseos* in the previous verse.

No prophecy was ever made by an act of human will -- Literally it says, "not by the will of man was prophecy borne along at any time." "Prophecy" in this verse refers to the same body of Old Testament Messianic prophecy that "prophetic word" (verse 19) and "prophecy of Scripture" (verse 20) did. "Made" translates the same verb ("borne along," *enechthe*, a form *phero*) which occurred in verses 17,18 of the voice from heaven, and which will be used again in the last phrase of this verse. "Not of human will" says the prophecies did not arise because some man wanted them to. The prophetic lamp "was neither fashioned nor lighted by the prophet himself."[147] The adverb *pote* ("ever," at any time) stands at the end of the clause in Greek for emphasis. Connected with a past tense verb it speaks of any time in the past.[148] False prophets may shape their prophecies to declare what they want to happen, but not at any time was this the way prophecies of Scripture originated! So just how did the prophetic Scriptures arise?

But men moved by the Holy Spirit spoke from God -- Literally, "as by the Holy Spirit they were borne along men spoke from God." It is because of the divine origin of prophecy that we can speak of an inerrant source of full knowledge about Jesus Christ. "Moved" is the verb used of a ship being borne along by a strong wind (Acts 27:15,17). By using a strong adversative "but" (*alla*) to contrast this with "by an act of human will," and by putting "men (were) moved by the Holy Spirit" first in this clause, Peter emphasizes that the Holy Spirit was the One who originated or produced the Old Testament prophecy. The Old Testament prophets, however, were not like inanimate ships. Those men[149] "spoke" as they were borne along by the Spirit. They remained conscious and in control of their powers of reason and choice of vocabulary words.[150] "From God" says that as they were speaking the message came from God. Peter recognizes both the divine and human element in the production of

---

[147] John Lillie, *Lectures on the First and Second Epistles of Peter* (Minneapolis: Klock and Klock, 1978 [reprint of an 1869 work]), p.428.

[148] The KJV has, "in old time." This rendering of the adverb was copied from the Geneva Bible.

[149] Whether the original reading was "men" or "holy men" is uncertain. The manuscripts at this place vary considerably. The Textus Receptus reads *elalesan hoi hagioi Theou anthropoi* while the Nestle-Aland Text has *elalesan apo Theou anthropoi*. These are but two of nearly half-a-dozen different readings found in the manuscripts here. See the United Bible Society's *Greek New Testament* (Stuttgart, W. Germany: Wurttemberg Bible Society, 1968), 2nd edition, p.807 for the manuscript evidence for each reading. It might be argued that since "holy" was a common adjective used of the prophets (Luke 1:70; Acts 3:21; 2 Peter 3:2), that some scribe added it at this place. Others argue it was accidentally omitted by a later copyist.

[150] See the Special Study on Revelation, Inspiration, and Illumination in the author's *New Testament History: Acts* (Moberly, MO: Scripture Exposition Books, 2002), p.127ff. Some critics have fancied that verses 10-21 reflect Montanism. Hardly! Montanists used stronger language, as readers of Tertullian know. With them prophecy was ecstasy and frenzy; prophets ceased to be men -- their reason left them and they became mere instruments on which, (as the Montanists explained it) the Spirit played. The wording of 2 Peter 1 points to an age previous to Montanism.

the prophetic Scriptures.[151] With such infallible sources for full knowledge about Christ, why would anyone listen for a moment to the foolish myths of the false teachers?

[151] Scripture elsewhere recognizes the dual authorship – divine and human elements – of Scripture. 2 Samuel 23:2; Jeremiah 1:7,9; Acts 4:25.

II. CONCERNING FALSE TEACHERS. 2:1-22

A. Prophetic Warning Portraying Coming False Teachers. 1:1-3

2:1 -- ***But false prophets also arose among the people, just as there will also be false teachers among you, who will secretly introduce destructive heresies, even denying the Master who bought them, bringing swift destruction upon themselves.***

But -- *De* seems to mark a transition to a new point of emphasis in Peter's letter. It is not quite right to say it is a transition to a new subject, for the false teachers here portrayed are the very ones chapter 1 talked about who proposed a path to full knowledge about Jesus different from the path of truth taught by the apostles and Scriptures, and are the very ones who will be depicted in chapter 3 as scoffing. But it is a new point of emphasis. Here in chapter 2, Peter draws a vivid and detailed picture of what the false teachers will teach, the methods they will use, and their lifestyles, so that when they do arrive on the scene, Peter's readers should have no trouble identifying them. Interspersed here and there in this description are encouragements and motivations for the Christians to be on their guard lest they be enticed and captured by these false teachers.

False prophets also arose among the people -- The transition is simple. Besides the true prophets mentioned in the last chapter who spoke as they were moved by the Holy Spirit, there were also false prophets on the scene at the same time. "The people" are the people of Old Testament Israel.[1] Even though God sent true prophets from time to time, Israel seemed to be plagued with false prophets (*pseudoprophetai*).[2] Some of them are characterized as "false" because they falsely claimed to be prophets of God; some were "false" because they made false predictions. Either way, there was an absence of a divine mission.

Just as there will also be false teachers among you -- "Also" says in view of Old Testament history, it ought not be thought strange, says Peter, if false teachers should arise to plague the church. "Will also be" reminds us there is a strange mixture of future, present, and past tense verbs in chapter 2. Typical of prophets who can "see" the future as though it were happening in the present, Peter uses various verb tenses in his descriptive denunciation of these coming

---

[1] *Laos* (singular) was a common designation for Israel, as contrasted with *laoi* (plural) which referred to all the other nations in the Gentile world. See Luke 2:32, Acts 26:17,23, and compare how Psalm 47:1 reads in the KJV and NASB. See also the article on *laos* in *TNDT*, Vol.4, p.52-54.

[2] One example of false prophets in the Old Testament would be the pretenders in the court of Ahab who contended with God's prophet Micaiah (1 Kings 22:8-20; 2 Chronicles 18:8-34). We could point to the old prophet who caused the destruction of the young man sent to warn the king of Israel (2 Kings 13); or to Zedekiah, who led Jehoshaphat to a fatal war (1 Kings 22); and to Hananiah, who opposed Jeremiah's prediction that Babylon would destroy Jerusalem (Jeremiah 28). The Old Testament abounds with denunciations of false prophets and their false motives and their degenerate lives (Micah 3:11; Isaiah 28:7; Jeremiah 5:31, 6:13, 23:14; Deuteronomy 13:1-5, 18:20).

false teachers (*pseudodidaskaloi*).[3] For the same reasons some ancient prophets were called "false," so these men are denounced by Peter as "false." Either they would falsely claim to hold the office of teacher, or what they taught would be false and perverse. This is the only place *pseudodidaskaloi* occurs in the New Testament,[4] but there are numerous predictions warning of the coming of false teachers. Christ, in the Sermon on the Mount (Matthew 7:15) warned, Beware of wolves coming in sheep's clothing! Paul warned the Ephesian elders that savage wolves would enter the flock and would speak perverse things to draw away disciples after them (Acts 20:28-32). The problem is that by the time Peter writes some of those predictions had already painfully come true, while others were on the immediate horizon. "Among you" contrasts with "among the people"[5] earlier in the verse and warns that the false teachers will infiltrate the churches as they try to win followers to their false way of life.[6]

Who will secretly introduce destructive heresies -- With *hoitines* ("who are of such a kind, or class, that ...") Peter introduces two identifying marks that will characterize the false teachers. One of those marks is that they will "secretly introduce" or stealthily smuggle in (*pareisaxousin*[7]) their doctrines; that is, while teaching some true doctrine, they would cleverly sneak in alongside the true much that was false. Another way to secretly introduce false doctrine is to use Biblical words but give them a new and strange definition. "Destructive heresies" is *haireseis apoleias*, which could also be translated "heresies of de-

---

[3] The Old Testament prophets often used past tense verbs when predicting the future because their vision of the future had been so vivid. Or, because what they were predicting was so certain, they could speak of it as though it were past. When it is remembered that a similar variation of verbs is found in (1) 2 Thessalonians 2:3-7 in the prediction about the "man of lawlessness," (2) in 1 Timothy 4:1-4 in a prediction about some who will fall away from the faith because of the influence of false teachers, and (3) in 2 Timothy 3:1-9 in a prediction about "difficult times," we should not be hasty to find in these verb tense variations evidences of pseudonymous authorship for 2 Peter. See this whole matter discussed in the Introductory Studies.

[4] In the Introductory Studies we called attention to Justin Martyr's allusion to this verse.

[5] In the background is Peter's idea of Christians as the New Testament counterpart of the Old Testament chosen people (1 Peter 2:9; 2 Peter 1:10).

[6] Galatians 2:4 contains similar language about "false brethren" (they were actually still members of the sect of the Pharisees, Acts 15:5) who had sneaked into Christian congregations in order to convert them to the lifestyle of the Pharisees. 2 Corinthians 11:13-15 tells how false apostles masqueraded as apostles of Christ in order to get a hearing.

[7] The verb *pareisaxousin* ("secretly introduce") is found only here in the New Testament, though the adjective derived from the same root is used by Paul in Galatians 2:4. It is a compound word made up of *ago* ("to bring") + *eis* ("into") + *para* ("alongside"). Vincent (*op. cit.*, p.328) says "the metaphor in the word is that of a *spies* or *traitors* introducing themselves into an enemy's camp." While the idea of stealth or secrecy is only implied in *para*, the idea of stealthy or underhanded means is plainly involved in the kindred word used in Jude 4. The only difference is that whereas Peter uses a future tense verb (making a prediction), Jude uses a past tense verb (the prediction has come true).

struction,"[8] or "heresies that lead to destruction."[9] The primary meaning of the word *hairesis* is "choice, a deliberate, self-chosen belief or position." By a natural transition it came to be used of the opinions held by a group of like-minded individuals, and then came to be used as a designation for the group itself.[10] The beliefs and teachings of the false teachers whom Peter had in view in this warning are obviously contrary to the teachings of Christ and the apostles. They were alien to the truth. The genitive word *apoleias* translated "destructive"[11] can be either objective or subjective. If we treat it as subjective, then the "heresies" come from "destruction" (hell or the devil). In Revelation 9:11, demonic locusts who come out of the abyss have a king over them (the devil) who is named "destruction" or "destroyer." Perhaps when he calls them "heresies of destruction" (Greek), Peter means something very similar to the "doctrines of demons" Paul wrote in 1 Timothy 4:1, i.e., that the heretical doctrines were learned from the devil or demons. If we treat *apoleias* as an objective genitive, there are several viable possibilities for the meaning of "destruction." Perhaps the heresies lead to the destruction and ruin the spiritual lives of all who embrace them, teachers and followers alike. Perhaps the heresies destroy the harmony of the congregations into which these heresies are smuggled. Perhaps the eternal destiny of the heretics is destruction (i.e., hell).[12] Tragically, all three possibilities are true.

Even denying the Master who bought them -- This is a second identifying mark that is characteristic of the false teachers. Since in Scripture "Master"[13] is used of both the Father (Luke 2:29; Acts 4:24) and the Son, we will have to let Jude 4 guide us at this place. Jude,

---

[8] "'Damnable heresies' came into the KJV from the Geneva Bible, and the KJV rendering is a change for the worse" (Plummer, *op. cit.*, p.151).

[9] This was R.C. Foster's preference expressed in a 1950's class at The Cincinnati Bible Seminary.

[10] For example, when we read in our Bibles of the "sect" of the Pharisees (Acts 15:5), or the "sect" of the Sadducees (Acts 5:17), or the "sect" of the Nazarenes (Acts 24:5,14), the word in the original is *hairesis*. The same word is sometimes translated factions or heresies. Splits in a congregation along party lines are factions or heresies (1 Corinthians 11:19), and factions are listed among the works of the flesh (Galatians 5:20). After Christianity had become established in the world, it became common to use the word heresy for any self-chosen view that was contrary to the truth Christianity taught. Thus the word heresy came to have a pejorative sense.

[11] Plummer (*ibid.*) has written, "The Greek word for 'destruction' occurs 6 times in the Greek text behind the KJV (5 times in the better text) -- and is rendered by them in no less than five ways -- 'damnable' and 'destructive' in this verse, 'pernicious' in verse 2, 'damnation' in verse 3, 'perdition' in 2:7, and 'destruction' in 3:16."

[12] Hell is the destiny of those who adopt "heresies" and thereby reject God's truth. Destruction is the opposite of salvation (cf. Matthew 7:13,14; Philippians 1:28; 2 Thessalonians 1:9). Hiebert is correct when he calls attention to the fact that destruction "does not mean extinction but ruination, not loss of being but loss of well-being" (*op. cit.*, p.89). The word speaks of the loss of everything that makes human existence worthwhile. In other words, it is not legitimate to use *apōleia* as a proof that annihilation is what the wicked have in store after the judgment.

[13] The word is *despotes* and denotes one who has supreme authority.

who records the fulfillment of Peter's prophecy, shows it was Jesus who was being denied. "Bought them" reminds us man's salvation was purchased with the blood of Christ (1 Peter 1:18,19; 1 John 2:2), and Romans 3:22-25 makes it clear this redemption is effective only for those who are faithful to the Lord. *Agoradzo* is one of three words in the New Testament translated "redeem." In classical Greek, this word spoke of purchasing something in the slave market.

"Who bought them" is a phrase over which theological battles have been fought.[14] The issue is the Calvinistic doctrine of eternal security.[15] Some insist verse 1 depicts the false teachers as persons who were once redeemed (i.e., bought by Christ) who then turn around and deny Him, only to be lost (as the close of verse 1 says).[16] Others insist the teachers who will habitually deny the Lord were never Christians in the first place since Jude 4 calls them "ungodly persons." We probably do not have enough information given in these verses to decide whether the heretics were once Christians or were just masquerading as Christians.[17] Their method of denial is not defined. How they denied the Lord, Peter does not say. Perhaps it was by their doctrine and/or perhaps by their lives. The incipient Gnostics about whom John wrote denied the Lord by their doctrine (1 John 2:22,23, 4:2,3). In Gnosticism, as it developed, the doctrinal denial of the Lord took one of two avenues: in the rush of things, it was Simon of Cyrene who was crucified, while Jesus stood by and watched; or the "Christ" came on Jesus at His baptism and departed from Jesus before He said "Father, into Thy hands I commend my spirit," leaving only the human Jesus to die. In either case, there was a denial of the atoning death of Christ. Perhaps they were denying the Lord by their lives. He bought them for His service but they were serving their own lusts (2:10). They were leading new converts astray (2:18,20). One of the most terrible ways to deny Christ is to seek to undo all He has done by influencing for evil the men for whom He died.

Bringing swift destruction upon themselves -- "The two participles, 'denying' and 'bringing,' without any conjunction to connect them, are awkward, and show that the writer's

---

[14] In the Introductory Studies we commented concerning the identity of the false teachers. Does "who bought them" indicate the false teachers were once Christians (actually redeemed) or does the verse simply say Christ's death was a ransom for all men's sins (potentially even theirs), but that they didn't accept such a doctrine?

[15] See the author's Special Study "Once Saved, Am I Always Saved?" in his *New Testament Epistles: Romans* (Moberly, MO: Scripture Exposition Books, 1996), p.397ff. (Pagination is different in the 1987 edition.)

[16] We recall Paul's prediction to the Ephesian elders that some of those very Christian leaders would go bad (Acts 20:28-32). So it is not impossible Peter's false teachers were once good men who went bad.

[17] The truth or falsity of the doctrine of the perseverance of the saints does not depend on this verse, but Bible students should be cognizant of the fact that many comments offered at this place are a rather obvious (and in some cases tortured) attempt to explain what 2 Peter must mean while at the same time not compromising or impinging on the doctrine of unconditional eternal security.

strong feeling is already beginning to ruffle the smoothness of his language."[18] The false teachers are introducing heresies of destruction into the church, denying the Lord, and by doing so are bringing upon themselves swift[19] destruction. There is no more certain way to ultimate condemnation than to deny the Lord and to teach others to sin! The false teachers bring this destruction[20] "upon themselves." No one compels them to deny the Lord who bought them. No one forces them to embrace religious error. They themselves chose these dangerous beliefs. If men perish, they perish by their own fault, for ample provision was made for their salvation, as well as for others, and they were freely invited to be saved. "Destruction ... destruction ... destruction!" Peter's hammering repetition of this word was intended to make a memorable impression on his readers. What happens if I embrace the heresy? I remember what Peter said, "destruction."

2:2 -- ***And many will follow their sensuality, and because of them the way of the truth will be maligned*;**

And many will follow their sensuality -- Verse 2 delineates two disastrous results of the work of the false teachers among the Christians: many will follow them, and others are led to speak evil of Christianity. Peter's prediction is the false teachers will be popular with many followers.[21] The tragic thing is these many followers will come from among people who were once members of Christ's church. Peter has used the verb *exakoloutheo* before (2 Peter 1:16), which means "to follow out to a conclusion, to pursue a line of thought to its termination." What a man teaches, or what he does, will often be carried way beyond what the teacher himself believes or does. "Sensuality" translates *aselgeiais*, a word that is plural in the Greek.[22] Perhaps the plural stands for habitual and repeated acts of sexual debauchery.

---

[18] Plummer, *ibid.* As we read on, because of the lack of smoothness of language, we will have difficulty deciding where sentences begin and end, and difficulty with punctuation and interpretation. But we can actually feel Peter's indignation as he hastens from thought to thought without careful grammatical connection.

[19] *Tachinos* can have here either of the two meanings ("swift" or "violent") explained at 1:14. If we take the "violent" connotation, we are immediately reminded of the doctrine of degrees of punishment in Hell.

[20] Here we see Peter's habit of repetition of key words. He repeats "destruction" three times in verses 1-3, "righteous" three times in verses 7,8, the verb "looking for" three times in 3:12-14. What the false teachers bring on themselves could be "destruction of health, property, and their own spiritual lives in this present world. That, of course, results in punishment in hell in the future world, including banishment from the presence of the Lord (2 Thessalonians 1:9). Involved in "destruction" is the loss of eternal life with God, and results in eternal misery and perdition, the lot of those excluded from the eternal kingdom of God. (See Thayer, *A Greek-English Lexicon of the New Testament* [New York: American Book Co., 1899], p.71).

[21] John also speaks of the popularity of the Gnostics he encountered. "The world listens to them," he wrote (1 John 4:5).

[22] See the word explained in notes at 1 Peter 4:3. There is a manuscript variation at this place. It is the sixth place in the Textus Receptus where the word *apoleia* occurs (see notes above on "destruction"). The KJV was translating the "when it offered "pernicious ways" as the reading for this verse. *Aselgeiais* is the better attested reading at this place.

The false teachers defended and practiced a wide spectrum of lascivious excesses,[23] feeling no shame even when committing wanton acts in public.

And because of them the way of the truth will be maligned -- This is a second disastrous result of the work of the false teachers among the Christians. Observers on the outside, watching how the followers[24] of the false teachers behaved, would speak contemptuously of Christianity. "The way" (*he hodos*, the road) is the path down which a person travels, in this case through life.[25] By calling it "the way" of truth Peter highlights the fact that each Christian's life is to be in total harmony with the "truth" taught by and embodied in Christ. The false teacher's converts had quit traveling the path of truth, but the outsiders, watching their sensuous lifestyle, did not know that. Those observers falsely assumed that what they saw was what Christianity actually was and so spoke contemptuously[26] of the way of truth. As he expressed in 1 Peter 1:12, where he said he wanted their behavior to be winsome or attractive to outsiders, so here Peter is concerned that Christians have a good reputation among outsiders.[27] What Peter here predicted regarding outsiders speaking reproachfully of Christianity because of observed evil behavior did come true.[28]

2:3 -- ***And in* their *greed they will exploit you with false words; their judgment from long ago is not idle, and their destruction is not asleep.***

And in *their* greed they will exploit you with false words -- Here is a third identifying mark of the false teachers whom Peter predicts will be coming. It is an honorable thing when Christian teachers are given a living wage (1 Corinthians 9:1-14; 1 Timothy 5:17,18), but

---

[23] See 2 Peter 2:10-15,18,19, 3:3, and Jude 4,8,12,13,16,18.

[24] The antecedent of "them" seems to be the "many" who follow the bad example of the false teachers in verse 2a, rather than the "false teachers" spoken of in verse 1.

[25] In the New Testament "the Way" was a common name for the Christian religion (since the way of salvation is found through the cross of Christ). Christ spoke of the narrow "way" of salvation (Matthew 7:13,14); the messengers of the Pharisees and Herodians acknowledged Christ taught "the way of God" (Mark 12:14); and Christ answered Thomas' question, "How do we know the way?" (John 14:5) by pointing to Himself, "I am the way" (John 14:6). People both inside and outside the early church used the designation of "the Way" to refer to Christianity (Acts 9:2, 19:9,23, 22:4, 24:14,22). It is the "way of salvation" (Acts 16:17), the "way of the Lord" (Acts 18:25), the "right way" (2 Peter 2:15), and the "way of righteousness" (2 Peter 2:21).

[26] "Maligned" translates *blasphemeo*, "to blaspheme, speak reproachfully of, rail at, revile."

[27] Similar thoughts are expressed in Romans 2:24 and Titus 2:5.

[28] Christians were said by some to be cannibals (a garbling of "eating His flesh and drinking His blood"). They committed incest ("brothers" and "sisters" lived together). They were atheists (they refused to honor the gods the heathen honored). Add to these misunderstandings the actual orgies promoted by the false teachers (2:13) and outsiders had a whole arsenal of ammunition against the Christians. In *Homily* xiii of 2 Clement, there is a remarkable amplification of this statement. It is likely 2 Peter was known to the writer of that homily. A different Clement, Clement of Alexandria (*Exhortation to the Heathen*, x) uses the expression "way of truth" and it may be an allusion to the existence of 2 Peter.

there was nothing honorable in what the false teachers would do. They were going to turn religion into a racket. Their motivation was greed or avarice[29] and they were going to take all the money they could get from the church members. There is deception in all rackets else the victims would never be fooled. "False words" would be the deception used by the false teachers. The word translated "false" (*plastois*, "plastic, feigned, molded") occurs nowhere else in the New Testament, but we think it is reminiscent of the "cunningly devised myths" of 1:16. Falsehood is easily resisted when it is an obvious falsehood. It is when it is cunningly dressed up and disguised as truth that it becomes threatening and menacing. It takes a devilish skill to put a spin on words so people think they are hearing the truth while at the same time the speaker is hiding his or her real motive and intent. That motive was to gain followers and then fleece them.[30] Peter can know such motives, of course, only by prophetic insight, and by the same means he can foresee that many of his readers ("you") will be the exploited ones.

Their judgment from long ago is not idle -- With this clause and the next, which Hiebert styles as sort of "Hebrew parallelism,"[31] Peter predicts what will happen to the false teachers and their followers.[32] "The sentence passed long ago on such false teachers will be carried out" is the gist of this first half of the parallel. *Krima* can be translated "condemnation, judgment, verdict, sentence." The word rendered "from long ago" (*ekpalai*) occurs only here and in 3:5 and takes us back to Old Testament times. "From the beginning God has condemned sin and inflicted suitable punishment on transgressors; and has promised in His word, from the earliest ages, to pour out His indignation on the wicked."[33] The Old Testament is full of pronouncements of doom on people who live like the false teachers and their followers (Deuteronomy 13:1-5; Jeremiah 14:14,15, 23:30-32, 27:10,14,15; Psalm 1:5-6). Jesus, too, had pronounced the certain doom of such teachers (Matthew 7:15-19). As surely as God lives the judgment is on its way ("is not idle").[34] The punishment, long ago predicted, will fall on these impure false teachers.

---

[29] *Pleonexia* is a compound from two words which mean "more" and "to have." The word is often translated covetousness, a greedy desire to have more.

[30] The literal meaning of *emporeuomai* is to travel, especially as a merchant on business, to go on a business trip. Sellers tried to gain customers, and buyers tried to curry a special relationship with sellers. Because shady deals often were involved in such trips, the word came to denote the selfish deception both buyer and seller tried to practice. So the false teachers worked to build a special relationship with their converts in order to take advantage of it for their own personal monetary benefit. "Exploit" is a good word to catch both ideas.

[31] Hiebert, *op. cit.*, p.93

[32] *Ois* is a dative plural and it can include both the false teachers and their dupes.

[33] Adam Clarke, "2 Peter," in *Clarke's Commentary on the New Testament* (Cincinnati: Methodist Book Concern, 1832), Vol.2, p.885.

[34] A cognate adjective for "idle" was used at 1 Peter 1:8. God has told men how He will judge the wicked, and men can be sure God will do what He has said. It is something like a sealed indictment handed down by a grand jury. The wheels of justice are moving, and the day will come when an arrest is made, a trial held, and a sentence imposed.

And their destruction is not asleep -- In the second half of the parallelism, "destruction" (*apoleia,* used twice in verse 1) is personified as "not drowsy."[35] "Perdition waits for them with unsleeping eyes" is how the NEB translates it. Perhaps there is personification here. The one assigned to do the punishing is not going to get drowsy and fall asleep and so fail to do his duty.[36] Punishment in hell is the ultimate end of the false teacher and his followers.

B. Historical Proof that God's Judgment is Not Idle. 2:4-10a

1. Angels who sinned were punished. 2:4

2:4 -- ***For if God did not spare angels when they sinned, but cast them into hell and committed them to pits of darkness, reserved for judgment;***

For if -- With "for" Peter introduces an explanation of something just said, namely that "judgment is not idle and destruction is not asleep." Some accuse Peter of writing another broken sentence here, starting out with an "if" and failing to write a proper conclusion.[37] We think Peter did not write a broken sentence. He wrote a very long sentence (verses 4-10a are one sentence in the Greek), and after three "if" clauses (verses 4,5,6), he writes his conclusion beginning in verse 9.[38] Each one of the "if" clauses is an example that God's judgment is not idle. Here in 2 Peter, the three examples (angels, flood, Sodom) appear to be in chronological order.[39]

God did not spare angels when they sinned -- The implication in Peter's words is this – if God did not spare (i.e., withhold punishment from) angels when they sinned, what makes you think He will spare men who are false teachers? Angels, like men, are specifically created beings.[40] Angels (at one time) were moral creatures who could choose between right and

---

35 The only other place in the New Testament the word *nustazo* ("asleep," became drowsy) occurs is in Matthew 25:5 in the parable of the wise and foolish bridesmaids.

36 Earthly judges may pronounce sentences that do not get carried out, but God does not. Though there is an appearance of delay, God does not forget (2 Peter 3:4-10).

37 "The sentence has no proper conclusion," wrote Plummer, *op. cit.*, p.153.

38 The NIV repeats the "if" four more times (verses 5,6,7,9). In the Greek it occurs only in verse 4, but it does govern what is said in verses 5 and 6, too.

39 In Jude the instances of God's judgment on the wicked are not in chronological order (unbelievers in the wilderness, angels, Sodom).

40 Colossians 1:16; Hebrews 1:7; Psalm 148:2,5, show that angels are created beings. They were present at the creation of the world (Job 38:7), so presumably their creation antedated Genesis 1:1. In the author's *New Testament Epistles: Hebrews* (Moberly, MO: Scripture Exposition Books, 1992), p.7-17, in the comments on Hebrews 1, there are a number of truths highlighted about the nature and work of angels.

wrong.[41] When they sinned, they were punished by God. Unlike men, angels do not seem to be subject to redemption from their sin (Hebrews 2:15). The fallen angels are also known as demons. The time when angels sinned is not specifically mentioned in the Old Testament, nor is it specified here in 2 Peter. It may be that not even Jude 6,7 helps us in regard to this timing since the meaning of that passage is disputed; others wonder if Jude is even a parallel to 2 Peter. We probably have three options from which to choose:

(1) There was *a rebellion in heaven*, evidently prior to the fall of man. A few details about this war in heaven resulting in Satan and his angels being cast out are found in Revelation 12:7-9.[42] Apparently, one-third of all the angels were involved in the rebellion led by Satan, (Revelation 12:4). Perhaps this is the "sin" Peter alludes to. Defenders of this view argue: (a) If we believe Peter gives illustrations in chronological order, then the fall of evil angels fits well since his second illustration is the flood in Noah's time. (b) There is no reason to interpret 2 Peter 2:4 in the light of Jude 6,7, for Jude's order (angels punished after the flood) doesn't match Peter's order (with angels punished before the flood). (c) While the Old Testament may not specifically tell of the rebellion in heaven and the origin of Satan, it is certainly implied. After all, there is a tradition about the fall of angels in all countries and in all religions, though the accounts given are various and contradictory.[43] Opponents of this view argue: (i) The rebellion in heaven option cannot be referred to here in 2 Peter. There is "no record of that rebellion in the Old Testament, and such a record in the Old Testament is implied in "judgment long ago is not idle." (ii) It affords no close analogy with the conduct of the false teachers."[44] (iii) Is "no longer a place for them in heaven" and "thrown down to the earth" (Revelation 12:8,9) anything like what Peter says happened in the instance he has in mind – "cast into Tartarus" (Greek) and "reserved in pits of darkness"? (iv) If fallen angels were, as Peter says, Tartarized and "committed to pits of darkness" until the judgment, how do we account for the demons' freedom to harass people, especially during the ministry of Jesus? Did they somehow get out of solitary confinement?

(2) Some think Peter refers to Jesus' summary *dismissal of the demons* during His earthly ministry. After the 70 returned from their memorable mission trip, they said, "Even the de-

---

[41] Job 4:18 and 15:15 imply that there was a time when angels were on probation. They were tested to see whether they would obey or rebel.

[42] This commentator interprets Revelation 12:7-9 to be a description of the origin of the devil's work in the world. The devil's rebellion (and subsequent "thrown down," verses 7-9) also precipitated God's plan for salvation to be provided, for the kingdom of our God and the authority of His Christ to be introduced, because God intended to counteract whatever accusations the devil might make against Christians on earth (Revelation 12:10). The devil's activity in the world also explains the opposition the radiant woman (Old Testament Israel?) and her son (the Christ) encountered (Revelation 12:1-6).

[43] Clarke, *ibid.*

[44] Plummer, *ibid.*, p.153

mons are subject to us." And Jesus replies, "I was watching Satan fall from heaven as lightening ..." (Luke 10:18). Opponents of this view argue: (i) If we accept this option, we must affirm Peter's illustrations are not chronological. (ii) Would demons being subject to us and even Jesus' personal casting out of demons be anything like the "judgment from long ago" which Peter is illustrating? (iii) Would Peter's readers know about it? Defenders of this view argue: (a) Yes, Peter's readers could know about the judgment on demons, for they have heard the gospel story (2 Peter 3:2) and they would get the idea that evil angels are judged and punished as the story unfolds. (b) It is only the commentators who have insisted Peter's illustrations are chronological. This second option, while fascinating, is hardly accepted by anyone as being what Peter had in mind.

(3) Some think Peter has in mind what is recorded at Genesis 6:2, where *the sons of God married the daughters of men.* This, they think, refers to some angels ("sons of God") who indulged in a sensual sin, similar to the sensuality of the false teachers in 2 Peter. Defenders of this view argue: (a) Angels are sometimes called "sons of God" in the Old Testament (Job 1:6, 7:1, 38:7). (b) We keep our "chronological" order – 2 Peter's three examples (angels, flood, cities of the plain) all come one after another in the early chapters of Genesis. (c) The sins of the false teachers and the angels would be analogous, i.e., sensuality. (d) The "angels" interpretation of Genesis 6:2 was held by first-century Jews, by Justin Martyr, Athenagoras, Cyprian, the Syrian Church, the Hellenistic and Palestinian synagogue.[45] (e) The appeal to Matthew 22:30/Luke 20:34-36 by opponents of the angelic view is misguided, putting a twist on the passage Jesus never intended.[46] (f) This view allows us to explain the demonic activ-

---

[45] G.F.C. Fronmüller, "The Second Epistle General of Peter," *Lange's Commentary* (Grand Rapids: Zondervan, reprint of 1867 ed.), p.27. That first-century Jews generally held the "angelic" interpretation of Genesis 6:2 can be seen from references in Tobit 6:14 (angels can have amatory desires towards women, it is implied); Josephus, *Ant.* i.3.1 (the history of Genesis 6:2 is described as a sin committed by angels cohabiting with mortal women, though nothing is said in Josephus about the punishment of the angels); 1 Enoch ch. 7:1,2 and ch. 5.13 (angels are said to have sinned by having sexual intercourse with women, and allusions to the doom of the sinning angels are numerous [see examples in a later footnote]; and the *Genesis Apocryphon (1QapGen col.2)* found among the Dead Sea Scrolls, in which Lamech (Noah's father) is concerned his son was conceived by one of the "Watchers." His wife assures him this was not the case. A translation of column 2 of *Gen. Apoc.* can be found in Theod. Gaster, *Dead Sea Scriptures* (New York: Doubleday, rev. and exp. ed., 1964), p. 257. (This volume, found at Qumran among the DSS, is intriguing. The scrolls were, it appears, Essene writings. Essene doctrine has been identified with the Colossian Heresy [J.B. Lightfoot, *St. Paul's Epistles to the Colossians and to Philemon* {Grand Rapids: Zondervan, reprint of 1879 ed.}, p. 349-419] -- i.e., it is not greatly differentiated from incipient Jewish Gnosticism which is repudiated in 2 Timothy, the Johannine epistles, and [we believe] in 2 Peter. The Qumran literature would reflect pre-Petrine Jewish ideas, at least among the Essene sectarians.)

[46] What are we to think of the argument based on Matthew 22:30/Luke 20:34-36 -- "they neither marry, nor are given in marriage, but are like the angels in heaven" -- that any idea that angels might have sex with human beings is out the question, so such an interpretation just cannot be the meaning of Genesis 6:1-4 or Jude 6,7? In the world of the occult, do we not hear of incubi and succubi? Does it really happen? Or, is this just titillating propaganda, devoid of any truth -- part of the devil's deception about his demonic helpers? And what is the point of Jesus' words in Matthew 22:30/Luke 20:34-36? When we let Luke's record guide us, it becomes evident in what sense resurrected men are like the angels, and thus there is no need for marriage between men and women in heaven. The likeness is this: they are no longer subject to the penalty of physical death since they are "sons of God, having participated in the resurrection." What Jesus is saying is that in the next world there is no need for reproducing offspring -- because the people counted worthy to attain that age are deathless like the angels. There is no need to marry and propagate to keep heaven populated. Seen in this light, the passage may say precisely nothing about whether or not angels could cohabit with humans.

ity in Jesus' time since we hold to the facticity of the pre-Adamic rebellion of all the angels who fell when Satan rebelled, but postulate that only some of the fallen angels were involved in Genesis 6. Those involved with women are now imprisoned, but the others were not so limited.[47] Opponents of this view argue: (i) "We deny that the angelic view is a proper interpretation of Genesis 6," said R.C. Foster.[48] (ii) "Angels" (there is no article before "angels" in 2 Peter) is not used of evil angels elsewhere in Scripture,[49] so it is doubtful 2 Peter refers to evil angels. (iii) Fronmüller wrote "as to Genesis 6:2, we are unable to abandon the view that it relates to the amalgamation of the Sethites ["sons of God"] and Cainites ["daughters of men"]." Cp. Luke 20:34-36, which is supposed to indicate angels could not be involved in sexual relationships.[50] (d) Peter's "angels when they sinned" probably would never have been interpreted otherwise than as setting forth the first fall in the realm of spirits [i.e., the rebellion in heaven] unless the parallel passage in Jude 6,7 had been believed to contain a reference to a *porneia* ("fornication") on the part of angels.[51] (e) While we have some idea of what happened to the men involved at Genesis 6, would the judgment or punish-

---

[47] C. Fred Dickason, *Demon Possession and the Christian* (Chicago: Moody, 1987), p.24, gives his opinion that fallen angels may be classified as "either confined or free." "The free," he writes, "have their abode in the heavenlies and have access to earth and its inhabitants (Ephesians 3:10, 6:12). Others are confined in several places. Some are in the abyss, or pit (Revelation 9:1-11). [Some demons in Christ's time entreated Him to refrain from sending them to the abyss, Luke 8:31] ... A particularly wicked group are kept in eternal bonds under darkness [reserved] for the judgment of the great day, Jude 6, 2 Peter 2:4."

[48] Foster, *ibid.* Several steps are needed to make Jude a reference to angels sinning with women. (1) At Jude 6,7, we will be told that angels "did not keep their own domain" or "abandoned their proper abode." This is then tied to Genesis 6:2. Once this connection is made, it is then affirmed that Jude is evidence that angels had relations with human women. Jude recognizes Peter's allusion and makes it more plain, it is argued by defenders of this view. (2) Since these presuppositions (what "proper abode" means and that it should be tied to Genesis 6:2) can be and have been disputed, defenders of the angel view appeal to *toutois* in Jude 7 and assert that it points back to the mention of angels in the previous verse. Having thus tied angels and Sodom and Gomorrah together, they can affirm that the angels of Genesis 6 acted sensuously, just as did the Sodomites. Keil has replied that *toutois* in verse 7 clearly points back, not to angels in verse 6, but to the inhabitants of Sodom and Gomorrah (earlier in this very verse 7), and he also affirmed this reference to Sodom and Gomorrah explains why the pronoun *toutois* (in verse 7) is masculine (quoted by Fronmüller, *op. cit.*, p.27).

[49] Before the Bible student accepts this categorical statement, attention will have to be given to 1 Corinthians 6:3 -- where "angels" is anarthrous, and evil angels may be intended.

[50] The problem of the interpretation of Luke 20 has already been alluded to in a previous footnote. "The Sethite interpretation (of Genesis 6:2) was held by writers of the Middle ages, by Julius Africanus, Ephraem the Syrian, Luther, Melanchthon, Calvin." Fronmüller, *ibid.*

[51] Fronmüller, *ibid.* Henry Alford (*Commentary on Jude* [London: Rivingtons, 1871], Vol.4, p.533) wonders whether Jude 6,7 was ever intended to be taken as a parallel to 2 Peter 2:4.

ment of angels who allegedly sinned at that time then been known to readers?[52]

This commentator knows of no way to decide between the first and the third views. He accepted view #1 as correct years ago, but now wonders if view #3 isn't the correct one.

But cast them into hell -- Marshall's interlinear gives "consigned to Tartarus" as a translation for *tartarosas*, the word Peter uses here.[53] It is an aorist participle grammatically dependent on the verb "committed." This consignment to Tartarus apparently does not refer to the final punishment of the devil and his angels;[54] that will occur when they are cast into the lake of fire after the final judgment (Revelation 20:10; Matthew 25:41). Instead, Tartarus[55] is a place of preliminary confinement for the angels who sinned, for before this verse is ended Peter will specifically say the fallen angels are "reserved for judgment."[56]

---

[52] Popular opinion certainly had it that the angels were punished. J.R. Lumby, "The General Epistle of Jude," in *The Bible Commentary*, edited by F.C. Cook (New York: Scribners, 1904), p.394, has written this: "The offenders are called at first angels, sons of heaven (1 Enoch vii.2), and after their transgression Azazel, one of their leaders, is described as bound hand and foot and cast into darkness (x.6); there shall he remain forever, cover his face that he may not see the light -- and in the great day of judgment let him be cast into the fire. And of the others who were with him it is afterwards said (x.15), 'Bind them for seventy generations underneath the earth even to the day of judgment.' And similar mention is made (xxi.6) of the prison of the angels. In the Midrash Ruth (quoted as a marginal note in Zohar ed. Cremona, 1559, col. 184), it is said, 'After the sons of God had begotten children, God took them and led them to a mountain of darkness, and bound them in iron chains which stretch to the middle of the great abyss'."

[53] The verb form of the word occurs only here in the Bible, though the noun form is found in the LXX at Job 40:15 and 41:23.

[54] Since *geenna* (Gehenna) is the usual word translated "hell" (the final place of punishment for the wicked), the "cast them down to hell" reading of the KJV and the "cast them into hell" reading of the NASB both can give a wrong idea at this verse if in fact we are trying to sort out in our minds what the unseen spiritual world looks like. See the author's *Commentary on Acts* in the Special Study on "Hades and The Intermediate Place of the Dead," for explanations of the places that in the Bible are called Hades, Tartarus, and Hell. If the use of "Hell" here is simply to give English readers an approximate idea of the horrible conditions of the confinement then it may be a permissible rendering. The marginal note in the ASV (Gr. *Tartarus*) could well have been repeated in the NASB to let the readers know the Greek word at this place is not *geenna* (hell).

[55] Not only is the word "Tartarus" found in the LXX and in 2 Peter, it is also found in Greek mythology. It may be saying too much to say the word "originated in Greek mythology" (Hiebert, *op. cit.*, p.97), but we certainly can agree it was used in Greek mythology, where Tartarus was pictured as a place beneath Hades where "divine punishment was meted out" (Arndt and Gingrich, *op. cit.*, p.813). It was a place of darkness and gloom, and the Titans and the giants who had rebelled against Zeus were confined there. Josephus (*Contra Apion*, ii.33) speaks of the oldest heathen gods as fettered in Tartarus. Clarke (*op. cit.*, p.885,886), has a number of citations from Greek writers on "Tartarus."

[56] Peter puts angels who sinned in Tartarus. The idea of some Bible students that Tartarus also is a place for the souls of wicked men is an interpretation formed by comparing what is said of wicked angels in this verse and what is said concerning wicked men in verse 9. It may not be quite "calling Bible things by Bible names" to say that the intermediate abode of wicked men is "Tartarus." Hades would be a better term for the place where the souls of wicked men are since Jesus rose from the dead (Revelation 20:14).

And committed them to pits of darkness -- In harmony with His long-revealed promise of what would happen to the wicked (verse 3), God delivered the angels who sinned to pits of darkness, consigning them to Tartarus.[57] "Committed" is to give over into the hands of another, to deliver to someone to keep, and is often used of handing someone over for imprisonment (Acts 8:3, 12:4). The KJV reads "chains of darkness;" Jude 6 also speaks of "chains;" and the manuscripts are pretty well divided here in 2 Peter between *seirois* (or *sirois*),[58] "pits," and *seirais* (or *sirais*),[59] "chains." A "pit" was an underground silo for holding grain. Such pits were used as prisons in Bible times,[60] and "pits" were sometimes dug to trap wolves or other wild animals. The word translated "chains" could also be of cords or of ropes. If we read "chains" the verse probably says the darkness itself is the chain that keeps the fallen angels prisoners. If we read "pits" it probably says that inside the pits of Tartarus it is dark and gloomy. There are several Greek words for "darkness,"[61] and the one used here is the synonym for the gloom of twilight.

Reserved for judgment -- "Reserved" (*teroumenous*, "kept, guarded") is a present participle, the guarding is going on right now.[62] This guarding is "for" (*eis*, "unto, with a view to") the judgment. It is merely temporal, until the judgment. No definite allusion to the time of the judgment is found here in chapter 2; Peter does refer to the day of the Lord (i.e., the final judgment) in chapter 3. Jude speaks of the "judgment of the great day."

---

[57] The subject and object of "committed" are understood from the context. This is one place where the action of the aorist participle ("tartarized") may be simultaneous with the action of the main verb which is also aorist tense. See J.G. Machen, *New Testament Greek for Beginners* (New York: Macmillan, 1969 reprinting), p.206, where he discusses how the aorist participle is sometimes used to denote the same act as the leading verb.

[58] The codices named Sinaiticus, Alexandrinus, Vaticanus, and Ephraemi all read "pits."

[59] P[72] and most of the Byzantine manuscripts read "chains." Metzger (*op. cit.*, p.702) argues that "chains is both the oldest [attested reading] and the most widespread, being supported by many versional and patristic witnesses, as well as by almost all minuscules," and therefore he thinks it is what Peter wrote.

[60] Genesis 37:20; Isaiah 24:22; Zechariah 9:11.

[61] There is *gnophos* which describes the darkness that accompanies a storm, *achlus* which is a misty darkness, and *zophos* the gloom of twilight.

[62] Again the question must be asked, If the demons are "committed to pits of darkness, tartarized, and reserved unto the judgment," how can the present world be demonized? Bengel (*op. cit.*, p.96,97) thinks it is possible for prisoners in Tartarus to dwell also on the earth (Luke 8:31; Ephesians 2:2; Revelation 9:11,13, 12:9, just as it is possible for one taken captive in war to walk beyond the place of his captivity. If we have outlined Revelation correctly, seeing several cycles through history to the final judgment, then Revelation 9 is something that happens during the church age. Revelation 9:1ff has a "star from heaven" opening the "shaft of the abyss" and letting out the demonic locusts. Perhaps this is how some demons get out of Tartarus to demonize the earth. It happens only when heaven permits. Grotius thinks the "guarding" indicates their inability to go beyond the confines of the place assigned to them, or to do anything without God's permission. Merrill F. Unger (*Biblical Demonology* [Wheaton, IL: Scripture Press, 1952], p.52) believes there are two classes of wicked angels. One class that sinned with women (Genesis 6, see above), and one class that rebelled but did not get involved with mortal women. Those not involved with women are still able to demonize the world. Those involved with women are out of circulation, reserved in Tartarus, and not able to go elsewhere.

The point of verse 4 is this: just as God said He would handle those who sin, God punished angels who sinned. Where those angels are now is a place of punishment, and they have the final judgment yet to face. From an example like this, it is certain that God will keep His Word and will also punish the false teachers who are in a state of rebellion against Him.

2. Ungodly people in Noah's time were punished. 2:5

2:5 -- ***And did not spare the ancient world, but preserved Noah, a preacher of righteousness, with seven others, when He brought a flood upon the world of the ungodly;***

And did not spare the ancient world -- This is Peter's second historical proof that God's "judgment from long ago is not idle" (verse 3). Again, God's divine sentence passed long ago on the wicked was carried out in history. As in verse 4, "did not spare" means God did not withhold punishment when it was deserved. The "ancient world" describes how things were before the flood in Noah's time. "World" is often used of the generation or races of men living at a given time; perhaps "world" is defined by "ungodly" at the close of verse 5, showing it is limited to men in this context. "World" is also used in Scripture to include the physical creation as well as man; perhaps "world" in this context is distinguished from the "ungodly" at the close of the verse.[63]

But preserved Noah ... with seven others -- Here, for the first time, comes the idea of the preservation of the righteous, which is further worked out in the next verses. Peter desires to encourage as well as to warn, so he calls attention to God's mercy in preserving Noah and his family. "Preserved" means to "guard a person so that he remains safe, that is, lest he suffer violence, or be despoiled."[64] It is not a reference to spiritual salvation, for Noah was a saved man before he entered the ark. It speaks of preservation from the kind of punishment that befell the ungodly. The Greek, *ogdoon Noe*, "an eighth, Noah," is a common classical idiom, generally with the pronoun *autos*, for "with seven others."[65] The others were Noah's wife, his three sons and their wives. Peter thus shows that the wicked world would be punished,

---

[63] This commentator is a catastrophist. He believes there were some marked changes on our globe, and perhaps in the universe, at the time of the flood. (For this, see more at 2 Peter 3:6,7.) Was it a universal flood? "If not, why two of every kind of animals?" asked R.C. Foster. He also called attention to the Code of Hammurabi. If there were such a thing as a universal flood, you would expect to find references to such in ancient writings besides the Bible. And you do, in places like the Code and the Gilgamesh Epic. Professor Foster then asked, "What about the argument against the flood being universal, that if it were you would have to bring animals from all over the world (like from North America, etc.) to the Ark?" He forcefully replied to his own question, "You couldn't move the animals six inches without the help of Almighty God. Did Noah climb up into the trees and set traps for all the birds? Noah didn't have to go catch or round up the animals. God brought them to the ark and Noah loaded them aboard." Do we have a renovated earth after the flood? We think so. See 2 Peter 3.

[64] Kenneth S. Wuest, *In These Last Days: II Peter, I,II,III John and Jude in the Greek New Testament* (Grand Rapids: Eerdmans, 1954), p.50.

[65] 1 Peter 3:20 also gives the number of those saved from the flood.

however numerous they might be. And the righteous, however few, would be saved. "The point is that the punishment must have been signal indeed, if only eight persons out of the whole world escaped."[66]

A preacher of righteousness -- The Genesis record (Genesis 6:9) tells us that Noah himself was a righteous man, who walked with God, but we do not read about his preaching in the Old Testament. Josephus (*Ant.* i.3.1) reflects Jewish tradition that Noah tried to persuade his neighbors to change their minds and their actions for the better. Peter's Greek word for "preacher" is herald. A herald in ancient times was a highly honored person, frequently a spokesman for the emperor, or an ambassador from one country to another. Noah was an ambassador for God. He brought an announcement and a proclamation from God. "Righteousness" can be either right relationships with God, or right relationships with one's fellow man. We can see Noah preaching both. We presume Noah preached the whole 120 years he was engaged in building the ark, warning people about the coming judgment of the flood and showing the way to personal salvation. We suppose Peter has deliberately made this rather pointed contrast between Noah, who preached and practiced righteousness, and the false teachers, who did the exact opposite. And who was it that was preserved?

When He brought a flood upon the world of the ungodly -- In verse 1, the ungodly are represented as bringing upon themselves swift destruction. Here God brings the punishment upon the ungodly. The same Greek word *epago* is used in both places.[67] "Flood" translates *kataclusmos*; transliterated, it is "cataclysm." The flood was a momentous and violent event marked with overwhelming upheaval and demolition.[68] "The ungodly" are men who have no reverential awe for God. These men lost their physical lives as they drowned in the rising waters, and then what happened to their souls? Was drowning their only punishment? No. 1 Peter 3:19,20 has already told us those "who were disobedient in the days of Noah" are also "in prison," i.e., the intermediate place of punishment. They too are waiting the final judgment and the eternal punishment to be meted out to the ungodly. In harmony with His announced judgment against wickedness, God cut off the wicked antediluvian race. This serves as a warning that He will punish the ungodly, no matter how many they are or when they live. The false teachers and their followers ought not to fool themselves that they can continue in sin with impunity. Those struggling to resist the temptations to quit living righteous lives should take courage from what happened to Noah and the seven others.

---

[66] Plummer, *op. cit.*, p.154.

[67] The verb means "to cause something to befall one," usually something evil. It is used of setting or letting loose the dogs.

[68] There are flood tides (*plemmura*, Luke 6:48) triggered by storms, and river floods (*potamos*, Matthew 7:25,27) following a downpour of rain, but what happened in Noah's day dwarfs these acts of God. Peter uses the same word for flood found in the LXX at Genesis 6:17. In the New Testament and early Christian literature *kataclusmos* is used "only for the flood in Noah's time" (Arndt and Gingrich, *op. cit.*, p.412).

3. The ungodly in Sodom and Gomorrah were punished. 2:6-8

2:6 -- *And* if *He condemned the cities of Sodom and Gomorrah to destruction by reducing* them *to ashes, having made them an example to those who would live ungodly thereafter;*

And *if* -- This is Peter's third historical proof that God's "judgment from long ago is not idle" (verse 3).[69] He acted in harmony with His long-stated policy in His dealings with Sodom and Gomorrah.

God condemned the cities of Sodom and Gomorrah to destruction -- The Biblical account of the destruction of Sodom and Gomorrah and the cities of the plain is found in Genesis 18,19. The messenger of God foretells the fate of the cities. Abraham then pleads with God for the city, asking that if even 10 righteous souls are found in it that the cities be spared. But when the angels visit Lot, they are made the intended object of the abominable lust of the Sodomites. This seals the fate of the city and God calls Lot and his family from the city. They are saved, except the wife of Lot, who, seemingly because she cannot make a clean break with the city, looks back and is turned into a pillar of salt. It was the gross immorality of the people in these ancient cities which brought about their overthrow. We suppose Peter picked this example as a lesson to those who were thinking of listening to the sensual false teachers. *Katastrophe*, the very word used in the LXX for what happened to the cities (Genesis 19:29), is translated "overthrow" in the ASV and "destruction" in the NASB.[70] The destruction of the cities was so thorough that their very location has been a matter of uncertainty.[71]

By reducing *them* to ashes -- The striking word *tephrosas*, occurring nowhere else in the New Testament, means either "reduce to ashes" or "cover with ashes." The same word is found in a description of what happened to a nearby town in the eruption of Mt. Vesuvius.[72] The Old Testament account reads, "The Lord rained on Sodom and Gomorrah brimstone and

---

[69] On the "if" in italics, see notes at the beginning of verse 4.

[70] The word also is used at 2 Timothy 2:14, where wrangling about words results in the "ruin" of some Christians. P^{72} and Codex Vaticanus omit the noun *katastrophe*. While some think it was not part of the original text, most of our critical Greek texts contain it. See the evidence in the apparatus of UBS^2 or Nestle-Aland, or in Metzger (*op. cit.*, p.702) who argues the word was accidentally omitted by a scribe.

[71] There was a time when scholars supposed the cities were located in what is now the southern end of the Dead Sea, south of the Lisan peninsula (see Ralph E. Baney, *The Search for Sodom and Gomorrah* [Kansas City: CAM Press, 1962]). In the late 1970's, when the water level of the Dead Sea dropped because the Jordan River water was being diverted to irrigate the Shepelah, archaeologists were able to explore the exposed sea floor, but failed to find evidence the cities were located in that area. However, two scholars have proposed that along what would have been the southeast shore of the sea, and along the east side of the Ghor south of the shore line, there are ruins of five cities that just might be the ancient cities of the plain. ("Have Sodom and Gomorrah Been Found?" *Biblical Archaeology Review*, 5/6 [Sep.-Oct. 1980], p.26-36.)

[72] Moulton and Milligan, *The Vocabulary of the Greek Testament* (London: Hodder and Stoughton, 1963), p.632, where it is translated "being overwhelmed with ashes."

fire" (Genesis 19:24, cf. Luke 17:29).[73] "Judgment" of Sodom and Gomorrah by fire is a fitting prelude to 2 Peter 3:6,7 where the whole world is to be "destroyed" by fire.

Having made them an example to those who would live ungodly thereafter -- To Peter, this is the abiding significance of what happened to Sodom and Gomorrah. It was God's intention that His destruction of those cities should serve as a warning to anyone who was about to live an ungodly life in future ages. "Having made" is a perfect tense participle, marking an event which has a continuing result – i.e., it is still an abiding example[74] to coming generations of the ruin which ungodliness brings. "Let our age take notice!"[75] Of course, the destruction of their town and their physical lives was not the end of their punishment. By the overthrow they were hurled into "eternity" where there will be abiding torment.

2:7 -- ***And if He rescued righteous Lot, oppressed by the sensual conduct of unprincipled men***

And if he rescued righteous Lot -- Just as was true in the time of the flood, so it was when the ungodly in Sodom and Gomorrah were being destroyed. At that very same time God was rescuing the righteous. The verb "rescued" (*errusato*) stands at the end of the verse for emphasis. Peter's readers who would, like Lot, remain "righteous" in the face of serious sensual temptations, would find themselves the objects of God's mercy just as Lot did.[76] Lot's escape was not the result of a last minute decision to repent and quit any further personal participation in the sins of his neighbors; he has been a righteous man all along,[77] though it wasn't always easy to stand for the right. The Old Testament record of Lot's rescue is found

---

[73] We are not excited by certain naturalistic explanations of what happened to the cities of the plain. One author notes that "the area is rich in bitumen, salt, and sulfur, and has been geologically active in historical times" (Blum, *op. cit.*, p.278). Luke 17:29 says God rained fire and brimstone "from heaven." If we accept what Jesus said, we hardly think one can posit a volcano erupting as the whole cause of what happened.

[74] Three words are translated "example," *hupodeigma* (an example to be shunned), *paradeigma* (an example to be followed), and *deigma* (a simple exhibition), though the differences are not always observed. The word here is *hupodeigma*, an example for imitation or warning, a different word from the one translated "example" at 1 Peter 2:21. *Hupodeigma* is used in this sense at John 13:15, Hebrews 4:11, and James 5:10. (G.R. Berry, *A New Greek-English Lexicon to the New Testament* [Chicago: Wilcox and Follett, 1948], p.103.)

[75] Hiebert, *op. cit.*, p.102.

[76] This brighter side of rescue of the righteous while the wicked are being judged is not included in Jude. By the time he writes, many of his readers have chosen to join the false teachers and are abandoning the way of righteousness.

[77] Peter's evaluation of Lot as being "righteous," at first sight, seems at variance with Lot's willingness to remain for the sake of earthly advantage in the valley where the five cities were located. "Righteous" does not say a man is sinless perfect, but it does say the tenor of his life is right, regularly in harmony with what God has revealed. He showed hospitality to the messengers from God (Genesis 19:2,3,8). Compare his rescue from the city in light of Abraham's appeal concerning just "10 righteous people" (Genesis 18:32). If Lot wasn't "righteous," why was he tormented and distressed by the filthy lives of his neighbors? See also his belief and obedience when told to leave all and flee. Zoar was saved at his intercession (Genesis 19:21). For Peter to call Lot "righteous" is not without warrant.

in Genesis 19:1-29. Not only was Lot "righteous," Abraham's intercession (Genesis 18:16-23) also had something to do with Lot's being rescued. "Righteous" is a word used three times of Lot in these verses.[78] If he had not been righteous, there would have been no rescue! When they find someone who objects to their sensuous lifestyle, will the false teachers use Lot[79] as an example to show it is OK to live in Sodom? Were they going to say, 'You'll still be rescued from any danger?' If so, Peter anticipates their twisted argument, insisting Lot was rescued because he was righteous. He was not at all like his debauched neighbors, not at all like the false teachers.

Oppressed by the sensual conduct of unprincipled men -- "Oppressed" represents *kataponoumenon*, "worn out, worn down and exhausted by the toil."[80] "Sensual" is the same word used in verses 2 and 18 for unbridled lust, wantonness, shamelessness. "Conduct" translates *anastrophe*, "manner of life."[81] "Unprincipled" is *athesmon*, found elsewhere in the New Testament only at 2 Peter 3:17, and is related to the *athemitois* ("abominable") of 1 Peter 4:3. The noun *thesmos* denotes a custom which was regarded as having divine approval,[82] so *athesmon* speaks of breaking and trampling the restraints and expectations of one's contemporary society. A man has to be pretty bad when he plunges ahead to do what even a pagan society thinks is taboo. That is how life was in Sodom and Gomorrah.

---

[78] These repetitions of the same word, of which Peter was fond in 2 Peter, and of which there are several examples in this epistle ("destruction" used three times, 2:1-3; "looking for" three times in 3:12-14), and which have been stigmatized as showing the paucity of Peter's vocabulary, are perfectly normal in Peter or any one who is speaking out of strong emotions. A person writing under strong emotion does not stop to pick his words. He uses the same word over and over to get across the point he is trying to make. Perhaps the audience will at least remember the words that were repeatedly emphasized.

[79] Many of the rabbinical interpreters, measuring Lot by the standard of the Law, regarded him as a notorious sinner (Hermann L. Strack and Paul Billerbeck, *Kommentar zum Neuen Testament aus Talmud und Midrasch* [Munchen: Beck, 1926], Vol.3, p. 769-771). Would the Jewish Gnostics follow the rabbi's lead and paint Lot with the same dirty brush as they tried to use him as a Biblical example to show that what they were doing was not condemned by God?

[80] The only other place the word occurs in the New Testament is Acts 7:24, where it describes how the Israelites in Egyptian captivity were "oppressed."

[81] This is a favorite word of Peter's. It appears 6 times in 1 Peter, and twice in 2 Peter (here and 3:11). Elsewhere it occurs in the New Testament only 5 times.

[82] In the beginning, God revealed Himself and His rules to men. Some of these were handed down orally from generation to generation, so that society had certain mores that everyone accepted (cp. Acts 10:28).

2:8 -- *(for by what he saw and heard* that *righteous man, while living among them, felt* his *righteous soul tormented day after day with* their *lawless deeds),*

(For -- *Gar* tells us that verse 8 is an explanation of what it was that caused Lot to feel oppressed. Some versions put the verse in parentheses; some set it off with a dash to help modern readers see that it is a further explanation. "Peter's illustration did not demand this explanation, but he apparently added it to encourage his readers, knowing they would face a similar situation when the false teachers assailed them with their libertine excesses."[83]

By what he saw and heard *that* righteous man, while living among them -- It was through his own choice that he had settled down and was living in Sodom (Genesis 13:11), but it was not a good neighborhood in which to live. He was a righteous man,[84] and what he personally saw and heard, day in and day out, was painful to him. He "saw and heard" because the townspeople had no shame or sense of decency; they didn't care who saw them as they committed their "sensual" (see verses 2 and 7) acts. Because the corruption of Sodom was open and shameless, though Lot did not go looking for it, he could not help but see and hear.

Felt *his* righteous soul tormented day after day with *their* lawless deeds) -- *Basanidzo*, "mental torture," is an active voice verb. Rather than the lawless tormenting his soul, it was he, the righteous man, who tormented his own soul. Some suggest Lot's mental anguish resulted from his sustained effort to resist the temptation of falling into the like vices himself.[85] Day in and day out, for upward of twenty years, just in normal contact with his neighbors, he observed their "lawless" deeds.[86] If he had not been shocked and horrified by what he saw, he likely soon would have joined them.[87]

---

[83] Hiebert, *op. cit.*, p.104.

[84] See notes on verse 7 on this assessment of Lot's own lifestyle.

[85] "Soul" is not an easy word to define. Sometimes it speaks of the center of one's feelings and emotions. Sometimes "soul" is that part of a man that animates the body, giving directions to the various parts of the body regarding how they are to function (step here, pick that up, touch that, avoid that, go there, look at this, eat that).

[86] "Lawless" here (*anomos*, a different word than *athesmos* used in the previous verse) indicates the inhabitants of Sodom and Gomorrah were acting in defiance of God's laws, not just in defiance of cultural mores. In every age, Patriarchal, Mosaic, and Christian, men have had a specific revelation from God of His laws for that age, though they were not always written as was the Mosaic Law. In comments on Acts 15:20 (see the author's commentary, *in loc.*), we speak about the Noachide Laws, which, according to rabbinic interpretation of Genesis, the whole race was commanded to observe. Such oral laws were what the people of Sodom and Gomorrah were transgressing.

[87] Cardinal Newman once said, "Our great security against sin lies in being shocked at it." "Herein is something very significant. It often happens that, when evils first emerge, people are shocked and disturbed at them; but, as time goes on, they begin to cease to be shocked and to accept them as a matter of course. There are many things at which we ought to be shocked and horror-stricken. In our own generation there is the problem of prostitution, promiscuity, drunkenness, the extraordinary gambling fever, the breakdown of the marriage bond,

4. Peter's conclusion drawn from the three examples. 2:9-10a

2:9 -- Then *the Lord knows how to rescue the godly from temptation, and to keep the unrighteous under punishment for the day of judgment,*

Then -- We have come to the conclusion of the long sentence begun with "if" in verse 4. From the three examples of God's judgment on the wicked and the two examples of His mercy upon the righteous, Peter draws this conclusion.

The Lord knows how to rescue the godly from temptation -- The "Lord" is God the Father, according to verse 4.[88] "Knows" carries the idea that He has the power to do it. "Rescue" is the same verb used in verse 7. He can send an angel to take the tempted by the hand. He can interpose and destroy the power of the tempter. He can raise up earthly friends. He can deliver His people completely and forever from temptation by their removal to heaven. The "godly" are the people like Noah and Lot who walk in faith with the living God, and who give God His due respect and reverence. Note who gets delivered – godly people, not the deliberately licentious. Peter promises God will rescue godly people "from temptation."[89] When a man is determined to be godly, God will interpose and remove the solicitations to evil, just as He did in Lot's case.[90]

And to keep the unrighteous under punishment for the day of judgment -- Whether they be wicked angels in Tartarus or wicked men in the prison of Hades, it can be seen from Peter's examples that God knows how – and has the power "to keep" or reserve[91] – the "unright-

---

violence, crime, death on the roads [caused by drunken drivers, random drive-by shootings, child abuse, murders of children by children, drug related crimes affecting both the addicts and their victims,flaunting of gay lifestyles], etc. And in many cases the tragedy is these things have ceased to shock in any real sense of the term." Barclay, *op. cit.*, p.387.

88 Because of the long "if" clause, Peter restates the subject as he draws his conclusion. Calling God "Lord" indicates His authority to treat both the righteous and the wicked as He does.

89 See notes at 1 Peter 1:6 on the word *peirasmos*. The Greek may be translated either "from temptation," i.e., God can put limits on how much the devil is allowed to tempt Christians (Matthew 6:13), or it may be "out of temptation," i.e., when a person is tempted God makes the way of escape evident to the Christian (1 Corinthians 10:13).

90 There are promises elsewhere that God will put limitations on what the tempter (the Devil) can do (Matthew 6:13). He will, when His children are tempted, also make the way of escape (1 Corinthians 10:13). "The illustrations of Noah and Lot make clear that God determines the time and manner of their rescue. He may for long years sustain them amid their trials before He intervenes to rescue them out of the difficulty." Hiebert, *op. cit.*, p.106.

91 The same root word was translated "reserved" in verse 4. While the grammar in Peter's concluding statement may not be the smoothest, this "keeping under punishment" is what he specially wishes to drive home.

eous"[92] until the day of final judgment, while continuing their punishment[93] during all the time intervening until then. Certainly included among those whom God classifies as "unrighteous" would be the false teachers and their duped followers.

2:10a -- ***And especially those who indulge the flesh in*** **its** ***corrupt desires and despise authority.***

And especially -- "Especially" is *malista,* meaning "chiefly, most of all, particularly." If God will punish sinners of all kinds, He will certainly and above all punish such as are about to be described. Peter has his eye on the coming false teachers and wishes to stress the enormity of their sin. Perhaps God's punishment falls on this class of sinners with a special severity.

Those who indulge the flesh in ***its*** **corrupt desires** -- *Poreuomai* ("to walk, journey, go"), translated "indulge" in the NASB, pictures the ungodly as persistently following a certain trail or course of life.[94] Peter uses *opiso sarkos* ("after the flesh") to name that course of life. *Opiso* is used of the act of joining a certain person as an attendant or follower, or running after the thing one lusts for.[95] *Sarkos* ("flesh") has no article, so is qualitative. The false teachers are pictured as following what "flesh" prompts them to do rather than what their spirits or the Spirit of God prompts them to do.[96] Peter's next words are *en epithumia miasmou*, "in passionate desires of defilement" or "that cause defilement."[97] The false teachers

---

[92] Both the Greek words for "godly" and "unrighteous" are without an article in the Greek. This shows that a class of beings, whoever they be, is intended.

[93] *Kolazomenous* is a present tense participle. The punishment is already going on, long before the day of final judgment dawns. Men do not have to wait until the final judgment to find out where they are going to spend eternity. Whether a man is "perishing" or has "eternal life" is something knowable in this present life (John 3:16,36). The final judgment is a vindication of God for the rewards and punishments already in part bestowed while those souls were in the intermediate state. Luke 16 (the rich man and Lazarus) shows that when physical death occurs, a soul in the intermediate state is either in bliss or torment. Temporal death (even violent death like the antediluvians and the residents of Sodom and Gomorrah experienced) does not exhaust the wrath of God, nor does the punishment in the intermediate state. The great judgment day is followed by the lake of fire for the wicked (Revelation 20:11-15).

[94] We observe that Peter's verb tenses change from future to present in this verse.

[95] Wuest, *op. cit.*, p.53.

[96] At this place extreme care must be taken lest our explanations suggest or imply inherited total depravity is a Biblical doctrine. (See "The Doctrine of Original Sin," in the author's *New Testament Epistles: Romans* [Moberly, MO: Scripture Exposition Books, 1996] p.231ff [pagination is different in the 1987 printing]; and his "Total Hereditary Depravity -- The Big Lie," in *Trust God: A Symposium on Calvinism* [Cincinnati, OH: Christian Restoration Association, 1998.) The devil has the ability to plant thoughts in our minds (Acts 5:3) and to stir up the desires of our bodies (Paul describes this as living in a "body of sin," Romans 6:6). Such temptations are the source of evil desires we all experience from time to time.

[97] The NASB's addition of "its" and the rendering "corrupt desires" is a bad example of writing a translators' theology into the translation, for it is the language of total hereditary depravity, and is not what Peter wrote at all! The NIV is even worse with its "who follow the corrupt desire of the sinful nature." *Miasmos* ("defilement") refers to the act of defiling; it pictures a process going on (Thayer, *op. cit.*, p.414; W.E. Vine, *An Expository Dictionary of New Testament Words with Their Precise Meanings for English Readers* [Westwood, NJ: Revell, 1965 reprinting], p.286). If the word pictures a process, with what justification can it be translated as if it were in the past, the result of Adam's sin, rather than the present, the result of the false teachers' own personal sins?

were desiring the very things that would defile them.[98]

And despise authority -- The present participle "despise"[99] denotes an habitual attitude towards "authority" all the while they are indulging the flesh. *Kuriotetos* is "lordship, dominion, or authority." Jude has the same word in verse 8. Perhaps they were despising the Lordship of Christ. Peter has previously said they were denying the Master who bought them (2:1). Perhaps it speaks of despising angelic dignities (as in Colossians 1:16 and Ephesians 1:21). Perhaps it speaks of despising civil authorities who try to enforce laws against sexual perversion. Perhaps it speaks of despising church leaders, who try to discipline sinning members. Any effort to govern and control their excesses is looked on with contempt and disregard. These are the ones especially on whom God's punishment will fall.

C. Further Description of the False Teachers. 2:10b-19

1. Their negative attitude toward "glories." 2:10b,11

2:10b -- *Daring, self-willed, they do not tremble when they revile angelic majesties,*

Daring, self-willed -- The NASB begins a new sentence here; Plummer long ago suggested a fresh verse should begin here since the Greek construction is entirely changed and a fresh subject is begun. No longer are we developing the idea that "their judgment from long ago is not idle." Now we enter into a colorful and scathing description of the false teachers. Peter starts with two exclamations. "Daring" (*tolmetai*), found only here in the New Testament, means bold, brazen, audacious, recklessly presumptuous as they defy the authority of God and man. There are two kinds of daring: there is the daring to do a noble thing, the mark of true courage and bravery; and there is the daring to do things a man has no right to dare to do. To do the latter means to defy the conscience and to defy the law of God. Despite the fact that they know the penalty for their conduct, they go ahead and sin, all the while daring God to do anything about it. "Self-willed" (*authades*, "self-pleasing") describes a person to whom the only thing that matters is pleasing himself and having his own way. Such persons will not respond to appeals to logic, common sense, or decency. They are going to do what they want to do and when they want to!

---

[98] Compare what Peter said about the "corruption that is in the world through lust" at 1:4. The noun translated "defilement" in verse 10 occurs nowhere else except in verse 20 below, though the corresponding verb is found at Titus 1:15, Hebrews 12:15, and Jude 8. Alongside Peter's word "defilement" we might place 1 Corinthians 6:18 which seems to say something very similar about what immorality does to a man.

[99] *Kataphroneo* means "to think down, to think little or nothing of, to disdain or despise."

They do not tremble when they revile angelic majesties -- "Tremble" means to fear, to be afraid. "Even while speaking evil of[100] ..." they feel no fear, no anxiety about what they are doing, no worry about what God thinks. The exact meaning of *doxas* ("dignities, glories," the word is plural) both here and in Jude 8 is not clear. The commentaries have offered a host of options. (1) Perhaps it speaks of an attitude toward the angels of God.[101] In light of what the next verse says, it is affirmed that "angels" are on Peter's mind. Strachan suggested the false teachers may have scoffed at the idea of both angelic help and diabolic temptation.[102] Plummer suggested the false teachers may have "denied the existence of, or irreverently spoke slightingly of, those spiritual agencies by means of which God conducts the government of the world."[103] When it is remembered that later Gnostics had a whole host of angelic beings ("aeons") in their Pleroma,[104] perhaps Peter is alluding to the false teacher's downgrading of God's angels to lesser and lesser beings as they tried to match the creation of the physical world to their dualistic ideas. (2) Perhaps "dignities" (*doxas*) speaks of the same thing "authority" did in verse 10a. (3) Perhaps "glories" (*doxas*) speaks of future glories, the resurrection of the body, and heaven. (4) Perhaps the false teachers rail against the "glories" of our Lord Jesus Christ, to which Peter referred in 1 Peter 1:11.[105] (5) Perhaps the plural "glories" is broad enough to cover all these suggestions.[106]

---

[100] *Blasphemeo* is "to rail at, attack, insult, blaspheme." The same word is translated "maligned" in 2:2.

[101] So the NASB translators understood it, "angelic majesties." So did the NIV, "celestial beings."

[102] Strachan, *op. cit.*, p.137. Ken Taylor, *The Living Bible* (Wheaton, IL: Tyndale House, 1976), p.1329, finds a reference to demons in verses 10-12. Raymond C. Kelcy, *The Letters of Peter and Jude* (Austin, TX: R.B. Sweet Co., 1972), p.143, raises the objection that "it is hard to think of Peter calling 'fallen angels' by the term 'glorious ones' (dignities)." Bauckham (*op. cit.*, p.262) holds that the reference in *doxas* is to demonic powers and that the immoral false teachers derided the idea they were under the control of such supernatural beings. Eugeniusz Szewc, "False Prophets in the Letter to Jude and the Second Letter of Peter," *Qumran Chronicle* 8/1-2 (August 1998), p.111, documents that the War Scroll (1QM 13:4,5) contains injunctions to the Essenes at Qumran to curse Satan and all the spirits of his company. It was one of the fundamental rules of the sect.

[103] Plummer, *op. cit.*, p.157.

[104] See Giovanni Filoramo, *A History of Gnosticism* (Cambridge, MA: Blackwell, 1990), p.17,55,56-69,63-67, for an explanation of "pleroma." In Gnostic thought, the "pleroma" was the upper spirit world consisting of seven heavens, each a higher one more glorious than the one below, with an angelic being ("aeon") guarding the entrance of each. By joining the Gnostics, and learning their secret knowledge, one might learn the passwords needed to get by the respective guards and enter the next level of existence. After a number of reincarnations, one might enter the seventh heaven, after which no more reincarnations were needed. When it came to creation, since spirit was good and matter evil, there was no way God (a spirit) could have created the world. What the Gnostics said He did was create a whole series of lesser beings (the angels), who then created another series of lesser beings (demiurges), one of whom created Jesus, who then created the devil, who created this evil world. Paul responds to this bewildering bunch of ideas by saying "in Him (Christ) dwells all the fulness (*pleroma*) of deity dwells in bodily form" (Colossians 2:9).

[105] Lenski and Hiebert both develop this idea in their comments. It requires "angels" in verse 11 to be the angels who sinned (verse 4), and it requires "them" in verse 11 to refer back to "glories," all of which is possible. What is attractive about this explanation is that it expresses a climax in the false teachers' activities -- namely a making light of everything the Lord Jesus did and does to redeem man.

[106] The Latin Vulgate strangely translates *doxas* by *sectas*, which the Douay translates "they do not fear to bring in sects, blaspheming."

2:11 -- ***Whereas angels who are greater in might and power do not bring a reviling judgment against them before the Lord.***

Whereas angels who are greater in might and power -- "Whereas" represents *hopou*, "in circumstances where." The false teachers rail at glories in circumstances where angels would not presume to rail, even though angels are greater in might and power than men and who therefore might be thought to be able to get away with it. Angels are greater than men since men were "made a little lower than the angels" (Hebrews 2:9). "Might" (*ischui*) denotes an inherent strength or ability, whereas "power" (*dunamei*) denotes ability to perform. Whether it is good angels or evil angels who do not rail will depend on how the rest of the passage is interpreted.

Do not bring a reviling judgment against them before the Lord -- It is best to begin our comments by addressing the matter of whether or not "before the Lord" was part of what Peter wrote.[107] The manuscripts that do carry the words read differently, some having *para kurio* (dative)[108] and some *para kuriou* (genitive).[109] *Para* with the genitive means "*from* the side of" whilst *para* with the dative means "*at* the side of." If the genitive is correct, this phrase would deny that the reviling judgment came from the Lord. If the dative is correct, it says that the reviling judgment was not spoken while the angels were "at the side of the Lord." The dative is the best supported reading. The angels remember they are in the presence of God and they are careful about their language.

The second difficult issue in this verse is the question, who is "them"? Perhaps "them" refers to the false teachers. Angels watch what is happening on earth and see men like the false teachers, but the angels do not rail against wicked men; they leave it to God to decide judgment.[110] Perhaps "them" refers back to "angelic majesties." As we have done before – in light of their prophecy and fulfillment relationship – we should allow Jude to help us explain what is meant.[111] Jude 9 refers to a contest between Michael the archangel and the devil over the body of Moses. While engaged in the struggle, Michael did not rail at the devil.

---

[107] Codex Alexandrinus, a number of cursive manuscripts, the Vulgate, and several other ancient versions omit the words. The words do not occur in Jude 9 either, but whether this has any bearing on the text of 2 Peter depends on whether or not Jude 9 and 2 Peter 2:11 are dealing with the same event.

[108] This is the way that Sinaiticus, Vaticanus, Ephraemi, and the whole Byzantine family reads.

[109] This is how P^{72} and several cursives and a few other witnesses read.

[110] Barclay's explanation is very similar. He thinks good angels went to report the Genesis 6 episode to God but did not condemn the evil angels. They let God do that. Barclay appeals to the *Book of Enoch* for corroboration of his interpretation. Do good angels appear in the heavenly courts to make reports concerning men? Apparently so, Job 1-2.

[111] To support this explanation, we are not limited to the passage in Jude alone; there has been more than one contest between angels of God and Satan. For example, there was a contest between Satan and the angel of the Lord about Joshua, the high priest (Zechariah 3:1,2).

If angels do not bad-mouth angels, men shouldn't either, would be Peter's point. Perhaps "them" refers back to "glories" and we should accept the idea that it speaks of the "glories" of the Lord Jesus Christ. Wicked angels are not brave enough to rail against Him before the Lord. How then could wicked men such as the false teachers be bold enough to speak against Jesus? Perhaps it says that good angels who are at the side of the Lord do not revile the fallen angels like the false teachers do. No wonder Peter calls them "brazen"!

2. Like mad animals, they will be destroyed for the harm they do. 2:12,13a

2:12 -- ***But these, like unreasoning animals, born as creatures of instinct to be captured and killed, reviling where they have no knowledge, will in the destruction of those creatures also be destroyed,***

But these – *Houtoi de* calls our attention away from the angels and back to the false teachers whom Peter began to describe in verse 10b.

Like unreasoning animals -- When it comes to conduct, the false teachers are not much different from unreasoning animals. Animals do not have true intelligence or reason; they are *alogoi*.[112] A bull in a china shop is not using any brains. It just plunges on, destroying whatever is in its path. Even less, when an animal is mad, or savage, does it demonstrate any sense or control over its appetites. Therein lies Peter's comparison of the false teachers to mad animals. The false teachers live as if satisfying the physical desire of the moment is all there is to life.

Born as creatures of instinct -- The NASB does not quite catch the idea in *gegennemena phusika*. "Born" is a perfect participle, indicating the creatures were born that way and are still in this state. *Phusika* indicates "physical, natural, under the guidance of nature;" there is no spirit to give direction to their souls. They are not led by reason. They are mere animals. Peter does not say the false teachers are born this way. He is talking about animals being born this way.

To be captured and killed -- Peter is describing a predatory animal which men deliberately capture and destroy for the harm it does. Such is the destiny of the false teachers who are acting like unreasoning animals, interested only in the gratification of their fleshly appetites.[113] "Killed" is the NASB's translation of *phthoran*, a word that can have a double

---

112 What evidence is there that a dog has a reasoning ability? Did you ever see a dog sit down and reason out a problem? Or laugh at a joke? A dog baying at the moon illustrates what it means when Peter speaks of "animals without reason."

113 Calvinistic commentators understand this verse to say that "the false teachers were born to be taken and destroyed." It becomes one of the favorite proof texts for God's eternal predestination of some to damnation. Non-Calvinists skirt being dragged into such a conclusion in one of several fashions: One writes that animals were created by God to be caught and taken by man, and to be killed for men's use. Another observes that the

meaning, either corruption (see 2 Peter 1:4) or perish.

Reviling where they have no knowledge -- The context, and the parallel passage in Jude, show that the *doxas* ("glories") of verse 10 are the things which the false teachers do not understand and which they revile.[114] "No knowledge" (*agnoousin*, "ignorance") would be a direct slap at people like the incipient Gnostics who were insisting they had knowledge others didn't have.

Will in the destruction of those creatures also be destroyed -- Two forms of *phthora* (a noun and a verb) occur in this phrase. Since the word has a double meaning, we suppose both should be employed here. When Peter uses *phthora* the first time, he is using the word (as he did in 1:4) of the corruption of faith and morals which the false teachers cause.[115] When Peter uses the verb *phtharesontai*, he must mean something similar to "killed" earlier in the verse. Because they corrupt others and cause them to be lost, the false teachers would themselves (like in the mad-animal examples[116]) eventually meet with the destruction which God has long ago (2:3) revealed will be the eternal destiny of such wicked men. They bring the destruction on themselves (compare verse 1). "As animals are trapped through their eagerness to satisfy their appetite, so self-indulgence betrays these men to their ruin."[117]

2:13a -- *Suffering wrong as the wages of doing wrong.*

Suffering wrong as the wages of doing wrong -- As it reads in the NASB, this participial phrase (*adikoumenoi misthon adikias*) is an explanation of the last clause in verse 12.[118] The false teachers will "suffer harm" as "fitting wages" for the "injury" they cause. It is a further threat of eternal punishment at the end of a life of sinning.

---

participle "born" can be either middle or passive. If we take it as middle, the verse says the false teachers "begat themselves" for this capture and killing. None of these expedients is needful. The last part of this verse, "shall in their corruption be destroyed," relieves us from being forced to adopt the Calvinistic predestination doctrine.

[114] "Revile" again translates *blasphemeo*, as it did in verses 10 and 11. Three times in three verses Peter has used "blasphemy," "blasphemy," "blasphemy"!

[115] The Greek reads "in the corruption of them." We are treating "them" to mean the corruption they cause. The *Living Bible* ("and [false teachers] will be destroyed along with the demons and the powers of Hell") treats "them" as a reference to demons, just as it has treated the whole paragraph.

[116] It is doubtful that Peter is saying irrational animals will be destroyed in hell and that the false teachers will be destroyed there at the same time.

[117] W. H. Bennett, "The General Epistles, James, Peter, John, and Jude," in *The Century Bible* (London: Blackwood, 1903), p.274.

[118] There is a manuscript variation at this place, resulting in translators punctuating the verses differently, and commentators offering widely different explanations. When it comes to punctuation, some translators treat 13a as

3. Their vices and sins. 2:13b-16

2:13b -- ***They count it a pleasure to revel in the daytime. They are stains and blemishes, reveling in their deceptions, as they carouse with you,***

They count it a pleasure to revel in the daytime -- The NASB begins a new sentence here and we shall follow its lead.[119] Peter is describing some of the vices and sins the false teachers will engage in. "Pleasure" translates *hedonen* (compare "hedonism"), a word that denotes the enjoyment they derive from fulfilling their sensual desires.[120] We have difficulty finding the right English word for *truphen* ("reveling"). The KJV's "riot" is too strong.[121] The word means "delicate fair, dainty living, luxury." The false teachers are pictured as not working for a living during the day time, the time when honest men typically were busy at their daily occupations. Instead, they would spend the day "taking it easy."[122]

---

part of what precedes (see the period in the middle of verse 13 in the NASB). Some treat 13a as part of what follows and interpret it similarly to a like expression in verse 15, as though it speaks of receiving financial rewards for doing wrong, like in the case of Balaam; the false teachers intended to profit from what Peter calls their wrongdoing. As for the manuscript variation, instead of *adikoumenoi* ("suffering wrong," found in P[72], Sinaiticus and Vaticanus), we find *komioumenoi* ("receiving") in Sinaiticus in the third hand, Alexandrinus, Ephraemi, and the Byzantine family. (*Komioumenoi* is a future tense participle, and commentators explain "receiving, as they shall [in the world to come], the reward of unrighteousness," cp. KJV at this place). Textual critics conjecture that some scribe reading *adikoumenoi* in his exemplar mistakenly thought it implied that God was treating the false teachers unjustly, and so deliberately changed the reading to *komioumenoi* as he made a copy. Bauckham (*op. cit.*, p.280) says the *adikoumenoi* reading "makes good sense and preserves a word play in Greek that is quite characteristic of Peter's style in this epistle." Kelcy (*op. cit.*, p.145), having observed that in the papyri *adikeo* means "to be defrauded" or "to be deprived of," thinks the false teachers are going to be deprived of the gain they thought they would make. He wrote, "Sin promises much, but the life of the sinner ends in destruction. He is deprived of the rewards which licentiousness promised."

[119] We still have the problem of punctuation. The only verb form in this phrase is a participle in the nominative plural. Normally, a participle cannot function as a main verb; it needs a main verb to complete its meaning. The KJV adds the word "as" at the beginning of this phrase, so that verse 13 reads "and (they) shall receive the reward of unrighteousness, *as* they that count it pleasure to riot in the day time." (Note the period in the middle of verse 13.) Others, as the NASB does, begin a fresh sentence with this phrase, and treat the participle as though it were a verb. "Their idea of pleasure is to carouse in broad daylight," NIV.

[120] The word as used in the New Testament has a bad connotation. See Luke 8:14; Titus 3:3; James 4:1,3, and a compound form of the word at 2 Timothy 3:4.

[121] Commentaries based on the KJV ("riot in the day time") often describe the false teachers as being so abandoned to sin that they extended their revelings into the day light hours, in bold contrast to the way most wicked men lived, confining their excesses to the night time. (Cp. 1 Thessalonians 5:7; and on Pentecost Peter refuted the charge of drunkenness by saying, "It's only 9 AM!")

[122] A number of writers have interpreted the Greek "for a day" to mean the false teachers' pleasure would be temporal and short lived. Fronmüller (*op. cit.*, p.34) cites a comment about "the time of the present life, which compared with eternity is only as one day." In the Shepherd of Hermas (*Sim.* vi.4.4) there is a passage which some suppose is an echo of this: "The time of luxury and deceit is one hour, but the hours of torment have the power of 30 days; if then a man luxuriates for one day ...." Alford (*op. cit.*, p.408) and Plummer (*op. cit.*, p.454,455) treat it as meaning "for a day," i.e., they have no thought for the future. They are concerned only about the present moment.

They are stains and blemishes -- It looks as if Peter has inserted two words of exclamation to express his personal disgust. "Stains and blemishes!"[123] A "stain" ruins what otherwise is pleasant and beautiful. Think of a big glob of grease on a white wedding dress. These false teachers will just ruin the beauty of the local church, the bride of Christ.[124] The word "blemishes" (*momoi*) occurs nowhere else in the New Testament. In the LXX (Leviticus 21:16ff) it describes a physical defect which disqualified a man for service before God. It then came to denote anything that is a disgrace or causes shame. The false teachers in the churches would result in Jesus being ashamed of those churches. The Lord who was a "lamb without blemish and without spot" (1 Peter 1:19) desires His body, the church, to be "without spot or wrinkle, or any such thing" (Ephesians 5:27).

Reveling in their deceptions, as they carouse with you -- The ASV reads, "While they feast with you," a much better rendering of *suneuocheo*.[125] As the false teachers live in luxury[126] or take it easy, they will even use church meetings to keep from working. The manuscripts, both here and in Jude 12, vary between *apatais* ("deceptions") and *agapais* ("love feasts"[127]). The better attested word at this place is *apatais*. In light of the word that follows "as they carouse with you," one wonders if Peter didn't make a deliberate play on words. Rather than using the honorable name for church banquets, Peter calls them "deceptions" – at least that is what the false teachers will make of them. The false teachers will join in these banquets, but only because these feasts give them another opportunity for self-indulgence and taking it easy. There is no love in their hearts being expressed for others as they participate.

---

[123] There is no verb or particle to connect these words with the surrounding words. These words stand out here just like "daring, self-willed" at verse 10 did. The translators of the NASB connected them with the following participle ("reviling") which is also in the nominative plural.

[124] Where Peter uses "stains" (*spiloi*), Jude uses a different figure of speech, *spilades* ("hidden reefs" on which ships would founder).

[125] This Greek word occurs elsewhere in the Bible only at Jude 12.

[126] The verb translated "reveling" is *entruphao*, a compound form of the root *truphen* used in a previous phrase in this verse.

[127] The love feasts (cp. 1 Corinthians 11:17-22) were similar to the basket dinners with which we are familiar. They were intended, in the early church, to give the poorer members an opportunity for a nutritious meal. Each church member brought what food they could to share with others but, of course, the wealthier members could bring more, thus benefitting the poorer members. Peter pictures the false teachers as being spots and blemishes on such occasions, feasting at the expense of others, thrilled that they were able to do so.

2:14 -- ***Having eyes full of adultery and that never cease from sin; enticing unstable souls, having a heart trained in greed, accursed children;***

Having eyes full of adultery -- If we tie this participial phrase together with "as they carouse with you," what Peter pictures is what the false teachers will be doing as they look around at the women who are at the banquet. The Greek should probably be rendered "having eyes full of an adulteress," and vividly pictures a man who cannot look at a woman without lascivious thoughts toward her. They regard every woman with the eye of lustful calculation, wondering if and how she can be persuaded to agree to gratify their lusts.

And that never cease from sin -- Peter seems to have in mind Christ's words in the Sermon on the Mount (Matthew 5:27,28), "everyone who looks on a woman to lust for her has committed adultery with her already in his heart." Just as "full of" indicated how completely impure passions can come to occupy one's mind, so "never cease" (*akatapauo*, "unable to stop") vividly portrays the enslaving power of lust. A man who allows himself to think lustful thoughts enough times slips into a rut so that all his thoughts turn to lust and all his actions are motivated by that same lust!

Enticing unstable souls -- "Enticing" (*deleazontes*) comes from *delear* ("bait"). Fowlers use bait to catch birds; fishermen use bait to catch fish. There is something deceptive about the bait.[128] Verse 18 describes the "bait" that will be used by the false teachers as sensual indulgence. The NIV reads "They seduce the unstable." "Women will be lured to commit adultery with them or men enticed to join them in their lewdness."[129] "Unstable souls" (*asteriktous*, from *steridzo*, is "to make stable, place firmly, set fast," plus an alpha-privative which negates the rest of the word) describes persons who are "not anchored securely, who are not solidly on a foundation, here doctrinally and experientially."[130] In verse 18 it is recent converts who are enticed. Perhaps that is the reason the victims of the false teachers are described as "unstable."[131]

---

[128] This verse may throw light on Peter's use of "deception" in the previous verse. Someone has observed that "all of Satan's worms have hooks in them."

[129] Hiebert, *op. cit.*, p.118.

[130] Wuest, *op. cit.*, p.57.

[131] We recall that in 2 Peter 1:12, Peter had described his readers as already stable (*esterigmenous*, "established" in the truth). In the future, it will be "unstable" ones who are caught by the false teachers' bait.

Having a heart trained in greed -- The next in the list of vices Peter charges against the false teachers is covetousness. Deep within them, the thoughts of the false teachers are starkly and simply "a desire to have more" (*pleonexias*). "Trained" or "exercised" (ASV) are translations of *gumnazo*, a word that indicates training in a gymnasium. Athletes practiced and trained and exercised until they got their desired skills mastered. The idea here is the false teachers have made a study and had become learned in the way in which men could be induced to part with their money under religious pretenses.

Accursed children -- We think this is another of Peter's exclamations.[132] Peter is not using a swear word as he describes the children; rather, he is using a Hebraism which means God's curse rests on them.[133] "They are devoted to execration; malediction has adopted them as its own."[134]

2:15 -- ***Forsaking the right way they have gone astray, having followed the way of Balaam, the* son *of Beor, who loved the wages of unrighteousness,***

Forsaking the right way they have gone astray -- "They have gone astray" is the only main verb in this long sentence that began in the middle of verse 13 and extends through verse 16. Peter is explaining how the false teachers will come to their position,[135] and as he does so he says the false teachers resemble that infamous Old Testament character Balaam, the classic example of a false teacher who, for the sake of personal gain, gets other people into sin. As the false teachers go astray, they "abandon the right way." What was described in verse 2 as the "way of truth" is here described as "the right (*eutheian*, "straight") way."[136] "Gone astray" is an aorist passive form. It may say they were led astray or caused to go astray or it may simply mean they wandered away, took a wrong path. The language says the persons were

---

[132] Lenski (*op. cit.*, p.331) wrote, "'Darers, self-pleasing!' in verse 10 is what they are for themselves; 'spots and blemishes!' in verse 13 is what they are in and for the Church; 'children of curse!' is what they are for God."

[133] Literally, the Greek says children of a curse. Compare "son of perdition" at John 17:12 and 2 Thessalonians 2:3. He is devoted to perdition, and worthy of being sent to perdition.

[134] Plummer, *op. cit.*, p.161.

[135] The past tense verbs in this verse are quite in harmony with the view that this passage is a prophecy (cp. Genesis 49:9,15,23,24). The future being foretold with such confidence as to be spoken of as already past is common language in Biblical prophecy.

[136] There is the way of revealed truth, the way of righteousness. It is called the way of the Lord (Genesis 18:19), the way of peace (Romans 3:7), the way of life (Proverbs 10:17), the way of salvation (Acts 16:17). Compare notes at 2 Peter 2:2. The word Peter uses for "straight" is not quite the same word Jesus used when He spoke of the "straight and narrow way" (Matthew 7:14), but the idea is similar.

at one time on the right road, but now had lost their way. One cannot forsake a way on which he has never been.[137]

Having followed the way of Balaam, the *son* of Beor -- The false teachers who will come and Balaam have several characteristics in common:[138] covetousness, running counter to the will of God for the sake of money, and encouraging people to sin, thus bringing ruin on the community. For the Biblical record of Balaam and his effort to get money see Numbers 22:1-41.

> Balak, the king of Moab, was alarmed at the steady and apparently irresistible advance of the Israelites [following their exodus from Egypt]. In an attempt to check this advance, he sent for Balaam to come and curse the Israelites for him, offering Balaam very great rewards if he would come. To the end of the day Balaam refused to curse the Israelites, but the story makes one thing quite clear, that Balaam's covetous heart longed after the rich rewards which Balak was offering, even if he was afraid to take them. Balaam, at Balak's second request, played with fire enough to agree to meet Balak. It was on that journey that the ass [he was riding] stopped in the way, because it saw the angel of the Lord standing in its path, and rebuked Balaam. As we have said, it is true that on this occasion Balaam did not succumb to Balak's bribes, but if ever a man desperately wanted to accept a bribe, that man was Balaam.
>
> A later account, in Numbers 25, tells how the Israelites were seduced into the worship of Baal, and into lustful alliances with Moabite women ... [Numbers 31:16 makes it clear] that Balaam was behind this seduction and was responsible for leading the children of Israel astray. And when the Israelites entered into possession of the land, "Balaam, the son of Beor, they slew with the sword" (Numbers 31:8). In view of all this, Balaam became increasingly the type and example of the false and misleading prophet.[139]

It must have been common knowledge that Balaam accepted money in return for his services in the arts of divination or Balak would not have persisted in his appeal to him on this basis. There is a manuscript variation concerning the name of Balaam's father. Some read "Beor"

[137] Does this verse say the false teachers abandoned Christianity? Not necessarily. If the false teachers are Jewish Gnostics, then the "right way" they forsake could well be the way of God as taught in the Jewish Scriptures. Those Scriptures pointed men to the Messiah and demanded right living, neither of which the false teachers showed any further interest in. We still have not settled the question of whether the false teachers were ever Christians, though certainly some of their followers had embraced Christianity before being enticed over to the ways of the false teachers (verse 18).

[138] *Exakoloutheo* ("followed") is the same word used at 1:16 and 2:2. It means "to tread in one's steps, to imitate one's way of acting." Years after Peter wrote this prediction, John the apostle wrote Revelation to, among other things, counteract the inroads of Gnosticism. In Revelation 2:14,15 John apparently compares the practice of the Nicolaitans (a false sect troubling the church) with what Balaam taught. In Revelation 2:6, Jesus indicates he hates the deeds of the Nicolaitans. A sect of Nicolaitans existed among the Gnostics in the third century, as is known from church fathers of the time (Irenaeus, Clement of Alexandria, Tertullian). It probably had its origin in the group condemned in Revelation.

[139] Barclay, *op. cit.*, p.393,394. Revelation 2:14 certainly is Biblical evidence that Balaam is the one who suggested to Balak that what he needed to do is have someone seduce the Israelites and God would stop blessing them.

and some read "Bosor,"[140] and recent critical editions of the text are accepting "Bosor" as the original reading. Various attempts have been made to explain the variation. One suggestion is "Bosor" was the Galilean mispronunciation of the guttural "ayin" in the name "Be'or."[141] Another suggestion is the letters "ayin" and "sadhe" were often interchanged by scribes copying Hebrew manuscripts, and that such a change (Be'or to Bosor) happened when some scribe was working on the copy of Numbers that Peter is alluding to when he tells about Balaam. A third suggestion is Balaam's father had two names, Beor and Bosor.[142] A fourth suggestion is that we have another deliberate play on words here. The word "Bosor" closely resembles the Hebrew word for flesh (*basar*), and Balaam is called "son of the flesh" in an allusion to the sins of the flesh into which Balaam lured the Israelites.[143]

Who loved the wages of unrighteousness -- Balaam is not specifically accused of covetousness in the Old Testament accounts, but his conduct can be explained by no other motive. The generous financial reward which the Moabite messengers carried in their hands (Numbers 22:7) is here called "the wages of unrighteousness."[144] It was money that would be received for doing something wrong. Balaam made the trip, confident he could not and would not pronounce a curse upon Israel, but he was all the time hoping he could find some way to get the money, even if he had to do something not right to get it. "The verb 'loved' indicates Balaam intelligently mapped out his course of action to achieve his purpose."[145] His covetousness caused him to suppress his better convictions.

2:16 -- ***But he received a rebuke for his own transgression;*** **for** ***a dumb donkey, speaking with a voice of a man, restrained the madness of the prophet.***

But he received a rebuke for his own transgression -- The sort of rebuke it was is shown in the next phrases. "His own" transgression distinguishes what Balaam did from what Balak

[140] *Beor* is the reading of Vaticanus and many Vulgate manuscripts. It is also how the LXX reads at Numbers 22:5, 31:8, and Deuteronomy 23:4. *Beōorsor* is the spelling found in Sinaiticus. *Bosor* is found in P^{72}, Sinaiticus in the third hand, Alexandrinus, Ephraemi, and the Byzantine text.

[141] Galileans did have trouble pronouncing the Hebrew letter "ayin." Some have supposed that the spelling "Bosor" is confirmation of the Petrine authorship of this letter. Peter was a Galilean and his speech betrayed him on the night Jesus was arrested and tried. Perhaps his speech betrayed him here in 2 Peter.

[142] Writers who believe Peter's letters were written in Babylon suppose that while Peter was in Babylon he learned the Babylonian form of Balaam's father's name. Balaam's home was Pethor on the River Euphrates in Mesopotamia (Deuteronomy 23:4).

[143] Compare the Jewish use of such names as *Ishbosheth* in derision for *Ishbaal* ("the son of shame" for "the man of Baal"), and *Jerubbesheth* (2 Samuel 11:21) for *Jerubbaal.*

[144] The same phrase was used in verse 13.

[145] Hiebert, *op. cit.*, p.121.

did. The guilt of offering wages of unrighteousness rested with Balak. Balaam's transgression lay in his readiness to accept the wages of unrighteousness, in his eager attempts to get at the money. "Transgression" (*paranomias*) speaks of one who acts contrary to a particular law. Balaam was willing to break the law of God to get the money. Peter, by parity of reasoning, is accusing the coming false teachers of behaving the same way.

***For* a dumb donkey, speaking with a voice of a man** -- The word for "donkey" is *hupozugion*, "under a yoke, a beast of burden."[146] "Dumb" (*aphonon*) means without the faculty of speech. It could bray, but it could not speak words until God put words in its mouth. "Speaking" translates *phthegxamenon*, "to utter a loud sound." Balaam heard the animal yelling at him in a man's voice, exactly what we read in Numbers 22:28. The beast spoke; it spoke with the voice of a man; it spoke audibly, and its words have been recorded and preserved. It complained that Balaam was acting unjustly when he applied the whip to the animal which had balked on seeing the angel. It is significant that Peter accepted and made use of the narrative in Numbers 22 regarding Balaam and the donkey as authentic. It was, to him, no imaginary incident, no fictitious account. Modernistic scholars, in seeking to eliminate the supernatural from the sacred writings entirely, alleged that Balaam merely heard the promptings of an uneasy conscience on this occasion and that the beast did not really speak, but only brayed. Such a view not only impeaches Moses as a historian; it also convicts Peter, an apostle of the Lord, as an unreliable writer. According to the account in Numbers, Balaam was rebuked twice, first by the donkey (to which Peter here alludes), then by the angel.

Restrained the madness of the prophet -- The KJV reads "forbad" as though Balaam was stopped altogether from going the wrong way. *Ekolusen* means simply "to hinder, check, restrain." Balaam was not stopped from his folly but he was slowed down for a moment.[147] The word for "madness" (*paraphronian*) occurs nowhere else in the New Testament. Some suppose Peter coined it and used it for the sake of alliteration with the word "prophet" and *paranomia* ("transgression"). The word means "senseless." Balaam was engaged in an enterprise which indicated he was out of his right mind. Balaam is called a "prophet." Was he a prophet of God? Obviously so, as God put words into his mouth (Numbers 23:38). Balaam was not a Jew, but he was made a prophet, much as Melchizedek, not a Jew, was made a priest of the Most High God.[148]

---

[146] The more common Greek word for "ass" or "donkey" is *onos* (cp. Matthew 21:5; Exodus 4:20; Joshua 6:21.)

[147] The donkey checked the prophet's folly by shrinking from the angel, and by speaking in a man's voice. The angel, while permitting Balaam to expose himself to the danger into which he had fallen by tempting the Lord, forbade any deviation from the word to be put into his mouth by God. Balaam obeyed to the letter, but afterwards, the madness which had been checked for the moment led him into deadly sin (Numbers 31:16).

[148] Hebrews 7:1. Samson, the judge, did not end his life too well. He was a broken stick, but he was the best man God had at the time. Perhaps, like Samson's, the latter part of Balaam's life was not as spiritual as the first.

4. The worthlessness, emptiness, and unprofitableness of their teaching. 2:17-19

2:17 -- ***These are springs without water, and mists driven by a storm, for whom the black darkness has been reserved.***

These are springs without water -- Peter's descriptive prediction of these coming false teachers "is a powerful piece of writing that gains momentum as it reaches its climax."[149] Peter uses some vivid word pictures. They will be like "springs without water."[150] A spring where there was no water was a great disappointment to a thirsty traveler (Jeremiah 14:3). Dried-up watering places in the desert can prove fatal to the traveler.[151] Some writers have appealed to Jesus' words in John 4:10-14 and 7:39 to explain what the "water" is that the false teachers cannot produce. To the woman at the well living water brings satisfaction. In the other place, Jesus has reference to the indwelling Holy Spirit. Followers of the false teachers were to find emptiness and disappointment in both these areas. The Living New Testament says the false teachers are "as useless as dried-up springs."

And mists driven by a storm -- "Mists" and dew[152] were both valuable for helping to raise vegetation in the Negeb, where average rainfall is less than two inches a year. Some grape vines there have very large leaves which catch and store the dampness in the air until the plant can use it. *Elauno* is used of the wind driving ships or clouds, and in Ephesians 4:14 for being "carried about by every wind of doctrine." *Lailaps* is a strong wind like those which signal to people on land that a storm front is passing through. It is the word used by Mark and Luke in their account of the fierce gale winds that raised huge waves which threatened the disciples in the boat on the Sea of Galilee (Mark 4:37; Luke 8:23). It looks to the worried farmer like his crops will get some moisture, but his expectations are disappointed. High winds drive the moisture away and only make conditions worse. So it would be with the false teachers. People were thirsting for the knowledge of salvation and the freedom from slavery to sin promised them in Christ. The false teachers with their great swelling words would blow away any chance people had to get some "moisture."

---

149 Blum, *op. cit.*, p.281.

150 The KJV reads "wells without water," but the word for well is *phrear*. The word here is *pege* and speaks of a stream of running water gushing out of the ground or the hillside.

151 In "Cool Water," a once-popular Country and Western ballad, the traveler is crossing the desert and is talking to his horse as he sees in the distance what looks like a watering hole. "Don't you listen to him, Dan; he's a devil, not a man, as he spreads the burning sand with water." He is telling the horse it is just a mirage. Don't go there! There's no water there!

152 *Homichlai* is the word for cloud, misty air, steam, fog rising from the ground. *Drosos* is the word for dew. The KJV reads *nephelai* ("clouds") here, but the reading is not well supported. The words for "clouds" and "carried along" in Jude 12 are quite different, and the KJV creates a false impression of great similarity.

For whom the black darkness has been reserved -- "Darkness" is the same word used at 2:4. The phrase "black darkness" denotes intense darkness. If the word "forever," which is found in some manuscripts and the KJV ("reserved forever"), is not part of what Peter wrote,[153] then we suppose 2 Peter 2:17 deals with the intermediate state. The verse then says a place of "black darkness" is reserved[154] in the intermediate world for the false teachers[155] just like there was a place of darkness for the angels who sinned (Jude 6). The place of darkness has been prepared and is being kept in a state of readiness, ready to receive them. It is like a jail or prison house which is built in anticipation there will be criminals, and therefore a use for the prison.

2:18 -- ***For speaking out arrogant* words *of vanity they entice by fleshly desires, by sensuality, those who barely escape from the ones who live in error,***

For speaking out arrogant *words* of vanity -- In the preceding verse, the false teachers are described as dried-up springs and mists. Here is the reason: All they say is worthless! "Great swelling words" (ASV) is one word in the Greek (*huperogka*, from *huper*, "over," and *ogkos*, "swelling"). It pictures something of excessive bulk, swollen far beyond normal size. Peter says their words will be extravagant, bloated, immoderate, exaggerated. Perhaps it describes great oratorical flair to impress the listeners, or great pretension to wisdom and learning that were hollow. "Speaking" translates the same word used of Balaam's donkey speaking. When they speak it will be a lot of loud talk. "Vanity" says their boasts are empty; what their high-sounding words promise won't be accomplished.[156] They boast what their doctrine will do in the liberation of their listeners. The exact opposite is true; the listeners will become more enslaved in their sins.

They entice by fleshly desires, by sensuality – *Deleazousin en epithumiais sarkos aselgeiais* is how the original reads. "Entice" is the word we had in verse 14, "to entice by bait." Probably *aselgeiais* ("sensuality, lasciviousness") should be taken as a dative of means, thus describing the bait used to entice men's "fleshly desires."[157] *Aselgeiais* is also plural and may

---

[153] "Forever" is supported only by Alexandrinus, Ephraemi, and the Textus Receptus. Vaticanus and Sinaiticus omit the words, as does the UBS[2] and Nestle-Aland texts. (However, see notes at Jude 13.)

[154] "Reserved" is the same verb used in the inheritance "reserved" for the saints (1 Peter 1:4), and of the fallen angels in pits of darkness "reserved" for the judgment (2 Peter 2:4).

[155] We are reminded of the verses about "utter darkness where there shall be weeping and gnashing of teeth." Some of those passages seem to refer to the final place of punishment for the wicked, and some ask how there can be a fire in hell and "utter darkness" at the same time. Perhaps it is not a literal fire, but something more terrible. Or perhaps there are several analogies used by Bible writers to try to describe hell, and we should not try to combine them.

[156] *Mataios* ("vanity") indicates they are not fulfilling the purpose for which speech is intended.

[157] The NIV's reading ("by appealing to the lustful desires of sinful human nature") unnecessarily thrusts the Calvinistic theology of the translators at the English readers. See comments on "flesh" above at verse 10a.

point to acts of lasciviousness. "By sensual propaganda they ensnare" new followers. They promised unlimited indulgence to fleshly appetites, or taught such doctrines that their followers would feel themselves free to give unrestrained liberty to such passions.

Those who barely escape from the ones who live in error -- Here Peter identifies the group of potential victims, the same folk who were called "unstable souls" in verse 14. It is the recent converts to Christianity, folk who just quit their old pagan ways, whom these false teachers bait.[158] "Live in error" (*en plane anastrephomenous*[159]) describes a wandering about in error, following wrong beliefs in the area of morals and religion. The people designated by this description are Gentiles who knew not God. People who become Christians escape the ways of error lived out by the unconverted.

2:19 -- *Promising them freedom while they themselves are slaves of corruption; for by what a man is overcome, by this he is enslaved.*

Promising them freedom -- In this verse, Peter makes it quite clear why he labels the false teachers' claims "great swelling words." "Freedom" would be their subject. They would talk loudly. But what they would say would have a hollow ring to it. It appears they were going to tell the recent converts that they had lost their liberty. They would tell them, 'You do not have to grow in the way set out in 2 Peter 1:3-11. Why don't you do what you want to any longer? What you have been taught are just a bunch of stupid, confining rules.' Writing in the late AD 60's, Peter is warning about the advent of incipient Gnosticism with their pleas to antinomianism and libertinism. To justify their teachings, the false teachers would take a true Christian doctrine – the freedom we have in Christ – and twist it into something perverse. Kelcy has nicely summarized what the commentaries say at this place:

---

[158] This identification of "recent converts" depends on several preliminary decisions made about the text and the meaning of words in the text. There is a manuscript variation here. Some read *tous ontos apopheugontas*, "those that were clean [really, actually] escaped," a reading represented in the KJV, and expressing a strong degree of spiritual attainment before they became victims of the false teachers' bait. Other manuscripts read *tous oligos apopheugontas*, "those who are just escaping," the reading translated in the NASB. When written in all capital letters, the words *ontos* and *oligos* look very similar; some copyist simply made a mistake copying. *Oligos* is a rare word, and if genuine, this is the only place it is found in the New Testament. The scribe may have substituted a familiar word for an unfamiliar one. A second decision concerns the tense of the participle: is it present tense or aorist tense? The present tense participle *apopheugontas* has the stronger textual support; the "escape" is in the process of happening. The final decision concerns the meaning of the adverb *oligos*, which is evidently the correct reading here. It may be understood of time ("a little time, just recently"); that is, they are recent converts. Calvinism understood this as expressing measure (escaping just a little way); that is, they had just begun to break many of their old evil habits. There was hope they would, after repentance, decide to become Christians, but before they did they were allured again into the sins they indulged in for so long (see further at footnote #119). We have opted to explain it as expressing time.

[159] *Anastrepho* is one of Peter's favorite words (see 1 Peter 1:1,5,18, 2:12, 3:1,2,16). *Plane* is from the same root word used in "gone astray" at 2:15.

> Jesus had promised freedom to His disciples, but it was surely not a freedom to follow the dictates of the flesh (John 8:32,34,36). Paul gave great emphasis to Christian liberty, but with Paul Christian freedom is freedom from the Law [of Moses], freedom from [slavery to] sin, and freedom to serve one's Master from the compulsion of love (cf. Romans 6:6,12-14,22, 7:6, 8:2; 2 Corinthians 3:17; Galatians 2:4, 5:1,13). The false teachers were insisting upon license rather than true Christian liberty. Perhaps this was one of the areas in which they twisted Paul's writings (see 3:16). They are doing the very thing which Peter himself has previously warned against, using "freedom as a pretext for evil" (cf. 1 Peter 2:16).[160]

While they themselves are slaves of corruption -- Peter is saying, 'They are fine experts to be talking about freedom! Why, they themselves are in the worst kind of bondage!' "Slaves" here is *douloi* and it is used with its abject and servile connotation. When a man throws away all moral restraints, he becomes a slave of all sorts of horrible vices. The vices in turn corrupt[161] the man in body and soul, not only for this life, but for the life to come. The participle *huparchontes*, translated "are," is present tense, indicating the false teachers all along have been such slaves.[162]

For by what a man is overcome, by this he is enslaved -- This clause, as "for" shows, is intended to be an explanation of "slaves of corruption" just preceding. "They ... are slaves," says Peter, and here is the reason he can say that. They have been overcome and enslaved.[163] Both Jesus and Paul made similar statements. Jesus said that everyone who continues to commit sin is a slave of sin (John 8:34). Paul's statement was, "when you present yourselves to someone as slaves for obedience, you are slaves of the one whom you obey, either of sin resulting in death, or of obedience resulting in righteousness" (Romans 6:16-20). Both Peter and Paul are reflecting what Jesus Himself had said. The writer of the lesson entitled "True Freedom" had this to say:

> W. Somerset Maugham wrote a long novel with the title "Of Human Bondage." It does, indeed, tell of a young man who was enmeshed in the net of a heartless and acquisitive society and who was also enslaved by the drives of his own desires and impulses. It is a fact of historic record and of contemporary observation that men continually commit themselves to various types of servitude. They voluntarily "sell themselves" to a condition of dependence and permit their actions to be dictated by desires they have deliberately cultivated ...

---

[160] Kelcy, *op. cit.*, p.149.

[161] Peter has used the word *phthora*, "corruption, destruction," before at 2:12.

[162] The question "Had the false teachers ever been Christians before they became false teachers?" is still on the table. The participle used here might indicate the false teachers never were free from their old slavery to sin. On the other hand, it must be taken into consideration that Romans 6:16,19 shows that by continued sinning after a man becomes a Christian, he can revert to the condition of slavery.

[163] The genitive pronoun that indicates the mastering agent can be either masculine or neuter. It could be "of whom" or "by what." If we take it as masculine, the Devil is in the background. If we take it neuter, the sensuous acts and desires are what have enslaved. One can be defeated and enslaved both by something and by somebody. Both verbs in this clause are perfect tense, denoting past completed action with present abiding results.

> Let us look at some of the areas of bondage that exist among "free" people today. The slavery to alcohol ... the slavery to drugs ... the slavery of gambling ... the slavery of immorality ... the slavery of "busyness" and superficiality ...
>
> The Scripture text for today's lesson presents one of the greatest and most basic Scriptural, theological, and moral truths, yet one that is little recognized. That truth is that there is but one absolute freedom, namely the freedom of choice that God gave man by creation in the granting of freedom of the will to the human personality ...
>
> This principle is perhaps best illustrated in Jesus' parable of the prodigal son. The prodigal son chose to free himself from the restraints of his father's house with the regulations and duties imposed upon him there, in order to enjoy the pleasures of the world with its freedom. This choice, which he was free to make, was the only absolute freedom he possessed. For in his attempt to free himself from the bondage of his father's will, he bound himself to the inevitable results of a wasteful and sinful life -- poverty, loneliness, remorse, guilt, and shame.[164]

Overcome by their vices, the false teachers were in bondage to them. They had become servants of the devil, a master who was using them to enslave others, and would eventually destroy them.

D. The Condition of Those Who Listen to the False Teachers. 2:20-22

2:20 -- ***For if after they have escaped the defilements of the world by the knowledge of the Lord and Savior Jesus Christ, they are again entangled in them and are overcome, the last state has become worse for them than the first.***

For if -- Of whom is Peter speaking in these verses? Perhaps he is still referring to the false teachers.[165] While much can be said for the view that Peter still has the false teachers in view, perhaps he is referring to those whom the false teachers would try to entice.[166] Perhaps both. We have chosen to explain verses 20-22 as though new Christians who are potential victims are in view. Peter perhaps can help them resist by showing them in vivid terms what a tragic position they would be getting themselves into. There is not much reason to address the false

---

164 James I. Fehl, ed., *Standard Lesson Commentary, 1973-1974* (Cincinnati, OH: Standard Publishing, 1973), p.65-69.

165 Defenders of this view make the following points: (a) False teachers were the topic in the immediately preceding verse; it is likely they still are the topic in this verse. The "for" which begins verse 20 connects it with something just said, and the same root word (translated "overcome") occurs in both verses 19 and 20. (b) Verse 15 has shown the false teachers were once in the right way.

166 The defenders of this view make the following points: (1) The *apophugontes* ("those having escaped") of this verse must be the same as the *apopheugontas* ("those who barely escape") of verse 18. (2) "For" does show this verse explains something said earlier, namely what was said in verse 18. (3) The hypothetical language in verse 20 is how you would speak to people exposed to severe temptation but who have not yet succumbed. That does describe the potential victims, but not the false teachers.

teachers here, for there is not much Peter can do for them. What Peter is doing is laying out in plain terms the dangerous condition of apostates from the gospel. An apostate is worse off than if he had never known the truth.

After they have escaped the defilements of the world -- "Defilements" is *miasmata*, moral corruption, shameful deeds, crimes.[167] "World" here stands for how people who are not saved live. Earlier Peter wrote of this "world of the ungodly" (2:5). Peter has previously described how, when a man becomes a Christian, he escapes "the corruption that is in the world" (1:4, 2:19).[168] The new converts who are being herein warned have "escaped," they have become new Christians.

By the knowledge of the Lord and Savior Jesus Christ -- We are here reminded how a man becomes liberated from the defilements of the world: it is through a relationship with Jesus Christ as Lord and Savior. The word translated "knowledge" is *epignosis*, full knowledge. 2 Peter 1:3-11 tells how to get this "true (full) knowledge," while 1:12-21 indicated the inerrant sources of this saving knowledge. The new converts had owned Jesus as both "savior" and "Lord," something the false teachers would object to. Gnostics found no saving significance in Calvary, and they certainly were not going to take orders from Jesus. They repudiated authority (2:10).

They are again entangled in them and are overcome -- The "defilements" from which they have escaped and in which they again become "entangled" are the corrupting sins of the heathen world. This is a clear passage teaching the possibility of apostasy.[169] They may be new converts (2:18) and "unstable souls" (2:14), but they were converts and had escaped the old way of living. "Entangled" is a figure of speech from the world of fishing, where fishes can become entangled in a gill net. The fish stick their heads through the fine mesh and their gills catch them so they cannot back out and get away. The "entangling," the going back to immoral former lifestyles, was not one act, but a gradual process. The aorist tense here describes the result of the process. "Overcome" is a figure of speech from the battle-

---

[167] A kindred noun was used at 2:10a.

[168] Some think the Shepherd of Hermas (I *Vis*. iv.3.2) is an echo of this verse, "you who have escaped this world."

[169] Calvinism struggles at this place. It is often claimed that those of whom Peter speaks were not truly converted, else they never would have apostatized. This is a cherished dogma of Calvinism. So we are told confidently this passage uses no terminology that would affirm they are Christians in reality (expressions like, "sons of God," "children," "born again," "regenerate," or "redeemed"). We are reminded that these folk have escaped only a little way (2:18); that is, they were not yet actual converts, but were just thinking about becoming Christians. Or the false teachers were merely posing as Christians, when in reality they were nothing of the kind. But is one who has "escaped the defilements of the world by the knowledge of ... Christ" just posing as a Christian? Is he just thinking about becoming a convert? How much more satisfying just to let the Bible speak, rather than trying to impose our doctrines upon the pages of Holy Writ.

field.[170] They have been defeated, overpowered. If the new converts defect, they will find out there is no freedom such as the false teachers have been promising. Instead, they will be entrapped by the very bait which allured them.

The last state has become worse for them than the first -- This is a distinct quotation of Jesus' words which are recorded in Matthew 12:45 and Luke 11:26,[171] about the unclean spirit who was cast out only to return with seven other spirits more wicked than himself. It is possible for a man's life to be clean and swept and later to be re-infested with filth. Jesus said so! "The first" is the condition of the man before conversion. "The last state" denotes their present state where they are entangled in the very things they had once abandoned, defeated and entrapped again in sin and its corruption. "Worse" – why worse? (1) Perhaps because apostates are usually more abandoned in sin than those who had never had left it to walk in the ways of righteousness. It is true that if a drunkard reforms and then goes back to his drink, he's a worse drunkard than before. A sensual, profligate man who goes back to the old way of life will be more abandoned to sin than he was before conversion. (2) Perhaps because there is no more hope of redemption is why Peter says "worse." Before conversion there was hope of being saved. But after apostasy, there is no hope. They are past redemption.[172] (3) Perhaps involved is the process called hardening of the heart. A Christian who forsakes his first love becomes more and more insensitive to the voice of God and the voice of conscience. (4) Perhaps because there are degrees of punishment in hell.[173] There would be greater punishment in store for those who have once obeyed the gospel and then apostatized than for those who never obeyed will receive. They were lost and liable to punishment before hearing and obeying the gospel, but their punishment will be greater after they have heard and then apostatized.

2:21 -- ***For it would be better for them not to have known the way of righteousness, than having known it, to turn away from the holy commandment delivered to them.***

For it would be better for them not to have known the way of righteousness -- With "for" Peter introduces an explanation of "worse" in the previous verse. He reinforces what he has just written. Ignorance of the way of salvation is to be preferred over apostasy from that way. "It would be[174] better" because they would not have dishonored the cause of Christ as

---

170 *Hettontai* is the same root found in the word "overcome" in verse 19.

171 "The spontaneous adoption of our Lord's words without marks of quotation is not like the work of a forger." Caffin, *op. cit.*, p.49.

172 Compare also Hebrews 6:4-6, 10:26-31 and 1 John 5:16.

173 Verses that imply degrees of punishment include Matthew 5:21,22, 10:15, 11:21-24, 12:47,48, 18:6; Hebrews 10:29; and James 3:1.

174 The Greek verb is an imperfect tense. As has been noted earlier, it is not unusual for prophecy of the future to be couched in past tense verbs.

they have now done by going away from Christ back to their former ways; because they would not have sunk so deep in sin as they now have; because they would not have incurred so aggravated a condemnation in the world of woe as they now have. The verb "known" is, like the noun "knowledge" in the preceding verse, from *epignosis*, the fullest form of knowledge, and he emphasizes the fact that these new converts had once had a full knowledge or experience of the principles of Christ which they now have repudiated. "Way of righteousness" (way of right living) is another name for the Christian life. "That which from a doctrinal point of view is 'the way of truth' (2 Peter 2:2), from a moral point of view is 'the way of righteousness'."[175] When they bit on the bait of sensuality (2:18), they were no longer living as a "righteous" man was taught to live.

Than having known it, to turn away from the holy commandment delivered to them -- These people had not only "known" (*epignosko*) the way, they had walked in it and enjoyed its benefits and pleasures. Despite this, through yielding to temptations aimed at their sensuous desires, they turned back to the manner of thinking and living already abandoned. Their "turn away" was a voluntary thing, a thing done after they were fully aware of God's expectations. "The holy commandment" (*hagias entoles*) refers to the authoritative, apostolic message in this passage, with special emphasis on the particular command dealing with purity of lifestyle.[176] It was "holy" because of its origin, substance, and end; because of its contrast to the pollutions of the world; and because it is the means to man's holiness. Peter has already spoken of "everything pertaining to life and godliness" which God had delivered to the apostles, and which the apostles had delivered to others (2 Peter 1:3,4). Jude 3 speaks of the faith once for all "delivered to the saints." That is the doctrinal equivalent to what Peter here writes, "delivered to them."[177]

2:22 -- ***It has happened to them according to the true proverb,*** **"A DOG RETURNS TO ITS OWN VOMIT,"** ***and "A sow, after washing,*** **returns** ***to wallowing in the mire."***

It has happened to them according to the true proverb -- Their relapse into their old ways of living is illustrated by two similes taken from the animal world. "True" stamps the message conveyed in these proverbs as being how things really are. The first one, indicated

---

175 Plummer, *op. cit.*, p.165. We agree that "righteousness" in this place speaks of how men live (rather than referring to the way of acquiring righteousness, i.e., having it imputed to him by God) since the context speaks of the "defilements of the world," i.e., the way sinners live.

176 Some writers think Peter's "holy commandment" is a reference to the Old Testament moral law. The Mosaic Scriptures gave God's laws to Old Testament Israel. The moral laws (laws relating to man's relationship with man) the Christian lives by are found in the new covenant Scriptures. The new covenant has abrogated and replaced the Mosaic covenant (Hebrews 7:12,18, 10:9).

177 *Paradidomi* ("delivered") marks the divine origin of the commandment, and its method of transmission. Concerning its origin, it was received from Christ Himself. Concerning its transmission, *paradidomi* is the regular term for oral transmission of Christian teaching in the first decades of the gospel era (cp. 1 Corinthians 15:3, also 1 Peter 1:18). What was at first delivered orally eventually came to be written in the books and letters that make up the New Testament Scriptures.

by the small capital letters in the NASB, may be Biblical (Proverbs 26:11),[178] while the second is extrabiblical. The word *paroimias*, translated here as "proverb," is three times rendered "figure" or "speech" (John 10:6, 16:25,29).[179] It has been suggested that the English word "allegory" would be a better English equivalent of *paroimias*. The point of the allegories is that what the animals are doing is repulsive. Will those recent converts, when tempted by the false teachers, see that following their lead is just as repulsive?

"A DOG RETURNS TO ITS OWN VOMIT" -- The construction is participial, a dog having returned.[180] The words are spoken, as it were, with reference to a case actually being observed. This proverb may come from Proverbs 26:11; but if it does, it is an independent translation of the Hebrew, for when the LXX and 2 Peter are compared, "dog" is the only word common to the two passages. It must be considered a possibility Peter is repeating a saying commonly used by his readers. The nauseating part of the picture in this proverb is that the dog is not just sniffing its vomit, it is pictured as lapping it up. It had poison or something spoiled in its stomach that it disgorged.[181] If it eats the poison again, it often kills the dog. That's exactly the point of the allegory when compared to people forsaking their old ways, only to go back and embrace them.[182]

And, "A sow, after washing, *returns* to wallowing in the mire" -- There is no saying even close to this in Scripture,[183] so it must have come from popular parlance. "Mire" is a mud hole, often slimy and filled with urine.[184] This commentator has seen prize sows washed or

---

178 When it is recalled that in 1 Peter the book of Proverbs is cited no less than four times (1:7, 2:17, 4:8,18), to have a citation from Proverbs here in 2 Peter would be one of those little marks of similar authorship for the two letters, since not many New Testament writers were in the habit of citing Proverbs.

179 In the ASV it is also translated as "parable," which can cause confusion since another word (*parabole*) is also translated "parable."

180 In the Greek of 2 Peter, neither proverb has a verb. We often say just part of a proverb, for example, "like a fool and his money ...."

181 The Greek word "vomit" (*exerama*) here may have been coined by Peter as he writes.

182 Once more we must object to Calvinism's handling of these proverbs. Advocates of the doctrine of the impossibility of apostasy, in an effort to avoid the obvious force of this passage, insist the dog remained a dog and the sow remained a sow. The natures of these unclean animals never were changed. Likewise, the people described by Peter never became Christians in the first place. Such is not the point of the proverb. The dog had ejected that which was foul; the sow had been washed! There was a change, and then the old ways reverted to.

183 Some have supposed that Jesus' use of "dog" and "swine" (Matthew 7:6) to describe those who are opposed to God and His word may have been the beginning of such proverbs as Peter here quotes.

184 The word for "mire," *borboros*, not a very common one (not being found elsewhere in the New Testament), is used by Irenaeus (*Against Heresies*, i.6.2) of the Gnostic teachers of his day, who taught that their fine spiritual natures could no more be hurt by sensuality than gold by mire.

bathed in preparation for showing at the county fair.[185] He has seen muddy sows hosed down so their young will have clean nipples to suck on, so there will be less chance of contracting filth-borne diseases. But they do not stay clean very long. On hot days, pigs often lie down and wallow around[186] in such muddy spots to help stay cool. The disgusting part of the analogy is that when the young pigs come to suck the sow, all they get is a mouthful of mud. That is about all the victims of the false teachers get from them, too!

---

[185] It might be overpressing the details of the analogy to make "washing" of the pigs a reference to the baptism of the folk being converted.

[186] *Kulismos*, "wallowing," is found only here in the New Testament.

III. CONCERNING CHRIST'S SECOND COMING. 3:1-16

A. The Certainty of Christ's Return in Spite of Mockers. 3:1-10

1. A Call to remember the Word of God. 1:1,2

3:1 -- ***This is now, beloved, the second letter I am writing to you in which I am stirring up your sincere mind by way of reminder,***

This is now, beloved, the second letter I am writing to you -- "Now" (*ede*) could as well be translated "already," and it would imply that the interval between the letters has been surprisingly short. "Beloved," used in 1 Peter 2:11, will be repeated three more times in this chapter.[1] If God didn't love them, and if Peter didn't love them so much, this letter would not have been written, nor would it have been written so quickly after the last one. He is worried about them, and is anxious that they not abandon Christianity when the false teachers finally arrive on the scene with the peculiar doctrines they will smuggle in (2:1) and the sensuous bait they will dangle before the Christians (2:18). In addition to what he has already warned them about in this letter, there is one more serious doctrinal deviation which the false teachers will attempt to spread. It will have to do with Christology, in particular a denial of His second coming (3:4).[2] What Peter writes in chapter 3 is intended to insulate their minds against what the mockers will have to say.

In the Introductory Studies we called attention to the fact commentators are not at all agreed as to the identity of the "first letter." The natural thing would be to think Peter speaks of the book in our Bibles known as "1 Peter."[3] As indicated also in the Introductory Studies,

---

[1] 3:8,14,17.

[2] From what Peter has written, it is obvious the false teachers will deny the Lordship of Jesus. They will deny that Calvary had anything to do with men's salvation. They will distinguish between "Jesus" and the "Christ." They will deny the Master who bought them. They will deny that Jesus is God. It is obvious they will have a sub-biblical view of Jesus Messiah. To anticipate and counteract their disparagement of Jesus, Peter writes some very lofty Christology as he works toward the climax of this short letter.

[3] We have not been convinced by the arguments for a possible lost letter from an inspired apostle to a church. While admitting the possibility (but not the probability) of a letter to an *individual* being lost, we doubt that any *church* would let an apostolic letter just pass into oblivion. The strongest argument, in this commentator's opinion, that 3:1 refers to some letter other than our 1 Peter has to do with the statement regarding the thrust of the two letters – that both are 'reminders;' this will be addressed in due time in the comments. A second argument sometimes used, that 2 Peter 1:12,16 implies a personal ministry to the recipients of the second letter while 1 Peter gives no such indication of a personal ministry, has been shown in notes on page xxv of the Introductory Studies for 1 Peter and in notes at 1 Peter 1:1 to be an overstatement of the case. Nor have we been convinced by the arguments that chapters 1 and 2 of our present 2 Peter were once a separate letter (Peter's "first" one). Such a view that two letters somehow got combined into the letter we now have requires us to suppose the close (personal allusions, doxology) of one letter was lost, and the opening signature, address, and greetings were lost from the other, before someone mistakenly put the pieces that were left together. There is not one shred of external evidence that something like this ever happened with these three chapters. Besides, it could rightly be affirmed that Peter's language "I am writing" includes all of what has already been written in chapters 1 and 2 rather than what he is just now beginning to write as he dictates what we call 3:1 and the few verses following. Finally, in the Introductory Studies we rejected the hypothesis that Peter didn't write what we call "2 Peter," such that therefore

if the first letter is our "1 Peter," then the "you (plural)" to whom this letter is addressed are the same Christians addressed in 1 Peter, namely those living in Pontus, Galatia, Cappadocia, Asia, and Bithynia (1 Peter 1:1).

In which I am stirring up your sincere mind by way of reminder -- Peter's words "to stir you up by way of reminder" here are almost identical with what he wrote in 1:13.[4] "Stir up" speaks of "arousing thoroughly." "Mind," as in 1:15, is the reflective faculty where moral decisions are made and understanding is stored. The thoughts that pass through the Christian's mind should be holy thoughts; his mind should be kept pure and full of thoughts learned from God's revelation. Here the mind is described as pure or "sincere."[5] The word *eilikrines* ("sincere") is of disputed derivation. Some think it pictures grain that is well sifted so there is no admixture of chaff left. Others talk about troops that have been judged and in the review were seen to be free from disentanglement with civilian interests so they are fixed in mind on just one thing, fighting and winning. Others think it means something that is held up to the light of the sun and is still seen to be flawless.[6] Peter is expressing his expectations that their minds will be free from wrong thoughts,[7] the kinds of thoughts they would learn if they listened to the false teachers. This is a powerful way to appeal to people, to let them know he believes in them and has high expectations for them. In fact, the singular "mind," used when speaking to all the people who will hear this letter read out loud in their public assemblies, suggests he wants them to continue to be of one "mind" on the topics he is warning about. "In which" says that in both his letters Peter was reminding them of important truths

---

we have no real idea what letter is alluded to in the language "this is ... the second letter I am writing." By a process of elimination of the other options, we have arrived at the likelihood the reference is to 1 Peter.

[4] What was written earlier in this letter (1:12) about the value of repetition to make sure certain ideas become fixed in men's minds is here reinforced. It is by continued repetition that the rudiments of knowledge are in the end settled in the mind of a child. It is by continued repetition that the great doctrines of Christianity become fixed in the mind of the believer. Again and again the New Testament makes it clear that preaching and teaching are so often not the *introducing* of new truth but the *reminding* of a man of that which he already knows, and the summoning of him to be that which he already has promised God he would be. An effective antidote against false doctrine is to remember and dwell on teaching already received from Jesus' apostles and prophets.

[5] "Can you stir up an insincere mind?" asked R.C. Foster. He answered, "Yes, to evil!"

[6] The only other place this adjective occurs in the New Testament is Philippians 1:10, where it is translated "sincere." A corresponding noun is found in 1 Corinthians 5:8 and 2 Corinthians 1:12, 2:17, where it is explained as being judged in the light of the sun, as a vase which, when held up to the sun light reveals no hidden flaws. Since such flaws were often concealed by skillful patching with wax, the word "sincere" (Latin, *sine cere*, "without wax") is well chosen.

[7] Peter appeals to them as being people whose minds are uncontaminated by heresy and untainted by deceit or sensuality, so far. Recall what was said in 2:14 about how habits take over the mind.

of the gospel which they were in danger of forgetting.[8]

3:2 -- *That you should remember the words spoken beforehand by the holy prophets and the commandment of the Lord and Savior* spoken *by your apostles.*

That you should remember -- Verse 2 continues the sentence begun in verse 1. After the word "remember"[9] there is a long string of words in the genitive case and they express two different bodies of teaching the readers are to keep in mind for their own spiritual welfare. One body is comprised of the words of the Old Testament prophets; the other body is made up of the words of the apostles of Jesus Christ.[10]

The words spoken beforehand by the holy prophets -- The word order in this verse seems to show it is God's Old Testament prophets that Peter has in mind.[11] "Spoken beforehand" then means the body of teaching was spoken before the present Christian dispensation began. Most of the Old Testament prophets flourished between the years of 850 BC to 400 BC.[12] Calling them "holy" prophets sets them apart by light-years from the unholy false teachers who were about to infiltrate the churches. The topic Peter is now writing about, as the following verses show, is the second coming of Christ. So the "words" he has in mind that can be found in the Old Testament prophets would be predictions of what the last days would be like, the appearance of scoffers, the return of Christ, the day of the Lord.[13] In the verses following, as we come to particular topics which Peter says were prophesied, we will call at-

---

[8] In 1 Peter, as the Christians were facing persecution, Peter bases his exhortations to faithfulness on certain great doctrinal truths. When those doctrinal sections of 1 Peter are recalled and compared to the important truths Peter calls to the readers' memory in this letter, it can be said in both he has been pursuing the same course of instruction. The one warns against the danger of being turned away from the faith by persecution; the other warns against the danger of false teachers. In both he reminds them of the great foundational truths on which their faith and practice rest. This summary of the two letters should not be thought to militate against the idea that our 1 Peter is the "first" letter to which 3:1 alludes. Furthermore, if we limit what is to be remembered to material about the second coming of Jesus, even that is emphasized in 1 Peter -- see 1:5,7-10, 4:13, 5:1,4,10.

[9] *Mnesthenai* is the exact word used in Luke 1:72 where God is said to remember His holy covenant.

[10] Note that we have here, side by side, the Old Testament and New Testament, treated as equally being the "Word of God." This would be a refutation of the liberal teaching that the early Christians did not know they had inspired writings in their hands when they were reading the letters and books from the apostles.

[11] While it is true there are New Testament prophets whose writings have been included in our New Covenant Scriptures, it seems appropriate to think that if the New Testament prophets were intended, Peter's word order would have been "apostles and prophets" as we find in Ephesians 2:20 and 4:11.

[12] The perfect tense verb "spoken" emphasizes the message that was completed in the past still has abiding significance. God not only inspired the prophets to speak in the first place, but still speaks through their words to the hearts and minds of people who read the written Scriptures they produced (Hebrews 3:7).

[13] The unity of 2 Peter as a whole comes out strongly in this last chapter. Verse 1 recalls 1:12,13; 3:17 recalls 1:10-12; 3:18 recalls 1:5-8. Great stress is laid on the word of prophecy in both 1 and 2 Peter (see 1 Peter 1:10-12 and 2 Peter 1:19).

tention to some of the relevant prophecies in both the Old and New Testaments.

And the commandment of the Lord and Savior *spoken* by your apostles -- There is a double possessive genitive in the Greek, and this makes it difficult to express all of Peter's ideas and to get a smooth translation at the same time. Mayor offers an illustration from English, as if we were to say "Shakespeare's speech of Mark Antony," by which we mean "the speech put into Mark Antony's mouth by Shakespeare."[14] In this phrase, Peter thinks of the commandment put into the apostles' mouths by the Lord and Savior.[15] In 2:21, Peter used "commandment" (*entole*) to express the teaching of our Lord.[16] By "your apostles"[17] Peter does not mean all the twelve, just the apostles of Jesus[18] from whom the readers received their first knowledge of the gospel. In 1:16, the writer of this epistle claims to have been one

---

[14] Mayor, *op. cit.*, p.146.

[15] The word order in the KJV involves a disturbance of the Greek word order, leaving us to think that "of the Lord Jesus" modifies "apostles" rather than "commandment." That is not what Peter wrote. The commandment was announced by the apostles but it came from the Lord Himself (cp. ASV, "the commandment of the Lord and Savior through your apostles"). We think what Peter here wrote needs to be spotlighted in this 21st century, when it is the almost universal practice of redaction critics to say the apostles took Jesus' teachings and modified them to fit the different audiences and life situations they were addressing. Peter here says the words the apostles spoke were the Lord's words with no admixture, no editing, no addition or deletion.

[16] Just what "commandment" Jesus gave to the apostles is open to a difference of opinion. Perhaps Peter has in mind Christ's commands to beware of the coming of false teachers (cp. Matthew 7:15; Romans 16:17; Mark 13:22, Ephesians 5:6; 2 Timothy 4:3). Perhaps Peter has in mind the main subject of this third chapter -- to be ready for Christ's second coming (cp. Matthew 24:36-39; Mark 13:35-37; Luke 12:40; 1 Thessalonians 5:2-4).

[17] All the better manuscripts read "your apostles," not "our" as the KJV has it. In one sense, it is a surprising expression, but Christ's personally chosen apostles can be rightly called the apostles of those to whom He sent them, for they were to be their teachers and were sent to benefit them. The expression "your apostles" is much like the expression "their angels" (Matthew 18:10) -- they serve at the beck and call of Jesus, yet they are sent to minister to the little ones. In like manner the "angels of the churches" whom Christ holds in His right hand (Revelation 1:20) are sent to benefit the churches when they deliver the letters from Christ to the respective churches, 2:1ff.

Kelly (*op. cit.*, p.354) claims that the expression "your apostles" could not possibly have been penned by the historical Peter, but that it is an inadvertent slip that gives away the fact this is a forged letter by someone other than Peter. That is not right. That claim is based on an erroneous premise; namely, that the apostles were not personally conscious of having the kind of authority that verse 2 implies, and that it was not until the second century that the apostles as a body were elevated to a venerated group by their credulous followers. Not only had Jesus promised His apostles special guidance from the Holy Spirit, that empowering occurred on Pentecost following His resurrection (cf. 1 Peter 1:3), and as a result, apostles claimed for themselves the right to speak on Christ's behalf (Romans 1:1,5; 1 Corinthians 2:10-16, 14:37; 1 John 1:1-5, 4:6; Revelation 22:18).

[18] "Your apostles" should not be demoted to mean "your missionaries," as though the folk who evangelized the readers were simply apostles of churches rather than apostles of Jesus Christ. See notes at 1 Peter 1:1. When "apostles" means "apostles sent by churches" the passage says so, either specifically or in the context, as in Philippians 2:25, where Epaphroditus was a "messenger" who carried the church's "living-link" offering to Paul.

of "your apostles".[19] Peter's description of Jesus as "Lord and Savior" is the same as in 1:11 and reminds Peter's readers they must recognize Christ as Lord of their lives as well as Savior.

2. A prophecy about mockers who will deny Christ's second coming. 3:3,4

3:3 -- ***Know this first of all, that in the last days mockers will come with*** **their** ***mocking, following after their own lusts,***

Knowing this first of all -- The same language as used in 1:20 indicates that here is something Peter thinks demands his readers' special attention.[20]

That in the last days -- "Last days" are the days that come between the first coming of Jesus Christ into the world and His second coming.[21]

Mockers will come with *their* mocking -- The "mockers" or "scoffers" (KJV) are the same false teachers introduced in chapter 2:1.[22] "With their mocking" (*en empaigmone*, found in nearly all the better manuscripts) has Peter emphasizing the mockers' scorn using a Hebraism,

---

[19] In 1 Peter, Peter shows an intimate knowledge of several of Paul's epistles and that of James. In this second letter he is writing to churches addressed in 1 Peter, and we have noted that some of them were planted by Paul. We must therefore understand, even before we get to 3:15, that Peter recognized the apostleship of Paul, just as Paul did that of Peter (cp. Galatians 2:9). The New Testament gives little evidence of an alleged Petrine vs. Pauline split in theological emphases, or of a lasting personal animosity that allegedly colored all their later dealings with each other.

[20] "Knowing" is actually a participle in the nominative case. Participles usually need another verb form to lean upon, and we might have expected an accusative participle leaning on the infinitive "remember" with which verse 2 began. Instead, Peter uses a nominative so we know it is the readers, the "beloved" of verse 1, who are to pay special attention to what he now has to say from Scripture. It is a little difficult to get a smooth English translation, so some of our versions (cp. NASB) treat the participle as though it were an imperative verb. Treating it as a circumstantial participle, we could translate, "Remember the words of the apostles and prophets while keeping this thought uppermost in your minds ...."

[21] Peter quoted Joel 2:28-32 in his first recorded sermon (Acts 2:16-21) and there it shows that "last days" covers both the beginning of the church age when God would pour out His spirit on all mankind and also the close of the age when cosmological changes would introduce the great and glorious day of the Lord. In 1 Peter 1:20, Peter used a different expression, the last of the times. When Jude (verse 18) alludes to what Peter here wrote, he uses "in the last times" as synonymous with "last days." Commentators often let their eschatology determine their theology at this place. Some write about the "time of trouble" (or the Great Tribulation, as it is called) as they offer comments in this place. We think it to be hardly believable that by "last days" Peter is alluding to a time 2000 years after his readers were dead. "Beloved, beware of false teachers -- they'll get here in 2000 years!" is hardly the point Peter is making. His readers would themselves still be living on earth when they would see the false teachers arrive, about whom he was warning them.

[22] Fronmüller (*op. cit.*, p.40) sees here another class of adversaries of Christ, different from the false prophets and teachers described in 2:1. As in the Introductory Studies, so here, the position is taken that chapters 2 and 3 are descriptions of the same group of false teachers, the difference being only concerning which of their false teachings the writer is calling attention to at the moment.

a Hebrew manner of speech.[23] Peter is saying the mockers will hold up to scathing contempt and ridicule any idea that Jesus might return to earth again.[24] Peter here prophetically asserts "the mockers will come!"

Following after their own lusts -- As they did their mocking, they were but walking after their own desires,[25] thus revealing that this was the real cause of their cynicism and denial. Peter has already described how the false teachers would live in sensuality (2:18) and be slaves of corruption (2:19).[26] He is here reminding his readers of the character description he has already written. "After" (*kata,* "down"), pictures the downward course along which they are proceeding.

3:4 -- *And saying, "Where is the promise of His coming? For* ever *since the fathers fell asleep, all continues just as it was from the beginning of creation."*

And saying -- The participle "saying" joins closely with the participle "following," and both of them lean on "mockers will come." Living according to their own desires, they mock any incentive to holy living – especially any idea there might be a second coming of Christ and a judgment to be faced.

"Where is the promise of His coming? -- The mockers were not asking, 'In what passages of Scripture does one read about it?' but they were asking, 'Where is the accomplishment of what was promised?' "His" instead of "the Lord's" probably reflects the irreverent way in which the scoffers will speak of Jesus. The word translated "coming" here is *parousia*, the regular word for the visit of a royal personage.[27] Back of our Greek text may be another He-

---

[23] There are other repetitions of this kind (Hebraisms) in the New Testament which have been translated by strengthening the verb in some way or another -- John 3:29; Acts 4:17, 5:28; James 5:17. Compare how repetition intensifies the meaning in Luke 22:15; Ephesians 1:3; Revelation 19:2. The word *empaigmone* ("mocking") occurs nowhere else in the New Testament, and *empaiktai* ("mockers") occurs only in the parallel passage at Jude 18. *Empaiktai*, which comes from "to play with, to sport with," does occur in the LXX of Isaiah 3:4, where the Hebrew has *ta'alulim*, "babes" (KJV), petulant (i.e., people who jest about or carelessly play with things of the greatest importance).

[24] Not a few writers call attention to Psalm 1:1, where we hear there will be some who "sit in the seat of scoffers" and who will be the opposite of the "righteous."

[25] *Epithumias* ("lusts, desires") has been explained at 2:18.

[26] How many times persons living in self-indulgence, in an effort to justify their own behavior, will deny great Biblical truths, and not only deny them personally, but broadcast their denial to anyone who will listen.

[27] At least three different Greek words, *apokalusis* ("revelation"), *epiphaneia* ("appearance, to be visible to human eyes") and *parousia* ("presence"), are used to refer to Christ's second advent. When we compare what is said to transpire when those comings occur, we conclude that all three words are but different figures of speech describing the same return of Christ at the end of the age. (Some systems of eschatology have 7 years of time between the *parousia* and the revelation, and perhaps another 1000 years transpiring before the appearance happens. This author is not convinced those systems present a true picture of second coming prophecies. See his *Let's Study Prophecy: Guidelines for Harmonizing Bible Prophecies about the Second Coming of Christ* [Moberly, MO: Scripture Exposition Books, 1982 reprint].) Fronmüller (*ibid.*) is correct, we believe, when he says that *parousia* is used of "the visible coming of Christ to the judgment of the wicked and the consummation of His kingdom" as 2 Peter 3:12 goes on to speak about.

braism – the traditional Jewish way of stating that the questioner thinks the thing questioned does not exist or is not true. Compare the question asked by evil men in Malachi's day, "Where is the God of justice?" (Malachi 2:17). Compare what the heathen demanded of the Psalmist, "Where is your God?" (Psalm 42:3, 79:10), with its implied answer "Isn't it true He is nowhere?" Compare what the enemies asked Jeremiah, "Where is the Word of the Lord?" (Jeremiah 17:15). "In every case, the implication of the question, and the belief of the questioner is that the thing or person asked about is a delusion and does not exist."[28] By the way he words their question, Peter is predicting that when the heretics appear, they will deny altogether that Jesus will ever come again.[29] Peter's words also indicate a general knowledge among the false teachers, a knowledge also held by the church members, that such a second coming had long been predicted by both the prophets and the apostles.[30]

For ever since the fathers fell asleep -- Peter here anticipates by prophetic insight the reason the mockers will give for denying the actuality of any second coming of Jesus. "Fell asleep" is a euphemism for physical death, a pleasant way of speaking of something that is itself not always pleasant.[31] Physical death is like a sleep; the body lies "sleeping"(as it were) in the

---

[28] Barclay, *op. cit.*, p.400.

[29] What was true at the beginning of the "last days" (Jude 3) and experienced by Peter's readers, we, too, who are also living in the same last days, can identify with. Certain contemporary preterist interpreters insist the prophecies about the return of Christ were all fulfilled in the destruction of Jerusalem in AD 70. They are denying there is any second advent yet to be experienced. Certain Neo-liberals project a similar doubt about any supernatural return of Christ. (See for example, Barclay's last full paragraph on page 408, where he indicates this is a doctrine we will have to lay aside.) How sad that men are still skeptical of what Jesus and writers of both Old and New Testaments indicated the future would certainly hold. With no second coming, there would be no resurrection. With no resurrection, there would be no consummation of history. With no consummation of history, everything God has been trying to do in His world would have come to naught. That is the thrust of 1 Corinthians 15:22ff.

[30] The second coming of Christ was taught in the Old Testament, see Daniel 7:13,14; Psalm 110:1 (cp. Hebrews 1:13, 10:13); Isaiah 26:11; Habakkuk 2:3,4 (cp. Hebrews 10:36-38). In a few verses, we shall call attention to other Old Testament verses dealing with the consummation of the age. That Jesus predicted His reign in heaven followed by His own return, see Matthew 16:27, 24:36-44ff, 26:64; John 14:1-3, 21:22. That His apostles took up the same glad refrain, see Acts 1:11, 3:20, 17:31; 1 Corinthians 15:23,51; 2 Corinthians 5:4; Titus 2:12,13; 1 Thessalonians 4:15-17, 5:2; 2 Thessalonians 1:7-10; 1 Peter 1:11; Revelation 1:7. Even the Lord's Supper is a weekly announcement of the return of Jesus ("you proclaim the Lord's death until He comes," 1 Corinthians 11:26). Members of the early church greeted one another with the glad news that "Our Lord is coming!" (*marana tha*, 1 Corinthians 16:22).

[31] The expression "fell asleep" is used of Stephen's death (Acts 7:60, NASB). Compare Matthew 27:52; Mark 5:39; John 11:11,13 (where Jesus says "Our friend Lazarus has fallen asleep" and John explains Jesus was talking about his physical death); 1 Corinthians 7:39, 15:6,18; 1 Thessalonians 4:13,14. The Bible does not teach soul sleep. See notes at Acts 7:60 in the author's *New Testament History: Acts*, p.305. The thoroughly Christian term "cemetery" (i.e., "sleeping place"), in the sense of a place where the dead body is at rest, comes from the same Greek root. Just as Jesus was able to raise sleeping Lazarus with a word, so it will be for all the dead on the great resurrection morning. Those who sleep in the tombs will be awakened, some to everlasting life, and some to everlasting condemnation. Thus, early Christians, having learned it from Jesus, readily embraced the term "asleep" as being perfectly in keeping with their well-founded conviction of the future resurrection of dead bodies. Of course, all this is a hopeless delusion if there is no second coming of Jesus and thus no resurrection.

grave. Commentators have disagreed when it comes to trying to identify the persons the false teachers call "the fathers." Is it the ancestors of the human race?[32] Is it the patriarchs and Old Testament prophets?[33] Is it the first generation of Christians?[34] Since Peter goes on to quote the false teachers concerning how all things have continued "from the beginning of creation," there is no reason to believe "the fathers" must be limited to the first generation of Christians.[35] The reference to the death of "the fathers" is spoken of from the mockers' perspective after they arrive on the scene, not from Peter's perspective some years before the mockers arrive.

All things continue just as it was from the beginning of creation." -- The mockers were going to argue against the idea of a second advent from the alleged uniformitarianism of nature. Things are going on[36] just as they have from the beginning;[37] there have been no sud-

---

[32] This suggestion may have arisen from an attempt to get rid of the difficulty of two dates (see footnote #36 below) by making both clauses in the verse mean virtually the same thing. Plummer argued that the second date might just be an afterthought. "Frequent is such language in Thucydides. The second [date] strengthens the first. 'Since the fathers fell asleep all things continue as they are -- nay more, since the beginning of creation [they continue as they are].'" *Op. cit.*, p.168.

[33] The term "fathers" is often used in the New Testament for the Old Testament patriarchs and for the generation of Hebrews who came out Egypt at the end of the captivity there (John 6:31; Romans 9:5; Acts 3:13; Hebrews 1:1).

[34] Peter is writing 37 years after the ascension of Jesus. Stephen has died (Acts 7:60). James the son of Zebedee has died (Acts 12:2). James the brother of the Lord has died. Not only have leaders died, but many of the first generation of Christians have also died by the time Peter wrote (cp. 1 Thessalonians 4:13, written 15 years before Peter wrote 2 Peter, and Hebrews 13:7, also written before Peter wrote). While we opt for "fathers" as far back as Old Testament times being the meaning intended by the false teachers, we note that similar language in 1 Clement about "our fathers" refutes the idea of some that the first generation of Christians could not be the meaning of what is here predicted by Peter, as though such scoffing would not be possible within Peter's lifetime or shortly thereafter. I Clement xxiii uses "our fathers" to speak of the first generation of Christians, and this was written before the close of the first century. Clement shows the argument Peter predicted the scoffers would use actually was used, and that it happened before the end of the first century.

[35] Those writers who have scoured internal evidence for proof Peter didn't write this letter have seized upon this statement about "the fathers" as proof the epistle was written after Peter died. Blum (*op. cit.*, p.285) observes that since "fathers" is normal New Testament language for Old Testament "fathers," the forger had to be rather clumsy to have missed so obvious a blunder in his use of words.

[36] This is another place the KJV translators went backwards. The Greek is present tense, "just as they are," not past tense "as they were." Perhaps the KJV translators made the change in wording from a mistaken desire to get rid of a slight difficulty of two supposed dates being given: (1) from the death of the fathers, (2) from the beginning of creation.

[37] How long ago creation occurred has divided Biblical scholars into two camps: those who believe the earth to be relatively young (9000 years or less), and those who hold to a very long history for the earth. Austin Robbins, "A Question of Time: Old or Young Earth?" *Bible and Spade* 15/2 (2002), p.57-63, has a very good overview of the whole debate.

den catastrophes; the laws of nature are still working with their changeless monotony.[38] When the false teachers allude to "all things" (ASV), they apparently have in mind the entire observable cosmic system. The sun rises, the sun sets. Tides ebb, tides flow. Seasons follow each other in their usual order, seed time then harvest. A generation is born, a generation dies, to be followed by yet another generation. Is there not every indication things will continue to operate as they have always done? Peter's answer to this question is, 'Yes, nature is uniform,[39] except where God steps in! When the record is studied, it can be seen that God has stepped into history in the past. That being so, He can do it again!'

3. Refutation of the mockers' arguments. 3:5-9

3:5 -- *For when they maintain this, it escapes their notice that by the word of God* the *heavens existed long ago and* the *earth was formed out of water and by water,*

For when they maintain this -- The mockers will make two arguments, Peter has said. One, a lot of time has passed, and nothing has happened. Two, the observed uniformity of nature argues against a second coming. Peter answers the second argument first (verses 5-7) and then (verses 8,9) deals with the claim of a long time. Peter's reply to their argument about uniformity is this: when the mockers say "from the beginning of creation all things continue as they are," they are flatly contradicting the account in Genesis. That is the point which Peter will flesh out in this and the verses following.

It escapes their notice -- "This they willfully forget" (ASV).[40] This thing escapes them willingly; that is, as they argue for the uniformity of nature, they will purposefully allow some things taught in Genesis[41] to go unnoticed.[42] False teachers, as they use Scripture to uphold

---

[38] Earlier, we have noted that arguments as old as the first-century mockers' arguments are still being used today. The same can be said about an argument from the uniformitarianism of nature. Charles Lyell (1797-1875) propounded a theory about the uniformity of nature that became the basis of later evolutionary attacks against supernaturalism.

[39] Care must be taken lest we press Peter's popular language too far. We are aware that at one time our world tried to base a view of nature on Newtonian physics. Science tried to show that our world was fixed with mathematical precision and predictable regularity. Then came along Heisenberg's theory of indeterminacy. Some properties of atoms are relative rather than fixed, and certain components of atoms do not react in the predictable way as was thought they would under Newtonian laws.

[40] There is a considerable variety in the translation of this passage in our English versions. The general idea is clear: there was a willful, deliberate attempt to make sure something escapes people's notice.

[41] The Greek word translated "this" (ASV) refers to what follows, namely, the changes that have happened since the beginning of Creation, changes that are plainly recorded in the chapters of Genesis for all to see.

[42] To see a modern example of deliberate exclusion of evidence to the contrary in the field of geology, see Bolton Davidheiser, *Science and the Bible* (Grand Rapids: Baker, 1971), chapter 23.

their views, will often omit some known Scriptures which contradict the views they are teaching. This is a part of wresting of the Scripture that 2 Peter 3:16 talks about.

That by the word of God *the* heavens existed long ago -- In the Greek, "by the word of God" stands last for emphasis. "By the word of God!" "Not by some fortuitous concourse of already existing atoms, not by spontaneous generation."[43] Instead of all things continuing from the beginning just as they are, there was a creation – a great and stupendous change, wrought by the word of God. Peter's language reminds us of what we read in Genesis 1:3, "Then God said ...."[44] God spoke and it was done! "Heavens" is plural, speaking of the atmosphere (Heb. *Rakiah*) and the starry heavens (Heb. *Shamayim*). "Long ago" or "from of old" (ASV) points back to the very first origin of all things. It is not true that things have always existed as they are. There was a time when heavens and earth were not. They were called into being by the word of God.[45] Don't you forget it!

And *the* earth was formed out of water and by water -- This is a difficult phrase to understand. Most writers believe Peter is referring to what is recorded in Genesis 1:6-10, a second passage in Genesis which shows that there has been a great change in how things are. His point? If there has been such a great change once, there is no reason to say there will be no change again! God has stepped into history. Jesus can step in again as He returns! The thrust of Peter's argument is clear enough.

The problem is in the details. The Greek reads *kai ge ex hudatos kai di' hudatos sunestosa*, and Marshall in his interlinear offers "and earth out of water and through water having been held together."[46] Comparing this to the NASB, the problems are fairly obvious. What translation shall we give *sunistemi*? The NASB has "formed"; the KJV has "standing

---

[43] Plummer, *op. cit.*, p.169.

[44] Some think "Word" is a reference to Jesus Christ, as in John 1:1,14. We acknowledge that Jesus was active in creation (Colossians 1:16). We also recognize that such a creation by Jesus was flatly denied by the Gnostics. "The world was not made by angels, nor by powers separated from God, but by his Word -- Christ," wrote Irenaeus as he contended against the Gnostics of his day (*Adv. Haer.*, II.2). A case certainly could be made for Peter also making reference to Jesus' work in creation. However, we tend to think Peter is referring to what can be plainly read in the pages of the Genesis record. Cp. Hebrews 11:3. (In the Shepherd of Hermas [*Vis.* i.3.4] we read, "Behold the God of virtues [powers] ... by His mighty word has fixed the heaven, and laid the foundation of the earth upon the waters." In an *Apology* of Melito of Sardis, addressed to Antonius Caesar about AD 170, there is a passage bearing considerable resemblances to verses 3-5 [see it quoted in the Introductory Studies].)

[45] "Existed" translates the imperfect tense form *hesan*. The word marks a continued existence. There was a time between creation and the flood that there was a continuity like that to which the mockers were appealing. But it wasn't a permanent, eternal continuity.

[46] Alfred Marshall, "Literal English translation," in *The Interlinear Greek-English New Testament* (London: Bagster, 1958), p.929.

out of" with a marginal note "consisting of."[47] Does the participle built off the verb *sunistemi* go with both prepositional phrases ("out of ..." and "by ..."), or with only the second one? What does "out of water" mean? Some think it denotes the material out of which the earth was made. Others think it pictures the earth rising up like an island in the ocean. What does "by water" mean?[48] Some think it says that water is the thing (a kind of glue) that helps hold together the earth (i.e., without a certain amount of moisture, all you have are loose particles of sand and dust).[49] Others think there is some reference to the waters above the firmament that Genesis 1 talks about. Whatever the meaning of the details, up until we begin verse 6, Peter is describing the world as it was before the flood.

3:6 -- *Through which the world at that time was destroyed, being flooded with water.*

Through which – *Di' hon* is plural in the Greek, "by means of which things." What things? To what does the plural refer? It might refer to "heavens ... and earth" (3:5); that is, these things contained in themselves the instruments of their own renovation. It might refer to the two words "water" in the previous verse. Compare Genesis 7:11, "the fountains of the great deep (the waters beneath) burst open," and "the floodgates of the sky were opened (waters from above)" when the deluge came. It might be explained the plural refers both to the waters and to the word of God. The flood waters destroyed the world because that was how the word of God directed things to happen. Verse 7 will connect the same "word of God" to the future judgment of the world when Christ returns.

The world at that time was destroyed -- The "world at that time" is the world as it stood in Noah's day, the pre-flood world.[50] "Destroyed" translates *apoleto*. It does not teach annihi-

---

[47] The same word is translated "consist" (KJV) or "hold together" (NASB) at Colossians 1:17. "The notion is that of coherence, solidarity, and order, as distinct from chaos" (Plummer, *op. cit.*, p.169). The perfect tense here indicates past completed action with present continuing results. When God was done creating, for a while, until the flood, things stood just as God made them.

[48] The KJV "in water" came from either the Genevan or Tyndale Bibles. It is difficult to see how *dia* can be translated "in" when *dia* and the genitive indicates intermediate agent, "by means of water."

[49] The NASB translators seemed to think that "by water" refers either to the action of the waters that gave the earth form and shape, or that water sustains life on earth.

[50] At 2 Peter 2:5 the meaning of the word *kosmos*, "world," has been discussed. The globe called "earth" was not destroyed, only its inhabitants and its outward form.

lation, but a change or breaking up of a previously existing order.[51] "The world that then was ... perished" (KJV) is equivalent to "God did not spare the ancient world" of 2 Peter 2:5.[52]

Being flooded with water -- "Flooded" translates *kataklustheis*, "cataclysm," the regular word for the Flood both in the New Testament and in classical Greek (see notes at 2 Peter 2:5). Peter has answered the uniformitarianism-of-nature argument of the mockers. It is absurd to say all things continue unchanged from the creation. There were huge changes as creation occurred and dry land appeared. There was a great catastrophe that ended the pre-flood world.[53] The flood was a catastrophe of such magnitude that no one can claim the earth has continued as it was from the beginning![54] The world previous to the flood perished; chaos for the moment returned, and a new world issued from the crisis.

3:7 -- *But the present heavens and earth by His word are being reserved for fire, kept for the day of judgment and destruction of ungodly men.*

---

[51] If "world" speaks of wicked men, 1 Peter 3:18 shows they were not annihilated; instead, their souls are imprisoned in another place waiting the final judgment. If "world" speaks of the globe, it was not annihilated, for we are still living on it. It was the face of the earth that was altered or "destroyed" by the flood.

(Our definition of "the world that then was" [KJV] depends on how we answer another question. Does 2 Peter 3:6 refer to a creation-ruination-recreation at Genesis 1:2 [the Gap Theory], or does verse 6 refer to the flood in Noah's time? In comments on verse 5, "from of old," we have indicated our preference for the time of the flood. Those who hold the Gap Theory teach that when the devil and his sinning angels were cast out of heaven, the whole pre-Adamic world -- including a race of men who lived on earth -- was destroyed because the world was contaminated by the sins of the devil and those pre-Adamic men. This ruination happened between Genesis 1:1 and 1:2. God then started all over to bring order out of chaos, Genesis 1:2. Wuest [*op. cit.*, p.67] teaches the Gap Theory as he comments on verse 5. A good rebuttal of the Gap Theory is found in Bernard Ramm, *The Christian View of Science and Scripture* [Grand Rapids: Eerdmans, 1955], p.195ff]. This commentator doubts the Gap Theory is taught anywhere in Scripture.)

[52] In the Introductory Studies, we called attention to the fact that Peter mentions three worlds (or shall we say three different conditions for this world) in this chapter (verses 6,7,13).

[53] These verses in 2 Peter form a considerable part of the commentator's Biblical worldview. It has a far-reaching significance for harmonizing the Bible and science and for judging certain current scientific theories. In this commentator's biblical worldview are included: (1) The real fact of **creation**. By the Word of God there was a creation *ex nihilo*. The things created were created with the appearance of age. The creation was accomplished by processes no longer in operation (Genesis 2:2). With this the first law of thermodynamics agrees, that nothing is now being created. (2) The **curse**. When God made it, everything was pronounced "very good" (Genesis 1:31). But Adam sinned, and physical death entered the world because of it (1 Corinthians 15:21,22; Romans 5:12), and the creation was subjected by its Creator to futility/corruption (Romans 8:20). This is the Biblical way of stating what is called the second law of thermodynamics, that the universe is running down. (3) The **flood**. This commentator is a catastrophist. In a global flood, the world that then was perished. The heavens, too, were changed by the removal of the canopy of waters that used to be above the earth and protected it. The world that now is (2 Peter 3:7) is different. Absolute uniformitarianism of nature since the earth began is a rejected hypothesis. At most, what can be said is that there has been an observable uniformity since the flood. (4) History is being moved to a **goal** by the God Who made it. That goal includes the return of Jesus, the final judgment, the consummation, and the ushering in of the states known as heaven and hell.

[54] In passing, Barclay makes the flood just a legend (*op. cit.*, p.402). Such a treatment eviscerates any argument Peter might be thought to give in rebuttal to the mockers. If it never really happened, then the earth has continued from the beginning just as the mockers claimed, has it not?

But the present heavens and earth -- The contrast in "now are" (i.e., "present") is to the earth before the flood in Noah's time. The heavens and earth that "now are" are different than they were before the flood.[55] Alford explains that Noah stepped out of the ark onto an earth that had a new face, and into a "starry heavens" that had a different appearance.[56]

By His word -- Some manuscripts read "by the same word."[57] If that reading is accepted as being correct, it refers to the original word of creation (verse 5), and this verse says that at the time of creation it was determined by God how the world would be destroyed. If we adopt "by His word," the reference could be to what God has said in the pages of Old Testament Scripture since the flood. See Joel 2:3; Psalm 50:3; Isaiah 29:6, 30:30, 66:15,16; Daniel 7:9,10; Micah 1:4; Nahum 1:5,6; and Malachi 4:1, for statements that the world will be destroyed the next time by fire.

Are being reserved for fire -- The words translated "are being reserved," (*tethesaurismenoi eisin*) are in the perfect tense. They were treasured up or kept in store in the past, and are still being kept. The word "fire" is in the dative and could be translated *with* fire or *for* fire. If we take it to be *with* fire, then the earth contains, stored up in its inner depths, the flammable materials (e.g., coal, oil, gas, the earth's molten core) which will finally be set afire. If we take it to be *for* fire, then the idea is that in the counsels of God the plans are to destroy (renovate) the earth with fire, when Jesus returns and the day of judgment takes place. This fire might be pictured as being rained from heaven, just as it happened when He rained fire and brimstone on Sodom and Gomorrah (Luke 17:29). The verses following seem to show this second idea is the correct one. This is one of the clearest prophecies in Scripture of the final conflagration of the universe, though John the Baptist (Matthew 3:11,12) and Paul both also spoke of it (2 Thessalonians 1:8).[58]

---

[55] It would not serve Peter's argument to make the contrast between the heavens and earth as they now are, and the new heavens and earth as they will be. That was the very thing being denied by the mockers.

[56] Alford, *op. cit.*, p.414. What were the physical changes made on this globe called "earth" by the flood? Were hills leveled or raised? Did some marine life become fossilized? Were layers of water laid rock produced by the huge tides and rolling billows that swished over the face of the globe while it was covered with water? See Donald Patten, *The Biblical Flood and the Ice Epoch* (Seattle : Pacific Meridian Publishing, 1966) and John C. Whitcomb and Henry M. Morris, *The Genesis Flood: The Biblical Record and Its Scientific Implications* (Philadelphia, PA: Presbyterian and Reformed Publishing Co., 1964) and a video by Steve Austin, *Mount St. Helens: Explosive Evidence for Catastrophe* (El Cajon, CA: Institute for Creation Research, 198?) showing pictorial evidence of geological strata being formed quickly by mud and water slides. Canyons, strata, the face of the landscape are changed in just hours.

[57] Sinaiticus, Ephraemi, and the Byzantine family generally, read "by His word."

[58] Because the Stoics and Persians had a doctrine about how the world would end, and because something similar is found in the *Book of Enoch*, source critics have supposed the writer of 2 Peter was influenced by one of these views. Gordon H. Clark points out the Stoics and Peter have far different ideas about the final conflagration. He gives two reasons why we should not seek among the Stoics for Peter's sources. "The first has to do with physics and the second is very strictly religious. In Stoicism the final conflagration is a gradual, natural process inherent in the constitution of matter. The process is cyclical and continuous ... Peter, on the other hand, announces a sudden, non-cyclical, virtually instantaneous cataclysm. This ends world history. There is no repeat. The second reason why Stoicism cannot be the source of the apostle's ideas is strictly religious. Whereas the Stoic

Kept for the day of judgment and the destruction of ungodly men -- "Kept" (present tense, *teroumenoi*) indicates that God's watchful providence and hands-on control is the only thing that keeps the fire from being kindled immediately. Biblical theism is not deism, where God just wound up the universe and then went off to leave it run on its own. Heaven and earth have not been released from His divine control, free to go on their own way forever just as they are now.[59] He is holding off the fire till the judgment day dawns. The Bible seems to teach that there will be one general judgment,[60] followed by the casting of the wicked into Hell.[61] Peter has described the false teachers and their duped followers as being "ungodly men" (2:6, cp. Jude 4), i.e., people who have no reverential awe towards God. If "destruction" is going to happen to those who follow the false teachers, and – contrary to what they affirm – that destruction happens when Christ's second advent occurs,[62] should not Peter's readers think twice about following them?

Peter's first argument is that the mockers were wrong because they were deliberately avoiding some of the Biblical evidence in the early chapters of Genesis. When all the evidence is studied, it is obvious that nature has not continued as it is from the beginning. We do not live in a closed universe! God has stepped into history in the past with cataclysmic results. It will happen again! Jesus is coming!

3:8 -- ***But do not let this one*** **fact** ***escape your notice, beloved, that with the Lord one day is as a thousand years, and a thousand years as one day.***

---

conflagration is purely natural, Peter's is a divine judgment and punishment of a sinful human race. This idea is as absent from Stoicism as theirs is from Peter." *II Peter. A Short Commentary* (Nutley, NJ: Presbyterian and Reformed Pub. Co., 1972), p.69.

[59] This same verb "kept" or "reserved" was used in 1 Peter 1:4 of the final destiny of the redeemed. Here in 2 Peter the verb has already been used three times (2:4,9,17), and each time it speaks about what God has "reserved" for wicked men and angels.

[60] Some systems of eschatology have a plurality of judgments following Christ's return, some of them separated by many years. However, if we run the references of the passages that speak of the judgment, we will see that though different classes of people are spoken about, yet the things that accompany the judgment – like the taking of the righteous to heaven, the casting of the wicked into hell, and the consummation – all take place *following* the judgment, regardless of what class of people is being judged. Further, it would appear from chapter 3 of 2 Peter that the "day of judgment" follows the *parousia* (see "coming" in verse 4, and "judgment" in verse 7). So readers should be careful here, for the commentator's eschatology (i.e., his millennial theories in particular) can greatly color the explanations offered at this place.

[61] The word "destruction" here and the verb "destroyed" in verse 6 come from the same root and have identical meanings. The Bible does not teach the wicked will be annihilated anymore than the earth ceased to exist when it was "destroyed" by the flood. What is meant is there will be a great change in the condition of the wicked, attended by penal consequences.

[62] The destruction of ungodly men takes place at the second coming of Christ. Paul says it happens at the "revelation" of Christ (2 Thessalonians 1:7-10). Peter says it happens at the *parousia* and the day of judgment (2 Peter 3:4,7). How do the premillennialists make their theory (a theory which says the *parousia* and Revelation comings are two different things) jibe with this amazing fact? We are convinced that a comparison of 2 Thessalonians and 2 Peter indicates that "parousia" and "revelation" are two different words for Christ's same second advent.

But -- Peter now begins to answer the mocker's second argument; namely, that a lot of time has passed and nothing has happened. In verses 8 and 9, Peter explains that we are not to judge the Lord by the same time constraints we use to judge men, nor accuse Him of being slow.

Do not let this one *fact* escape your notice, beloved -- As he answered the first argument which Peter predicts the mockers would advance to deny any second coming, Peter accused them of deliberately ignoring some pertinent Biblical evidence (verse 5). Now he calls on his beloved[63] readers to stop ignoring[64] similar pertinent Biblical evidence. Stop allowing "this one fact (to) escape your notice!" The Greek construction is the kind that forbids the continuance of an action already going on.[65] What the one fact is, the next verses go on to state.

That with the Lord one day is as a thousand years, and a thousand years as one day -- The language Peter uses reminds us of Psalm 90:4.[66] From that Old Testament passage we learn that distinctions of long and short time are nothing in the sight of God. A lot of time passing is a purely human concept.[67] God doesn't look at the passing of time like we human

---

[63] See notes on "beloved" at 3:1.

[64] Peter uses the same word, *lanthano*, that he used in verse 5 of the mockers' purposefully allowing some things to go unnoticed.

[65] It is just possible that some Christians inadvertently gave the mockers a fertile seed bed into which seeds of doubt could be planted. Already, years earlier, when Paul wrote his two letters to the Thessalonians, it is evident that some Christians entertained erroneous views regarding the time and the nature of the Lord's return (see 1 Thessalonians 4:13-18, 5:13; 2 Thessalonians 2:1-7). Observe carefully what has been said here. It has not been said the apostles and prophets who gave us the New Testament writings changed their ideas about when the return of the Lord would occur, shifting emphases from an imminent return to an emphasis on explaining the apparent delay. We have said it is possible some of their *readers* misunderstood what the apostles and prophets wrote as they urged a lifestyle in harmony with a constant expectation of Jesus' return. Peter's imperative to stop thinking that way would be a corrective to the readers' mindsets, and once their thinking was right, the false teachers would get nowhere with their "It's been a long time and nothing has happened yet" arguments.

[66] The ideas expressed both in Psalm 90:4 and here in 2 Peter 3:8 are the same, but the language Peter uses is not a word-for-word quotation (the NASB did not put any of verse 8 in small capital letters, though Westcott and Hort did put some of the words in caps). Justin Martyr's language (*Dial. c. Trypho*, lxxxi) is much closer to 2 Peter 3:8 than to Psalm 90:4. As another possible allusion to 2 Peter follows in the next chapter of Justin, it is altogether possible Justin knew the letter we call 2 Peter. In any case, since Psalm 90 is cited in its heading as being by Moses, we have Peter appealing to Moses both to answer the mockers (an appeal to Genesis) and to correct the thinking of his readers (an appeal to Psalm 90).

[67] Negative critics have used the term "delay" to express a view that, as the years passed since Christ's ascension and the second coming had not happened yet, somehow the early apostles and preachers had to come up with a plausible explanation that did not obviously contradict what they had preached earlier, or otherwise risk losing their followers (or at the least cause their followers to doubt the truthfulness of what they were saying). Therefore, we hesitate to use the term "delay" in our commentary. We have no wish to give any aid or comfort to those who insist there are mistakes in our Bibles! If we have interpreted John 21:18-23 correctly, Peter would have understood Christ to be saying the *parousia* would not occur in Peter's own lifetime. Therefore, it would be improper to accuse a young Peter of ever preaching that Christ would return during his lifetime only to have to change his message as he got older.

beings do, and the passing of time does not affect the promises or threatenings of God. Whether it be a day or a thousand years between the time of the promise and the reward, or between the threatening and the retribution, God will perform it. He keeps His word! Peter's comment on the equivalence between one day and a thousand years with God is a beautiful statement of God's eternality, His superiority to time-space limitations.[68] And it is exciting to think how such a concept contracts the period of waiting for Christ's return. We accomplish quickly enough our years of this pilgrimage. But then, once "with the Lord" and freed from space-time limitations, it is but a day or two – figured even from apostolic times – until His kingdom comes with all its joys.[69]

3:9 -- ***The Lord is not slow about His promise, as some count slowness, but is patient toward you, not wishing for any to perish but for all to come to repentance.***

The Lord is not slow about His promise -- Having called on his beloved readers to stop judging the Lord using the same time constraints we apply to men, he now calls on them to stop thinking the Lord might be "slow." It is difficult to know whether "the Lord" refers to Jesus Christ or to the Father. In verse 8, it appears "the Lord" referred to God the Father. That would be in favor of the same meaning here. So would Mark 13:32, where we are told that only God the Father knows of the day and hour when the second coming will occur. On the other hand, "about His promise" naturally refers to Jesus Christ's promise that He will return. The same doubt (i.e., is it the Father or the Son?) also occurs in verse 15 below. *Bradutes* means "slow, to linger, to be tardy." No one should think the Lord is late beyond the appointed time. "Promise" in the genitive case could be tied to "the Lord" so that it would read "the Lord of promise is not slow ...." More likely, though, the way the ASV/NASB trans-

---

[68] God can take a thousand years to do a job we might expect Him to do in a day. He can do in a day what we might expect Him to take a thousand years to do. God, who has all of eternity and who is guided by His infinite wisdom, can do things as quickly or as slowly as He sees best.

[69] Several warning signs must be erected so people passing this way will avoid some dangers. (1) The early church fathers, as is well known, drew from this passage in Peter the inference that the world is to last 6000 years from the time of creation until the second coming, with the second coming followed by one more 1000-year-long "day," the "day of the Lord." Hebrews 4:9 was also enlisted as a proof text, since it speaks of a "sabbath rest" for the people of God. God created in six days and rested on the seventh. (Actually, the book of Hebrews argues God's rest is already available and Christians could miss the rest if they left Christianity to go back to Judaism.) Ignoring the application made by the Hebrews writer, the early church fathers drew from this the idea that the six days of creation (i.e., 6000 years of history) are to be followed by a seventh day (i.e., 1000 years), called in Hebrews a "sabbath rest." Examples of those second-century and later writings include the *Epistle of Barnabas* (xv.4) where we read, "For a day means with Him a thousand years, as He himself witnesseth, saying, Behold, today shall be as a thousand years." That same epistle, as it appears in Codex Sinaiticus, reads, "The Day of the Lord shall be as a thousand years." Irenaeus has the same language twice (*Adv. Haer.*, v.23.2; 28.3). Hippolytus has it once (*Comm. on Daniel*), and Methodius once (*Photius Bibliotheca*, cod. 235). None of this extravagance is found in 2 Peter. How did the alleged second-century forger miss it when it was the *zeitgeist* of the time? (2) A second warning sign: this verse in Peter should not be used to prove God will punish the wicked a thousand years in hell for every day they have sinned on this earth. Nor does it say God can punish in one day the sins of a thousand years.

lates it is correct.[70] So translated, it speaks of the promise made time after time that Jesus will return, the earth will be renovated, and the day of judgment will dawn. The Lord who made such a definite promise is not tardy or slack about doing what He promised.[71] He has not backed off from doing what He promised.

As some count slowness -- When men, after a considerable lapse of time, fail to keep their promises, we infer it is because they have changed their plans, or because they have forgotten their promises, or because they have no ability to perform them, or because they lack the honor which makes them keep their promises, or because they have died, or because some other conditions have arisen which make it impossible to perform what they had promised. No such inference can be drawn when it is the Lord who has made a promise. None of these contingencies characteristic of men is ever the characteristic of the Lord. If a long time passes, it is not evidence the Lord has forgotten or has changed His plans. If what seems like a long time passes, it is because the Lord, who can take all the time He wants to, has some good motive for waiting.[72]

But is patient toward you -- If what seems to men to be a long time passes between when the promise was made and its fulfillment, the long time is not due to some shortcoming in the Lord or from procrastination. It is because of His longsuffering. Peter uses the same word here he did in 1 Peter 3:20 when he wrote about how the patience of God waited while the ark was being built. *Makrothumia* ("putting up with people"[73]) calls to mind God's infinite patience with sinners who put Him to the test and provoke Him. He puts off the punishment due sin for a long time, hoping the sinner will take the opportunity to repent. The startling and sobering thing about this verse is that it is Christians ("you"[74]), Peter's beloved readers, with whom God is being patient.

---

[70] Strict grammar would have had an accusative after the verb rather than a genitive. The genitive suggests holding back *from* the promise, so that it will not be fulfilled.

[71] In notes at verse 4 and in footnote #30, we called attention to Jesus' own personal promise of His second advent. Statements made by some modern interpreters, that Jesus promised His return would be during the generation immediately following His resurrection and ascension, are not acceptable. Interpreters who treat Matthew 10:23, 16:28, 24:34, and Mark 9:1 as though Jesus mistakenly thought His second advent would happen within just a few years have put a wrong meaning on His words. Those verses evidently had reference to coming destruction of Jerusalem which occurred in AD 70.

[72] Whether Peter has some first-century people in mind who were accusing the Lord of "slowness," we cannot be sure. Perhaps, as indicated earlier, some of the church members to whom this verse is addressed had drawn some wrong conclusions. Perhaps the false teachers were going to use the apparent lapse of time as part of their mockery.

[73] A Greek synonym for "patience," *hupomone*, speaks of putting up with *things*.

[74] *Eis humas*, "toward you" (NASB) is a better supported reading than *eis hemas*, "to usward" (KJV), or *di' humas*, "because of you" found in some manuscripts. Peter's exclusion of himself (in "toward you") is no proof that Peter by now is living a sinless perfect life and so needs no repentance from time to time. Peter knows and appreciates the Lord's patience towards him, but he is calling on his readers to quit forgetting that it is longsuffering toward them that motivates the Lord to wait before fulfilling His promise about Jesus' return.

Not wishing for any to perish -- The Lord has no pleasure in the death of the wicked (Ezekiel 18:23,32, 33:11). "Perish" is the same word used in verses 6 and 7 where it was translated "destruction" or "destroyed." It speaks of being delivered up to eternal misery in hell. Peter knew very well many were on the broad way that leads to destruction (Matthew 7:13). They were going to perish as a result of the choices they made. But it was not God's original or personal desire that they perish. In fact, God in His goodness tries to lead men to repentance (Romans 2:4). Whether or not they respond positively to God's overtures is up to them. The translation of *boulomai* ("wishing") at this place is a matter of theological controversy between Arminian and Calvinistic interpreters. Does it talk about the Lord's *will* or the Lord's *wish*?[75] God has endowed man with the freedom to choose; if he wants to, man can resist and oppose all God wills or wishes. Of course, in the end, man will find that rebellious behavior carries with it a large penalty.

But for all to come to repentance -- The Greek word for "come" is *choresai* and means "to go in, to enter."[76] "Repentance" is a change of mind and a change of action resulting from Godly sorrow for sin, and includes restitution where possible.[77] This is what God wants Christians to do.[78] The fact that He gives them ample time to repent is not to be taken as evi-

---

[75] Two Greek words can be translated either "will" or "wish." They are *boulomai* and *thelo*. When writers of Greek "dictionaries" give explanations of the two words, they are not always free of theological bias. (Examples can be found in Berry, "New Testament Synonyms #32," *op. cit.*, p.128,129. See, too, the author's comments on *boulomai* and *thelo* at 1 Timothy 2:4 in *New Testament Epistles: Timothy and Titus* [Moberly, MO: Scripture Exposition Books, 1999], p. 49,50.) Strict predestinarians would be likely to argue that if the sovereign God "wills" something, it is going to happen. They therefore tend to want to make a distinction between God's "desirative" will and His "decretive" will, and attempt to make one of the Greek words refer to the first and the other to the second of these two kinds of will. Not feeling compelled to defend such nice theological distinctions, this commentator sees no reason why *boulomai* in this place means anything other than something that is the result of serious deliberation on God's part, just as Thayer (*op. cit.*, p.105, 285-286) defines the word.

One other thought could be added in passing. If this passage says that it is the Lord's decretive will that Christ not return until all of the elect have come to repentance (and this is surely how Calvinist interpreters would handle it), then this passage cannot be harmonized with premillennialism. Premillennial scholars usually teach there will be people saved during the millennium alleged to follow Christ's return. Since premillennialism must be defended, *boulomai* in this passage must speak of the Lord's "desirative" will, while at 1 Timothy 2:4 it is *thelo* that is His "desirative" will. We think the words are used pretty much interchangeably, and that no theological doctrine should be made to hinge on which word appears in any given passage.

[76] Thayer (*op. cit.*, p.252) gives as synonyms *erchomai*, *baino*, *poreuomai*, and *choreo*. He notes *choreo* always indicates the idea of separation, or change of place. Compare its use at Matthew 15:17. Calvin translated this word "willing to *receive* all to repentance," but Alford (*op. cit.*, p.415) says Calvin's translation is wrong, and quotes an exact parallel to Peter's language from Plutarch to prove how the Greek word was used.

[77] See the Special Study on "Repentance," in the author's *New Testament History: Acts* (*op. cit.*), p.145-149.

[78] Of course, each day Jesus doesn't return also gives the ungodly an opportunity to repent. Barclay (*op. cit.*, p.406) calls "each day which comes to us ... a gift of mercy." It is a day of opportunity granted to us by God to repent of our sins, to develop and purify ourselves, to render some service to our fellow-men, to grow in the expected qualities identified in 2 Peter 1:5-7.

dence that He will never send Jesus into the world again or that he will fail to renovate the earth by fire as He has promised He will do.[79]

4. Emphatic affirmation that the day of the Lord will come. 3:10

3:10 -- ***But the day of the Lord will come like a thief, in which the heavens will pass away with a roar and the elements will be destroyed with intense heat, and the earth and its works will be burned up.***

But the day of the Lord will come -- Peter leaves no uncertainty about the fulfillment of the promise. He flatly affirms it will be fulfilled, whatever may be the lapse of time until it occurs. The word "will come" (*hexei*) stands emphatically at the beginning of the clause. The "day of the Lord" is the day when Jesus shall appear on the clouds of heaven on the occasion of His second coming, for the purpose of raising the dead and instituting the general judgment.[80] "Day of the Lord" is a phrase found frequently in the Old Testament,[81] where it usually denotes God's decisive intervention in history for the purpose of judgment. By using familiar Old Testament language, Peter is saying the New Testament doctrine of the second coming of Jesus Christ is the same thing which was described in the Old Testament terminology "day of the Lord."[82] The absence of any article before "day of the Lord" stresses

---

[79] Advocates of universalism appeal not only to 1 Timothy 2:3,4 but also to Peter's "God desires all men to come to the knowledge of the truth." Barclay (*op. cit.*, p.406.) cites the usual proof texts supposed to teach universalism, and then expresses his own feelings, "We are not forbidden to believe that somehow and some time the God who loved the world will bring the whole world to Himself." Barclay's wishful embrace of universalism contradicts all Peter has written about destruction and perishing. If every one is going to be saved, why worry what the false teachers say, or whether or not young Christians may be persuaded to defect back to their sensual lifestyles and their old way of living? The plain truth is that after the second coming, there will be no further opportunity for repentance. That is why God in His longsuffering is giving men as long as possible to repent before the great and terrible day of the Lord dawns.

[80] 1 Thessalonians 5:2; 1 Corinthians 1:8; Philippians 1:6; and 2 Thessalonians 2:1-2 all connect the second coming and the judgment. What Peter highlights as happening on the "day of the Lord" is written with the arguments of the mockers in mind. They had asserted that "things continue as they are." Peter emphasizes the change that will occur when this material creation is "set free from its slavery to corruption into the freedom of the glory of the children of God" (Romans 8:21).

[81] See Isaiah 2:12, 13:6,9, 34:8; Ezekiel 13:5, 20:3; Joel 1:15, 2:11; Amos 5:18; Zephaniah 1:14; Zechariah 14:1.

[82] This conclusion is somewhat contradictory to certain modern premillennialists who distinguish four different "days" in their scheme of things. They speak of the "day of man" (1 Corinthians 4:3, Greek), which is supposed to speak of life here and now; the "day of Christ" (Philippians 1:6), which is supposed to speak of the rapture; the "day of the Lord" (Isaiah 13:9, 2 Peter 3:10), which is supposed to speak of the millennium; and "the day of God" (2 Peter 3:12) which is supposed to speak of heaven. Before one adopts such a scheme of things, it should be observed that in 2 Peter 3:12, the *parousia* is used of the "day of God" whereas on the premillennial scheme of things it should refer to the rapture, not to the day of God.

the character of the "day" as one belonging especially to the "Lord."[83]

Like a thief -- The point of the comparison is that the Lord's second coming will be sudden, unexpected, without warning. Peter's words here echo Jesus' own words spoken in His Olivet Discourse, a sermon which Peter himself heard (Matthew 24:42-44). Over and over in that sermon, Jesus indicated there were no signs by which one could ascertain the near approach of the second coming.[84] The analogy "like a thief" is commonly repeated in the New Testament (cp. Luke 12:39; 1 Thessalonians 5:2,4; Revelation 3:3, 16:15).[85] Though the day will come unexpectedly, Christians who are constantly prepared and living in continued expectation of the day will not suffer any loss (1 Thessalonians 5:4-10).

In which the heavens will pass away with a roar -- "In which" means during "the day of the Lord." "The heavens" refer to the atmosphere around the earth and the starry heavens (the universe we see with our eyes, and that beyond, with telescopes).[86] The word translated "pass away," *parerchomai*, is the same word used by Jesus when He predicted "Heaven and earth will pass away" (Matthew 24:35).[87] The verb does not assert annihilation (see verse 13), but rather that the heavens will pass from one state of existence to another.[88] They will

---

[83] While the Old Testament Hebrew passages use the four-letter sacred name ("Jehovah") in the phrase "day of the Lord," the New Testament clearly uses the language of Jesus Christ. This is one of many places where Old Testament "Jehovah" passages are applied to Christ. That can be done rightly only if Jesus is God! In fact, it is impossible to witness correctly about "Jehovah" and at the same time treat Jesus as though He is not self-existent deity.

[84] Matthew 24:42 (we do not know the day or the hour precisely because there are no signs), 24:43 (the owner of the house did not know when the thief was coming, for the same reason), 24:50 (the master of the house returns when the slave does not expect him), 25:13 (you do not know the day nor the hour), 24:36 ("Of that day and hour no one knows" -- Why not? Because there are no signs!). It is misapplying Scripture to find in Matthew 24:3-28 "signs of the times" of the second coming. Those were signs of the approaching destruction of Jerusalem, AD 70, as Luke 21:20, a parallel passage, plainly shows. To interpret Matthew in such a way as to have Jesus say "there are signs" for the second coming in the first half of His sermon, and "no signs" for the second coming in the second half would be to make Jesus contradict Himself. But if there were signs for the coming destruction of Jerusalem and no signs for the second coming, there is no reason to charge Jesus with inconsistency or human frailty.

[85] The additional words "in the night," found in some versions, are not in the best manuscripts.

[86] "Heaven" is also used to refer to the place where God dwells, but that is not likely the meaning here, even though heaven as it now is (Revelation 4-8) will change in appearance and location (Revelation 21,22) when the second coming and renovation of the universe take place. A floor plan of heaven as it now is, after which the Old Testament tabernacle was modeled (Hebrews 8:5), will give way to "the holy city, New Jerusalem." While there is a "temple" in heaven now (Revelation 11:1, cp. the description in Revelation 4-8), there will be no temple in New Jerusalem (Revelation 21:22).

[87] This seems to be a third reminiscence of Jesus' Olivet Discourse in this chapter 3 of 2 Peter.

[88] Peter's statement about a conflagration contradicts what the Gnostics would teach. Gnostic ideas about a "fire which lies hidden in the world" that "would blaze forth and burn" "destroying all matter ... so that it has no further existence" after men's souls had entered into the Pleroma was a doctrine Irenaeus rejected (*Adv. Haer.* i.7.1). While 2 Peter 3:7 ("reserved for fire") might cause some to think Peter's doctrine about the coming conflagration and that of the Gnostics are just alike, there is no way the rest of Peter's words can be stigmatized as

be renovated so that their form and structure, their appearance, change radically. Compare Jesus' graphic description in Matthew 24:29,30 with John's language at Revelation 6:12ff and 20:11. *Hroizedon* is an onomatopoetic word meaning "a rushing noise, to whiz, to crackle." The noun form of this word occurs in classical Greek of the whizzing of an arrow through the air, the whistling sound of shepherd's pipe, the rustle of wings when a covey of birds takes flight, the splash of water, the hissing of a snake, the noise of a huge waterfall, or the roar of a mighty wind. It might be understood of the crash of the ruins of a burning building, or the crackling roar of the destroying flames (e.g., forest fires make a huge noise).

And the elements will be destroyed with intense heat -- The meaning of *stoicheia*, "elements," is much disputed. The word speaks of the minute parts of which anything is composed.[89] Since Peter inserts this statement between his reference to the "heavens" and his reference to "earth" in the next phrase, it seems reasonable to assume that Peter is calling attention to what happens to the sun, moon, stars, and other heavenly bodies. Elsewhere in Scripture, predictions of what happens when Christ returns make frequent mention of the sun, moon, and stars (cp. Matthew 24:29 and parallel passages, Isaiah 13:10, 14:13; Joel 2:31).[90] The verb translated "destroyed" here is *luo*, not the same word used in verses 6 and 7. *Luo* can be translated "loose, break, destroy, dissolve." This dissolution is contrasted with the con-

---

being pro-Gnostic. Peter is not speaking of annihilation but renovation. Yet the similarity of what Peter writes to those later Gnostic ideas may be a reason why Irenaeus regarded 2 Peter with suspicion. The same may be said for Origen (*Cont. Cels.* iv. 11.79).

[89] Individual letters that make up words are the "elements" of those words. Scholars have searched for parallel ideas in Scripture and in the first century world. In Colossians 2:8, when Paul writes about "elements of the world" (Greek), in light of the Colossian heresy there is something to be said for the idea Paul is refuting the heretics' astrological superstitions about certain powerful spirits living on the planets who attempt to control man's future. There is not much enthusiasm among commentators for the idea Peter is saying those elemental spirits are going to be dissolved by fire. In Revelation 7:1, "angels" are in charge of some physical elements of nature. There is not much enthusiasm for the idea that Peter is saying these angels are going to be destroyed by fire. In certain philosophical circles in the first century, the four "elements" which were basic to everything else were earth, air, fire, and water. Some commentators have supposed Peter has reference to these four "elements" being burned up, but the difficulty with this is how are we to explain that fire is destroyed by fire? Moreover, "earth" is mentioned separately in the next clause of 2 Peter 3:10. The Bible nowhere says or implies there are just four elements. Had it done so, devotees of modern science would surely have used that as another argument to show there are errors in our Bibles. The word "elements" is not used in Peter in the sense it is used in modern chemistry, where elements are also spoken of.

[90] Justin Martyr calls the sun, moon, and stars "heavenly elements" (*Apol.* ii.5; *Dial. c. Try.* xxiii).

stancy verse 5 speaks of.[91] The Greek here is *stoicheia de kausoumena luthesetai. Kausoumena*, used only here and in verse 12, means "to set fire to, to burn up," and the present participle could be rendered "while burning," describing the manner of dissolution. It was the term doctors used to describe a burning fever. Verse 7 has already spoken of the "fire" that accompanies the day of judgment. The elements are going to suffer from excessive heat, a burning fever.

And the earth and its works will be burned up -- The face of the earth seems to be what is in Peter's mind. In his first letter to Corinth, Paul spoke about the outward fashion or "form" (*schema*) of this earth passing away (7:31). The "works" belonging to earth can be either the things God made (e.g., works of nature, trees, plants, minerals, geological features), or things men made (e.g., art, architecture, houses, cities, instruments), or both. There is a puzzling manuscript difference here.[92] Most modern critical texts opt for *heurethesetai* and punctuate it with a question mark. When this reading is followed, the clause is translated, "Shall the earth and the works that are therein be found?" That is, it is a question addressed to the mockers, 'Are things going to continue as they always have?' (Cp. 2 Peter 3:4.) The only possible answer to this question is, "No!" The universe is to be renovated (i.e., purified) by fire when the day of the Lord comes.[93] The Bible doctrine is always more optimistic than heathen mythology. Heathen mythology is extremely pessimistic. The last act in Wagner's play is entitled "The Destruction of the Gods." In this play, man, gods, and heaven itself are simply annihilated. There is no such pessimism in the Word of God. Jesus, Paul, John, and Peter say the most important thing about the second coming is not what happens to the heavens or the earth, but that man is prepared for what that day holds in store for him.

B. Exhortations With Reference to the Approaching Day of the Lord. 3:11-16

1. A call to holy living. 3:11

---

[91] Some modern commentators have supposed Peter here predicts the splitting of the atom and of atomic fusion. While an atomic blast triggered by men and the dissolving of the elements triggered by God are hardly the same things, it is thought provoking to consider what would happen if the cohesive force holding atoms together were to be released or what would happen when constellations were no longer held in their proper places, or what would happen if "gravity" were loosed and everything became weightless.

[92] Instead of *katakaesetai*, "will be burned up, will be consumed by fire," some manuscripts read *heurethesetai*, "shall be discovered;" and one reads *aphanisthesontai*, "will not be visible." Some versions have *ouch heurethesetai*, "will not be found." In fact, three other variants also occur at this place. As a result, translators do not know quite which English word to use, nor whether to punctuate with a period or a question mark, and commentators have to offer several options. Richard Bauckham, "Jude, 2 Peter," *Word Biblical Commentary* (Waco, TX: Word Books, 1983), Vol.50, p.316-321, has an exhaustive study of the variant readings and proposed interpretations.

[93] See the extended notes on "renovation" versus "annihilation" in the author's *New Testament Epistles: Romans* (Moberly, MO: Scripture Exposition Books, 1996), at Romans 8:19ff.

3:11 -- ***Since all these things are to be destroyed in this way, what sort of people ought you to be in holy conduct and godliness,***

Since all these things are to be destroyed in this way -- Having set forth the Biblical certainty of the second coming and the cosmological changes that will accompany that event, Peter now comes to some exhortations to his readers to help them be prepared for the judgment of the day of the Lord. In the Greek, the first half of verse 11 is a construction known as a genitive absolute. It sets forth in summary fashion the facts already affirmed in verse 10. "These things" would be the heavens, the elements, the earth, and the works therein, all of which have been identified in the previous verse. The better manuscripts read *houtos*,[94] "thus, in this way," again as described in the previous verse (i.e., intense heat, fire, dissolved). The present tense participle translated "are to be destroyed" is a form of *luo*, the same word used in the previous verse describing what would happen to the "elements." Perhaps the present tense is an example of a prophetic present, i.e., the future is so certain to happen it can be prophetically regarded as already present. Perhaps this verse says that when the final conflagration comes, it will be a process, rather than an instantaneous flash. Some understand that the process of dissolution is already under way and has been ever since the creation was subjected to vanity when Adam sinned (Romans 8:20). The song writer has said it well, "change and decay in all around, I see." We don't have to wait for years to see that the process has already begun. Since we can see it already beginning to happen, that ought to be an incentive to holy living right now.

What sort of people ought you to be in holy conduct and godliness -- *Potapos* (derived either from *topos*, "place," or *dapedon*, "land, soil") may have literally meant, 'From what country, what race, or what tribe?' Then it came to mean, 'Of what sort or of what quality?' Peter may not so much be asking a question as he is making an exclamation.[95] If Christians are citizens of the commonwealth of heaven, should they not behave like citizens? "Ought to be" translates *dei huparchein*, "it is necessary to be."[96] *Huparchein*, a present tense infinitive, implies that the state of holy conduct and godliness is one that has continued for some time in the life of the Christian. "Holy" means separated from evil and set apart for

---

[94] The KJV translates a text (supported by Sinaiticus and Alexandrinus) that reads *oun*, "therefore," the idea being that Peter is drawing a conclusion from what has been previously written. "Thus" is found in P^{72} and Vaticanus.

[95] The Greek word *potapos* seems to be used in the New Testament as an exclamation only, not as an interrogative particle. The NIV's punctuation is therefore hardly right. It reads "What kind of people ought you to be? You ought to live holy and godly lives ...." The NIV is not alone, however, in treating "holy and godly lives" as though these words should be connected with what is written following in verse 12.

[96] Some manuscripts read "you" (*humas*) and some read "we" (*hemas*) and some, including P^{72} and Vaticanus, omit altogether any subject for the infinitive. See notes at 2 Peter 1:8 at the word "are" for the connotation of *huparchein*.

God's service. "Conduct" or manner of life is *anastrophe*, one of Peter's favorite words.[97] "Godliness" is reverence toward God, or reverently seeking to do what pleases Him.[98] The lives of Peter's readers must be a marked contrast to what the false teachers practiced and encouraged. Now the noteworthy thing is that both "conduct" and "godliness" are plural words in the Greek, "livings and godlinesses."[99] The plurals may point to behavior and piety in all its different forms and examples, or they may remind the readers they will have numerous opportunities to put holy living and godliness into practice. As surely as the Biblical worldview is correct, man is a morally responsible creature. He did not arise by chance and he does not live by chance. He will give an account of his deeds to the God who created him. If a man is living on the brink of eternity, which he will spend either in happiness or torment – depending upon how he has lived his days here on earth – he certainly should not have any trouble responding positively to the exclamation Peter here makes.

2. A call for an attitude of expectation. 3:12,13

3:12 -- ***Looking for and hastening the coming of the day of God, on account of which the heavens will be destroyed by burning, and the elements will melt with intense heat.***

Looking for and hastening the coming of the day of God -- With no date announced, another aspect of "what sort of people ought you to be" (verse 11) is to live in an attitude of expectancy. Peter uses two participles to describe the Christian's attitude. The first, "looking for," is *prosdokao*, from *pros*, "toward" (in this case speaking of mental direction) and *dokao*, "to expect, to look for, to wait for."[100] It is the verb used to describe Joseph of Arimathea who was "waiting (looking) for the kingdom of God" (Mark 15:43). It is the Christian's attitude that says, 'My life is in order. I'm ready for Him to come anytime, and I'm anxious to see Him.' The second participle, *speudontas*, has two different possible meanings. The ASV reads "earnestly desiring." The NASB has "hastening."[101] If we adopt the ASV reading, Peter is using another word to express the proper expectancy – you are awaiting the day with eager desire.[102] If we adopt the NASB reading, Peter is saying that

---

[97] See the word explained in notes at 1 Peter 1:15 and at 2 Peter 2:7.

[98] See the word explained at 2 Peter 1:3,6,7.

[99] These nouns are not used in the plural elsewhere in the New Testament. (1 Peter 1:15 does have an expression that is practically synonymous with these plurals.)

[100] As the contestants in a race round the last turn, the spectators lean out to see if their favorite is in the lead. It is an expectant look, an expectant waiting. There is an eagerness akin to desiring.

[101] The KJV reads "hastening unto the coming of the day of God," but there is no "unto" in the Greek.

[102] We might compare this translation with Peter's statement about "fix your hope completely on the grace to be brought to you at the revelation of Jesus Christ" (1 Peter 1:13). Perhaps our attachment to this world and how little we think about and long for the coming of the Lord are indications we need to give this subject much more study and thought!

Christians can cause the day of the Lord to come more quickly by helping to fulfill the conditions without which it cannot come. The Father has put the times and seasons in His own power, but as the longsuffering of God waited in the days of Noah, so now He "is patient toward you, not wishing for any to perish but for all to come to repentance" (3:9). In His gracious mercy he waits for the Christians to repent. When enough of them have, Jesus will come.[103] "Coming" translates *ten parousian*. It is very striking to find the particular word used elsewhere for the coming of Christ Himself used here for the coming of the day of God. The expression "day of God" cannot excite surprise if respect is had for the Old Testament and for what Peter has written earlier in chapter 3. The "day of God" and the "day of the Lord" (verse 10) are two designations for the same day.[104] Peter has already called Jesus "God" in 2 Peter 1:1, and by modifying his language he reminds his readers of the divine nature of the One with whom they would have to deal at the end of time. It is a perilous thing to deny the Lord (cp. 2:1).

On account of which – *Di' hen* speaks either of the day of God or the coming of the day. Old things must pass away because of the coming of the Lord. The old order must give place to the new (verse 10).

The heavens will be destroyed by burning, and the elements will melt with intense heat -- The heavens being set on fire will be dissolved. Peter repeats the thought of verse 10 without enumerating all the details. What he meant by "reserved for fire" (verse 7) now becomes more apparent: "The elements will melt." "Elements" here are the same "elements" identified in verse 10. The Greek word here for "will melt" is *teketai*; it pictures the elements melting like wax.[105] The present tense is another of Peter's prophetic present

---

[103] In Peter's second recorded sermon (Acts 3:19,20, ASV), his invitation and promise was this, "Repent and turn again that your sins may be blotted out and that there may come seasons of refreshing ... *and that He may send the Christ ....*" The thought is so striking and unusual, found nowhere else in the New Testament save here in 2 Peter, that "hastening the coming of the day" furnishes an argument of considerable weight in favor of Peter's authorship of this letter. In one of His parables, Jesus indicated the Father wanted His house full of guests (Luke 14:23). Romans 11:25 speaks of the "fulness" of the Gentiles coming in to the "olive tree"; Romans 11:12 speaks of the "fulness" of the Jews, with their "acceptance" (Romans 11:15) being followed by "life from the dead" (likely a reference to the final resurrection). This passage, too, seems to point to a huge number of redeemed that God wants in His family. Conversions of lost souls and faithful living by redeemed souls helps the number to be reached. It hastens the day when Jesus will return. (Note: These comments have been worded carefully and deliberately, lest any get the idea that we are implying a belief that from all eternity certain people are predestined to be saved and certain ones predestined to be lost, and that the number is fixed and unalterable in God's mind.)

[104] That this is so, see the references where the two designations occur and compare what happens on those days. For example, the elements are to be dissolved on both, and the wrath of God is poured out on the wicked on both days. Therefore, we believe the expressions are but two different designations for the same day. Compare 1 Thessalonians 5:1-9, 2 Peter 3:10 and 3:12. (Some would also treat Revelation 16:14 as describing the same "day of God.")

[105] Isaiah 34:4 (in the LXX) has a similar prediction, "and all the powers (i.e., celestial bodies) of the heavens will melt," even using the same Greek word for "melt." *2 Clement* (xvi) speaks of "The day of judgment comes ... and the heavens shall melt, and all the earth as lead melting on the fire."

tenses. Peter seems to envision the heavenly bodies which appear to us to be solid masses simply liquefying in the intense heat. The core of our earth is hot, molten rock. Igneous rocks were once in a liquid state. Why not have them returned to a liquid state as God renovates the universe by fire? We think this summary recapitulation is one more attempt by Peter to insulate his readers against what the mockers will teach about the future.

3:13 -- *But according to His promise we are looking for new heavens and a new earth, in which righteousness dwells.*

But -- This additional statement following Peter's recapitulation is a flat contradiction of what the Gnostics would teach. They would teach the future conflagration would annihilate this present order of things and that good people would be absorbed into the Pleroma (the series of seven heavens).[106] In contrast, Peter now stresses the Christian's expectations.

According to His promise -- The promise of the new heavens and new earth had been a theme of the Old Testament prophets.[107] God had promised it. It was a hope and vision shared by Abraham and the patriarchs (Hebrews 11:10). It would happen just as God said it would. It is that which makes God's people of all ages "strangers and aliens."

We are looking for new heavens and a new earth -- One might put emphasis on "*we* are looking for."[108] We believers in God's promises as found in Scripture (in contrast to the mockers who have a low view of God's written word) – *we* look for a new heavens and a new earth. Or we might put emphasis on "new" – there is a *new* world coming.[109] Based on God's promises, Bible believers anticipate a renovation of the universe,[110] not annihilation,

---

[106] See footnote #104 in chapter 2, and footnote #88 in chapter 3.

[107] Isaiah 2:4, 11:6-9, 65:17, 66:22, 30:26, 32:16; Micah 4:1-5. The same thing will be recorded by John in Revelation 21:1,9. Here is another place where Peter's conviction about the more sure word of prophecy (cf. 2 Peter 1:19) shines through.

[108] This is the third time we have had the word "look for" in 2 Peter. See 2:8 and 3:12.

[109] There are several Greek words that can be translated "new." One is *neos*, which means new *in time*, brand new as never existing before. Another is *kainos*, which means new *in quality*, in the sense of renewed or refreshed, in contrast to that which is old and worn out. The latter is the word used here and in Revelation 21:1,9 to describe the "new heavens and new earth." The "heavens and earth" Peter describes are not brand new but renewed, renovated.

[110] Romans 8:19-21 teaches the creation (all of non-rational nature, animate and inanimate) has been subjected to vanity (not fulfilling the purpose for which God created it) because of man's sin. When Jesus comes the second time, all this is going to be changed. Creation will be delivered from the bondage of corruption (the decay and death to which it is now subjected). What Paul says in Romans 8:19-21 settles the question raised by other passages (Psalm 102:27; 2 Peter 3:10,13; Revelation 20:11; Isaiah 34:4; Job 14:12) as to whether the physical (creature) world will be annihilated or renovated. The "freedom of the glory" (Romans 8:21) cannot have a double meaning -- blessed, eternal life for the children of God (Romans 8:17,18) but annihilation for the creation. Romans teaches renovation. So does 2 Peter when read carefully. It has been well said that not the earth itself

when the conflagration takes place. Just like the time after the flood when Noah stepped out of the ark onto a "new world" (the present heavens and earth that now are, 3:7), when the conflagration has transformed and refined the universe, the redeemed will step out into a new world.[111] Peter is here describing what is elsewhere called "My Father's house" (John 14:2), "heaven" (Philippians 3:20), "the city which has the foundations" (Hebrews 11:10, cf. Revelation 21:10-27), "the kingdom of their Father" (Matthew 13:43), and "the eternal kingdom of our Lord and Savior" (2 Peter 1: 10).[112]

In which righteousness dwells -- "In which" is plural. It refers to both in the "new heavens" and the "new earth." It may well be asked, how could righteousness dwell therein if righteous people were not there? The "new heavens and a new earth" are to be the abode of righteous and obedient people, Peter is saying.[113] Jesus' redeemed people are going to settle down[114] and live in the renovated universe. Compare Isaiah 60:21, "Then all your people will

will pass away, but only the "form of this world" (1 Corinthians 7:31). So the fire mentioned by Peter must be the fire of purification (2 Peter 3:10). The "new heavens and new earth" are not *neos*, newly created and never having existed before, but *kainos*, fresh, new in contrast with the old, different from what heaven and earth formerly were. Many questions regarding details confront us in this connection. Will the animals, plants, insects, be raised to life? What about the noxious creatures, the bacilli, for instance? Perhaps Revelation 5:13 gives some help. But we must not let our lack of answers dim our hope. He who made paradise for Adam will, in the consummation, make heaven and earth new, far beyond the glory of paradise. In that new paradise, "the tabernacle of God is among men, and shall dwell among them" (Revelation 21:3) in a way far beyond anything Adam ever knew. The new heavens and new earth, new in quality, purified by fire from any curse, will surely be beautiful beyond the wildest expectation of man. Peter presents the heavens and earth as destined, not to total destruction (annihilation), but to hereafter being transformed to a more glorious condition. What will happen to the heavens and earth at the second coming is not greatly different from what will happen to our mortal bodies which shall become glorified, heavenly, spiritual bodies (1 Corinthians 15:42-49).

[111] This much is certain, "new heavens and a new earth" speak of a new order of things, different from what we know now. And the differences between what now is and what shall be will be as great or greater than the differences after the change at the time of creation, or the change at the time of the flood.

[112] With this whole 13th verse in 2 Peter 3, we should compare 1 Peter 1:4 where a similar thought is expressed with equal beauty, and 1 Peter 1:13 where a similar conclusion is drawn.

[113] Even Revelation 21 and 22 do not picture all the redeemed as being city-dwellers, living within the confines of new Jerusalem. Revelation 21:24 pictures "nations" walking into its light, and the kings of earth bringing their glory into it. This can be done day or night, for the gates of the city will never be closed. Visitors to the heavenly city will bring the glory and honor of the nations into it (Revelation 21:26).

[114] The word "dwells" is *katoikeo*, which means "to settle down, to be permanently at home." We may be pilgrims and sojourners now, but we shall have a permanent home in the new heavens and new earth.

be righteous."[115] John saw a new heavens and a new earth in which there was nothing impure (Revelation 21:1,8,27). There will be no sin there (Revelation 22:15). There will be no one like the false teachers or their followers there. Because only righteous people will dwell there, that is why our lives, as we here prepare to dwell there, must be right.[116]

3. A call for diligence. 3:14

3:14 -- ***Therefore, beloved, since you look for these things, be diligent to be found by Him in peace, spotless and blameless,***

Therefore, beloved -- *Dio* means "for this reason." If it is only righteousness that can dwell in the new heavens and earth, then the proper thing for a man to do is to be diligent to be righteous.[117] The nouns and verbs in this verse are all plural, showing this call is intended for all Peter's readers.

Since you look for these things -- "These things" are the coming of the Lord, the renovation of the universe by fire, with the resultant new heavens and earth; in short, all that Peter has presented in verses 10-13. Peter here displays a personal knowledge about his readers' beliefs. He knows they are looking for these things in harmony with the promises of Scripture and the preaching of their apostles. "Look for" is the same word used in verse 12. Such an expectancy calls for a certain type of life, not the least of which is to assiduously avoid all that the false teachers will teach and promote.

Be diligent -- Peter uses one of his favorite terms as he writes this command.[118] We use similar commands to express the need for immediate action and intense effort; we say, Hop to it! or Get at it! What he expected his readers to be diligent about is expressed in the remainder of the verse.

To be found by Him in peace -- "Found" implies there is an examination to be made when

---

[115] The Old Testament prophets had looked forward to a time when all would be righteous. See Jeremiah 23:5,6, 33:16; Psalm 9:8; Isaiah 11:4-5, 45:8. "The Lord our righteousness" was going to usher in righteousness. Not only do these verses look forward to the redemption at Calvary, but they also look forward to their ultimate fulfillment in the new heavens and new earth (Isaiah 65:17-25).

[116] Even Jesus spoke about the redeemed living on the new earth, we believe, when He promised, "Blessed are the gentle, for they shall inherit the earth."

[117] On "beloved," see notes at 3:1. It is not just Peter who is said to love the recipients of this letter, although he does, but God does also. Peter has expressed his own heart-felt affection for the readers, and he has also told them how God loves them and because of that love is longsuffering toward them, wishing them all to come to repentance.

[118] Peter has used the verb at 1:10,15, and a related noun at 1:5. Make every effort, be eager, be zealous are possible translations for the word translated "be diligent."

Jesus returns. Jesus Himself[119] will serve as the examiner (cp. 2 Corinthians 5:10; Philippians 3:9; Jude 24). Exactly with whom men are to be at peace must often be determined by the context.[120] "There is no peace for the wicked, says the Lord" (Isaiah 48:22, 57:21). Christ warns the impenitent that He will "make war against them with the sword of My mouth" (Revelation 2:16). So those who will be "found at peace by Him" will be those who have repented and put out of their lives everything He hates. This is one area where Christians are commanded to be diligent.

Spotless and blameless -- Here we have two more areas in the readers' lives requiring diligence. We have had the same two words, though in reverse order, at 1 Peter 1:19, where they were used to describe Jesus. These qualities are the exact opposite of the false teachers, who were called "stains and blemishes" at 2 Peter 2:13. Paul, too, indicated Christians are to be "holy and blameless" (Ephesians 1:4). Christians are "spotless," not because they are sinless perfect, but because, having repented and confessed their sins, those sins have been forgiven. "Blameless" means one against whom no charge of moral or religious defect can be substantiated. How pointed this word is can be seen when it is remembered the false teachers were going to use immorality as bait (2:18), and their religion was anything but genuine (2:1, 3:16). It pictures a man who has so lived that his whole life is a fit offering to God.[121] A deep awareness that we are soon to stand in the presence of our Judge, the spotless and unblemished One, cannot but have a happy influence motivating us to "be diligent" in our efforts to be like Him.

4. A call to make proper use of the Lord's patience. 3:15,16.

3:15 -- *And regard the patience of our Lord* to be *salvation; just as our beloved brother Paul, according to the wisdom given him, wrote to you,*

And regard the patience of our Lord *to be* salvation -- This is a second command based on

---

[119] The NASB, in our opinion, is correct when it takes the personal pronoun *auto* with the infinitive that follows, treating it as a dative of agent just before a passive voice infinitive. This is more satisfactory than trying to connect the pronoun with the nouns "spotless and blameless" which immediately precede it.

[120] Sometimes it speaks of peace with God, because sins (which produced enmity) have been forgiven. Sometimes it speaks of being at peace with one's fellow men. "In peace" can hardly refer to differences between Jewish and Gentile Christians, a subject foreign to this epistle. It might refer to the discord ("heresies," 2:1) that was going to be caused by the false teachers.

[121] *Amomos* was a sacrificial word in the Old Testament. Under the Law of Moses, before an animal could be offered as a sacrifice to God, it had to be inspected and examined. If any blemish was found it was to be rejected as unfit to offer to God. Only the best could be offered as sacrifices. By parity of reasoning, to say a man is "blameless" is to say that in every area of life -- work, pleasure, sport, home life, interpersonal relations -- he has so lived that what he does could be taken and offered to God. There can be nothing in any of those area that would disqualify our lives as a fit offering to make to God.

their looking for all these things (verse 14).[122] The verb is *hegeomai* and the present imperative indicates constant consideration, constant thought, constant estimation is required. The "patience" of the Lord has been unfolded in verse 9 along with the reason for it. Instead of regarding the passing of time as evidence of slackness on God's part, Christians should take advantage of whatever time they are given to get their lives right. Jesus Christ is evidently the one referred to in this verse by the title "our Lord."[123] If this is correct, then "throughout this weighty passage the Lord Jesus is invested with the full attributes of deity."[124] That may be exactly what was needed to refute the false teachers' denial of "the Master who bought them" (2:1). "Salvation" must be used as somehow synonymous with "repentance" in verse 9. In both verses it is something Christians are expected to do.[125] Paul wrote to some of his Christian readers that they had need to "work out [their] salvation with fear and trembling" (Philippians 2:12). Peter hardly can be thought of as having his readers' initial salvation from sin in mind since he has already spoken about how they had "escaped the corruption that is in the world" (2 Peter 1:4) and were among the called and chosen (1:10). Both Paul and Peter are emphasizing the expected lifestyle that complements and corresponds to such a salvation. So, Peter commands, instead of thinking the Lord's longsuffering is "slowness" and that no cataclysm or conflagration is ever going to happen, think of His patience as "salvation"! That is, make use of whatever time you have yet by repenting when needed, and by daily practicing all holy livings and godlinesses. A failure to make good use of the time would be to presume on the Lord's patience.

Just as also our beloved brother Paul -- Peter appeals to Paul's writings for confirmation of what he has just said. The plural pronoun "our" may imply Paul was known to the churches to which Peter was writing and was loved by them just as he was known and loved by Peter.[126] "Beloved brother" was a designation quite commonly used in that day (1 Corinthians 4:17; Ephesians 6:21; Colossians 4:7,9; Philemon 16).[127] *Kathos* (even as, just as, in full accord

---

[122] The "and" with which this verse begins ties it to the previous one.

[123] Actually, as in verse 9, a case can be made for either God the Father or Jesus Christ being the one whom Peter calls "Lord." In neither verse is absolute certainty obtainable, but here the balance seems to be in favor of "Lord" being a reference to Jesus. In verse 8, "the Lord" certainly meant God, not the Lord Jesus (cp. 2:9,11). In verse 18, "our Lord" is expressly stated to be Jesus Christ. In the two verses in between (verses 9 and 15), the identification is open to dispute. The fact that "our" appears before "Lord" in both verses 15 and 18 seems to point in the direction of Jesus when "Lord" is used in those two verses.

[124] Alford, *op. cit.*, p.418.

[125] Because Peter did not write "your salvation" but simply "salvation," some broaden this passage into an evangelistic thrust. They reason this way: since the Father wants His house full, and since conversions will hasten the coming of Christ (Acts 3:19,20), perhaps Peter intends for his readers to take advantage of Christ's patience to get busy winning more souls.

[126] Some have used Peter's language here as proof that when Peter writes, Paul is still living, and if so, we have another indication that 2 Peter must be dated before AD 68.

[127] Alford (*ibid.*) thinks the term "beloved brother" is used here in a sense narrower than merely signifying a

with) and "also ... Paul" indicates that Paul is in complete agreement with Peter concerning the subject at hand. It may be the false teachers will try to enlist Paul as agreeing with them against what Peter here writes (see what Peter says about distorted interpretations in 3:16). Peter torpedoes that attempt by saying there is no contradiction between him and Paul.[128]

According to the wisdom given him -- There is emphasis on "given [to] him." It wasn't Paul's own wisdom. This is the apostle Peter's way of saying Paul's theology was not of human origin but was of divine origin, the product of divine revelation. Paul claims the same revelatory source for his own teachings and writings.[129] We may even appeal to 1 Corinthians 1:30 where Paul says the "wisdom from God" includes such matters as "righteousness, and sanctification, and redemption."

Wrote to you -- What did Paul write to the recipients of 2 Peter? Where? To whom? What epistle or epistles are here meant? Few points have been more debated. Following are some of the attempts that have been made to identify exactly what source Peter alluded to. (1) Peter refers to a now-lost letter of Paul's.[130] (2) Peter alludes to the book of Hebrews.[131] (3) Peter has 1 Corinthians in mind.[132] (4) It is 1 and 2 Thessalonians, with

---

"fellow Christian." He thinks it means "our beloved fellow-apostle." Whether or not Alford is right, the designation "beloved brother" is a mark of the genuineness of 2 Peter. In the Introductory Studies we have called attention to the extravagant and gushing terms used when referring to Paul in the late first and early second century by writers (e.g., Ignatius, who calls him, "Paul the sanctified, the martyred, worthily called blessed" [*Ad Eph.* vii.2]). A second-century imitator forging "2 Peter" would scarcely have used the simple but warm expression "our beloved brother."

[128] This verse has a bearing on certain theologically liberal theories concerning the background of the New Testament. F.C. Baur of the Tubingen School, over a century ago, affirmed there were Pauline and Petrine factions in the early church. This idea, though discredited, still forms the foundation of much Biblical scholarship to this day. Just as the mockers had to avoid certain verses that contradicted their views (2 Peter 3:5) so did the Tubingen School. Baur had to deny the Petrine authorship of this 2 Peter 3:15, saying that Peter would never have referred to Paul in such loving and approving terms. Baur also had to reject Galatians 2:9, which says that Peter gave Paul the right hand of fellowship. It is true that, on a later occasion, Paul had to rebuke Peter (Galatians 2:11-16), but the two did not head radical factions of Christianity, nor did they stand opposed to each other as Baur and his followers have alleged.

[129] 1 Corinthians 2:7-14, 3:10; Galatians 1:11, 2:9; Ephesians 3:2,7,8; Colossians 1:25.

[130] This can neither be proved nor disproved. But such a hypothesis is not necessary to find a passage in Paul to which Peter may be referring. What was written in a footnote on 2 Peter 3:1 about the possibility, but not the probability, of inspired letters to churches being lost needs to be reviewed before this option is even considered, let alone accepted.

[131] What is written in Hebrews 9:26-28 and 10:23-25,27 is what advocates of this view think Peter had in mind.

[132] 1 Corinthians 1:8 does speak of being blameless until the day of our Lord Jesus Christ. Chapter 15 speaks about the final resurrection and consummation.

their references to the day of the Lord, that Peter speaks of.[133] (5) It is Paul's letter to the Romans to which Peter alludes.[134] (6) Since he says Paul wrote "to you," and since 2 Peter is addressed to churches in the provinces of Asia Minor, Peter has reference to Pauline letters addressed to the same provinces – e.g., Galatians, Ephesians, and Colossians.[135] This view allows us to take "to you" literally, and preserves the distinction between what "Paul ... wrote to you" (verse 15), and "all his letters" (verse 16).

3:16 -- ***As also in all* his *letters, speaking in them of these things, in which are some things hard to understand, which the untaught and unstable distort, as* they do *also the rest of the Scriptures, to their own destruction.***

As also in all *his* letters -- In the previous verse, Peter made reference to one or more of Paul's writings. Now he widens his reference from a particular letter (or letters) written by Paul to other writings by him. The language assumes a collection of Paul's letters that was known at least to Peter,[136] if not also to the readers of Peter's epistle as well. There are indications the epistles of Paul were at this time being read in the churches generally and were thus enjoying a much wider circulation than only among the brethren to whom they were originally sent.[137]

---

[133] If we accept this option, we will have to modify our conclusions concerning the destination of 2 Peter, and also our conclusions about the "first letter" alluded to in 2 Peter 3:1. What makes this idea attractive is what is said in 1 Thessalonians 4:14-18, 5:1-11,23, and the fact that 2 Peter 3:10 recalls 1 Thessalonians 5:2. Not only that, but there are things "hard to understand" in 2 Thessalonians 2, yet what Paul there writes indicates that the *parousia* is not going to happen immediately. There will be some time until there is a rebellion and a revelation of the man of lawlessness, and only after that will the *parousia* and the day of the Lord occur.

[134] Defenders of this view appeal to Romans 2:4, 3:25, 6:1-11, and 9:22,23, as being what Peter might well have in mind. Romans 6:16 was recalled in 2 Peter 2:19. Romans 6:1 (which indicates Paul's doctrine of grace was grossly misunderstood) may well have been a favorite Gnostic proof text for a libertine life-style. If we accept this view, we will be forced to modify our conclusions concerning either the destination of "Romans" or the destination of 2 Peter (are we to suppose 2 Peter was addressed to Rome?)

[135] Both Ephesians (which in all probability was a circular letter for all the churches in the province of Asia) and Galatians (addressed to the "churches" of Galatia) were intended for wide readership. So was Colossians, as Colossians 4:16 indicates.

[136] In our study of 1 Peter, we have noted Peter shows a certain familiarity with a number of Paul's letters.

[137] This matter of early circulation and collection of New Testament books has already been addressed in the Introductory Studies, p.xvii. More can be said on the matter. "From the first, the churches read the Pauline Epistles as authoritative messages for the Christian faith and practice, and this attitude obtained even in those churches which were not the direct recipients (Colossians 4:16, 1 Thessalonians 5:27). Like the books of the Old Testament, his epistles were accepted as revealing the mind of God" (Hiebert, *op. cit.*, p.175). The letters from the apostles and prophets were intended to be read out loud in the public assemblies. To keep from hearing the same letter Sunday after Sunday, churches very quickly would make collections of known letters, thus allowing for variety while at the same time contributing to a wider knowledge of the expectations of Christianity. Each congregation made a collection of Paul's letters (and any other new covenant Scriptures that were available) for their own use as soon as they became known to the church, and as soon as they could afford copies. The larger churches would likely have collections before the smaller ones did. Lewis A. Foster ("The Earliest Collection of Paul's Epistles," *The Seminary Review* 14/2 [Winter, 1968], p.41-56) has argued cogently that Luke made a collection of Paul's letters about the same time he published his two volumes of history (Luke and Acts). If Foster is right, and there is no reason to doubt it, then all of Paul's letters (save for those to Timothy and Titus) were available for col-

Speaking in them of these things -- What things? The exhortation to holiness in view of the Lord's coming (verse 14)? The Lord's patience or longsuffering (verses 9,15)? All the major topics in 2 Peter (the lordship and deity of Jesus, the return of Christ, the Day of the Lord, the fiery renovation of the universe, the new heavens and earth)? Anti-Gnostic teaching?[138] The participle "speaking" could be translated "when speaking." Peter would thus be saying that when Paul touches on these matters in any of his epistles, what he says is in complete agreement with what Peter says.[139]

In which are some things hard to understand -- The manuscripts vary between the masculine/neuter *en hois* and the feminine *en hais* for the words translated "in which." If we read the masculine/neuter, the reference is back to Paul's sayings. If we read the feminine, the reference is back to Paul's letters. The word *dusnoetos*, "hard to understand, difficult to comprehend, obscure," occurs nowhere else in the New Testament and only a few places in the classics[140] and patristic writings.[141] Paul's readers may have difficulty either because the topic is lofty or because, while the statement was sufficient to communicate with the original readers, it does not give enough details for us to know precisely what was being talked about, or because (taken in isolation) it is capable of misinterpretation. It is no criticism to say some things in Paul's letters are hard to understand.[142] This is a fact in all books of the Bible, including those written by Peter himself.[143] Peter does not tell us what difficult "things" were in his thoughts. Commentators have hazarded guesses and made lists of possible teachings

---

lection and copying before the mid-60's AD. Thus, there is no reason to believe Peter's readers were unfamiliar with most of Paul's letters. Many of them could pick up and read the very letters Peter alludes to as he writes about "all his [Paul's] letters."

This mention of Paul's epistles as a group has been used as an argument for a second-century date for 2 Peter. Barclay (*op. cit.*, p.412), for example, affirms Paul's epistles were not collected and published until AD 90 or later. But this is all theory, and denies the evidence that appears in the pages of the New Testament itself.

138 Compare Ephesians 2:5,6; Colossians 2:12; and 2 Timothy 2:18.

139 The bearing of this passage as a solid refutation of certain theories of the development of New Testament theology should not be missed. It essentially shows that presentations of New Testament theology like that of George B. Stevens (*The Theology of the New Testament* [New York: Scribners, 1953]), in which each New Testament writer is supposed to have had his own peculiar theology different from all the rest, is just flat contradictory to what the Bible writers themselves wrote.

140 Liddell, Henry G., and Scott, Robert, *A Greek-English Lexicon*, revised by Henry S. Jones (Oxford: Clarendon Press, 1961), p.459.

141 G.W.H. Lampe, *A Patristic Lexicon* (Oxford: Clarendon Press, 1961), p.393.

142 It was this passage that made John Calvin certain that Peter himself did not write 2 Peter, because, he believed, no apostle would ever have "criticized" what Paul wrote like this. (See *Commentary on 2 Peter,* in notes on 3:15.)

143 That we may come across some things that will challenge our minds, or ideas that will be difficult to grasp, is no excuse to avoid reading and meditating upon the Word of God. Peter has already told his readers they would do well to pay attention to the sure word of prophecy (1:19). He has told them of his expectation that they would remember the words spoken beforehand by the holy prophets and the commandment of the Lord and Savior spoken through the apostles (3:2).

in Paul which are "hard to understand" and which can be twisted. Included in the list are Paul's teachings about the man of lawlessness; the Lord's Supper; the doctrine of justification by faith; the doctrine of Christian liberty (which might be perverted into antinomianism); the whole matter of eschatology; the doctrine of faith and works; and the topics that have come to be identified as the five points of Calvinism. This passage says "*some* things", so it does not give countenance to the old Roman Catholic doctrine that *all* Scripture is too hard for the average church member to understand, and therefore must be explained by an official church interpreter.[144]

Which the untaught and unstable distort -- According to Sharp's rule of grammar, the two adjectives denote one group which has both characteristics. "Untaught" comes from *amatheis*, "without ordinary instruction."[145] We have had the word "unstable" (*asteriktoi*) at 2:14. It pictures a person without definite convictions, one who has no clear principles of Christian doctrine in mind on which to stand. It is not the Bible writers' fault their works are distorted. The fault lies with the people handling those sacred writings. The verb translated "distort" (*streblousin*) is found only here in the New Testament. It means "to twist with a windlass, to torture, to put to the rack, to twist or dislocate the limbs on a rack." Victims of torture are often forced to say what their torturers want them to say. When applied to Scripture, this very graphic word pictures forcing the Scriptures in order to yield a meaning never intended by Paul or the Holy Spirit.[146] Is it the false teachers who are stigmatized as being untaught and unstable or (as in 2:14) their converts?

---

[144] Until the doctrine was somewhat relaxed by Vatican II, the Roman Church discouraged the reading of the Bible by the common people. Peter said nothing like "Do not read!" or "Pass over the hard parts!" He did say to be on your guard against being led astray by interpretations that distort the gospel.

[145] It is not the same word translated "uneducated" at Acts 4:13. That word means "unlettered," because they have not been to the Rabbis' schools. In His great commission, Jesus instructed that new converts be taught to observe all things He had commanded. When congregations who lead people to become new converts fail to carry out Jesus' teaching mandate, those poor souls are "untaught" and are vulnerable to every wind of doctrine that comes along. Out of sheer spiritual hunger they may swallow anything that is attractively packaged and sounds right from any teacher who comes along, either on foot, or on radio, or TV, or the internet.

[146] After commentators earlier in the verse have hazarded a guess about the identification of the "some things," it is then common to find additional comments showing how those "things" have been twisted, even in New Testament times. Paul's doctrine of grace was, in fact, twisted into an excuse and a justification to go on committing sins (Romans 6). Paul's doctrine of Christian liberty was, in fact, twisted into an excuse for unchristian license (Galatians 5:13). Paul's doctrine of faith was twisted into an argument that Christian action and obedience were unimportant (James 2:14-26). The Thessalonian epistles show how some of Paul's readers twisted Paul's teaching about the second coming.

As *they do* also the rest of the Scriptures -- Not only did the untaught and unstable wrest Paul's letters, they also treated the "rest of the Scriptures" in the same way. The word "Scriptures," as used by a Jew, had a technical significance; it meant inspired writings and its use was reserved and applied only to the sacred writings in the Old Testament canon. So the question is asked, By "rest of the Scriptures" does Peter have in mind only the 39 books of the Old Testament? Or, since he here equates Paul's writings with "Scripture,"[147] is it possible Peter also had in mind the non-Pauline New Testament writings which were already in existence?[148] It is well known that a later generation of Gnostics treated the Scriptures with disdain. "They objected to proofs from Scripture on the grounds that the living voice was more authoritative. By 'living voice' they meant their own secret traditions, which led them to deny the validity of the orthodox apostolic writings and to substitute their own."[149] Like Satan did (Matthew 4:6), false teachers and their followers can quote Scripture out of context, or quote only part of a verse for their own purposes. That's torturing and twisting the Scritpures.[150]

To their own destruction -- On the meaning of the word "destruction," see notes at 2:1,3 and 3:7. The Greek "their own," an adjective and a pronoun together, is very emphatic. The de-

---

[147] The normal understanding of the Greek word "other" (*loipas*) is that Paul's writings are just like the "others." (Arndt and Gingrich, *op. cit.*, p.481, cite numerous references where "other" means "of the same category.") This passage shows Paul's epistles (those already written when Peter wrote) had by this time taken their place in the estimate of Christians by the side of the sacred books of the Old Testament and were regarded as holy Scripture. Peter is not starting the idea that Paul's writings should be regarded as Scripture. He is simply reflecting the common belief in the churches, especially those who received Paul's letters. In fact, in 2 Peter 3:1,2, Peter has already treated the Old Testament prophets and the apostles of Jesus as being equally sources of the authoritative word of God. Paul himself claimed for his own writings that they were the Word of God (see 1 Corinthians 14:37; 1 Thessalonians 2:13; 2 Thessalonians 2:15; Ephesians 3:3-5; cp. Acts 15:28). He made claims that he was now God's mouthpiece ("bond-servant") just as were the Old Testament prophets (Romans 1:1; Philippians 1:1; Titus 1:1). From the moment of their composition, Paul's writings were considered Scripture -- inspired words from the Lord through His apostle (1 Corinthians 1:1; Galatians 1:1). In 1 Peter 1:12, New Testament inspired preachers are made superior to Old Testament prophets, a statement which harmonizes well with 2 Peter 1:15-19, and with the view set forth here in chapter 3.

[148] By AD 67 when Peter writes, all of the New Testament books except Jude and the Johannine literature (the Gospel, the Epistles, and Revelation) are already in existence. (For details about the dating of the New Testament books, see G.L. Reese, *New Testament Survey Notes* [Moberly, MO: Scripture Exposition Books, 1993].) Concerning Luke's Gospel being called Scripture at 1 Timothy 5:18, and the technical nature of the word "Scripture," see the Introductory Studies to 2 Peter, p.xii-xvii.

[149] Donald H. Guthrie, *New Testament Introduction* (Downers Grove, IL: InterVarsity, 1970), Vol.3, p.177. Guthrie adds, "Irenaeus frequently charges the Gnostics with dishonesty in the treatment of Scripture (cf. *Adv. Haer.* i.3.6; viii.1; ix.1)."

[150] Peter has certainly implied that the difficult passages do have a correct and proper interpretation. "In a time when the Christian church is plagued by heretical cults and false teaching, Peter's warning about the irresponsible use of Scripture is important. [Sound hermeneutics and] correct exegesis must be a continuing concern of the church" (Blum, *op. cit.*, p.289). Even the most basic rules for interpreting Scripture must constantly be emphasized. A good place to start is with C.J. Sharp's "fundamental rules for studying the Scriptures" in *New Training for Service* (Cincinnati, OH: Standard, 1934), p.10ff.

struction is their own doing. Paul and the other writers of Scripture are not to blame. The wicked men's own behavior – in spite of God's goodness and patience, in spite of God sending His only begotten Son, yea including their active opposition to all God has done to try to save them – has triggered God's condemnatory judgment. God has given Scripture to be a lamp and a light to illumine the way to pleasing Him. No wonder twisting Scripture brings condemnation. One of the most tragic things in life is when a man twists Christian truth and holy Scripture into an excuse and a defense, and even a reason, for doing what he wants to do rather than accepting that Scripture as a guide for doing what God wants him to do. Such actions will place men face to face (*pros*) with their own eternal ruination.

Concluding Exhortations and Doxology. 3:17,18

A. Exhortation to Guard Against the Error of the Wicked. 3:17

3:17 -- ***You therefore, beloved, knowing* this *beforehand, be on your guard lest, being carried away by the error of unprincipled men, you fall from your own steadfastness,***

You therefore, beloved -- The pronoun "you" is emphatic. Others have gone astray. You – YOU beware! YOU continue faithful! "Therefore" bases this exhortation on what happens to unprincipled men, the twisters of Scripture. Once more Peter tells his readers they are special to him and to God.[151] In these concluding verses Peter will touch once more on the main themes of the letter as he summarizes what he has written.

Knowing *this* beforehand -- The Greek participle *proginoskontes* has no object. The ASV has supplied "these things" while the NASB has supplied "this." What Peter has in mind becomes clear as we read on. He has reference to the false teachers/mockers who are going to arise and trouble the churches. His readers know about this beforehand precisely because of what Peter has just written in this letter. They have been given a vivid picture of how those false teachers will live, what they will teach, and the tricky, underhanded, and sensual methods they will use to try to gain converts to their heresy.

Be on your guard -- The verb Peter uses is a present tense imperative in the middle voice. This is something that calls for constantly being on guard, and they are to do it for their own benefit. To be forewarned is to be forearmed. If any of Peter's readers are taken in by the false teachers, they cannot plead ignorance when they stand before the judgment seat of Christ. They have been given clear warnings. They know the wrong way and its disasters and its ultimate end. In fact, to be forewarned is a grave responsibility, for he who knows the right and does the wrong is under a double condemnation.

---

[151] See notes at 3:1,8,14 on "beloved."

Lest, being carried away by the error of unprincipled men -- The same word *sunapago* was used in Galatians 2:13 (of Barnabas, who, along with Peter, was then carried away by the dissimulation of the Judaizers) with the same meaning as it is used here. It means "to accommodate one's self to what others expect, to keep close company with." "Error" recalls the use of the same word in 2:18, a wandering from the path of truth. "Unprincipled" was used at 2:7 to describe the conduct of the inhabitants of Sodom and Gomorrah. Here it is used of the Gnostic false teachers/mockers who are coming, about whom he has written in this letter of warning. No fraternization, no close company with people of that sort!

You fall from your own steadfastness -- *Ekpipto* means "to fall out of." If, as some allege, it is impossible for a child of God to fall from grace, this warning about being on guard lest you fall is without force. The conclusion is irresistible that Peter's readers would escape the *destructio*n of the wicked only by being constantly on guard against the *seductions* of the wicked.[152] The word *sterigmos* ("steadfastness") occurs in its noun form only here in the New Testament. However, the verb *steridzo*, which has the same root, occurs in several places, including Luke 22:32 (Jesus' command to Peter), 1 Peter 5:10, and 2 Peter 1:12 (where it describes Peter's present readers). Steadfast believers are the opposite of "unstable souls" mentioned in 2:14 and 3:16. Such steadfastness comes from a solid belief in the powerful coming of Jesus Christ the first time based on the Old Testament prophecies and the historicity of the apostolic message (chapter 1), from a wholesome lifestyle in harmony with God's revealed will in the Scriptures and in submission to the lordship of Christ (chapter 2), and from an expectation and anticipation of the Lord's return and the accompanying day of the Lord (with its fiery renovation of the universe and its awesome judgment) strong enough to be the deciding and motivating factor in everyday behavior (chapter 3). The unprincipled men will attempt to shift the Christians off their sure spiritual foundations.

B. Exhortation to Grow in Grace and Knowledge. 3:18a

3:18a -- ***But grow in the grace and knowledge of our Lord and Savior Jesus Christ.***

But grow -- The force of the present imperative verb form is that they are to keep on growing. By such continual growth they will be safeguarded against falling from their own steadfastness. Scripture elsewhere presents "spiritual growth" as a condition of persever-

[152] "The entire absence of directions -- which Jude gives rather elaborately -- as to how these evil men and their victims are to be treated by sound Christians, is in favor of the priority of 2 Peter. When evil men begin to arise, the first impulse is to avoid them and their ways, and to this course Peter exhorts his readers. But when such men have established themselves and gained followers, people begin to consider how to deal with the seducers and to win back the seduced, and to these points Jude directs his readers." Plummer, *op. cit.*, p.178.

ance.[153] The Great Commission, "teaching them to observe all that I commanded you," is an exhortation to help men grow. In this very letter Peter has previously urged his readers to supplement their faith with virtue, *knowledge*, etc. (2 Peter 1:5-10).[154] The command to keep on growing is an appeal to the will. Peter's readers can decide whether or not they want to grow; if they want to, they can do something to stimulate that growth.

In the grace ... of our Lord and Savior Jesus Christ -- Peter wrote "in" not into. His readers are already within the sphere of grace and knowledge. Now they need to grow. Before we can explain what "grace" is, we must first decide whether the genitive phrase ("of the Lord ... Jesus Christ") is connected with it or whether the genitive is connected only with the word "knowledge." Caffin objects to connecting the genitive with grace. "This connection forces us to regard [the genitive] first as subjective, then as objective – the grace which Christ gives [or of which He is the author], and the knowledge of which He is the object – and so seems somewhat forced."[155] But, in reply to Caffin, Peter has already written (3:9,14,15) of the need to constantly be in the Lord's favor and good will.[156]

And in the knowledge ... of our Lord and Savior Jesus Christ -- To grow in knowledge (it is *gnosei* here) about the Lord Jesus Christ is to become better informed concerning what the Scriptures, both Old and New, teach about Him, to enter more fully and sympathetically into His cause. Peter insists, both at the beginning and at the end of this letter, that correct knowledge about Jesus Christ is absolutely imperative for the Christian. With such knowledge the Christian will do well. Without it, the Christian is easily led away into error and destruction. In His high priestly prayer, Jesus Himself called attention to the fact that knowledge of God and of Himself were the way to eternal life (John 17:3). Each one of the words, "Lord," "Jesus," "Christ," and "Savior" is an important topic of study and learning.[157] An emphasis on high Christology is an apt way for Peter to close this letter.

---

[153] Hebrews 5:11-14; 2 Timothy 2:15. See also Philippians 3:10-14 and Ephesians 1:17.

[154] Michael Green (*op. cit.*, p.150) has well illustrated Peter's point. "The Christian life ... is like riding a bicycle. Unless you keep moving, you fall off!"

[155] Caffin, *op. cit.*, p.71. Lenski (*op. cit.*, p.365) thinks we should treat the genitive as subjective with both nouns -- thus saying Jesus is the source of both the grace and the knowledge that men need to live by. That knowledge from Jesus would be mediated by the New Testament apostles and prophets, one of the very topics this letter has repeatedly emphasized.

[156] Another option is to explain this as the grace for daily Christian living, i.e., the help the Holy Spirit gives to live the Christian life (cp. Romans 8).

[157] This is the fourth time Peter has used this full confessional title. (See also 1:11, 2:20, 3:2.)

C. Doxology to Jesus. 3:18b

3:18b -- ***To Him*** **be** ***the glory, both now and to the day of eternity. Amen.***

To Him *be* the glory -- There is no verb in this doxology, but it is the common way a writer expressed a prayer for his readers. Peter prays his readers will give "the glory" to Jesus Christ. To ask his readers to ascribe "the glory" to Jesus is a notable thing. For one like Peter, who grew up as a Jew, and who certainly knew the great words of Isaiah 42:8 ("I am the LORD [Jehovah]; that is my name; I will not give My glory to another"), this doxology is a clear confession of the deity of Jesus.[158] Peter opens (1:1) and closes (3:18b) his letter by emphasizing Jesus' deity. That is exactly the knowledge his readers need to keep in mind, and ascribing the glory to Jesus is a practice they need to be in the habit of doing, as they anticipate and prepare themselves to resist the coming of the false teachers.

Both now and to the day of eternity -- "Now" speaks of what goes on daily in this life. They are to join Peter and Thomas in the acclamation, "My Lord and my God!" (John 20:28). The remarkable expression *eis hemeron aionos* ("to the day of eternity") occurs only here and has been variously explained. One opines it means the day which marks the end of time and the beginning of eternity. Another says eternity is only one day, but it is an everlasting day. There is no tomorrow to follow it. Since *aion* can also mean "age" (as well as "day"), some have said it describes "eternity" as being an unending age. However we interpret this unusual expression, Peter is not saying Jesus should be praised only until that day begins. He is to be ascribed "the glory" both now and throughout all eternity. "Through all eternity I'll sing His praises," says Peter, and he wishes for his readers to do the same!

Amen -- There is some question about whether Peter wrote this "Amen" or whether it was added by a later copyist.[159] When one examines the last page of P^{72} it appears like the word "amen" was perhaps penned in the margin as a sort of afterthought. Whether it expresses Peter's agreement with what the Spirit has prompted him to write, or some copyist's endorsement, it certainly should be the sentiment and the appropriate response of all who read 2 Peter.

---

158 Peter is claiming no more for Jesus than what Jesus Himself expressed, as recorded in John 5:23. Men are to honor Him just as they honor the Father.

159 Manuscripts which include it are P^{72}, Sinaiticus, Alexandrinus, Ephraemi, and the Byzantine text family. The Vulgate includes it. Vaticanus and a few other manuscripts omit it, as did Augustine. (Cp. the comments on "Amen" at 1 Peter 4:11, 5:11 and 5:14.)

In most of the epistles in the New Testament, we are accustomed to read some personal remarks as the letters are brought to a close. There have been none in 2 Peter. We think Plummer's explanation is right on the mark:

> The epistle comes to a most abrupt conclusion, without any personal remarks or greetings. This is so unlike the First Epistle, so unusual in Apostolic letters generally, that an imitator, and so accomplished an imitator as the writer of this epistle must have been, would scarcely have omitted so usual and natural an addition. The addition would have been doubly natural here, for the personator (if the writer of the letter be such) is personating Peter near the end of his life, writing to congregations whom he is not likely to see or address again. Surely such circumstances would have seemed to him to demand some words of personal greeting and tender farewell (and Acts 20:18-34 and 2 Timothy 4:6-18 could have supplied him with models). But nothing of the kind is inserted.
>
> Assume that Peter himself is the writer, and we can understand how he came to disappoint such natural expectations. His heart is too full of the fatal dangers which threaten the whole Christian community to think of himself and his personal friends. Perhaps already having been sentenced to death (2 Peter 1:14), his chief fear is lest he be killed before he has left on record these words of exhortation and warning. Therefore, at the beginning he hurries to his subject at once, and presses on, without pause or break, until it is exhausted; and now that he has unburdened his heart, he cares to say no more, but ends at once with a tribute of praise to the Master that bought him![160]

Peter's second letter is, to this commentator, one of the great expressions of the Christian faith. It is surprising that so many modern students of the Bible seem to have had so little appreciation for this magnificent epistle. It is both elevating and inspiring. In imagery and execution it is one of the best-done epistles in the New Testament.

We conclude by reading again 3:17,18:

You therefore, beloved, knowing this beforehand, be on your guard lest, being carried away by the error of unprincipled men, you fall from your own steadfastness, but grow in the grace and knowledge of our Lord and Savior Jesus Christ. To Him be the glory, both now and to the day of eternity. Amen.

[160] Plummer, *op. cit.*, p.179.

Commentary On

Jude

JUDE

INTRODUCTORY STUDIES

I. Preliminaries

This short epistle has a singular place among New Testament books. Its authorship, date, circle of readers, the evils against which it is directed, and indeed almost all points connected with its literary history are the subjects of keen dispute among Bible scholars and students. The most opposite verdicts have been pronounced, and continue to be pronounced, on its right to a position in the canon, on its doctrinal value, on its worth as a mirror of the condition of the primitive church. It is not too much to say that the New Testament nowhere else presents so many strange phenomena, or raises so many curious questions within so narrow a space.

In the Introductory Studies to 2 Peter, we noted how that book is a very neglected book among contemporary readers. Jude has had even less interest shown in it. In fact, it has been called "the most neglected book in the New Testament."[1] Various reasons have been suggested for this neglect. Some have called attention to the fact that Jude is such a short book. Some in an earlier age neglected it because they thought it cited non-canonical (pseudepigraphical) Jewish writings. Some postmodern readers are offended by its claim that there is absolute truth for which a man should take a definite stand. Nevertheless, Jude's emphasis on a fixed body of truth, designated by him as "the faith," needs to be pondered and incorporated into every Christian's thinking and action! Guthrie concludes his paragraph on the value of the epistle with these words, "Its neglect reflects more the superficiality of the generation that neglects it than the irrelevance of its burning message."[2]

Restoration Movement folk have tended to make more use of Jude than many of their religious neighbors. Jude 3, "Contend earnestly for the faith which was once for all delivered to the saints," has been a verse the brethren have been expected to memorize and quote regularly.[3] They have been taught to use it to show that "faith" includes a body of doctrine

---

[1] Douglas J. Rowston, "The Most Neglected Book in the New Testament," *New Testament Studies* 21 (July 1975), p.554-563.

[2] Donald F. Guthrie, "The Epistle of Jude," in *New Testament Introduction: Hebrews to Revelation* (Chicago: Inter-Varsity Press, 1966), p.249.

[3] While it is sadly true some have used Jude 3 to justify an intolerantly dogmatic stance about relatively minor theological issues, there has also been a well-placed warning about the great danger of accepting uncritically any doctrinal position as valid even when such acceptance means compromising God's final and complete revelation as disclosed by Jesus and His apostles.

that is expected to be uniformly held by all followers of Christ, and to show that the revelation given through Jesus and His apostles has a finality to it (versus modern claims to more recent revelation from God). Not a few preachers have used the words of Jude 24-25 as their regular prayer of benediction at the close of Sunday worship services. Indeed, as long as men need stern rebukes for their evil and ungodly practices, Jude's epistle will be of permanent value.

In the early twenty-first century, when new-age ideas – which, after all, differ little from the old Gnostic ideas – are bombarding the consciousness of people, the warnings and correctives of Jude need again to be emphasized. We Christians may continue to ignore the little book of Jude only at our own risk!

II. AUTHORSHIP AND ATTESTATION

A. Internal Evidence. One evidence is the "title" of this epistle.[4] It appears in a variety of forms. Yet, in general, this fact is true: the older the document, the simpler the title. The two most ancient uncial manuscripts, Sinaiticus and Vaticanus, have a single word title, "Jude." Codex Alexandrinus and a few others have the title "The Epistle of Jude." These ancient manuscripts leave the question of the author's identity untouched. In more recent manuscripts, the title expands into such forms as these: "The Epistle of Jude the Apostle," "The Catholic Epistle of the Apostle Jude," "The Epistle of Jude the Brother of James," and one very late manuscript ventures to give Jude the designation "brother of God."

When we study the verses of this letter for clues about authorship, several things come to our attention. In verse 1, the writer signs his name as "Jude, a bond-servant of Jesus Christ, and brother of James." In verses 17 and 18 the writer seems to distinguish himself from the apostles of Jesus. Verses 3 and 4, and following, indicate the writer has personal knowledge of the situation (i.e., the acute dangers from false teachers) his readers are facing.

What can be made of these scant clues? There are at least seven Judes[5] in the New Testament: (1) Judas Iscariot, Mark 3:19; (2) the apostle Judas (not Iscariot), one of the

---

[4] Of course, we must remember the title was most probably added some years after the epistle itself was written, and likely it was added by someone other than the actual writer of the book.

[5] "Jude" and "Judas" are simply English variants for the one Greek form *Ioudas*. The name Jude or Judas was a common one in New Testament times. It was the name of one of the Twelve patriarchs, and it was more recently popularized because of the exploits of Judas the Maccabean. Since our translators had the choice of Jude or Judas for the title of the book, and for the author's name, it is probably because of the perfidy of Judas Iscariot that "Jude" became the accepted title rather than "Judas." Our English versions use the shortened form of "Jude" only in connection with this epistle, using the longer form "Judas" for all its other occurrences in the New Testament.

Twelve, John 14:22;[6] (3) Jude, the brother of Jesus, Matthew 13:55, Mark 6:3; (4) Judas, called Barsabbas, a Christian prophet, well respected in the Jerusalem church, Acts 15:22; (5) Judah, an ancestor of Jesus, Luke 3:30; (6) Judas, the Galilean, who led an insurrection against Rome in the time of Quirinius "in the days of the census," Acts 5:37; and (7) Judas, with whom Paul lodged in Damascus, Acts 9:11. Which of these is the author of the epistle? Not Iscariot who betrayed Jesus, for he was dead long before any New Testament books were written. All the other "Judes" except the apostle and the brother of the Lord are too insignificant to be considered.[7]

Before we can determine which of the two was the author, we must study the matter of whether or not the "apostle Jude" and the "Lord's brother" were the same person.[8] Arguments that they were the same person include: (a) One of the brothers of Jesus was named James (Matthew 13:55); in several places in the KJV (Luke 6:16; Acts 1:13), the apostle Jude is called "Jude *the brother* of James."[9] (b) If the two Judes were distinct, then one of them (the apostle Jude) disappears altogether from the New Testament after Acts 1:13.[10] (c) If the two are distinct, we have certainly <u>*two*</u>, and in all probability <u>*three*</u>, sets of

---

[6] The apostle Jude also seems to have been called by the names of Lebbaeus and Thaddeus (Matthew 10:3; Mark 3:18).

[7] Of these others, only Judas Barsabbas has been proposed as being the possible writer of our epistle. His being a "prophet" (Acts 15:22,32) would be evidence of his ability to speak and write by inspiration, and thus would have helped the whole matter of the canonicity of Jude (since inspiration was the chief criterion for inclusion in the canon). This identification would help explain the prominence in the church of the writer of this letter as implied from Jude 1. Defenders of this idea that Judas Barsabbas is the author of "Jude" (see for example, E. H. Plumptre, "The General Epistles of St. Peter and St. Jude," *Cambridge Bible for Schools*, p.85-86) have had to explain away either "brother of James" (e.g., "brother" is an interpolation; he was actually the "son of James") or the meaning of "Barsabbas" (e.g., it is not patronymic, but a nickname descriptive of character similar to what "Barnabas" was for Joseph the Levite, Acts 4:36). Both of these matters have proven so difficult to accept that scholars have largely rejected the hypothesis that Judas Barsabbas could be the author of our letter.

[8] In a Special Study #2 ("The Brothers of the Lord") in the author's *New Testament History: Acts*, it is concluded that the "brothers of Jesus" and the "apostles of Jesus" were two separate groups of men. See also J.B. Mayor's article on the "Brethren of the Lord" in *Hasting's Dictionary of the Bible* (New York: Scribners, 1908), Vol.2, p.320-326.

[9] Note that the words "the brother" are in italics, indicating that there is no word in the Greek for "brother" in this place. In the ASV/NASB, Jude is called "*the son* of James." *Ioudas Iakobou* ("Jude of James [or Jacob]") is how the Greek reads, and the regular method of translating this particular genitive construction elsewhere in the New Testament is "son of." The Peshitto Syriac version (at Luke and Acts) reads "son" rather than "brother." (Admittedly, Arndt-Gingrich offers examples of this genitive construction being translated "brother of" in certain extra-Biblical Greek references, so we cannot be dogmatic in the affirmation that the KJV "brother of" is totally out of the question.)

[10] Jude is not the only apostle to "disappear" after Acts 1:13. So too do Simon the Zealot, Nathanael (Bartholomew), and Thomas. Acts never was intended to be a comprehensive history of all the apostles.

brothers bearing the same names.[11] Hidden behind the scenes in this ongoing debate is the question of the perpetual virginity of Mary. Those who defend that dogma are accustomed to identify the "apostle Jude" and the "Lord's brother" as being the same person.[12] Arguments that they were not the same person include: (a) Distinguishing between the two allows us to give the term *adelphos* ("brother") its natural meaning. (b) The New Testament clearly shows a distinction between the "brothers of the Lord" and "the apostles of the Lord" (John 2:12, 7:5; Mark 3:21,31; and Jude 1 compared with Jude 17,18).[13]

Having decided the apostle Jude and the Lord's brother are two different people, may we conclude the apostle Jude is the author of this letter? Few commentators, unless they identify the apostle Jude and the Lord's brother as being the same person, have defended the view the apostle Jude is the author. The fact that the writer of this epistle distinguishes himself from the apostles (Jude 17,18) is fairly convincing evidence that we should not consider the apostle Jude as being the author.

By the process of elimination, we have come to the conclusion that Jude, the brother of the Lord, is the author of this epistle.[14] There can be no doubt that the author wanted his

[11] One set would be James, Joseph, Simon, and Judas, the brothers of Jesus (Matthew 13:55). A second set would be James, Joses, and Symeon, the sons of Clopas (John 19:25 cp. with Matthew 27:56 and Mark 15:40,47). If Clopas and Alphaeus (in the New Testament) are distinct personalities, then Alphaeus also has sons with the same names (Mark 3:18), and we have three sets of children with the same names. [J.W. McGarvey, *Fourfold Gospel*, p.224 has affirmed that Clopas and Alphaeus are but different ways to transliterate the Aramaic name '*Chalphai*.' J.H. Ropes, "James," *ICC*, p.58, has argued that such an identification of names as McGarvey made is "linguistically unsound." The weight of scholarly opinion in the lexicons and Bible dictionaries is that Clopas and Alphaeus are different people.]

[12] Jerome's theory that the brothers of Jesus were our Lord's cousins (children of Alphaeus) is contradicted by John 7:5. The brother of the Lord could not have been one of His original disciples, for until after Jesus' resurrection, His "brothers did not believe on Him." Though popularized in the West by Jerome's influence, the identification of James the Lord's brother with James the son of Alphaeus has never prevailed in the Eastern church.

[13] Jude not only does not claim to be an apostle but seems to regard the apostles as apart from himself (Jude 17,18). This mitigates against "Jude" (the brother of James, the brother of the Lord) as being the same as the apostle Jude.

[14] Other hypotheses have proven unacceptable. Not many contemporary writers argue "Jude" is an assumed name (pseudonymous). Using an obscure name is not how pseudonymity was done among ancient writers. In pseudepigraphic works written under a pen name, the names attached to the writings are those of well-known persons in order to lend "weight" to their alleged prophecies. Those writers hardy enough to espouse pseudonymity for Jude, if they even make an attempt to explain, have given lame and desperate explanations about how an obscure name like "Jude" came to be chosen. The hypothesis of Grotius, Moffatt, and Streeter, that the "Jude" who wrote this letter was the second-century bishop of Jerusalem who bore that name, requires some fanciful stepping. The words "brother of James" must be treated as an episcopal title at Jerusalem, though no evidence of such a title is produced. The passage in the *Apostolic Constitutions* on which the idea rests is hardly convincing evidence. Such a late date for Jude that this hypothesis would require is against the believability of the hypothesis (see notes below). E.F. Scott's view (*The Literature of the New Testament*, p.225) that "brother" at Jude 1 is an interpolation, and that the author of our letter is an unknown Jude who was the *son* of an unknown James, has pushed the envelope to its limits. There is no textual evidence that "brother" is an interpolation, and an unknown authorship would have made it difficult for the book to ever have been considered to be canonical.

readers to think of "James of Jerusalem" when he identified himself as "the brother of James" (Jude 1). After the death of James the son of Zebedee, AD 44 (Acts 12:2), James of Jerusalem (the Lord's brother, Galatians 1:19; Acts 12:17, 15:13ff, 21:18ff, and now himself an apostle, though he was not one of the original Twelve) is the only James as well known as the language of Jude 1 implies "James" is.[15] Jude commends himself to his readers as a "servant of Jesus Christ" and through his brother James's reputation.[16]

B. External Evidence. *Allusions.*[17] There are possible allusions to Jude in Clement of Rome,[18] the *Shepherd of Hermas*,[19] Polycarp,[20] Athenagoras,[21] *The Epistle of Barnabas*,[22] Theophilus of Antioch,[23] and perhaps the *Didache*.[24]

---

[15] "James" is well-enough known to Jude's readers that all that was needed to identify him was the name "James." The brother of the Lord is the only famous "James" we know whose name would be so instantly recognizable.

[16] If the writer is the brother of Jesus, his identification of himself is exactly what we would expect. Why did he not say "brother of the Lord" if that is what he was? It is likely neither James nor Jude ever called themselves "brother of the Lord" after Jesus' ascension. His resurrection and ascension and glorification had altered all of Jesus' human relationships. His atoning death and resurrection broke all earthly relationships. Thereafter, if any man wanted a part of Jesus Christ, they must be believers in Him. "Servant of Jesus Christ" is what the "brothers" called themselves (see Jude 1, and cp. James 1:1), and as comments below at verse 1 will indicate, this expression is a claim of special position and of inspiration. Instead of claiming physical relationship to Jesus as a reason they should be heard, "servant of Christ" is exactly what we would expect from a church leader who expects his words to carry unquestioned authority.

[17] See the first two footnotes on the introduction to 2 Peter for an explanation of the four kinds of external evidence one may find for New Testament books -- allusions, quotations, annotated quotations, and canonical listings.

[18] Twice Clement (*I Clem.* xx.12, lix.2) uses language ("glory" and "majesty") that reminds us of Jude 25. We date I Clement at AD 96.

[19] In *Sim.* v.7.2 is an expression ("defile the flesh") that reflects Jude 8. We date the writing of Hermas in the early second century, c. AD 140.

[20] In the address of Polycarp's letter *To the Philippians* we have language ("mercy to you and peace be multiplied") similar to Jude 2. Only in Jude 3 and Jude 20 do we find the figure of building on or into the faith such as we read in *To the Philippians* iii.2. The Greek text behind *To the Philippians* x is a match for Jude 21 ("waiting anxiously for the mercy of the Lord"). The same two thoughts ("building yourselves up" and "snatching them out of the fire") found in juxtaposition in Jude 20,23 are found in *To the Philippians* xi.4. Polycarp died in AD 155.

[21] Athenagoras, about AD 177, in *A Plea for the Christians* xxiv and xxv, speaks of fallen angels in a manner which suggests acquaintance with Jude 6 and 8-10.

[22] Chapter ii.10 uses language "crept in unnoticed" that occurs only in Jude 3,4. We date the writing of Barnabas at c. AD 130.

[23] In Book 2, chap.15, at the end, Theophilus (d. AD 183-185) in his *To Autolycus* speaks of the planets as a type of fallen man. That language is comparable to Jude 13, "wandering stars."

[24] Compare ii.7 with Jude 22ff, and iii.6 with Jude 8-10. The date for this writing is c. AD 120.

Quotations. Clement of Alexandria (c. AD 190) several times quotes Jude in his works. "For I would have you know, says Jude, that God once ...."[25] "It was respecting these, I suppose, and similar heresies, that Jude in his epistle said prophetically ...."[26] Eusebius informs us that Clement of Alexandria, in his work called *Hypotyposes*, "made short explanations of all the canonical Scriptures, not omitting those which are disputed, I mean that of Jude, and the other general [catholic] epistles."[27] Tertullian, in North Africa, about AD 200, spoke of Jude as the author of the epistle,[28] calls it Scripture, and argued that its quotation from *Enoch* upheld the authority of that book. Origen, AD 210, did not appear himself to question the authenticity of Jude, though he observes that some of his contemporaries had doubts about the book. In his *Commentary on Matthew* (Book x,17), he wrote, "Jude, who wrote a letter of few lines, it is true, but full of powerful words and heavenly grace, said in the preface, 'Jude, the servant of Jesus Christ and the brother of James'." Origen several times quotes Jude 6 in his commentaries on Matthew and John.[29] In the Latin versions of Origen's works, Jude 6 and Jude 8 are quoted and attributed to Jude.[30] Eusebius (AD 325), in his *Ecclesiastical History*, classified Jude among the *Antilegomena*. He wrote, "Among the disputed books, although they are well known and approved by many, is that one called the Epistle of James, and that of Jude ... " (iii.25.3). *Antilegomena* were writings "some people in some places spoke against" but which Eusebius himself recognized as canonical. A few lines earlier, Eusebius gave his reason for classifying James and Jude as "disputed." "There are not many of the ancients who have made mention of it [that is, quote it by name], as neither of that called Jude's, which likewise is one of the epistles called *catholic*. We know, however, that these also are publicly read in most churches, together with the rest" (ii.23.25). Jerome (AD 385) wrote, "Jude, the brother of James, left a small epistle, which is reckoned among the seven catholic epistles. And because in it he quotes from the apocryphal *Book of Enoch*, it is rejected by many. However, it has acquired such authority by age and use that it is reckoned among the sacred Scriptures."[31]

---

[25] *Paedagog.* lib. iii.

[26] *Stromata* iii.

[27] *H.E.*, vi.14.

[28] In his work, *On the Apparel of Women*, Tertullian wrote, "Enoch possesses a testimony in Jude the apostle." Tertullian was of the opinion that Jude was written by an "apostle."

[29] See Matthew, Book xvii.30, where Jude's epistle is named as the source of the words about angels "being kept in everlasting chains of darkness unto the judgment of the great day." See also his commentary on John, Book xiii.37.

[30] The title "apostle" is given to Jude in the Latin versions of Origen. It appears that in his Greek originals, Origen did not use the title "apostle" for Jude.

[31] *Lives of Illustrious Men*, chap.4.

Canonical Listings. Although direct proof is lacking, Jude seems to have been in the Old Latin Version (before AD 170). Tertullian's language (quoted above) indicates Jude was an acknowledged part of the canon in North Africa.[32] The epistle of Jude was included in the Muratorian Canon (c. AD 170). The Latin words are fragmentary, *"Epistolae sane Judae et ... in catholica habentur."* The broken sentence is usually completed in this fashion, *"Epistolae sane Judae et superscripti Johannis duas in catholica habentur."* The meaning thus given to the passage is that the writer of this fragment wished to give the two epistles of John and the epistle of Jude a place in the canon of the church.

The external evidence for authorship, though not exceedingly strong, points to the same person, Jude, as does the internal evidence.

C. Modern objections to Jude's authorship. Critics have pointed to certain features within the letter which they claim point to a time outside the possible lifetime of Jude. For example, some have argued the language of Jude seems too Hellenistic for someone who supposedly grew up in Galilee (like the traditional author Jude did). There are thirteen Greek words in Jude not found elsewhere in the New Testament. Other critics pick up on what some of the ancients were also troubled by – namely, the possible use of pseudepigraphical sources (the *Assumption of Moses* in verse 9,and of the *Book of Enoch* in verse 14) – and argue the half-brother of the Lord, growing up in Galilee, would not have had access to such sources. Still others object that Jude can not have written the letter because in its appeal to contend for "the faith" it bears the marks of "early Catholicism." Such *Fruhkatholizismus* which began to emphasize formalized creeds, it is asserted, is a second-century development. Another calls attention to the allusion to "the apostles of our Lord" in Jude 17,18 and affirms the writer of the letter belongs to a generation removed from the apostles so that the memory of them is a mere tradition. Again, some critics have maintained the type of Gnosticism attacked in the epistle did not come into existence until considerably after apostolic times, and therefore Jude could not be the author.

Each of these objections has been answered. For example, "faith" is used of a body of doctrine in Paul's epistles (e.g., Galatians 1:23, 3:23) and before that at Acts 6:7. One does not have to posit a late date for Jude because of Jude 3. Galilee was not a rural backwater whose citizens were culturally ingrown. James, the brother of the Lord, writes excellent Greek in his epistle. Why can't his brother Jude also have had a good vocabulary

---

[32] Chase, "Jude" in *Hasting's Dictionary of the Bible*, argues that Jude was not in Cassiodorus' listing of ancient Latin translations. It was also omitted from the *Canon Mommsenianus* of about AD 350. However, by the time of the third Council of Carthage in AD 397, it was included in the canon recognized in North Africa (Westcott, *Canon*, p.542).

and a command of the Greek? There is nothing in Jude 17,18 to show the author and the "apostles" lived generations apart. All that is required in the word "beforehand" is that Jude is writing at a later date than when some of them spoke and wrote. We have already commented on incipient Gnosticism in our introduction to 2 Peter, and while what Jude writes reflects what we know of incipient Gnosticism in the last third of the first century, there is no reason to suppose the writer of Jude had in view the definite Gnostic sects of the second century, say the Carpocratians, the Cainites, or the Ophites.[33] Salmon, arguing for the possibility the letter was written during the lifetime of "Jude ... brother of James," said this, "On the whole, I conclude that the evils under which Jude's Epistle reveals the Church to be suffering are not essentially different from those the existence of which we learn from Paul's Epistles, and therefore we are not forced to bring the authorship down to the second century."[34] Indeed, if the Pastoral Epistles, written by Paul before his death in AD 68, deal with incipient Gnosticism (and we think they do), there is no reason to use Gnosticism as an argument for such a late date that Jude could not be alive to write this book.

There is no external evidence which militates against Jude being the author, and since the arguments against his authorship gleaned from internal evidence have proven to be less than convincing, we see no reason to do anything but agree with the traditional view that Jude, the brother of James, the one whose signature is on the letter, is the author of this short letter.

III. THE LIFE OF JUDE

Neither Scripture nor early tradition tells us much about this man's life. He was one of the children of Joseph and Mary, born after the virgin Mary gave birth to Jesus.[35] Unless he was an exception to the statement in John 7:5 (of which there is no intimation), Jude was

---

[33] The Carpocratians were a mid-second-century sect noted for their immoral practices, particularly their advocacy of promiscuous sexual indulgence. Clement of Alexandria (*Stromata* iii.6-10) noted the close connection between Jude's false teachers and this sect, but regarded Jude's references as prophetic. Bigg, "Introduction to the Epistle of St. Jude," *ICC*, p.312-323, gives a concise summary of Carpocratian beliefs and practices. The Ophites and Cainites appear to have reversed good and evil, so their behavior also conformed to immoral patterns.

[34] George F. Salmon, *An Historical Introduction to the Study of the Books of the New Testament*, 4th edition (New York: Dutton, 1889), p.525.

[35] If the Epiphanian view is correct, that Jesus' "brothers" were Joseph's children from a marriage previous to his union with Mary, then the "brothers" would be physically older than Jesus by several years. See this matter discussed in the author's Special Study entitled "The Brothers of Jesus" referred to above in footnote #8. We have accepted the view that Jesus' brothers and sisters were the actual children of Joseph and Mary, born subsequent to the time when Jesus was born, in what are the early years of the first century AD.

not a believer in Jesus during His earthly ministry. For a long time Jude was staggered by the Messianic claims of Jesus, and not until after Jesus' resurrection and His personal appearance to Jude's older brother, James, did Jude come within the circle of believers (Acts 1:14). From what is said about Jesus' brothers in 1 Corinthians 9:5, and from what we read in Hegesippus, we may presume Jude was married, that he was a traveling preacher, and that his wife accompanied him on his preaching tours. Indeed, his claim to be a "bond-servant of Jesus Christ" implies a call into the ministry and a special empowerment to serve as an inspired mouthpiece who makes God's revelations known to men.

Tradition, which often delighted in furnishing details respecting the apostles and early leaders of the church, is almost completely silent concerning the life and ministry of Jude. The apocryphal Gospels do not mention his name. The lone story connected with the name of Jude, as told by Hegesippus, has been preserved for us by Eusebius in his *Ecclesiastical History* (iii.19,20). As related there, Domitian, about AD 95, near the end of his reign, had given orders that the descendants of David should be slain.[36] Certain heretical informers attempted to excite the jealousy of the emperor Domitian against Jude's two grandsons on the ground they were of the lineage of David. Hegesippus related the facts in these words:

> Of the family of the Lord there were still living the grandchildren of Jude, who is said to have been the Lord's brother according to the flesh. Information was given that they belonged to the family of David, and they were brought to the Emperor Domitian by the Evocatus [a retired soldier who was called on to do military duty as a volunteer]. For Domitian feared the coming of Christ as Herod also had feared it. And he asked them if they were descendants of David, and they confessed that they were. Then he asked them how much property they had, or how much money they owned. And both of them answered that they had only nine thousand denarii, half of which belonged to each of them; and this property did not consist of silver, but of a piece of land which contained only thirty-nine acres, and from which they raised their taxes and supported themselves by their own labor. Then they showed their hands, exhibiting the hardness of their bodies and the callousness produced upon their hands by continuous toil as evidence of their labor. And when they were asked concerning Christ and His kingdom, of what sort it was and where and when it was to appear, they answered that it was not a temporal nor an earthly kingdom, but a heavenly and angelic one, which would appear at the end of the world, when He should come in glory to judge the living and the dead, and to give unto every one according to his works. Upon hearing this, Domitian did not pass judgment against them, but disdaining them as harmless peasants, he let them go, and by a decree put a stop to the persecution of the Church. But when they were released they were honored in the churches, because they were witnesses and were also relatives of the Lord. And peace being established, they lived until the time of Trajan.

[36] Domitian, emperor of the Roman empire, after some years of rule, had become an old man, and he was much worried about being assassinated. He was especially worried that one "Christ" – or some of his followers – would try to see that this "Christ" was made king. Especially the descendants of David were sought out, and if they were men of any consequence, they were put out of the way.

IV. DESTINATION OF THE LETTER

The address in verse 1 is general – "to those who are the called, beloved in God the Father, and kept for Jesus Christ." I.e., the destination is to Christians. No geographic location where the addressees live is indicated, though there are internal indications the author knew of the conditions within the church or churches to whom he writes. According to verse 4, Jude is aware that certain false teachers had infiltrated the churches and were a dangerous threat to the continuing faithfulness of the readers. According to verses 22 and 23, some church members were already in need of being rescued from the clutches of these false teachers. According to verses 17 and 18, the readers were aware of the letter we call 2 Peter, which was addressed to Christians in Asia Minor, in particular in the provinces of Pontus, Galatia, Cappadocia, Asia, and Bithynia.[37]

Using this scant bit of information, commentators have suggested various places as possible destinations.

(1) Alexandria in Egypt has been suggested. This is suggested because Clement of Alexandria is the first one who bears specific, annotated information about the authorship of this epistle; because the *Book of Enoch* (which is alleged to be quoted in Jude 14) was in favor there; and because it is affirmed Jude contains certain images and figures taken from the natural objects which agree with the physical features of Egypt, such as "clouds without water" and "raging waves of the sea." Against this hypothesis are the questions of whether there is any evidence of Christians in Egypt during Jude's lifetime, and what did the folk in Egypt know of 2 Peter this early?

(2) Corinth has been suggested. It is asserted the known wickedness of Corinth fits what is condemned in Jude. Against this hypothesis is the question of whether incipient Gnosticism was flourishing in Corinth as early as the time of Jude.[38]

(3) A popular opinion is Jude was originally an encyclical letter addressed to the churches of Palestine and perhaps Syria.[39] In support of this view it is affirmed that Jude 17 and 18 suggest the readers have personally heard the original apostles preach. This would argue for Palestine, or a place close to Palestine, as the destination. Furthermore, it is affirmed that Hegesippus describes the condition of the churches in Palestine about AD 80, and his descrip-

---

[37] See notes at 1 Peter 1:1, 2 Peter 3:1, and the Introductory Studies to both books included earlier in this volume.

[38] See this matter discussed in the author's *New Testament Epistles: 2 Corinthians and Galatians* (Moberly, MO: Scripture Exposition Books, 2011), p.xxiii. Were the false teachers attacked in those letters Judaizers, or were they Jews who were beginning to embrace Gnostic ideas?

[39] F.H. Chase ("Jude, Epistle of" in *Hasting's Bible Dictionary*, Vol.2, p.805) has argued for Syrian Antioch as being the original destination. He bases his decision on three points: the Christians addressed were mainly Gentiles; they were men among whom Paul had worked; and they had received oral instruction from Jesus' original apostles. He thinks Antioch would satisfy all these points.

tion matches what we find in Jude. It is also affirmed that Hegesippus implies neither Jude nor his children or grandchildren ever left the Holy Land (save when the grandchildren were taken for trial before Domitian). If Jude were writing to churches he personally knew about, they would *ipso facto* be located in Palestine or Syria. It was in Palestine that "James of Jerusalem" (the writer's brother) was well known, not only among the Christians but also among the Jewish people who were unconverted. Moreover, the illustrations used in the letter are those familiar to a Jew writing to Jews. The deliverance from Egypt, the fallen angels, the destruction of the cities of the plain, the legend of Michael's contention with Satan, the references to Cain, Balaam, and Korah, as well as the prophecy ascribed to Enoch, are all found in a very brief space and are touched upon in such a manner (it is affirmed) as could be edifying to none save those who were familiar not only with Old Testament Scripture but also with Jewish traditions. Against this presentation it has been proposed that the Jewish coloring of the epistle is an argument *ad hominem* – since Gnosticism was a Jewish heresy to begin with, the writer appeals to Jewish Scriptures to condemn the heresy. Such an appeal does not necessarily demonstrate that the readers were Jews who lived in Palestine. Jude 17 and 18 do not require that the readers have personally heard the original apostles preach. Acquaintance with the letters of Peter and Paul would satisfy this historical allusion.

(4) We tend to believe the letter was an encyclical addressed to the churches of Asia Minor, just as were Peter's letters and some of Paul's (e.g., Colossians and the letters to Timothy, which refute false teachings similar to those addressed in 2 Peter and Jude). When we recall that incipient Gnosticism began as a Jewish heresy, then spread among the Gentiles, we have satisfied the references in the letter that seem to call for a Jewish milieu and those referenced that seem to suggest some of the readers were of Gentile background. Jude has been a traveling preacher. What is to keep us from supposing he has visited the countries in Asia Minor to which, because he is concerned for their spiritual well-being, he now sends this very urgent and heart-felt letter? Furthermore, when the New Testament apocryphal and pseudepigraphical letters came to be written, a majority of them were written by Gnostics to defend Gnostic teachings. Because that heresy began among the Jews, this would explain the acquaintance with old Jewish legends and writings that were incorporated eventually into the Gnostic writings that are still extant to us.

V. OCCASION AND PURPOSE OF WRITING

The occasion for Jude's writing of this letter is clearly stated in verse 4, and his purpose is stated in verse 3.[40] Because of what was happening in the churches, he felt the need to write to them to appeal to them to "contend earnestly for the faith which was once for all delivered to the saints." The inroads the false teachers are making must be vigorously op-

[40] As will be explained in the comments on this verse, verse 3 is capable of two different interpretations. One has Jude changing the topic he feels a necessity to write about, the other has him writing on the very topic he all along intended to emphasize.

posed. Believers must be warned lest they be caught in the insidious errors being promulgated among them.

Who these false teachers are has been thoroughly discussed in our Introductory Studies on 2 Peter. The conclusion there reached is that incipient Gnosticism is troubling the churches. Jude does tell us some of their doctrinal deviations and he identifies some of their wrong lifestyles. Concerning their erroneous doctrine, verse 4 tells us they "deny our only Master and Lord, Jesus Christ." They do not believe the articles of "the faith" once for all delivered to the saints (verse 5). The greatest threat of Gnosticism toward Christianity lay in its denial of God's revelation through Jesus Christ. "To follow the Gnostic path led to a radical rejection of all God's Word to man, and to a substitution of a different salvation."[41] To the Gnostics, the way of salvation rested on esoteric teaching rather than on the truth that is in Jesus Christ. Verse 4 says that they turn the grace of God into lasciviousness. To them, apparently, God's grace was an excuse to sin more. Verse 8 indicates they "reject authority and revile angelic majesties." Their doctrine about angels is wrong. Their teachings produce no spiritually profitable results either for themselves or their hearers (verses 12,13). Rather than being initiates into a higher state of spirituality (as Gnostics claimed to be), they are devoid of the Spirit and teach wrong doctrine about the Holy Spirit (verses 19, 20). They continually speak ungodly things against the Lord (verse 15). Perhaps they get some of their teachings while in self-induced altered states of consciousness (verse 8). They were "psychic" and not "spiritual" (verse 19).[42] Concerning their dangerous lifestyles, verse 4 indicates they have pretended to become Christians and have under false colors (they actually were "ungodly persons") crept into the church. Verse 7 indicates that they indulge in gross immorality and go after strange flesh. Verse 8 indicates that their thoughts are constantly such as defile the flesh. Their behavior at the love feasts ruins those occasions (verse 12). They are into religion just for the money (verse 11) and flatter people for the sake of their own advantage (verse 16); they were promulgating the errors they did simply in order to further their own financial situation. They are grumblers, fault finders, and are following their own ungodly lusts (verses 16, 18). They act worse than irrational animals (verse 10), they indulge in unnatural lust (verses 4,7,16), and they are consequently defiled (verses 8, 23). Their behavior is the very same kind that in days gone by resulted in judgment and punishment from God.

If Jude's readers continue to offer the false teachers no resistance, these false teachers will destroy the church and cause the damnation of any of Jude's readers who embrace their false system. Jude's strong language is now understandable. The influence of these false

---

[41] Edwin A Blum, "Jude" in *Expositor's Bible Commentary*, edited by F.C. Gaebelein (Grand Rapids: Zondervan, 1981), Vol.12, p.385.

[42] It has been observed that while Jude's description of the false teachers matches rather closely the one given in 2 Peter, nevertheless Peter calls attention to some distinct characteristics not mentioned in Jude. Peter notes that the false teachers' special targets are the newly converted (2 Peter 2:18,19). Peter calls attention to the false teachers' wrong handling of the Scriptures (2 Peter 3:15,16). Peter also calls attention to their erroneous teaching concerning Christ's second coming (2 Peter 3:1-7).

teachers must be stopped! Each individual reader is responsible for his or her own repudiation of what is so dangerously false and perniciously misleading. Believers are also responsible to attempt to rescue those who have already been duped, snatching them like brands from the fire (verse 23). And all alike are assured the judgment and punishment promised by God will befall both those who smuggle the false teaching into the church, and those who are swept away by it.

VI. THE PLACE OF WRITING

There is nothing in the letter or in early church tradition that helps us determine where Jude was when he composed this letter. Scholarly guesses include Alexandria in Egypt or Jerusalem in Palestine. The reasons given for these guesses are speculative. Alexandria is chosen because of Clement of Alexandria's knowledge of and strong endorsement of the letter. Jerusalem is picked on the supposition that, like James, Jude made Jerusalem his headquarters. But if Jude were a traveling preacher as 1 Corinthians 9:5 implies, there is little that ties him to Jerusalem. The fact of the matter is, we just do not know where Jude was when he wrote this letter.

VII. DATE OF WRITING

The date we assign for the writing of this letter depends largely on decisions already made on other matters – i.e., the decisions reached concerning authorship, concerning the relationship of Jude to 2 Peter,[43] concerning Jude's alleged use of biblical (e.g., Pauline letters) and non-biblical (e.g., pseudepigraphic) sources, and concerning whether or not Jude would have included the destruction of Jerusalem (AD 70) as an example of God's punishment of wicked people had that event already happened before he wrote.

Those who regard the epistle as pseudonymous are apt to date it around AD 150. Those who regard Jude (the Lord's brother, and James' brother) as the author will opt for a date in the AD 60's or 70's, for the dating must naturally be confined to the reasonable limits of his life. Those who believe the Lord's brothers were older physically than He (because they were Joseph's children by a previous marriage) will date the book in the AD 60's. Those who believe the Lord's brothers were younger than He (because they were born to Joseph and Mary after Jesus was born) tend to date the book in the AD 70's. Mayor, who accepts the view that Jude was younger than Jesus, has calculated Jude would have been in his 70s when Domitian began to reign (AD 81). Jude apparently was dead by AD 95, the time of the trials of Jude's grandchildren by Domitian. For had Jude still been living, would not he too have

---

[43] See the Introductory Studies to 2 Peter for a discussion of the alleged literary dependence of Peter on Jude, or Jude on Peter. The conclusion reached is that there is no copying or editing by either writer of the other writer's work, but that Peter *predicts* the coming of false teachers, while Jude (calling attention to Peter's prediction) says that that prophecy has been *fulfilled* by the time he writes. What Peter predicted would happen is a painful present reality when Jude writes.

been dragged before Domitian as his grandchildren were? That he was not implies he has died before AD 95, and this would be the latest possible date for the writing of Jude.

Those who think Peter copied Jude will date Jude in the early AD 60's (Peter died in AD 68; if he copied Jude, Jude must be earlier). Those who think Jude copied Peter will date the letter after Peter's death (in the late AD 60's, or in the AD 70's). While we have rejected any literary dependence between the two letters (see introduction to 2 Peter), we have nevertheless accepted the view (based on Jude 17 and 18) that the relation between 2 Peter and Jude is that of prophecy (2 Peter) and fulfillment (Jude). We would date Jude later than 2 Peter.

We have yet to study the matter of Jude's alleged use of sources, but this much can be said. Even if we were to admit Jude made use of materials from the *Book of Enoch* or the *Assumption of Moses*, it would be of little help for ascertaining the date of Jude for this simple reason – the date of those pseudepigraphic works is far from certain. For example, the dates given to the *Book of Enoch* vary from 100 BC to AD 150.[44] The dates given to the *Assumption of Moses* are "late first century AD." When it comes to the question of whether or not Jude shows familiarity with some of Paul's letters (which were written between AD 51 and AD 68), if evidence from this line of study proves a familiarity, we still could date Jude in the late AD 60's or even in the AD 70's.

Not a few scholars are swayed in their dating of Jude by the fact there is no mention of the destruction of Jerusalem in Jude. Plummer has written, "The fact that the destruction of Jerusalem and consequent ruin of the Jewish nation is not mentioned among the instances of divine vengeance (verses 5-7) is a strong reason for believing that the Epistle was written before AD 70."[45] This argument may be flawed. The wicked men whose punishment Jude calls attention to were guilty of the same kind of wickedness as are the false teachers about whom Jude is writing. So, only if Jerusalem were destroyed for the same reason the wilderness wanderers, the angels, and Sodom and Gomorrah were destroyed might Jude be expected to allude to it.

Based on the allusion to the apostles' words being in the past (Jude 17) and on the predictions of 2 Peter that Jude says are fulfilled by the time he writes, we tend to date the writing of Jude about AD 75, a date well within the possible limits of Jude's lifetime and a date that reflects that many of the original apostles of Jesus may well have finished their earthly lives and ministry.

---

[44] Eleven manuscripts of parts of the *Book of Enoch* were found among the Dead Sea Scrolls. Those manuscripts were produced before AD 70, when Qumran was destroyed by the Romans. Since scholars conclude that the *Book of Enoch* is full of interpolations, some parts of the book (those not found at Qumran) may date later than AD 70.

[45] Alfred Plummer, "The General Epistle Jude," *Ellicott's Commentary on the Whole Bible* (Grand Rapids: Zondervan, [reprint, no date]), p.265.

VIII. THE CANONICITY OF THE EPISTLE OF JUDE

The history of the canon of the New Testament is an interesting study. We have outlined that history on this fashion: (1) The making and accepting of the books of the New Testament, AD 45-96. (2) The collecting of the books of the New Testament, c. AD 60-140. (3) The guarding of the books of the New Testament canon, AD 140-400. (4) The copying [by hand] of the books of the New Testament, AD 50 [?] to 1600.[46]

In the author's *New Testament Survey* notes, it is documented that the *writing* of the New Testament books took place between the years AD 45 and AD 96. It is also asserted the books were *accepted* as authoritative (or not) the moment they were received by those to whom they were written. Those recognized as authoritative Scripture were regularly read out loud at public worship assemblies and were quoted as the basis of doctrinal viewpoints.[47] The period we have called the *guarding* of the canon is not the first time early Christians were attempting to decide which books were authoritative. Rather, at this period, because of the clamor by more recently-written heretical books to be recognized as authoritative, they were reassessing what had already been done by an earlier generation.[48]

It is from this period of the guarding of the canon that we have the references from early Christian literature which we call canonical listings. We have earlier cited the inclusion of Jude in the Old Latin version and the fact that Origen, Eusebius, and Jerome record that some folk "spoke against" Jude's inclusion in the canon. As the early church was guarding the canon in the West, quite early Jude was accepted, being known in Italy, North Africa, and Egypt. Some have concluded Jude was not included in the Old Syriac Version or in the Peshitto Syriac version[49] and then have used this as proof Jude was not accepted as canonical in the Syriac church. Additionally, it appears Jude was excluded from the canon drawn up by Lucian of Antioch (d. AD 312), nor was Jude mentioned in the writings of John Chrysostom (AD 347-400). On the other hand, there are a few quotations from Jude in the Latin translations of Ephraem the Syrian, the most distinguished leader in the Syrian Church in the fourth century.

---

[46] These handwritten copies are called "manuscripts." They are now classified into three groups called Papyri, Uncials, and Minuscules. Their age, their family history, and the history of the transmission of the text of these New Testament writings are areas of study concerning which we are still learning.

[47] For examples of this use of the authoritative New Testament writings, see above, what we have called "allusions" and "quotations."

[48] "Inspiration" was the criterion for inclusion in the canon. Three tests were applied in an attempt to determine the possibility of inspiration: (1) Was the book written by an apostle or a close associate of an apostle? (2) Are the contents of this work in harmony with the contents of those works already accepted as canonical? (3) Was the work accepted as canonical by both the Eastern and Western churches?

[49] It is true that the extant manuscripts of the Old Syriac and the Peshitto Syriac do not include Jude. But the manuscripts are few and there are other New Testament books about which there never was any question of canonical authority that also are not represented in the Old Syriac manuscripts. By AD 508, when another revision of the Syriac Bible was made (which we call it the Philoxenian Syriac), Jude was included.

It is not quite right to say Jude's epistle won its way to canonical position by slow and uncertain steps. Rather, we should say that when the Christians were guarding the books that should continue to be recognized as authoritative, they were very careful in their decision making, lest they inadvertently include a heretical work along with the true writings. There is awareness that some of the people responsible for making such decisions had certain reservations about Jude,[50] but the evidence for continuing to include it in the New Testament canon, after full and ample testing, was considered to be convincing. By the close of the period of the guarding of the canon, Jude continued to be recognized as canonical by the Councils of Laodicea (AD 363), and Carthage (AD 397).

IX. DOES JUDE USE SOURCES?

From whence did Jude get his information about Sodom and Gomorrah (verse 7)? Or the prophecy of Enoch (verses 14, 15)? Or his information about Michael the archangel (verse 9)? Or his quotation about what the apostles said at an earlier time (verses 17, 18)?

There is little doubt other New Testament writers alluded to or quoted writings other than Scripture. Paul, for example, includes some quotations from Greek poets. In Acts 17:28, "some of your own poets have said, 'for we are His offspring'" is a quotation of Cleanthes' "Hymn of Zeus," and is also found in Aratus of Sol. 1 Corinthians 15:33, "bad company corrupts good morals" is a statement found in Menander. Titus 1:12, "Cretans are always liars" is from a Cretan poet named Epimenides, and is also found in Collimachus' "Hymn to Zeus." If Paul's quoting of an uninspired work does not impinge on the truthfulness of what he writes, why should we be unduly upset if it should prove true that Jude also quoted uninspired works?

In a number of passages that allude to Old Testament events, the New Testament includes information not included in the Old. At 2 Timothy 3:8, "Jannes and Jambres" are named as the Egyptian magicians whom Moses confronted. In Acts 7:4-6, we are told Abraham was called by God to leave kindred and home while he was still in Ur, before he lived in Haran; this is something we do not read in Genesis 12. Acts 7:23 and 42 both mention a period of "40 years," a fact we are not told in the Old Testament. Hebrews 11:24 tells us Moses refused to be called the son of Pharaoh's daughter. James 5:17 tells us it didn't rain in Elijah's time for "3 years and 6 months." Did the New Testament writers quote Jewish oral tradition in these instances where the Old Testament Scriptures do not have the information? Did the New Testament writers get their information by revelation and inspiration, and therefore did not have to rely on uninspired tradition?

---

[50] Those reservations, for the most part, centered not on who was the author but on the issue of whether or not Jude contains quotations from pseudepigraphical works. Those who thought Jude does quote such non-canonical works were apt to argue that Jude should not continue to be included among the books accepted and read in the churches. Instead, it should be excluded just as the apocryphal and pseudepigraphical works were excluded. See this whole matter of Jude's alleged use of sources discussed below.

Where did Jude get his information about Sodom and Gomorrah? From the Old Testament, from the words of Jesus, from oral tradition, or by revelation and inspiration?

Where did Jude get his information about the prophecy of Enoch? These words are not in the Old Testament. Some have said he is drawing material from the *Book of Enoch.* What is that book? To answer this question, we must become acquainted with those bodies of literature called Apocrypha and Pseudepigrapha. In the 400-year silent period between the writing of Malachi and the beginning of the earthly life and ministry of Jesus, Jewish people were writing books to attempt to explain (in the absence of any voice from God) why the Jewish people were still suffering persecution at the hands of their enemies. In certain editions of our English Bibles there are 12 or 14 books included that make up the Old Testament Apocrypha. These books did not pass the tests that were required for inclusion in the Old Testament Canon.[51] Books that did not pass the tests required for inclusion in the Apocrypha were included in a third category called Pseudepigrapha.[52]

The *Book of Enoch*, the longest of the surviving Jewish pseudepigraphical writings,[53] consists of revelations purporting to have been given by Enoch to Noah. Its object is to vindicate the ways of divine providence, to set forth the retribution reserved for sinners, and to show that the world is under the immediate government of God. Such writings were the oppressed Jewish people's way of expressing hope in the future.

1 Enoch 1:9 contains a story similar to what we read in Jude 14,15: "Behold he comes with ten thousands of his saints, to execute judgment upon them, and to destroy the

---

[51] After Malachi, we have 400 silent years. The gift of prophecy or the office of prophet was unknown. Thus, any books written during these 400 years could not be inspired and so were not included in the Old Testament canon. Books like Maccabees may be legitimate and factual secular history, but they are not inspired.

The Septuagint version we possess today includes the Old Testament Apocrypha, but the editions of the LXX current in Jesus' day probably did not include the Apocrypha. None of the Apocrypha was written before 200 BC, whereas the LXX was completed in 285 BC. The Jews considered only the inspired Holy Scriptures as writings worthy to be saved. They burned and destroyed all the copies of the Apocrypha they could get their hands on. It was the Christians of a later generation who preserved the Apocryphal books.

[52] Pseudepigrapha means works of forged authorship, false writings. All the Jewish writings of the intertestamental period which were considered not of good enough quality to be included in the Apocrypha are called Pseudepigrapha. The *Book of Enoch, The Ascension of Isaiah, The Assumption of Moses, the Book of Jubilees, Greek Apocalypse of Baruch, Letters of Aristeas, III and IV Maccabees, Psalms of Solomon, Secrets of Enoch* are some of the books included in the Pseudepigrapha.

[53] After acquaintance with the book seems to be indicated in the *Epistle of Barnabas*, the *Book of Jubilees*, and the *Testament of the Twelve Patriarchs*, and after certain early church fathers indicated their knowledge of the book, evidence of its existence nearly disappeared after Augustine's time until a copy of it was found in an Ethiopic Bible in 1773 and translated into English in 1821. Since then it has been the object of intense study by numerous scholars. There is a scholarly consensus that the work as it now stands is the product of several different writers who lived in several different decades or centuries. That the pseudonymous work was ascribed to Enoch is not surprising given what is said of him in Genesis 5:21-24. The few words in Genesis would give a writer with a vivid imagination ample room to rewrite ancient history as though it were a prophecy made by that man of God.

wicked, and to strive [at law] with all the carnal for everything which the sinful and ungodly have done and committed against him." While there are sharp variations between this story and Jude 14,15, was Jude perhaps influenced by this passage?[54] Was Jude, as some early Christian writers have alleged, drawing information from 1 Enoch? Some have supposed Jude expected his readers to be familiar with the story found in this pseudepigraphical work, and also to respect it as being historically accurate. Some have even suggested Jude, by using the story and by using the word "prophesied," was indicating his belief that the *Book of Enoch* was Scripture.[55] These suppositions and suggestions, if true, certainly raise doubts in modern readers' minds about the inspiration and truthfulness of Jude.

Some commentators, wishing to protect Jude from any appearance of giving a false or misleading testimony about the value of the *Book of Enoch,* have proposed that what Jude is doing is quoting from oral tradition which had preserved a true saying of Enoch down through the centuries since Enoch lived. The story in 1 Enoch is explained by saying that whoever wrote the *Book of Enoch* got his information from Jude, or the oral tradition.

In any case, Jude claims to quote Enoch himself, not the *Book of Enoch.* There is nothing to hinder us from the belief that as Jude was writing, his writing was an inspired writing of what he had learned by revelation.[56]

Where did Jude get his information about Michael, the archangel (verse 9)? This information is not in the Old Testament. Some have held the information about Michael the archangel and the devil contesting about the body of Moses is taken from the pseudepigraph-

---

[54] F.H. Chase, "Jude, Epistle of" in *Hasting's Dictionary of the Bible* (New York: Scribners, 1909), Vol.2, p.801-802, calls attention to words and phrases from fourteen other verses in Jude that he thinks are evidence of the influence of the *Book of Enoch* on Jude's mind. If his parallels do prove literary dependence, what is to keep us from concluding that the pseudonymous author of Enoch was influenced by the Epistle of Jude, rather than the other way around? Let it be remembered that the date of the writing of *Enoch* is very uncertain. It is certainly a live possibility that portions of *Enoch* were written after Jude. Furthermore, contemporary scholars insist the *Book of Enoch*, as we have it today, is full of interpolations (i.e., additions to the original work). Perhaps 1 Enoch 1:9 is an interpolation added after Jude was written. Some scholars, Lenski among them (*The Interpretation of the Epistles of St. Peter, St. John and St. Jude* [Minneapolis: Augsburg, 1966], p.628-630, 640-642), vigorously dispute the idea Jude quoted from pseudepigraphical books.

[55] The idea that Jude treats Enoch as Scripture has far-reaching ramifications. Roman Catholics, who wish to include the Old Testament Apocrypha in their Bibles, argue the canon was not closed until late in the first or early in the second century AD. We have alluded to the Jewish idea of 400 silent years since Malachi's time. That argues for a closed canon. Jews and Christians in the first century treated the Old Testament canon as closed. Jesus spoke of the "Law of Moses, and the Prophets, and the Psalms" (Luke 24:44) as though the canon were closed. Now the *Book of Enoch* (whatever date we assign to its writing [see page xiv above in these Introductory Studies]) was written after 400 BC. If Jude regarded the *Book of Enoch* as canonical, then the whole idea of a closed canon is called into question. This clearly will not do in face of the evidence to the contrary!

[56] See 1 Corinthians 2:6-15, where the steps (revelation, inspiration, illumination) by which information gets from the mind of God to the mind of man are set forth.

ical *Assumption of Moses*.[57] The arguments pro and con concerning Jude's possible use of the *Assumption of Moses* are similar to those for his alleged use of the *Book of Enoch*. Again, the date of the *Assumption* is uncertain; late in the first century AD is the usual date assigned to it.[58] Since the original text of the *Assumption* is not available to us, there are no means of verifying whether Jude copied, or even the extent of his copying. And as for Jude even having to copy some already pre-existing material, the writers of Scripture are not dependent merely on natural origins for the material they wrote.[59]

Where did Jude get his information about what the apostles preached (verse 17)? It is very likely he has before him a copy of 2 Peter to which he refers when he speaks about how the apostles predicted "mockers" would come. 2 Peter refers to the writings of Paul wherein the same things were predicted. We may assume Jude and his readers have also heard some of the apostles preach in person while they were still alive.

While we are not convinced Jude did use pseudepigraphical sources for any of his information, we would find no objection to the canonicity of his book if it were actually determined he did make use of some traditional materials in his record.

X. CHARACTERISTICS AND OUTLINE

One of the striking characteristics of Jude is his fondness for the use of triplets. Hiebert calls attention to a dozen examples of triplets in the twenty-five verses of the epistle.

> "Jude, servant, brother" verse 1; "called, beloved, kept" verse 1; "mercy, peace, love" verse 2; "certain persons, those ..., ungodly persons" verse 4; "Israelites, angels, cities of the plain" verses 5-8; "Cain, Balaam, Korah" verse 11; "cause divisions, worldly minded,

---

[57] Origen, it will be recalled, attributes this to a book he calls *Ascensio Mosis* in his *de Princip*, iii.2. Only a few fragments of the book are still in existence, and none of the fragments contains the account of the dispute over the body of Moses. The book purported to be a record of the final commands given by Moses to Joshua for the people of Israel. What follows is a history of the Jewish people (down to the time of Herod, his children, and the Roman destruction of Jerusalem) written after the fact, but written as though it were a prophecy of the future. The extant fragments end with Moses telling Joshua his death is imminent, and Joshua rends his garments, wondering who will lead the people after Moses is dead.

[58] R.H. Charles, *The Apocrypha and Pseudepigrapha* (Oxford: Clarendon Press, 1963) dated the *Assumption of Moses* "before AD 26." Others date it in the first decade after the death of Herod the Great. R.C. Foster dated it early in the second century AD since Josephus, who wrote his last works about AD 100 and who loved the kind of imaginative material one finds in the *Assumption of Moses,* makes no use of it.

[59] Bible writers could do independent research, such as Luke claims to have done before he wrote his Gospel (Luke 1:1-4), but much of the Bible materials comes from the mind of God through revelation rather than through unaided human research (1 Corinthians 2:6-13).

devoid of the Spirit" verse 19; "defile, reject, revile" verse 8; "on some, others, on some" verses 22,23; "before all time, and now, and forevermore" verse 25.[60]

Such a frequent use of triplets has no parallel in any other portion of the Word of God. "Its style," says Salmond, "is broken and rugged, bold and picturesque, energetic, vehement, glowing with the fires of passion."[61] Jude's religious indignation against the false teachers who have wormed their way into church circles is expressed in a severity of tone almost without parallel in the New Testament Scriptures.

We offer this outline for Jude's letter.[62]

INTRODUCTION. 1:1-4

A. Signature, Address, and Prayer of Blessing. 1,2
B. Purpose of this Letter. 3
  To exhort the readers to contend for the faith
C. Immediate Occasion of Writing of this Letter. 4
  Certain dangerous men have stealthily infiltrated the churches.

I. A REMINDER OF EXAMPLES OF GOD'S PUNISHMENT OF WRONG-DOERS. 1:5-7

A. Unbelieving Children of Israel. 5
B. Angels Who Sinned. 6
C. Immoral Sodom and Gomorrah. 7

II. A SOLEMN PREDICTION OF COMING PUNISHMENT ON THE UNGODLY MEN WHO HAVE INFILTRATED THE CHURCHES. 1:8-16

A. The Punishable Behavior the Ungodly Men Have Exhibited. 8-10
B. Biblical Examples of Wickedness Like Theirs Being Punished. 11
  1. Cain, an example of disobedience
  2. Balaam, an example of greed
  3. Korah, an example of insubordination
C. Metaphorical Pictures (reminiscent of Old Testament Warnings) of the Harm Caused by These Infiltrators. 12,13
D. As Long Ago as Enoch, God Revealed He Would Punish the Ungodly. 14-16

---

[60] Hiebert, *An Introduction to the Non-Pauline Epistles* (Chicago: Moody, 1962), p.182.

[61] S.D.F. Salmond, "The General Epistle of Jude" in *The Pulpit Commentary* (Grand Rapids: Eerdmans, 1962 reprint), p.i.

[62] See footnote #56 in the commentary section on Jude for a different way of outlining the letter.

III. EXHORTATIONS AND INSTRUCTIONS TO BELIEVERS WHO ARE FACED WITH THE CHALLENGES TO THEIR FAITH POSED BY THE FALSE TEACHERS. 1:17-23

A. They Were to Pay Attention to the Words of Prophecy Concerning the Coming of Such False Teachers. 17-19

B. Personally, Each One was Responsible to Keep Himself (or Herself) in the Love of God. 20-21

1. By building themselves up on their most holy faith
2. By praying in the Spirit
3. By waiting anxiously for the mercy to be received by the faithful when Jesus returns

C. They were to Exhibit Loving Compassion for Their Deceived Brethren. 22-23

1. On some, have mercy!
2. On some, snatch them out of the fire!
3. On some, have mercy with fear!

CONCLUDING DOXOLOGY TO GOD. 1:24,25

A. His Assistance Keeping Faithful Men from Stumbling. 24a
B. His Actions to Make them Blameless at the Judgment. 24b
C. Glory and Majesty to be Given to Him Through Jesus Christ. 25

JUDE

INTRODUCTION. 1:1-4

A. Signature, Address, and Prayer of Blessing. 1:1,2

1:1 -- ***Jude, a bond-servant of Jesus Christ, and brother of James, to those who are the called, beloved in God the Father, and kept for Jesus Christ:***

1. The writer. 1:1a

Jude -- This brief letter follows the typical first-century letter-writing convention, where the author signs his name and identifies himself. As shown in the Introductory Studies, this Jude is one of the Lord's younger brothers. In the Hebrew, his name means "the praised, the confessor, the renowned." There was a time when, like his brothers, Jude did not believe in Jesus (John 7:5), but all that has changed because of Jesus' resurrection and His post-resurrection ministry. As he writes, Jude is now a leader in the churches, a "bond-servant of Jesus Christ."

A bond-servant of Jesus Christ -- "Jude" was a very common Jewish name,[1] so more identification is needed than simply his name. Jude writes two qualifying expressions. There are times in Scripture when "servant of Jesus Christ" is used as a general description of any Christian believer (e.g., 1 Corinthians 7:22; Ephesians 6:6). However, we are convinced that here the term is used in a special sense, just as it was in 2 Peter 1:1 (i.e., I am a special mouthpiece speaking for Jesus Christ). "Jude uses this title to establish his right to address the churches with an authoritative word from the Lord."[2] When there is any question about to whom the readers should listen – the false teachers who recently infiltrated the churches or Jude the "bond-servant of Jesus Christ" – calling attention to his special commission as a preacher of the gospel should settle the matter! Perhaps Jude also means to convey the idea that he is about to write what his Master wants him to say.

---

[1] See the Introductory Studies.

[2] Douglas J. Moo, "Jude" in *The NIV Application Commentary* (Grand Rapids: Zondervan, 1996), p.222. Whereas the Old Testament leaders spoke of themselves as "servants of God," in the New Testament "Jesus Christ" is substituted for "God." Jude and others were convinced by the evidence that Jesus is God and are not ashamed to say so. It did not take generations before the Christians gave Jesus this exalted status. It was something recognized from before Peter's Pentecost sermon (Acts 2:36) where he calls Him "Lord" (i.e., a term used to translate the Old Testament sacred name "YHWH").

And brother of James -- Jude the writer has a brother named James. This is the well-known James, the brother of the Lord,[3] an apostle (Galatians 1:19), and for years a leader of the church at Jerusalem (Acts 12:17, 15:13ff, 21:18ff) until his death in AD 62. Jude certainly did not need to do any name-dropping as though he needed the prestige of James in order to give himself a strong recommendation. Rather, let the false teachers and their followers consider this: both Jude and James lived with the earthly Jesus for years and knew Him intimately. If anyone could give a testimony concerning who Jesus was, it was His earthly brothers.[4] Their testimony agreed exactly. In light of that fact, any claims[5] made by the false teachers about Jesus that differed from those of James and Jude – who were bond-servants of Jesus Christ – were obviously wrong.

2. The address. 1:1b

To those who are called -- It was part of the common first-century letter form, after the signature, to indicate the reader(s) to whom the letter was addressed. The term "the called" is practically synonymous with "Christians." The readers were "called" or invited to become followers of Jesus through the gospel.[6] No geographical location where these "called" ones live is identified, so Jude is usually said to be a general, or circular, letter. If Jude is addressed to the same audience as 2 Peter, the Christians lived in the provinces of Pontus, Galatia, Cappadocia, Asia, and Bithynia.[7] The following phrases, "beloved in God the Father, and kept for Jesus Christ" further describe the readers.[8]

---

[3] It appears to be true that neither James (who does not use the title "brother of the Lord" in his letter) nor Jude ever referred to themselves as "the Lord's brother," though others did (Galatians 1:19). Perhaps the brothers were reflecting the teaching of Jesus who had insisted that those who did His will were possessed of greater distinction than any fleshly relationship might have afforded (Matthew 12:46-50).

[4] 1 Corinthians 9:5 indicates the brothers of the Lord went on evangelistic tours of the Mediterranean world. There is little reason to doubt that both James and Jude had visited and preached to the very people addressed in this letter, and that they should remember what the "brothers" had said about Jesus and the Christian faith.

[5] We are assuming the conclusions reached in our notes on 2 Peter that the false teachers opposed by both Peter and Jude were teaching and embracing incipient Gnosticism. As we studied 2 Peter, we learned these things about these false teachers: they denied Jesus had come in the flesh, they denigrated Scripture's presentation of God's truth, they lived Godless life-styles, they had sub-scriptural ideas about angels and spirits.

[6] 2 Thessalonians 2:14; Romans 8:28; 1 Corinthians 1:24,26; 1 Peter 1:15; 2 Peter 1:3. "Many are called but few are chosen" (Matthew 22:14). The reason they are not "chosen" is because they don't heed, hearken to, and obey the gospel. We reject the Calvinistic view that "call" is nearly synonymous with God's election, and therefore folk respond because they have received what Calvinists identify as an "effectual call."

[7] See Introductory Studies for details on the question of destination.

[8] The KJV treats the three clauses as co-ordinates, "to them that are sanctified ... and preserved ... and called." It is better, in our opinion, to take "called" (which occurs last in the Greek verse, for emphasis) as the subject, and the two participles as qualifying epithets.

Beloved in God the Father -- The text of the NASB is better attested in the manuscripts than is the reading of the KJV ("sanctified by God the Father").[9] The word *egapemenois* is a perfect passive participle, denoting a past completed act that has present, continuing results, "have been and are loved." "In God" is an unusual expression. From Paul's epistles we are used to "in Christ" and "in the Lord," but "in God" is not found elsewhere in Scripture except at 1 Thessalonians 1:1 and 2 Thessalonians 1:1. The dative is likely a dative of sphere.[10] Because the readers have responded positively to the gospel call they are "in God" (the sphere of spiritual life)[11] and are therefore the objects of God's special love for them.[12] "Beloved in God" is similar to the exhortation in verse 21, "keep yourselves in the love of God." Christians, who have been born again and adopted into God's family, think of God as being their Father.[13] This reminder of the exalted position the readers already enjoy "in God" may well be intended to insulate them from any temptation to think they can gain a better position by listening to the alluring presentations of the false teachers who are among them.

And kept for Jesus Christ -- With this clause, Jude further describes the position of those who have been "called." According to Jude 24,25, it is God the Father who guards them and keeps them for Jesus.[14] "Kept" (*teteremenois*) is a perfect passive participle. It too expresses a past act with present continuing results. It is something God has been doing for the faithful ever since they obeyed the invitation (call) to become Christians. The word "kept" expresses the idea of watchful care, to guard, to hold firmly as one's present possession. It is a word both Jude and Peter use.[15] This keeping is not unconditional in its nature (see

---

[9] The Greek text behind the NASB is supported by P^{72}, Sinaiticus, A, B, the Vulgate, the Syriac. It is adopted by Nestle, Westcott and Hort, Tishchendorf, Lachmann. Zane C. Hodges and Arthur Farstad, eds., retain "sanctified" as the reading in their *The New Testament According to the Majority Text* (Nashville: Thomas Nelson, 1982).

[10] The KJV, which rendered the preposition as "by," treated it as a dative of agent. The NIV treats both phrases that modify "called" as being datives of agent: "who are loved by God the Father and [who are] kept by Jesus Christ." This translation causes Jude to speak of two Who do the "keeping" (Jesus in verse 1, and God the Father in verses 24,25).

[11] See Romans 3:24, 6:11, 8:39 and 1 John 2:24, where being "in Christ" also puts a person in the sphere where he is a recipient of the love of God.

[12] Some understand that the readers are here described as objects of Jude's love -- a love which is no mere natural affection, but inspired by God and of spiritual motive.

[13] Paul ordinarily wrote "God *our* Father" (Romans 1:7; 1 Corinthians 1;3), but he also used the same expression "God *the* Father" (Galatians 1:1,3) that Jude here uses.

[14] See 1 Peter 1:5 and 2 Timothy 1:12. Jesus, while praying for His apostles, said "Holy Father, keep (*tereo*) them in Thy name, the name which Thou hast given me ..." (John 17:11,12,15).

[15] The evil angels are preserved or kept for judgment (Jude 6); Christians are to "keep" themselves in the love of God (Jude 21). In 1 Peter 1:4, there is an inheritance "reserved" in heaven for Peter's faithful Christian readers. In 1 Peter 1:5 Peter has spoken of how Christians are "protected" through faith (*faithfulness* is the condition of God's continual "keeping"). The heavens are "preserved" or kept for fire (2 Peter 3:7).

Jude 21), and hence does not suggest the impossibility of falling away from the grace of God and the divine favor.[16] "Jesus Christ" is in the dative case in the Greek. There is no preposition in the Greek, such as is translated "in" (KJV) or "for" (NASB), but the NASB translators appear to be more nearly correct here.[17] God the Father is keeping Christians, guarding them, preserving them for Jesus Christ – that is, for His honor and glory.[18] Jesus paid a great price for them, and God is at work making sure that the called and redeemed continue to be Jesus' prized spiritual brethren. It cannot be claimed by the false teachers that they are being "kept for Jesus Christ"!

We noted in the Introductory Studies that Jude is fond of using triplets. We have had several of these in verse 1. Jude used three terms to identify himself; he used three terms to identify his readers. In the next verse, Jude will use a triplet in his prayer of blessing for his readers.

3. The prayer of blessing. 1:2

1:2 -- ***May mercy and peace and love be multiplied to you.***

May mercy and peace and love -- Typical of first-century letters, after the address comes a greeting. Jude's greeting speaks of something more than good wishes for his friends. Each of the words he uses is full of spiritual meaning. This is not quite the way salutations or prayers of blessing are worded by other New Testament writers,[19] but this is one of the most

---

[16] "Compare the comments on 1 Peter 1:4. Though the divine guardianship is here marvelously set forth, there is the corresponding thought of faithfulness and fidelity. Though we are 'kept' for Jesus Christ, we must 'keep' ourselves (the same Greek verb is employed) in His love." Guy N. Woods, *A Commentary on the New Testament Epistles of Peter, John, and Jude* (Nashville, TN: Gospel Advocate Co., 1954), p.383. The whole epistle of Jude is about the readers' desperate need to be faithful rather than surrender to the teachings of the intruders who have stealthily entered their congregations. If faithfulness were not a condition of being "kept for Jesus Christ," why write this letter?

[17] While the simple dative "Jesus Christ" could be translated with a helping preposition "by" or "in," the usual helper with the simple dative is "to" or "for." Some have supposed that the "in" that precedes "God the Father" is to be carried over and mentally repeated before "Jesus Christ," but there is no instance elsewhere of the carrying over of a preposition from one clause to another.

[18] Expressing a very similar idea, we read of Paul's prayer that the Thessalonian Christians may be kept blameless unto the second coming of Christ (1 Thessalonians 5:23).

[19] Paul on occasion speaks of "grace, mercy, and peace" (1 Timothy 1:2; 2 Timothy 1:2), and these usually proceed "from God the Father and the Lord Jesus Christ." Peter's salutation spoke of "grace and peace" being "multiplied" to the readers. "What Jude prays for is not that his readers may be helped to exhibit in large measure a merciful, peaceful, and loving disposition to others, but that they may enjoy in liberal degree the great blessings of God's mercy, peace, and love bestowed upon themselves." S.D.F. Salmond, "The General Epistle of Jude" in the *Pulpit Commentary* [Grand Rapids: Eerdmans, 1950 reprint], p.3.

beautiful of them, full of the choicest blessings. Each of the blessings Jude prays for is exactly what the troubled readers (being besieged by Gnostic false teachers) need more of. "Mercy" is "pardon of all their sins and acceptance with God;"[20] it is God's compassion and goodness toward the miserable and afflicted, joined with a desire to relieve them. "Peace" is the "tranquil state of the soul assured of its salvation through Jesus Christ, and so fearing nothing from God and content with its earthly lot, of whatever sort it is."[21] God is not at peace with the unrepentant sinner.[22] Jude prays the readers will continue in their presently enjoyed restored relationship with God. "Love" indicates an attitude of God toward man which, when realized, results in the man exhibiting the same quality toward others (1 John 4:16-19). The word speaks of doing what is spiritually best for the other person.

Each of these blessings is something to which the false teachers were strangers, as Jude's continuing description and denunciation of them plainly show. They were unpardoned. They were not content with their lot, and they had plenty to fear from God's judgments. They certainly were not (without repentance) going to be in the sphere of God's love. And they certainly did not act out of love toward the readers.

Be multiplied to you -- See comments on the same optative mood prayer wish in 1 Peter 1:2 and 2 Peter 1:2. As the readers stay with the faith once for all delivered to the saints, it is Jude's prayer that God will multiply these three blessings in their lives. They will experience them in an ever-increasing measure.

B. Purpose of this Letter. 1:3

1:3 -- *Beloved, while I was making every effort to write you about our common salvation, I felt the necessity to write to you appealing that you contend earnestly for the faith which was once for all delivered to the saints.*

Beloved -- This word may be an indication of Jude's love for the readers. They have a special place in Jude's heart. If this is the meaning, we have the implication Jude knows his readers and has interacted with them personally before this (e.g., during an evangelistic tour among them). He is writing to them now because he loves them. "Beloved" also may be expressive

[20] Albert Barnes, *Notes on the New Testament, Explanatory and Practical -- James, Peter, John, and Jude*, edited by Robert Frew (Grand Rapids: Baker Book House, 1951 reprint), p.387.

[21] Joseph Henry Thayer, *A Greek English Lexicon of the New Testament* (New York: American Book Co., reprint of 1889 ed.), p.182.

[22] Such impenitent souls are said to be "enemies" of God -- at war with God (Romans 5:10, 11:28; Hebrews 10:13).

of God's love for the readers, just as "love" was in verses 1 and 2. It is not very often we find the term used so early in any of the New Testament books.[23] What we do often find at this spot in first-century letters is a word of thanksgiving, but Jude skips this and moves right into the heart of his letter.

While I was making every effort to write to you -- Jude informs us a letter to the readers was already in the incubation process before he actually sat down to put his pen to the papyrus with this letter being the result.[24] Some think Jude means he had been actively in the process of writing a different letter and scrapped it in favor of this one.[25] Others suppose Jude means that for some time now he had been seriously thinking about the important place a letter from him to the readers could play in their spiritual lives, but had not yet begun to actually write it.[26]

About our common salvation -- Which particular facet of "salvation" Jude was going to write about is not stated. Since the incipient Gnostic heresy was beginning to trouble the churches, we suppose he was intending to write a letter he hoped would blunt the Gnostic teachings and influence among the brethren. Perhaps he was going to emphasize the fact that our common salvation was brought about by the atoning death of Christ, something the Gnostics denied. Perhaps he was going to highlight the conditions for continuing to participate in that salvation; namely, by faithfulness to the revelation from God through Jesus Christ, again something the Gnostics downplayed. Perhaps in opposition to the Gnostics, he was going to highlight the doctrines and practices by which Christianity ("our common salvation") is forwarded. Just as "common" had an anti-Gnostic emphasis to it in Titus 1:4 and 2 Peter 1:1, we suppose it also does here. Jude and his readers (the "called" of 1:1) already

---

[23] See the term used by Paul in Romans 1:7; 2 Corinthians 7:1; Philippians 2:12; by Peter in 1 Peter 2:11, 4:12; 2 Peter 3:1,8,14,15,17; by James at James 1:16; and by John at 1 John 2:7 and 3 John 1:2.

[24] The language "all diligence" has been seen in Peter's letters at 2 Peter 1:5,10,15, 3:14. Both the Greek participle ("making") and the infinitive ("to write") used here are in the present tense, indicating continuing action, a process going on for some time. He had them in his thoughts and would have written even if he had not heard of the immediate danger threatening them (verse 4).

[25] The NIV so interprets: "Dear friends, although I was very eager to write to you about the salvation we share, I felt I had to write and urge you to contend for the faith ...." "Very eager" translates a circumstantial participle, and "although" is one helping word we can use to translate such a construction.

[26] The NRSV reflects this way of understanding this verse: "Beloved, while eagerly preparing to write ... I find it necessary to write and appeal to you." "Preparing" is a circumstantial participle, and we could use the helper "while" to translate it.

Whichever way we decide to interpret it, this verse does give us some insight into the way inspiration worked. When under the power of the Holy Spirit, the man's own self-control, the man's own vocabulary, the man's own initiative was not overwhelmed. Compare notes at 1 Corinthians 2:13 (about "combining spiritual thoughts with spiritual words") and 1 Corinthians 14:32 ("the spirits of the prophets are subject to the prophets").

share in the salvation (it is common to all[27]); they do not need to embrace anything the Gnostics were teaching in order to participate in it.[28]

I felt the necessity to write to you -- Jude says he felt a prompting, an inward constraint, a sense of necessity, to write what he is about to pen in this letter. Was it the prompting of the Holy Spirit? Was it a sense of necessity arising from circumstances affecting the readers he has just learned about?[29] Do Jude's words indicate a change of topics?[30] Whereas he had intended to write on general grounds, did the emergency circumstances cause him to zero in on a different thrust for his letter? In our opinion, the letter we have is not so much a complete change of topic as perhaps a change of emphasis to one particular facet of "our common salvation;" namely, the need to resist what is false, and to heed especially the admonitions Jude writes in verses 17-23. It is likely that Jude's language here indicates he clearly "felt there was no one else who could step in and do what needed to be done."[31]

Appealing that you contend earnestly for the faith -- Jude's letter is an appeal; it is a letter of exhortation. The Greek verb translated "contend earnestly" (*epagonidzesthai*) is a compound verb not found elsewhere in the New Testament. The addition of the preposition *epi* (which makes it what is called a compound verb) serves to strengthen what the rest of the word says. *Agonidzomai* denotes extreme effort, expending all one's energy in order to prevail. We might render it "struggle, wrestle, or agonize" – i.e., a vigorous, intense, determined effort to defeat the opposition. Some even suppose it pictures the defender standing over a wounded and fallen comrade to fight in his or her defense. The verb is used to describe the intense, strenuous efforts athletes exert to win the contest they are in (1 Corin-

---

[27] The KJV reads "*the* common salvation" whereas the NASB reads "*our* common salvation." Jude has styled himself a "bond-servant of Jesus Christ," thus claiming to speak for Christ. "Common salvation" says "You readers and I alike are on the same page religiously." The salvation he shares with them (and perhaps even taught them) is what Jesus wanted taught and lived. There is no reason to look at some new, strange, esoteric thing like the Gnostics were advocating, as though their "common salvation" were somehow deficient. (A few commentators think the "our" in the phrase "our common salvation" refers to Jews and Gentiles sharing in the same Messianic salvation. While that is a true doctrine [see notes at 2 Peter 1:1], we are not convinced that is the emphasis here.)

[28] Gnosticism claimed certain secret knowledge that people in the world could learn only after being initiated into their select group. "Common salvation" says that claim is totally false. You can fully participate in what God wants you to know and do without joining that heretical group.

[29] If this is the meaning, Jude does not tell us how he learned of the critical situation resulting from the presence of false teachers (verse 4) in their midst.

[30] It is rather common to read among the commentaries that Jude suspended his planned letter and wrote on this topic instead. The commentators even speculate about what happened to the interrupted letter -- never finished, lost, etc.

[31] D. Edmund Hiebert, *Second Peter and Jude* (Greenville, SC: Unusual Publications, 1989), p.218.

thians 9:25).[32] That's the kind of effort Jude wants his readers to put forth in the defense and propagation of "the faith," i.e., the truths of Christianity.[33] The present tense Greek verb indicates such a fight for the faith is a continuing duty rather than an occasional or one-time thing.

Of course, Jude is not calling for physical violence or for his readers to take up arms. Such a course of action would be contrary to the true spirit of Christianity.[34] Jude 20-23 will give some of the specific ways by which the readers can contend for the faith. Others look to 1 Peter 3:15 as another way of defending the faith. The intensity of the defense must be adjusted to the intensity of the opposition. Sometimes the contention will be by argument, by reasoning, by debate. Sometimes it becomes necessary to draw the faithful away and meet by themselves, as Paul did at Philippi (Acts 18:6,7) and at Ephesus (Acts 19:8,9).[35] To contend for the faith is costly and agonizing, and may not be the popular thing to do, but it is what is expected of "saints."

---

[32] Paul used this same term to describe his and his fellow-workers' "striving" for the gospel (Colossians 1:29; 1 Timothy 4:10, 6:12; 2 Timothy 4:7).

[33] "Faith" sometimes in Scripture refers to the believer's subjective trust, as when we speak of a person's "faith" in Christ. However, "the faith" here – within a context that speaks of "our common salvation" – denotes a body of doctrine. There is a definite article in the Greek before "faith" -- it is "*the* faith". It is called "your most holy faith" in Jude 20. Some critics doubt that there was, this early in church history, a fixed body of doctrine which believers were expected to embrace, but Acts 2:42, 6:7, 13:8; Romans 6:17; Galatians 1:23; Ephesians 4:5; and 1 Timothy 4:1 all indicate that from the time Jesus taught His apostles and from the time they first began preaching, "faith" took on a definite form. In the author's commentary on Romans, in a footnote at 1:16, is a listing of things the Scriptures call "gospel," and the proposition is there advanced that what the Bible calls "gospel" and "the faith" are interchangeable terms. It certainly behooves Jude's readers to have some list, derived from Scripture, of those absolute truths for which they are willing to fight.

Let it be observed, too, that Jude's language is hardly compatible with modern redaction criticism which sees several layers of information in our Scriptures. Jude's language can only mean that what he urges them to contend for is the same as the apostles delivered, and they delivered what Jesus told them to, without additions, subtractions, or modifications.

[34] The night Jesus was arrested, Peter sought to defend Him with a sword, but was rebuked by Jesus for his attempt. "In bidding Peter to sheathe his sword, He forevermore made it clear that His followers were not to fight with carnal weapons in His behalf." Woods, *op. cit.* p.385.

[35] "Jude writes with urgency; we need to sense that urgency and pick some of it up as we read the letter. For false teachers are all about in our day, and the 'faith once for all entrusted to the saints' is battered and attacked on every side. Do we care? Jude sure did!" (Moo, *op. cit.* p.235). This commentator has lived through a half a century of struggle between conservatives and theological liberals. He has seen congregations and colleges that years ago were true to the "faith once for all delivered to the saints" slowly drift to the place where they have jettisoned many of the cardinal doctrines of the faith and have quit evangelizing and growing. If you ask church members what the teachers in their nearby Bible college are teaching, usually they do not know. If you quote some of the current teachers' ideas and writings that are inimical to the faith, the church members simply refuse to believe you, or they treat it as of no great moment. If you raise a question about the local leaders' beliefs on certain cardinal truths of the Christian religion, you are treated as being narrow-minded and judgmental. It seems our current generation is not taking to heart the theme of the epistle of Jude. No wonder our churches and colleges are infiltrated with unbelief!

Which was once for all delivered to the saints -- Any "faith" which does not have this characteristic is not worth contending for. The "faith" for which they are to contend is something that has been delivered to them; it is "not something which the preachers manufactured or discovered for themselves."[36] The word here used (*hapax*) may mean "once for all" in the sense that it was then complete and not to be repeated. Or it may mean "once" (see KJV), in the sense of "at some previous time" before Jude writes his letter. Since the verb "delivered" is an aorist tense and speaks of completed action, most modern translations prefer the first option, "once for all." Each successive generation is responsible to transmit the faith just as they have received it. "One is accursed who dares to preach a message different from that which was originally delivered (Galatians 1:9,10). The faith once delivered is not to be supplemented [or subtracted from] in any way."[37]

"Delivered" is the regular term for the oral transmission of religious instruction. The line of transmission starts with God and continues through His inspired mouth pieces (apostles and prophets).[38] Jude's burden for his readers is that they maintain the truth of the Christian faith just as it has been handed down to them from Christ through the apostles. Since not all the books of the New Testament had been written before Jude penned this verse, some are surprised that he says the faith has already been delivered. What we must understand is that Jesus promised His apostles they would be led into all truth (John 16:13). By the time Jude writes, many of the apostles have already died. That fact necessitates belief in an already-completed revelation if we are to maintain that Jesus' promise came true. Those few apostles, contemporary with Jude and who were still living and preaching and writing, were not introducing any new truths. "The faith" (the truth) – a completed revelation – had already been delivered. They were simply repeating and emphasizing the body of doctrine already revealed and disseminated before Jude wrote.

There are two emphases in this description of "the faith" that are anti-Gnostic. If "the faith" has already been delivered, there is no place for any new revelations that the Gnostics might claim access to. Their claims to continuing revelations are lies. Further, "the faith" was delivered "to the saints." Gnostics, with their irreverent, ungodly, insubordinate, sensual lifestyles, were hardly "saints."[39] This should warn Jude's readers to go to "saints" rather than to the Gnostics if they wish to learn more about "the faith," for it has not been delivered to such as the latter.

---

[36] William Barclay, *The Letters of John and Jude* (Philadelphia: Westminster, 1960), p.209.

[37] Raymond C. Kelcy, *The Letters of Peter and Jude* in The Living Word Commentary Series (Austin, TX: R.B. Sweet Co., 1972), p.173. The "faith" was put in the hands of God's messengers as a sacred trust, a precious deposit.

[38] See comments on 2 Peter 2:21 ("the holy commandment delivered to them"). See Acts 16:4; 1 Corinthians 11:2,23 and 15:3. Consider also Jude 17 and 18 which indicates Jude's readers are acquainted with what the apostles have taught.

[39] A "saint" is some one who has been separated from the world and set apart for holy living. See Acts 9:13,32,41; Romans 12:13; Hebrews 6:10. In the Scriptures a saint is a living Christian. The Roman Catholic idea of a saint -- someone now dead, but who, while living, was extremely better than he needed to be to be saved, and who has now been canonized -- is not in harmony with the Scriptures.

C. Immediate Occasion of Writing of this Letter. 1:4

1:4 -- ***For certain persons have crept in unnoticed, those who were long beforehand marked out for this condemnation, ungodly persons who turn the grace of our God into licentiousness and deny our only Master and Lord, Jesus Christ.***

For -- Verse 4, beginning with "for," gives a reason for Jude's felt necessity for writing this appeal he makes to his readers to contend for the faith. He is writing for their spiritual good because he loves them.

Certain persons -- These persons are the false teachers Peter warned were coming, and who Jude now indicates have arrived. In the commentary on 2 Peter, these false teachers, also described as "mockers," were identified as being the beginning of the Gnostic heresy with which the church would have to contend for years. Perhaps Jude is expressing his disgust when he identifies them only as "certain persons."

Have crept in unnoticed -- Peter, warning about the coming of these same false teachers, predicted they would "secretly introduce destructive heresies" (2 Peter 2:1). Jude says they "crept in unnoticed;" we might render *pareisedusan* as "stealthily," meaning they sneaked in by a side door.[40] It is an insidious invasion into the life of the church, an entrance under false colors. They gained admission into the life of the congregations by pretending to be something they were not (like ravenous wolves in sheep's clothing, Matthew 7:15). "They had not made a bold and open avowal of their real sentiments. They professed to teach the Christian religion, when in fact they denied some of its fundamental doctrines and ethics."[41] Once they have gained the confidence of the group, and perhaps have even worked their way into leadership positions, then they will no longer pretend to be what they are not. Their strange doctrines will be taught openly. It is because evil men will deliberately attempt to deceive them that Christians need to be on the watch!

Those who were long beforehand marked out for this condemnation -- It should not have been a surprise to Jude's readers that these men have now actually shown up. The readers had had ample warning such men would be coming,. Not only that, those men's sentence of

[40] Jesus warned of people who would enter the sheepfold by some way other than the door (John 10:1). The behavior of these men with their incipient Gnostic tendencies was very similar to the behavior, a generation earlier, of the Pharisaic Judaizers who invaded the Galatian churches, and whom Paul identified as "false brethren who had sneaked in to spy out our liberty which we have in Christ Jesus" (Galatians 2:4). The false teachers Jude describes are not Christians either -- they do not hold to the faith once for all delivered to the saints, and they are ungodly men. See also 2 Timothy 3:6, which antedates Jude, plus 1 John 4:1-3 and 2 John 7, which were written at a later time than Jude. Such sneaky deceivers were a constant worry in the early church, and their kin are still at work in the current century.

[41] Barnes, *op. cit.*, p.388.

condemnation had already been announced.[42] The implication of the fact that the false teachers already stand condemned is that Jude's Christian readers would associate with the false teachers at their own peril. Instead of "beforehand marked out," the NASB margin reads "written about beforehand." Either of these translations is preferable to "before of old ordained," which is how the KJV rendered the verb *prographo*. Needless to say, predestinarians have had a field day with this verse. Beza, for example, commented, "This eternal decree of God comprehended not only the event, but even principally the persons themselves involved in it."[43] What is wrong with this is that "ordained" is not a good translation for the verb,[44] and "of old" (*palai*) is not applied in the New Testament to something God did as far back as eternity before creation.[45] So where had it been written "beforehand" that such evil men would be condemned? Jude might have in mind 2 Peter (if our dating is correct, about 8 years before Jude wrote), or Paul's warnings about such false teachers, or the Gospels which contain Jesus' predictions about the coming of false teachers and false prophets,[46] or even the Old Testament examples he is about to quote (as far back as Cain [verse 11] and Enoch [verse 14]).[47] Jude now begins a characterization of these persons whose condemnation was written down beforehand.

---

[42] The Greek word is *krima*, which literally means "sentence or judgment." Since this context shows the judgment is an adverse one against them, "condemnation" conveys the right idea. "This condemnation" is stated and illustrated by the fate of those mentioned in verses 5-7. 2 Peter 2:3 would certainly be called to the readers' minds since Jude's language is so similar. It would have been clear to the readers what the sentence of the Judge would be.

[43] Cited by Henry Alford, *The New Testament for English Readers* (Chicago: Moody, nd), p.1770.

[44] The KJV translation here is very poor, and is even inconsistent. The same version translates the same verb as "written aforetime" when it occurs in Romans 15:4. In Galatians 3:1 it is rendered "set forth," and in Ephesians 3:3 it is translated "I wrote before." The KJV translation "ordained" at Jude 4 is one of several places where the Calvinistic theology of the KJV translators was written into their translation. Acts 2:47 is another. While "ordained" is not a defensible translation (Calvinists have nothing to justify their doctrine that the condemnation was unconditional, or, that it was announced in eternity, or that it was determined without regard to the moral character of those thus condemned), one might use "proscribed" as a possible rendering. That word pictures the posting up in a public place of names of people who were to be tried, or the posting of the sentence of condemnation long before it was carried out.

[45] *Palai* means "long ago," or "in time past." It indicates some time has elapsed, but doesn't indicate how much. It may be fairly recent, or long ago. The same term is used in Matthew 11:21, "they would have repented *long ago*"; in Mark 15:44, where Pilate wonders whether Jesus "were dead *by this time*"; in Hebrews 1:1, where "God spoke *long ago* to the fathers"; and in 2 Peter 1:9, "purified from his *former* sins."

[46] If we have dated the Gospels correctly, Matthew (AD 45-50), Luke (AD 60), and Mark (AD 68) have all been written and were circulating before Jude wrote his letter.

[47] We doubt the correctness of the suggestion that the false teachers had been entered in a heavenly book in which God enters the names of the damned. There is a "book of life" in which men's names are entered when they become Christians (Philippians 4:3), and whose names can be blotted out if they apostatize (Revelation 3:5), but we know of no Biblical passage that has a similar book containing the names of the lost. The only book of names to be checked at the final judgment is the book of life (Revelation 20:15).

Ungodly persons -- The men who had sneaked into the churches were not Christians, they were "ungodly men." *Asebes* was used at 1 Peter 4:18 and at 2 Peter 2:5 and 3:7. It describes a person as being destitute of reverential awe toward God, as being without true piety or religion. This general word (which occurs often enough that it has been called "the keynote to the epistle"[48]) is followed by two participial phrases that specify some of what was involved in their ungodliness.

Who turn the grace of our God into licentiousness -- The verb translated "turn" is *metatithemi*, "to transpose or put one thing in the place of another." The gospel offers grace[49] and the false teachers use that doctrine as a justification for a licentious lifestyle.[50] These false teachers were apparently actually doing what some accused Paul of falsely teaching, "Let us continue in sin that grace may increase!" (Romans 6:1).[51] Instead of practicing self-control so as to limit how much they sin (which is what the "grace of our God" actually requires), these men were presumptuously insisting that it is perfectly proper to satisfy every wanton desire because, after all, God forgives! That's one of the horrible things the "ungodly persons" were habitually doing. R.C. Foster said, "There is no quicker way to jump head-first into hell than through lasciviousness."

And deny our only Master and Lord, Jesus Christ -- This is the second participial phrase intended to define what was involved in the false teachers' behavior that justified Jude's calling them "ungodly." Peter warned (2 Peter 2:1) that false teachers would do exactly what Jude says they are doing – denying Jesus the Messiah as their Lord and Master.[52] Jude does not specifically say how the ungodly persons were repeatedly denying (present tense) Jesus

---

[48] J.B. Mayor, *The Epistle of St. Jude and the Second Epistle of St. Peter* (Grand Rapids: Baker, 1965 reprint), p.26.

[49] "Grace" is a term that covers a wide area. We have defined it as unmerited favor, or all that God thinks and does to save a man. Here we suppose it speaks in particular of the forgiveness of sins which God generously offers to penitent men on the basis of Christ's atoning sacrifice. It is a glorious freedom in Christ which the children of God enjoy (Romans 8:21; 2 Corinthians 3:17), but it is not a freedom to indulge the flesh (Galatians 5:13).

[50] The Greek word *aselgeia*, translated "licentiousness," is of wide and evil application, describing every species of unbridled conduct, but specially unblushing lasciviousness. See 2 Peter 2:18; Galatians 5:19; Romans 3:5-8.

[51] Compare what Peter wrote as he warned what these false teachers would do when they came (2 Peter 2:18-21). See also what John wrote at a later time about the Gnostics his readers faced (1 John 3:7-10). Starting with a dualistic philosophy that disparaged the body, antinomianism and libertinism was to be a characteristic of certain forms of second-century Gnosticism (see Irenaeus, *Haer.* i.6.2-4 and Clement of Alexandria, *Strom.* iii.30). That later practice had its roots in the teachings of the false teachers whom Jude warns against.

[52] The KJV, which reads "denying the only Lord God, and our Saviour Jesus Christ," reflects a different manuscript reading than is reflected in the NASB. If the KJV is correct, the false teachers would deny both the Father and the Son, and 1 John 2:22 would be a parallel passage. If the NASB reflects what Jude wrote (and the better manuscript evidence supports this reading), then the false teachers deny Jesus, who is described as both Lord and Master. (In the Greek there is one article ["the"] with two nouns in the same case connected by "and."

Christ.[53] A few years later, incipient Gnosticism denied Christ had come in the flesh (1 John 4:2,3), i.e., Jesus did not have a physical body like other men do. Jude does indicate that somehow the ungodly men denied His lordship (i.e., they do not submit to Him or to His authority) and they denied His sovereignty.[54] Calling Jesus the "only Master" is not in distinction from the Father (see Jude 25) but from all false masters such as were advocated by the false teachers.[55] It is possible the ungodly men's denial of Jesus was as much moral as it was theological. (Cp. Titus 1:16, "They profess to know God, but by their deeds they deny Him.") Jesus is presented in Scripture as "King of kings and Lord of lords." It is the height of ungodliness to deny by word or action either His perfect humanity or His deity.

I. A REMINDER OF EXAMPLES OF GOD'S PUNISHMENT OF WRONGDOERS. 1:5-7

A. Unbelieving Children of Israel. 1:5

1:5 -- ***Now I desire to remind you, though you know all things once for all, that the Lord, after saving a people out of the land of Egypt, subsequently destroyed those who did not believe.***

Now I desire to remind you -- The verse begins with *de* in the Greek, and could be translated "but." It indicates a direct contrast between Peter's readers and the "ungodly persons" just mentioned. Jude is not giving new information; instead, just as Peter did in 2 Peter 1:12-15, he is calling his reader's attention to three well-known Biblical examples of a sentence of con-

---

Sharp's rule of grammar says that in such a construction both nouns refer to the same thing, with the second being a further description).

[53] We suppose that all four words, "Master," "Lord," "Jesus," and "Christ (Messiah)," are used by Jude because the idea represented in each was repudiated by the false teachers.

[54] "Master" translates *despotes*, which means "sovereign" or "ruler." In some passages, the term is used of God the Father (Luke 2:29; Acts 4:24; Jeremiah 4:10). Peter applied the term to Jesus (2 Peter 2:1), likely deliberately anticipating and trying to guard against the very denial the false teachers would make. If both "Master" and "Lord" apply to Jesus Christ, the terms are hardly distinguishable. Using language of Jesus that elsewhere is used only of God is a strong argument for the deity of Jesus.

[55] Gnosticism came to distinguish between the Supreme God who created a lower being, and the lower being who created several more generations of lower beings (Demiurges), until eventually an even lower being, Jesus, was created. Jesus then created the devil, and the devil created the world, and that is how Gnostics accounted for the evil in the world, when the Supreme God was spirit (and spirit is good).

demnation being passed by God upon the ungodly.[56] His "desire" to remind them may have sprung from his love for them or from the prompting of the Holy Spirit as he writes. Whereas Peter's examples were apparently in chronological order, Jude's list is not.

Though you know all things once for all -- There is considerable manuscript variation at this place.[57] We shall comment on the text as it stands in the NASB because it appears to be as close to certain what Jude wrote as we can get. "Know"[58] has the force of a present tense; it does not imply they once knew these things but have forgotten them. "All things" is not a claim the readers are omniscient; rather their knowledge on the pertinent point in question is not deficient. They are already cognizant of "the faith once for all delivered to the saints." They know God punishes those who are evil. In particular, they already are familiar with the examples Jude is going to bring to their memory. "Once for all" (*hapax*, the same word used in verse 3, and with the same anti-Gnostic emphasis) might well be expressed here "you have known all along." Or, if we may ignore the Greek word order, it might be translated "remember," so that it reads "I will remind you once for all." Probably, in light of Old and New Testament Scriptures with which the readers were familiar, what Jude means is they had already been taught all Jude intends to say, so that he needs only to remind them. He is encouraging them to use their knowledge of Scripture, a vital spiritual resource, to face the serious problem that has arisen among them because of the entrance of the false teachers.

---

[56] During the last quarter of the 20th century, many writers called attention to insights from rhetorical criticism as they attempted to explain the source and message of the Biblical books. In the ancient world, since Aristotle's *The Art of Rhetoric*, anyone who wanted to persuade and move an audience made deliberate use of all the tools of the trade. Modern critics who have tried to fit Biblical books into the first-century rhetorical mold often must manipulate the Scriptures in order to get a corresponding match. It is not very convincing when it becomes obvious the material must be forced to fit the alleged rhetorical form. We have not been convinced by F. Duane Watson's attempt (*Invention, Arrangement, and Style: Rhetorical Criticism of Jude and 2 Peter* [Atlanta: Scholars Press, 1988]) to show Jude follows typical ancient rhetorical procedures. Were we to force Jude into a rhetorical mold, we would have a four-point outline for the whole book. Verse 3 would be the *exordium*, which makes the "case" that the speaker is going to try to make. Verse 4 would be the *narratio*, which sets forth the concerns that have led to the issue being addressed. Verses 5-16 would be the *probation*, which attempts to persuade the audience to accept the speaker's point of view by arguments and proofs. Verse 17-23 would be the *peroratio*, which repeats the basic case and appeals to the emotions of the audience in order to effect the wanted change. This suspicion of the validity of rhetorical criticism as a tool for interpreting Scripture does not mean Jude was not trying to persuade his audience; he certainly was. But we must allow for the Holy Spirit to produce conviction in the hearts of the hearers (John 16:8-11) rather than attributing the persuasion to the elocutionary and rhetorical flourishes that the wisdom of men could produce.

[57] UBS^3 lists nine different readings. Some manuscripts read "you all know" instead of "you know." Some have "once for all" after "Lord." Some read "God" instead of "Lord." Some read "the Lord" rather than "Lord." Some insert "Jesus" after "Lord." Some read "this" instead of "all things." Scribes apparently felt quite uncertain that the exemplar they were copying was accurate at this place, and so offered changes hoping to fix what to them looked to be a problem.

[58] *Oida* is a second perfect tense in the Greek. It has a present meaning.

That the Lord -- This is a construction in the Greek called indirect discourse. "That" introduces "that" about which Jude wishes to remind them. Is "the Lord" (there is a "the" in the Greek) a reference to the Father[59] or to Jesus? Paul tells us that the pre-existent Jesus did have something to do with providing manna and water during Israel's wilderness wanderings (1 Corinthians 10:4,9). Is Jude now telling us the pre-existent Jesus had something to do with arranging the exodus out of the land of Egypt?[60]

After saving a people out of the land of Egypt -- "*A* people" is what the Greek says, not "*the* people" as the KJV translates it. "The idea is not simply that the ancient Israelites experienced both redemption and judgment at the hands of their Lord, but that Israel's Lord, by bringing Israel out of Egypt, secured a people for Himself, though He had also to destroy unbelievers among them."[61] Jude treats the exodus from Egypt (see Exodus 6-14; Psalm 68, 78:10-24) as an historical event.[62]

Subsequently destroyed those who did not believe -- As the NASB margin shows, the words translated "subsequently" literally mean "the second time" (*to deuteron*). "It marks a sharp contrast and sharpens the point of the warning."[63] The first thing the Lord did was deliver them. The second thing He did was destroy the unbelievers among them (Numbers 13-14).[64] The Savior can also be a destroyer. Those unbelievers who perished numbered over half a million people. Most writers see "destroyed" as a reference to what happened in

---

[59] Observe that the same person who delivered the Israelites (verse 5) has kept the angels in eternal bonds (verse 6). Observe, too, the manuscript differences here: some read "Lord"; some read "God"; some read "Jesus"; and P^{72} reads "God Christ." Bruce M. Metzger. *A Textual Commentary on the Greek New Testament* (London: United Bible Society, 1971), p.724, insists that according to the usually accepted critical principles, "Jesus" was the original reading. The UBS^2 adopted the reading "Jesus."

[60] If the variant reading "Lord Jesus" is correct, then here is another place where we have an act attributed to Jehovah in the Old Testament ascribed to Jesus in the New Testament. That can be done only if Jesus is Jehovah (one of the self-existent members of the Godhead).

[61] Salmond, *op. cit.*, p.6.

[62] Some preachers have treated the historical event in an allegorical fashion, making the deliverance from Egypt parallel to the Christian's deliverance from sin. The Israelites had to believe (i.e., that God would deliver them; that Moses was their leader); they had to repent (i.e., they had to be so sick of Egypt they would gladly leave); there had to be a confession (i.e., this is found in the Passover -- in the celebration of which they showed to the world their intention of leaving Egypt); there was a type of baptism (cp. 1 Corinthians 10:1,2); there had to be steadfastness and faithfulness (i.e., there were perils in the wilderness -- the people had to prove faithful through all the years, even after the deliverance from Egypt, before they could enter the Promised Land).

[63] Charles Bigg, "A Critical and Exegetical Commentary on the Epistles of St. Peter and St. Jude," *International Critical Commentary* (Edinburgh: T&T Clark, 1910), p.228.

[64] Defenders of unconditional eternal security are quick to point out, 'Obviously, this is not an instance of people being saved and then losing their salvation.' All they lost, it is affirmed, was their physical lives. We think God's sentence of condemnation involves more than just how long or how short we live upon this earth.

the wilderness[65] to the Israelites who were unbelievers (cp. Psalm 95:7c-11; 1 Corinthians 10:1-11; and Hebrews 3:16-4:2). Perhaps the point of this illustration is to warn the readers not to become unbelievers by following the lead of the ungodly infiltrators. For if they do, they shall as surely perish as did unbelieving Israel.

> The sins of the people of Israel during this period were exceedingly numerous and grave. Their constant and determined murmuring; their faithlessness in the promises of Jehovah; their unwillingness to go into the land of Canaan; the idolatry of the golden calf; their gross fleshly corruption, are matters duly recorded in great detail by the sacred historian. All of this is summed up under the basic sin of unbelief.[66]

Jude is arguing from the punishment which befell the unbelieving Israelites for the abiding truth that punishment certainly awaits Christians who depart from God. The punishment (*apollumi*) for unbelieving Christians includes more than physical death (see notes at 2 Peter 3:9).

B. Angels Who Sinned. 1:6

1:6 -- ***And angels who did not keep their own domain, but abandoned their proper abode, He has kept in eternal bonds under darkness for the judgment of the great day.***

And angels -- The origin and nature of angels is explained in notes at 2 Peter 2:4. This is the second example Jude alludes to in order to help the readers remember the Biblical truth that God punishes those who do evil.

Who did not keep their own domain -- This implies angels were once on probation and that some chose to rebel; that is, they failed to exercise watchful care and transgressed the limits that had been placed on them, thus misusing the freedom they had been granted by God their Maker. The word translated "domain" is *arche*, which can mean "beginning"[67] or "rule, pow-

---

65 The adverb "second time" has been explained another way, as though Jude had reference to two acts of destruction. G.F.C. Fronmüller ("The Epistle General of Jude," in *Commentary on the Holy Scriptures*, ed. by J.P. Lange [Grand Rapids: Zondervan, 1950 reprint], p.17) urges that the two destructions were the one in the wilderness and then the Babylonian captivity. Theodor Zahn urges the second one was the destruction of Jerusalem in AD 70 (*Introduction to the New Testament* [Grand Rapids: Kregel, 1953], Vol.2, p.253-55, 261-62). Those who think a second punishment is in view make the text treat someone other than those delivered as being the ones punished. That would rob the illustration of its warning force to Jude's living readers. How would it deter their unbelief to warn them that a later generation was going to be punished? It is better to see a reference to what Numbers 14:1-38 and other Old Testament passages portray as happening during Israel's wilderness wanderings.

66 Woods, *op. cit.*, p.388.

67 The KJV's "first estate" seems to be an attempt to give this possible meaning of the word.

er, sovereignty, dominion, principality,"[68] and then "rank, pre-eminence, priority." Used of angels, the word can be descriptive of either an office or a responsibility or a dignity assigned to them. Sadly, they did not "keep" it; they did not fulfill their God-given obligation of carefully guarding and maintaining their high position in God's scheme of things. It may even mean they refused to be governed by their Creator.[69]

But abandoned their proper abode -- The aorist tense verb "abandoned" means to leave once and for all. Their departure was of their own accord; it was done with determination. "Proper" translates *idion*, which means "one's own, private, personal, unique possession."[70] "Abode" is *oiketerion*, "a dwelling place, a home." According to most commentators, heaven is the home the sinning angels abandoned. Barnes supposes they became dissatisfied with where they were living and voluntarily chose to leave. They did not like God's rules so they left home.

He has kept in eternal bonds under darkness -- They were not free of restraint just because they abandoned their proper home. The Lord (verse 5) has kept or guarded or reserved[71] these rebellious angels in chains and in darkness where they are awaiting the final judgment. The word for "eternal" is *aidios*, not the usual word for "eternal" but the one also used at Romans 1:20. It is a peculiarly strong word, describing the "bonds" as being bonds from which there never can be escape. Jude uses *desmos* for "bonds," a different word than Peter used at 2 Peter 2:4. Jude does not picture the fallen angels as chained, but as in custody, detained in a certain place. There is an awesome darkness and gloom[72] that covers the whole place where the fallen angels are in custody.[73]

---

[68] There are orders of angels -- cherubim, seraphim, archangels, principalities, world powers, etc. The word translated "principalities" in Romans 8:38; Ephesians 1:21, 3:10, 6:12; Colossians 1:16, 2:10,15; and Titus 3:1 is the same word Jude uses here. The word is translated "rule" at 1 Corinthians 15:24. According to Deuteronomy 32:8 in the LXX, when God "divided to the nations their inheritance, when He separated the sons of Adam, he set the bounds of the people *according to the number of the angels of God*." This verse apparently indicates that nations were assigned guardian angels. Some suppose it was this responsibility to guard the nation assigned to the angels that certain angels rebelled against.

[69] Neither Jude nor Peter specifies the time when the angels sinned. See notes at 2 Peter 2:4 for several options suggested by commentators. One view is that Jude has in mind the original fall of some angels who, influenced by Satan, rebelled against God. The second view is that Jude is alluding to the event recorded in Genesis 6:1-4 (as though the "sons of God" in that passage were angels). We tend to opt for the former, though Judaism and some in the early church opted for the latter.

[70] Kenneth S. Wuest, *In These Last Days: 2 Peter, 1,2,3 John, and Jude in the Greek New Testament* (Grand Rapids: Eerdmans, 1954), p.240.

[71] The verb form is a perfect tense, indicating a completed action in the past time, with present continuing results. Their confinement took place in the past and is still continuing.

[72] See notes at 2 Peter 2:4 for the meaning of *zophos*, translated "darkness." It is the densest, blackest darkness. Commentators are not agreed whether it is a literal or figurative darkness. If literal, the idea is the darkness broods around and over them. There is no light for the duration of their custody in the intermediate prison house. If it is figurative, Jude says these angels are separated from any inward spiritual light, separated from any guidance or direction to a more positive existence that holy people can expect from their Creator.

[73] In notes on 2 Peter 2:4 we addressed the question of how to harmonize the verses about the wicked angels

For the judgment of the great day -- The present detention of the fallen angels is but a prelude to a still more-awful doom. The devil and his angels will be cast into the lake of fire (Matthew 25:41) when the final judgment occurs.[74] The point Jude is making is that if God did not spare angels who sinned (i.e., who did not keep their own domain), He will not spare men who behave in the same ungodly way.

C. Immoral Sodom and Gomorrah. 1:7

1:7 -- ***Just as Sodom and Gomorrah and the cities around them, since they in the same way as these indulged in gross immorality and went after strange flesh, are exhibited as an example, in undergoing the punishment of eternal fire.***

Just as Sodom and Gomorrah -- This is the third example of God's punishment of wrong doers that Jude calls to the readers' memory.[75] The first Greek word in this verse (*hos*) is translated variously in the New Testament – "about, according as, as, even like, like as, to wit, while, and how." We might translate it "how" and connect it with "remind you" (verse 5), so that the thought runs, "I remind you *how* Sodom and Gomorrah ... are set forth as an example."[76] If we think "just as" introduces a comparison showing a likeness between the angels (verse 6) and Sodom and Gomorrah (verse 7), we must be cautious in our identification of that likeness. There is no question that both were guilty of committing sin, but it might be more than the author intended if we were to affirm that both the angels and the people of Sodom were guilty of the *same* sin. The similarity lies in the fact that both sinned and both were punished.

And the cities around them -- The cities of the plain included Sodom, Gomorrah, Admah, Zeboim, and Zoar (Genesis 14:2; Deuteronomy 29:23; Hosea 11:8). Zoar was spared from the judgment visited upon the other cities (Genesis 19:22).

---

being in custody with the Scriptural affirmation elsewhere that demons are at work in the world.

[74] The final judgment is designated by a number of terms in Scripture. In Revelation 6:17 the terminology is just like Jude's. Elsewhere we read of "the last day," "the day of judgment," "the day of the Lord," and "the great and glorious day of the Lord."

[75] Bible students have noted that Jude's examples are not in chronological order like Peter's were (2 Peter 2). Some have supposed Jude introduces his examples in the order he does in order to emphasize the growing severity of punishment on the wrong doers -- from physical death (verse 5) to punishment in the intermediate state (verse 6) to condemnation to everlasting punishment (verse 7).

[76] Henry Alford, "Jude" in *Alford's Greek Testament* (London: Rivingtons, 1871), Vol.4, p.533.

Since they in the same way as these indulged in gross immorality -- Jude has already alluded to the gross immorality committed by the false teachers (verse 4). We suppose "they" refers to the inhabitants of the cities of the plain, and "these" refers to the false teachers about whom Jude writes.[77] God is consistent in His punishment of immorality, whether it be Sodom and Gomorrah or the false teachers of the first century AD. How the people of Sodom and Gomorrah acted immorally is set forth in Genesis 19:1-5. The verb *ekporneuo* speaks of unreserved surrender to or indulgence in fornication.

And went after strange flesh -- Not only were the people of Sodom and Gomorrah guilty of immorality, they also "went after strange flesh." The words translated "went after" (*apelthousai opiso*) indicates they were addicted to this vice. The reference in "strange flesh" seems to be "to the particular sin which, from the name Sodom, has been called sodomy."[78]

Are exhibited as an example -- Here is the reason why God visited such a memorable punishment on the cities of the plain. He wanted to make an example of them and thereby warn others to stay away from such ungodly behavior. Attention is drawn to what happened to Sodom and Gomorrah with remarkable frequency in Scripture.[79] "Exhibited" (it is right before your eyes![80]) reminds us that one only had to look at the southern end of the Dead Sea area in order to have continuing evidence of what happens to those who disobey God. The area that used to be lush and abundant (Genesis 13:10) is completely desolate as a result of God raining fire and brimstone on the cities. "Example" is something that is held up to view as a warning.

In undergoing the punishment of eternal fire -- Vincent has observed that the participle "undergoing" is present tense, indicating the people of the cities are suffering to this day the punishment which came upon them when God destroyed the city, raining fire and brimstone

---

[77] There has been much diversity of interpretation of "these." A popular explanation is that it refers to the angels of verse 6 and says the angels committed the same immoralities which Sodom and Gomorrah did. It is not unusual to see Genesis 6:2 alleged to be the particular instance Jude has in mind. See all this discussed in notes at 2 Peter 2:4.

[78] Barnes, *op. cit.*, p.392. "Strange" translates *heteros*, "of a different kind." The modern terms are lesbianism, homosexuality, pederasty, and perhaps bestiality. All of those sexual unions are "different" than what God intended. In passing, it should be noted God must have given His verdict that such behavior is sin long before the cities of the plain indulged in it. Modern defenders of this "alternative lifestyle" are as wrong about their behavior being acceptable to God as were the people of Sodom, or the false teachers of Jude's time. Romans 1:27,28 show that people indulge in this sin only after they have been "given up" by God (1:24,26). Moo, *op. cit.*, p.250-255, has a balanced presentation of the Biblical teaching and the struggle Christians have (as they try to uphold Biblical standards) against a society and culture that increasingly accepts such behavior.

[79] Isaiah 1:9, 13:19; Jeremiah 23:14, 49:18, 50:40; Hosea 11:8; Amos 4:11; Matthew 10:15, 11:24; Luke 10:12, 17:29; 2 Peter 2:6-8.

[80] The word *prokeimai* ("to lie exposed") is used in classical Greek of food laid out on a table ready for the guests, and of a corpse laid out for burial.

on them. "Eternal fire" does not mean the fires that consumed the cities are still burning. Rather "their punishment was so utter and so permanent that the nearest approach to it will be seen in the destruction which shall be characteristic of those who suffer the eternal fire [of hell]. Their destruction thus stands as a symbol of that which shall eventually be the lot of all ungodly men."[81] They may not be in hell yet, but like the wicked angels were "kept for the judgment of the great day," so the wicked inhabitants of Sodom and Gomorrah and the cities of the plain are in the intermediate place of torment where they are being held until the time when wicked men are hurled into the lake of fire (Revelation 20:14).

II. A SOLEMN PREDICTION OF COMING PUNISHMENT ON THE UNGODLY MEN WHO HAVE INFILTRATED THE CHURCHES. 1:8-16

A. The Punishable Behavior the Ungodly Men have Exhibited. 1:8-10

1:8 -- ***Yet in the same manner these men also by dreaming defile the flesh, and reject authority, and revile angelic majesties.***

Yet in the same manner these men also -- "Yet"[82] means despite such clear Biblical warnings that God punishes wicked ones, these men go right ahead with their ungodliness. In case the false teachers (i.e., "these men") should protest saying, 'We are not like those sinners whom God destroyed,' Jude shows in this and the following verses that indeed they are. The "ungodly persons" (Jude 4) are sinners "also" and "in the same manner."

By dreaming -- There are several possible ways to understand the participle *enupniazomenoi*. Perhaps it says the false teachers are full of empty speculations, they are "just dreaming."[83] Perhaps it says they sit around thinking filthy thoughts.[84] Perhaps it implies they are deep in spiritual slumber, the slumber of sin (cp. Romans 13:11). Perhaps it says the false teachers,

---

[81] Woods, *op. cit.*, p.391.

[82] The KJV does not translate the Greek word *mentoi*.

[83] This seems to be how the Latin translators understood the word, since they used *somnium*, a word that can mean vain imagination. This was also how Clement of Alexandria (*Strom.* iii.2.11, and *Adumb. en Ep. Judae* ii) explained the passage. "They just imagined God was not displeased with them for their behavior." Moo, *op. cit.*, p.245.

[84] The KJV supplied the word "filthy" to describe the dreamers. Perhaps instead of supplying "filthy" from the next clause, our English translation should reflect the fact that all three clauses following are somehow related to the "dreaming." We might translate this circumstantial participle with the helper "because" so that the verse reads, "because they are dreaming they defile ... reject ... and revile ...."

after having a vision while in a self-induced trance, make claims of having a prophecy as the source of their teaching and behavior.[85] As a result of their "dreaming" Jude specifies in the following clauses three forms of wickedness of which the false teachers are guilty.

Defile the flesh -- *Miaino* means "to pollute, sully, contaminate, soil." Thayer tells us the word is used in both a physical and a moral sense.[86] If we take "flesh" as a reference to their physical bodies, this verse alludes to the polluting nature of the sin of licentiousness (verse 4). The false teachers pollute their own bodies by various sexual sins. 1 Corinthians 6:18 does seem to suggest fornication does something to the sinner's physical body that no other sin does. Homosexuality is not less harmful. If we take "flesh" to refer to their inner natures, then this phrase speaks of the result of indulging in an immoral lifestyle: their very passions, desires, and appetites become polluted or addicted to the sin. Plummer has observed, "Some of the earliest forms of Gnosticism, on its antinomian as distinct from its ascetic side, exhibit the licentiousness inveighed against here; e.g., the Simonians, Nicolaitanes, Cainites, Carpocratians."[87]

And reject authority -- There are some untranslatable particles (*men* and *de*) in the Greek, one before the previous clause, the other introducing these last two clauses in the verse. The point is this, the sins of rejection and reviling are sharply contrasted with the fleshly indulgence of the previous clause. *Atheteo* is a little stronger than "reject." "Despise" or "show contempt for" would come closer to catching the nuance. Jude's brief statement does not tell us whether the authority (*kuriotes*, "dominion," see notes at 2 Peter 2:10) they set at nought is civil, church,[88] or divine (God's rules, or Christ's "lordship"). When people reject Christ's authority over the lives of men, they may exhibit contempt for any and all "authority" which would interfere with their own desires and will.

And revile angelic majesties -- "Revile" represents *blasphemeo* ("blaspheme, rail against") in the original. The other Greek word in this clause is *doxas* ("glories"), which was commented on at 2 Peter 2:10. Our translators, influenced by the following verse in Jude

[85] Compare Colossians 2:18, "taking his stand on visions he has seen." There are genuine dreams from the Lord that are revelations (Acts 2:17), and there are self-induced trances that result in the dreamer hearing a message, but it is not from the Lord. Deuteronomy 13:1,3,5 shows that false prophets will try to support their evil doctrines and practices by pretended revelations. In the 4th century, Epiphanius reports the Gnostics claimed such visions to justify their doctrines and practices (*Pan. Haer.* xxvi.3).

[86] Thayer, *op. cit.*, p.414. A paragraph on the same page calls attention to the connotation of two synonyms: *miaino*, "to stain," differs from *moluno*, "to smear." One affects the very fiber, the other can be just external.

[87] Alfred Plummer, "The General Epistle of Jude," in *Layman's Handy Commentary on the Bible* (Grand Rapids: Zondervan, 1957 reprint), p.276. Plummer names those later Gnostic sects as illustrations of what he supposes the false teachers contemporary with Jude are likely to have taught.

[88] J.N.D. Kelly, *A Commentary on the Epistles of Peter and Jude* (Grand Rapids: Baker, 1981 reprint), p.262, has argued that *kuriotes* did not mean "civil" or "ecclesiastical" authority until Byzantine times.

(which has one angel not railing against another angel), opt for the suggestion that Jude has in mind "glorious angels."[89]

1:9 -- ***But Michael the archangel, when he disputed with the devil and argued about the body of Moses, did not dare pronounce against him a railing judgment, but said,*** **"THE LORD REBUKE YOU."**

But -- In contrast to the blatant treatment accorded to the angels by the false teachers, Jude now presents the case of Michael the archangel and his restrained treatment of a fallen angel, Satan. The inference is the false teachers should have learned from, and emulated, the example of Michael.

Michael the archangel -- "Michael" means "who is like God?" His name is mentioned several times in Scripture – at Daniel 10:13,21 and 12:1 where he is the guardian angel of the people of Israel, and at Revelation 12:7-9 where he is described as the leader of the unfallen angels who warred against and conquered Satan and his angels. "Archangel" means ruling angel, chief of angels, captain of angels. The word occurs only one other place in the New Testament (1 Thessalonians 4:16).[90]

When he disputed with the devil -- What Jude presents in this verse is not found in the Old Testament Scriptures. As a result, this verse has given great perplexity to those who would comment upon it. In fact, it is not unheard of to read some commentators have decided on the basis of verse 9 that the whole letter of Jude should be regarded as uninspired and of doubtful historical facticity. However, just because it is not recorded in the Old Testament Scriptures is no reason to treat what Jude says as being fanciful imagination on his part, or as being a foolish incorporation into his letter of some science-fiction story that may have been current in the first century AD.[91] Do not forgot that Jude identified himself as a "bond-servant

---

[89] "Glory" is a term used to describe the sphere of brilliant light which surrounds God (1 Timothy 6:16), and angels who surround Him are regarded as sharing that light, or as reflecting it (Hebrews 9:5). In the second century, certain Gnostics despised the angels because they thought of them as the agents (working for an inferior creator-God) who brought the universe into existence (Irenaeus, *Haer.* i.25.1ff). Perhaps we may suppose the false teachers contemporary with Jude held a similar low view of angels.

[90] Michael is also one of the characters introduced in the pseudepigraphical *Book of Enoch*. In the pseudepigraphical works we find a hierarchy with seven archangels, including Michael, Gabriel, Raphael, and Uriel. Because these books were written *after* the Old Testament canonical books, higher critics (embracing an evolutionary scheme of things) have said, "He (Michael) belongs to that developed form which the doctrine of angels took toward the close of the Old Testament age, when the ideas of distinction in dignity and office were added to the simpler conception of earlier times." We have argued elsewhere that while Old Testament revelation was indeed progressive, the hypothesis that all the ideas presented therein are simply naturalistic growths added to older beliefs is not warranted. There is a God and He does reveal Himself!

There is no convincing proof Michael is ever to be identified with Christ Himself, as some modern sects have affirmed. See George C.M. Douglas, "Michael," in *Fairbairn's Imperial Standard Bible Dictionary* (Grand Rapids: Zondervan, 1957 reprint), Vol.4, p.238-241, and J.E. Rosscup, "Michael," in *The Zondervan Pictorial Encyclopedia of the Bible* (Grand Rapids: Zondervan, 1975), Vol.4, p.217,218.

[91] In the Introductory Studies, we have called attention to those writers who have supposed Jude draws some of his information here written from the *Assumption of Moses*.

of Jesus Christ" (Jude 1), and this is a claim to inspiration. If that is true, and we find no reason to doubt it, there is nothing to keep us from understanding that Jude received his information about Michael by revelation and wrote it by inspiration.[92] The word "disputed" speaks of a contention with words, rather than a hand-to-hand physical struggle. The "devil" is a fallen angel (Revelation 12:7-9) and the chief antagonist of God, doing all he can to thwart what God is doing in His world with His people.[93]

And argued about the body of Moses -- The Old Testament record of the death and burial of Moses is found in Deuteronomy 34:5,6, but there is nothing in that account like what Jude tells us about a dispute over Moses' body. All it says is the Lord buried him in a valley in the land of Moab, over against Beth-peor. There is a statement in the Targum of Jonathan at Deuteronomy 34:6 which says Michael was appointed guardian of Moses' grave.[94] Beyond this we have nothing but some claims by early Christian writers, none of which we can verify.[95]

> The strange question, "What did the devil want with the body of Moses?" has been asked and answered in more than one way: -- (1) to make it an object of idolatry, as the Israelites would be very likely to worship it; (2) to keep it as his own [i.e, deprive Moses of the honor of burial], as that of a murderer, because Moses killed the Egyptian (Ex. 2:12).[96]

---

92 See "Did Jude Use Sources?" in the Introductory Studies to this epistle. We see no reason to treat Jude's words other than as a literal record of what happened between Michael and the devil at the burial of Moses. However, some scholars have tried to interpret Jude's words figuratively -- as though the body of Moses were a figure of speech for the Mosaic Law, and the dispute between Michael and the devil is located at Mt. Sinai at the time of the giving of the Law -- or the body of Moses refers to the Jewish polity, and the contest occurred at the time of the siege when Hezekiah was king (Michael, the defender of Israel, won, so Hezekiah was not defeated).

93 See Arthur B. Fowler's article on the "Devil" in the *Zondervan Pictorial Bible Dictionary* (Grand Rapids: Zondervan, 1963), p.215. Also see notes at 1 Peter 5:8.

94 The Targum was not written down until the third century AD or later. We have no way of knowing how old a tradition it reflects, or whether it might have been based on what Jude wrote a hundred or more years before the Targum was committed to writing.

95 As documented in the Introductory Studies, Clement of Alexandria, Origen, and Didymus of Alexandria all gave us their understanding that Jude was quoting from the pseudepigraphical *Assumption of Moses*. The fragments of that writing still extant do not include any statement about a contention over the body of Moses, so we cannot compare the accounts to see if their conclusions about Jude copying were correct or not. R.H. Charles has published a two-volume work on *The Apocrypha and Pseudepigrapha* (Oxford: Clarendon Press, 1963) and the extant fragments of the *Assumption of Moses* can be referred to there.

96 Plummer, *op. cit.*, p.277.

Did not dare pronounce against him a railing judgment -- Archangels are certainly superior to human beings since men were made a little lower than the angels (Psalm 8:5; Hebrews 2:7). That being true, if an archangel is not brave enough to rail against a fallen angel, how do the false teachers dare to blaspheme angelic dignities? We are not told why it is said Michael did not dare to do it. Certainly not because he feared the devil. Perhaps it was because he feared the Lord. Perhaps it is because he knew that such behavior was wrong in God's sight. A "railing judgment" is "a judgment pronounced in reproachful terms."[97] The implication is the false teachers have been accustomed to utter such reproachful speech, just as Peter predicted they would do (2 Peter 2:10).

But said, "THE LORD REBUKE YOU" -- What Michael was saying is "May the Lord rebuke you (devil) for your blasphemy."[98] The devil used opprobrious language during his verbal contention with Michael. Michael did not reply in kind, but turned the whole matter over to the Lord. He understood it is the Lord's job to censure[99] the wrongdoer.

1:10 -- *But these men revile the things which they do not understand; and the things which they know by instinct, like unreasoning animals, by these things they are destroyed.*

But these men -- The adversative "but" shows that in verse 10 we have a contrast of the behavior of the false teachers and that of Michael (verse 9). The old proverb, "Fools rush in where angels fear to tread," is true in their case. The two halves of the verse make these points: what they cannot know they rail at; what they do know they abuse.

Revile the things which they do not understand -- Jude says the false teachers are totally ignorant about the things of which they contemptuously speak. In the context (verse 8), "the things" they do not know and speak contemptuously about are "authority" (*kuriotes*) and "angelic majesties" (*doxas*). These things belong to the world of the spirit, the world of God's hidden wisdom; unless men listen to what God reveals about them, they are unknowable.[100] The false teachers have not had their spiritual antennae attuned, so there is no way for them

---

[97] Thayer, *op. cit.*, p.102.

[98] The verb "rebuke" is in the optative mood in the Greek, expressing a wish or a desire or a prayer. Michael expressed this rebuke because the actions and conduct of the devil were wrong. "The same rebuke was administered to Satan by the angel of Jehovah when Satan appeared as the adversary of Joshua, the high priest, the restorer of the temple and of the daily sacrifice, and one of the Old Testament types of Christ (Zechariah 3:2)." Plummer, *ibid.* While that is true, we certainly are not encouraged to have any confidence in what else some writer may say who suggests that, here in verse 9, Jude made use of Zechariah, either accidentally or deliberately putting the words in the mouth of Michael as he made up this story about the dispute with the devil.

[99] The word translated "rebuke" (*epitimao*) has a number of shades of meaning. In Matthew 8:26 it is used of commanding or restraining the winds and waves. In Matthew 18:18, Mark 1:25, and Luke 4:34, 35, it is used of admonishing strongly or censuring.

[100] Those commentators who understand "authority" (dominion) and "glories" (verse 8) to refer to human authorities are at a loss here to explain this phrase. The false teachers certainly would know earthly rulers.

to understand.[101] Is there a veiled attack on the false teachers' claim to superior knowledge? We think so. When it comes to the divine majesty and true status of angels, the false teachers don't have a clue!

And the things which they know by instinct -- "Know" here translates *epistamai*, which means "to know well." "By instinct" is *phusikos* which, transliterated, is "physical." The knowledge which can be gained simply from human (physical) existence, but using no spiritual faculties, is what the false teachers are expert at. Their knowledge is a based on human appetites and sensual pleasures.

Like unreasoning animals -- Jude (just as Peter did in 2 Peter 2:12) is saying the false teachers are on no greater level than brute creation. They are not using their ability to reason. They live by no greater instincts and impulses than those instincts and impulses that men share in common with the animals.

By these things they are destroyed -- The verb tense here is not future, but present. The corruption – the word translated "destroyed" is *phtheiro*, "corruption" – is already happening.[102] "These things" are the things of the flesh, the appetites and passions that men and animals have in common. When people surrender to the appetites of the flesh and thereby descend to the level of animals, they have begun the process by which they forfeit their spiritual standing and their eternal destiny. What becomes their greatest pleasure becomes the occasion of their corruption.

B. Biblical Examples of Wickedness Like Theirs Being Punished. 1:11

1:11 -- ***Woe to them! For they have gone the way of Cain, and for pay they have rushed headlong into the error of Balaam, and perished in the rebellion of Korah.***

Woe to them! -- "Woe" (*ouai*) is an interjection that can express either pity or condemnation, depending on the tone of voice with which it is spoken. It is a word Old Testament prophets used to announce the punishment coming on unrepentant people (e.g., Isaiah 3:11). It is the same word Jesus often used (Luke 6:24-26; Matthew 23:13,15-16,23,25,27,29, 24: 19). It can be either the indicative or the optative mood in Greek. If the former, it is a simple statement of the misery that is descending on the false teachers. If the latter, it is a wish, "Let

---

101 The word translated "understand" is *oida*, a Greek word meaning "to know," and speaks of mental comprehension and knowledge that comes by instruction, as compared to the verb *ginosko*, which speaks of knowledge that is gained by personal experience. The false teachers have not listened to the instructions given by the apostles of Jesus -- this is why they do not understand.

102 The verb form may be either middle (they are bringing themselves to ruin) or passive (by these things they are brought to ruin). God has so arranged it!

woe be to them!" Jude knows such a sad fate awaits them because of what happened to people with similar sin problems in the three examples he is about to cite from the Old Testament – Cain, Balaam, and Korah.

1. Cain, an example of disobedience

For they have gone the way of Cain -- The verb tense Jude uses as he introduces these three Old Testament examples is the past tense. This is typical of prophetic language[103] where the punishment of their sins is so certain that one can speak of it as having already happened. "To go the way of" is familiar language for an habitual course of conduct, either moral or religious. We can read about Cain in Genesis 4:5-12; 1 John 3:12; and Hebrews 11:4.[104] The point of comparison between Cain and the false teachers apparently is this: disobedience. Just as Cain did not faithfully carry out God's revealed will, so neither are the false teachers.[105] Such disobedience and rebellion, a determination to do things their own way rather than God's way, results in divine punishment. It did for Cain, and it will for the false teachers, for God is consistent in His behavior.

2. Balaam, an example of greed

And for pay they have rushed headlong into the error of Balaam -- We read about Balaam in Numbers 22-24, 31:16-19, and 2 Peter 2:15,16. "Rushed headlong" translates *ekcheo*, a word used of the water rushing over a falls, or a swift current. The false teachers are pictured as exercising no restraint as with reckless abandon they poured themselves into the same evil behavior Balaam exhibited, and like him, they did it because of the money they hoped to get.[106] "Error" translates *plane*, "wandering, straying about, roaming hither and thither having been led astray from the right way." Metaphorically, it indicates an "error, a wrong opinion relative to morals or religion."[107] The point of the comparison between Balaam and the false teachers is apparently this: greed. Balaam is the prototype of all greedy religious

---

[103] It is well known that many of the Old Testament prophecies of the coming Messiah are spoken of using past tense verbs.

[104] Abel offered his sacrifice "by faith," which implies Cain did not. "Faith" is doing what God says. God had revealed the kind of sacrifice that would be acceptable to Him, and this Cain refused to bring.

[105] Moo (*op. cit.*, p.257) calls attention to a statement attributed to Cain in the Jerusalem Targum that may reflect the same attitudes taught by the false teachers Jude is warning about. According to the Targum, Cain affirms, "There is no judgment, no judge, no future life; no reward will be given to the righteous, and no judgment will be imposed on the wicked."

[106] *Misthos*, translated "pay," can refer to wages paid for work, or it can speak of popularity or men's applause. Jude apparently is charging the false teachers with covetousness and greed and a love of money.

[107] Thayer, *op. cit.*, p.514.

teachers who lead God's people into false religion and immorality because they know they can make money by it.

> Balaam went wrong because he allowed himself to hanker after gain, and so lost communion with God. He not only went wrong himself, but he abused his great influence and his reputation as a prophet, to lead astray the Israelites by drawing them away from the holy worship of Jehovah to the impure worship of Baal Peor.[108]

3. Korah, an example of insubordination

And perished in the rebellion of Korah -- Korah "rose up" against Moses, objecting to the selection of the family of Aaron to be the priests in Israel, and Korah led others into the same attitude of rebellion (Numbers 16:1-35, 26:9-11; Psalm 106:16-18). The point of comparison between Korah and the false teachers is apparently this: insubordination. Like Korah objected to God's appointed leaders, they, too, are objecting to the local church leaders and the authority vested in them. The false teachers want to be the recognized leaders and so are encouraging others to follow their leading while at the same time rebelling against and ignoring the true spiritual leadership of the congregations they have infiltrated. For their refusal to obey what God's appointed leader (Moses) commanded, Korah and his two companions, Dathan and Abiram, and their followers were swallowed up by the earth. Then 250 rebellious Levites were consumed by fire from the Lord. "Perished" (*apollumi*) is often used in Scripture to denote future punishment in hell.[109] Jude, using a past tense verb to make a prediction, says that just as sure as Korah perished, the same destiny awaits the false teachers because they are guilty of the same sin.

C. Metaphorical Pictures, Reminiscent of Old Testament Warnings, of the Harm Caused by These Infiltrators. 1:12-13

1:12 -- ***These men are those who are hidden reefs in your love feasts when they feast with you without fear, caring for themselves; clouds without water, carried along by winds; autumn trees without fruit, doubly dead, uprooted;***

These men -- Ever since he spoke of "certain ungodly persons" (verse 4), Jude has referred to them again and again as "these men" (verses 8,10). Jude now piles up six metaphorical pictures to describe the harm caused by the false teachers, offered as further reason they deserve to perish.

---

[108] Joseph B. Mayor, *The Epistles of Jude and II Peter* (Grand Rapids: Baker, 1965 reprint), p.39.

[109] Matthew 10:28,39, 18:14; Mark 1:24; Luke 13:3,5; John 3:15,16, 10:28; 2 Thessalonians 2:10; 2 Peter 3:9.

Are those who are hidden reefs in your love feasts -- "Love feasts" were a kind of basket dinner in which all of the saints shared as they met together on the first day of the week.[110] Those who had food to share provided it and the poorer brethren were invited to eat together with the wealthier members. For some of the have-nots, this might be the only decent meal they would have in a week's time. The false teachers loved to come to these dinners and gorge themselves on what others had provided. But their presence in the congregation was as treacherous as sunken reefs[111] were to ancient sailors. Those reefs could not be seen, but any ship that struck one had its bottom ripped open and many inevitably sank along with all its cargo, frequently with loss of life. Jude is alluding to the fact that the people who unsuspectingly got too close to these false teachers would make shipwreck of their faith.

When they feast with you without fear -- "Feast with you" (*suneuocheo*) perhaps could better be translated "feasting together with themselves." There is no word in the Greek for "you." We don't know the original word order here. Shall we connect "without fear" to "feast with you" (as the NASB does), or shall we connect it with "caring for themselves" (as the KJV and ASV did)? The false teachers misbehaved without any fear of the consequences for themselves. The NASB translators thought the false teachers should have something to fear as a result of their behavior at the "love feasts." Did their behavior at the love feast carry over into the observance of the Lord's Supper, so that they were mocking Christ's death, and by sitting apart in their own little group were they showing disdain for the idea that the congregation participates together as the body of Christ? Instead of using the love feasts to realize the unity of Christians and to exhibit brotherly love, they were using them selfishly for their own purposes. Behavior like that is something that ought to put the fear of the Lord into those men (cp. Hebrews 10:26-31 and 1 Corinthians 11:27-32).

Caring for themselves -- The word *poimaino* means "to feed, to tend a flock of sheep." The ASV therefore translated this phrase "Shepherds that ... feed [only] themselves." This figure of speech recalls all the Biblical warnings (such as Isaiah 56:11 and Ezekiel 34:2,8) about false shepherds who care nothing for the flock. Jesus Himself, whose lordship the false teachers rejected, spoke of hireling shepherds who cared nothing for the flock (John 10:12,13). If we take "without fear" with this clause, Jude tells us the false teachers behave

---

[110] See comments on the "love feast" at 2 Peter 2:13, Acts 2:46, and at 1 Corinthians 11:17-34. At the close of the dinner, the early Christians would observe the Lord's Supper. At Corinth, the behavior of some at the love feast made a meaningful observance of the Lord's Supper impossible. As a result of improper participation in the Lord's Supper, many were "weak, sick, and not a few were asleep" (1 Corinthians 11:30). May we also read between the lines here in Jude the implication that the behavior of the false teachers not only ruined the love feast but also made proper observance of the Lord's Supper impossible, thus resulting in harm to the participants?

[111] The rendering "spots" (KJV) or "blemishes" (NIV) is borrowed from 2 Peter 2:13. Plummer (*op. cit.*, p.279) tells us that just as Peter's word *spiloi* may mean either "spots" (KJV) or "rocks" (ASV), usually the former, so Jude's word *spilades* may mean either "spots" or "rocks" (usually the latter). Bigg (*op. cit.*, p.333) has a helpful study of how lexicographers arrive at the possible meaning of *spilades*. He also explains how the Greek construction ("these" is masculine, and "rocks" is feminine) requires us to supply a verb.

as they do, acting without the slightest qualm, because they imagined they had no consequences to fear from God who had His eyes on them. Instead of tending to the flock of God, these false teachers set themselves up as the true shepherds of the flock, their true motive being to feed only themselves and further their own schemes and lusts.

Clouds without water, carried along by winds -- Here is the third metaphor Jude uses to describe the harm done by these false teachers. Perhaps Jude reflects Proverbs 25:14 (NIV), "Like clouds and wind without rain is one who boasts of gifts never given." How disappointed people in a drought area are when the clouds promise rain but the rain doesn't come, and soon the winds drive the clouds on[112] past the drought area. "In a land of little rainfall such as Palestine, indeed, in much of the East, the appearance of clouds offering refreshing rain are eagerly watched by the farmer, but when the cloud is borne along by the wind leaving no moisture, hope yields to despair."[113] These false teachers will leave only spiritual disappointment behind when they are gone. There will have been no showers of blessing resulting from their ministry.

Autumn trees without fruit, doubly dead, uprooted -- "Autumn trees" brings to mind the image of trees whose limbs are bare after the leaves have fallen.[114] A fruit tree that produces no fruit is not of much benefit. We wonder if Jude remembered Jesus' cursing of the barren fig tree (Matthew 21:18-22), or His parable of the barren fig tree (Luke 13:6-9), both of which teach a lesson about legitimate expectation which is unfulfilled. Anyone who goes to the false teachers looking for some useful spiritual fruit will come away with, at best, a mouth full of dirt but nothing sweet or refreshing or nourishing.[115] Exegetes differ about the meaning of "doubly dead" or, as the marginal note reads, "twice dead." Some suppose the trees are pictured as being dead in two successive seasons. Some suppose it means no more than utterly dead. Others suppose these men, having once been dead in trespasses and sins (Ephesians 2:1), were raised to life in baptism (Romans 6:1-4; Colossians 2:13), only to relapse and apostatize back into the death of sin – so that it can be said they were twice dead.[116] Still others suggest there is a reference to the "second death" (Revelation 2:11, 20:6,14, 21:8).

---

[112] Instead of *paraphero* ("carried along, borne along") there is a weakly attested variant, *peripheromenai* ("tossed about"), perhaps suggested by Ephesians 4:14, an image which would suggest instability.

[113] Woods, *op. cit.*, p.396. Jude is doing more here than simply accusing the false teachers of bringing no food to the love feasts and so having nothing to share. It seems obvious there is no longer any allusion to the love feast as we move through this series of metaphorical descriptions.

[114] The KJV translation here ("trees whose fruit withereth, without fruit ...") results in a strange contradiction. The word *phthinoporina* is a compound made up of *phthino* ("to waste away, to pine away") and *opora* ("autumn").

[115] Compare notes at 2 Peter 1:8.

[116] While it is possible for a man to be born again and then fall away (Romans 6:15-16,23; Hebrews 6:4-6; 2 Peter 2:18-20), we are not sure that the false teachers Jude is describing were once Christians who have relapsed, their apostasy causing them to have died spiritually again. Study in this connection the comments at 2 Peter 1:9 and 2:20.

First, they died because of their trespasses and sins; secondly, they die the second death.[117] The tree being described was not only leafless, barren, and twice dead; it has also been blown over (or drug out by the husbandman) so that its roots are no longer in the soil.[118] There was no possibility for any fruit from such a source, in this life or the life to come. In fact, such uprooted trees were disposed of by burning (Matthew 3:10, 7:19, 15:13).

1:13 -- ***Wild waves of the sea, casting up their own shame like foam; wandering stars, for whom the black darkness has been reserved forever.***

Wild waves of the sea, casting up their own shame like foam -- The fifth metaphor Jude uses to describe the harm the false teachers do is taken from the restless ocean waves as they break upon the shore. Jude's language is reminiscent of Isaiah 57:20, "But the wicked are like the tossing sea; for it cannot be quiet, and its waters toss up refuse and mud." Along the seashore the waves are lashed into foam as they break and dash upon the shore. It is amazing the amount of flotsam and jetsam cast upon the shore in the foam. Thus it is with the false teachers. What they impart is as unsubstantial and valueless as what is in the foam of the ocean waves. "Wild" may be a glance at the false teachers' lack of self-control. The word translated "shame" is plural in the Greek, perhaps speaking of their shameful deeds or degrading lusts.

Wandering stars -- The word "wandering" (*planetai*) is that from which we derive our word "planet." When the ancients looked up into the night sky, the stars seemed to keep their place night after night. But a few points of light – today we know these as the planets Venus, Mars, Jupiter, Saturn – seemed to shift positions nightly. To the ancients, the planets seemed to wander about the heavens. Mariners and other ancient travelers could use the stars as an aid to navigation, but the planets and comets were of little help. The false teachers could not be depended upon for guidance either. Whether Jude is alluding to the false teachers wandering from town to town, or whether he is describing them as vacillating in their teaching, all they did was mislead those who listened to them.

For whom the black darkness has been reserved forever -- With nearly the same words, Peter (2 Peter 2:17) declared the punishment God has in store for these false teachers. Jude used the same words before at verse 6 to speak of the intermediate state from which, following the final judgment, those confined therein will be cast into hell.[119] Christ Himself spoke of

---

[117] If we accept the conclusion the false teachers never were Christians, then this "second death" option is the one preferred.

[118] Jesus did speak of the necessity of "abiding in Him" if one wishes to bear fruit (John 15:5-8).

[119] People have used alleged conflicting descriptions of hell as a proof that "fire" is an image of judgment, rather than a description of what hell is like. For example, "the punishment of eternal fire" (Jude 7) is supposed to be contradictory to "black darkness" (Jude 13). The flaw in this argument is that the first term speaks of punishment *after* the final judgment, whereas the former speaks of punishment in the intermediate state *before* the final judgment. Other people have espoused the view that the wicked are not punished eternally but rather they are annihilated. Two helpful sources on this are William Crockett, ed., *Four Views of Hell* (Grand Rapids: Zondervan, 1992), and for a work against annihilationism see Moses Stuart, *Exegetical Essays on Several Words*

how the place of punishment had been prepared since the creation of the world (Matthew 25:41).

D. As Long Ago as Enoch, God Revealed He Would Punish the Ungodly. 1:14-16

1:14 -- ***And about these also Enoch,*** **in** ***the seventh*** **generation** ***from Adam, prophesied, saying, "Behold, the Lord came with many thousands of His holy ones,***

And about these also -- Having spoken in the previous verse about a punishment awaiting the false teachers of his day, Jude now documents his claim by reference to a prophecy made long ago by Enoch.[120] "Jude's use of the word *also* indicates Enoch's prophecy includes the fate of the false teachers of Jude's day as well as the fate of the ungodly who lived in Enoch's day."[121]

Enoch, *in* the seventh *generation* from Adam, prophesied -- There were two men named "Enoch" listed in the genealogies in Genesis 5:3-18 and 1 Chronicles 1:1-3, one a son of Seth in the third generation from Adam, and the other, the son of Jared, in the seventh generation. The "seventh from Adam" identifies the Enoch to which Jude is referring. When he wrote "the seventh from Adam" instead of "the son of Jared," this may be Jude's way of indicating the extreme antiquity to this prophecy. To "prophesy" means to speak by inspiration in the language of the people. Enoch is one of the prophets God used to speak to the people living in the Patriarchal Age (Hebrews 1:1). It appears that even that early in human history, men needed a warning about what happens to the ungodly, as well as a promise of the coming of the Lord for judgment. Hebrews 11:5,6 tells us Enoch was a man who was pleasing to God because of his faithfulness, and that he was transported directly into heaven rather than experiencing physical death as do other mortal men.

Saying, "Behold, the Lord came with many thousands of His holy ones -- Enoch prophesied about what Christians now call the second coming of Christ. "Came" is a prophetic past tense, common in prophetic language. The "holy ones"[122] may be angels (Matthew 25:31; 2 Thessalonians 1:7; Psalm 68:17; Deuteronomy 33:2) or the souls of the

---

Relating to Future Punishment (Rosemead, CA: Old Paths Book Club, 1954 reprint).

[120] How Jude could have known the words of Enoch which he quotes has been discussed in the Introductory Studies. Some have supposed Jude is using an *ad hominem* argument here -- that Enoch was a favorite with the Gnostics, and Jude uses the very words of one of their heroes to condemn them.

[121] Raymond C. Kelcy, *The Letters of Peter and Jude* (Austin, TX: R.B. Sweet, 1972), p.182.

[122] The KJV reads "saints." We commonly apply the name "saints" to redeemed people. However, the plural word in the Greek ("holy ones") can apply to all who are holy, angels as well as men.

redeemed (1 Thessalonians 4:14), or both (1 Thessalonians 3:13), who accompany Jesus as He returns to consummate earth's history and to judge all men. The "many thousand holy ones" (literally, "His Holy ten thousands," NASB mg.) are "His;" that is, they belong to Him, stand before His throne, and wait for His commands. False teachers are not "holy ones," so will not be included in the group who get to accompany Jesus as He comes again.

1:15 -- ***To execute judgment upon all, and to convict all the ungodly of their ungodly deeds which they have done in an ungodly way, and of all the harsh things which ungodly sinners have spoken against Him."***

To execute judgment upon all -- This continues Enoch's prophecy, telling what Jesus will do when He returns.[123] "To execute judgment" is a phrase found only here and in John 5:27. Men have known about a coming judgment,[124] with its rewards and punishments, as long ago as Enoch, the seventh from Adam.[125] "Judgment" speaks of a process of examining the evidence and making a resultant decision, then pronouncing the verdict upon those judged. "Upon all" indicates that none are exempt from the judgment, none will be accidentally overlooked.

And to convict all the ungodly of all their ungodly deeds which they have done in an ungodly way -- Being repeated four times, the words "all" and "ungodly"[126] are emphasized. Who will be "convicted" and of what they will be convicted have been plainly revealed. The Bible elsewhere speaks of men being judged for the deeds done in the body, whether good or bad. The verb "convict" implies an authoritative examination, unassailable proof, decisive judgment, and punitive power. It says sentence will be pronounced on the guilty as a result of the evidence of their guilt, and the sentence will be carried out.

And of all the harsh things which ungodly sinners have spoken against Him." – Elsewhere the Bible teaches men will be called into judgment for the words they speak, as well as for their deeds. They will be convicted and condemned because of words and deeds which

---

[123] It may not have been obvious to Old Testament people that the judgment occurs at the second coming, rather than the first coming, of the Lord. But New Testament references have helped us understand what the Old Testament prophets were saying (e.g., 2 Thessalonians 1:5-10; 2 Timothy 1:10).

[124] While some popular eschatological schemes have separate judgments for the righteous and the wicked, Enoch's language seems to picture one general judgment which occurs when Jesus returns accompanied by all his holy ones. Not only will the righteous be present at the judgment seat of Christ, but so will the wicked.

[125] Romans 1:32 indicates that Gentiles, without access to the Law of Moses, knew about the ordinance of God, and that those who practice the kinds of sins enumerated in verses 29-31 of that same chapter are "worthy of death." People in the Patriarchal Age once had a clear understanding of what God expected, but they "exchanged the truth of God for a lie" (Romans 1:25) and the world was soon engulfed in ignorance and sin because they had lost the knowledge of Jehovah.

[126] This word has been explained at Jude 4.

result from their lack of piety toward and fear of God. The adjective "harsh" or "repulsive" applied to words or speeches is not difficult to understand. One day, some people in Jesus' audience accused Him of uttering "difficult statements" (John 6:60). That is the railing speech like the false teachers used (Jude 8,10). It is the "harsh and evil" language Nabal used (1 Samuel 25:3). It is mocking things said against the Lord (2 Peter 3:3,4). In the Greek text, the words "ungodly sinners" stand at the end of the verse so that there is emphasis on them. "*Ungodly sinners*" – that is who Jesus will convict!

1:16 -- *These are grumblers, finding fault, following after their* own *lusts, they speak arrogantly, flattering people for the sake of* gaining an *advantage.*

These are grumblers -- The words in verse 16 are not part of Enoch's prophecy, but are Jude's way of showing the false teachers are "ungodly" men, the very kind who were warned by Enoch about the Lord's judgment against them. The Greek word *gogguzo* is onomatopoeic. "The word is used of the cooing of doves. It refers not to loud, outspoken dissatisfaction, but to an undertone muttering."[127] In 1 Corinthians 10:10 Paul uses the word to describe what the rebels in the wilderness did as they complained against God and Moses (cp. Exodus 15:24, 17:3; Numbers 14:29). "They were finding fault with God's plans and purposes and doings."[128] Or, as later Gnostics did, they were perhaps complaining about their soul's being imprisoned in a material body.

Finding fault -- Some older versions read "complainers." The Greek word is a compound made up of *memphomai* ("to find fault with") and *moira* ("a part, or lot, or circumstances"). The false teachers were constantly complaining of their lot, were discontented with and critical of their circumstances. Perhaps there is allusion to their grumbling against their superiors, especially in the congregations into which they had infiltrated. People who spend all their time trying to satisfy their lusts "can never be content, for (1) the means of gratifying them are not always present, and (2) the lusts are insatiable."[129]

Following after their *own* lusts -- Perhaps this clause declares the reason for their discontent. Or, perhaps this clause is another example of ungodly behavior. We have commented on the meaning of this language in 2 Peter 2:18. When a person disregards God and the needs of their fellow man, and gives unlimited indulgence to human appetites and passions, there results a life of dissoluteness, licentiousness, lasciviousness.

They speak arrogantly -- While pursuing such a course of life as "following their own lusts" describes, they are loud-mouthed boasters (cp. 2 Peter 2:18,19). They boast about them-

---

[127] Wuest, *op. cit.*, p.252.

[128] Barnes, *op. cit.*, p.401.

[129] Plummer, *op. cit.*, p.281.

selves. They boast about what they are doing. They boast about how good it is. They boast about how important their teachings are. And all these boasts are hot air spoken not so much to express their sincere inner convictions as to impress their listeners!

Flattering people for the sake of *getting an* advantage -- The Greek literally reads "honoring faces" or "they admire faces." It is a highly picturesque way of expressing their "open and unconcealed adulation of such people in the community to whom it might be of advantage to attach themselves."[130] They played favorites; they courted the rich and influential and prominent people in the community; they curried favor, because they hoped thereby to derive some benefit for themselves. "As the fear of God drives out the fear of men, so defiance of God tends to put man in His place, as the chief source of good or evil to his fellows."[131] Jude's condemnation implies such behavior is wrong. All such partiality or showing favoritism is flatly condemned in James 2:1-9.

III. EXHORTATIONS & INSTRUCTIONS TO BELIEVERS FACED WITH THE CHALLENGES TO THEIR FAITH POSED BY THE FALSE TEACHERS. 1:17-23

A. They Were to Pay Attention to the Words of Prophecy Concerning the Coming of Such False Teachers. 1:17-19

1:17 -- *But you, beloved, ought to remember the words that were spoken beforehand by the apostles of our Lord Jesus Christ,*

But you, beloved -- The emphatic "you" puts Jude's readers in sharpest contrast to the grumblers and fault-finders.[132] With "beloved" he again expresses either the Father's or his love for them (compare Jude 1 and 3). It is because they are "beloved" that Jude now addresses his words of counsel and guidance to them so they will not be deceived and ruined by the false teachers already in their midst. In this very important part of the letter, Jude points out three things he wants his readers to do as they "contend earnestly for the faith" (verse 3): (1) Pay careful attention to the words of the apostles who predicted the coming of the false teachers; (2) Maintain personal responsibility for keeping themselves in the love of God; (3) Rescue as many of their deceived brethren as they can.

---

[130] Salmond, *op. cit.*, p.13.

[131] Mayor, *op. cit.*, p.46.

[132] Letters like this were intended to be read out loud at the public assembly. We wonder if the false teachers were present when this public denunciation and condemnation was read. Christians, too, were present. We hope they responded positively to the exhortations we are about to hear.

Ought to remember the words that were spoken beforehand by the apostles of our Lord Jesus Christ -- One protection against false teachers is to know the word of God so well that it serves as a shield and insulation against anything that is false. When one knows the Word, he will not be carried about by every wind of false doctrine that blows his way. "From a human standpoint, these false teachers have 'secretly slipped in' (verse 4), but God knew all along they were coming."[133] He even tried to warn the Christians about them. Jude points in particular to prophetic messages[134] the apostles of Jesus Christ[135] had delivered. Whether the language of this verse and the next ("they were saying to you") points to evangelistic tours among the readers by some of the apostles (Peter among them[136]), or whether it points to already circulating apostolic writings[137] with which the readers were familiar, we cannot determine with certainty. By whichever way the readers became acquainted with the words of the apostles, likely the thing Jude wants them to remember is that those prophecies not only described what the false teachers would teach, but also described their character and lifestyle so it would be easy to recognize and avoid them when they appeared.

1:18 -- ***That they were saying to you, "In the last time there shall be mockers, following after their own ungodly lusts."***

That they were saying to you -- When Jude says "*they* were saying to you," he seems to indicate that he himself is not an apostle of Jesus.[138] He also tells us the warnings delivered by the apostles were many and often; "were saying" is an imperfect tense verb, indicating the predictions had been repeated over a period of time. With repeated sermons or epistles on this very topic, the apostles had tried to prepare their listeners to resist and defeat the false teachers when those ungodly men finally began to arrive on the scene. Jude now repeats the very heart of their predictions.

---

133 Moo, *op. cit.*, p.280.

134 The Greek is *hrema* ("a word or a message") and *proeiremenon* (from *pro*, "before" + *eipon*, "to say"). It is not possible to determine if Jude had oral messages or written books in mind. *Hrema* is used of Scripture.

135 See notes at 1 Peter 1:1 on apostles of Jesus Christ. There were 16 or 17 different men in the early days who were apostles of Jesus, some of them called by Jesus during His earthly ministry, and some called after His resurrection and ascension.

136 There must have been some reason for Jude to allude to James, his brother, in the opening of the letter. May we suppose that the brother of the Lord, who eventually became an apostle of Jesus (Galatians 1:19), has also preached in the communities where the readers of this letter lived? That might account for Jude's plural "apostles" if he has in mind orally-delivered messages with which the readers are familiar.

137 Those who understand Jude to be addressed to churches in Asia Minor look to the writings of Paul and Peter to supply us with these prophecies concerning the false teachers (e.g., Acts 20:29,30; 1 Timothy 4:1-5; 2 Timothy 3:1-9, 4:1-8; 2 Peter 3:2,15,16). It does not seem probable that 1 John 4:1ff would be in Jude's mind, for traditionally 1 John is not written until after Jude was.

138 It is not surprising many writers think Jude's language implies he himself was writing toward the close of the apostolic age. "The apostles of our Lord Jesus Christ" were a well-known group of leaders in the past.

"In the last time there shall be mockers, following after their own ungodly lusts" -- What catches our attention here is Jude's use of the word "mockers" to describe the false teachers. It is the very same unusual word that occurred in 2 Peter 3:3, and is one of the reasons we treat the relationship between 2 Peter and Jude as that of prophecy and fulfillment.[139] We infer from Jude's use of the word that the mockers were sneering at the idea of a second coming of Christ, just as Peter predicted the mockers would do. Jude's reminder about the mockers' "ungodly lusts"[140] being predicted reminds us of 2 Peter 2:2. "Ungodly" (as at verse 15) is the last word in the Greek. There is emphasis on it. "Last time" is an expression that covers the final dispensation, the whole church age, the final period of time which shall be ended when Christ returns.[141]

1:19 -- ***These are the ones who cause divisions, worldly-minded, devoid of the Spirit.***

These are the ones who cause divisions -- Just as he did in verses 12 and 16 – the Greek is exactly alike – Jude once more drives home the point that there can be no doubt the false teachers now present in the churches are the very ones about whom the apostles warned beforehand. In this verse, Jude uses his favorite pattern of triplets to characterize the infiltrators and thus drive the point home. The word *apodiorizontes* ("cause divisions") is an extremely rare word, used only here in the New Testament.[142] Perhaps Jude alludes to the fact that these men cause divisions within the congregations (especially at the love feasts, Jude 12). Perhaps Jude alludes to the fact already mentioned (verse 16) that these men attached themselves to the rich and influential members, ignoring those who obviously had nothing with which to enrich the greedy false teachers. Perhaps these men, like the Gnostics of a later generation, "divided Christians by classifying them into groups of initiates ('spiritual') and lesser ones ('natural' which translates *psuchikoi*) who may by strenuous effort qualify for salvation."[143] Jude would be countering their claim by affirming that if there were

---

[139] See the Introductory Studies on 2 Peter.

[140] The Greek is literally translated "desires of ungodlinesses," and is best understood as an objective genitive, indicating the things lusted after. The rendering "ungodly lusts" treats the phrase as being the way the Greek would handle a Hebraism, as at 2 Peter 2:1 ("heresies of destruction"). Jude, growing up in the Holy Land, may well have, at times, thought and spoken like a Hebrew.

[141] Compare notes on Peter's equivalent expression "the last days" in 2 Peter 3:3. See also 2 Timothy 3:1,2,6, 1 Peter 1:5,20, and Hebrews 1:2. It was a Hebrew idea that time is divided into two great periods: "this age" (Old Testament times) and "the age to come" (introduced by the coming of the long-promised Messiah). It is to totally misunderstand the words "the last times" to interpret them as though Jude mistakenly expected history to end shortly.

[142] The Textus Receptus adds "themselves" to the text here. Thus, the KJV reads "they separate themselves." Commentaries based on the KJV speak about how these men separate themselves from the church, an idea that would hardly be in agreement with Jude 12.

[143] Edwin A. Blum, "Jude" in *Expositor's Bible Commentary*, edited by F.C. Gaebelein (Grand Rapids: Eerdmans, 1981), p.394. Second century Gnostics claimed that, in contrast to ordinary Christians who were "natural," they themselves were enlightened and had become aware of that higher "spiritual" element in man.

elite spiritual persons, they were not to be found among the Gnostics! Perhaps the rare word should be translated "making definitions," which would allude to esoteric and unusual definitions for Biblical words, typical of many Gnostic-like cults,[144] by which they try to give their heretical teachings a Biblical veneer. Perhaps Jude is accusing them of founding heretical sects as they dupe willing listeners into following them.

Worldly-minded -- The Greek word is *psuchikos* (the root of which is *psuche*, "soul") for which we have no precisely equivalent English word. The same word is translated "natural man" at 1 Corinthians 2:14. The soul stands midway between the body and the spirit of a man, and is something a man shares in common with animals (Genesis 2:7,19; Psalm 78:50). Perhaps Jude is describing the individual who lives on the plane of the soul – a lower nature than that of spirit, though higher than that of the body; i.e., a man who lives according to no higher impulses than those by which "unreasoning animals" live (cp. verse 10). Since Jude's description here is pejorative, perhaps in this place "psychic" would be a good translation. It would then refer to altered states of consciousness into which the false teachers entered in order to get their visions and revelations from the spirit world. In this context, such behavior is indulged in by the "ungodly."

Devoid of the Spirit – Since *pneuma* here has no article in the Greek, perhaps it should be translated with a small "s" – "not having a spirit." Scriptures do seem to teach that when a man commits his first sin, the spirit part of him ceases to be able to function as God intended. Having died "spiritually," he lives as he is prompted by the desires of his body (he is fleshly or carnal) and soul (he is a natural or sensual man). Jude may be saying the false teachers are dead spiritually. They are "ungodly" because they have not been born again. Being without the guidance and direction of the spirit, their lives are sensual, earthly, devilish (James 3:15 ASV). If we read capital "s" (Spirit), we will have to give a different explanation to what Jude here says about the false teachers. When a man is born again, his spirit becomes alive[145] and he receives the gift of the Holy Spirit who indwells him and helps him live the Christian life.[146] Perhaps Jude is saying the false teachers don't even have the indwelling gift of the Holy Spirit, let alone any special gifts of the Spirit such as equipped men for service and credentialed the message they delivered.

---

[144] Compare the folk who explained away the doctrine of future resurrection of the body by saying "the resurrection has already occurred" (2 Timothy 2:18) when people "rose to walk in newness of life" (Romans 6:4). Compare the occult claim that their practice of clairvoyance is the same thing as Biblical visions seen by the prophets of God.

[145] John 3:6; Romans 8:10.

[146] Acts 2:38; Romans 8:13-17.

B. Personally, Each One was Responsible to Keep Himself (or Herself) in the Love of God. 1:20,21

1. By building themselves up on their most holy faith

1:20 -- ***But you, beloved, building yourselves up on your most holy faith; praying in the Holy Spirit;***

But you, beloved -- Verses 20 and 21 form one sentence in the Greek, the main verb of which is a command, "keep yourselves in the love of God." The rest of the sentence is made up of three participial phrases ("building," "praying," "waiting") which tell how one keeps one's self in the love of God. Once more Jude reminds his readers that he loves them and God loves them. They are in stark and vivid contrast ("you" is emphatic here exactly as it was in verse 17) to the false teachers.

Building yourselves up on your most holy faith -- This participial phrase expresses one of the conditions by which his readers could keep themselves in the love of God. "Faith" reminds us of "the faith once for all delivered to the saints" (verse 3). It is called "holy" because it comes to us from God, reveals God to us, tells us about God's "holy servant Jesus" (Acts 4:27,30), is the means by which men are set apart to sacred service, and calls for a lifestyle radically different from that exemplified by the ungodly false teachers. The "faith" has been set apart, sanctified, by God in a special way and for a holy purpose. "Most holy faith"[147] is surely contrasted to the unholy Gnostic teachings and practices the false teachers presented. 'Don't suppose you can keep yourselves in the love of God by building on Gnostic ideas,' is what Jude is saying. Only when our own personal faith is based on and in harmony with "the faith," is it a suitable place to do our spiritual building.

"*On* your most holy faith" is the foundation on which the Christians were to build.[148] That "holy faith" is already possessed by the readers; they do not have to go to the Gnostics to get something that was missing or left out when it was delivered to them by the apostles of Jesus (verse 3). Jude is saying they should start from where they are in their understanding and practice of what they learned from the apostles of Jesus and build on that![149] The metaphor of "building" is a common figure used to represent growth in Christianity (Matthew 7:24-27; 1 Corinthians 3:9-17; Ephesians 2:19-22; 1 Peter 2:5). "Building yourselves up"

---

147 "Most holy" is a superlative degree adjective in the Greek. There is nothing to compare to the "faith" once for all delivered to the saints.

148 There is no preposition in the Greek before the dative case "most holy faith." Some think "by" should be supplied, making this a dative of means, "by your most holy faith." We think the NASB translators were correct when they suggested "on" as the proper preposition, making this a dative of respect, indicating the respect in which something exists or is true.

149 We suppose that Acts 20:32 is a parallel passage that makes clear the Word of God is able to build a man up.

underlines the reader's personal responsibility (i.e., they were to act as moral and responsible agents) to oppose the influences and temptations presented by the false teachers.[150] There is more to contending earnestly for the faith (verse 3) than just opposition to what is false. There must also be growth in the understanding of Christian knowledge and in the practice of that which conforms thereto. Christians will have to fight the temptation to be satisfied with where they are in their spiritual lives. There is something devilish in an attitude which takes one's own spiritual condition for granted. 2 Peter 1:5-11 spoke of starting with your own personal "faith" and developing certain qualities of character as being the secret of remaining neither barren nor unfruitful. The present participle "building" indicates this is to be continuous action on their parts.

2. By praying in the Spirit

Praying in the Holy Spirit -- This is the second of three participial phrases in verses 20 and 21 that show how the readers can keep themselves in the love of God. "Praying" also is present tense, something Christians are to do constantly. "In the Holy Spirit" may be either a dative of sphere or a dative of agent.[151] If we treat it as agent, it says the Holy Spirit is the agent who motivates or empowers the Christian to pray.[152] If we treat it as sphere, it says believers are to pray "according to the Spirit's will (as set forth in the written Word and as made known by inner promptings) to accomplish God's work by God's power."[153] Ephesians 6:18 seems to refer to the same kind of prayer. Such true prayer would be unknown and totally foreign to the ungodly false teachers.

3. By waiting anxiously for the mercy to be received by the faithful when Jesus returns

[150] Jude's presentation of each reader's own personal responsibility reminds us of Philippians 2:12, "work out your salvation with fear and trembling."

[151] Our translators have taken "in the Holy Spirit" with praying, which makes this second participial phrase nicely balance the first one. However, it is possible to translate the verse as did Luther, "building yourselves up by (or on) faith, in the Holy Spirit, through prayer." If we interpret the verse in this manner, then Romans 8:12-17 explains how the indwelling Holy Spirit helps Christians to live consistent Christian lives. It takes the prompting of the Spirit, and prayer.

[152] Writers have looked for parallel passages to help explain what Jude has written. Some appeal to Romans 8:26, some to 1 Corinthians 14:15. We are not certain either of these passages is helpful. The Romans passage does say the Holy Spirit helps our weaknesses, causing us to yearn or sigh (a feeling or expression which God can read and understand), but the passage specifically says there are no words spoken. Jude seems to be indicating more than "groanings" or sighing as one habitually prays. In the NASB, the passage in 1 Corinthians is written (correctly we believe) with a small "s" -- "I shall pray with the spirit ...." It seems to refer, not to a prayer in language prompted by the Holy Spirit, but a prayer in which the believer's "spirit" actively participates. Jude's language is different; he is not speaking of "spirit" but of "Holy Spirit."

[153] Blum, *op. cit.*, p.395.

1:21 -- ***Keep yourselves in the love of God, waiting anxiously for the mercy of our Lord Jesus Christ to eternal life.***

Keep yourselves in the love of God -- This exhortation is the main clause of verses 20 and 21. Jude uses the same word for "keep" that he did in verse 1. Other Bible writers have also appealed to their readers to "keep themselves ..." (1 Timothy 5:22; James 1:27). The "love of God" in this context is doubtless God's love for man.[154] His love is pictured as a sphere within which faithful Christians bask and live. The three participles in verses 20 and 21 tell how the Christian keeps himself in that sphere where he can continue to enjoy God's love.[155] Jesus told the apostles how they could keep themselves in His love, just as He had remained in the Father's love (John 15:9,10). In the same way, for Jude's readers, abiding in the Father's love is conditional.

> In admonishing his readers to *keep* themselves in the love of God, human agency in salvation is thus clearly indicated by the inspired writer. While God provides the sphere of salvation -- His love -- it is man's function to keep himself, through faithfulness, in that sphere; and a failure to so do is to exclude one from the provisions of salvation.[156]

> God's protective love for His children is invulnerable to attack from outside forces (Romans 8:38,39). But Christians can so conduct themselves as to remove themselves from within the beneficent sphere of God's merciful provisions. The example of angels who 'did not keep their own position' (verse 6) is fresh in the minds of Jude's readers.[157]

Jude is anxious that his readers make sure their own spiritual position is secure. That is the first step when false teaching rears its ugly head. Once your own position is secure, then you can reach out to help others (verses 22,23).

Waiting anxiously for the mercy of our Lord Jesus Christ to eternal life -- This is the third participial phrase Jude used to explain how a person keeps himself or herself in the love of God. *Prosdechomai* ("waiting anxiously") is a present participle (as in Titus 2:13).[158] This confident anticipation of, this looking for, the coming of Christ is to be a habit of life.

---

[154] Some commentaries take the words to mean "love for God" as in 2 Thessalonians 3:5. While the Greek could speak of God's love for man, or man's love for God, the "love of God" appears to be in a sense parallel to what is said in the next clause about the "mercy of Christ." If "of Christ" is a subjective genitive, then so, it would seem, is "of God."

[155] The Scriptures say that we love God because He first loved us. It is also true that "God takes the initiative in salvation and in keeping His own (Jude 1), but in order for His initiative to be effective He must have the co-operation of man" responding in the positive way God has indicated He expects man to respond. Kelcy, *op. cit.* p.186.

[156] Woods, *op. cit.*, p.405.

[157] Kelcy, *ibid.*

[158] Peter uses a different word when he discusses the same idea mentioned by Jude, that of awaiting or looking

Hope can cause a man to change his behavior. If a man lives in constant expectation of the appearance of Christ in glory, he will be encouraged and motivated to keep himself in the love of God. "Eternal life" in this context refers to the future, joyous, blessed, heavenly aspects of the salvation Christians currently enjoy.

When we think of the final judgment, we typically think of God's justice and condemnation on the wicked, so Jude's unexpected emphasis on "mercy" being displayed at the second coming captures our attention. The "mercy" Christians are anticipating and keeping their attention fixed upon is the mercy Jesus Christ will show as Judge at the final judgment.[159] No man lives a sinless perfect life (1 John 1:8), so even the faithful Christian stands in need of mercy.[160] In mercy He will say to those on His right hand, "Come, you who are blessed of My Father, inherit the kingdom prepared for you from the foundation of the world" (Matthew 25:34). Those who have been faithful to Him will be the recipients of His mercy. When men stand in the final judgment, what a happy contrast awaits the Christian as compared to what Jude has warned about in this whole letter – namely, that those who have taught and behaved like the false teachers are doing will not be shown mercy. Each of the words – Lord, Jesus, Christ – has a certain anti-Gnostic ring. And Jude, who loves triplets, has referred to the three members of the Godhead as he wrote this exhortation to his beloved readers.

C. They Were to Exhibit Loving Compassion for Their Deceived Brethren. 1:22,23

1. On some, have mercy!

1:22 -- ***And have mercy on some, who are doubting;***

And -- The manuscripts have variant readings at verses 22 and 23 so diverse and so difficult to determine that "some of our best [textual] critics take this to be one of the passages in which

---

for the second coming of Christ (2 Peter 3:12). Jude does not use the word *parousia* as he writes this passage, but he clearly has that return of Christ in mind. Jude, like Peter, affirms what the mockers questioned: there will be a coming that God has promised, what the mockers say notwithstanding!

[159] "To eternal life" is a prepositional phrase (*eis* + the accusative), which interpreters have struggled to explain in this context. Of the three options (i.e., take "to eternal life" with either "keep yourselves" or with "anxiously waiting" or with "mercy"), the translators of the NASB have chosen to take it with "mercy." If we construe "eternal life" with "keep yourselves in the love of God," it means keep yourselves in the love of God and it will bring eternal life to you. Either of the other two options results in the same explanation of this participial phrase. Whereas Peter spoke of the mercy of God which made possible the *beginning* of the Christian life (1 Peter 1:3-7), Jude here emphasizes the mercy which *crowns* the Christian life, the mercy which leads to eternal life.

[160] Note, 1 John is an anti-Gnostic writing. The errorists he attacks, as he writes a few years later, evidently claimed they had no sins. Perhaps the Gnostics of Jude's day did too, and this verse is another refutation of their wrong claims.

we have to recognize a corruption of the primitive text, now past certain correction."[161] The first phrase of verse 22 varies between "have mercy on some" and "convict some." The second phrase varies between "who are doubting," "making a difference," "when they are contending with you," and "when they separate from you." There is also a question in the manuscripts as to whether there are two or three classes of persons designated in verses 22 and 23.[162] Our comments will explain the verses as they appear in the NASB, which has followed the text that has three classes of persons designated (three times we read "on some," "on some," "on some").

We would not be surprised if these two verses give another means by which Jude's readers are to "contend earnestly for the faith which was once and for all delivered to the saints." Not only do they have a responsibility for themselves (verses 20,21), they also need to be aware of, and reach out redemptively to meet, the needs of their brethren.[163]

Have mercy on some -- Jude turns his attention to his readers' responsibilities towards their brethren who have foolishly allowed themselves to be victimized by the false teachers.[164] The readings in the manuscripts vary here, some reading "mercy" (compassion) and some reading "convict" (refute). If we read "convict," what Jude is asking his readers to do as they attempt to salvage this first group of victims is to bring their sins home to them, or refute their errors (cp. Matthew 18:15; Titus 1:13). If we read "mercy," what Jude is asking is that the approach to the victims be tenderly affectionate and kind (cp. Galatians 6:1).

---

[161] Salmond, *op. cit.*, p.16. The epistle of Jude, or portions of it, are found in 3 papyri and 12 uncial manuscripts. From these copies the textual critics must try to determine what was in the autograph.

[162] According to Westcott and Hort, Hodges and Farstad, and Nestle's 25th edition, two groups were in view. According to the text printed in Nestle's 26th edition there are three groups in view. This same change from two groups to three can be seen in some of the latest editions of certain English versions -- such as RSV (two) and NRSV (three); Jerusalem Bible (two) and NJB (three); NEB (two) and REB (three). Sakae Kubo has defended the text that has three classes in "Jude 22-23: Two Division Form or Three? in *New Testament Criticism: Its Significance for Exegesis*, edited by Eldon J. Epp and Gordon D. Fee (Oxford: Clarendon, 1981), p.239-253. Jude's normal pattern of triplets leads us to find three groups here. But whether we read it as two groups or three, it should be stated such serious manuscript differences as occur at this place should not cause us to conclude that we cannot trust our Bibles, whether in the form of a critically reconstructed Greek text, or in the form of a translation into our native language. If all the verses on which there is any doubt concerning what was in the original autographs were put together, they would fill less than 1/2 of one page if the total text contained 1000 total pages. And whether we have two groups of persons or three, the general thrust of the passage ("Use discretion as you reach out to try to rescue them!") is the same.

[163] It seems obvious Jude is speaking of the victims of the false teachers. Jude apparently views the teachers themselves as incorrigible (verses 12, 13).

[164] Peter warned of an approaching storm of false teaching. Jude indicates the storm has now broken in all its fury. Christians have not fulfilled their responsibility if they simply batten down the hatches and attempt to ride out the storm. They must try to rescue those who are in peril on the sea. Jesus spoke this beatitude, "Blessed are the merciful, for they shall receive mercy" (Matthew 5:7). Jude's readers may expect to receive mercy at the Judgment (verse 21) if they will now show mercy toward their misled brethren (verses 22, 23).

Who are doubting -- If we accept "making a difference" (KJV) as the original reading here, Jude is asking his readers[165] to make a judgment about the spiritual state of the victims. Which are incorrigible and which are perhaps redeemable? If we accept "while they dispute with you" (ASV mg) as the original reading, Jude is saying "have mercy on (or refute) those misled church members (or false teachers) who contend or argue with you."[166] If we read "who are doubting," then Jude is telling his readers how to approach the least hopeless class in the hopes of winning them. This class of victims is "doubting" or "wavering" or "confused" because the teaching and example of the false teachers has caused them to be uncertain where they stand.[167] They are still trying to decide whether to follow the false teachers or not. This group is to be dealt with mercifully and kindly and patiently, as they are tenderly escorted away from the false teachers and back to the truth.

2. On some, snatching them out of the fire!

1:23 -- ***Save others, snatching them out of the fire; and on some have mercy with fear, hating even the garment polluted by the flesh.***

Save others, snatching them out of the fire -- As Jude's readers deal with their erring brethren in a manner called for by the condition of those in error, this second group will be treated differently from the first group (the ones "who are doubting"), because this second group has progressed further into the belief system taught by the false teachers. Strongly influenced by the false teachers, they are about to leave the faith they once embraced. It takes vigorous, firm, and decisive action to rescue someone from a fire. No patient talking, no time spent in reasoning and persuasion. You take ahold of them and, if it is in your power to do so, you get them out of danger.[168] The "fire" that threatens to burn this second group ultimately may well refer to eternal fire (verse 7). If this second group of believers continues on with their unquestioning and deliberate acceptance of what the false teachers are advocating (in spite of Scripture's warnings), they will spend eternity where we have already been told the false teachers will spend it.

---

[165] There is a manuscript difference as to the case of the participle. In some manuscripts the word is in the nominative case (*diakrinomenoi*); in some it is in the accusative case (*diakrinomenous*). If we read the nominative as the Textus Receptus and KJV do, it is something the readers are to do. If accusative, as Nestle[26] and NASB do, it is something the victims or the false teachers are doing.

[166] See Jude 9 for a similar use of *diakrino*. Those who accept this reading think the "disputers" are the false teachers rather than their converts, the worst of the different groups the Christians will encounter. 1 Timothy 5:20 and Titus 1:9 are then thought to teach Christians a similar behavior to that which Jude commands.

[167] For this use of *diakrino* see Matthew 21:21; Mark 11:22; Romans 4:20; and James 1:6.

[168] One writer uses the vivid picture of a person about to fall into a volcano. Some suppose the figure in Jude's mind is a rescue from a burning building. Others suppose he has Zechariah 3:2 in mind, which speaks of a "brand plucked from the fire." When you are trying to retrieve something from the fire, you don't keep your hand in the fire very long. If you do, you are in danger of being burned and losing your hand.

3. On some, have mercy with fear!

And on some have mercy with fear, hating even the garment polluted by the flesh -- Perhaps this third group of victims is the most hopeless,[169] yet attempts are to be made to rescue them from the beliefs and practices into which the false teachers have led them. They need pity or mercy because they have become contaminated.[170] This group appears to not only have accepted the false teachers' belief system but also are involved deeply in the polluting, licentious, immoral lifestyle those people encouraged.[171] This group will be the hardest to win back.[172] Perhaps what Jude instructs is that the readers are to demonstrate mercy because they themselves stand in awe of God (cp. 1 Peter 1:17); they know this is what God expects of them. Perhaps what Jude instructs the Christians to do is to try to rescue the victims by appeals adapted to produce fear in them.[173] Perhaps Jude instructs Christians themselves to "fear" lest while spending time with the sinners they are trying to win, they themselves become involved in the contagious, polluting sins of the body.[174] Those who attempt to rescue others are to take every precaution to preserve their own purity.[175]

---

[169] Some treat the third class as the best; others treat it as the worst and most hopeless. The addition of "with fear" and "hating even the garment polluted by the flesh" suggests this group is the worst.

[170] In the on-going struggle between conservatism and liberalism among the churches, this verse has been used by some middle-of-the-roaders to justify their position. Said one man, 'It is a matter of opinion how far we are to go in fellowshipping with unbelievers and false teachers in our effort to win them.' Did Jude write that we are to have "mercy" on them, or that we are to "convict" them (verse 22)? Did Jude write "have mercy" in verse 23, or is the KJV correct? Did Jude treat the false teachers (leaders) as hopeless, while giving instructions about trying to rescue their victims?

[171] Care should be exercised here lest "flesh" be taken to refer to an old sinful nature. The doctrine of hereditary total depravity is not a Biblical doctrine. See the Special Study on "The Doctrine of Original Sin" in the author's *New Testament Epistles: Romans* (Moberly, MO: Scripture Exposition Books, 1996), p.231ff.

[172] R.C.H. Lenski (*The Interpretation of the Epistles of St. Peter, St. John, and St. Jude* [Minneapolis: Augsburg, 1966], p.648), following Luther's lead, has suggested Jude means that faithful Christians are to do no more toward these than to show mercy in the sense of feeling pity for them. Christians do not even get close to this third class because of fear of contamination by their sins. What they do instead is simply sorrowfully avoid any company with these men. However, it seems more likely the "mercy" shown to the victims is more than mere feeling, but is instead an active, anxious interest in their rescue, if possible.

[173] It may not be the best motive to get a person to change his behavior, but "fear" – whether of ruin in this life or hell in the next – can be a useful motivation. This is what the KJV translators understood Jude's command to mean.

[174] This is how the translators of the NASB interpreted Jude's words to mean.

[175] "Garment" (*chiton*) usually denotes the tunic, the inner robe (or underclothes) worn next to the skin. Sometimes, however, it denotes the outer garment also. Jude's language may allude to a garment worn by a leper, thought to be infected (cp. Leviticus 13:47-52), or by someone who has the plague or a highly communicable disease. He may be alluding to the case mentioned in Leviticus 15:4,10,17. Or he may be alluding to the "filthy (the Hebrew word here means human excrement) garments" of Joshua, the high priest in Zechariah 3:3. In contrast, those who continue faithful to Jesus are "people who have not soiled their garments" (Revelation 3:4, 7:14). Whatever the word picture, note Jude says "*hating* even the garment polluted" -- don't touch even the clothing they had worn. We suppose this is a metaphor for not just the clothing they wear, but anything connected

CONCLUDING DOXOLOGY TO GOD. 1:24,25

A. His Assistance Keeping Faithful Men from Stumbling. 24a

1:24 -- ***Now to Him who is able to keep you from stumbling, and to make you stand in the presence of His glory blameless with great joy,***

Now to Him -- This doxology has been called one of the grandest in all the New Testament. The way the doxology reads in the KJV, it could be addressed to Jesus. But the way it reads in the NASB, it is addressed to the Father.[176] As it reads in the NASB, it calls attention to God's assistance in keeping faithful men from stumbling (verse 24a) and His actions to make them blameless at the judgment (verse 24b). It closes with an exhortation to give glory, majesty, dominion, and authority to Him through Jesus Christ (verse 25). A common feature of doxologies in the New Testament is that they pick up important themes covered in the letter. Jude's doxology is no different in this respect. Closing his letter with a doxology shows that Jude anticipated this letter would be read to assembled congregations of readers.

Who is able to keep you from stumbling -- Jude has said much about God's "keeping" in this letter, both in regard to the wicked (verses 6,13) and to the righteous (verses 1,24). Those readers who keep themselves in His love, God guards or protects from stumbling over the dangers (as written about in this letter) of being led away by the allurements and examples of the false teachers. God is able or powerful enough to do that! The Scriptures show that, for the faithful, God puts limitations on what the devil can do (Romans 8:1-3; Matthew 6:13) so that the faithful will not be tempted above what they are able to resist if they want to resist (1 Corinthians 10:13). With this divine aid, there is no reason, external to themselves, for the readers to stumble,[177] or to fail to keep themselves in the love of God.[178]

---

with the impure lifestyle of this third group. It gives greater emphasis to the need for "fear" as this group is dealt with.

[176] Jude's doxology is similar to the one Paul wrote in Romans 16:25-27. Romans has been in circulation for over 15 years before Jude was written, and Jude may well have seen Romans. But we need not accuse Jude of borrowing or paraphrasing Romans. Men of God, speaking on the same subject, may well use the same language, without borrowing or copying.

[177] What Jude promises is a protection against "stumbling" (not against "falling" as the KJV reads). There is a difference between stumbling and falling: stumbling is a step short of falling, a condition that could result in falling. The Greek here is *aptaistous* (from *ptaio*, "to stumble, to trip," + an *alpha*-privative which negates the rest of the word). It is used in classical Greek of a sure-footed horse that does not stumble, and of a good man who does not make moral stumbles.

[178] "The passage does not teach the impossibility of apostasy; it is not affirmed that God guards all whether they keep themselves in His love or not. On the contrary, only those who avail themselves of the means of escape provided (1 Corinthians 10:12,13) are thus protected." Woods, *op. cit.*, p.407. "If Christians stumble and fall, it will be due to their refusal to appropriate that which God so graciously offers and not due to any lack of ability or willingness on the part of God (cf. John 17:12,15; Romans 8:38,39; Ephesians 6:10-18)." Kelcy, *op. cit.*, p.189.

B. His Actions to Make them Blameless at the Judgment. 24b

And to make you stand in the presence of His glory blameless with great joy -- Jude has already called attention to the "judgment of the great day," and Scriptures elsewhere speak of the dead, small and great, standing before the great white throne, to be judged by the things written in the books, according to their deeds (Revelation 20:12). The "glory" of both Father and Son will be awesome.[179] On that decisive day, the "blameless" will be standing on His right hand and He will claim them as His own.[180] The saved are "blameless" (faultless, pure) – not because they were sinless perfect (for all have sinned), but because they have a Savior.[181] So if Jude's readers deliberately pursue a lifestyle like the one the false teachers were living, including a denial of Jesus as Lord and Master (verse 4), there is little chance they will be "without blemish." God doesn't forgive or justify the impenitent. It is not easy to decide whether the "great joy"[182] is what the Christians experience as they hear "Well done!" or whether it speaks of God's joy and delight to be able to grant eternal life (Matthew 25:21, 23).

C. Glory and Majesty to Given to Him Through Jesus Christ. 25

1:25 -- ***To the only God our Savior, through Jesus Christ our Lord,*** **be** ***glory, majesty, dominion and authority, before all time and now and forever. Amen.***

To the only God our Savior -- As Jude continues this doxology he designates God as the one of whom he speaks in the preceding verse.[183] Jude deliberately contradicts another Gnostic doctrine when he recognizes Jehovah as the "only" God (cp. John 5:44 and 1 Timothy 1:17).[184] He also describes God as "our Savior," and this too has an anti-Gnostic thrust to it.[185]

---

179 See Matthew 25:31; Luke 9:26; Titus 2:13; 1 Peter 1:7, 4:13, 5:1,4.

180 See Matthew 25:33; 2 Thessalonians 1:7,10; Revelation 3:21.

181 Ephesians 5:27; Colossians 1:22; 1 Thessalonians 3:13.

182 *Agalliaō* is onomatopoetic and denotes jubilation.

183 The way the verse reads in the KJV appears as though Jesus is here called "God." Not only that, the KJV calls Him "the only wise God." However, manuscript evidence requires that we omit the word "wise" and add the following clause "through Jesus Christ our Lord." Thus the doxology is addressed to God the Father. (We suppose some copyist, familiar with other well-known doxologies, like Romans 16:27, which reads "only wise God," might easily change the reading here to match what was familiar to his mind. The same manuscripts that add "wise" here in Jude also add it at 1 Timothy 1:17.)

184 Before "only God" is used to deny deity to Jesus, it should be remembered that in verse 4 Jesus was called "only Master and Lord." Jude is contradicting Gnostic ideas of a distinction between an inferior creator-God and an unknowable supreme God.

185 While the Scriptures commonly call Jesus "Savior" (e.g., Luke 2:11; Acts 5:31, 13:23; Ephesians 5:23; Philippians 3:20; 2 Timothy 1:10; Titus 1:4), the designation of God the Father as "Savior" is common in the letters to Timothy and Titus (1 Timothy 1:1, 2:3; Titus 1:3, 2:10, 3:4). There, just as here in Jude, the language is deliber-

Through Jesus Christ our Lord -- On the evidence of the earliest manuscripts we must add this phrase which does not occur in the KJV. *Dia* ("through") with the genitive indicates Jesus is pictured as being an intermediate agent between the one offering the doxology and the One who receives it. Jude includes himself among the readers by his use of the intimate pronouns "our ... our." For Jesus to serve as a person's mediator, He must be confessed and obeyed as "Lord" (Romans 10:9; Philippians 2:11). A person who repudiates the lordship of Jesus Christ (see verse 4) will have no mediator through whom to offer any doxology or word of praise to God the Father.[186]

***Be* glory, majesty, dominion and authority** -- If Jude's readers give God the glory, majesty, dominion, and authority He rightly deserves, there will be no problem for Him to keep them from stumbling (verse 24). "Glory" here might be synonymous with "praise," the largest possible ascription of praise to God.[187] "Majesty" speaks of the royal greatness of God; He is transcendent; He is the highest and most high God.[188] "Dominion" translates *kratos*, "power." It calls to mind the essential, immovable strength of the Divine Being, which faints not, neither grows weary.[189] It calls to mind "the sovereign freedom of action He enjoys as Creator"[190] to exert His control over the universe. It speaks of the absolute power of God which ensures His ultimate victory. "Authority" (*exousia*) says God has an intrinsic right to rule over all, and He has every right to expect our submission to His authority. Contrast this attitude with that of the false teachers who "rejected authority" (verse 8).

Before all time and now and forever -- Jude says these four qualities, which were ascribed to God back in eternity before the ages of time began, should be given to Him now in this time, and should be ascribed to Him to all the ages future (i.e., eternity, when time is no more).[191] God was worthy of being adored before time began. Perhaps "before all time" is an allusion to evil angels who were greatly in error when they rebelled before time began

---

ate, we believe, to contradict a Gnostic teaching. Gnostics tended to teach auto-salvation (a man saves himself), and this is manifestly contrary to Biblical teaching.

[186] Instead of thinking of Jesus' mediatorship, some would translate this clause "God who is our Savior through Jesus Christ." While this is barely possible, if this is what Jude intended we would have expected a dative participial clause (*to sosanti hemas*) rather than the noun *soteri*.

[187] "Glory" is a word with many shades of meaning and many connotations difficult to express in a few words. See Thayer, *op. cit.*, p.155,156.

[188] There is an anti-Gnostic ring to this term. Many Gnostics spoke of Jehovah as being a lesser god than the devil. Not so, says Jude.

[189] For "power" see 1 Timothy 6:16; 1 Peter 4:11, 5:11; Revelation 1:6, 5:13.

[190] W. Kelly, *Lectures on the Epistle of Jude* (London: Hammond, 1939 reprint), p.293.

[191] There is no verb in the Greek, as the word "be" in italics in the previous phrase indicates. In a sense, this doxology cannot be a prayer, since it would be difficult to pray for something in the past.

(verse 6).[192] God is worthy of being adored all the days of our lives. "Now" may be an allusion to the terrible errors of the false teachers at the present time, who, because they do not honor the Son, do not honor the Father (John 5:23). In contrast to what the false teachers are doing "now," Jude and his readers will continue to acknowledge His right to our adoration. God is worthy to be adored all through the ages to come after the salvation of His people has been completed.

> These ungodly men may "despise dominion, and speak evil of dignities," may utter "great swelling words" about their own knowledge and liberty, and scoff at those who walk not with them; but still, ages before they were born, and ages after they have ceased to be, glory, majesty, dominion, and power belong to Him who saves us, and would save even them, through Jesus Christ our Lord.[193]

In contrast to these evil ones, Jude pleads with his readers to continue to have the proper submissive attitude to God so as to offer Him – through the Lord Jesus Christ – the proper regard and praise and honor that are rightly His due. If they do it now, they will get to do it while the ages of eternity roll, after standing in the final judgment, and time is no more.

Amen -- On "Amen," see notes at 1 Peter 4:11. Having written all the above verses as he was moved by the Holy Spirit, Jude now adds his own hearty approval to the message he has just heard from God.[194]

Now that we have worked through the verses of this short letter, we have come to realize what a shame it is that this book has been so neglected. There are some valuable warnings, some moving exhortations, and some very precious promises to believers found in it. It is a shame for today's Christians to be unaware of them and unmoved by them.

We close this commentary on Jude (and on 1 and 2 Peter) with an expression of the same desire Jude expressed. **"To Him be glory, majesty, dominion, and authority ... both now and forever."** In all our affections and aspirations, may God be supreme! If while living in this world we continually practice offering our praise to God through Jesus Christ our Lord, we will be right at home when it comes time to cast every crown at His feet and say, **"You are worthy, O Lord, to receive glory, and honor, and power; for you created all things, and for your pleasure they are and were created. Hallelujah! Salvation and glory and honor and power unto the Lord our God!"**

---

[192] If glory and majesty were offered to God through Jesus back in eternity before time began, this language expresses clearly Jude's belief in the pre-existence and eternality of Jesus Christ. It was before creation was ever begun, when it was still in the planning stage, that Jesus volunteered to become the Savior if one were needed by the men who were about to be created. Perhaps the rebellion of the angels, even then, was a rebellion against "all authority" in heaven and earth being given to the Son.

[193] Plummer, *op. cit.*, p.286,287.

[194] Our Scriptural precedent for saying "Amen," when we approve of what is being sung or said, is 1 Corinthians 14:16.

SELECTED BIBLIOGRAPHY FOR 1 AND 2 PETER

Commentaries

Achtemeier, Paul J., *1 Peter*, in the HERMENEIA series. Minneapolis, MN: Fortress, 1996.

Intended for scholars who have kept up on their Greek. Little is given in the way of devotional or homiletical suggestions. In his 75-page introduction (including 744 notes), Achtemeier defends the idea that 1 Peter is a pseudonymous letter, written between AD 80 and 100 from Rome. It was addressed to mixed Jewish-Gentile congregations in Asia Minor whose members represent a broad spectrum of social and economic characteristics. Suffering is a prominent theme in the letter, and the persecution is not an official state persecution, but "unofficial harassment." The appropriation of the language of Israel to refer to the Christian community is no indication that the church has superseded the chosen people Israel. 1 Peter has its share of difficult passages to exegete. Achtemeier discusses the alternative interpretations concisely and indicates his preferred solution. He is hesitant to follow the currently popular view that many of Peter's verses reflect 1st century creedal or liturgical formulae. He does not find the instructions to wives and husbands in chapter 3 to be normative for today's church or home. The readiness to present a defense in 1 Peter 3:15 is seen as preparation to give account to informal demands of inquirers during daily social activities. Christ's preaching to the spirits in prison (1 Peter 3:18ff) is a proclamation to evil spirits of His victory over them. The "dead" of 4:6 are a different group -- Christians who died after hearing the Gospel. "Strangers" and "aliens" describe the Christian's relationship to their own hostile cultural environment. "Meddler" (1 Peter 4:15) is an embezzler. Achtemeier finds little value in using what linguists call verbal "aspect" and he has little in common with recent rhetorical methods of interpretation.

Alford, Henry, "The First Epistle General of Peter," "The Second Epistle General of Peter," and "Jude" in *Alford's Greek Testament.* London: Rivingtons, 1871. Vol.4. (A reprint edition is bound 4 volumes in two.)

A delightful tool for the student who knows Greek and who wishes to work through Peter's letters in the Greek text.

Barclay, William, *The Letters of James and Peter* in the DAILY STUDY BIBLE Series. Philadelphia: Westminster, 1961.

Barclay's notes are helpful for illustrations, for literary quotations, historical background materials, and for Greek word studies scattered throughout the book. Barclay, a Neo-liberal, must be read with care, for he denies miracles, rejects Peter's authorship of 2 Peter, and regularly attempts to explain away any supernatural intervention in men's lives. (The 1970s imprint of this series has American illustrations rather than English.)

Barnes, Albert, "James, Peter, John and Jude" in *Barnes' Notes on the New Testament.* Grand Rapids: Baker Book House, 1953.

His comments are often very lucid yet simple to understand. The author is faith-only, espouses original sin, and eternal security in the Calvinistic sense.

Barnett, Albert E., and Elmer G. Homrighausen, "The Second Epistle of Peter" in *The Interpreter's Bible*. New York: Abingdon, 1957. Vol.XII.

A treatment of 2 Peter from a liberal theological position. Introduction by Barnett, exposition by Homrighausen. The letter is treated as being Petrine in character and spirit, but not from the hand or dictation of Peter.

Bauckham, Richard J., *Jude, 2 Peter* in the WORD BIBLICAL COMMENTARY. Waco, TX: Word, 1983.

According to Bauckham, 2 Peter is pseudepigraphical and belongs to two literary genres, the epistle and the testament or farewell speech. (Bauckham claims that first century readers recognized such testaments as fictional literature that tried to prove a point. At the same time Bauckham admits that none of the other examples of the testament genre are entirely comparable with 2 Peter!) He says the author is an unknown Christian leader in the church at Rome, perhaps a member of a Petrine circle who considered Peter to be their most authoritative member, present and past. Bauckham even offers an attempt to make pseudonymity to be compatible with canonicity (p.161ff). Written about AD 80-90 (2 Peter 3:4 is a key verse to him for dating), the letter used most of Jude and is a polemical document directed against theologically unaware Christians who had compromised with ideas current in the pagan world around them. Interpretations which find the false teachers to be Gnostics are rejected. E. Kasemann, a few years previous, had insisted that 2 Peter was an example of an early catholic document, and Bauckham's commentary is intended to rehabilitate 2 Peter from this charge. Bauckham finds that hope of the *parousia* was not fading; he finds no increased institutionalization evidenced or appeal to ecclesiastical authority and interpretation, nor is there any evidence of a crystallization of the faith or insistence upon formal creedal orthodoxy. Bauckham's treatment of 2 Peter 1:16-21 is an interpretation all his own, ending with a denial of the inspiration of the Old Testament prophets.

Beare, F.W., *The First Epistle of Peter: The Greek Text with Introduction and Notes*. Oxford: Blackwell, 1947. Second edition with supplement, 1958. 3rd ed, 1970.

A liberal exegete who is often extreme. This is the first time the idea (now widely accepted) that 1 Peter is a pseudonymous work is presented in a commentary. He accepts the theory that the letter is a composite made up of a baptismal sermon and a warning about persecution. A good commentary to read if one would learn the modern problems of the book. Though Beare wrote for those who can read Greek, the reader who is without Greek can, with effort, generally understand the points being made.

Bengel, James A., "On the First Epistle of Peter" and "On the Second Epistle of Peter" in *Gnomon of the New Testament*. Edinburgh: T&T Clark, 1860. Vol.5. (Kregel reprint, 1971, in 2 volumes.)

Greek word studies. An old classic.

Bennett, W.H., "The General Epistles" in *The New Century Bible*. Edinburgh: T.C. & E.C. Jack, 1901.

A good, moderate commentary on the English text.

Best, Ernest, *1 Peter* in the NEW CENTURY BIBLE Series. London: Oliphants Ltd., 1971.
A liberal commentary. Denies the Petrine authorship, but does see the book as containing encouragement to Christians who are undergoing persecution. The reader must constantly beware of the author's liberal theological biases.

Bigg, Charles, *The Epistles of St. Peter and St. Jude* in THE INTERNATIONAL CRITICAL COMMENTARY Series. Edinburgh: T&T Clark, 1901. Reprinted many times.
The introductory studies are helpful and informative. Second Peter is dated after the close of the New Testament canon, and while looked upon as having practical value, is not regarded as authentic. For six decades, this was the definitive commentary on First Peter. This one is only for those readers who have expertise in Greek. Oriented to historical and grammatical issues.

Black, Allen, and Mark C. Black, *1 and 2 Peter*, in COLLEGE PRESS NIV COMMENTARY. Joplin, MO: College Press, 1998.
Intended for Sunday School teachers and serious Bible students. Comments are concise.

Blenkin, G.W., *The First Epistle General of Peter* in the CAMBRIDGE GREEK TESTAMENT. Cambridge: University Press, 1914.

Blum, Edward W., *1 and 2 Peter* in EXPOSITOR'S BIBLE COMMENTARY, edited by F.E. Gaebelein. Grand Rapids: Zondervan, 1981.
Solid exposition.

Brown, John, *Expository Discourses on 1 Peter*. Third Edition. Three Volumes. Edinburgh: Oliphants, 1886. Reprinted many times.
First published in 1848, this commentary has stood the test of time. Full and complete expository outlines. Three volumes in two.

Caffin, B.C., *The First Epistle General of Peter*, and *The Second Epistle General of Peter* in PULPIT COMMENTARY. Grand Rapids: Eerdmans, 1950.
This set of commentaries is one of the first to be studied when this present commentator begins an in-depth set of comments and explanations of any Bible book.

Caton, N.T., *A Commentary and an Exposition of the Epistles of James, Peter, John and Jude*. 1879. Reprinted. Delight, AR: Gospel Light, nd.
One of the old Restoration Reprint Library titles. Intended to help Sunday School teachers in their weekly preparation.

Cedar, P.A., *James, 1, 2 Peter, Jude* in COMMUNICATOR'S COMMENTARY. Waco, TX: Word Books, 1984. Vol.11.
Cedar, senior minister of Lake Avenue Congregational Church in Pasadena, CA, provides introductions, outlines, and exegetical-homiletic expositions of James through Jude. The topics treated include how to live with faith and works (James 2:1-26), what suffering is all about (1 Peter 4:12-19), encouragement to keep on following Jesus (2 Peter 1:1-21), and a strong warning against nominal Christianity (Jude 1-25).

Chase, F.H., "Peter, First Epistle of" and "Peter, Second Epistle of" in *Hasting's Dictionary of the Bible*. New York: Scribners, 1908. Vol.3.

Theologically liberal in its conclusions.

Clark, Gordon H., *II Peter. A Short Commentary*. Nutley, NJ: Presbyterian & and Reformed, 1972.

Strongly Calvinistic in emphasis.

Clowney, Edmund, *The Message of 1 Peter: The Way of the Cross* in THE BIBLE SPEAKS TODAY series. Downers Grove, IL: InterVarsity Press, 1988.

Based on the NIV, with footnotes giving more precise information and detailed explanation of the Greek text, the intent of this series is to provide expositions of Biblical texts that relate their meaning to contemporary life and are also written in a readable style. Clowney considers 1 Peter to be a "traveler's guide for Christian Pilgrims." A brief introduction informs the reader that 1 Peter is a "pastoral letter" written around AD 63 in Rome by the apostle Peter and addressed primarily to Gentile Christians scattered throughout the region of northern Asia Minor. Peter reminds these believers of the "true grace of God" that has provided for their salvation, has given them new birth in Christ, is sustaining them through their present sufferings, and will bring them to experience the glory of God fully. The result of Peter's work is a manual of instruction to believers about their social and political duties as members of the Christian church. Over and over again, Clowney appeals to Peter's experience as Jesus' disciple in Palestine. Clowney also demonstrates that Peter's theological concepts are similar to those of other New Testament writers. As for 1 Peter 3:18-22, after explaining three major interpretations of the passage, Clowney opts for Augustine's interpretation that "Christ's preaching was done in the Spirit through Noah." Clowney does from time to time reflect his theological commitment to the Reformed tradition, as for example, when it comes to baptism (to him it is an "outward sign of an inward grace").

Cook, F.C., *The First Epistle General of Peter* in volume 10 of THE BIBLE COMMENTARY, ed. by F.C. Cook. New York: Scribners, 1904.

Cranfield, C.E.B., *The First Epistle of Peter*. London: SCM Press, 1950.

Might be used for getting an overview of the epistle, but too brief for the expository preacher. Reflects influence of recent higher critical views.

Cullmann, Oscar, *Peter: Disciple, Apostle, Martyr*. London: SCM Press, 1953.

Dalton, William J., *Christ's Proclamation to the Spirits*. Second edition. Rome: Pontifical Biblical Institute, 1989.

This reprint of the 1965 edition reflects a significant change in the author's convictions. He no longer believes that the theme of "preached" in 3:19 relates to condemnation of evil spirits, but has human salvation in its sights. Perhaps his earlier treatment may be judged more satisfactory, though we are not in total harmony with it, either.

Davids, P.H., *The First Epistle of Peter* in THE NEW INTERNATIONAL COMMENTARY ON THE NEW TESTAMENT, edited by G.D. Fee. Grand Rapids, MI: Eerdmans, 1990.

Good exegesis of 1 Peter, and helpful introductory essays. (Petrine authorship is defended, as is a date of writing from the Neronian persecution. The letter is written from Rome. It is not a baptismal homily, but more likely [as Selwyn earlier argued] a catechetical training tool. Interacting with the issue of sources, Davids notes many citations and allusions to the Old Testament, and also to the teaching of Jesus.) Davids' essays on theology and "pastoral care" and on "suffering in 1 Peter and the New Testament" are especially useful for the expositor. The footnotes contain David's reaction with contemporary scholarship on disputed issues.

Davidson, Samuel, "Introductions to the First and Second Epistles of Peter and Jude" in *New Testament Introduction*. London: Bagster, 1851.

Elliott, John H., *A Home for the Homeless: A Social-Scientific Criticism of 1 Peter, Its Situation and Strategy*. Minneapolis: Fortress, 1990.

One of the newer tools the critics are trying to use to "explain" the Bible is social-scientific criticism. The social context of Asia Minor is examined. Its study of "aliens and strangers" is given a societal twist in keeping with the general thrust of the volume. Elliott has 1 Peter written from Rome by the Petrine circle who were expressing concern for their brethren in Asia.

-----, "Peter, First Epistle of" and "Peter, Second Epistle of" in *Abingdon Bible Dictionary*. New York: Doubleday, 1992. Vol.5, p.282-287.

Social science critical handling of Peter's letters.

Fronmüller, G.F.C., "The Epistles General of Peter," in *Lange's Commentary: Critical, Doctrinal and Homiletical*. Grand Rapids: Zondervan, nd. With additions by J. Isidor Mombert.

One of the better older English commentaries. A mass of material of both practical and homiletical nature. Tends to reflect Lutheran views.

Goppelt, L.A., *A Commentary on 1 Peter*, translated by J.E. Alsup. Grand Rapids, MI: Eerdmans, 1993.

The beginning of attempts to use social science criticism as a tool to interpret 1 Peter, he tries to identify the social dimension of the reader's needs as a major item. His thesis is that the letter addresses systematically and thematically the matter of Christian alien residence within the structure of contemporary society that is not Christian. He has the letter written from Rome between AD 65 and 80. Christians were facing growing persecution, not from the police (cf. Kelly) or the state (cf. Beare), but from non-Christian neighbors. Occasionally it relates items in 1 Peter to discoveries in the Dead Sea Scrolls.

Green, E.M.B., *2 Peter Reconsidered*. London: Tyndale, 1961.

Outstanding defense of the Petrine authorship of 2 Peter.

-----, *The Second Epistle General of Peter and the General Epistle of Jude. An Introduction and Commentary*. Grand Rapids: Eerdmans, 1968. (Second edition, 1987.)

The second edition is based on the NIV. Handles the problems of textual criticism and the problems of authorship with rare ability. An English Anglican conservative, he has produced a detailed exegesis and application to present needs. The excellent defense of the Petrine authorship of 2 Peter found in his earlier volume (*2 Peter Reconsidered*) is repeated.

Grudem, W.A., *The First Epistle of Peter. An Introduction and Commentary* in TYNDALE NEW TESTAMENT COMMENTARIES. Grand Rapids: Eerdmans, 1988.

The 23-page introduction to 1 Peter deals with author (Peter the apostle: "by Silvanus" at 5:12 means Silvanus was the bearer of the letter, not an amanuensis), place of writing (Rome), date (between AD 62 and 64), destination and readers, purpose, nature and possible sources (it is not a baptismal sermon, nor is there any literary dependence on other New Testament writings), and prominent themes. He outlines the book in two major points: the greatness of your salvation (1:3-2:10), and specific ethical teachings -- how to be holy in the midst of unbelievers (2:11-5:11). A 37-page appendix discusses Christ preaching to the spirits through Noah (1 Peter 3:19-20) in the light of dominant themes in Jewish literature.

Guthrie, Donald, *New Testament Introduction*. Vol.3. London: Tyndale, 1964.

Pages 95-136 cover 1 Peter. Pages 137-185 cover 2 Peter. Pages 226-250 cover Jude.

Hart, J.H.A., "The First Epistle General of Peter" in *The Expositor's Greek Testament*, edited by W. Robertson Nicoll. Grand Rapids: Eerdmans, 1956 reprint.

Defends the Petrine authorship and dates the letter at AD 64. Cites rabbinical sources while giving technical information and Greek word studies.

Hiebert, D. Edmond, *An Introduction to the New Testament*. Vol.3 (The Non-Pauline Epistles and Revelation). Revised and enlarged edition. Chicago: Moody Press, 1977.

In addition to covering the standard introductory matters, Hiebert also includes a bibliography of commentaries on each book. Conservative in outlook.

-----, *First Peter*. Chicago: Moody Press, 1984.

This commentary is based on the ASV. In his 20-page introduction to 1 Peter, Hiebert concludes that the letter was written by Peter from Rome in AD 64. After discussing its title and presenting a 6-page outline of contents, he offers expositions of its seventeen pericopes: opening salutation (1:1-2), thanksgiving for our salvation (1:3-12), Christian life in relation to God (1:13-21), etc. Hiebert has incorporated material from his articles which originally appeared in *Bibliotheca Sacra* and *Studia Missionalia*.

-----, *Second Peter and Jude: An Expositional Commentary*. Greenville, SC: Unusual Publications, 1989.

A scholarly defense of the Petrine authorship of 2 Peter, and dates Jude after 2 Peter. Explains the nuances of the Greek text, with the Greek words transliterated.

Hillyer, N., *1 and 2 Peter, Jude* in NEW INTERNATIONAL BIBLE COMMENTARY 16. Peabody, MA: Hendricksen, 1992.

Hillyer contends there are no irrefutable reasons for rejecting the claims of the letters themselves to have been written by the apostle Peter, and by Jude, the brother of James who was also a brother of Jesus.

Hort, F.J.A., *The First Epistle of St. Peter*. London: Macmillan, 1898. Reprinted Grand Rapids: Eerdmans, 1956.

A critical and exegetical study of 1 Peter 1:1 to 2:17.

Hunter, Archibald M., and Elmer G. Homrighausen, "The First Epistle of Peter" in *The Interpreter's Bible*. New York: Abingdon, 1956. Vol. XII.

A treatment of 1 Peter from a liberal theological position. Introduction by Hunter, exposition by Homrighausen.

Huther, Joh. Ed., *Critical and Exegetical Handbook to the General Epistles of James, Peter, John, and Jude* in MEYER'S COMMENTARY ON THE NEW TESTAMENT. Winona Lake, IN: Alpha Publications, 1979. Vol.10. (Reprint of 1883 edition).

James, M.R., "The Second Epistle General of Peter and the General Epistle of Jude" in *Cambridge Greek Testament for Schools and Colleges*. Cambridge: University Press, 1912.

Kelcy, Raymond C., *The Letters of Peter and Jude* in LIVING WORD COMMENTARY. Austin, TX: R.B. Sweet Co., 1972.

This commentary is based on the RSV. The introductory studies are well outlined and generally satisfactory, though one might wish for more specific statements on the authorship of 2 Peter and the dates of both Petrine letters. This is a good text to use, since it gives the reader a good preview and introduction to the two letters of Peter.

Kelly, J.N.D., *A Commentary on the Epistles of Peter and Jude* in HARPER NEW TESTAMENT COMMENTARIES Series. New York: Harper and Row, 1969.

Does not adhere to the Petrine authorship of 2 Peter. Kelly was influenced to some degree by the baptismal theory of 1 Peter's origins and (as one might expect from a patristics specialist like Kelly) often finds tantalizing parallels in early Christian writings and Qumran literature.

Kelly, William, *The Epistles of Peter*. London: C. A. Hammond, reprint, nd.

A Plymouth Brethren scholar, Kelly handles even the difficult passages in a clear manner. He had finished notes up to 2 Peter 3:7 before his death.

-----, *The Preaching to the Spirits in Prison. 1 Peter 3:18-20*. Denver: Wilson Foundation, 1970. Reprint.

Kistemaker, Simon J., *Exposition of the Epistles of Peter and the Epistle of Jude* in NEW TESTAMENT COMMENTARY series. Grand Rapids: Baker, 1987.

This commentary is based on the NIV. It tends to emphasize matters that are of interest to Reformed theology (foreknowledge, election, eternal security) more than it emphasizes what Peter himself had to say. It does have useful paragraphs on Greek constructions and word meanings at the close of each section. The conclusions reached in the introductory studies are in harmony with conservative views on the Scripture.

Kruger, Michael J., "The Authenticity of 2 Peter," *Journal of the Evangelical Theological Society* 42:2 (Dec. 1999), p. 645-671.

A vigorous reply to contemporary scholarship's arguments for the pseudonymity of 2 Peter.

Leighton, Robert, *A Practical Commentary Upon the First Epistle General of Peter.* Grand Rapids: Kregel, 1972.

One of the better older expository works on 1 Peter. Devotional in nature, Anglican in theology. First printed in 1853.

Lenski, R.C.H., *The Interpretation of the Epistles of St. Peter, St. John, and St. Jude.* Minneapolis: Augsburg Publishing House, 1966.

A thorough exposition by a conservative scholar in the Lutheran tradition.

Lillie, John, *Lectures on the First and Second Epistles of Peter.* Minneapolis: Klock and Klock, 1978. (Reprint of an 1869 edition)

A classical as well as a Biblical scholar, Lillie's notes are an enduring example of the care with which critical research and exegetical work was done in the mid-nineteenth century. There is regard for the truth and accuracy of the text; to Lillie, every word was significant. On the passage about baptism, he tells us that baptism is "a Divine institution, whereby God ordinarily dispenses His grace." The Petrine epistles abound with well-known "difficult" passages, and Lillie never evades them (though we may not always agree with his explanations).

Lumby, J. Rawson, "The First Epistle of St. Peter" in *The Expositor's Bible*, edited by W. Robertson Nicoll. Grand Rapids: Eerdmans, 1947.

Conservative treatment, with homiletical usefulness.

-----, "The Second Epistle General of Peter" in volume 10 of *The Bible Commentary*, edited by F.C. Cook. New York: Scribners, 1904.

Luther, Martin, *Commentary on the Epistles of Peter and Jude.* Grand Rapids, MI: Kregel Publications, 1982.

First published in the German language in 1523, this is one of Luther's better writings. Luther deals hard with sin, and shows the way of salvation through Christ, plus an emphasis with practical advice for how a Christian may grow spiritually. In a stirring way, Luther presents the eternal hope of the believer with a reminder that he is but a pilgrim and stranger here on his way to an eternal rest with the Lord. Paul W. Bennehoff, editor of this printing, combines Luther's 1523 and 1539 editions. The 1539 edition had supplementary notes by George Roerer and an analysis of each chapter by J.G. Walsh. The commentary is hard to use because Luther did not make a distinction between an explanation of the text and theologizing for his churches.

Marshall, I. Howard, "1 Peter" in *InterVarsity Press NT Commentary*, ed. by G. R. Osborne. Downers Grove, IL: InterVarsity, 1991.

A readable commentary that both explains 1 Peter and applies it to our world. Marshall is one of the best evangelical scholars in Great Britain.

Martin, R.P., "Peter, First Epistle of" in the *New International Standard Bible Encyclopedia*, edited by G. W. Bromiley. Grand Rapids: Eerdmans, 1986. Vol.3, p.807-815.

Mason, A.J., "The First Epistle of Peter" in *Ellicott's Commentary on the Whole Bible*. Grand Rapids: Zondervan, 1959.

This set of commentaries is also one of the first this present commentator checks when wanting to know in depth what one of the New Testament letters likely means. It has a number of notes based on the Greek text, including the meaning of words and the impact of verb tenses. The handling of the difficult passages in 1 Peter 3:19ff and 4:6 deserves attention, as well as the introductory studies.

Mayor, Joseph B., *The Epistle of St. Jude and the Second Epistle of St. Peter*. Grand Rapids: Baker Book House, 1965. (Originally published in 1907.)

Denies the Petrine authorship of 2 Peter, but is inclined to accept its canonicity. Also holds to the priority of Jude before 2 Peter. Should be read on this topic along with Ellicott's Commentary, which holds the priority of 2 Peter.

McKnight, Scot, "1 Peter" in *The NIV Application Commentary*. Grand Rapids, MI: Zondervan, 1996.

After briefly listing the major views on introductory matters, with their pros and cons, McKnight opts for the Petrine authorship, and dates the writing at the time of Nero's persecution. He offers a three point outline for the letter -- exhortations based on salvation, on social groups, and on the church. He offers three views for 1 Peter 3:18ff (the descent into hell, the pre-existent Christ, and the triumphal proclamation by Christ), and shows how each can be made to fit the overall theme of the book, and then opts for the third view. The "dead" in 4:6 are Christians who have died after they heard and obeyed the gospel. Typical of the NIV Application volumes, comments on each paragraph of text deal with original meaning, bridging contexts, and contemporary significance (which is useful for ideas and applications for contemporary preaching).

McNab, Andrew, "The General Epistles of Peter" in *The New Bible Commentary*, edited by F. Davidson. Grand Rapids: Eerdmans, 1953.

Michaels, J. Ramsey, "1 Peter", in *Dictionary of the Later New Testament and its Development*, ed. by Ralph Martin and Peter Davids. Downers Grove, IL: InterVarsity, 1997. p.914-922.

A presentation of and defense of social scientific criticism of 1 Peter.

-----, "1 Peter" in the *Word Biblical Commentary* series. Waco, TX: Word Books, 1988.

Conservative Bible students will not be encouraged by the conclusions reached by this commentary on 1 Peter. He thinks "the living Peter was personally responsible for the letter as it stands," though Michaels dates the letter as late as AD 70 or 80 (arguing that the tradition of a lengthy residence of Peter in Rome is hard to reconcile with the common belief that Peter died in the Neronian persecution: the early evidence for the martyrdom of Peter is more ambiguous than is generally assumed). Michaels does hold the integrity of the letter, rejecting the modern scholarly notion that 1 Peter 4:12ff reflects a different situation from that implied by what precedes it. He describes the letter as an all-purpose circular letter to a number of distant congregations largely unknown by the author, who assumes that some of them, like his own, have elders and that others do not, and thinks that, wherever there are authority structures based on seniority, it is helpful to appeal to them and build on them. Michaels thinks the audience addressed is predominantly Gentile Christian, though the writer has chosen to address these Gentiles "as if they were Jews." To Michaels, this identification of Christians with Israel (which is a characteristic of Peter) is something quite distinct from the Judaizing which Paul opposes in Galatians, and also from the theory of the displacement of the Jews as the people of God. (Both these conclusions, plus Michael's efforts to play to the modern feminism movement's audience [p.83], is perplexing.) The most useful feature conservative scholars will find in this volume (as indeed in all the WBC series) is the exhaustive bibliographical references; e.g., nearly 50 modern commentaries are listed in the main bibliography, all but two from this century. Some have designated this volume as the best scholarly commentary available on 1 Peter today.

-----, "Peter, Second Epistle of" in the *New International Standard Bible Encyclopedia*, edited by G.W. Bromiley. Grand Rapids: Eerdmans, 1986. Vol.3, p.815-819.

Moffatt, James, "The General Epistles" in *The Moffatt New Testament Commentaries*. New York: Harper, 1928.

The author is theologically liberal (he rejects the traditional authorship of James, 2 Peter and Jude, etc.), and the reader must beware of his modernistic presuppositions. Still, it is a good historical and exegetical help. Based on Moffatt's Bible translation.

Moo, Douglas J., "2 Peter and Jude," in *The NIV Application Commentary*. Grand Rapids, MI: Zondervan, 1996.

In the introductory studies, Moo tackles the usual problems (i.e., the relation of 2 Peter to Jude -- did Peter copy Jude, did Jude copy Peter, did Peter and Jude make use of a common [but now lost] document, or did they use common oral tradition) and comes to no conclusion on who "redacted" whom. He does opt for the Petrine (not pseudonymous) authorship for 2 Peter. He dates Jude after 2 Peter. He indicates that we cannot be sure who the false teachers were that Peter and Jude write about. Typical of the NIV Application volumes, comments on each paragraph of text deal with original meaning, bridging contexts, and contemporary significance (which is useful for ideas and applications for contemporary preaching).

Morehead, William G., "Peter, First Epistle to" and "Peter, Second Epistle to" in *International Standard Bible Encyclopedia*, edited by James Orr. Grand Rapids: Eerdmans, 1949. Vol.4, p.2351-2358.

Mounce, Robert H., *Born Anew to a Living Hope: A Commentary on 1 and 2 Peter*. Grand Rapids: Eerdmans, 1982.

"These epistles are indispensable antidotes to two chronic ailments which threaten the church. 1 Peter is a prescription to face suffering, while 2 Peter is medicine to stave off heresy." Mounce sees the keynote of the letters as hope, but the main purpose is hortatory -- that is, they were written "to encourage believers in Asia Minor to expect and endure hardship as a result of their commitment to the Christian faith" and "to stimulate them to wholesome thinking" *vis-a-vis* false teachers who had risen within the church itself. The purpose of the doctrine taught in each of the letters is to provide the theological basis for the exhortations Peter has to offer.

Neyrey, Jerome H., *2 Peter, Jude: A New Translation with Introduction and Commentary* in the ANCHOR BIBLE series. New York: Doubleday, 1993.

This recent English-language technical commentary incorporates social-critical and literary approaches as it tries to "explain" the text for modern readers.

Oberst, Bruce, *Letters from Peter* in the BIBLE STUDY TEXTBOOK series. Joplin, MO: College Press, 1962.

Intended for use by Bible students making their own personal study of the books, one of the strong features of this series is the set of questions included with each chapter, which will help the reader recall the important points in the text and commentary. The series is very useful for preparation for mid-week lessons, or even Bible School lessons.

Paine, Stephen W., "The Second Epistle of Peter" in *The Wycliffe Bible Commentary.* Edited by Charles F. Pfeiffer and Everett F. Harrison. Chicago: Moody Press, 1962.

Patterson, Paige, *A Pilgrim Priesthood: An Exposition of the Epistle of First Peter.* Nashville: Thomas Nelson, 1982.

Written in easy-to-read sentences, the author does pay careful attention to the Greek words (transliterated) and what they picture. The first sentence on each verse usually explains how this new verse contributes to the flow of the thought. One may even find help with wording the points of a sermon or lesson outline (e.g., "Earlier verses have noted the enemies of the soul and the equanimity of the sufferer. The final verses of the chapter focus on the example of the Savior.")

Payne, David F., "The Second Letter of Peter" in *The International Bible Commentary,* Revised edition ed. by F.F. Bruce. Grand Rapids: Zondervan, 1986.

Brief introduction. Concise notes.

Plummer, Alfred, "The Second Epistle of Peter" in *Ellicott's Commentary on the Whole Bible.* Grand Rapids: Zondervan, 1959.

An able defense of the genuineness of 2 Peter, with excellent comments on the verses. Has a number of notes based on the Greek text, including the meaning of words and the impact of verb tenses.

Plumptre, E.H. "The General Epistles of St. Peter & St. Jude" in the *Cambridge Bible for Schools and Colleges.* Cambridge: University Press, 1893.

For the lay student, written from a conservative standpoint. Valuable introductions to the epistles, and concise comments on the text.

Polkinghorne, G.J., "The First Letter of Peter" in *The International Bible Commentary.* Revised edition ed. by F.F. Bruce. Grand Rapids: Zondervan, 1986.

Brief introduction. Concise comments.

Reicke, Bo, "The Epistles of James, Peter, and Jude" in the *Anchor Bible Commentary*. Garden City, NY: Doubleday, 1964.

Robertson, A.T., "The First Epistle General of Peter" and "The Second Epistle General of Peter" in *Word Pictures in the New Testament*. Nashville: Broadman Press, 1933.

Robertson is typically Baptist in his handling of 1 Peter 3:19ff, insisting that baptism only symbolically saves. Still, his introductory studies and his comments on key Greek words and phrases are always interesting and instructive.

Salmon, George, "The First Epistle of Peter" and "The Second Epistle of Peter" in *A Historical Introduction to the Study of the Books of the New Testament*. New York: E. and J.B. Young, 1889. 4th ed. p.475ff (1 Peter), p.529ff (2 Peter).

Selwyn, E.G., *The First Epistle of St. Peter*. London: Macmillan, 2nd ed. 1946.

A work which is regarded by many as the finest treatment of the Greek text extant. And for years, this was the only serious commentary in English -- though it has now been somewhat pushed aside by Michaels and Goppelt. The essays in Selwyn are permanently useful. Supports the Petrine authorship with Silvanus having an influence on the Greek text.

Senior, D., "1 and 2 Peter" in *New Testament Message 20*. Wilmington, DE: Michael Glazier, 1980.

The hand of an historical critic is everywhere in view: e.g., the non-Petrine authorship of 1 Peter and the non-martyrdom situation of the readers addressed. The approach, as is typical of this series, is pastoral. Relevance for Christian living is insisted upon throughout. Has a running glossary of key Biblical terms. In the short introduction, the importance of 1-2 Peter as a witness to the tradition surrounding Peter after his death is emphasized, as is the letters' insistence that Christians have a strong sense of the future.

Stibbs, Alan M., "The First Epistle General of Peter" in the *Tyndale Bible Commentaries* Series. Grand Rapids: Eerdmans, 1959.

The excellent introductory studies are written by Arthur F. Walls. Both men's works are representative of the finest in British evangelical scholarship.

Strachan, R.H., "The Second Epistle General of Peter" in *The Expositor's Greek Testament*. Grand Rapids: Eerdmans, 1967.

Rejects the Petrine authorship, dating the epistle about AD 110-115.

Summers, Ray, "1 Peter and 2 Peter" in *The Broadman Bible Commentary*, edited by C.J. Allen. Nashville: Broadman, 1972.

Thiessen, Henry C., *Introduction to the New Testament*. Grand Rapids: Eerdmans, 1954. p.279-292.

Van Elderen, B., "Peter, First Epistle" in *Zondervan Pictorial Encyclopedia of the Bible.* Grand Rapids: Zondervan, 1975. Vol.4, p.723-726.

Wheaton, David H., "2 Peter" in *The New Bible Commentary, Revised.* Edited by D. Guthrie and J.A. Motyer. Downers Grove, IL: InterVarsity, 1970.

White, W., "Peter, Second Epistle of" in *Zondervan Pictorial Encyclopedia of the Bible.* Grand Rapids: Zondervan, 1975. Vol.4, p.726-732.

Williams, N.M., "Commentary on the Epistles of Peter" in *An American Commentary.* Philadelphia: American Baptist Publication Society, 1888.

Woods, Guy N., *A Commentary on the New Testament Epistles of Peter, John and Jude.* Nashville: Gospel Advocate Co., 1958.

A Church of Christ preacher has produced this commentary, intended for Sunday School teachers. Uses the ASV text.

Wuest, Kenneth S., *First Peter in the Greek New Testament.* Grand Rapids: Eerdmans, 1942.

This book is a simplified Greek commentary, intended for the student who is not acquainted with Greek. It is flawed in that at times the author inserts a Calvinistic bias into his comments on the meanings of Greek words. Still, it is a useful work to consult when working through 1 Peter.

-----, *In These Last Days. II Peter, I, II, III John, and Jude in the Greek New Testament for the English Reader.* Grand Rapids: Eerdmans, 1954.

A simplified commentary on the Greek text, intended to help the English reader by means of exegetical comments, word studies, and expanded translations. Tends at times to reflect Calvinism and modern pre-millennialism.

Zahn, Theo.H., *Introduction to the New Testament.* Grand Rapids: Kregel, 1953. Vol.2, p.134-292.

Sermon and Lesson Outline Ideas

Bible students should be saving their yearly bound issues of Sunday School lessons, such as *Standard Lesson Commentary* and *Peloubet's Select Notes*, for in these will be found explanations of the text, outlines, illustrations, and applications, that will greatly reduce the time needed to prepare a sermon, once a personally-produced commentary on 1 and 2 Peter has been completed.

Adams, Jay E., *Trust and Obey: A Practical Commentary on First Peter*. Phillipsburg, NJ: Presbyterian and Reformed, 1978.

Containing exegetical and explanatory notes together with applicatory helps for preaching and counseling. There are 24 sections of exegetical notes, each followed with a sermon outline based on that section.

Caffin, B.C., "First Peter" and "Second Peter" in *Pulpit Commentary*. Grand Rapids: Eerdmans, 1950.

Pulpit Commentary offers multiple sermon outlines by several great preachers of the past.

Criswell, W.A., *Expository Sermons on the Epistles of Peter*. Grand Rapids: Zondervan, 1976.

27 sermons based on 1 and 2 Peter.

Faust, David, *Faith Under Fire*. Joplin, MO: College Press, 2002.

13 studies on 1 and 2 Peter that would lend themselves either to lessons or sermons. Includes questions for further discussion.

Fickett, Harold L., *Peter's Principles*. Glendale, Cal.: Regal Books, 1974.

A series of 13 sermons on 1 and 2 Peter. Intended to help Christians apply Peter's principles to their day-to-day struggles, and to discover, as Peter did, that victory is available in Christ.

Ironside, H.A., *Expository Notes on the Epistles of Peter*. New York: Loizeaux Brothers, 1947.

Knowles, Victor, "13 Lessons on 1 and 2 Peter" in *Bible Student Study Guide* Series. Joplin, MO: College Press, 1985.

Brief exposition of key verses, plus study and discussion questions for each lesson.

Lloyd-Jones, D.M., *Expository Sermons on 2 Peter*. London: Banner of Truth, 1983.

Theological and practical application of the text or of points from within the text.

Meyer, F.B., *Tried by Fire: Expositions of the First Epistle of Peter*. London: Marshall, Morgan and Scott, 1955.

A full devotional exposition of 1 Peter. Reprinted from the edition published in 1890.

Neiboer, J., *A Practical Exposition of 1 Peter*. Erie, PA: Our Daily Walk, 1951.

-----, *A Practical Exposition of 2 Peter*. Erie, PA: Our Daily Walk, 1952.
An American Plymouth Brethren preacher, his volumes are practical, and abound in apt illustrations and applications.

Roth, Robert P., "1 Peter" in *The Bible Expositor*, Carl F.H. Henry, ed. Vol.3. Philadelphia: Holman, 1960

Shelly, Rubel, *Something to Hold On To*. Nashville, TN: Christian Teacher Bookstore, 1979.
Christians of the first three centuries of the church had to endure physical abuse, imprisonment, and even death; Christians of the present time are more likely to suffer social pressures, verbal abuse, and a sense of alienation from a world which is becoming more and more anti-Christian every day. The Christian needs something "unmoved" and "unchanging." He needs an anchor for his soul. Shelly concludes that the epistles of 1 and 2 Peter were written to emphasize this truth. Each sermon is followed with a list of things to "take thought" and a list of suggestions to "take action."

Wiersbe, Warren W., *Be Hopeful*. Wheaton, IL: Victor Books (Scripture Press), 1982.
Twelve sermons based on 1 Peter. Intended to help people who are experiencing suffering and persecution because of their loyalty to Christ. Though the Christian can expect to suffer for his faith, he can prepare for the best of God's blessings rather than be fearful of the worst of man's hatred.

-----, *Be Alert*. Wheaton, IL: Victor Books (Scripture Press), 1984.
Twelve sermons based on 2 Peter, 2 and 3 John and Jude. The theme is "Don't be fooled by the merchandisers of error!" Religious deception is on the rise. Who are the false teachers? How can the Christian recognize them? Wiersbe uncovers the disguises of today's religious impostors. He wants to sharpen the Christian's spiritual discernment, so the Christian won't be fooled by the masquerade.

SELECTED BIBLIOGRAPHY FOR JUDE

Commentaries, Introductions

Alford, Henry, "Jude" in *The Greek New Testament.* London: Rivingtons, 1871, Vol.4.
(See annotation in bibliography for 1 and 2 Peter)

Barclay, William, *The Letters of John and Jude.* Philadelphia: Westminster Press, 1960.
Helpful for word studies and historical background information. Barclay is Neo-liberal in his theology. He does accept the view Jude was probably written by Jude, the brother of the Lord.

Barnes, Albert, *Notes on the New Testament, Explanatory and Practical -- James, Peter, John, and Jude.* Edited by Robert Frew. Grand Rapids: Baker, 1951 reprint.
(See annotation in bibliography for 1 and 2 Peter)

Barnett, Albert E., and Elmer G. Homrighausen, "The Epistle of Jude" in *The Interpreter's Bible.* New York: Abingdon, 1957, Vol.12.
Barnett, who is responsible for the introductory studies and exegesis, rejects the traditional authorship, dating the epistle about AD 125. Homrighausen handles the exposition.

Bauckham, Richard J., "Jude, 2 Peter" in *Word Biblical Commentary.* Waco, TX: Word Books, 1983, Vol.50.
(See annotation in bibliography for 1 and 2 Peter)

Bigg, Charles, *A Critical and Exegetical Commentary on the Epistles of St. Peter and St. Jude* in INTERNATIONAL CRITICAL COMMENTARY series. Edinburgh: T&T Clark, 1910.
(See annotation in bibliography for 1 and 2 Peter)

Blum, Edwin A., "Jude" in *Expositor's Bible Commentary*, edited by F.C. Gaebelein. Grand Rapids: Zondervan, 1981.
The *Expositor's Bible Commentary* has proven to be fairly conservative in the positions espoused, and this volume is no exception. He dates the letter in the early AD 60's. Disappointingly, he treats Enoch's prophecy as being a quotation of the *Book of Enoch*, and the dispute between Michael and the devil as being a quotation from the *Assumption of Moses*.

Caton, N.T., *A Commentary and an Exposition of the Epistles of James, Peter, John and Jude.* Delight, AR: Gospel Light Publishing, reprint of 1897 edition.
Intended to help Sunday school teachers teach through the books. The whole Restoration Commentary series, of which this volume is one, was prepared by Christian Church scholars of a previous century.

Chase, F.H., "Jude, Epistle of" in *Hasting's Dictionary of the Bible.* New York: Scribners, 1909, Vol.2.

Theologically liberal.

Fronmüller, G.F.C., "The Epistle General of Jude" in *Lange's Commentary on the Holy Scriptures: Critical, Doctrinal, and Homiletical*, with additions by J. Isidor Mombert. Grand Rapids: Zondervan, 1950 reprint of 1872 edition.

(See annotation in bibliography for 1 and 2 Peter)

Green, Michael, *The Second Epistle of Peter and the Epistle of Jude* in TYNDALE NEW TESTAMENT COMMENTARIES series. Grand Rapids: Eerdmans, 1979.

(See annotation in bibliography for 1 and 2 Peter)

Guthrie, Donald F., "The Epistle of Jude" in *New Testament Introduction: Hebrews to Revelation*. Chicago: InterVarsity Press, 1966.

Guthrie's introductory studies are thorough and present a conservative conclusion to all the critical problems.

Hiebert, D. Edmund, *Second Peter and Jude.* Greenville, SC: Unusual Publications, 1989.

A very readable commentary, carefully explaining each Greek word, before showing the probable meaning of the phrase or verse in which the words occur. A scholarly defense of the Petrine authorship of 2 Peter, and dates Jude after 2 Peter.

Kelcy, Raymond C., *The Letters of Peter and Jude* in the LIVING WORD COMMENTARY series. Austin, TX: R.B. Sweet, 1972.

Produced by a Churches of Christ publishing house, this volume helps readers grasp the train of thought which the Bible writers were intending to convey.

Kelly, J.N.D., *A Commentary on the Epistles of Peter and Jude.* Grand Rapids: Baker, 1981 reprint.

Dates Jude before 2 Peter.

Kelly, W., *Lectures on the Epistle of Jude.* London: Hammond, 1939 reprint.

A series of expository lectures by a Plymouth Brethren scholar.

Kistemaker, Simon J., *Exposition of the Epistles of Peter and the Epistle of Jude* in NEW TESTAMENT COMMENTARY series. Grand Rapids: Baker, 1987.

(See annotation in bibliography for 1 and 2 Peter)

Lenski, R.C.H., *The Interpretation of the Epistles of St. Peter, St. John and St. Jude*. Minneapolis: Augsburg, 1966.

(See annotation in bibliography for 1 and 2 Peter)

Lumby, J. Rawson, "The General Epistle of Jude" in *The Bible Commentary*, edited by F.C. Cook. New York: Scribners, 1904. Vol.10.

Manton, Thomas, *An Exposition of the Epistle of Jude*. London: Banner of Truth Trust, 1958 reprint.

An old Puritan work whose style modern readers may find difficult, but rewarding to the diligent student.

Mayor, J.B., *The Epistle of St. Jude and the Second Epistle of St. Peter*. Grand Rapids: Baker, 1965 reprint.

Based on the Greek text. (See annotation in bibliography for 1 and 2 Peter)

Moo, Douglas J., "2 Peter, Jude" in *The NIV Application Commentary* series. Grand Rapids: Zondervan, 1996.

(See annotation in bibliography for 1 and 2 Peter)

Plummer, Alfred, "The General Epistle of Jude," in *Layman's Handy Commentary on the Bible*, edited by C.J. Ellicott. Grand Rapids: Zondervan, 1957 reprint.

A concise and informative commentary on the epistle. Gives a list of parallels between the Book of Enoch, 2 Peter and Jude.

Plumptre, E.H., "The General Epistles of St. Peter and St. Jude" in *Cambridge Bible for Schools and Colleges*. Cambridge: University Press, 1893.

(See annotation in bibliography for 1 and 2 Peter)

Salmon, George F., "Jude" in *An Historical Introduction to the Study of the Books of the New Testament*, 4th edition. New York: Dutton, 1889.

Salmond, S.D.F., "The General Epistle of Jude," in *The Pulpit Commentary* Series. Grand Rapids: Eerdmans, 1962 reprint.

Introductory studies and exposition in the *Pulpit Commentary* are always a good primary source when beginning a study of any Biblical book.

Summers, Ray, "Jude" in *The Broadman Bible Commentary*. Nashville: Broadman, 1972. Vol. 12.

Webb, R.L., "Jude" in *Dictionary of the Later New Testament and its Development*, ed. by Ralph Martin and Peter Davids. Downers Grove, IL: InterVarsity, 1997, p.611-621.

Over two pages of bibliographical references pointing to books and articles in scholarly journals. Gives a brief overview of contemporary scholarship's handling of the letter (genre, rhetorical structure, midrashic style, literary relationships, pseudonymity, redaction criticism, identity of the false teachers).

Woods, Guy N., *A Commentary on the New Testament Epistles of Peter, John, and Jude*. Nashville, TN: Gospel Advocate Co., 1954.

Intended to help Sunday school teachers prepare to teach through the books. The Gospel Advocate Company is a Churches of Christ publishing house. Uses the ASV text.

Kenneth S. Wuest, *In These Last Days: 2 Peter, 1,2,3 John and Jude in the Greek New Testament*. Grand Rapids: Eerdmans, 1954.

Word studies and exposition, understandable even if the student is not fluent in Greek. (See annotation in bibliography for 1 and 2 Peter)

Sermon and Lesson Ideas

Hesselgrave, David J., and Ronald P. Hesselgrave, *What in the World Has Gotten Into the Church?* Chicago, IL: Moody, 1981.

Twelve studies in the book of Jude for contemporary Christians. Irreverence, sensuality, lawlessness, falling away, are some of the bad things; work out your own salvation and work for the salvation of others, and give praise to God, are some of the good things that have gotten into the church. Few portions of the Word of God are more relevant to our troubled times than the book of Jude.

Wiersbe, Warren W., *Be Alert!* Wheaton, IL: Victor Books (Scripture Press), 1984.

(See annotation in the bibliography for 1 and 2 Peter.)

1 PETER INDEX

(Roman numerals indicate pages in the Introductory Studies. Chapter and verses are given for notes in the commentary pages.)

Abominable idolatries -- 4:3
Abraham -- 3:5,6
Abstain from fleshly lusts -- 2:11
Account,
    of the hope that is in you -- 3:15
    they shall give, to Him who judges -- 4:5
Acts, Book of -- x
Acts of Paul and Thecla -- xviii
Adam -- 3:21
Adornment of the wife -- 3:5
Adversary, the devil -- 5:8
After you have suffered a while, He will make you perfect -- 5:10
Alert, be on the -- 5:8
Aliens and strangers -- *see* Strangers and pilgrims
All things,
    end of, at hand -- 4:8
    in, God may be glorified -- 4:11
Allusions -- x, xi, xviii
Amanuensis -- iii, xiii, 5:12
Amen -- xxxi, 4:11, 5:11,14
Andrew -- v, xxv
Angels (*see also*, Spirits, the)
    and authorities subject to Christ – 3:22
    created beings -- 1:12
    evil -- 3:22
    fallen -- 3:19
    good -- 3:22
    hierarchical ranking of -- 3:22
    Jewish apocryphal beliefs -- 3:19
    powers -- 1:5
    sons of God -- *see* Sons of God
    things angels desire to look into – 1:10,12
Annotated quotations -- xi, xii, xviii
Anonymity -- xviii
Answer,
    of a good conscience toward God -- 3:21
    be ready to make a defense (apology) – xxviii, xxx, 3:15
Antediluvians, disobedient -- 3:20
Antioch of Syria -- xxii
Antitype -- 3:21
Anxiety, cast all, on Him -- 5:7
Apocryphal books -- xviii
Apostles' Creed -- xxxii, 3:19
Apostles of churches -- 1:1
Apostles of Jesus, 1:1
    born again to a living hope -- 1:3
    good men selected to be -- v
    higher office includes functions of lower – 5:1
    the twelve -- v
    sphere of authority -- xxv
Apparel -- *see* Dresses
Appeal to God for a good conscience -- 3:21
Appear -- 1:20, 5:4
Appointed, to this they were -- 2:8
Ark, Noah's,
    being constructed -- 3:20
Aristion of Smyrna -- xxvii
Arm yourselves with the same purpose -- 4:1
Ascension -- *see* Christ
Ashamed, let him not feel -- 4:16
Asia,
    Roman province of -- ii, xxv, 1:1
    evangelized by Paul -- xxv
Atonement (*see also* under Christ, Sacrifice)
Augustine -- 3:19
Authority,
    civil -- 2:13
    of angels -- 3:22
    of apostles -- xxv
Authorship, 1 Peter
    reasons for such a study -- viii
    arguments for Peter's authorship -- ix
    internal evidence -- ix
    external evidence -- xi
    arguments against Peter's authorship – xiii-xviii, xxiv
    alternatives to Petrine authorship not credible -- xviii

Babylon -- iv, xix, 5:13
    church(es) in -- iv, xx, xxiii, 5:13
    metaphorical use – xxii

Babylon, continued
figurative for Jerusalem -- xxii
figurative for Rome -- xxiii, 5:13
in Egypt -- xx
in Mesopotamia -- xx
Jews expelled from Babylon, AD 40 -- xxi
Baptism -- xxvii, xxxiii, 1:22
an appeal to God for a good conscience – 3:21
dying to sin in -- 4:1
immersion -- 3:21
not removal of dirt from the flesh -- 3:21
now saves you -- 3:21
typified by the flood -- 3:20
of the Holy Spirit -- ix, 3:21
Baptismal homily -- xviii, xxvii, xxxii
Baptismal liturgy -- xxxii, xxxiii
Barnabas, xxv, xxix
Mark travels with -- iv
Barnabas, Epistle of -- xi
Baruch, Apocalypse of -- xxiii
Begotten again -- *see* Born again
Behavior,
act as free men -- 2:16
be holy in all your -- 1:15
conduct yourselves in fear -- 1:17
chaste -- 3:2
good, in Christ -- 3:16
respectful -- 3:2
winsome among the Gentiles -- xxviii, 1:9, 2:11,12,17, 3:1,7
of husbands -- 3:7
of wives -- 3:1
Believe in Him -- 1:8, 2:6
Believers, in God -- 1:21
Beloved -- 2:1, 4:12
Better, to suffer for doing right -- 3:17
Bishop,
Christ described as a -- 2:25
elder and, synonymous -- x, 5:1
Bithynia -- ii, xxiii, 1:1
Blessed, blessing -- 1:3
giving a -- 3:9
inherit a -- 2:9
you are -- 3:13, 4:14
Blood,
precious, of Christ -- *see* Precious blood
sprinkled with His -- ii, 1:2
Body, soul, spirit -- 1:9,23, 3:4
Bond-slaves -- 2:16
Born again -- 1:3,23
of imperishable seed -- 1:23
see also, regeneration
Bring us to God -- 3:18
British Israelism -- xxv
Brotherhood -- 2:17, 5:9
Brotherly love,
exhortation to -- 1:22, 3:8
see also, love
Buffeted for faults -- 2:20
Busybody -- *see* Troublesome meddler

Caligula -- xxii
Called, calling
for this purpose -- 3:9
Holy One called you -- 1:15
out of darkness into His marvelous light -- 2:9
unto His eternal glory -- 5:10
you have been, for this purpose -- 2:21
Calvin -- xx, 3:19
Calvinism -- 2:8
Canon, New Testament
making and accepting of the books -- xviii
books collected early - i, xv
canonical listings -- xi, xii
guarding of the canon -- xviii
when were Paul's letters collected -- xv
Cappadocia -- ii, xxv, 1:1
Cares
cast all, on Him -- 5:7
He, for you -- 5:7
Carousals -- 4:3
Casting all your care upon Him -- 5:7
Catalogues (of vices and virtues) -- *see* Codes
Catechism
instructions -- xxxii
primitive Christian -- xxxii
Catholic epistles - i
Ceased from sin -- 4:1
Ceremonial washings, Jewish -- 3:21
Chapter divisions -- 2:1
Charges, not lording it over the -- 5:3
Charity, its covering power -- 4:8
Chaste behavior -- *see* Behavior

Child, children (in figurative sense) -- 5:13
Chosen -- ii, 1:1, 5:13
race -- 2:9
people -- 1:1,2
of God, precious -- 1:2,
see also, Elect, election
Christ -- 1:1
angels, authorities, powers subject to – 3:22
appeared in these last times -- 1:20
ascension -- 1:11, 3:19,22
at the right hand of God -- 3:22
blood of, redemption by -- 2:19
blood of, Precious -- *see* Precious blood
bore our sins in His own body -- 2:24
chief Shepherd -- 5:4
choice and precious in sight of God – 2:4,6
committed Himself to Him who judges righteously -- 2:23
coronation -- 1:11
death -- ii, 3:18
deity of -- 1:3, 4:11
descent into Hades -- *see* descent
died for sins once -- 3:18
domination over supernatural beings – 3:22
doxologies addressed to -- 4:11
entrusted Himself to God -- 2:23
example -- *see* Example, Christ's
foreknown before the foundation of the world -- 1:19
glorification -- 1:11
glory given to -- 1:21
gone into heaven -- 3:22
"in Christ" -- 3:16, 5:10
incarnation -- 1:1,3,19, 3:18
Jesus -- 1:1
Judge of all -- 4:5
lamb, unblemished and spotless -- 1:19
living stone -- *see* Stone, cornerstone
Lord, lordship -- 1:3,25, 2:3, 3:15
made a little lower than the angels -- 3:22
made alive (quickened in spirit) -- 3:18
Messiah -- 1:1,3
not seen, but loved -- 1:8
Parousia -- *see* Second Advent
Passion -- *see* Sufferings
Christ, *continued*
physical body -- 3:18
preaching to spirits in prison -- 3:19
pre-existence -- 1:11,19, 3:19
put to death in flesh -- 3:18
resurrection -- ii, iii, x, 1:3,21, 3:18,21
reviled -- 2:23
sacrifice -- 3:18
sayings of -- 3:18, 4:5
scourged -- 2:24
second advent -- *see* Second advent
Shepherd and Guardian of souls -- x, 2:25
sinlessness -- x, 1:19, 2:22, 3:18
Son of God -- 1:3
Stone -- *see* Stone, cornerstone
Suffering Servant -- *see* Suffering Servant
sufferings -- x, 2:23, 5:1
benefit of -- 2:24
an example -- *see* Example, Christ's
in the flesh -- 3:18, 4:1
once, for all -- 3:18
predicted by Old Testament prophets -- 1:11
vicarious -- 2:21, 3:18
temporary subordination to the Father – 1:3
temptations of -- 5:9
trials of -- v, x, 2:20, 5:1
virgin birth -- 1:3
without spot or blemish -- x, 1:19
Christian(s)
believers in God -- 1:21
bond-slaves of God -- 2:16
derivation of the term -- 4:16
disciples called, at Antioch -- xxix, 4:16
glorify God in this name -- iv
living stones -- 2:5
not a nickname -- 4:16
priesthood -- 2:5
protected by the power of God -- 1:5
so called by Suetonius -- xvii
slandered as being evildoers -- 2:12
suffering as a -- iv, xvii, 1:1, 4:16, 5:9
virtues -- *see* Spiritual qualities
Christianity
the true grace of God -- 5:12
Church -- *see also*, People of God

Church, *continued*
conceived of as "God's house" or temple -- 2:5, 4:17
God's own possession -- 2:9
a holy priesthood -- 2:5
a royal priesthood -- 2:9
a chosen race -- 2:9
a brotherhood -- 2:17
a flock -- x
living stones -- 2:5
mixed character of churches in Asia Minor -- xxvi
OT terms applied to Israel now applied to church -- iii, 1:1, 2:3,9
organization (polity) -- x, 2:17, 5:1,2,3
relationship to civil government -- 2:13
a spiritual house -- 2:5
Circumcision,
a paraphrase for "Hebrews" -- viii
Circus Maximus -- iii
Civic duties
Peter's teaching on -- 2:14, 4:15
comparison with Paul's teaching on – 2:13
submission to civil rulers -- 2:13
Claudius, emperor -- vii, xxii
Clement of Alexandria -- xii, xxiii
Clement of Rome -- xi, xviii
1 Clement -- xi, xxii
Cloak of maliciousness -- *see* Covering for evil
Codes
standard ethical (*haustafel*) -- xv, xxxi
Codex Angelicus -- ii
Codex Sinaiticus -- xx
Colossians -- xxi
Coming to the Lord -- 2:4
Complaint, without -- 4:9
Compulsion, not of -- 5:2
Conditional sentences -- 2:3
Confirm, God will, you -- 5:10
Conjectural emendation -- 3:19
Conscience
good, answer of a -- 3:21
good, exhortation to keep a -- 3:16
toward God -- 2:19
Conversation -- *see* Behavior
Coptic church -- xx
Covenant
blood of the -- 1:2
New -- 1:2
Covering for evil -- xii, 2:16
Creator -- *see* God
Credit, what is there -- 2:20
Crown, crowns
of glory, unfading -- 5:4
several types of, in Scripture -- 5:5

Darkness, called out of -- 2:9
Date of letter -- *see* 1 Peter
Dative case
means -- 3:18
sphere -- 3:18
Day, days
of the Lord -- 4:6,7
of Noah -- 3:20
of visitation -- 2:12
Dead, the
Gospel preached to the -- 3:19, 4:6
in trespasses and sins -- 4:5
judge the living and the -- 4:5
Deceit, none found in Christ -- 2:22
Decree, Apostolic (Acts 15) -- *see* Jerusalem Conference
Deeds, good -- 2:12
Defense, ready to make a -- 3:15
Deluge -- *see* Flood, Noah's
Descent into Hades -- xxii, 3:19
Desire
of the Gentiles -- 4:3
to look into -- 1:12
Destination of 1 Peter -- iii, 1:1
the place -- xxv
the origin of the churches -- xxv
the ethnic background of the readers – xxvi, 1:14,18
Devil
adversary -- x, 5:8
can stir up desires of the body -- 1:22, 2:11
prowls as a roaring lion -- iii, xxviii, 5:8
resist him, firm in your faith -- iii, xxviii, 5:9
seeks someone to devour -- 5:8

Devil, *continued*
    war in heaven -- *see* War in heaven
Diaspora – *see* Dispersion
Didache -- viii, xi
Die to sin -- 2:24
Difficulty, with, the righteous saved -- 4:18
Dignities -- *see* Angelic majesties
Dirt, removal of, from the flesh -- 3:21
Disappointed, not -- 2:6
Disbelieve, those who -- 2:7
Disobedient -- 2:7
    spirits, Christ preaches to -- 3:20
    to the Word -- xxxi, 2:8, 3:1
Dispensationalism -- 1:12
Dispersion -- iii, vii, viii, xxvi, 1:1
Dissipation, excess of -- 4:4
Distress, distressed -- 1:6
Docetists -- 2:24, 3:18
Doing good -- 2:15, 3:11
    see also, Deeds, good
Doing right -- iv, 2:14,15,20, 3:6, 4:19
Dominion -- 4:11, 5:11
Domitian -- xvi
Doxologies -- xxxi, 4:11, 5:11
Dresses -- 3:3
Drinking parties -- 4:3
Drunkenness -- 4:3

Eagerness, shepherd the flock with -- 5:2
Early Christian literature -- xi
Earth, your stay (sojourn) upon -- 1:17
Earthly rulers, obedience to --
    see Authority, civil
Easter sermon -- xxvii
Eight souls saved -- 3:20
Elder, elders
    a paid position -- 5:2
    examples to the flock -- 5:3
    not lording it over your charges -- 5:3
    Peter, a fellow-elder -- ix, 5:1
    and "bishops" synonymous terms - x, 5:1
    shepherds -- 5:1,2
    submission to, enjoined -- 5:5
Elect, election -- 1:1
    Calvinistic vs. Arminian views -- 1:1
    for service -- 1:1
Elect, election, *continued*
    involves obedience -- 1:2
    term used for Christians -- 1:1
Elijah -- 1:12
Encyclical letters - i
End, of all things at hand -- xxviii, 4:7
Enoch -- 3:19
    1 Enoch -- 3:19
Envy, put aside -- 2:1
Ephesians
    addressed to churches in Asia Minor -- xv
    "in Ephesus" missing from some manuscripts -- ii
    resemblances to in 1 Peter -- xv
Ephesus -- 1:1
Epistle, meaning of the word -- ii
Epistle of Barnabas -- *see* Barnabas
Epistolary framework,
    of first-century letters -- 1:2
    of 1 Peter -- xix, xxvi, 1:1
Erasmus -- xx
Eschatology, systems of -- 4:6,7
Establish, God will, you -- 5:10
Eternal purpose, God's -- 1:1,2,19, 2:8
Eternal security –
    see Faith, protected by power of God through
Eucharist – *see* Lord's Supper
Eusebius -- viii, xii, xiv, xxii
Evangelists -- 5:1
Evil
    a covering for -- 2:16
    face of the Lord against those who do – 3:12
    refrain the tongue from -- 3:10
    turn away from -- 3:11
Evildoers
    punishment of -- 2:14
    suffer not as -- 4:15
    they slander you as -- 2:12
Evil for evil, not repaying -- 3:9
Exalt you, God will -- 5:6
Example, Christ's -- 2:21, 4:1
    Imitatio Christi, a central theme of 1 Peter -- 2:21
Excess of dissipation -- 4:4
Exhort, exhortation -- xxvii, 5:12
    grounded on doctrine -- 1:1

Exhort, *continued*
I, the elders -- 5:1
Exiles -- *see* Strangers and pilgrims
Exultation, rejoice with -- 4:13

Face of the Lord, against those who do evil – 3:12
Faith
and hope in God -- 1:21
comes by hearing God's Word -- 1:2, 2:8
created by God (?) -- 1:2
defense of -- 3:15
end (goal, outcome) of your -- 1:9
hope, and love -- xxvii
obedience to the truth -- 1:22
obtained a like precious -- *see* Obtained
personal response to Gospel -- 1:7
proof of -- 1:7
protected by power of God through -- 1:5
resist the devil, firm in your -- 5:9
trial of -- 1:6
testing of -- 1:6,7
Faithful, faithfulness -- iii, 1:5
False teachers and scoffers -- 4:7
Father,
calling on God as -- 1:17
power -- 3:1
Favor with God -- 2:20
this finds -- 2:19,20
Fear,
do not, their intimidation -- 3:14
God -- 2:17
pass the time of your sojourning in -- 1:17
see also, Reverence
without being frightened by -- 3:6
Fellow-elder -- 5:1
Fellow heir -- 3:7
Fervent -- 4:8
Fiery trial -- iv, xxviii, xxix, 4:12
First fruits -- 1:21
Flesh,
all, is as grass -- 1:24
Christ suffered in the -- 3:18
he who has suffered in the -- 4:1
judged in the, as men -- 4:6
no longer live in the -- 4:2
Flesh, *continued*
put to death in the, quickened in spirit – 3:18
sinful nature? *see* Sinful nature
Fleshly lusts,
abstain from -- 2:11
wage war against the soul -- 2:11
Flock, feed the, of God -- x, 5:2
Flood, Noah's
type of baptism -- *see* Baptism
eight persons saved -- 3:20
Flower of grass -- 1:24
Foolish men -- 2:15
Forever and ever -- 4:11, 5:11
Forefathers -- 1:18
Foreknowledge of God -- *see* God
Foreordained, what was -- 1:2
Form Criticism -- xxx, xxxiii
Former,
lusts -- 1:14
times -- 3:5
Foundation laid in Zion –
see Stone, cornerstone
Free men -- 2:16
Freedom, not a covering for evil -- 2:16
Futile way of life -- 1:18

Galatia -- ii, xxv, 1:1
northern -- xxv, 1:1
southern -- xxv
Roman province of -- 1:1
Galilee, bilingual -- xiii
General letters - i
Genitive case
objective genitive -- 1:2, 3:14,21
subjective genitive -- 1:2,11, 3:14,21
Genre -- xxx, xxxiii
Gentile Christians -- xxv, 1:1
Gentiles -- 2:10
desire of -- 4:3
included in the Gospel -- 1:10
sins of the -- 4:3
will of the, wrought -- 4:3
Gentleness -- 3:15
Genuineness of 1 Peter -- ix
strength of evidence for -- xii

Gifts, Spiritual -- *see* Spiritual gifts
Gird,
your minds for action -- 1:13
yourselves with humility -- x, 5:5
Glorify God
because of your good works -- 2:12
in that name -- 4:16
on the day of visitation -- 2:12
through Jesus Christ -- 4:11
Glory -- 1:7
God called you to eternal -- 5:10
like the flower of grass -- 1:24
of God -- 5:10
partaker of the, to be revealed -- 5:1
shared by Christ -- 5:1
crown of -- *see* Crown of glory
the revelation of His -- 4:13
Spirit of, rests on you -- 4:14
that follows Christ's sufferings -- 1:11
to Him be, for ever and ever -- 4:11
Glories to follow -- 1:11
God
all seeing -- 1:17, 2:19
believers in, through Him -- 1:21
called you to eternal glory -- 5:10
cares for you -- iii
eternal purpose -- *see* Eternal purpose, God's
excellencies of -- 2:9
faithful creator -- iv, 4:19
Father -- 1:2,17
Father of our Lord Jesus Christ -- 1:3
foreknowledge -- 1:2,20
His grace -- 5:10
Holy one -- 1:15
judges righteously -- 2:23
impartial love towards all -- x
impartially judges men's work -- x, 1:17
mercy -- 1:3
mighty hand of -- xxviii, 5:6
moving history to a goal -- 1:13
openness of -- 1:2
opposed to the proud -- 5:5
patience -- 3:20
power of -- 1:5
providence -- 1:3,5, 4:19
resists the proud -- 5:5
right hand of -- 3:22
God, *continued*
not slack about His promises -- *see* Promises
virtues -- *see* God, excellencies
will of -- *see* Will of God
will perfect, confirm, strengthen, you – 5:10
Godless man, what will become of -- 4:18
Gold,
jewelry -- 3:3
more precious than -- 1:7
not redeemed with -- 1:18
Good,
conscience -- *see* Conscience
days, see -- 3:10
deeds -- *see* Deeds, good
zealous for the -- 3:13
Gospel,
of God -- 4:17
preached to the dead (?) -- 3:19, 4:6
the outcome of those who obey not the – 4:17
was preached to you -- 1:25
Governors -- xvii, 2:14
Grace,
and peace be multiplied -- 1:2
brought to you at the revelation of Jesus – 1:13
God gives, to the humble -- 5:5, 5:10
manifold, of God -- 4:10
of God, stand firm in it -- iii, xxvi, 5:12
of life, fellow-heir of the -- *see* Life
prophecy of the, that should come to you -- 1:10
unmerited favor -- 1:10
Grass,
all flesh is as -- 1:24
withers -- 1:24
Great Days with Jesus -- *see* Peter, reminiscences
Greek Language
commonly spoken in Galilee -- xiii
1 Peter is excellent Greek -- xiii
Epistle of James is excellent Greek -- xiii
a participial loving language -- xiii
Greetings -- 1:2, 5:13,14
Growth, spiritual, continuous, essential to life – 2:2

Guardian -- 2:25
Guile,
  none found in Christ -- 2:21
  put aside all -- 2:1
  refrain from speaking – 3:10

Hades -- 3:19
  Descent into -- 3:19
  Harrowing of, in medieval thought -- 3:19
Hair, braiding of -- 3:3
Hand, mighty, of God -- 5:6
Hannibal -- viii
Harm, who will, you -- 3:13
Harmonious, let all be -- 3:8
Harshly treated -- 2:20
Haustafel – *see* Codes.
Healed, by His wounds -- 2:24
Healing in the atonement -- 2:24
Heart,
  hidden person of the -- 3:4
  inner man -- 3:4
  love one another from the -- 1:22
  sanctify Christ as Lord in your -- 3:15
Heaven, heavens
  Christ has gone into -- *see* Christ
    inheritance reserved in -- 1:4
  Jesus went to prepare a place in -- 1:4
  New, and earth -- *see* New heavens and earth
  shall pass away with a great noise
Hebraisms -- 1:14
Hell -- 4:1
Hereditary depravity -- *see* Sinful nature
Heretics -- xviii
Hermas, Shepherd of -- xi
Hermeneutics -- 4:6
Hidden person of the heart -- 3:4
Higher criticism -- ix, 1:11, 4:7
Hindered, prayers not -- 3:7
Hippolytus -- xxii
Historical allusions, 1 Peter,
  beginning - ii
  ending -- iii
  elsewhere in the letter -- iv
Historical criticism -- xxvii-xxxiv
Holiness -- 1:15
Holiness, *continued*
  Christians called to (be holy) -- 1:15
  Exhortation to -- 1:14
  Incitements to -- 1:14,15
  see also, Sanctification
Holy,
  kiss -- 5:14
  nation -- 2:9
  priesthood -- 2:5
  women -- 3:5
Holy Spirit -- *see* Spirit of God
Honor -- xxxiv
  all men -- 2:17
  give, to the wife -- 3:7
  received at the second coming -- 1:7, 2:7
  the king -- 2:17
Hope,
  an account of the, that is in you -- 3:15
  born again to a living -- 1:3
  exhortation to -- 1:13
  in God -- 1:21, 3:5
  reason for the, that is in you -- 3:15
  set your, completely on the grace -- 1:13
Hosea's children,
  names of, enshrine prophecy -- 2:10
Hospitality, encouraged -- 4:9
Hostility, prudent rules for meeting -- 4:14ff
House, household
  the church as a spiritual -- 2:5
  of God -- 4:17
Human institutions (civil authorities) -- 2:13
Humble,
  in spirit -- 3:8
  yourselves under the mighty hand of God --iii, 5:6
Humility -- x, 5:5
Husbands -- 3:1
  in the Hellenistic World -- 3:1
  disobedient to the Word -- 3:1
  duties of -- 3:7
  understanding toward wives -- 3:7
  unsaved, how attracted -- 3:2,3,4
  won by the behavior of their wives -- 3:1
Hymns,
  Jewish and early Christian -- xxxii
  in 1 Peter? -- xxx, xxxi, xxxiii, 1:20, 3:18
  in 1 Timothy? -- xxxii
Hypocrisy, put aside -- 2:1

Idolatry -- 1:18
Ignatius -- xi, xxii
Ignorance,
former lusts in your -- 1:14
of foolish men, silence the -- 2:15
Imperative
future tense verb used as -- 1:16
participial -- 2:4,18, 3:1
mood -- 1:15
Imperishable -- 1:4,23
quality of a gentle spirit -- 3:4
"In" Christ -- *see* Christ
Incarnation -- *see* Christ
Inheritance -- 1:4
incorruptible, undefiled -- iii, 1:4
reserved in heaven -- *see* Heaven
Inspiration -- 5:11
attacked and denied -- xi, xxvii
of apostles and prophets -- ix, xiii, xiv,1:10, 11,12, 3:19
tests for, as New Testament canon was guarded -- ix
Insult for insult, not returning -- 3:9
Intermediate state -- 3:19
souls are conscious -- 1:12
Interpreter, Mark was Peter's -- xiii
Intimidation, do not fear their -- 3:14
Irenaeus -- xii
Israel,
chosen to keep monotheism alive -- 1:1
church is spiritual Israel -- 1:1
of God -- 1:1

James, Letter of,
resemblances to, in 1 Peter -- xiv
Jerome,
on the epistles of Peter -- vii, xxiii
Jerusalem,
destruction of, AD 70 – xxi, 2:13
Jerusalem Conference -- vii, xiv, xviii, xxv, 5:12
Jewelry -- 3:3
Jewish Christians -- xxiv, 1:1
Jews,
expelled from Babylon -- xxi
expelled from Rome -- xxi
Job, Book of - i

John, the apostle -- v, xxv, 5:1
John the Baptist -- v, x, 1:11
Joy,
inexpressible and full of joy -- 1:8
Judas Iscariot -- v
Judge, judged
in the flesh as men -- 4:6
the living and the dead -- 4:5
Judgment
begins at the house of God -- 4:17
daily -- 1:17
final -- 1:7, 4:5,6
persecution in relation to -- 4:17
without respect of persons -- 1:17
Just for the unjust,
Christ suffered, the -- 3:18
Justification -- 2:24
Justin Martyr -- viii, xvii, 3:15

Kept through faith -- *see* Faith, protected by power of God through
Kerygma and didache -- xi
Kindhearted, let all be -- 3:8
Kindness of the Lord,
if you have tasted the -- 2:3
King James Version,
"church in Babylon" -- iv, 5:13
King(s) -- 2:13,17
Kiss of love -- *see* Holy Kiss
Knowledge -- 3:7

Lamb,
without spot or blemish -- 1:19
Passover -- 1:19
Last time(s)
Christ appeared in these -- 1:20
salvation, ready to be revealed in the – 1:5
Latin Versions
Latin Vulgate -- xx, 5:13
Letters, New Testament
to be read in the churches - i
collections of -- *see* Canon

Liberal theology -- xxiv
Life,
  a life you can love -- 3:10
  fellow-heir of the grace of -- 3:7
  walking in newness of -- 3:21
Light, marvelous -- 2:9
Lion -- 5:8
Literary structure -- *see* 1 Peter
Liturgy, baptismal -- xxxii
Live,
  for the will of God -- 4:2
  in the spirit -- 4:6
  the rest of the time in the flesh -- 4:2
  unto righteousness -- 2:24
Living
  hope -- 1:3
  judge the, and the dead -- 4:5
  stone, coming to -- 2:4
  stones, believers are -- 2:5
  word -- 1:23
Local autonomy -- 2:17
Lord
  angry with the wicked -- 3:12
  eyes of the, upon the righteous -- 3:12
  face of, against those who do evil -- 3:12
  Jesus Christ: *see* Jesus Christ, Lord
  regular word used to translate "Yahweh" --1:25
  Sarah called Abraham -- 3:6
  word of the -- 1:25
Love,
  covers a multitude of sins -- 4:8
  fervently, one another -- 1:22, 4:8
  Him, without seeing Him -- 1:8
  life -- 3:10
  the brotherhood -- 2:17
  unfeigned, of the brethren -- 1:22
Lusts,
  desires -- 1:14, 4:3
  former, stop being conformed to -- 1:14
  in your ignorance -- 1:14
  of men -- 4:2
Lutheran theology -- 3:19
LXX -- *see* Septuagint

Malice, put aside all -- 2:1
Malign you -- 4:4
Manuscript variations -- 1:16,21,22
  2:2,6,7,24
  3:1,6,7,8,13,18,21
  4:1,3,7,14,16
  5:2,10, 13,14
Mark, John -- iv, ix, xx, xxi
  commended by Paul -- iv
  Eusebius' allusions to -- xix
  my son -- xxi, 5:13
  traditional connection with Alexandria – xx
  traditional connection with Peter -- vii, xxiii
  Paul's helper -- xxi
  Peter's interpreter -- xiii
Marriage -- 3:1
Masters,
  good and gentle -- 2:18
  servants' submission to earthly -- 2:18
  unreasonable -- 2:18
Meek and quiet spirit -- 3:4
Men, judged in the flesh as -- 4:6
Mercy,
  received -- 2:10
  two different words translated -- 1:3
Messianic prophecies -- 1:11, 2:4,6
Mind,
  gird up your, for action -- 1:13
Mithradates -- 1:1
Mixed marriages -- 3:1,7
  Peter's and Paul's directions the same – 3:1,7
Modern revelations -- 1:25
Moses -- 1:12
Muratorian Canon -- xiv
Murderer, suffer not as a -- 4:15
Mystery -- 1:11
Mystery Religions -- 3:18

Nation, holy -- *see* Holy nation
Neo-liberalism -- xi
Nero -- iii, iv, xv, 2:5,13, 4:12, 5:8
  falsely accused Christians of burning Rome -- 2:12

Nero, *continued*
Peter's death in Nero's 14th year of reign -- vii
New birth -- *see* Born again
Newborn babes -- 2:2
New Testament Canon -- *see* Canon
Noah -- 3:19,20

Obey, Obedience -- 1:14, 3:19
Jesus Christ -- ii, 1:2
to the gospel of God -- 4:17
obedient faith -- 1:8, 2:6,8
to the truth -- 1:22
Obedient children -- 1:14
Oecumenius -- xxiii
Offer up -- 2:5,24
Old Testament,
allusions to in 1 Peter -- 4:8
Optative mood,
expresses possibility -- xxviii
expresses a wish -- 1:2
rare in New Testament -- 3:14
Oracles, of God -- 4:11
Origen -- viii, xii, xxv
Outline of 1 Peter -- *see* 1 Peter

Pacifism -- 3:9
Papias -- xi, xviii, xxiii
Paraenesis -- *see* Exhort, exhortations
Parousia -- *see* Christ
Participles, circumstantial -- 1:6, 2:4
Participial imperative -- *see* Imperative
Passion of Christ -- *see* Christ
Passover -- 1:19
Patience -- 2:20
Paul,
first missionary journey -- ii, iv
wrote 2 Timothy -- iv
Paulinisms -- xv, xxiii, 1:3
Paul's epistles
Peter's reference to -- xv
Peace,
be to all who are in Christ -- 5:14
may peace be multiplied -- 1:2

Peace, *continued*
seek, and pursue it -- 3:11
Peculiar people -- *see* People
Pentecost -- xxii, xxvi
People
for God's own possession -- 2:9
of God (*see also*, Church) -- 2:10
in time past you were not a -- 2:10
Perfect, God will, you -- iii, xxix, 5:10
Perfect tense, implication of -- 1:9
Persecution
of Christians -- xvi
nature of, suffered by readers -- xvi, xxviii-xxx
Neronian -- iii, iv, xv, xxiv, xxix, 4:12, 5:8
not yet systematic in the provinces -- xvii, 1:6, 4:12,19
Peter's teaching on -- 4:12ff
how to face -- iv, 4:12
time of testing -- 4:12
Persecution literature - i
Peshitto Syriac -- *see* Syriac
Peter
at Antioch -- vii, viii, xxii
life and character -- v, vi
name change, Simon to Peter -- v, 1:1
call to be an apostle -- v, ix
fellow elder -- 5:1
first recorded sermon -- ii
good confession -- vi
witness of sufferings of Jesus -- ix
reminiscences of Great Days with Jesus – x, xvii, 1:6,8,19,22, 2:4,12,13,16,23,24, 3:9,12,14,22, 4:5,6, 5:1,2,3,4,5,6,8,9,10
at the Transfiguration -- vi
fisherman on Sea of Galilee -- v
his speeches in Acts -- ii, x, 1:7
his missionary travels -- vii, xx, xxi, xxiii, xxv, 1:1
housetop experience -- v
languages spoken by -- xiii
was married -- 5:13
miracles -- vii
publicly rebuked by Paul -- vii
his manner of death foretold by Christ – vi

Peter, *continued*
tradition about his death -- vii, viii
walking on the water -- vi
was Peter ever in Rome? -- viii, xxiii, xxiv
witness of the sufferings of Christ -- 5:1
Peter, Acts of -- viii
Peter, Apocalypse of -- viii
Peter, Gospel of -- viii
Peter, Judgment of -- viii
1 Peter,
authorship -- *see* Authorship, 1 Peter
composite theory, evaluation of -- xxxiii
date of -- ii, xxii, xxiv
destination of -- *see* Destination of 1 Peter
influenced by writings of Paul -- xiv, xv
sense of rhythm -- xiii
good Greek -- xiii, 5:12
full of reminiscences of Jesus' life -- *see* Peter, reminiscences
literary structure -- xxx-xxxiv
occasion -- xv
outline -- xxviii, 1:3, 2:4, 5:5b
place of writing -- xx-xxiv
purpose for which written -- xxvii
references to the Holy Spirit -- xvii
signed by Peter -- ix, 1:1
translation of Aramaic original? -- xiii
unity of -- *see* Unity of 1 Peter
2 Peter,
Petrine authorship denied by some -- xv, 5:12
rugged Greek -- xiii, xiv
written from Rome -- xxiv
Petrine sermons in Acts -- 1:7
Pilgrimage, Christian life a -- *see* Strangers and pilgrims
Pledge of a good conscience -- 3:21
Pliny, the younger -- 1:1
letter to Trajan -- xvi, xxiv, 1:1, 3:15, 4:16
Polemon, kingdom of -- xxv, 1:1
Polycarp -- xi, xviii
Polycarp, letter to Philippians -- xi
Pontus -- ii, xxiii, xxv, xxvi, 1:1
evangelized by Andrew and Thaddeus – xxv
Possession, a people for God's own -- 2:9
Power and coming of our Lord Jesus -- *see* Christ
Powers, angelic -- 3:22
Praise
and glory and honor -- iii, 1:7
of those who do right -- 2:14
Prayer, prayers -- 2:4
addressed to the Father -- 1:17
be sober, for the purpose of -- 4:7
His ears attend to their prayer -- 3:12
not hindered -- 3:7
Preach, preaching -- 1:12, 4:6
inspired -- 1:12
Precious,
blood of Christ -- 1:19
Christ is, in sight of God -- 2:4
quiet spirit is, in God's sight -- 3:4
testing of faith is, 1:7
value -- 2:7
Predestination -- 1:2
double -- 2:8
Priesthood,
holy -- *see* Holy priesthood
royal -- 2:9
Prison, spirits in -- 3:19
Private interpretation -- *see* Prophets, prophecy
Proclaim, proclamation
the excellencies of Him who called you – 2:9
made, to spirits in prison -- 3:19
Prohibitions -- 1:14
Promised land -- 1:4
Proof of your faith -- 1:7
Prophets, prophecy
consciousness of -- 1:11
"to speak by inspiration" -- xiii
inspiration of -- *see* Inspiration
made careful search in inquiry -- 1:10
New Testament prophets -- xiv
not serving themselves -- 1:12
of the grace that should come -- 1:10
Old Testament prophets -- 1:10
Proud, God resists -- *see* God
Providence of God -- *see* God
Psalm 34 -- 2:3, 3:10
Psalm 118 -- 2:4,7
Pseudepigrapha -- xviii

Pseudepigraphy,
condemned by early Christians -- xviii
serious problems inherent in -- ix
Pseudonymity -- xviii, xxvii
what is involved in claims of -- ix
not a harmless literary device -- xviii
Punishment of evildoers -- 2:14
Pure,
Conscience -- *see* Conscience
milk -- 2:2
Purify, purification
your souls in obeying the truth -- 1:22
Purpose,
arm yourselves with the same -- 4:1
God's eternal -- *see* Eternal purpose
of the letter -- *see* 1 Peter purpose

Qualities, spiritual, *see* Spiritual qualities
Quiet spirit -- 3:4
Quotations,
of 1 Peter in early Christian literature -- xi
Peter's, of OT, not always from LXX – 2:6, 4:8
of early Christian hymns, alleged -- 3:18
Rabbinical writers -- 2:6
Rebecca -- 3:3
Rebirth -- *see* Regeneration
Recipients, of the letter -- *see* Destination of 1 Peter
Reconciliation -- 3:18
Redeemed, not with corruptible things -- 1:18
Regeneration -- 1:23
Rejected by men, stone -- 2:4
Rejoice,
as you share the sufferings of Christ – 4:13
you greatly rejoice -- 1:6,8
with exultation -- 4:13
Religio illicita -- xv
Religio licita -- xv
Reserved, in heaven for you -- 1:4
Resist the devil -- 5:9
Rests upon you, Spirit -- 4:14
Resurrection -- *see* Christ
Resurrection, *continued*
its relation to redemption, regeneration, and baptism -- 3:21
Retaliation, to be avoided -- 3:9
Revealed, it was revealed to them (Old Testament prophets) -- 1:12
Revelation of Jesus Christ -- *see* Second Advent
Reverence
exhortation to -- 1:17
make your defense with -- 3:15
see also, Fear
Revile your good behavior -- 3:16
Reviled,
for the name of Christ -- xxviii, 4:14
not again -- x, 2:23
Reward, degrees of -- 1:7
Righteous,
eyes of the Lord are upon the -- 3:12
saved with difficulty -- 4:18
Righteousness,
live unto -- 2:24
suffer for the sake of -- 3:13
Roaring Lion, *see* Devil
Reformation -- xxii
Roman Catholic Church - i
good works a deposit -- 4:19
25-year episcopate of Peter -- viii
indulgences -- 4:8
Peter's papacy -- xx
Romans, epistle to
resemblances to in 1 Peter -- xv
Rome
burning of, AD 64 -- viii, xv
Christians falsely blamed for burning of – viii, xvi
Peter in Rome -- viii
typified by Babylon -- xxii
Royal priesthood -- *see* Priesthood
Run with them, you no longer -- xxviii, 4:4

Sacrifice, Christ's, conceived as vicarious – 3:18
Sacrifices
acceptable to God through Jesus -- 2:5
spiritual sacrifices of Christians -- 2:5

Sacrifices, *continued*
to the emperor -- xvi
Salutations, Peter's -- 1:2
Salvation -- 1:1
God's part and man's part -- 1:22, 2:12
grow in respect to -- 2:2
used with different meanings -- 1:5
of your souls -- 1:9
past, present, and future -- 1:5, 2:2
ready to be revealed in the last time -- 1:5
subject of OT prophecy -- 1:10
Same afflictions,
are accomplished in your brethren -- 5:9
Samson and Delilah -- 2:11
Sanctification -- 1:15
not synonymous with sinless perfection – 1:2
word used in different senses -- 1:2
see also, Holiness
Sanctify Christ as Lord -- 3:15
Sarah,
example of -- 3:6
obeyed Abraham -- 3:6
whose daughters you are -- xxvi, 3:6
Satan -- *see* Devil
Saved, if righteous is, with difficulty -- 4:18
Scripture,
contained in -- 2:6
inerrancy -- 1:25
preservation of -- 1:25
Second Advent -- 1:5
chief Shepherd shall appear -- 5:4
Greek words used for -- 1:7
mistakenly supposed to be near -- 4:5,7
revelation of Jesus Christ -- iii, 1:7,13
revelation of His glory -- 4:13
Second chance, post-mortem -- 4:6
Second work of grace -- 1;2
Secretaries -- *see* Amanuensis
Seed,
corruptible -- 1:23
incorruptible -- 1:23
Semo Saneus (Sabine god) -- viii
Sensual conduct, sensuality,
having followed a course of -- 4:3
Septuagint,
quoted in 1 Peter -- xviii, 1:24,25, 2:6, 4:18
Septuagint, *continued*
widely used in Palestine -- xviii
Servant, Suffering -- *see* Suffering Servant
Servants
and Masters -- 2:18
household -- 2:18
slaves -- *see* Slaves
Serve, serving
employ your special gift in, one another – 4:10
in the strength which God supplies -- 4:11
Shame -- xxxiv
believer not put to -- 2:6
slanderers put to -- 3:16
Sharp's rule of grammar -- 1:3
Sheep,
lost -- 5:4
straying like -- 2:25
returned to Shepherd and Guardian -- 2:25
Shepherd of Hermas – *see* Hermas, Shepherd of
Shepherding program -- 5:3
Sheol -- *see* Hades
Shepherd, Chief -- 5:4
Sibylline Oracles -- xxiii
Sight of God, choice and precious in the -- 2:4
Signature -- *see* 1 Peter
Silas, Silvanus -- xix, 5:12
a faithful brother -- 5:12
a chief man among the brethren -- xiv
a prophet -- xiv, 5:12
"By" Silas, I have written -- iii, ix, xiii, xiv, 5:12
Silver -- 1:18
Simon Magus -- vii, viii, xxiii
Sinope -- 1:1
Sin, sins
Christ died for, of others -- 3:18
he who has suffered ... has ceased from – 4:1
love covers a multitude of -- 4:8
offering -- 3:18
Sinner, what will become of the -- 4:18
Sinful nature -- 2:11,24
Slander, slandered -- 3:16
as evil-doers -- 2:12
put aside all -- 2:1
Slaves (servants),
in the Roman empire -- 2:17

Sober, Sobriety
be, for the purpose of prayer -- 4:7
keep sober in spirit -- xxviii, 1:13, 5:8
Social science criticism -- xxvii, xxxiv-xxxvi
Sons of God, how explained -- 3:19
Sordid gain -- 5:2
Sorrows -- 2:19
Soul -- 1:9
commit your, to a faithful Creator -- iv, 4:19
eight, saved -- 3:20
fleshly lusts war against the -- *see* Fleshly lusts
purified, in obeying the truth -- 1:22
returned to the Shepherd and Guardian of your -- 2:25
salvation of your -- 1:9
Sound judgment, be of -- 4:7
Source criticism -- xxxi, 3:18
Speak, speaks
whoever, let him speak as the oracles of God -- 4:11
Speeches, Peter's in Acts -- x
Spirit (Holy)
of Christ -- 1:11
of God -- 4:14
and glory rests on you -- 4:14
baptism of -- *see* Baptism of the Holy Spirit
doctrine of, in 1 Peter, meager? -- xvii
Source of sanctification -- 1:2
operative in obedience -- 1:2
a person -- 1:11
present with Christians when they are persecuted -- 4:14
power -- 1:5
sanctifying work of -- 1:2
sent from heaven -- 1:12
Spirit of Christ in the prophets -- 1:11
spiritual gifts -- *see* Spiritual gifts
works through the Word in conversion – 3:1
Spirit, human -- 1:2,22
is born again -- 1:2,22,23
dead in trespasses and sins -- 1:2
gentle and quiet -- 3:4
keep sober in -- 1:13, 4:7, 5:8
live in the -- 4:6
Spirit, human, *continued*
nourishment for -- 2:2
made alive (quickened) in spirit -- *see* Christ
Spirits, the -- 3:19
disembodied -- 3:20
Christ's conflict with evil spirits -- 3:22
the "spirits in prison" -- 3:19
see also, Intermediate state
Spiritual,
applied to the milk of the Word -- 2:2
applied to the church as "house" of God – 2:5
applied to Christian sacrifices -- 2:5
Spiritual gifts (charisma) -- 3:15
as each has received a -- 4:10
employ it serving one another -- 4:10
received by laying on of apostles' hands – ix, 4:10
Special Study -- following chapter 4
temporary -- 3:15
Sprinkling of the blood of Jesus -- *see* Blood
Steadfastness, falling from -- *see* Falling from steadfastness
Stephanus, Greek text of - i
Stephen -- 4:14
Stewards, good,
of the manifold grace of God -- 4:10
Stone, cornerstone -- x
choice, precious -- 2:4,6
head of the corner -- x, 2:7
living -- 2:4
stone of stumbling -- 2:8
rock of offense -- 2:8
rejected by builders -- 2:7
rejected by men -- 2:4
Strangers -- 2:11
aliens -- iii, 1:1,4,17, 2:11
and pilgrims -- iii
scattered throughout Pontus -- 1:1
Strength, which God supplies -- 4:11
Strengthen, God will, you -- 5:10
Stripes, by whose, you are healed -- 2:24
Stumble at the word -- *see* Word
Subjection, submission
to civil authorities -- xxviii, 2:13
of slaves to masters -- 2:18

Subjection, submission, *continued*
- Of wives to husbands -- 3:1,5
- of younger to the elders -- 5:5

Subscriptions -- 5:12
Suetonius -- 2:12
Suffer, suffering
- according to the will of God -- 3:17, 4:19
- after you have, for a little -- xxviii, 5:10
- as a Christian -- 4:16
- for righteousness' sake -- 3:13, 4:12
- for doing right -- 2:20, 3:17
- testing -- 4:12
- sharing the sufferings of Christ -- 4:13
- purifying effect of -- 4:1,18
- in what sense a cure for sin -- 4:1
- not as a murderer or busybody -- 4:15
- others have same experiences -- 5:9
- paradox of joy in suffering -- 4:13
- suffering for the name -- 4:16
- Christians not to be surprised by -- 4:12
- unjustly -- 2:19
- wrongfully, blessedness of -- 2:20

Suffering Servant poems -- xxxi, 1:11, 2:21
Sufferings of Christ – *see* Christ
Sulpicius Severus -- xvi
Supplies -- 4:11
Surprised, that you no longer run with them – 4:4
Sympathetic, let all be -- 3:8
Syriac Versions
- Old Syriac -- xiv
- Peshitto Syriac -- xx, 5:13

Tacitus -- xv, 2:12
Talmud, Babylonian -- xxi, xxii, xxvi
Talmud, Jerusalem -- xxii
Tartarus -- 3:19
Tatian -- xiv
Temptations, to sin -- 2:11, 4:1
Ten lost tribes -- xxvi
Tertullian -- xii, xiv, xxii
Tested,
- by fire -- 1:7
- by fiery ordeal -- 4:12

Testimony, Peter's -- xxvii, 5:12
Textus Receptus -- 1:16
Thaddeus -- xxv
Theophilus of Antioch -- xi
Theophrastus -- 5:3
Thief, suffer not as -- 4:15
Thomas, apostle -- xxi
Three-storied universe (?) -- 3:19
Time already past is sufficient -- 4:3
Titles of New Testament books
- added by men - i
- older, are shorter - i
- reflected traditional beliefs of primitive churches - ii
- no reason to question truthfulness of traditional titles -- ii

Tongue, refrain from speaking evil -- 3:10
Total hereditary depravity -- *see* Sinful nature
Trajan -- xvi, 4:16
Transfiguration -- *see* Christ
"Tree" (cross of Jesus was a) -- x, 2:24
Trials,
- distressed by various -- 1:6
- tests -- xxviii, 1:6

Trinity, the -- 1:2
- *see also*, God

Troubled, do not be -- 3:14
Troublesome meddler, not suffer as a -- xxix, 4:15
Trustworthiness -- ix
Truth, Christianity as obedience to the -- 1:22
Tubingen school -- xiii
Twelve tribes -- xxvi

Ulpian -- 2:14
Unconditional election -- 1:2
Unconditional eternal security -- 1:5
Undefiled -- 1:4
Unfading -- 5:4
Ungodly and sinner, judgment on -- 4:18
Unity of 1 Peter -- xix, xxxi, xxxii-xxxiv
Unreasonable,
- masters may be -- 2:18

Unrighteous men -- 3:18

Verba Christi -- x
Verbal adjectives -- 1:1
Victory of Christ -- 3:19,22
Visitation, day of -- *see* Day of visitation
Voluntarily, shepherd the flock -- 5:2

Walking,
 after the flesh -- *see* Flesh
 in Jesus' steps -- 2:21
War in heaven -- 3:19
Way, of life, futile -- 1:18
Weaker vessel -- 3:7
Well-doing, suffering for -- 3:17
Wickedness -- *see* Malice
Will of God -- 2:15, 3:17, 4:2,6
Wine, excess of -- 4:3
Wives,
 be submissive to your own husbands -- 3:1
 position of in Hellenistic world -- 3:1
 duties of Christian -- 3:1
 fellow heirs of grace of life -- 3:7
 weaker vessel -- 3:7
 how to adorn themselves -- 3:3
Women, Christianity elevated the status of – 3:7
Won to Christ -- 3:1
 without a word -- 3:1
Word of God -- 2:8
 abides forever -- 1:25
 disobedient to the -- 2:8
 lamp and light -- 2:9
 living and abiding nature of -- 1:23
 pure milk of the -- 2:2
 seed, by which men are begotten again – 1:23
 stumble at the -- 2:8
 this is the word preached to you -- 1:25, 2:2
Work men's, judged by God -- 1:17
World -- 5:9
Worship -- 2:4
Written, it is -- 1:16
Wrong, suffering for -- 3:17

Younger, the -- 5:5
 be submissive to your elders -- 5:5

Zealots -- v, xxix, 2:13
Zealous for what is good -- 3:13
Zion, choice Stone laid in -- 2:6

2 PETER INDEX

(Roman numerals indicate pages in the Introductory Studies. Chapter and verses are given for notes in the commentary pages.)

Abraham,
  pleads for cities of Sodom and Gomorrah -- 2:6,7
  Testament of -- *see* Testament of Abraham
Abundantly -- 1:11
Abyss -- 2:4
Accursed children -- 2:14
Acts of Paul and Thecla -- x
Acts of Peter -- *see* Peter, Acts of
Adultery, eyes full of -- 2:14
Aeons -- 1:16, 2:10
Ages, three, of earth's history -- xxxvii, 3:6
Akhmim Fragment -- ii
All his (Paul's) letters -- xvii, 3:16
All things,
  continue as they were -- 3:4
  pertaining to life and godliness -- 1:1,3
Allusions to 2 Peter in early Christian literature -- ii-iv, xxx, 1:8,17, 2:2,20, 3:5,8
Amanuensis -- viii, xii, xiv
Amen -- 3:18
Anacoluthon -- xiv, 1:17, 2:4
Analogy of Scripture -- 1:20
Ancient world, God did not spare -- 2:5
Angelic majesties -- xl, 2:10
Angel, angels (*see also*, Spirits, the)
  Balaam's donkey shrank from an -- 2:16
  created beings -- 2:4
  do not bring railing accusations -- 2:11
  evil -- 2:4
    see also, Demons
  fallen -- xiii, xix, xxvii, 2:4,10
  greater in might and power -- 2:11
  imprisoned -- 2:4
  dignity of -- 2:10
  God did not spare, who sinned -- xl, 2:4
  neither marry nor given in marriage -- 2:4
  reserved unto judgment -- 2:4
  sons of God -- *see* Sons of God
  spirits -- *see also*, under Spirits
  who sinned were punished -- 2:4
Animals, like mad -- xl, 2:12
Annihilation -- xxxviii, 2:1, 3:6,10
Annotated quotations -- i, iv
Antilegomena -- iv, v-vii
Antinomianism -- 1:2, 2:19
Aorist tense,
  historical -- 1:17
  participle may denote same act as leading verb -- 2:4
  timeless -- 1:17
Apocalypse of Peter -- *see* Peter, Apocalypse of
Apocalyptic writings -- xviii, xxi
Apocryphal Acts -- xxxiv
Apocryphal books -- ii, xxiv, xxxiii
Apology of Phileas -- v
Apostates, apostasy -- 2:20,22
Apostles (of churches) -- 3:2
Apostles (of Jesus),
  authority of -- xxxvi, 2:21, 3:16
  called by Jesus -- x, 1:1,3
  empowered on Pentecost -- x, 1:3, 3:2
  faithfully delivered their message -- 1:1
  area of authority -- xvi, 3:16
  knowledge of Jesus Christ -- 1:3
  no change of doctrine about the second advent -- 3:8
  spoke on Jesus' behalf -- 3:2
  spoke the command of the Lord -- 3:1
  temporary office -- xvi
Apostolic,
  fathers -- xviii
  succession -- 1:15
Aristides -- 1:11
Aristotle -- 1:6
Ark, Noah's, being constructed -- 2:5
Article, Greek definite -- *see* Sharp's rule of grammar
Ascension -- *see* Christ
Asceticism -- 1:2
Ashes, reduced to -- 2:6
Asia Minor -- 1:1
Asleep, fallen -- *see* Death
Assumption of Moses -- xvii, xx
Astrology -- xxxii
Athenagoras -- 2:4
Atonement -- 1:1
  see also, Christ, Sacrifice

Augustine -- viii
Authenticity of 2 Peter -- iv, xxxiv, xxxv
Authority,
apostolic -- xi, xvi, xxxvi
civil -- 2:10
despised -- 2:10
Authorship
1 Peter -- iv, xiv
2 Peter -- *see* 2 Peter
Auto-salvation -- xxxii, 1:2

Balaam -- xix
a prophet -- 2:16
rebuked for his iniquity -- xxvii
way of -- 2:15
Balak -- 2:15
Baptism,
for the remission of sins -- 1:9
immersion -- 1:9
Barnabas -- 3:17
Barnabas, Epistle of -- 3:9
Basilides -- xxxiii
Beforehand -- 3:2
Beginning, just as it was from the -- 3:4
Behavior,
favorite word with Peter -- 2:7, 3:11
winsome among the Gentiles -- 2:2
Beloved -- 3:1,8,14,17
Beor -- 2:15
Better, not to have known the way of righteousness -- 2:21
Bible and science -- 3:6
Blameless -- 3:14
Blaspheme, the way of righteousness -- ii
Blemishes -- xix, 2:13
Blessing,
pronounced on readers of canonical books -- v, vi
Blind or short-sighted -- 1:9
Bodmer VIII Papyrus -- *see* P^{72}
Body,
physical -- 1:13
resurrection -- 3:13
Bohairic Coptic -- *see* Coptic versions
Bond-servant -- xi, 1:1
Book of Enoch -- *see* 1 Enoch
Books of New Testament,
arranged according to length -- xxx
Born again -- 1:3
Brethren -- 1:10
Brotherly kindness, add -- 1:7
Brotherly love inculcated -- xiii
see also, love
Byzantine text -- 2:4,13,15, 3:7

Cain -- xix
Called, calling
and election sure -- 1:10
many are, but few chosen -- 1:10
to become Christians -- 1:3,10
Calvin, Calvinism -- viii, 2:4,18, 3:9
doubted Peter's authorship of 2 Peter – 3:16
election precedes the call -- 1:10
eternal security -- 2:1,20,22
God's "desirative" and "decretive" will – 3:9
perseverance of the saints -- 1:9, 2:1
predestination to damnation -- 2:12, 3:12
predestination to salvation -- 3:12
total depravity – *see* Total depravity
Canon, New Testament
collecting of the New Testament books -- xii, xvi, xvii, xxii, 3:16
completed -- 1:19
criteria for canonicity -- i
evidence for 2 Peter's inclusion in -- i, viii
guarding of the books -- ix, xvi, xvii, xxxix
listings of canonical books -- v-viii
making and accepting of New Testament books -- xvii
Capitulations -- vii
Captured, to be -- 2:12
Carpocrates, the Gnostic -- xxxiii
Carried away by error -- 3:17
Catholic epistles -- iv, vii
Cephas -- *see* Peter
Cerinthus -- 1:2
Certain,
make His calling and choosing -- 1:10
Word of God is more -- 1:19

Chains of darkness -- 2:4
Chester Beatty Papyrus II -- *see* P[46]
Chiliasm -- xxxviii
Choosing of you, make His sure -- 1:10
Christ -- xxxvii
  active in creation -- 3:5
  all power in heaven and earth granted to – 1:16
  ascension -- xxxvii
  beloved son, This is My -- 1:17
  blood of, redemption by -- xxxvii, 2:1
  deity -- xviii, 1:1,3, 3:12,15,18
  divine power -- 1:3
  doxologies addressed to -- xl, 3:18
  God's beloved Son -- 1:17
  eternal -- xxxvii
  first advent (a powerful coming) – 1:16,18,19
  glory and virtue of -- 1:3,16, 2:10
  glory given to -- xviii, xxxvii, 1:1,17, 3:18
  God in the flesh -- 1:3,19
  incarnation -- xxxvii, 1:18
  Jehovah passages applied to -- 3:10
  Judge of all -- 3:14
  King -- 1:16
  Lord, lordship -- xxxvi, xxxvii, 1:2,11, 2:10, 3:2,18
  majesty -- 1:16
  Master -- xxxvii
  Messiah -- 1:3
  miracles -- 1:16
  parables -- 3:12
  parousia -- xxxvi, xxxviii, 1:11,16
  patience -- 3:15
  portrayal of, in 2 Peter -- xxxvi
  power over demons -- 2:4
  promised Messiah -- 1:1
  received honor and glory -- xviii, xxxvii
  reign of -- 3:4
  resurrection -- xxxvii, xxxviii, 1:16
  at right hand of God -- 1:11
  sacrifice -- 1:1
  Savior -- xiii, xxxvii, 1:1,11, 3:2
  second advent -- *see* Second advent
  sermon on the mount -- 2:1
  sinlessness -- 2:13
Christ, *continued*
  spotless and blameless -- 3:14
  transfiguration -- ii, xi, xxxvii, xxxviii, 1:15,16
    accounts of, compared -- 1:16,17
  virtue of -- 1:3,5
Christian(s)
  liberty -- xxxii, 2:19, 3:16
  virtues -- *see* Spiritual qualities
Christianity
  way of truth, evil spoken of -- 2:2
Christology,
  high, of 2 Peter -- *see* 2 Peter
Church (*see also*, people of God)
  a chosen people -- 2:1
Clement of Alexandria -- iv, v, 2:2,15
Clement of Rome,
  account of Peter's martyrdom -- xxiv
  allusions to 2 Peter -- ii, 1:17
1 Clement -- ii, xxiv, 3:4
2 Clement -- iii, 2:2
Cleverly devised tales -- xxxii
Clouds,
  carried by a tempest -- 2:17
  without water -- xix
Codex Alexandrinus -- 1:10, 2:4,13,15,17, 3:11,18
Codex Ephraemi -- 2:4,13,15,17, 3:7,18
Codex Sinaiticus -- vii, 1:1,10, 2:4,13,15,17, 3:7,11,18
Codex Vaticanus -- vii, 1:1, 2:4,6,13,15,17, 3:11,18
Colossian heresy -- 2:4, 3:10
Commandment
  holy -- 2:21
  of the Lord through His apostles -- 1:3
  of the Lord spoken by your apostles -- 3:2
Common salvation -- xxii
Compendium, compilation -- *see* 2 Peter
Condemnation of ungodly men -- xix
Conditional sentences -- 2:4
Conduct -- 2:7, 3:11
Confession -- 1:1
Conflagration, final -- v, xxxvii, xxxviii, 3:7,10,12
    Gnostic beliefs -- 3:10
    Stoic beliefs -- 3:7
Consummation of the age -- 3:4,6

Continue, all things, as from the beginning – 3:4
Conversation -- *see* Behavior
Coptic versions,
Bohairic -- v
Sahidic -- v
2 Peter and Jude included in -- v
Corrupt, desires -- 2:10
Corruption,
in the world -- xxxii, 1:4, 2:10
slaves of -- 2:19
Cosmological changes -- 3:3,11
Councils of Hippo, Laodicea, Carthage -- vii
Covenant,
Noahic -- 2:8
New -- 2:21, 3:16
Old has been abrogated -- 2:21
Covetousness -- 2:15
Creator -- *see* God
Creation,
by the Word of God -- 3:5,6
the beginning of -- 3:4
subjected to futility when man sinned – 3:6,13
Creatures without reason -- xix, 2:12
Curse, when man sinned -- 3:6
Cyprian -- 2:4

Daring, false teachers are -- 2:10
Dark place, a lamp shining in a -- 1:19
Darkness,
black, reserved for false teachers -- 2:17
chains of -- 2:4
outer -- 2:17
prison of demons -- 2:4
Date of writing -- *see* 2 Peter
Dative case -- 3:7
denotes means -- 1:1, 2:18
denotes sphere -- 1:1
of agent -- 3:14
Daughters of men -- 2:4
David's throne, Christ now sits on -- 1:11
Day,
as a thousand years -- iii, 3:8
of eternity -- 3:18
Day, *continued*
of God -- 3:12
of Judgment -- 2:9
of the Lord -- xxxviii, 3:10,15
Day dawn -- 1:19
Daytime, revel in the -- 2:13
Dead Sea Scrolls -- 2:4,10
Death,
called an "exodus" -- iii, xxiii, 1:15
entered the world when man sinned -- 3:6
fallen asleep -- xviii, 3:4
putting off bodily tent -- xiii
of Peter, predicted -- *see* Peter, death of
Deceivers, appearance of -- *see* False Teachers
Deceptions, reveling in their -- 2:13
Defilements of the world -- 2:20
escaped by the knowledge of the Lord – 2:20
entangled again therein -- 2:20
Degrees,
of punishment -- 2:20
of reward -- 1:11
Deism -- 3:7
Delivered,
faith was once for all -- 2:21
holy commandment was -- 2:21
Deluge -- *see* Flood, Noah's
Demiurge -- 2:10
Demons -- 2:1,4,10
if imprisoned, how can world be demonized? -- 2:4
two classes of? -- 2:4
Denunciation of ungodly men -- xix
Deny the Lord who bought them -- xxxii, 1:1, 2,17, 2:1, 3:15
Departure -- *see* Death
Desires,
corrupt -- 2:10
entice by fleshly -- 2:18
Despise authority -- 2:10
Destination of 2 Peter -- *see* 2 Peter
Destructive heresies -- xix, xxxii, 2:1
Destruction, destroyed -- 3:9
all these things to be -- 3:11
bring swift, on themselves -- 2:1,12
cities of Sodom and Gomorrah condemned to -- 2:6
heavens will be -- 3:12

Destruction, destroyed, *continued*
of Jerusalem (AD 70) -- *see* Jerusalem, destruction of (AD 70)
of the earth, by fire -- iii
of ungodly men -- 3:7
is not asleep -- 2:3
the world at that time was -- 3:6
word does not mean annihilation -- 3:6
wrest Scripture to their own -- 3:16
Deutero-Pauline epistles, so called -- xv
Devil,
cast out of heaven -- 3:6
led a rebellion in heaven -- 2:4
limitations placed on -- 2:9
power of -- xxxii
resist him, firm in your faith
Diaspora -- *see* Dispersion
Dignities -- *see* Angelic majesties
Diligent, diligence,
applying all -- 1:5
be all the more -- 1:10, 3:14
Peter promises to be -- 1:15
Dispersion -- xiii
Divine nature -- xxiii
partakers of the -- xiii, xxxviii, 1:1,4
Divine power -- xiii, xxxvii, 1:3
Docetists, docetism -- x, xxvi, 1:2
Doctrines,
of demons -- 2:1
of perdition -- *see* Destructive heresies
Dog, returns to its vomit -- 2:22
Donkey,
dumb -- 2:16
restrained Balaam's madness -- 2:16
speaking with a voice of a man -- 2:16
Double negative -- 1:10
Doubts as to authenticity of 2 Peter -- xi-xxvii
how explained -- xi-xxvii
Doxologies -- xxxv, xl, 3:18
Drowsy -- 2:3
Dualism, Greek -- xxxiii. 1:2
Dumb ass -- *see* Donkey
Dwell -- 3:13

Earnestly desiring the day of God -- 3:12
Early catholicism -- xv, xvi, 1:13
Early Christian literature -- iv, viii
Earth,
burning -- 3:10
formed out of water and by water -- 3:5
the heavens and, that now are -- xxxvii, 3:7
and its works will be burned up -- 3:10
Earthly dwelling -- 1:13
Ecstasy and frenzy -- 1:21
Eight souls saved -- 2:5
Eirenikon -- xii
see also, Tubingen school
Elemental spirits -- 3:10
Elements melt with fervent heat -- 3:10,12
1 Enoch -- xx, 2:4
Entangled again, in defilements -- 2:20
Entice,
by fleshly desires -- 2:18
unstable souls -- 2:14
Entrance into the eternal kingdom -- 1:11
Epaphroditus -- 3:2
Ephraem Syrus -- vii, 2:4
Epiphanius -- viii
Epistle of Barnabas -- *see* Barnabas
Epistle of the Churches of Vienne and Lyon – iii
Epistle to the Alexandrines -- x
Epistle to the Laodiceans -- x
Erasmus -- viii
Error, carried away by the, of unprincipled men -- 3:17
Escape, escaped,
do not let this one fact, notice -- 3:8
the corruption that is in the world -- 1:4, 2:20
the pollutions of the world -- xiii, xxxviii, 2:20
Essenes -- 2:4,10
Established in the truth -- *see* Truth
Eternal bonds -- 2:4
Eternal,
kingdom -- 1:11
punishment -- 2:13
security -- *see* Faith, protected by power of God through
Eternity, day of -- 3:18
Eusebius -- v, vi

Example,
different Greek words for -- 2:6
Sodom and Gomorrah made an -- 2:6
Exhortation -- xxxvi
to grow in grace and knowledge -- 3:18
to guard against the error of the wicked – 3:17
External evidence -- *see* 2 Peter, authorship
Eyes full of adultery -- 2:14
Eyewitness -- xiii
Peter as -- x, 1:18
of Christ's majesty -- 1:16
of Christ's transfiguration -- x 1:15,16,18

Fables -- xxiii, xxiv
not followed cunningly devised -- xiii, xxxii, 1:16
Faith -- 1:5
and works -- 3:16
body of doctrine -- 1:1
comes by hearing the Word -- 1:1
once for all delivered to the saints -- 1:3
personal conviction -- 1:1
received a like precious -- 1:1
Fallen asleep -- *see* Death
Falling from steadfastness -- 3:17
False doctrine -- x
False prophets -- ii, iii, 1:21, 2:1
False teachers and scoffers -- iii, xiv, xvi, xviii, xix, xxxii, 2:1-22
bring destruction on themselves -- 2:12
claims and teachings -- xxxii, xxxvii, 3:1
deliberately omit known Scriptural teachings -- 3:5
denied any second coming -- 1:16, 3:1,4
denied the Lord who bought them – *see* Denied
denounced -- xxvii
despised authority -- 2:10
fallen Christians, or never converted? – 2:1,19,20
follow the way of Balaam -- 2:15
follow their own lusts - 3:3
forsaken the right way -- 2:15
greed of -- 2:3

False teachers, *continued*
have no knowledge -- 2:12
identified -- xvi, xxxi-xxxiii, xxxvi
their judgment is not idle -- 2:3
lifestyle encouraged by -- 1:3, 2:2,8,18, 3:1
like unreasoning animals -- 2:12
many will follow them -- 2:2
mocking -- 3:3
prediction of -- iii, xxii, xxv, xxxi, xl, 2:1-3,17, 3:3
promise their converts freedom -- 2:19
secretly introduce destructive heresies – 2:1, 3:1
sensuality of -- 2:2,4
slaves of corruption -- *see* Servants of corruption
speak arrogant words of vanity -- 2:18
spots and blemishes -- 2:13, 3:14
ungodly men – 3:7
vices and sins -- 2:13-16
worthlessness of their teaching -- 2:17-19
wrested Scripture -- 2:19, 3:5,15,16
False words -- 2:3
Father, God the -- 1:17
Fathers, have fallen asleep -- xvi, xviii, 3:4
Felix and Drusilla -- 1:6
Fire,
destruction of the earth by -- iii, xxxviii, 3:7
flaming -- xxxviii
present heavens and earth are reserved for -- 3:7
rained on Sodom and Gomorrah -- 2:6, 3:7
see also, Conflagration, final
stored up for -- xxxvii, 3:7
Firmillian -- iv
First, know this -- 1:20, 3:3
Flesh,
defiling desires of -- 2:10
indulge the -- 2:10
put to death the deeds of the -- 1:6
Flood, Noah's -- xxxvii, 2:5
a "catastrophe" -- 2:5, 3:6
eight persons saved -- 2:5
followed by a "new world" -- 3:13
Flooded with water -- 3:6

Follow, followed -- 1:16, 2:2,15
Forgery -- vi, viii, xxi, xxiv
Forgotten his purification -- 1:9
Formed, earth was -- 3:5
Forsaken the true way -- iii, 2:15
Freedom,
 not a covering for evil -- 2:19
 Paul's teaching about -- xxxii
 promised by false teachers -- 2:19
 see also, Christian liberty
Fullness of the Jews comes in -- 3:12

Gap theory -- 3:6
Genesis Apocryphon -- 2:4
Genitive,
 absolute -- 1:3, 3:11
 double possessive -- 3:2
 objective -- 1:2,3, 2:1, 3:18
 of source -- 1:20
 subjective -- 2:1, 3:18
Genre -- xxxiii
Gentiles, live in error -- 2:18
Genuineness -- x
 of 2 Peter -- i, iv, xi
Gift of prophecy -- 1:19
Gilgamesh Epic -- 2:5
Glories, railed at -- xl, 2:10
Glory,
 Christ's -- *see* Christ
 to Him be, for ever and ever -- 3:18
Gnossis, Gnostics, Gnosticism -- xxvi, xxxii, xxxiii, xxxviii, 1:2,3
 cleverly devised tales -- 1:16
 dishonest handling of Scripture -- xxxii, 2:7, 3:16
 esoteric knowledge claimed -- 1:3
 explanation of the creation -- 2:10, 3:5
 incipient -- xviii, xxv, xxxii, xxxiii, 1:2,16, 2:4
 Jewish -- xviii, xxix, xxxii, 1:16, 2:4
 flourishes -- ii, xvi
 heretical ideas -- xvi, xxxii, 1:1, 2:1
 libertine emphases -- 2:19, 3:16
 "living voice" preferred above Scripture – 3:16
Gnostics, *continued*
 major doctrines -- 1:2, 3:10
 Pleroma -- 2:10, 3:10,13
 seven heavens -- 2:10, 3:13
 unprincipled men -- 3:17
 wrote pseudepigraphical books -- ix, xvii
 see also, Knowledge
God,
 benefactor -- xiii
 brought a flood on the ungodly -- 2:5
 divine power -- *see* Divine power
 eternality -- 3:8
 Father – *see* Father
 goodness, leads men to repentance -- 3:9
 granted all things pertaining to life and godliness -- 1:1
 His judgment is not idle -- *see* Judgment
 knows how to rescue the godly -- 2:9
 majesty -- xxiii, 1:17
 patience -- *see* Patience
 providence -- xviii, 3:7
 righteousness of -- 1:1
 not slack about His promises – *see* Promises
 steps into history -- 3:4
 virtue -- xxiii, xxiv
 wish (or will) -- 3:9
Godliness -- xiii, xxxvii, 1:1,3, 3:11
 add -- 1:6
Godly (people) -- 2:9
Gods, pagan,
 involvement in human history (fables) – xiii
Gomorrah -- *see* Sodom and Gomorrah
Gone astray -- 2:15
Gospel,
 definite doctrinal content -- 1:12,13
 no embellishment -- 1:16
 power of God unto salvation -- 1:3
Gospel of Peter -- *see* Peter, Gospel of
Gospel of Truth (Gnostic) -- iii
Grace,
 and peace be multiplied -- 1:2
 grow in the, of the Lord -- xl, 3:18
Grammar, Sharp's rule of -- *see* Sharp's
Granted -- 1:3,4
Great Tribulation -- 3:3
Greed, a heart trained in -- 2:14

Greek philosophy -- xxxiii
Greetings -- 1:2
Growth,
in grace -- 3:18
in knowledge -- xxxvii, 3:18
spiritual, continuous, essential to life – 3:18
Guard, be on your -- 3:17

Hades -- 2:9
Hammurabi -- 2:5
Hananiah -- 2:1
Hapax Legomena -- xv, 2:1,13,16,18,22, 3:3,16
how number of is computed -- xv
Hastening the day of God -- 3:12
Heart,
day dawns in your -- 1:19
hardening of the -- 2:20
trained in greed -- 2:14
Heaven, heavens,
Christ has gone into -- *see* Christ
destroyed by burning -- 3:12
existed long ago, by Word of God -- 3:5
New, and earth – *see* New heavens and earth
the, and earth that now are -- xxxvii, 3:7
rebellion in -- *see* Rebellion
will pass away with a roar -- 3:10
Hebraism -- 2:14, 3:3,4
Hebrew letters,
Galileans had trouble pronouncing some – 2:15
Hebrews, epistle to -- vii
Heisenberg's theory of indeterminacy -- 3:4
Hell -- 2:1,3,10,17, 3:6,9
see also, Tartarus
Hellenism, Hellenistic
in 2 Peter -- xiii
language -- xiii, xv
Heresies -- x, xv, xvi, 2:1
destructive – *see* Destructive Heresies
of the first and second centuries – *see* Gnostics
Heretics -- iv, v
Hermas, Shepherd of -- iii, viii, 2:20, 3:5
Hermeneutics, rules of -- 3:16
Herodotus -- ix
Higher criticism -- i, viii, xi, xxxiv, 3:8
Hippolytus of Portus -- iv, 3:9
History, being moved to a goal -- 3:6
Holy commandment -- 2:21
Holy conduct -- 3:11
Holy living -- xxxii, xxxviii, xl, 1:1,11, 3:11
Holy men, inspiration of -- *see* Inspiration
Holy mount -- ii, xvi, xviii, 1:18
Holy prophets -- 3:2
Holy Spirit -- *see* Spirit of God
Homologoumena -- v, xxv
Honor received by Jesus -- 1:17
Hope, set your, on the revelation of Jesus Christ -- 3:12
Human will -- 1:21
Hymns, Jewish and early Christian -- vii

Idle -- 2:3
Ignatius -- xii, 1:8
Image of God -- 1:4
Imperfect tense,
signifies continuous action in the past – 3:5
Incarnation -- *see* Christ
Incubi -- 2:4
Inherited total depravity -- *see* Total depravity
Inspiration -- xxvii, xxxvi
important to canonicity -- i, xviii
Holy men of God spoke as they were moved by the Spirit -- iv, 1:21
of apostles and prophets -- xx
of Old Testament books -- xii, xviii, 1:1,19, 3:2
Integrity of the text -- xxviii, xxix
Intermediate state -- 2:5,9,10,17
Interpolations -- xxviii
Interpretation, no prophecy is of private – 1:20
Interpreter,
different one used for 2 Peter -- viii
Paul had Titus as his -- viii
Irenaeus -- iii, xxxii, xxxviii, 2:15,22, 3:5,9,10,16

Israelites,
destroyed in the wilderness -- xix
the people -- 2:1

James, Letter of -- vii
Jerome,
on the epistles of Peter -- viii, ix,
differences in style -- xii
Jerusalem, destruction of (AD 70) -- xxvi, 3:4,10
Jerusalem Conference -- 1:1
Job, Testament of -- *see* Testament of Job
John, Acts of -- xxxiv
John, apostle
writings of, opposed to Gnosticism – xxxiii
John, Gospel of,
alluded to in 2 Peter? -- xvi
1 John -- 1:7
2 John -- vii
3 John -- vii
Joseph of Arimathea -- 3:12
Josephus -- 1:1, 2:4,5
resemblances to 2 Peter, alleged -- xxiii
Judaizers -- 1:2, 3:17
Jude, epistle of -- iv, vii, 2:4
date of writing -- xix
rare words in -- xxi
rejected by some -- xvii
relation of, to 2 Peter -- i, viii, xviii, xix-xxiii, xxviii, xxxii, 2:1,4,7,13, 3:17
sources, alleged -- xx
Judgment,
day of -- 2:9, 3:7
Jesus is the judge -- 3:14
of the Great Day -- 2:4
on false teachers is not idle -- 2:3
final -- xxxviii, 2:10, 3:6
reviling, brought by false teachers -- 2:11
upon the ungodly -- xix
Julius Africanus -- 2:4
Jung Codex -- iii
Justification by faith -- 1:1
Justin Martyr -- iii, 2:4, 3:8,10

Kasemann, Ernst
alleged degenerate Christology in 2 Peter -- xxxvii
alleged defective soteriology in 2 Peter – xxxvii
alleged sub-Christian eschatology in 2 Peter -- xxxviii
Kept through faith -- *see* Faith, protected by power of God through
Killed, to be -- 2:12
King James Version,
use made of older translations -- xxxvi
went backwards in translation of 2 Peter – xxxv, 2:1, 3:4,5,12
Kingdom -- 1:11, 3;12
different connotations of the word -- 1:11
Know this first of all -- 1:20, 3:3
Knowledge -- xiii, xxxii, xl
add -- 1:5
full -- 1:1,2,8,12, 2:20,21
grow in, of our Lord Jesus Christ – xl, 1:2, 3:18
inerrant source of -- 1:3,12,18,19,21
of Jesus our Lord -- 1:2,8, 2:20
of God -- 1:2
true -- xxxvii, 1:2,8
Korah -- xix

Lamech -- 2:4
Lamp shining in a dark place -- 1:19
Laodiceans (pseudo-Pauline) -- xxv
Last days -- 3:3
Last state, worse than the first -- 2:20
Last times -- 3:3
Latin Versions
Old Latin -- 1:1
Latin Vulgate -- xxxvi, 1:1, 2:10, 3:18
Lawless deeds -- 2:8
Laws of nature -- 3:4
Lazarus, raised from the dead -- 3:4
Libertine lifestyle -- xxxii, 2:19
Life -- xxxvii, 1:3
Life after death,
Peter's language implies -- 1:14,15
Like precious -- 1:1

Literary dependence -- ii, xix, xxi, xxii
Live, in error -- 2:18
Looking for the day of God -- 3:12,13
Lord
    God the Father -- 2:9
    Jesus Christ -- 1:8, 2:20, 3:18
    knows how to rescue the godly -- 2:9
Lord's Supper -- 3:4
Lost letters (?) -- xxx, 3:1
Lot,
    deliverance of -- 2:6,7
    oppressed by the sensual conduct -- 2:7
    righteous man -- 2:7
Love, loved,
    add -- 1:7
    the wages of unrighteousness -- 2:15
Love feasts -- 2:13
Luke, made a collection of Paul's letters – 3:16
Lust, lusts,
    corruption in the world through -- xxxii, 1:4
    false teachers follow their own -- 3:3
Luther -- viii, 2:4
LXX -- *see* Septuagint

Madness, restrained -- 2:16
Magic -- xxxii
Magnificent promises -- *see* Promises
Majestic glory -- 1:17
Man of sin (lawlessness) -- 3:16
Manuscript variations -- 1:1,3,4,10,12,19,21
    2:1,2,4,6,10,12,15,17,18
    3:2,9,10,11,16,18
Maranatha -- 3:4
Marcion -- xxxiii
Mark, John,
    Gospel of, alluded to -- viii, xi, 1:15
    Peter's interpreter -- viii
    traditional connection with Peter -- 1:15
Martyrdom, glorified -- xxiv
Master, denial of the -- xxxvii
Mattathias -- 1:1
Melanchthon -- 2:4
Melchizedek -- 2:16
Melito of Sardis -- iii, 3:5
Melt, elements will, with intense heat -- 3:12
Messianic Prophecies -- xxxii, 1:19,20,21
Methodius -- iii, v, 3:9
Micaiah -- 2:1
Michael, archangel -- 2:11
Midrash Ruth -- 2:4
Milton -- xiv
Mind, stir up your sincere -- 3:1
Might, angels are greater in -- 2:11
Mire -- *see* Wallow
Mists driven by a storm (winds) -- xix, 2:17
Moab, Moabites -- 2:15
Mockers -- *see* False teachers and scoffers
Montanism -- 1:21
Moral excellence -- 1:5
Morning star -- 1:19
Moses -- xviii, xxiii
    Assumption of -- *see* Assumption
    author of Psalm 90 -- 3:8
    contest for his body -- 2:11
    Testament of -- *see* Testament of Moses
Mount Hermon -- 1:18
Mount Sinai -- 1:17
Mount Tabor -- 1:18
Muratorian Canon -- vii, x
    attempts to emend the text -- vii
Mystery Religions -- 1:16
Myths -- *see* Fables

Nag Hammadi -- iii
Nativity of Mary -- v
Neo-liberalism -- xv, 1:16, 3:4
Neronian persecution -- xxx
New Birth -- *see* Born again
New converts,
    escaped the defilements of the world – 2:20
    enticed by false teachers -- 2:18
New covenant -- *see* Covenant
New heavens and new earth -- xxxvii, 3:10,13
Newness of life -- 1:9
Newtonian physics -- 3:4
Nicolaitan heresy -- 1:2, 2:15
Noah -- xix, 2:4

Noah, *continued*
preacher of righteousness -- *see* Righteousness
preserved by God -- 2:5
Noahic Covenant -- *see* Covenant
Notice,
it escapes their -- 3:5
stop letting it escape your -- 3:8

Obtained a like precious faith -- 1:1,16
Old Testament,
accounts accepted as historical -- 2:5,6,16
allusions to in 2 Peter -- iii, xxxvi
pronounces doom on false teachers -- 2:3
prophecies -- 1:19, 3:13
Olivet Discourse -- 3:10
One day with the Lord,
as a thousand years -- 3:8
Ophites -- 1:2
Oppressed by sensual conduct -- 2:7
Optative mood -- 1:2
Oral tradition -- xx
Oral transmission of Christian teaching -- 2:21
Ordo salutis -- xxxvi
Origen -- iv, xxxviii
Ought, what sort, you to be -- 3:11
Overcome, by defilements of the world -- 2:20

P^{46} -- xvii
P^{72} -- v, vi, 1:1, 2:4,6,13,15, 3:11,18
Paradise -- 3:13
Parallels between 2 Peter,
and Book of Jude -- xix-xxv
and Josephus -- xxiii
and Philo -- xxiii
Parousia – *see* Christ
see also, Second advent
Partakers of the divine nature -- *see* Divine nature
Participles
circumstantial -- 3:3
Participles, *continued*
participial imperative – *see* Imperative
strange constructions -- xiv
Patience of the Lord -- xl, 3:15
Patient,
different words for --3:9
God is -- 3:9
Patriarchs -- xviii
Paul,
and Peter, execrated heretics -- v, xxx, 3:16
and Peter's theology in complete agreement -- 3:16
Peter's approving reference to -- xi, 3:2, 15
associated with Peter -- xi
bond-servant -- 3:16
difficult passages in -- 3:16
doctrine of grace -- 3;16
farewell speech to Ephesian elders – xxxiv
his letters called "Scripture" -- xi, 3:16
known to readers of 2 Peter -- xxx, 1:1, 3:2,15
our beloved brother -- xii, 3:15
Spirit led on 2nd missionary journey -- 1:1
when were his letters collected -- xvi, 3:16
wrote according to the wisdom given him -- 3:15
Paul, Acts of -- xxv
Paul, Apocalypse of -- xxv
Paul's Epistles -- xxx, 3:15
claimed to be the Word of God -- 3:16
early collection of -- xii, xvii, 3:16
Peter's reference to -- xi, xii, 3:16
read in churches as authoritative messages -- 3:16
some things in them twisted -- xvii, 3:16
Peace,
be diligent to be found in Him in -- 3:14
grace and, be multiplied -- 1:2
Pearl of great price -- 1:4
Pentecost -- x
People,
false prophets arose among the -- 2:1
of God (*see also*, Church) -- 2:1
what sort of, ought you to be -- 3:11

Perfect tense, implication of -- 1:12, 2:6,19, 3:2,5
Perish, God does not wish any to -- 3:9
Persecution
Diocletian's -- v
Neronian -- 1:14
Perseverance,
add -- 1:6
of the saints -- *see* Calvin, Calvinism
Peshitto Syriac -- *see* Syriac
Peter
and Paul's theology in complete agreement -- 3:16
an apostle -- xi, xvi
Cephas -- 1:1
name change, Simon to Peter -- 1:1
call to be an apostle -- x, 1:1
death of, predicted by Jesus -- x, xi, xviii, 1:14, 3:8
equal with apostle Paul -- xi
eyewitness to Jesus' ministry -- *see* Eyewitness
Hebrew name, Simeon -- 1:1
reminiscences of Great Days with Jesus – 1:1,15, 2:20,22, 3:2,8,10
at the Transfiguration -- x, 1:1,15
fisherman from Galilee -- xiii, 1:1
his speeches in Acts -- xxxviii, 1:3,9,10, 3:3,12
his missionary travels -- ix, 1:12,14,16, 3:1
personal allusions -- x, xi, 1:15
prophetic insight -- 2:3
tradition about his death -- xxiv, xxx, xxxi, 1:14
was Peter ever in Rome? -- xxiv
well acquainted with his readers – 1:12, 3:1,2
Peter, Acts of -- xxiv, xxv, xxxiv
Peter, Apocalypse of -- ii, vii, viii, xxv, xxxviii
Peter, Gospel of -- x, xxiv
Peter, Preaching of -- *see* Preaching of Peter
1 Peter,
authorship -- xiv
acknowledged by all -- vi
compared with 2 Peter -- xiv, xxx
exhortations to faithfulness -- 3:1
1 Peter, *continued*
good Greek -- xiv
2 Peter,
absence of personal remarks at close – 3:18
authorship,
internal evidence -- x, xxiv, xxv, xxviii, 1:1,14,17, 3:2,4,15,16,18
external evidence -- i-ix, xxii, xxiii, xxviii, 3:12
see also, Authorship
a compendium, compilation (?) -- xxvi
alleged testamental genre -- *see* Testament (farewell speech)
date of writing -- i, ii, xxiv, xxxi, xxxiii, 1:18,19, 3:4,15,16
destination -- ix, xxix, 1:1, 2:18, 3:1,15
early use and wide circulation of -- ix
an epistle -- xxxv
Greek text and syntax -- xxix, xxxvi
high Christology -- 1:11, 3:1
modern denial of Petrine authorship – xi-xxv, xxix, xxx
neglected book -- i
no anachronisms -- xxv
not 2nd-century Hellenistic words -- 1:4
outline -- xl
place of writing -- ix, xxx
purpose -- xxx, xxxi-xxxv, 3:17
Greek, quality of -- xiv, xv
reiteration in -- xiii, xiv, 2:1,7,12
rejected by some -- xviii
similarity to Jude -- *see* Jude, relation of to 2 Peter
sources, alleged -- xvi, xx, xxxvi
style of the epistle -- viii, ix, xii-xv
theology of -- xxvi-xxxix, 3:16
unity of the letter -- 3:1,2
verb tenses change -- xxi, xxii, xxvi, xxix, xxxiv, 2:1,10
vocabulary -- xii-xiv, 2:7
Petrine vs. Pauline factions, alleged -- xi, 3:15
see also, Tubingen school
Philo,
alleged resemblances in 2 Peter -- xxiii
legend that, visited Peter -- xxiv
Pits of darkness -- 2:4
Plagiarism -- *see* Forgery; Pseudonymity

Plato -- 1:13
Play on words -- 2:13,15
Pleasure to revel in the daytime -- 2:13
Pleroma -- *see* Gnostics
Pollutions of the world,
escaped -- 2:20
entangled again therein -- 2:20
Polycarp, letters of,
to Philippians -- xii
Power, angels are greater in -- 2:11
Power and coming of our Lord Jesus -- *see* Christ
Practice these things -- 1:10
Prayer of the Apostle Paul -- xxv
Preaching of Peter -- xxiv
Pre-Adamic world -- 3:6
Precious promises -- *see* Promises
Premillennialism -- 3:9,10
Present tense, prophetic -- 3:11,12
Present world -- *see* World
Preserved, God, Noah -- 2:5
Preterism -- 3:4
Private interpretation –
see Prophets, prophecy
Promise, promises,
according to His -- 3:13
exceeding great and precious -- xxxvii, 1:4
not slack concerning His -- 3:9
where is the, of His coming? -- 3:4
Prophets, prophecy -- xiii
came not in old time by the will of men – 1:21
fulfilled, a strong apologetic argument – 1:19
inspiration of -- *see* Inspiration
more sure word of -- 1:1,19, 3:13
not of private interpretation -- 1:20
New Testament -- 1:19
Old Testament, 1:1,19, 3:2
past tense verbs used in -- 2:1,15,21
Proverb true, it happened to them according to -- 2:22
Proverbs, Book of, quoted by Peter -- 2:22
Providence of God -- *see* God, providence
Psalm 90 -- iii, xxxviii, 3:8
Pseudepigrapha -- ii, xi, xvii, xxiv, xxv, 3:2
condemned by early Christians -- vi, x
forgeries with famous names attached -- ii, xi, xxvii, xxxiii
Pseudepigrapha, *continued*
see also, Spurious
Pseudonymity -- i, viii, xxv, xxxiv, 1:15, 2:1
and canonicity mutually exclusive -- xxvii
deception involved in -- xxvi, xxvii
not accepted by early church -- x, xxvii
2 Peter does not reflect 2nd century concerns -- xviii, xxxviii, 1:1, 3:9,15
reasons why, is unbelievable -- xxvi-xxviii
writings still extant are heretical -- xxvii
Pseudo-Petrine literature -- ix, 1:15
Purification from former sins -- xxxvii, 1:9

Q (Quelle) -- xix
Qualities, spiritual – *see* Spiritual qualities
Quotations -- ii
Qumran -- *see* Dead Sea Scrolls

Rail at dignities -- xix
Rapture -- 1:19
Reason, creatures without -- xix
Rebellion in heaven -- 2:4
Rebirth -- *see* Regeneration
Rebuke -- 2:16
Received (obtain by lot) -- 1:1
Recipients of the letter - *see* 2 Peter, destination
Redaction criticism -- xx, xxii, xxvi, 1:1, 3:2
Redeemed, Master bought them -- 2:1
Redemption -- xxxvii
Regeneration (rebirth) -- *see* Born again
Reincarnation -- 1:2
Remember,
the words of the holy prophets -- 3:2
the command of the Lord and Savior – 3:2
Remind you, I will -- 1:12
Reminder, by way of -- 1:13, 3:1
Renovation of the universe -- xxxviii, 3:10,13
Repent, repentance -- 3:9
God waits patiently for men to -- xxxvii, 3:9,12

Reserved,
black darkness has been -- 2:18
in heaven for you -- 1:4
for fire -- 3:7
for judgment, fallen angels are -- 2:4
for the day of judgment -- 3:7
under punishment -- 2:19
Resurrection,
body -- 1:4
Christ's -- *see* Christ
final -- xxxviii, 2:4, 3:4,12
its relation to the consummation -- 3:4
Revelation,
Book of -- 2:15
from God to men in every age -- 2:8
made to Paul -- 3:15
special one to Peter? -- 1:14
Revel, reveling,
in the daytime -- 2:13
in their deceivings -- 2:13
Rhythmic formulations -- xiii
Righteousness,
connotations of the word -- 1:1, 2:21
dwells in new heaven and earth -- xxxvii, 3:13
Noah, a preacher of -- xxxvii, 2:5
of God -- 1:1
Old Testament predictions of -- 3:13
River Euphrates -- 2:15
Roar, heavens pass away with a -- 3:10
Rome and Roman church
Peter in Rome -- xxx
Roman Catholic church
an official interpreter needed for Scripture -- 1:20, 3:16
intercession of the saints -- 1:15
Rufinus -- iv

Sahidic Coptic -- *see* Coptic versions
Salutation, Peter's -- 1:2
Salvation,
involves godliness -- xiii
regard the patience of our Lord to be – 3:15
Samson -- 2:16
Satan – *see* Devil
Scoffers -- *see* False teachers and scoffers
Scripture,
Luke's Gospel called -- xii
New Testament books accorded scriptural status -- xvii, 3:2,16
Old Testament writings called -- xii, xvii, 1:20
other -- 3:16
Paul's letters called -- xi, xii, 3:16
some things hard to understand -- 3:16
technical term -- xvii, 3:16
the Word of God -- 3:7
wrested by false teachers -- xxxii, 1:1, 2:19, 3:16
writers of, quote inspired works -- xxii
Second Advent -- xxxvii, 3:1-16
alleged change of thought about its imminence -- 3:8
alleged delay -- xviii, 3:8
an incentive to holy living -- 3:4,7,11
attitude of expectation called for -- 3:12
be ready for -- 3:2
certainty of -- xl, 3:1
comes as a thief -- 3:10
cosmological changes accompany -- 3:10
denied by scoffers -- *see* False teachers
different terms used for -- xxxviii, 3:4,7
emphasized in 1 Peter -- 3:1,10
hope of, being abandoned (?) -- xvi, xviii
idea of, rejected -- xvi, xviii, xxxii, 1:16, 3:3
immanence (?) -- 3:8
looking for and hastening the day -- 3:12
parousia -- 3:4,7,8,12,16
Paul's teaching on, misunderstood -- 3:8
signless -- 1:19, 3:10
taught in the Old Testament -- 3:4,13
time of, known only to the Father – 3:9,12
Second letter -- ix, x, xxvi, xxx, 3:1
Secretaries -- *see* Amanuensis
Secretly introduce destructive heresies -- 2:1
Security,
eternal -- 2:1
of the believer is conditional -- 1:10
Self-control, add -- 1:6
Self-willed, false teachers are -- 2:10

Sensual conduct, sensuality -- 1:2, 2:2,6,7,18
Septuagint -- iii, xxxvi, 2:5,6,13,15,22
Serapion -- x
Servants of corruption -- 1:1, 2:19
Sethite interpretation of Gen. 6:2 -- 2:4
Seven heavens -- *see* Gnostics
Seven others, preserved -- 2:5
Sharp's rule of grammar -- 1:1,10,16, 3:16
Shekinah -- 1:17
Sheol -- *see* Hades
Shepherd of Hermas – 2:13
  see Hermas, Shepherd of
Signs of the times -- 1:19
Silas, Silvanus -- xiv
Simon Magus -- xxiv, xxv
Sin, sins,
  never cease from -- 2:14
  purification from former -- 1:9
  slaves to -- 1:6, 2:19
Sincere -- 3:1
Sinless perfection -- 1:10, 3:9
Slow, slowness -- 3:9
Sodom and Gomorrah -- xix, xxvii, xxxvi, xl, 2:4,6
  location of -- 2:6
Sons of God,
  how explained -- 2:4
  married daughters of men -- 2:4
Soul, souls
  enticing unstable -- 2:14
  Lot's righteous, tormented -- 2:8
  sleep -- 1:14, 3:4
Source criticism -- 1:16, 3:7
Sow, returns to wallow -- iv, 2:22
Spared not,
  the old world -- 2:5
Speak evil of angelic majesties -- 2:10
Speeches, Peter's in Acts -- xv
Spirit, Holy
  divine power granted -- 1:3
  guides apostles into all truth -- 1:3
  Holy men of God spoke as they were moved by -- iv
  indwelling -- 1:19
Spirit, human -- 1:4
  fruit of -- 1:6
  once dead in trespasses and sins -- 1:3
Spirits, the
  good and evil -- 2:11
  the "spirits in prison" -- 2:5
Spiritual qualities or graces -- 1:1,5-7
Spotless -- 3:14
Spots -- xix
Springs without water -- *see* Water
Spurious (rejected) books -- vi, x
  2 Peter never included among -- ix, xxvii
  see also, Pseudepigrapha
Stains and blemishes -- 2:13
Standing out of water, earth was -- 3:5
Steadfastness, falling from -- *see* Falling from steadfastness
Stoicism -- 3:7
Storm, mists driven by a -- 2:17
Strangers and pilgrims -- 1:1
Stumble, never -- 1:10
Style of letter -- *see* 2 Peter
Succubi -- 2:4
Suffering Servant Passages – xxxi
Suffering wrong as the wages of wrongdoing -- 2:13
Supply -- 1:5,11
Symeon,
  for "Simon Peter" -- xi, 1:1
  several men named, in Scripture -- 1:1
Synonyms, pairs of -- xiii
Synoptic problem -- xix
Syriac Versions
  Old Syriac -- vii
  Palestinian -- 1:1
  Peshitto Syriac -- vii, xviii
  Philoxenian Syriac -- vii

Tabernacle,
  human body compared to a -- 1:13
  put off this tabernacle -- 1:14
Tacitus -- ix
Tales, cleverly devised -- *see* Fables
Tartarus -- xiii, 2:4,9
Tertullian -- ix, x, 1:21, 2:15
Testament (farewell speech) -- xxiv, xxvi, xxxiii-xxxv, 1:15
Testament of Abraham -- xxxiii
Testament of Job -- xxxiii

Testament of Moses -- xxxiii
Testaments of the Twelve Patriarchs -- xxxiii
Text of 2 Peter -- xxxvi
Theology,
  alleged development of New Testament – 3:16
Theophilus of Antioch -- iv
Thermodynamics, first and second laws of – 3:6
Thief, Day of the Lord will come as a -- 3:10
Thomas, Acts of -- xxxiv
Thousand years
  a day with the Lord is like a -- iii, 3:8
Thucydides -- ix
2 Timothy -- xvii
Tormented, righteous soul was -- 2:8
Total depravity, inherited -- 2:10
Trained in greed -- 2:14
Transfiguration -- *see* Christ
Transgression, rebuked for his own -- 2:16
Truth -- xxxvi
  established in the present truth -- xxiii, 1:12
  way of -- *see* Truth, Way of
Tubingen School -- xi, xxvi, 3:2,15
Turn away from the holy commandment – 2:21

Ungodly and sinner,
  judgment on -- xix, xl, 2:5,6
  destruction of -- 3:7
Uniformitarianism of nature, alleged -- 3:4,6
Universalism -- 3:9
Universe, renovation of the -- 3:6
Unlettered -- 3:16
Unprincipled men,
  carried away by error of -- 3:17
  oppressed by the conduct of -- 2:7
Unrighteous, kept under punishment -- 2:9
Unrighteousness, wages of -- 2:15
Unstable souls -- 2:14, 3:17
Untaught and unstable -- 3:16
Useless nor unfruitful -- 1:8

Valentinus -- xxxiii
Vanity, arrogant words of -- 2:18
Virtue,
  add -- 1:5
  Christ's – *see* Christ
  God's -- xxiii
Virtue and vice lists -- xiii
Vocabulary of 1 and 2 Peter compared – xii, xiii
Voice from the heavenly glory -- 1:17
Vomit, dog returns to its -- 2:22

Wages,
  of sin, is death -- 1:10
  of unrighteousness -- 2:15
Wallow, sow returns to -- 2:22
War in heaven -- *see* Rebellion in heaven
Washing, sow after, returns to wallow -- 2:22
Water,
  earth was formed out of and by -- 3:5
  wells (springs) without -- xix, 2:17
Way -- xxxvii, 2:2
  of life -- 2:15
  of righteousness -- xxxvii, 2:15,21
  of salvation -- 2:15
  of truth -- xxxvii, 2:21
    evil spoken of -- 2:2
  right -- xxxviii, 2:15
Well pleased -- 1:17
Will, human -- *see* Human will
Winds, mists driven by -- xix
Wisdom, given to Paul -- 3:15
Wish,
  God does not, for any to perish -- 3:9
  Greek words so translated -- 3:9
Wolves in sheep's clothing -- 2:1
Word, Word of God,
  by His, heavens and earth reserved for fire -- 3:7
  by the, the heavens existed long ago -- 3:5
  you do well to take heed to -- 1:19
  distorted -- xvii, xxxii
  divine preservation -- xviii
  God speaks and it happens -- 3:5,6,7
  inspiration -- *see* Inspiration

Word of God, *continued*
a lamp to our feet -- 1:19
prophetic, made more sure -- 1:19
Scripture is called -- 3:7
Works, earth's, burned up -- 3:10
World,
corruption in the -- 1:4, 2:18
defilements of the -- 2:20
of the ungodly -- 2:5
old -- xxxvii, 2:5, 3:6
the one that now is -- xxxvii, 3:6
was destroyed -- 3:6
Worldview -- 3:6
Worse, last state is, than the first -- 2:20
Wrest the Scriptures, to their own destruction –
- xxxii
Wrong, suffer -- 2:13
Wrong-doers, wrong doing -- 2:13

Young earth -- 3:4

Zedekiah -- 2:1

JUDE INDEX

(Roman numerals indicate pages in the Introductory Studies. Chapter and verses are given for notes in the commentary pages.)

Abel -- 26
Abiram -- 27
Able to keep you from falling -- 45
Abraham -- xvi
Adam -- 31
Admah -- 18
Alexandria - x, xiii
Alphaeus, sons of -- iv
Altered states of consciousness -- xii, 21, 37
Amen -- 48
Angels
abandoned their proper abode -- 17
fallen, not spared by God -- v, xi, 17, 18
dignity (majesty) of -- xii, 17, 21, 24
guardian -- 17
kept in everlasting chains -- vi, 4, 15, 17
kept not their own domain -- 16, 40
Lord comes with 10,000 -- 31
orders of -- 17
origin and nature of -- 16
rebellion of -- 48
sinned -- 16, 17
thousands of thousands -- 32
Animals, unreasoning -- xii, 25
Antilegomena -- vi, xv
Antinomianism -- *see* Libertinism
Antioch of Syria -- x
Aorist tense -- 9, 17
Apocrypha and Pseudepigrapha –
i, vii, xi,xiii, xiv, xvi, xvii, 22
Old Testament Apocrypha -- xvii, xviii
Apostles of Jesus Christ -- vii, 35
author of Jude not -- iv, 35
Jude (Lord's brother) not an apostle -- ii, iii
led into all truth -- 9
prayed for, by Jesus -- 3
prediction of coming mockers -- xvi, xix, 34, 35
Apostolic Constitutions -- iv
Aratus -- xvi
Archangel -- 17, 22
Aristotle -- 14
Article, definite -- 8, 12
Ascension, Christ's -- *see* Jesus Christ
Asceticism among Gnostics -- 21
Asia, Roman province -- x, 2
churches of -- xi, 35
Assumption of Moses -- *see* Moses
Athenagoras -- v
Augustine -- xvii
Authority -- 47
rejected -- 21, 24
Authorship of Jude -- *see* Jude, epistle of
Autumn trees -- *see* Trees

Babylonian Captivity -- 16
Balaam -- xi, 26
error of -- 26
Barnabas, Epistle of -- *see* Epistle of Barnabas
Before all time -- 47
Beforehand -- viii, 10, 35
Beloved -- x, 3, 5, 34, 38
Bithynia -- x, 2
Blameless in His presence -- 4, 45, 46
Blasphemy -- *see* Railing and Revile
Bond-servant of Jesus Christ -- v, ix, 1
Book of Enoch -- *see* Enoch, Book of
Book of Life -- 11
Both now and forever -- 47, 48
Brothers of the Lord -- xiii, 2
distinct from the apostles -- iii, iv
Epiphanian view -- viii
names of -- iii, iv
once were unbelievers -- iv, viii, 1
went on evangelistic tours -- 2
Build on your most holy faith -- 38

Cain -- xi, 26, 31
Cainites, Gnostics -- viii, 21
Call, called -- x, 2
Calvinism -- 2, 4, 11, 15
Canon
criteria for inclusion in -- xv
New Testament -- xiv-xvi
Old Testament, closed -- xvii, xviii

Canon Mommsenianus -- vii
Cappadocia -- x, 2
Carpocrates, the Gnostic -- viii, 21
Catholic epistles -- vi, vii
Chains of darkness -- vi
Children of Israel -- 13, 14
saved out of Egypt -- 15
sins of the -- 16
wilderness wanderings -- 15, 16, 33
Christ – *see* Jesus Christ
Christian liberty -- 10
Chrysostom -- xv
Cities of the plain -- xi, 18
Civil authorities -- 21
Cleanthes -- xvi
Clement of Alexandria -- vi, viii, xiii, 12, 20, 23
Clement of Rome -- v
Clouds without water -- 29
Codex
Alexandrinus -- ii, 3
Sinaiticus -- ii, 3
Vaticanus -- ii, 3
Collimachus -- xvi
Complainers -- 33
Condemnation
marked out for this -- 10
sentence of -- 10, 11, 15
Conservatives vs. liberals -- 8, 44
Contend for the faith -- *see* Faith
Contending, some who are -- 42
Convict -- 32, 42
Corinth -- x
Council of Carthage -- vii, xvi
Council of Laodicea -- xvi
Crept in unnoticed (unawares) -- vi, x, xii, 10, 35
Crisis
exhortations suggested by the -- 34
how Jude learned of it -- 7
Critics
on angels -- 22
on Jude -- 8, 14

Darkness -- 17
Blackness of -- 17, 30
Dathan -- 27
Dative -- 4
of agent -- 3,39
of means -- 38
of respect -- 38
of sphere -- 3, 39
Day of Judgment -- *see* Judgment, final
Dead in sins -- 29, 37
Dead Sea -- 19
Dead Sea Scrolls -- xiv
Deceivers, Appearance of predicted – *see* Mockers
Defile the flesh -- *see* Flesh
Demiurge --13
Deny the Lord -- xii, 12, 13
Destroyed
by these things -- 25
those who did not believe -- 15, 16
Devil -- 24
dispute with Michael -- xi, xviii, 22
limitations on, God puts -- 45
Didache -- vi
Didymus of Alexandria -- 23
Dignities, speak evil of -- 21, 22
Disobedience -- 26
Disputing about the body of Moses – *see* Moses
Domain -- 16
Dominion -- 17, 21, 47
Domitian -- ix, x, xiii
Doubting, some who are -- 42
Doubts as to authenticity of Jude -- xv
Doxology -- 45-48
Dreamers -- 20, 21
Dualism, Greek -- 12, 13

Early Catholicism -- vii, 8
Early Christian literature -- v-vii, xv
Eastern church -- iv
Egypt
Israel's deliverance from -- 13, 15
Jude thought to have been written from – xiii
Elijah -- xvi
Encyclical letter -- xi, 2

Enoch -- xvii
- Book of -- vi, vii, x, xiv, xvii, 22
- Prophecy of -- xi, xvi, xvii, 31
- Seventh from Adam -- 31

Ephraem Syrus -- xv
Epimenides -- xvi
Epiphanius -- 21
Epistle of Barnabas -- v
Eternal
- bonds -- 17
- fire -- 19, 43
- life -- 41

Ethiopic Version -- xvii
Eusebius -- vi, ix
Evil doers, punishment of -- *see* Punishment
Example -- 19
Exodus -- xi, 15

Faith -- 26
- body of doctrine -- i, ii, vii, 8
- build upon -- v, 38
- contend for the -- i, xi, 7, 34, 39, 42
- most holy -- 8, 38
- once for all delivered -- i, xii, 9, 38
- personal convictions -- 8

False teachers and scoffers
- cause divisions -- 10, 36
- characteristics -- xii, 11, 12, 20, 33
- confess not that Jesus Christ has come in the flesh -- 2, 13
- deny Jesus as Lord and Master -- 12, 13, 46
- devoid of the Spirit -- 37
- doctrines -- *see* Gnostics, doctrines
- harm caused by -- 27-31
- incorrigible -- 42
- infiltrated the churches -- *see* Crept in unawares
- prediction of -- 10, 34, 35
- pretend to be Christians -- xii, 10
- relapsed Christians (?) -- 29
- revile angelic majesties -- *see* Revile angelic majesties
- *see also*, Gnostics, Gnosticism
- speak arrogantly -- 33
- worldly minded -- 37

Fault finders -- xii, 33
Fear
- as a motive -- 44
- have mercy with -- 43, 44
- they feast with you without -- 28

Fire
- and brimstone -- 19
- Eternal -- *see* Eternal fire
- snatch them out of -- v, 43

Flattering people -- 34
Flesh
- defile the -- v, xii, 21
- garment polluted by the -- 43, 44

Foam -- 30
Forever
- black darkness has been reserved -- 30
- before all times, now, and -- 47

Fornication -- 19, 21

Gabriel, archangel -- 22
Galatia -- x, 2
Galilee
- first-century culture -- vii

Garment, polluted by the flesh -- 43, 44
Gentiles -- xi, 7
Glory -- ix, 4, 22, 41, 45, 46, 47
Gnostics, Gnosticism
- doctrines -- ii, xi, xii, 2, 7, 12, 13, 22, 25, 36, 38, 41, 46
- incipient -- viii, x, xi, 2, 10, 21
- practices -- 10, 26, 33, 38
- second century -- vii, viii, 12, 37

God
- Creator -- 17, 46, 48
- Father -- 3, 13, 45
- doxology addressed to -- 45
- glorified through Jesus Christ -- 46
- glory of -- 45, 46
- love of -- 40
- Only God -- 46
- providence of -- xvii, 45
- Savior -- 46

Gomorrah -- *see* Sodom and Gomorrah
Gospels, date of writing -- 11
Grace -- 12
- Turned into licentiousness -- xii, 12

Great Day -- vi, 18
Great joy -- 45, 46
Greed -- xii, 26
Growth, Spiritual -- *see* Spiritual growth
Grumblers -- xii, 33

Hebraism -- 36
Hegesippus -- ix, x
    testimony about Jude's grandchildren -- ix
Hell -- 20, 27, 30
    alleged conflicting description of -- 30
    not annihilation -- 31
Herod the Great -- ix, xix
Hezekiah -- 23
Hidden reefs -- 28
Holy
    faith -- 38
    ones -- 31, 32
Holy Spirit
    indwelling -- 38, 39
    praying in -- 39
Homosexuality -- 19, 21
Hope -- 41

Immorality, gross -- xii, 19
Imperfect tense -- 35
"In Christ" -- 3
"In God" -- 3
Inherited sin -- *see* Total hereditary depravity
Inspiration -- iii, xvi, xviii, 6, 7, 23
    chief criterion for canonicity -- iii, xv
Instinct -- 25
Insubordination -- 27
Intermediate state -- 17, 20, 30
Interpolation -- iii, v, xviii
Irenaeus -- 12
Italics, words in -- iii

James, the Lord's brother
    an apostle -- v, 2
    risen Christ's appearance to -- ix
    Epistle of -- vi
    known by the readers of Jude -- 35
James, Lord's brother, *continued*
    leader of Jerusalem church -- v, x, xiii, 2
    writes good Greek -- viii
Jannes and Jambres -- xvi
Jehovah -- 1, 15, 32
Jerome -- iv, vii
Jerusalem
    destruction of -- xiii, xiv, xix, 16
    possible place of writing -- xiii
Josephus -- xix
Jesus Christ
    active in Old Testament times -- 15
    ascension -- v
    atoning death -- 6
    comes with 10,000 holy ones – 31, 32
    death -- v, 28
    deity -- 1, 13, 46
    humanity -- 13
    intermediate agent between man and God -- 46
    judge -- 32, 41
    Lord -- 1, 12, 13, 15, 31
    only Master -- 12, 13
    mediator -- 47
    mercy of -- 40, 41
    Messiah -- 12
    pre-existent -- 15, 47
    resurrection -- v, ix, 1
    Savior -- 46
    Second Coming -- *see* Second Coming
Joy, great -- *see* Great joy
Jubilees, Book of -- xvii
Judaizers -- 10
Judas
    the apostle -- ii, iii
    Barsabbas -- iii
    Iscariot -- ii, iii
    the Galilean -- iii
    the name -- ii
Jude,
    brother of James -- ii, 2
    felt the necessity to write -- 7
    grandchildren -- ix, xiii
    knows his readers -- 5, 6
    life of -- viii-ix
    the Lord's brother -- iii, iv, 1
    the name -- ii, 1
    traveling preacher -- ix, xi, xiii, 2

Jude, epistle of
- authorship -- ii-viii
  - external evidence -- v
  - internal evidence -- ii
- canonicity -- iii, vi, vii, xiv-xvi
- date -- xiii-xiv
- destination -- x-xi, 2
- keynote of the epistle -- 12
- modern objections to Jude's authorship – vii-viii
- neglected -- i, 48
- occasion for writing -- xi, 10
- outline -- xx-xxi, 14
- place of writing -- xiii
- purpose for writing -- xi, 5
- relationship to 2 Peter -- xiii, xiv, 11, 13, 36, 42
- title -- ii
- triplets -- xix, 4, 41, 42
- use of sources (alleged) -- xiii, xiv, xvi-xix, 22, 23, 24

Judgment -- 18, 32
- Final -- vi, xii, 18, 31, 32, 41, 45
- one general judgment -- 32
- *see also*, Great Day

Keep
- you from stumbling -- 45
- yourselves in the love of God -- 3, 4, 34, 38, 39

Kept
- by God -- 4
- for Jesus Christ -- x, 2, 3
- in eternal bonds -- vi, 17
- kept not their own domain -- 16, 17

King James Version -- 2, 7, 11, 12, 15, 20, 28, 29, 31, 36, 42, 44, 45, 46

Know
- all things -- 14
- by instinct -- 25
- synonyms -- 25

Korah, rebellion of -- xi, 27

Lasciviousness -- xii, 12

Last days (times) -- 36

Latin Versions
- Old Latin -- vii, xv
- Vulgate -- 3, 20

Law of Moses -- 23

Letters, first-century form of -- 1, 4, 6

Libertinism -- 12

Licentiousness, 21
- Turning the grace of God into -- xii, 12

Lord's Supper -- 28

Love
- be multiplied -- 4, 5
- of God -- 40

Love Feast -- xii, 28, 36

Lucian of Antioch -- xv

Lust -- 29, 30, 33, 36
- following after their own -- 33
- ungodly -- 35, 36

Luther -- 39, 44

LXX -- *see* Septuagint

Majesty -- 21, 47

Manuscripts -- xv, 41
- *see also*, Variant readings

Master -- 12, 13

Menander -- xvi

Mercy
- be multiplied to you -- 4, 5
- have, on some -- 41, 42, 43
- waiting anxiously for -- v, 40

Michael, archangel -- xvi, xviii, 22
- dispute with the devil -- xi, xviii, 22
- not identified with Christ -- 22

Minuscules -- xv

Mockers -- 36, 40
- Jude's allusion to -- 36
- Peter's allusion to -- 36

Moses -- xvi, 23, 27, 33
- Assumption of -- vii, xiv, xix, 23
- dispute about his body –
  - *see* Michael and dispute with the devil
- murdered the Egyptian -- 23

Muratorian Canon -- vii

Nabal -- 33
Natural -- 36, 37
New Age Movement -- ii
New Birth -- *see* Regeneration
Nicolaitans -- 21
Noah -- xvii

Once for all -- 9, 14
Ophites -- viii
Optative Mood -- 5, 24, 25
Origen -- vi, xix, 23

P72 -- 3, 15
Palestine -- x
Papyri -- xv
Parallels between Jude and 2 Peter – *see* Jude, Epistle of
Partiality -- *see* Flattering people
Participles -- 38
  circumstantial -- 6
Patriarchs, Patriarchal Age -- ii, 31, 32
Paul
  Epistles of -- vii, viii, xi, xiv, 45
  quotes Greek poets -- xvi
Pay -- 26
Peace be multiplied -- 4,5
Perfect tense -- 3, 14, 17
Perish -- 27
Perpetual virginity of Mary -- iv
Peshitto Syriac -- *see* Syriac Versions
2 Peter -- i, viii, xi, xiii, xiv, xix, 1, 2, 4, 5, 6, 19, 11, 12, 13, 16, 21, 24, 25, 30, 33, 36, 39
  Jude's readers aware of -- x, xi, xix
  known in Egypt (?) -- x
Planets -- vi, 30
Polycarp -- v
Pontus -- x, 2
Postmodernism -- i
Prayer, praying -- 39
Predestination -- 11
Present tense -- 8, 13, 19, 39, 40
Preservation of believers
  conditional -- 4, 40
  see also, Security of believers
Principalities-- 17
Prophet, prophets, prophecy -- iii, xvii, 31
Prophetic past tense -- 26, 27
Pseudepigrapha -- *see* Apocrypha and Pseudepigrapha
Pseudonymity, problem of -- iv, xiii
Psychic -- xii, 37
Punishment -- xiv, 16
  Biblical examples of -- 14, 25-27
  upon ungodly -- xii, 13, 14, 18, 31

Railing
  judgment -- 24
  speech -- 24, 33
Raphael, archangel -- 22
Rebuke -- 24
Redaction criticism -- 8
Regeneration -- 3, 29, 37
Restoration Movement -- i
Revelation, God's -- 6, 21, 22, 24
  finality of -- i, ii, 9
  source of information for Bible writers – xvi, xviii, 23
Revile
  angelic majesties -- xii, 21, 24
  things they don't understand -- 24
Rhetorical criticism -- 14
Roman Catholic Doctrine -- xviii, 9

Saints -- i, 9, 31
Salutation -- 4
Salvation
  common -- 6
  Gnostic doctrine of -- xii, 6, 37, 46
  God's initiative in -- 40
  steps of -- 15
Sanctified, Sanctification -- 3
Satan -- *see* Devil
Save others -- 43
Scoffers -- *see* Mockers
Scripture
  mishandled by false teachers -- xii
  value of, combatting false teaching – 35, 38

Second Coming -- xii, 31, 32, 36, 40
Second death -- 29
"Second time" -- 15, 16
Security of the believer, conditional -- 40, 45
Sensual -- 9, 25, 37
Septuagint Version -- xvii
Servant of Christ -- *see* Bond-servant
Shame -- 30
Sharp's Rule of Grammar -- 13
Shepherd of Hermas -- v
Shepherds that feed themselves -- 28
Silent years, 400 -- xvii, xviii
Simonians, Gnostics -- 21
Sin
    if we say we have no -- 41
    inherited -- *see* Total hereditary depravity
Sodom and Gomorrah -- xvi, 18, 19
Sodomy -- 19
Soul -- 37
Spirit,
    have not the -- xii, 37
    man's -- 37, 39
Spiritual growth -- 38,39
Strange flesh -- xii, 19
Stumbling, keep you from -- 45
Superlative, use of -- 38
Syriac Versions -- 3
    Old Syriac -- xv
    Peshitto Syriac -- iii, xv
    Philoxenian Syriac -- xv

Targum of Jonathan -- 23, 26
Tertullian -- vi
Testament of the Twelve Patriarchs -- xvii
Textual variations -- *see* Variant readings
Theophilus of Antioch -- vi
Total hereditary depravity -- 44
Tradition, traditional teaching -- xviii
    apostolic (oral) - x, 9
    early church -- ix
    Jewish -- xi, xvi
Trance -- 21
Trees,
    autumn -- 29
    twice dead -- 29
    unfruitful -- 29
    uprooted -- 29
Truth -- 9
Twice dead -- *see* Trees

Unbelief -- 8, 15
Uncials -- xv
Unconditional eternal security -- 15
    see also, Security of the believer
Ungodly -- 12, 31, 32
    deeds -- 32
    lusts -- xii, 36
    speech -- 32
    sinners -- 32
Uriel, archangel -- 22

Valentinians, Valentinus
Variant readings -- 3, 7, 12, 14, 15, 41, 42, 46
Visions -- 21, 37
Vulgate -- *see* Latin Versions

Waiting anxiously -- 40
Wandering stars -- vi, 30
Waves of the sea -- 30
Winds, carried along by -- 29
Woe -- 25
Worldly minded -- 37

Zeboim -- 18
Zoar -- 18

www.ingramcontent.com/pod-product-compliance
Lightning Source LLC
Chambersburg PA
CBHW061957090426
42811CB00006B/970

* 9 7 8 0 9 7 1 7 6 5 2 4 5 *